P9-DFV-919

How to Use the Maps in *World History, Sixth Edition*

Here are some basic map concepts that will help you to get the most out of the maps in this textbook.

- Always look at the scale, which allows you to determine the distance in miles or kilometers between locations on the map.

- Examine the legend carefully. It explains the colors and symbols used on the map.

- Note the locations of mountains, rivers, oceans, and other geographic features, and consider how these would affect such human activities as agriculture, commerce, travel, and warfare.

- Read the map caption thoroughly. It provides important information, sometimes not covered in the text itself, and poses a thought question to encourage you to think beyond the mere appearance of the map and make connections across chapters, regions, and concepts.

- Several "spot maps" appear in each chapter, to allow you to view in detail smaller areas that may not be apparent in larger maps. For example, a spot map in Chapter 12 lets you zoom in on Charlemagne's Empire.

- Many of the text's maps also carry a globe icon, which indicates that they or similar maps appear in interactive form at www.cengage.com/history/Duiker/World6e

TO 1500

SIXTH EDITION

WORLD HISTORY

WILLIAM J. DUIKER

The Pennsylvania State University

JACKSON J. SPIELVOGEL

The Pennsylvania State University

WADSWORTH
CENGAGE Learning

Australia • Brazil • Japan • Korea • Mexico • Singapore • Spain • United Kingdom • United States

World History, To 1500, Sixth Edition
William J. Duiker and Jackson J. Spielvogel

Publishers: Clark Baxter and Suzanne Jeans

Senior Sponsoring Editor: Nancy Blaine

Senior Development Editor: Margaret McAndrew Beasley

Assistant Editors: Megan Curry and Lauren Bussard

Editorial Assistant: Megan Chrisman

Senior Media Editor: Lisa Ciccolo

Media Editor: Yevgeny Ioffe

Senior Marketing Managers: Diane Wenckebach and Katherine Bates

Marketing Communications Managers: Heather Baxley and Christine Dobberpuhl

Production Manager: Samantha Ross

Senior Content Project Manager: Lauren Wheelock

Senior Art Director: Cate Rickard Barr

Production Technology Analyst: Jamison MacLachlan

Senior Print Buyer: Mary Beth Hennebury

Sr. Rights Account Manager-Text: Bob Kauser

Production Service: John Orr, Orr Book Services

Text Designer: Kathleen Cunningham

Permissions Account Manager, Images: Don Schlotman

Photo Researcher: Abigail Baxter

Cover Designer: Kathleen Cunningham

Cover Image: "Commerce in the Gulf of Cambaye" from *Le Livre des Merveilles*, c.1410. Bibliotheque Nationale, Paris (Ms. fr. 2810), France//© Giraudon/Art Resource, NY

Compositor: International Typesetting and Composition

© 2010, 2007 Wadsworth, Cengage Learning

ALL RIGHTS RESERVED. No part of this work covered by the copyright herein may be reproduced, transmitted, stored, or used in any form or by any means graphic, electronic, or mechanical, including but not limited to photocopying, recording, scanning, digitizing, taping, Web distribution, information networks, or information storage and retrieval systems, except as permitted under Section 107 or 108 of the 1976 United States Copyright Act, without the prior written permission of the publisher.

For product information and technology assistance, contact us at
Cengage Learning Academic Resource Center, 1-800-423-0563

For permission to use material from this text or product,
submit all requests online at **www.cengage.com/permissions**
Further permissions questions can be e-mailed to
permissionrequest@cengage.com

Library of Congress Control Number: 2008941673

ISBN-13: 978-0-495-56904-6

ISBN-10: 0-495-56904-6

Wadsworth
25 Thomson Place
Boston, MA 02210-1202
USA

Cengage Learning products are represented in Canada by Nelson Education, Ltd.

For your course and learning solutions, visit **www.cengage.com**

Purchase any of our products at your local college store or at our preferred online store **www.ichapters.com**

Printed in Canada
1 2 3 4 5 6 7 12 11 10 09

ABOUT THE AUTHORS

WILLIAM J. DUIKER is liberal arts professor emeritus of East Asian studies at The Pennsylvania State University. A former U.S. diplomat with service in Taiwan, South Vietnam, and Washington, D.C., he received his doctorate in Far Eastern history from Georgetown University in 1968, where his dissertation dealt with the Chinese educator and reformer Cai Yuanpei. At Penn State, he has written widely on the history of Vietnam and modern China, including the highly acclaimed *The Communist Road to Power in Vietnam* (revised edition, Westview Press, 1996), which was selected for a Choice Outstanding Academic Book Award in 1982–1983 and 1996–1997. Other recent books are *China and Vietnam: The Roots of Conflict* (Berkeley, 1987), *Sacred War: Nationalism and Revolution in a Divided Vietnam* (McGraw-Hill, 1995), and *Ho Chi Minh* (Hyperion, 2000), which was nominated for a Pulitzer Prize in 2001. While his research specialization is in the field of nationalism and Asian revolutions, his intellectual interests are considerably more diverse. He has traveled widely and has taught courses on the history of communism and non-Western civilizations at Penn State, where he was awarded a Faculty Scholar Medal for Outstanding Achievement in the spring of 1996.

TO YVONNE,

FOR ADDING SPARKLE TO THIS BOOK AND TO MY LIFE

W.J.D.

JACKSON J. SPIELVOGEL is associate professor emeritus of history at The Pennsylvania State University. He received his Ph.D. from The Ohio State University, where he specialized in Reformation history under Harold J. Grimm. His articles and reviews have appeared in such journals as *Moreana, Journal of General Education, Catholic Historical Review, Archiv für Reformationsgeschichte,* and *American Historical Review.* He has also contributed chapters or articles to *The Social History of the Reformation, The Holy Roman Empire: A Dictionary Handbook, Simon Wiesenthal Center Annual of Holocaust Studies,* and *Utopian Studies.* His work has been supported by fellowships from the Fulbright Foundation and the Foundation for Reformation Research. At Penn State, he helped inaugurate the Western civilization course as well as a popular course on Nazi Germany. His book *Hitler and Nazi Germany* was published in 1987 (fifth edition, 2005). He is the author of *Western Civilization,* published in 1991 (seventh edition, 2009). Professor Spielvogel has won five major university-wide teaching awards. During the year 1988–1989, he held the Penn State Teaching Fellowship, the university's most prestigious teaching award. In 1996, he won the Dean Arthur Ray Warnock Award for Outstanding Faculty Member and in 2000 received the Schreyer Honors College Excellence in Teaching Award.

TO DIANE,

WHOSE LOVE AND SUPPORT MADE IT ALL POSSIBLE

J.J.S.

BRIEF CONTENTS

DETAILED CONTENTS

vii

MAPS

CHRONOLOGIES

DOCUMENTS

This page constitutes an extension of the copyright page. We have made every effort to trace the ownership of all copyrighted material and to secure permission from copyright holders. In the event of any question arising as to the use of any material, we will be pleased to make the necessary corrections in future printings. Thanks are due to the following authors, publishers, and agents for permission to use the material indicated.

THE LEGENDARY GRANDEUR OF MAJAPAHIT 267
From *The World of Southeast Asia: Selected Historical Readings* by Harry J. Benda and John J. Larkin, eds. Copyright © 1967 by Harper & Row, Publishers.

CHAPTER 10

ACTION OR INACTION: AN IDEOLOGICAL DISPUTE IN MEDIEVAL CHINA 276
From *Chinese Civilization and Bureaucracy*, by Etienne Balasz. Copyright © 1964 by Yale University Press. Used with permission. Han Yu selection from W. T. de Bary and I. Bloom *Sources of Chinese Tradition*, vol. I, 2nd ed. (New York, 1999), pp. 569–573.

THE SAINTLY MISS WU 287
From *The Inner Quarters: Marriage and the Lives of Chinese Women in the Sung Period*, Patricia Ebrey (Berkeley, University of California Press, 1993), pp. 197–198.

THE GOOD LIFE IN THE HIGH TANG 280
From *Perspectives on the T'ang*, by Arthur F. Wright and Denis Twitchett. Copyright © 1973 by Yale University Press. Used with permission.

A LETTER TO THE POPE 290
From Prawdin, Michael, *The Mongol Empire: Its Rise and Legacy* (Free Press, 1961), pp. 280–281.

KHANBALIQ, KHUBILAI KHAN'S CAPITAL 294
From *The Travels of Marco Polo* by Marco Polo, edited by Ronald Latham. Viking Press, 1958.

THE WAY OF THE GREAT BUDDHA 297
Excerpted from *Sources of Chinese Tradition*, by William Theodore de Bary. Copyright © 1960 by Columbia University Press. Reprinted with the permission of the publisher.

A CONFUCIAN WEDDING CEREMONY 299
Excerpted from *Confucianism and Family Rituals in Imperial China: A Social History of Writing About Rites*, "A Welcoming in Person," translated and edited by P. B. Ebrey. Copyright © Princeton University Press, 1991.

CHAPTER 11

THE EASTERN EXPEDITION OF EMPEROR JIMMU 309
Excerpt from *Sources of Japanese History*, David Lu, ed. (New York: McGraw-Hill, 1974), I, p. 7.

TWO TANG POETS 301
From Hucker, Charles O., *China's Imperial Past*. Copyright © 1965 by the Board of Trustees of the Leland Stanford Junior University. With the permission of Stanford University Press. www.sup.org.

THE SEVENTEEN-ARTICLE CONSTITUTION 311
Excerpt from *Sources of Japanese History*, David Lu, ed. (New York: McGraw-Hill, 1974), I, p. 7.

JAPAN'S WARRIOR CLASS 314
Excerpt from *Sources of Japanese Tradition*, by William Theodore de Bary. Copyright © 1958 by Columbia University Press. Reprinted with the permission of the publisher.

LIFE IN THE LAND OF WA 316
Excerpt from *Sources of Japanese History*, David Lu, ed. (New York: McGraw-Hill, 1974), I, p. 7.

SEDUCTION OF THE AKASHI LADY 318
From *The Tale of the Genji* by Lady Murasaki, translated by Edward G. Seidensticker, copyright © 1976 by Edward G. Seidensticker. Used by permission of Alfred A. Knopf, a division of Random House, Inc.

A SAMPLE OF LINKED VERSE 320
Excerpt from *The Cambridge History of Japan*, Vol. III, edited by Koza Yamamura, excerpt from "A Sample of Linked Verse" by H. Paul Varley from p. 480. Copyright © 1990. Reprinted with the permission of Cambridge University Press.

THE FIRST VIETNAM WAR 326
From Keith W. Taylor, *The Birth of Vietnam* (Berkeley, 1983), p. 18.

A PLEA TO THE EMPEROR 328
From *Translations and Reprints From the Original Sources of European History*, Series I, Vol. 4, No. 4, by A. C. Howland, © 1898 by Department of History, University of Pennsylvania Press.

CHAPTER 12

GERMANIC CUSTOMARY LAW: THE ORDEAL 335
From *Translations and Reprints from the Original Sources of European History*, Series I, Vol. 4, No. 4, by A. C. Howland, copyright 1898 by Department of History, University of Pennsylvania Press.

THE ACHIEVEMENTS OF CHARLEMAGNE 337
From Einhard, *The Life of Charlemagne*, translated by S. E. Turner, pp. 50–54. Copyright © 1960 by The University of Michigan. Translated from the Monumenta Germanie.

AN ITALIAN BANKER DISCUSSES TRADE BETWEEN EUROPE AND CHINA 344
Henry Yule and Henri Cordier, eds, *Cathay and the Way Thither*, 2d ed. (London: Hakluyt Society, 1913–16), vol. 3, pp. 151–155.

MURDER IN THE CATHEDRAL 348
From *The Letters of John of Salisbury*, Vol. II, W. J. Millar and C. N. L. Brooke, eds. (Oxford: Oxford at the Clarendon Press), 1979. Reprinted with Permission of Oxford University Press.

A MUSLIM'S DESCRIPTION OF THE RUS 351
From *The Vikings*, by Johannes Bronsted, translated by Kalle Skov (Penguin Books, 1965) copyright © Johannes Bronsted, 1960, 1965. Reproduced by permission of Penguin Books Ltd.

A MIRACLE OF SAINT BERNARD 353
From R.H.C. Davis, *A History of Medieval Europe*, 2nd ed. (London: Longman Group) 1988, pp. 265–266. Reprinted by permission of Pearson Education, UK.

UNIVERSITY STUDENTS AND VIOLENCE AT OXFORD 355
From *The Story of Oxford* by Cecil Headlam, 1907.

CHAPTER 13

A BYZANTINE EMPEROR GIVES MILITARY ADVICE 371
George T. Dennis, trans. *Maurice's Strategikon: Handbook of Byzantine Military Strategy*, Book 11 (Philadelphia: University of Pennsylvania Press, 1984), pp. 118–119.

This page constitutes an extension of the copyright page. We have made every effort to trace the ownership of all copyrighted material and to secure permission from copyright holders. In the event of any question arising as to the use of any material, we will be pleased to make the necessary corrections in future printings. We wish to thank the following copyright holders for permission to use the material indicated.

CHAPTER 1

1 Bibliothèque, Louvre, Paris, France//© Erich Lessing/Art Resource, NY 2 © Nik Wheeler/CORBIS 5 AP Images/Jean Clottes 7 Henri Lhote Collection, Musée de l'Homme, Paris, France//© Erich Lessing/Art Resource, NY 8 Archaeological Museum, Amman, Jordan//© Erich Lessing/Art Resource, NY 12 © British Museum, London, UK/The Bridgeman Art Library 13 Louvre, Paris, France//© Réunion des Musées Nationaux (Hervé Lewandowski)/Art Resource, NY 15 From Cultural Atlas of Mesopotamia & the Ancient Near East by Michael Roaf/Courtesy Andromeda Oxford Limited, Oxford, England 16 top left Louvre, Paris, France//© Réunion des Musées Nationaux (Hervé Lewandowski)/Art Resource, NY 16 bottom left © Sandro Vannini/CORBIS 16 right Kabah, Yucatan, Mexico//© Erich Lessing/Art Resource, NY 20 Museum of Fine Arts, Boston, USA//© Erich Lessing/Art Resource, NY 23 Bibliothèque, Louvre, Paris, France//© Erich Lessing/Art Resource, NY 25 © Adam Woolfitt/CORBIS 28 © British Museum, London, UK//Ancient Art and Architecture Collection Ltd./The Bridgeman Art Library 33 British Museum, London, UK//© Werner Forman/Art Resource, NY 35 Apadana, Persepolis, Iran//© The Art Archive/Gianni Dagli Orti

CHAPTER 2

39 © The Trustees of the Chester Beatty Library (InE 1479), Dublin, Ireland/The Bridgeman Art Library 41 left Mohenjo-Daro, Pakistan//© Borromeo/Art Resource, NY 41 right © William J. Duiker 42 © National Museum of India, New Delhi, India/The Bridgeman Art Library 43 © The Art Archive/Heraklion Museum, Crete, Greece/Gianni Dagli Orti 44 Archaeological Museum, New Delhi, India//© Scala/Art Resource, NY 52 © Atlantide Phototravel (Massimo Borchi)/CORBIS 54 © William J. Duiker 55 Elephanta, Bombay, India//© Charles & Josette Lenars/CORBIS 56 left © William J. Duiker 56 right St. Catherine Monastery, Mount Sinai, Sinai Desert, Egypt//© Erich Lessing/Art Resource, NY 57 Dhanek Stupa at Sarnath, Varanasi, Uttar Pradesh, India//© age fotostock/SuperStock 58 Great Stupa, Sanchi, India//© SuperStock 60 © Sarnath, Uttar Pradesh, India/The Bridgeman Art Library 63 left Ajanta. Cave No. 26, Maharashtra, India//© age fotostock/SuperStock 63 right © Abbey of Saint-Philibert, Tournus, France//Lauros/Giraudon/The Bridgeman Art Library 64 © William J. Duiker

CHAPTER 3

67 © Howard Sochurek/Time Life Pictures/Getty Images 69 left & right © William J. Duiker 70 British Museum, London, UK//© Werner Forman/Art Resource, NY 72 left Banpo Neolithic Archaeological Site and Museum, Chanyan, Shaanxi, China//© Lowell Georgia/CORBIS 72 top right © William J. Duiker 72 bottom right © Egyptian National Museum, Cairo, Egypt/The Bridgeman Art Library 73 © Ashmolean Museum, University of Oxford, UK/The Bridgeman Art Library 79 © Topham/The Image Works 86 top & bottom © William J. Duiker 87 left & right © William J. Duiker 89 © William J. Duiker 90 left © William J. Duiker 90 right © Martin Puddy/Getty Images 91 Ripley Center, Smithsonian Institution, Washington, DC//Photo © William J. Duiker 93 left & right © William J. Duiker

CHAPTER 4

96 © British Museum, London, UK/The Bridgeman Art Library 99 National Archaeological Museum, Athens, Greece//© Erich Lessing/Art Resource, NY 100 © AAAC/Topham/The Image Works 102 Museo Nazionale di Villa Giulia, Rome, Italy//© Scala/Art Resource, NY 106 left The Metropolitan Museum of Art, New York Fletcher Fund, 1932 (32.11.1)//Image copyright © The Metropolitan Museum of Art/Art Resource, NY 106 right Egyptian Museum, Cairo, Egypt//© Scala/Art Resource, NY 107 top © AAAC/Topham/The Image Works 107 bottom © The Art Archive/Acropolis Museum, Athens, Greece/Gianni Dagli Orti 111 top © Art Resource, NY 111 bottom © Adam Crowley/GettyImages 112 Museo Archeologico Nazionale, Naples, Italy//© Scala/Art Resource, NY 113 Museo Archeologico Nazionale, Naples, Italy//© Erich Lessing/Art Resource, NY 115 Image copyright © The Metropolitan Museum of Art/Art Resource, NY 117 © British Museum (GR, 1872.5-15.1), London, UK/HIP/Art Resource, NY 121 Warner Bros./The Kobal Collection/Jaap Buitendijk 124 The Metropolitan Museum of Art (09.39), New York, NY, USA//Image copyright © The Metropolitan Museum of Art/Art Resource, NY 125 left © The Art Archive/Kanellopoulos Museum, Athens, Greece/Gianni Dagli Orti 125 right National Museum of Pakistan, Karachi, Pakistan//© Borromeo/Art Resource, NY

CHAPTER 5

129 © Dulwich Picture Gallery, London, UK/The Bridgeman Art Library 133 top © Jon Arnold Images Ltd (Walter Bibikow)/Alamy 133 bottom © China Tourism Press/Getty Images 136 Louvre, Paris, France//© Erich Lessing/Art Resource, NY 137 Museo Archeologico Nazionale, Naples, Italy//© Scala/Art Resource, NY 138 Braccio Nuovo, Vatican Museums, Vatican State//© Scala/Art Resource, NY 141 © The Art Archive/Bardo Museum, Tunis, Tunisia/Gianni Dagli Orti 142 left © PictureNet/CORBIS 142 right © David Buffington/Getty Images

143 Museo Archeologico Nazionale, Naples, Italy//© Erich Lessing/Art Resource, NY 145 Bryna/Universal/The Kobal Collection 149 © Fitzwilliam Museum, University of Cambridge, UK/The Bridgeman Art Library 151 Catacomb of S. Domitilla, Rome, Italy//© Scala/Art Resource, NY 157 © William J. Duiker

CHAPTER 6

165 © Pierre Colombel/CORBIS 166 Museo Nacional de Antropologia e Historia, Mexico City, D.F., Mexico//© SEF/Art Resource, NY 169 © Claire L. Duiker 170 top © Will and Deni McIntyre/Photo Researchers, Inc. 170 bottom © SuperStock 171 © William J. Duiker 172 © William J. Duiker 173 From *Atlas of Ancient America* by Michael Coe, Dean Snow and Elizabeth Benson/Courtesy Andromeda Oxford Limited, Oxford, England 174 left © William J. Duiker 174 right © The Art Archive/National Anthropological Museum, Mexico/Gianni Dagli Orti 175 top © British Museum/Art Resource, NY 175 bottom © William J. Duiker 179 Museo Nacional de Antropologia e Historia, Mexico City, D.F., Mexico//© Werner Forman/Art Resource, NY 181 © Ann Ronan Picture Library/HIP/Art Resource, NY 182 © F. Ardito, UNEP/Peter Arnold Inc. 183 © The Art Archive/Museo del Oro, Lima, Peru/Gianni Dagli Orti 184 © Carol C. Coffin 186 © The Trustees of The British Museum, London/Art Resource, NY 187 © William J. Duiker

right © William J. Duiker 255 top and bottom © William J. Duiker 257 © William J. Duiker 260 left & right © William J. Duiker 261 left © William J. Duiker 261 right © Werner Forman/Art Resource, NY 262 © Lynn McLaren/Photo Researchers, Inc. 266 left & right © William J. Duiker 269 © William J. Duiker 270 left & right © William J. Duiker 271 © William J. Duiker

CHAPTER 10

274 © Pierre Colombel/CORBIS 277 top & bottom © William J. Duiker 279 © William J. Duiker 283 © Bibliothèque Nationale de Cartes et Plans, Paris, France/The Bridgeman Art Library 284 © Museum of Fine Arts, Boston, Massachusetts, USA, Special Chinese and Japanese Fund/The Bridgeman Art Library 285 © Claire L. Duiker 288 © The Art Archive/Topkapi Museum, Istanbul, Turkey/Gianni Dagli Orti 289 © National Palace Museum, Taipei, Taiwan/The Bridgeman Art Library 292 © Everett Collection 295 left & right © William J. Duiker 296 © William J. Duiker 298 © William J. Duiker 302 © The Art Archive/British Museum, London, UK 303 © The Art Archive/National Palace Museum, Taipei, Taiwan

CHAPTER 7

190 British Library, London, UK//© British Library Board. All Rights Reserved/The Bridgeman Art Library 193 top © John Bryson//Time Life Pictures/Getty Images 193 bottom © Mehmet Biber/Photo Researchers Inc. 199 Babylon, Iraq/© The Bridgeman Art Library 201 left Krak des Chevaliers, Syria//© Michael Nicholson/CORBIS 201 right Conwy Castle, Wales//© Fridmar Damm/zefa/CORBIS 204 top and bottom © William J. Duiker 206 Bibliothèque Nationale (Ms.arab. 5847) Paris, France//© Art Resource, NY 207 left & right © William J. Duiker 209 © Topkapi Palace Museum (Ms. Ahmet III, 3206), Istanbul, Turkey//The Bridgeman Art Library 210 Museum fuer Islamische Kunst, Staatliche Museen zu Berlin, Berlin, Germany//© Bildarchiv Preussischer Kulturbesitz (Georg Niedermeiser)/Art Resource, NY 214 © Scala/Art Resource, NY 215 top © William J. Duiker 215 bottom Mezquita Cathedral and Mosque in Cordoba//© Nik Wheeler/CORBIS 216 © William J. Duiker

CHAPTER 8

219 © Nick Greaves/Alamy 222 © Frans Lemmens/zefa/CORBIS 224 National Museum, Lagos, Nigeria//© Scala/Art Resource, NY 226 Musée de l'Homme, Paris, France//© Erich Lessing/Art Resource, NY 230 © William J. Duiker 232 top © William J. Duiker 232 bottom © British Library/HIP/Art Resource, NY 233 © The Art Archive/Musée des Arts Africains et Océaniens/Gianni Dagli Orti 236 © Ruth Petzold 238 National Museum of Ife, Ife, Nigeria//© Scala/Art Resource, NY 240 left © Werner Forman/Art Resource, NY 240 center © William J. Duiker 240 right © Borromeo/Art Resource, NY 241 © Jenny Pate/Getty Images

CHAPTER 9

245 © Thomas J. Abercrombie/National Geographic Image Collection 251 top & bottom © William J. Duiker 254 left &

CHAPTER 11

306 © William J. Duiker 308 left, center, right © William J. Duiker 311 © William J. Duiker 312 © Museum of Fine Arts, Boston, Massachusetts, USA, Fenollosa-Weld Collection/The Bridgeman Art Library 313 Eisei-bunko, Japan//© Sakamoto Photo Research Laboratory/CORBIS 317 Daiei/The Kobal Collection 321 left & right © William J. Duiker 322 left © William J. Duiker 322 right © Kaz Mori/Getty Images 324 © William J. Duiker 325 left © Bulguksa Temple, Mt. Tohamsan, Gyeongju, South Korea/The Bridgeman Art Library 325 right © William J. Duiker 327 top & bottom © William J. Duiker

CHAPTER 12

332 Bibliothèque de l'Arsenal, Paris, France//© Scala/Art Resource, NY 336 Bibliothèque Nationale, Paris, France//© Snark/Art Resource, NY 338 left © The Pierpont Morgan Library (MS M.736, f.9v.), New York, USA/Art Resource, NY 338 right © Robert Harding Picture Library Ltd (G. Richardson)/Alamy 341 left © The Art Archive/British Library, London, UK 341 right © The Art Archive/Freer Gallery of Art, Washington, DC, USA 343 Avco Embassy/The Kobal Collection 345 Bibliothèque de l'Arsenal, Paris, France//© Snark/Art Resource, NY 346 © British Library (Harley 4379, f.64), London, UK//HIP/Art Resource, NY 347 © Musée de la Tapisserie, Bayeux, France/With special authorisation of the city of Bayeux//The Bridgeman Art Library 354 © Musée de l'Assistance Publique, Hopitaux de Paris, France//Archives Charmet/The Bridgeman Art Library 357 left © The Art Archive/Gianni Dagli Orti 357 right © S. Grandadam/Photo Researchers, Inc. 358 left © Adam Woolfitt/CORBIS 358 right © Scala/Art Resource, NY

CHAPTER 13

363 S. Vitale, Ravenna, Italy//© Scala/Art Resource, NY 366 S. Vitale, Ravenna, Italy//© Scala/Art Resource, NY 367 S. Vitale, Ravenna, Italy//© Scala/Art Resource, NY 368 © Erich Lessing/Art Resource, NY 369 bottom Patio De Los Arrayanes (Patio of the Myrtles), Alhambra, Granada, Spain//© Vanni/Art Resource, NY 369 top left Trinity College (Ms. AI6, fol. 32v), Dublin, Ireland//© Art Resource, NY 369 top right St. Catherine Monastery, Mount Sinai, Sinai Desert, Egypt//© Erich Lessing/Art Resource, NY

374 Hagia Sophia, Istanbul, Turkey//© Erich Lessing/Art Resource, NY 380 Bibliothèque Royale Albert I (Ms. 13076-77, c.24t, Fol. 24v), Brussels, Belgium//© Snark/Art Resource, NY 383 © Bibliothèque Nationale (Fr 2643 f.165v), Paris, France/The Bridgeman Art Library 387 top © Scala/Art Resource, NY 387 bottom S. Maria delle Grazie, Milan, Italy//© Scala/Art Resource, NY 388 Accademia, Florence, Italy//© Scala/Art Resource, NY

FOR SEVERAL MILLION YEARS after primates first appeared on the surface of the earth, human beings lived in small communities, seeking to survive by hunting, fishing, and foraging in a frequently hostile environment. Then suddenly, in the space of a few thousand years, there was an abrupt change of direction as humans in a few widely scattered areas of the globe began to master the art of cultivating food crops. As food production increased, the population in those areas rose correspondingly, and people began to congregate in larger communities. Governments were formed to provide protection and other needed services to the local population. Cities appeared and became the focal point of cultural and religious development. Historians refer to this process as the beginnings of civilization.

For generations, historians in Europe and the United States pointed to the rise of such civilizations as marking the origins of the modern world. Courses on Western civilization conventionally began with a chapter or two on the emergence of advanced societies in Egypt and Mesopotamia and then proceeded to ancient Greece and the Roman Empire. From Greece and Rome, the road led directly to the rise of modern civilization in the West.

There is nothing inherently wrong with this approach. Important aspects of our world today can indeed be traced back to these early civilizations, and all human beings the world over owe a considerable debt to their achievements. But all too often this interpretation has been used to imply that the course of civilization has been linear, leading directly from the emergence of agricultural societies in ancient Mesopotamia to the rise of advanced industrial societies in Europe and North America. Until recently, most courses on world history taught in the United States routinely focused almost exclusively on the rise of the West, with only a passing glance at other parts of the world, such as Africa, India, and East Asia. The contributions made by those societies to the culture and technology of our own time were often passed over in silence.

Two major reasons have been advanced to justify this approach. Some people have argued that it is more important that young minds understand the roots of their own heritage than that of peoples elsewhere in the world. In many cases, however, the motivation for this Eurocentric approach has been the belief that since the time of Socrates and Aristotle, Western civilization has been the sole driving force in the evolution of human society.

Such an interpretation, however, represents a serious distortion of the process. During most of the course

of human history, the most advanced civilizations have been not in the West, but in East Asia or the Middle East. A relatively brief period of European dominance culminated with the era of imperialism in the late nineteenth century, when the political, military, and economic power of the advanced nations of the West spanned the globe. During recent generations, however, that dominance has gradually eroded, partly as the result of changes taking place in Western societies and partly because new centers of development are emerging elsewhere on the globe—notably in Asia, with the growing economic strength of China and India and many of their neighbors.

World history, then, has been a complex process in which many branches of the human community have taken an active part, and the dominance of any one area of the world has been a temporary rather than a permanent phenomenon. It will be our purpose in this book to present a balanced picture of this story, with all respect for the richness and diversity of the tapestry of the human experience. Due attention must be paid to the rise of the West, of course, since that has been the most dominant aspect of world history in recent centuries. But the contributions made by other peoples must be given adequate consideration as well, not only in the period prior to 1500, when the major centers of civilization were located in Asia, but also in our own day, where a multipolar picture of development is clearly beginning to emerge.

Anyone who wishes to teach or write about world history must decide whether to present the topic as an integrated whole or as a collection of different cultures. The world that we live in today, of course, is in many respects an interdependent one in terms of economics as well as culture and communications, a reality that is often expressed by the phrase "global village." The convergence of peoples across the surface of the earth into an integrated world system began in early times and intensified after the rise of capitalism in the early modern era. In growing recognition of this trend, historians trained in global history, as well as instructors in the growing number of world history courses, have now begun to speak and write of a "global approach" that turns attention away from the study of individual civilizations and focuses instead on the "big picture" or, as the world historian Fernand Braudel termed it, interpreting world history as a river with no banks.

On the whole, this development is to be welcomed as a means of bringing the common elements of the evolution of human society to our attention. But there is a problem involved in this approach. For the vast majority of their time on earth, human beings have often lived in partial or virtually total isolation from each other. Differences in climate, location, and geographical features have created human societies very different from each other in culture and historical experience. Only in relatively recent times (the commonly accepted date has long been the beginning of the age of European exploration at the end of the fifteenth century, but some would now push it back to the era of the Mongol Empire or even further) have cultural interchanges begun to create a common "world system," in which events taking place in one part of the world are rapidly transmitted throughout the globe, often with momentous consequences. In recent generations, of course, the process of global interdependence has been proceeding even more rapidly. Nevertheless, even now the process is by no means complete, as ethnic and regional differences continue to exist and to shape the course of world history. The tenacity of these differences and sensitivities is reflected not only in the rise of internecine conflicts in such divergent areas as Africa, India, and eastern Europe but also in the emergence in recent years of such regional organizations as the Organization of African Unity, the Association for the Southeast Asian Nations, and the European Union.

The second problem is a practical one. College students today are all too often not well informed about the distinctive character of civilizations such as China and India and, without sufficient exposure to the historical evolution of such societies, will assume all too readily that the peoples in these countries have had historical experiences similar to ours and will respond to various stimuli in a similar fashion to those living in western Europe or the United States. If it is a mistake to ignore those forces that link us together, it is equally a mistake to underestimate those factors that continue to divide us and to differentiate us into a world of diverse peoples.

Our response to this challenge has been to adopt a global approach to world history while at the same time attempting to do justice to the distinctive character and development of individual civilizations and regions of the world. The presentation of individual cultures is especially important in Parts I and II, which cover a time when it is generally agreed that the process of global integration was not yet far advanced. Later chapters adopt a more comparative and thematic approach, in deference to the greater number of connections that have been established among the world's peoples since the fifteenth and sixteenth centuries. Part V consists of a series of chapters that center on individual regions of the world while at the same time focusing on common problems related to the Cold War and the rise of global problems such as overproduction and environmental pollution.

We have sought balance in another way as well. Many textbooks tend to simplify the content of history courses by emphasizing an intellectual or political perspective or, most recently, a social perspective, often at the expense of sufficient details in a chronological framework. This approach is confusing to students whose high school social studies programs have often neglected a systematic study of world history. We have attempted to write a well-balanced work in which political, economic, social, religious, intellectual, cultural, and military history are integrated into a chronologically ordered synthesis.

Features of the Text

To enliven the past and let readers see for themselves the materials that historians use to create their pictures of the past, we have included **primary sources** (boxed documents) in each chapter that are keyed to the discussion in the text. The documents include examples of the religious, artistic, intellectual, social, economic, and political aspects of life in different societies and reveal in a vivid fashion what civilization meant to the individual men and women who shaped it by their actions. We have added questions to help guide students in analyzing the documents, as well as references to related documents that are available online.

Each chapter has a **lengthy introduction and conclusion** to help maintain the continuity of the narrative and to provide a synthesis of important themes. Anecdotes in the chapter introductions convey more dramatically the major theme or themes of each chapter. **Timelines**, with thumbnail images illustrating major events and figures, at the end of each chapter enable students to see the major developments of an era at a glance and within cross-cultural categories, while the more **detailed chronologies** reinforce the events discussed in the text. An **annotated bibliography** at the end of each chapter reviews the most recent literature on each period and also gives references to some of the older, "classic" works in each field.

Updated maps and extensive illustrations serve to deepen the reader's understanding of the text. **Map captions** are designed to enrich students' awareness of the importance of geography to history, and numerous **spot maps** enable students to see at a glance the region or subject being discussed in the text. Map captions also include a question to guide students' reading of the map, as well as references to online interactive versions of the maps. To facilitate understanding of cultural movements, illustrations of artistic works discussed in the text are placed near the discussions.

Chapter outlines and focus questions, including critical thinking questions, at the beginning of each chapter give students a useful overview and guide them to the main subjects of each chapter. The focus questions are then repeated at the beginning of each major section in the chapter. A **glossary of important terms** (now boldfaced in the text when they are introduced and defined) and a **pronunciation guide** are provided at the back of the book to maximize reader comprehension.

Comparative essays, keyed to the seven major themes of world history (see p. xxxi), enable us to more concretely draw comparisons and contrasts across geographical, cultural, and chronological lines. Some new essays as well as illustrations for every essay have been added to the sixth edition. **Comparative illustrations,** also keyed to the seven major themes of world history, continue to be a feature in each chapter. We have also added focus questions to both the comparative essays and the comparative illustrations to help students develop their analytical skills. We hope that both the comparative essays and the comparative illustrations will assist instructors who wish to encourage their students to adopt a comparative approach to their understanding of the human experience.

New to This Edition

After reexamining the entire book and analyzing the comments and reviews of many colleagues who have found the book to be a useful instrument for introducing their students to world history, we have also made a number of other changes for the sixth edition. In the first place, we have reorganized some of the material. Chapter 12, "The Making of Europe," now focuses entirely on medieval Europe to 1400. A new Chapter 13, "The Byzantine Empire and Crisis and Recovery in the West," covers the Byzantine Empire with new material as well as the crises in the fourteenth century and the Renaissance in Europe. Chapter 7 is devoted exclusively to the rise of Islam. Chapter 19 was reorganized and focuses now on "The Beginnings of Modernization: Industrialization and Nationalism in the Nineteenth Century." Chapter 20 now covers "The Americas and Society and Culture in the West" in the nineteenth century. Also new to the sixth edition is an Epilogue, "A Global Civilization," which focuses on the global economy, global culture, globalization and the environmental crisis, the social challenges of globalization, and new global movements.

We have also continued to strengthen the global framework of the book, but not at the expense of reducing the attention assigned to individual regions of the world. New material has been added to most chapters to help students be aware of similar developments globally, including new comparative sections.

The enthusiastic response to the primary sources (boxed documents) led us to evaluate the content of each document carefully and add new documents throughout the text, including a new feature called **Opposing Viewpoints,** which presents a comparison of two or three primary sources in order to facilitate student analysis of historical documents. This feature appears in nineteen chapters and includes such topics as "Women in Athens and Sparta," "The Siege of Jerusalem: Christian and Muslim Perspectives," "Three Voices of Peacemaking," "Action or Inaction: An Ideological Dispute in Medieval China," "White Man's Burden, Black Man's Sorrow," and "Who Started the Cold War: American and Soviet Perspectives." Focus questions are included to help students evaluate the documents.

An additional new feature is **Film & History,** which presents a brief analysis of the plot as well as the historical significance, value, and accuracy of sixteen films, including such movies as *Alexander, Marco Polo, The Mission,*

Khartoum, The Last Emperor, Gandhi, and The Lives of Others.

A number of new illustrations and maps have been added, and the bibliographies have been reorganized by topic and revised to take account of newly published material. The chronologies and maps have been fine-tuned as well, to help the reader locate in time and space the multitude of individuals and place names that appear in the book. To keep up with the ever-growing body of historical scholarship, new or revised material has been added throughout the book on many topics.

Chapter 1   New material on Neolithic Age, early civilizations around the world, and Sumerian social classes. New sections, "The Spread of Egyptian Influence: Nubia" and "Nomadic Peoples: Impact of the Indo-Europeans," with a new subsection on "The Hittites." Revisions to the section on the Code of Hammurabi and material on ancient Israel and Zoroastrianism. New spot maps on early civilizations in India and Peru. New Opposing Viewpoints feature on Akhenaten's *Hymn to Aten* and Psalm 104 of the Hebrew Bible.

Chapter 2   Added material on the arrival of Indo-European peoples. New boxed document on the role of women in ancient India. New Comparative Illustration "Buddha and Jesus."

Chapter 3   New material on the arrival of *Homo sapiens* in East Asia, the "mother culture" hypothesis and the origins of the Zhou dynasty, and jade, tea culture, and the role of women. Revised maps. New Comparative Illustration on the afterlife, rice culture, and bronze work. Coverage of the Han dynasty has been moved to Chapter 5.

Chapter 4   New material on the Greek way of war and a new section on "Foreign Influence on Early Greek Culture," emphasizing impact of Phoenicians and Egyptians on early Greek culture. New Opposing Viewpoints feature "Women in Athens and Sparta" and new Film & History feature, *Alexander.* New comparative essay, "The Axial Age."

Chapter 5   New section on "Evolution of the Roman Army" and new material on early Christianity. New Film & History feature, *Spartacus.* New Opposing Viewpoints feature "Roman Authorities and a Christian on Christianity."

Chapter 6   New introduction and new materials on the arrival of *Homo sapiens* in the Americas. Additional material on Zapotec culture, the Olmecs, the "mother culture" hypothesis, and the Maya, including the writing system, city-state rivalries, and the causes of collapse. Expanded coverage of Caral and early cultures in South America. All material on the arrival of the Spanish has been relocated to Chapter 14. Revised and new maps.

Chapter 7   Major expansion of material on Islamic culture, with relocation of Byzantine material to the new Chapter 13. New information on military tactics, political and economic institutions of the Arabic empire, and the role of the environment. Major expansion of material on Andalusian culture. New material on science and technology in the Islamic world. New Film & History feature, *The Message*, on the life of Muhammad. Opposing Viewpoints on differing views of the Crusades. New map.

Chapter 8 Additional material on the role of trade in ancient Africa. New boxes on gold trade and nomadic culture. New map on the expansion of Islam in China.

Chapter 9 Additional material on trade and missionary activity in South Asia and two early states of Southeast Asia, Funan and Angkor. Expansion of the section on science and technology. New section on the spread of Polynesian culture in the Pacific. New document on Ibn Battuta in India. New map on spread of religion. New Film & History feature, *Rashomon*.

Chapter 10 Major new section on the Mongol Empire, with boxed document and illustration of Genghis Khan. New Opposing Viewpoints on Taoist and Confucian attitudes.

Chapter 11 New introduction. New materials on the origins of Korean and Vietnamese civilizations and the universalist nature of Chinese civilization. New Film & History feature, *Marco Polo*.

Chapter 12 Reorganized chapter to focus entirely on medieval Europe to 1400. Sections on "The Crises of the Late Middle Ages and Recovery: The Renaissance" were placed in the new Chapter 13. New material on Arian Christians and kingdom of the Franks, technological changes in the High Middle Ages and their relationship to China and the Middle East, chivalry, England and the Holy Roman Empire in the High Middle Ages, and Viking expansion and the early Crusades. New sections on "Popular Religion in the High Middle Ages" and "Effects of the Crusades." New documents, "Murder in the Cathedral" and "University Students and Violence at Oxford." New Film & History feature, *The Lion in Winter*. New Comparative Essay, "Cities in the Medieval World."

Chapter 13 This is a new chapter, "The Byzantine Empire and Crisis and Recovery in the West," with the following major sections: "From Eastern Roman to Byzantine Empire"; "The Zenith of Byzantine Civilization (750–1025)"; "Decline and Fall of the Byzantine Empire (1025–1453)"; "The Crises of the Fourteenth Century"; and "Recovery: The Renaissance." New material on the Byzantine Empire and educated women in the Renaissance. New section, "The Black Death: From Asia to Europe," with a subsection on "The Role of the Mongols." New documents, "A Byzantine Emperor Gives Military Advice"; "The Achievements of Basil II"; "The Christian Crusaders Capture Constantinople," "The Fall of Constantinople," and "A Woman's Defense of Learning."

Chapter 14 New material on the role of Islamic traders and the Songhai empire. New Film & History feature, *Mutiny on the Bounty*.

Chapter 15 New material on Zwingli and the Zwinglian Reformation and a new section, "A Military Revolution?" New Opposing Viewpoints feature, "A Christian Reformation Debate: Conflict at Marburg."

Chapter 16 Additional material on the Ottoman Empire. New document from Babur's memoirs. Revised maps.

Chapter 17 Expanded material on Vietnam and additional information on technological developments in China.

Chapter 18 New material on the Haitian revolution and on Napoleon. New Opposing Viewpoints feature, "The Natural Rights of the French People: Two Views." New Film & History feature, *The Mission*.

Chapter 19 Reorganized to focus on "The Beginnings of Modernization: Industrialization and Nationalism in the Nineteenth Century," with the following major sections: "The Industrial Revolution and Its Impact"; "The Growth of Industrial Prosperity"; "Reaction and Revolution: The Growth of Nationalism"; "National Unification and the National State, 1848–1871"; and "The European State, 1871–1914." New material on urban living conditions, the principle of legitimacy, the nature of nationalism, and the Revolution of 1830. New Opposing Viewpoints feature, "Response to Revolution: Two Perspectives."

Chapter 20 Reorganized to focus on "The Americas and Society and Culture in the West," with the following major sections: "Latin America in the Nineteenth and Early Twentieth Centuries"; "The North American Neighbors: The United States and Canada"; "The Emergence of Mass Society"; "Cultural Life: Romanticism and Realism in the Western World"; and "Toward the Modern Consciousness: Intellectual and Cultural Developments." New material on Latin America, including new sections on "The Wars for Independence" and "The Difficulties of Nation Building." New material on the United States, especially a new section on "Slavery and the Coming of War" and new material on the Civil War and Reconstruction. New material on Canada, Charles Dickens, and realism in South America. New Opposing Viewpoints feature, "Advice to Women: Two Views." New document, "Simón Bolívar on Government in Latin America."

Chapter 21 Chapter revised to sharpen focus on various areas of Africa and Asia. New Film & History feature, *Khartoum*.

Chapter 22 Revised maps. New Film & History feature, *The Last Emperor*.

Chapter 23 Clarified points on the Russian Revolution. New material on the background to the Russian Revolution of 1917. New section on "The Impact of World War I" to provide better context on material of the 1920s. New Opposing Viewpoints feature, "Three Voices of Peacemaking," and new Film & History feature, *Paths of Glory*.

Chapter 24 Revised and expanded section on Palestine between the wars. Expanded coverage of Japanese literature, Mexico, and Latin American literature. New Film & History feature, *Gandhi*. Revised maps and new document on Japanese writer Nagai Kafu.

Chapter 25 New material on "Retreats from Democracy: Dictatorial Regimes" to provide background on the rise of dictatorial regimes, Hitler's invasion of Poland,

and the home front in the United States. New Opposing Viewpoints feature, "The Munich Conference: Two Views." New Film & History feature, *Europa, Europa.*

Chapter 26 Expanded coverage of the opening of the Cold War, the Middle East, the Vietnam War, and Cold War rivalry in the Third World. Revised section on who started the Cold War. New Comparative Essay. New Film & History feature, *Missiles of October.* New Opposing Viewpoints feature.

Chapter 27 Expanded and updated material on contemporary China and Soviet literature.

Chapter 28 New material on France, Germany, and Great Britain since 1995; eastern Europe after communism; immigrants to Europe; and Canada, the United States, and Latin America since 1995. Reorganized material on society in the Western world and added new material on antiwar protests. New section, "Art in the Age of Commerce: The 1980s and 1990s." New document, "A Child's Account of the Shelling of Sarajevo." New Film & History feature, *The Lives of Others.*

Chapter 29 Revised introduction. Additional material on the population problem, Africa in the Cold War, and the role of international organizations in Africa. Section on the question of Palestine has been reworked and expanded. Updated coverage on countries in Africa and the Middle East.

Chapter 30 All sections updated. New section focuses on the Little Tigers of Asia and the role of China. New Film & History feature, *The Year of Living Dangerously.*

Epilogue: A Global Civilization New to the sixth edition. Contains a new document, "A Warning to Humanity."

Because courses in world history at American and Canadian colleges and universities follow different chronological divisions, a one-volume comprehensive edition, a two-volume edition of this text, and a volume covering events to 1500 are being made available to fit the needs of instructors. Teaching and learning ancillaries include the following:

Instructor Resources PowerLecture with JoinIn® ISBN-10: 0495572632 This dual platform, all-in-one multimedia resource includes the Instructor's Manual, the Resource Integration Guide, and Microsoft® PowerPoint® slides with lecture outlines and images. Also included is ExamView, an easy-to-use assessment and tutorial system that allows you to create, deliver, and customize tests and study guides (both print and online) in minutes. ExamView guides you step-by-step through the process of creating tests; you can even see the test you are creating on the screen exactly as it will print or display online. You can build tests of up to 250 questions using up to 12 question types.

HistoryFinder This searchable online database allows instructors to quickly and easily download thousands of assets, including art, photographs, maps, primary sources,

and audio/video clips. Each asset downloads directly into a Microsoft® PowerPoint® slide, allowing instructors to quickly and easily create exciting PowerPoint presentations for their classrooms.

Instructor's Manual with Test Bank Prepared by Eugene Larson of Los Angeles Pierce College, this expanded and improved manual includes chapter outlines and summaries; suggested lecture topics; discussion questions pertaining to the primary source documents presented in the text; suggested student activities, map exercises and links to some of the best and most relevant websites available. Exam questions include essays, identifications, multiple choice, and true/false questions.

WebTutor™ for Blackboard® Printed Access Card: ISBN-10: 0495833754 Instant Access Code: ISBN-10: 049583372X With WebTutor's text-specific, pre-formatted content and total flexibility, you can easily create and manage your own custom course website! WebTutor's course management tool gives you the ability to provide virtual office hours, post syllabi, set up threaded discussions, track student progress with the quizzing material, and much more. For students, WebTutor offers real-time access to a full array of study tools, including animations and videos that bring the book's topics to life, plus chapter outlines, summaries, learning objectives, glossary flashcards (with audio), practice quizzes, and weblinks. Instructors can access password-protected Instructor Resources for lectures and class preparation. WebTutor also provides robust communication tools, such as a course calendar, asynchronous discussion, real-time chat, a whiteboard, and an integrated e-mail system.

WebTutor™ for WebCT® Printed Access Card: ISBN-10: 0495833746 Instant Access Code: ISBN-10: 0495833738 With WebTutor's text-specific, pre-formatted content and total flexibility, you can easily create and manage your own custom course website! WebTutor's course management tool gives you the ability to provide virtual office hours, post syllabi, set up threaded discussions, track student progress with the quizzing material, and much more. For students, WebTutor offers real-time access to a full array of study tools, including animations and videos that bring the book's topics to life, plus chapter outlines, summaries, learning objectives, glossary flashcards (with audio), practice quizzes, and weblinks. Instructors can access password-protected Instructor Resources for lectures and class preparation. WebTutor also provides robust communication tools, such as a course calendar, asynchronous discussion, real-time chat, a whiteboard, and an integrated e-mail system.

Transparency Acetates for World History ISBN-10: 0495128686 | ISBN-13: 9780495128687 Each package contains more than 100 four-color map images from the text and other accredited sources. Packages are three-hole punched and shrink-wrapped. Map commentary provided by James Harrison of Siena College.

Student Resources Document Exercise Workbook for World History, Volume 1, 3rd ISBN-10: 0534571778 | ISBN-13: 9780534571771 Prepared by Donna Van Raaphorst of Cuyahoga Community College, this workbook provides a collection of exercises based on primary sources in history. Contact your local sales representative for information on packaging this book with the text of your choice.

Document Exercise Workbook for World History, 3rd ISBN-10: 0534571786 | ISBN-13: 9780534571788 Prepared by Donna Van Raaphorst of Cuyahoga Community College, this workbook provides a collection of exercises based on primary sources in history. Contact your local sales representative for information on packaging this book with the text of your choice.

Journey of Civilization: The World and Western Traditions CD-ROM, Bundle Version (Windows/Macintosh) ISBN-10: 0314206205 | ISBN-13: 9780314206206 Prepared by David Redles of Cuyahoga Community College, this fully interactive CD-ROM covers six major time periods, addressing topics from a variety of themes and perspectives. It contains text, photos, video, audio, animations, interactive exercises, simulations, and graphics that present and explain topics in a visually exciting and stimulating manner. Students select the time period and country they want to explore from a map and timeline on the screen.

Magellan World History Atlas ISBN-10: 0534568661 | ISBN-13: 9780534568665 This atlas contains 45 four-color historical maps in a practical 8" × 10" format.

Map Exercise Workbook, Volume 1, 3rd ISBN-10: 0534571794 | ISBN-13: 9780534571795 Prepared by Cynthia Kosso of Northern Arizona University, this workbook features approximately 30 map exercises. It is designed to help students feel comfortable with maps by having them work with different kinds of maps to identify places and improve their geographic understanding of world history. Also includes critical thinking questions for each unit.

Map Exercise Workbook, Volume II ISBN-10: 0534571808 | ISBN-13: 9780534571801 Prepared by Cynthia Kosso of Northern Arizona University, this workbook features approximately 30 map exercises. It is designed to help students feel comfortable with maps by having them work with different kinds of maps to identify places and improve their geographic understanding of world history. Also includes critical thinking questions for each unit.

Scientific American—Ancient Civilizations ISBN-10: 0495008036 | ISBN-13: 9780495008033 Bring your students into current activity in the field with *Scientific American* magazine. As an exclusive offer from Cengage, this magazine is available as a bundle item for your course. This issue includes coverage by region, including such topics as the Iceman, Death Cults of Prehistoria Malta, Keys to the Lost Indus Cities, Woman and Men at Catalhoyuk, Rock Art in Southern Africa, Life and Death in Nabada, Tapestry of Power in a Mesopotamian City, Daily Life in Ancient Egypt, Great Zimbabwe, Precious Metal Objects of the Middle Sican, Life in the Provinces of the Aztec Empire, and Reading the Bones of La Florida.

Printed AP Instructor's Guide This instructor's guide is designed specifically for teachers of Advanced Placement World History courses. It includes correlations of the text and the test bank with the most recent released AP exam; sample syllabi; essays on "Making AP Accessible" and "Utilizing Library Resources"; "What to Do After the AP Exam"; learning objectives; lecture outlines; lesson plans keyed to the AP World History Standards; suggested class times; glossary items; lecture and discussion topics; group work suggestions and possible projects; and document-based questions (DBQs). Also available on the instructor's website.

Wadsworth World History Resource Center 2-Semester Instant Access Code Wadsworth's World History Resource Center gives your students access to a "virtual reader" with hundreds of primary sources such as speeches, letters, legal documents and transcripts, poems plus maps, simulations, timelines, and additional images that bring history to life, along with interactive assignable exercises. A map feature including Google Earth™ coordinates and exercises will aid in student comprehension of geography and use of maps. Students can compare the traditional textbook map with an aerial view of the location today. It's an ideal resource for study, review, and research.

ACKNOWLEDGMENTS

BOTH AUTHORS GRATEFULLY acknowledge that without the generosity of many others, this project could not have been completed.

William Duiker would like to thank Kumkum Chatterjee and On-cho Ng for their helpful comments about issues related to the history of India and premodern China. His longtime colleague Cyril Griffith, now deceased, was a cherished friend and a constant source of information about modern Africa. Art Goldschmidt has been of invaluable assistance in reading several chapters of the manuscript, as well as in unraveling many of the mysteries of Middle Eastern civilization. Ian Bell, Carol Coffin, and Ruth Petzold have provided illustrations, and Dale Peterson has been an unending source of useful news items. Finally, he remains profoundly grateful to his wife, Yvonne V. Duiker, Ph.D. She has not only given her usual measure of love and support when this appeared to be an insuperable task, but she has also contributed her own time and expertise to enrich the sections on art and literature, thereby adding life and sparkle to this, as well as the earlier editions of the book. To her, and to his daughters Laura and Claire, he will be forever thankful for bringing joy to his life.

Jackson Spielvogel would like to thank Art Goldschmidt, David Redles, and Christine Colin for their time and ideas. Daniel Haxall of Kutztown University and Kathryn Spielvogel of SUNY-Buffalo provided valuable assistance with materials on postwar art, popular culture, Postmodern art and thought, and the digital age. Above all, he thanks his family for their support. The gifts of love, laughter, and patience from his daughters, Jennifer and Kathryn; his sons, Eric and Christian; his daughters-in-law, Liz and Laurie; and his sons-in-law, Daniel and Eddie, were especially valuable. Diane, his wife and best friend, provided him with editorial assistance, wise counsel, and the loving support that made a project of this magnitude possible.

Thanks to Wadsworth's comprehensive review process, many historians were asked to evaluate our manuscript. We are grateful to the following for the innumerable suggestions that have greatly improved our work. Members of this edition's Editorial Review Board (asterisked) deserve our particular thanks.

Najia Aarim
SUNY College at Fredonia

Jacob Abadi
U.S. Air Force Academy

Henry Maurice Abramson
Florida Atlantic University

*Wayne Ackerson
Salisbury University

Charles F. Ames Jr.
Salem State College

Nancy Anderson
Loyola University

J. Lee Annis
Montgomery College

Monty Armstrong
Cerritos High School

Gloria M. Aronson
Normandale College

Charlotte Beahan
Murray State University

Doris Bergen
University of Vermont

*Martin Berger
Youngstown State University

Deborah Biffton
University of Wisconsin—LaCrosse

Charmarie Blaisdell
Northeastern University

Brian Bonhomme
Youngstown State University

Patricia J. Bradley
Auburn University at Montgomery

Dewey Browder
Austin Peay State University

Nancy Cade
Pikeville College

Antonio Calabria
University of Texas at San Antonio

Alice-Catherine Carls
University of Tennessee—Martin

*Harry Carpenter
Western Piedmont Community College

Yuan Ling Chao
Middle Tennessee State University

Mark W. Chavalas
University of Wisconsin

Hugh Clark
Ursinus College

Joan Coffey
Sam Houston State University

Eleanor A. Congdon
Youngstown State University

Jason P. Coy
College of Charleston

Edward R. Crowther
Adams State College

John Davis
Radford University

Ross Dunn
San Diego State University

Lane Earn
University of Wisconsin—Oshkosh

Roxanne Easley
Central Washington University

C. T. Evans
Northern Virginia Community College

Edward L. Farmer
University of Minnesota

William W. Farris
University of Tennessee

Ronald Fritze
Lamar University

Joe Fuhrmann
Murray State University

Robert Gerlich
Loyola University

Marc J. Gilbert
North Georgia College

xxviii

William J. Gilmore-Lehne
Richard Stockton College of New Jersey

Richard M. Golden
University of North Texas

Candice Goucher
Washington State University—Vancouver

Joseph M. Gowaskie
Rider College

Jonathan Grant
Florida State University

Don Gustafson
Augsburg College

Deanna Haney
Lansing Community College

Jason Hardgrave
University of Southern Indiana

Jay Harmon
Catholic High School

Ed Haynes
Winthrop College

Marilynn Jo Hitchens
University of Colorado—Denver

Tamara L. Hunt
University of Southern Indiana

Linda Kerr
University of Alberta at Edmonton

David Koeller
North Park University

Zoltan Kramar
Central Washington University

Douglas Lea
Kutztown University

David Leinweber
Emory University

Thomas T. Lewis
Mount Senario College

Craig A. Lockard
University of Wisconsin—Green Bay

George Longenecker
Norwich University

Norman D. Love
El Paso Community College

Robert Luczak
Vincennes University

Aran MacKinnon
State University of West Georgia

*Matthew Maher
Metropolitan State College of Denver

Patrick Manning
Northeastern University

Eric Mayer
Victor Valley College

Dolores Nason McBroome
Humboldt State University

John McDonald
Northern Essex Community College

Andrea McElderry
University of Louisville

Jeff McEwen
Chattanooga State Technical Community College

Margaret McKee
Castilleja High School

Nancy McKnight
Stockton High School

Robert McMichael
Wayland Baptist University

David L. McMullen
University of North Carolina at Charlotte

John A. Mears
Southern Methodist University

David A. Meier
Dickinson State University

Marc A. Meyer
Berry College

Stephen S. Michot
Mississippi County Community College

John Ashby Morton
Benedict College

William H. Mulligan
Murray State University

*Henry A. Myers
James Madison University

Marian P. Nelson
University of Nebraska at Omaha

Sandy Norman
Florida Atlantic University

Patrick M. O'Neill
Broome Community College

Roger Pauly
University of Central Arkansas

Norman G. Raiford
Greenville Technical College

Jane Rausch
University of Massachusetts—Amherst

Dianna K. Rhyan
Columbus State Community College

Merle Rife
Indiana University of Pennsylvania

Patrice C. Ross
Columbus State Community College

John Rossi
LaSalle University

Eric C. Rust
Baylor University

Maura M. Ryan
Springbrook High School

Jane Samson
University of Alberta

Keith Sandiford
University of Manitoba

Elizabeth Sarkinnen
Mount Hood Community College

Pamela Sayre
Henry Ford College

Bill Schell
Murray State University

*Linda Scherr
Mercer County Community College

Robert M. Seltzer
Hunter College

Patrick Shan
Grand Valley State University

David Shriver
Cuyahoga Community College

Amos E. Simpson
University of Southwestern Louisiana

Wendy Singer
Kenyon College

Marvin Slind
Washington State University

Paul Smith
Washington State University

John Snetsinger
California Polytechnic State University

George Stow
LaSalle University

John C. Swanson
Utica College of Syracuse

Patrick Tabor
Chemeketa Community College

Tom Taylor
Seattle University

John G. Tuthill
University of Guam

Salli Vaegis
Georgia Perimeter College

Joanne Van Horn
Fairmont State College

*Peter von Sivers
University of Utah

Christopher J. Ward
Clayton College and State University

Pat Weber
University of Texas—El Paso

Douglas L. Wheeler
University of New Hampshire

David L. White
Appalachian State University

Elmira B. Wicker
Southern University—Baton Rouge

Glee Wilson
Kent State University

Laura Matysek Wood
Tarrant County College

Harry Zee
Cumberland County College

The authors are truly grateful to the people who have helped us to produce this book. We especially want to thank Clark Baxter, whose faith in our ability to do this project was inspiring. Sue Gleason and Margaret McAndrew Beasley thoughtfully and cheerfully guided the overall development of the sixth edition. Bruce Emmer was, as usual, an outstanding copyeditor. Abbie Baxter provided valuable assistance in obtaining permissions for the illustrations. John Orr, of Orr Book Services, was as cooperative and cheerful as he was competent in matters of production management.

ONE OF THE MOST difficult challenges in studying world history is coming to grips with the multitude of names, words, and phrases in unfamiliar languages. Unfortunately, this problem has no easy solution. We have tried to alleviate the difficulty, where possible, by providing an English-language translation of foreign words or phrases, a glossary, and a pronunciation guide. The issue is especially complicated in the case of Chinese, since two separate systems are commonly used to transliterate the spoken Chinese language into the Roman alphabet. The Wade-Giles system, invented in the nineteenth century, was the most frequently used until recent years, when the pinyin system was adopted by the People's Republic of China as its own official form of transliteration. We have opted to use the latter, since it appears to be gaining acceptance in the United States, but the initial use of a Chinese word is accompanied by its Wade-Giles equivalent in parentheses for the benefit of those who may encounter the term in their outside reading.

In our examination of world history, we need also to be aware of the dating of time. In recording the past, historians try to determine the exact time when events occurred. World War II in Europe, for example, began on September 1, 1939, when Adolf Hitler sent German troops into Poland, and ended on May 7, 1945, when Germany surrendered. By using dates, historians can place events in order and try to determine the development of patterns over periods of time.

If someone asked you when you were born, you would reply with a number, such as 1990. In the United States, we would all accept that number without question, because it is part of the dating system followed in the Western world (Europe and the Western Hemisphere). In this system, events are dated by counting backward or forward from the birth of Jesus Christ (assumed to be the birth year 1). An event that took place 400 years before the birth of Christ would most commonly be dated 400 B.C. (before Christ). Dates after the birth of Christ are labeled as A.D. These letters stand for the Latin words *anno Domini*, which mean "in the year of the Lord" (the year since the birth of Christ). Thus an event that took place 250 years

after the birth of Christ is written A.D. 250. It can also be written as 250, just as you would not give your birth year as "A.D. 1990" but simply as "1990."

Some historians now prefer to use the abbreviations B.C.E. ("before the common era") and C.E. ("common era") instead of B.C. and A.D. This is especially true of world historians who prefer to use symbols that are not so Western- or Christian-oriented. The dates, of course, remain the same. Thus, 1950 B.C.E. and 1950 B.C. would be the same year, as would A.D. 40 and 40 C.E. In keeping with the current usage by many world historians, this book uses the terms B.C.E. and C.E.

Historians also make use of other terms to refer to time. A decade is 10 years, a century is 100 years, and a millennium is 1,000 years. The phrase "fourth century B.C.E." refers to the fourth period of 100 years counting backward from 1, the assumed date of the birth of Christ. Since the first century B.C.E. would be the years 100 B.C.E. to 1 B.C.E., the fourth century B.C.E. would be the years 400 B.C.E. to 301 B.C.E. We could say, then, that an event in 350 B.C.E. took place in the fourth century B.C.E.

The phrase "fourth century C.E." refers to the fourth period of 100 years after the birth of Christ. Since the first period of 100 years would be the years 1 to 100, the fourth period or fourth century would be the years 301 to 400. We could say, then, for example, that an event in 350 took place in the fourth century. Likewise, the first millennium B.C.E. refers to the years 1000 B.C.E. to 1 B.C.E.; the second millennium C.E. refers to the years 1001 to 2000; and so on.

The dating of events can also vary from people to people. Most people in the Western world use the Western calendar, also known as the Gregorian calendar after Pope Gregory XIII, who refined it in 1582. The Hebrew calendar uses a different system in which the year 1 is the equivalent of the Western year 3760 B.C.E., once calculated to be the date of the creation of the world, according to the Old Testament. Thus the Western year 2009 corresponds to the year 5769 on the Jewish calendar. The Islamic calendar begins year 1 on the day Muhammad fled Mecca, which is the year 622 on the Western calendar.

THEMES FOR UNDERSTANDING WORLD HISTORY

AS THEY PURSUE their craft, historians often organize their material on the basis of themes that enable them to ask and try to answer basic questions about the past. Such is our intention here. In preparing the sixth edition of this book, we have selected several major themes that we believe are especially important in understanding the course of world history. These themes transcend the boundaries of time and space and have relevance to all cultures since the beginning of the human experience.

In the chapters that follow, we will refer to these themes frequently as we advance from the prehistoric era to the present. Where appropriate, we shall make comparisons across cultural boundaries or across different time periods. To facilitate this process, we have included a comparative essay in each chapter that focuses on a particular theme within the specific time period dealt with in that section of the book. For example, the comparative essays in Chapters 1 and 6 deal with the human impact on the natural environment during the premodern era, while those in Chapters 22 and 26 discuss the issue during the age of imperialism and in the contemporary world. Each comparative essay is identified with a particular theme, although it will be noted that many essays deal with several themes at the same time.

We have sought to illustrate these themes through the use of comparative illustrations in each chapter. These illustrations are comparative in nature and seek to encourage the reader to think about thematic issues in cross-cultural terms, while not losing sight of the unique characteristics of individual societies. Our seven themes, each divided into two subtopics, are listed below.

1. *Politics and Government*   The study of politics seeks to answer certain basic questions that historians have about the structure of a society: How were people governed? What was the relationship between the ruler and the ruled? What political power? What actions did people take to guarantee their security or change their form of government?

2. *Arts and Ideas*   We cannot understand a society without looking at its culture, or the common ideas, beliefs, and patterns of behavior that are passed on from one generation to the next. Culture includes both high culture and popular culture. High culture consists of the writings of a society's thinkers and the works of its artists. A society's popular culture is the world

of ideas and experiences of ordinary people. Today the media have embraced the term popular culture to describe the current trends and fashionable styles.

3. *Religion and Philosophy*   Throughout history, people have sought to find a deeper meaning to human life. How have the world's great religions, such as Hinduism, Buddhism, Judaism, Christianity, and Islam, influenced people's lives? How have they spread to create new patterns of culture in other parts of the world?

4. *Family and Society*   The most basic social unit in human society has always been the family. From a study of family and social patterns, we learn about the different social classes that make up a society and their relationships with one another. We also learn about the role of gender in individual societies. What different roles did men and women play in their societies? How and why were those roles different?

5. *Science and Technology*   For thousands of years, people around the world have made scientific discoveries and technological innovations that have changed our world. From the creation of stone tools that made farming easier to advanced computers that guide our airplanes, science and technology have altered how humans have related to their world.

6. *Earth and the Environment*   Throughout history, peoples and societies have been affected by the physical world in which they live. Climatic changes alone have been an important factor in human history. Through their economic activities, peoples and societies, in turn, have also made an impact on their world. Human activities have affected the physical environment and even endangered the very existence of entire societies and species.

7. *Interaction and Exchange*   Many world historians believe that the exchange of ideas and innovations is the driving force behind the evolution of human societies. The introduction of agriculture, writing and printing, metal working, and navigational techniques, for example, spread gradually from one part of the world to other regions and eventually changed the face of the entire globe. The process of cultural and technological exchange took place in various ways, including trade, conquest, and the migration of peoples.

FOR HUNDREDS OF THOUSANDS of years, human beings lived in small groups or villages, seeking to survive by hunting, fishing, and foraging in an often hostile environment. Then, in the space of a few thousand years, an abrupt change occurred as people in a few areas of the globe began to master the art of cultivating food crops. As food production increased, the population in these areas grew, and people began to live in larger communities. Cities appeared and became centers of cultural and religious development. Historians refer to these changes as the beginnings of civilization.

How and why did the first civilizations arise? What role did cross-cultural contacts play in their development? What was the nature of the relationship between these permanent settlements and nonagricultural peoples living elsewhere in the world? Finally, what brought about the demise of these early civilizations, and what legacy did they leave for their successors in the region? The first civilizations that emerged in Mesopotamia, Egypt, India, and China in the fourth and third millennia B.C.E. all shared a number of basic characteristics. Perhaps most important was that each developed in a river valley that was able to provide the agricultural resources needed to maintain a large population.

The emergence of these sedentary societies had a major impact on the social organizations, religious beliefs, and ways of life of the peoples living in them. As population increased and cities sprang up, centralized authority became a necessity. And in the cities, new forms of livelihood arose to satisfy the growing demand for social services and consumer goods. Some people became artisans or merchants, while others became warriors, scholars, or priests. In some cases, the early cities reflected the hierarchical character of the society as a whole, with a central royal palace surrounded by an imposing wall to separate the rulers from the remainder of the urban population.

Although the emergence of the first civilizations led to the formation of cities governed by elites, the vast majority of the population consisted of peasants or slaves working on the lands of the wealthy. In general, rural peoples were less affected by the changes than their urban counterparts. Farmers continued to live in simple mud-and-thatch huts, and many continued to face legal restrictions on their freedom of action and movement. Slavery was common in virtually all ancient societies.

Within these civilizations, the nature of social organization and relationships also began to change. As the concept of private property spread, people were less likely to live in large kinship groups, and the nuclear family became increasingly prevalent. Gender roles came to be differentiated, with men working in the fields or at various specialized occupations and women remaining in the home. Wives were less likely to be viewed as partners than as possessions under the control of their husbands.

These new civilizations were also the sites of significant religious and cultural developments. All of them gave birth to new religions that sought to explain and even influence the forces of nature. Winning the approval of the gods was deemed crucial to a community's success, and a professional class of priests emerged to handle relations with the divine world.

Writing was an important development in the evolution of these new civilizations. Eventually, all of them used writing as both a means of communication and an avenue of creative expression.

From the beginnings of the first civilizations around 3000 B.C.E., the trend was toward the creation of larger territorial states with more sophisticated systems of control. This process reached a high point in the first millennium B.C.E. Between 1000 and 500 B.C.E., the Assyrians and Persians amassed empires that encompassed large areas of the Middle East. The conquests of Alexander the Great in the fourth century B.C.E. created an even larger, if short-lived, empire that soon divided into four kingdoms. Later, the western portion of these kingdoms, along with the Mediterranean world and much of western Europe, fell subject to the mighty empire of the Romans. At the same time, much of India became part of the Mauryan Empire. Finally, in the last few centuries B.C.E., the Qin and Han dynasties of China governed a unified Chinese empire.

At first, these new civilizations had relatively little contact with peoples in the surrounding regions. But evidence is growing that regional trade had started to take hold in the Middle East, and probably in southern and eastern Asia as well, at a very early date. As the population increased, the volume of trade rose with it, and the new civilizations moved outward to acquire new lands and access needed resources. As they expanded, they began to encounter peoples along the periphery of their empires.

Not much evidence has survived to chronicle the nature of these first encounters, but it is likely that the results varied according to time and place. In some cases, the growing civilizations found it relatively easy to absorb isolated communities of agricultural or food-gathering peoples whom they encountered. Such was the case in southern China and southern India. But in other instances, notably among the nomadic or seminomadic peoples in the central and northeastern parts of Asia, the problem was more complicated and often resulted in bitter and extended conflict.

Contacts between these nomadic or seminomadic peoples and settled civilizations probably developed gradually over a long period of time. Often the relationship, at least at the outset, was mutually beneficial, as each needed goods produced by the other. Nomadic peoples in Central Asia also served as an important link for goods and ideas transported over long distances between sedentary civilizations as early as 3000 B.C.E. Overland trade throughout southwestern Asia was already well established by the third millennium B.C.E.

Eventually, the relationship between the settled peoples and the nomadic peoples became increasingly characterized by conflict. Where conflict occurred, the governments of the sedentary civilizations used a variety of techniques to resolve the problem, including negotiations, conquest, or alliance with other pastoral peoples to isolate their primary tormentors.

In the end, these early civilizations collapsed not only as a result of nomadic invasions but also because of their own weaknesses, which made them increasingly vulnerable to attacks along the frontier. Some of their problems were political, and others were related to climatic change or environmental problems.

The fall of the ancient empires did not mark the end of civilization, of course, but rather a transition to a new stage of increasing complexity in the evolution of human society. ◆

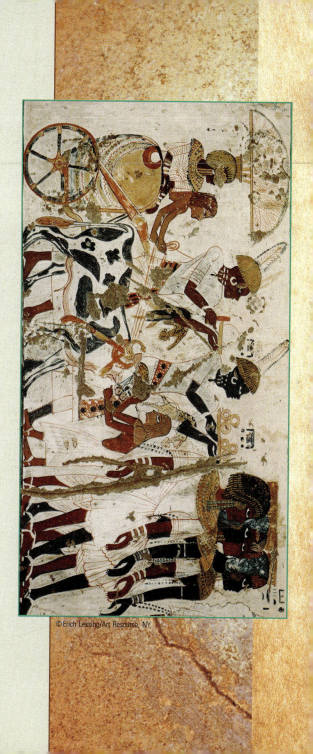

© Erich Lessing/Art Resource, NY

CHAPTER 1

THE FIRST CIVILIZATIONS: THE PEOPLES
OF WESTERN ASIA AND EGYPT

© Nik Wheeler/CORBIS

Ruins of the ancient Sumerian city of Uruk

CHAPTER OUTLINE
AND FOCUS QUESTIONS

The First Humans

Q How did the Paleolithic and Neolithic Ages differ, and how did the Neolithic Revolution affect the lives of men and women?

The Emergence of Civilization

Q What are the characteristics of civilization, and what are some explanations for why early civilizations emerged?

Civilization in Mesopotamia

Q How are the chief characteristics of civilization evident in ancient Mesopotamia?

Egyptian Civilization: "The Gift of the Nile"

Q What are the basic features of the three major periods of Egyptian history? What elements of continuity are there in the three periods? What are their major differences?

New Centers of Civilization

Q What was the significance of the Indo-Europeans? How did Judaism differ from the religions of Mesopotamia and Egypt?

The Rise of New Empires

Q What methods and institutions did the Assyrians and Persians use to amass and maintain their respective empires?

CRITICAL THINKING

Q In what ways were the civilizations of Mesopotamia and Egypt alike? In what ways were they different? What accounts for the similarities and differences?

IN 1849, A DARING YOUNG ENGLISHMAN made a hazardous journey into the deserts and swamps of southern Iraq. Braving high winds and temperatures that reached 120 degrees Fahrenheit, William Loftus led a small expedition southward along the banks of the Euphrates River in search of the roots of civilization. As he said, "From our childhood we have been led to regard this place as the cradle of the human race."

Guided by native Arabs into the southernmost reaches of Iraq, Loftus and his small band of explorers were soon overwhelmed by what they saw. He wrote, "I know of nothing more exciting or impressive than the first sight of one of these great piles, looming in solitary grandeur from the surrounding plains and marshes." One of these piles, known to the natives as the mound of Warka, contained the ruins of Uruk, one of the first cities in the world and part of the world's first civilization.

Southern Iraq, known to ancient peoples as Mesopotamia, was one of the areas in the world where civilization began. In the fertile valleys of large rivers—the Tigris and Euphrates in Mesopotamia, the Nile in Egypt, the Indus in India, and the Yellow River in China—intensive agriculture became capable of supporting large groups of people. In these regions, civilization was born. The first civilizations

2

emerged in western Asia (now known as the Middle East) and Egypt, where people developed organized societies and created the ideas and institutions that we associate with civilization.

Before considering the early civilizations of western Asia and Egypt, however, we must briefly examine our prehistory and observe how human beings made the shift from hunting and gathering to agricultural communities and ultimately to cities and civilization. ◆

The First Humans

Focus Question: How did the Paleolithic and Neolithic Ages differ, and how did the Neolithic Revolution affect the lives of men and women?

Historians rely mostly on documents to create their pictures of the past, but no written records exist for the prehistory of humankind. In their absence, the story of early humanity depends on archaeological and, more recently, biological information, which anthropologists and archaeologists use to formulate theories about our early past.

Although science has given us more precise methods for examining prehistory, much of our understanding of early humans still relies on considerable conjecture. Given the rate of new discoveries, the following account of the current theory of early human life might well be changed in a few years. As the great British archaeologist Louis Leakey reminded us years ago, "Theories on prehistory and early man constantly change as new evidence comes to light."

The earliest humanlike creatures—known as **hominids**—lived in Africa some three to four million years ago. Called Australopithecines, or "southern ape-men," by their discoverers, they flourished in eastern and southern Africa and were the first hominids to make simple stone tools. Australopithecines were also bipedal—that is, they walked upright on two legs, a trait that enabled them to move over long distances and make use of their arms and legs for different purposes.

In 1959, Louis and Mary Leakey discovered a new form of hominid in Africa that they labeled *Homo habilis* ("handy human"). The Leakeys believed that *Homo habilis* was the earliest toolmaking hominid, which had a brain almost 50 percent larger than that of the Australopithecines. Their larger brains and the ability to walk upright allowed these hominids to become more sophisticated in the search for meat, seeds, and nuts for nourishment.

A new phase in early human development occurred around 1.5 million years ago with the emergence of *Homo erectus* ("upright human"). A more advanced human form, *Homo erectus* made use of larger and more varied tools and was the first hominid to leave Africa and move into Europe and Asia.

CHRONOLOGY The First Humans	
Australopithecines	flourished c. 2–4 million years ago
Homo habilis	flourished c. 1–4 million years ago
Homo erectus	flourished c. 100,000–1.5 million years ago
Homo sapiens:	
Neanderthals	flourished c. 100,000–30,000 B.C.E.
Homo sapiens sapiens	emerged c. 200,000 B.C.E.

The Emergence of *Homo sapiens*

Around 250,000 years ago, a third and crucial phase in human development began with the emergence of *Homo sapiens* ("wise human"). By 100,000 B.C.E., two groups of *Homo sapiens* had developed. One type was the Neanderthal, whose remains were first found in the Neander valley in Germany. Neanderthal remains have since been found in both Europe and the Middle East and have been dated to between 100,000 and 30,000 B.C.E. Neanderthals relied on a variety of stone tools and were the first early people to bury their dead. (Some scientists maintain that burial of the dead indicates a belief in an afterlife.) Neanderthals in Europe made clothes from the skins of animals that they had killed for food.

The first anatomically modern humans, known as *Homo sapiens sapiens* ("wise, wise human"), appeared in Africa between 200,000 and 150,000 years ago. Recent evidence indicates that they began to spread outside Africa around 70,000 years ago. Map 1.1 shows probable dates for different movements, although many of these dates are still controversial. By 30,000 B.C.E., *Homo sapiens sapiens* had replaced the Neanderthals, who had largely become extinct.

The movement of the first modern humans was rarely deliberate. Groups of people advanced beyond their old hunting grounds at a rate of only 2 to 3 miles per generation. This was enough, however, to populate the world in some tens of thousands of years. Some scholars have suggested that such advanced human creatures may have emerged independently in different parts of the world, rather than in Africa alone, but the latest genetic evidence strongly supports the out-of-Africa theory as the most likely explanation of human origin. In any case, by 10,000 B.C.E., members of the *Homo sapiens sapiens* species could be found throughout the world. By that time, it was the only human species left. All humans today, be they Europeans, Australian Aborigines, or Africans, belong to the same subspecies of human being.

The Hunter-Gatherers of the Paleolithic Age

One of the basic distinguishing features of the human species is the ability to make tools. The earliest tools were made of stone, and so this early period of human history

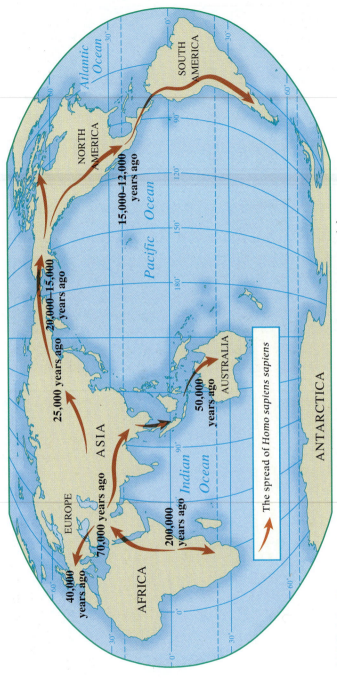

MAP 1.1 **The Spread of Homo sapiens sapiens.** *Homo sapiens sapiens* spread from Africa beginning about 70,000 years ago. Living and traveling in small groups, these anatomically modern humans were hunter-gatherers.

Q Given that some diffusion of humans occurred during ice ages, how would such climate change affect humans and their movements, especially from Asia to Australia and Asia to North America? **View an animated version of this map or related maps at www.cengage.com/history/Duiker/World6e**

(c. 2,500,000–10,000 B.C.E.) has been designated the **Paleolithic Age** (*paleolithic* is Greek for "old stone").

For hundreds of thousands of years, humans relied on hunting and gathering for their daily food. Paleolithic peoples had a close relationship with the world around them, and over a period of time, they came to know which animals to hunt and which plants to eat. They did not know how to grow crops or raise animals, however. They gathered wild nuts, berries, fruits, and a variety of wild grains and green plants. Around the world, they captured and consumed various animals, including buffalo, horses, bison, wild goats, reindeer, and fish.

The hunting of animals and the gathering of wild plants no doubt led to certain patterns of living. Archaeologists and anthropologists have speculated that Paleolithic people lived in small bands of twenty to thirty individuals. They were nomadic (they moved from place to place) because they had no choice but to follow animal migrations and vegetation cycles. Hunting depended on careful observation of animal behavior patterns and required a group effort for success. Over the years, tools became more refined and more useful. The invention of the spear and later the bow and arrow made hunting considerably easier. Harpoons and fishhooks made of bone increased the catch of fish.

Both men and women were responsible for finding food—the chief work of Paleolithic people. Since women bore and raised the children, they generally stayed close to the camps, but they played an important role in acquiring food by gathering berries, nuts, and grains. Men hunted for wild animals, an activity that often took them far from camp. Because both men and women played important roles in providing for the band's survival, scientists have argued that a rough equality existed between men and women. Indeed, some speculate that both men and women made the decisions that governed the activities of the Paleolithic band.

Some groups of Paleolithic peoples, especially those who lived in cold climates, found shelter in caves. Over time, they created new types of shelter as well. Perhaps the most common was a simple structure of wood poles or sticks covered with animal hides. Where wood was scarce, Paleolithic hunter-gatherers might use the bones of mammoths for the framework and cover it with animal hides. The systematic use of fire, which archaeologists believe began around 500,000 years ago, made it possible for the caves and human-made structures to have a source of light and heat. Fire also enabled early humans to cook their food, making it taste better, last longer, and in the case of some plants, such as wild grains, easier to chew and digest.

The making of tools and the use of fire—two important technological innovations of Paleolithic peoples—remind us how crucial the ability to adapt was to human survival. Changing physical conditions during periodic ice ages posed a considerable threat to human existence.

AP Images/Jean Clottes

Paleolithic peoples used their technological innovations to change their physical environment. By working together, they found a way to survive. And by passing on their common practices, skills, and material products to their children, they ensured that later generations, too, could survive in a harsh environment.

But Paleolithic peoples did more than just survive. The cave paintings of large animals found in southwestern France and northern Spain bear witness to the cultural activity of Paleolithic peoples. A cave discovered in southern France in 1994 (known as the Chauvet cave after the leader of the expedition that found it) contains more than three hundred paintings of lions, oxen, owls, bears, and other animals. Most of these are animals that Paleolithic people did not hunt, which suggests to some scholars that the paintings were made for religious or even decorative purposes. The discoverers were overwhelmed by what they saw: "There was a moment of ecstasy.... They overflowed with joy and emotion in their turn.... These were moments of indescribable madness."[1]

The Neolithic Revolution, c. 10,000–4000 B.C.E.

The end of the last ice age around 10,000 B.C.E. was followed by what is called the **Neolithic Revolution**, a significant change in living patterns that occurred in the New Stone Age (the word *neolithic* is Greek for "new stone"). The name New Stone Age is misleading, however. Although Neolithic peoples made a new type of polished stone axes, this was not the most significant change they introduced.

A Revolution in Agriculture   The biggest change was the shift from hunting animals and gathering plants for sustenance (food gathering) to producing food by systematic agriculture (food production; see Map 1.2). The planting of grains and vegetables provided a regular supply of food, while the domestication of animals, such as sheep, goats, cattle, and pigs, added a steady source of meat, milk, and fibers such as wool for clothing. Larger animals could also be used as beasts of burden. The growing of crops and the taming of food-producing animals created a new relationship between humans and nature. Historians like to speak of this as an agricultural revolution. Revolutionary change is dramatic and requires great effort, but the ability to acquire food on a regular basis gave humans greater control over their environment. It also enabled them to give up their nomadic ways of life and begin to live in settled communities.

The shift from hunting and gathering to food producing was not as sudden as was once believed, however. The **Mesolithic Age** ("Middle Stone Age," c. 10,000–7000 B.C.E.) saw a gradual transition from a food-gathering and hunting economy to a food-producing one and witnessed a gradual domestication of animals as well. Likewise, the movement toward the use of plants and their seeds as an important source of nourishment was also not as sudden. Evidence seems to support the possibility that the Paleolithic hunters and gatherers had already grown crops to supplement their traditional sources of food. Moreover, throughout the Neolithic period, hunting and gathering as well as nomadic herding remained ways of life for many people around the world.

Systematic agriculture developed independently in different areas of the world between 8000 and 5000 B.C.E. Inhabitants of the Middle East began cultivating wheat and barley and domesticating pigs, cattle, goats, and sheep by 8000 B.C.E. From the Middle East, farming spread into the Balkan region of Europe by 6500 B.C.E. By 4000 B.C.E., it was well established in the south of France, central Europe, and the coastal regions of the Mediterranean. The cultivation of wheat and barley also spread from western

Paleolithic Cave Painting: The Chauvet Cave. Cave paintings of large animals reveal the cultural creativity of Paleolithic peoples. This scene is part of a mural in a large underground chamber at Vallon-Pont-d'Arc, France, discovered in December 1994. It dates from around 30,000–28,000 B.C.E. and depicts aurochs (long-horned wild oxen), horses, and rhinoceroses. To make their paintings, Paleolithic artists used stone lamps in which they burned animal fat to illuminate the cave walls and combined powdered mineral ores with animal fat to create red, yellow, and black pigments. Some artists even made brushes out of animal hairs with which to apply the paints.

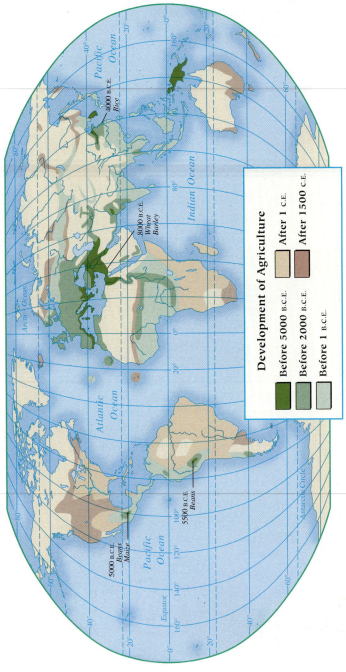

MAP 1.2 **The Development of Agriculture.** Agriculture first began between 8000 and 5000 B.C.E. in four different parts of the world. It allowed the establishment of permanent settlements where crops could be grown and domesticated animals that produced meat and milk could be easily tended.

Q What geographical and human factors might explain relationships between latitude and the beginning of agriculture? ● View an animated version of this map or related maps at **www.cengage.com/history/Duiker/World6e**

Asia into the Nile valley of Egypt by 6000 B.C.E. and soon spread up the Nile to other areas of Africa, especially Sudan and Ethiopia. In the woodlands and tropical forests of Central Africa, a separate agricultural system emerged, based on the cultivation of tubers or root crops such as yams and tree crops such as bananas. The cultivation of wheat and barley also eventually moved eastward into the highlands of northwestern and central India between 7000 and 5000 B.C.E. By 5000 B.C.E., rice was being cultivated in southeastern Asia, from where it spread into southern China. In northern China, the cultivation of millet and the domestication of pigs and dogs seem well established by 6000 B.C.E. In the Western Hemisphere, Mesoamericans (inhabitants of present-day Mexico and Central America) domesticated beans, squash, and maize (corn) as well as dogs and fowl between 7000 and 5000 B.C.E. (see the comparative essay "From Hunter-Gatherers and Herders to Farmers" on p. 7).

Neolithic Farming Villages The growing of crops on a regular basis gave rise to relatively permanent settlements, which historians refer to as Neolithic farming villages or towns. Although Neolithic villages appeared in Europe, India, Egypt, China, and Mesoamerica, the oldest and most extensive ones were located in the Middle East. Jericho, in Palestine near the Dead Sea, was in existence by 8000 B.C.E. and covered several acres by 7000 B.C.E. It had a

wall several feet thick that enclosed houses made of sun-dried mudbricks. Çatal Hüyük, located in modern Turkey, was an even larger community. Its walls enclosed 32 acres, and its population probably reached six thousand in-habitants during its high point from 6700 to 5700 B.C.E. People lived in simple mudbrick houses that were built so close to one another that there were few streets. To get to their homes, people would walk along the rooftops and enter the house through a hole in the roof.

Archaeologists have discovered twelve cultivated products in Çatal Hüyük, including fruits, nuts, and three kinds of wheat. People grew their own food and stored it in storerooms in their homes. Domesticated animals, especially cattle, yielded meat, milk, and hides. Hunting scenes on the walls indicate that the people of Çatal Hüyük hunted as well, but unlike earlier hunter-gatherers, they no longer relied on hunting for their survival. Food surpluses also made it possible for people to do things other than farming. Some people became artisans and made weapons and jewelry that were traded with neighboring peoples, thus connecting the inhabitants of Çatal Hüyük to the wider world around them.

Religious shrines housing figures of gods and god-desses have been found at Çatal Hüyük, as have a number of female statuettes. Molded with noticeably large breasts and buttocks, these "earth mothers" perhaps symbolically represented the fertility of both "our mother" earth and

COMPARATIVE ESSAY
FROM HUNTER-GATHERERS AND HERDERS TO FARMERS

About ten thousand years ago, human beings began to practice the cultivation of crops and the domestication of animals. The exact time and place that crops were first cultivated successfully is uncertain. The first farmers undoubtedly used simple techniques and still relied primarily on other forms of food production, such as hunting, foraging, and pastoralism (herding). The real breakthrough came when farmers began to cultivate crops along the floodplains of river systems. The advantage was that crops grown in such areas were not as dependent on rainfall and therefore produced a more reliable harvest. An additional benefit was that the sediment carried by the river waters deposited nutrients in the soil, enabling the farmer to cultivate a single plot of ground for many years without moving to a new location. Thus the first truly sedentary (nonmigratory) societies were born.

The spread of river valley agriculture in various parts of Asia and Africa was the decisive factor in the rise of the first civilizations. The increase in food production in these regions led to a significant growth in population, while efforts to control the flow of water to maximize the irrigation of cultivated areas and to protect the local inhabitants from hostile forces outside the community provoked the first steps toward cooperative activities on a large scale.

The need to oversee the entire process brought about the emergence of an elite that was eventually transformed into a government.

We shall investigate this process in the next several chapters as we explore the rise of civilizations in the Mediterranean, the Middle East, South Asia, China, and the Americas. We shall also raise a number of important questions: Why did human communities in some areas that had the capacity to support agriculture not take the leap to farming? Why did other groups that had managed to master the cultivation of crops not take the next step to create large and advanced societies? Finally, what happened to the existing communities of hunter-gatherers who were overrun or driven out as the agricultural revolution spread its way rapidly throughout the world?

Over the years, a number of possible reasons, some of them biological, others cultural or environmental, have been advanced to explain such phenomena. According to Jared Diamond, in *Guns, Germs, and Steel: The Fates of Human Societies*, the ultimate causes of such differences lie not within the character or cultural values of the resident population but in the nature of the local climate and topography. These influence the degree to which local crops and animals can be put to human use and then be transmitted to adjoining regions. In Mesopotamia, for example, the widespread availability of edible crops, such as wheat and barley, helped promote the transition to agriculture in the region. At the same time, the lack of land barriers between Mesopotamia and its neighbors to the east and west facilitated the rapid spread of agricultural techniques and crops to climatically similar regions in the Indus River valley and Egypt.

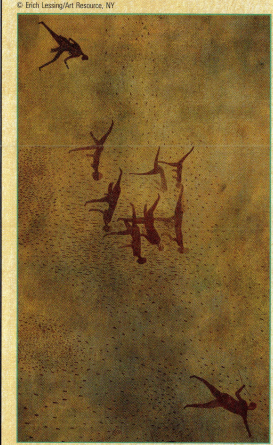

© Erich Lessing/Art Resource, NY

Women's Work. This rock painting from a cave in modern-day Algeria, dating from around the fourth millennium B.C.E., shows women harvesting grain.

human mothers. Both the shrines and the statues point to the growing role of religion in the lives of these Neolithic peoples.

Consequences of the Neolithic Revolution The Neolithic agricultural revolution had far-reaching consequences. Once people settled in villages or towns, they built houses for protection and other structures for the storage of goods. As organized communities stored food

and accumulated material goods, they began to engage in trade. In the Middle East, for example, the new communities exchanged such objects as shells, flint, and semiprecious stones. People also began to specialize in certain crafts, and a division of labor developed. Pottery was made from clay and baked in fire to make it hard. The pots were used for cooking and to store grains. Woven baskets were also used for storage. Stone tools became refined as flint blades were used to make sickles

more important than work done in the home, men came to play the more dominant role in human society, a basic pattern that has persisted to our own times.

Other patterns set in the Neolithic Age also proved to be enduring elements of human history. Fixed dwellings, domesticated animals, regular farming, a division of labor, men holding power—all of these are part of the human story. For all of our scientific and technological progress, human survival still depends on the growing and storing of food, an accomplishment of people in the Neolithic Age. The Neolithic Revolution was truly a turning point in human history.

Between 4000 and 3000 B.C.E., significant technical developments began to transform the Neolithic towns. The invention of writing enabled records to be kept, and the use of metals marked a new level of human control over the environment and its resources. Already before 4000 B.C.E., artisans had discovered that metal-bearing rocks could be heated to liquefy the metal, which could then be cast in molds to produce tools and weapons that were more useful than stone instruments. Although copper was the first metal to be used for producing tools, after 4000 B.C.E., metalworkers in western Asia discovered that a combination of copper and tin produced bronze, a much harder and more durable metal than copper. Its widespread use has led historians to call the period from around 3000 to 1200 B.C.E. the Bronze Age; thereafter, bronze was increasingly replaced by iron.

At first, Neolithic settlements were hardly more than villages. But as their inhabitants mastered the art of farming, more complex human societies gradually emerged. As wealth increased, these societies sought to protect it from being plundered by outsiders and so began to develop armies and to build walled cities. By the beginning of the Bronze Age, the concentration of larger numbers of people in river valleys was leading to a whole new pattern for human life.

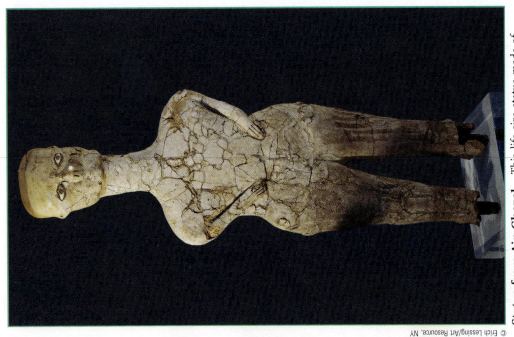

Statue from Ain Ghazal. This life-size statue made of plaster, sand, and crushed chalk, created around 6500 B.C.E., was discovered in 1984 at Ain Ghazal, an archaeological site near Amman, Jordan. It is among the oldest known statues of the human figure. Although it appears lifelike, its features are too generic to be a portrait of a particular individual. The purpose of this sculpture and the reason for its creation may never be known.

© Erich Lessing/Art Resource, NY

and hoes for use in the fields. Obsidian—a volcanic glass that was easily flaked—was also used to create very sharp tools. In the course of the Neolithic Age, many of the food plants still in use today came to be cultivated. Moreover, vegetable fibers from such plants as flax and cotton were used to make thread that was woven into cloth.

The change to systematic agriculture in the Neolithic Age also had consequences for the relationship between men and women. Men assumed the primary responsibility for working in the fields and herding animals, jobs that kept them away from the home. Women remained behind, caring for the children and weaving cloth, making cheese from milk, and performing other household tasks that required considerable labor. In time, as work outside the home was increasingly perceived as

The Emergence of Civilization

Focus Question: What are the characteristics of civilization, and what are some explanations for why early civilizations emerged?

As we have seen, early human beings formed small groups that developed a simple culture that enabled them to survive. As human societies grew and developed greater complexity, civilization came into being. A **civilization** is a complex culture in which large numbers of people share a variety of common elements. Historians have identified a number of basic characteristics of civilization, including the following:

1. *An urban focus.* Cities became the centers for political, economic, social, cultural, and religious development. The cities that emerged were much larger than the Neolithic towns that preceded them.

2. *New political and military structures.* An organized government bureaucracy arose to meet the administrative demands of the growing population, and armies were organized to gain land and power and for defense.

3. *A new social structure based on economic power.* While kings and an upper class of priests, political leaders, and warriors dominated, there also existed large groups of free common people (farmers, artisans, craftspeople) and, at the very bottom of the social hierarchy, a class of slaves.

4. *The development of more complexity in a material sense.* Surpluses of agricultural crops freed some people to work in occupations other than farming. Demand among ruling elites for luxury items encouraged the creation of new products. And as urban populations exported finished goods in exchange for raw materials from neighboring populations, organized trade grew substantially.

5. *A distinct religious structure.* The gods were deemed crucial to the community's success, and a professional priestly class, serving as stewards of the gods' property, regulated relations with the gods.

6. *The development of writing.* Kings, priests, merchants, and artisans used writing to keep records.

7. *New and significant artistic and intellectual activity.* For example, monumental architectural structures, usually religious, occupied a prominent place in urban environments.

Early Civilizations Around the World

The first civilizations that developed in Mesopotamia and Egypt will be examined in detail in this chapter. But civilizations also developed independently in other parts of the world. Between 3000 and 1500 B.C.E., the valleys of the Indus River in India supported a flourishing civilization that extended hundreds of miles from the Himalayas to the coast of the Arabian Sea (see Chapter 2). Two major cities—Harappa and Mohenjo-Daro—were at the heart of this advanced civilization, which flourished for hundreds of years. Many written records of this Harappan or Indus civilization, as it is called, exist, but their language has not yet been deciphered. As in the city-states that arose in Mesopotamia and along the Nile, the Harappan economy was based primarily on farming, but Harappan civilization also carried on extensive trade with Mesopotamia. Textiles and food were imported from the Mesopotamian city-states in exchange for copper, lumber, precious stones, cotton, and various types of luxury goods.

Another river valley civilization emerged along the Yellow River in northern China about four thousand years ago (see Chapter 3). Under the Shang dynasty of kings, which ruled from 1750 to 1122 B.C.E., this civilization contained impressive cities with huge city walls, royal palaces, and large royal tombs. A system of irrigation enabled early Chinese civilization to maintain a prosperous farming society ruled by an aristocratic class whose major concern was war.

Scholars have long believed that civilization emerged only in these four areas—the fertile river valleys of the Tigris and Euphrates, the Nile, the Indus, and the Yellow River. Recently, however, archaeologists have discovered other early civilizations. One of these flourished in Central Asia (in what are now the republics of Turkmenistan and Uzbekistan) around four thousand years ago. People in this civilization built mudbrick buildings, raised sheep and goats, had bronze tools, used a system of irrigation to grow wheat and barley, and had a writing system.

Another early civilization was discovered in the Supe River valley of Peru. At the center of this civilization was the city of Caral, which flourished around 2600 B.C.E. It contained buildings for officials, apartment buildings, and grand residences, all built of stone. The inhabitants of Caral

Harappa and Mohenjo-Daro

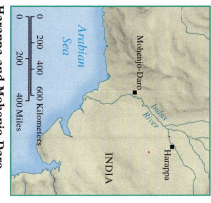

The Yellow River, China

Major regions of the late Shang state

Central Asian Civilization

(Modern state names are in parentheses)

Caral, Peru

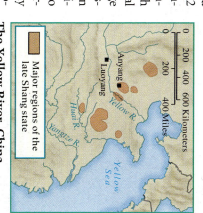

catastrophic. In such circumstances, farming could be accomplished only with human intervention in the form of irrigation and drainage ditches. A complex system was required to control the flow of the rivers and produce the crops. Large-scale irrigation made possible the expansion of agriculture in this region, and the abundant food provided the material base for the emergence of civilization in Mesopotamia.

CHRONOLOGY The Birth of Early Civilizations

Egypt	c. 3100 B.C.E.
Mesopotamia	c. 3000 B.C.E.
India	c. 3000 B.C.E.
Peru	c. 2600 B.C.E.
China	c. 2000 B.C.E.
Central Asia	c. 2000 B.C.E.

also developed a system of irrigation by diverting a river more than a mile upstream into their fields. This Peruvian culture reached its height during the first millennium B.C.E. with the emergence of the Chavín style, named for a settlement near the modern city of Chavín de Huántar (see Chapter 6).

Causes of Civilization

Why civilizations developed remains difficult to explain. Since civilizations developed independently in different parts of the world, can general causes be identified that would tell us why all of these civilizations emerged? A number of possible explanations have been suggested. A theory of challenge and response maintains that challenges forced human beings to make efforts that resulted in the rise of civilization. Some scholars have adhered to a material explanation. Material forces, such as the accumulation of food surpluses, made possible the specialization of labor and development of large communities with bureaucratic organization. But some areas were not naturally conducive to agriculture. Abundant food could be produced only through a massive human effort to manage the water, an effort that created the need for organization and bureaucratic control and led to civilized cities. Some historians have argued that nonmaterial forces, primarily religious, provided the sense of unity and purpose that made such organized activities possible. Finally, some scholars doubt that we are capable of ever discovering the actual causes of early civilization.

Civilization in Mesopotamia

Focus Question: How are the chief characteristics of civilization evident in ancient Mesopotamia?

The Greeks called the valley between the Tigris and Euphrates Rivers Mesopotamia, the land "between the rivers." The region receives little rain, but the soil of the plain of southern Mesopotamia was enlarged and enriched over the years by layers of silt deposited by the two rivers. In late spring, the Tigris and Euphrates overflow their banks and deposit their fertile silt, but since this flooding depends on the melting of snows in the upland mountains where the rivers begin, it is irregular and sometimes

The City-States of Ancient Mesopotamia

The creators of the first Mesopotamian civilization were the Sumerians, a people whose origins remain unclear. By 3000 B.C.E., they had established a number of independent cities in southern Mesopotamia, including Eridu, Ur, Uruk, Umma, and Lagash (see Map 1.3). As the cities expanded, they came to exercise political and economic control over the surrounding countryside, forming city-states, which were the basic units of Sumerian civilization.

Sumerian Cities Sumerian cities were surrounded by walls. Uruk, for example, was encircled by a wall 6 miles long with defense towers located along it every 30 to 35 feet. City dwellings, built of sun-dried bricks, included both the small flats of peasants and the larger dwellings of the civic and priestly officials. Although Mesopotamia had little stone or wood for building purposes, it did have plenty of mud. Mudbricks, easily shaped by hand, were left to bake in the hot sun until they were hard enough to use for building. People in Mesopotamia were remarkably innovative with mudbricks, inventing the arch and the dome and constructing some of the largest brick buildings in the world. Mudbricks are still used in rural areas of the Middle East today.

The most prominent building in a Sumerian city was the temple, which was dedicated to the chief god or goddess of the city and often built atop a massive stepped tower called a **ziggurat.** The Sumerians believed that gods and goddesses owned the cities, and much wealth was used to build temples as well as elaborate houses for the priests and priestesses who served the deities. Priests and priestesses, who supervised the temples and their property, had great power. In fact, historians believe that in the formative stages of certain city-states, priests and priestesses may have had an important role in governance. The Sumerians believed that the gods ruled the cities, making the state a **theocracy** (government by a divine authority). However, actual ruling power was primarily in the hands of worldly figures, known as kings.

Kingship Sumerians viewed kingship as divine in origin—kings, they believed, derived their power from the gods and were the agents of the gods. As one person said in a petition to his king, "You in your judgment, you are the son of Anu [god of the sky]; Your commands, like the

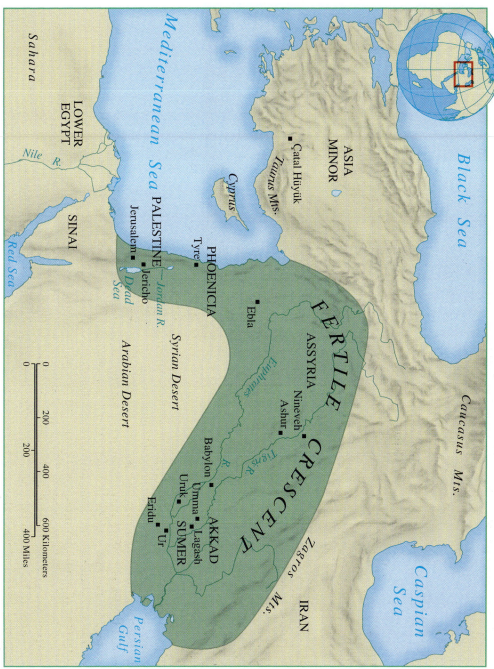

MAP 1.3 **The Ancient Near East.** The Fertile Crescent encompassed land with access to water. Employing flood management and irrigation systems, the peoples of the region established civilizations based on agriculture. These civilizations developed writing, law codes, and economic specialization.

Q What geographical aspects of the Mesopotamian city-states made conflict between them likely? **View an animated version of this map or related maps at** www.cengage.com/history/Duiker/World6e

word of a god, cannot be reversed: Your words, like rain pouring down from heaven, are without number."[2] Regardless of their origins, kings had power—they led armies and organized workers for the irrigation projects on which Mesopotamian farming depended. The army, the government bureaucracy, and the priests and priestesses all aided the kings in their rule. Befitting their power, Sumerian kings lived in large palaces with their wives and children.

Economy and Society The economy of the Sumerian city-states was primarily agricultural, but commerce and industry became important as well. The people of Mesopotamia produced woolen textiles, pottery, and metalwork. The Sumerians imported copper, tin, and timber in exchange for dried fish, wool, barley, wheat, and metal goods. Traders traveled by land to the eastern Mediterranean in the west and by sea to India in the east. The

introduction of the wheel, which had been invented around 3000 B.C.E. by nomadic people living in the region north of the Black Sea, led to carts with wheels that made the transport of goods easier.

Sumerian city-states probably contained four major social groups: elites, dependent commoners, free commoners, and slaves. Elites included royal and priestly officials and their families. Dependent commoners included the elites' clients, who worked for the palace and temple estates. Free commoners worked as farmers, merchants, fishers, scribes, and craftspeople. Probably 90 percent or more of the population were engaged in farming. Slaves belonged to palace officials, who used them in building projects; to temple officials, who used mostly female slaves to weave cloth and grind grain; and to rich landowners, who used them for agricultural and domestic work.

© British Museum, London, UK/The Bridgeman Art Library

The "Royal Standard" of Ur. This detail is from the "Royal Standard" of Ur, a box dating from around 2700 B.C.E. that was discovered in a stone tomb from the royal cemetery of the Sumerian city-state of Ur. The scenes on one side of the box depict the activities of the king and his military forces. Shown in the bottom panel are four Sumerian battle chariots. Each chariot held two men, one controlling the reins and the other armed with a spear for combat. A special compartment in the chariot held a number of spears. The charging chariots are seen defeating the enemy. In the middle band, the Sumerian soldiers round up captured enemies. In the top band, the captives are presented to the king, who has alighted from his chariot and is shown standing above all the others in the center of the panel.

Empires in Ancient Mesopotamia

As the number of Sumerian city-states grew and the states expanded, new conflicts arose as city-state fought city-state for control of land and water. The fortunes of various city-states rose and fell over the centuries. The constant wars, with their burning and sacking of cities, left many Sumerians in deep despair, as is evident in the words of this Sumerian poem from the city of Ur:

Ur is destroyed, bitter is its lament.
The country's blood now fills its holes like hot bronze
*   in a mold.*
Bodies dissolve like fat in the sun.
Our temple is destroyed, the gods have abandoned us,
*   like migrating birds.*
Smoke lies on our city like a shroud.

Sargon's Empire Located in the flat land of Mesopotamia, the Sumerian city-states were also open to invasion. To the north of the Sumerian city-states were the Akkadians. We call them a Semitic people because of the type of language they spoke (see Table 1.1). Around 2340 B.C.E., Sargon, leader of the Akkadians, overran the Sumerian city-states and established an empire that included most of Mesopotamia as well as lands westward to the Mediterranean. Even in the first millennium B.C.E., Sargon was still remembered in chronicles as a king of

TABLE 1.1 Some Semitic Languages

Akkadian	*Assyrian*	Hebrew
Arabic	Babylonian	Phoenician
Aramaic	Canaanitic	Syriac

NOTE: Languages in italic type are no longer spoken.

Akkad who "had no rival or equal, spread his splendor over all the lands, and crossed the sea in the east. In his eleventh year, he conquered the western land to its furthest point, and brought it under his sole authority."[3] Attacks from neighboring hill peoples eventually caused the Akkadian empire to fall, and its end by 2100 B.C.E. brought a return to the system of warring city-states. It was not until 1792 B.C.E. that a new empire came to control much of Mesopotamia under Hammurabi, who ruled over the Amorites or Old Babylonians, a large group of Semitic-speaking seminomads.

Hammurabi's Empire Hammurabi (1792–1750 B.C.E.) employed a well-disciplined army of foot soldiers who carried axes, spears, and copper or bronze daggers. He learned to divide his opponents and subdue them one by one. Using such methods, he gained control of Sumer and Akkad, creating a new Mesopotamian kingdom. After his conquests, he called himself "the sun of Babylon, the king who has made the four quarters of the world subservient," and established a new capital at Babylon.

Hammurabi's Empire

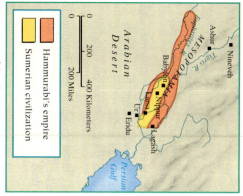

Hammurabi, the man of war, was also a man of peace. A collection of his letters, found by archaeologists, reveals that he took a strong interest in state affairs. He built temples, defensive walls, and irrigation canals; encouraged trade; and brought about an economic revival. Indeed, Hammurabi saw himself as a shepherd to his people: "I am indeed the shepherd who brings peace, whose scepter is just. My benevolent shade was spread over my city. I held the people of the lands of Sumer and Akkad safely on my lap."[4] After his death, however, a series of weak kings were unable to keep Hammurabi's empire united, and it finally fell to new invaders.

The Code of Hammurabi: Society in Mesopotamia

Hammurabi is best remembered for his law code, a collection of 282 laws. Although many scholars today view Hammurabi's collection less as a code of laws and more as an attempt by Hammurabi to portray himself as the source of justice to his people, the code still gives us a glimpse of the Mesopotamian society of his time (see the box on p. 14).

The Code of Hammurabi reveals a society with a system of strict justice. Penalties for criminal offenses were severe and varied according to the social class of the victim. A crime against a member of the upper class (a noble) by a member of the lower class (a commoner) was punished more severely than the same offense against a member of the lower class. Moreover, the principle of "an eye for an eye, a tooth for a tooth" was fundamental to this system of justice. This meant that punishments should fit the crime: "If a freeman has destroyed the eye of a member of the aristocracy, they shall destroy his eye" (Code of Hammurabi, %196). Hammurabi's code reflected legal and social ideas prevailing in southwestern Asia at the time, as the following verse from the Hebrew Bible demonstrates: "If anyone injures his neighbor, whatever he has done must be done to him: fracture for fracture, eye for eye, tooth for tooth. As he has injured the other, so he is to be injured" (Leviticus 24:19–20).

The largest category of laws in the Code of Hammurabi focused on marriage and the family. Parents arranged marriages for their children. After marriage, the parties involved signed a marriage contract; without it, no one was considered legally married. While the husband provided a bridal payment to the bride's parents, the woman's parents were responsible for a dowry to the new husband.

As in many patriarchal societies, women possessed far fewer privileges and rights in the married relationship than men. A woman's place was in the home, and failure to fulfill her expected duties was grounds for divorce. If she was not able to bear children, her husband could divorce her. Furthermore, a wife who was a "gadabout, . . . neglecting her house [and] humiliating her husband, shall be prosecuted" (%143). We do know that in practice, not all women remained at home. Some worked in the fields and others in business, where they were especially prominent running taverns.

Women were guaranteed some rights, however. If a woman was divorced without good reason, she received the dowry back. A woman could seek divorce and get her dowry back if her husband was unable to show that she had done anything wrong. In theory, a wife was guaranteed the use of her husband's legal property in the event of his death. A mother could also decide which of her sons would receive an inheritance.

Sexual relations were strictly regulated as well. Husbands, but not wives, were permitted sexual activity outside

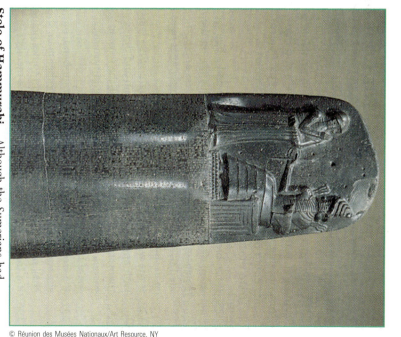

Stele of Hammurabi. Although the Sumerians had compiled earlier law codes, the Code of Hammurabi, king of Babylonia, was the most famous in early Mesopotamian history. The upper part of the stele depicts Hammurabi standing in front of the seated sun god, Shamash. The king raises his hand in deference to the god, who gives Hammurabi the power to rule and orders the king to record the law. The lower portion of the stele contains the actual code, a collection of 282 laws.

© Réunion des Musées Nationaux/Art Resource, NY

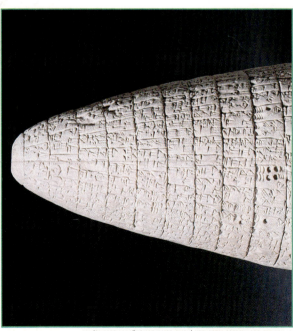

© Réunion des Musées Nationaux (Hervé Lewandowski)/Art Resource, NY

© Erich Lessing/Art Resource, NY

© Sandro Vannini/CORBIS

ARTS & IDEAS

Early Writing. Pictured at left is the upper part of the cone of Uruinimgina, covered in cuneiform script from an early Sumerian dynasty. The first Egyptian writing was also pictographic, as shown in the hieroglyphs in the detail from the mural in the tomb of Rameses I at bottom left. In Central America, the Mayan civilization had a well-developed writing system, also based on hieroglyphs, as seen below in the text carved on a stone platform in front of the Palace of the Large Masks in Kabah, Mexico.
Q What common feature is evident in these early writing systems? How might you explain that?

In astronomy, the Sumerians made use of units of 60 and charted the heavenly constellations. Their calendar was based on twelve lunar months and was brought into harmony with the solar year by adding an extra month from time to time.

Egyptian Civilization: "The Gift of the Nile"

Q **Focus Questions:** What are the basic features of the three major periods of Egyptian history? What elements of continuity are there in the three periods? What are their major differences?

"The Egyptian Nile," wrote one Arab traveler, "surpasses all the rivers of the world in sweetness of taste, in length of course and usefulness. No other river in the world can show such a continuous series of towns and villages along its banks." The Nile River was crucial to the development of Egyptian civilization (see the box on p. 18). Egypt, like Mesopotamia, was a river valley civilization.

The Impact of Geography

The Nile is a unique river, beginning in the heart of Africa and coursing northward for thousands of miles. It is the longest river in the world. The Nile was responsible for creating an area several miles wide on both banks of the river that was fertile and capable of producing abundant harvests. The "miracle" of the Nile was its annual flooding. The river rose in the summer from rains in Central Africa, crested in Egypt in September and October, and left a deposit of silt that enriched the soil. The Egyptians called this fertile land the "Black Land" because it was dark in color from the silt and the crops that grew on it so densely. Beyond these narrow strips of fertile fields lay the deserts (the "Red Land"). About 100 miles before it empties into the Mediterranean, the river splits into two major branches, forming the delta, a triangular-shaped territory called Lower Egypt to distinguish it from Upper Egypt, the land upstream to the south (see Map 1.4 on p.19). Egypt's important cities developed at the tip of the delta. Even today, most of Egypt's people are crowded along the banks of the Nile River.

Unlike Mesopotamia's rivers, the flooding of the Nile was gradual and usually predictable, and the river itself was seen as life-enhancing, not life-threatening. Although a system of organized irrigation was still necessary, the small villages along the Nile could create such systems without the massive state intervention that was required in Mesopotamia. Egyptian civilization consequently tended to remain more rural, with many small population centers congregated along a narrow band on both sides of the Nile.

The surpluses of food that Egyptian farmers grew in the fertile Nile valley made Egypt prosperous. But the Nile also served as a unifying factor in Egyptian history. In ancient times, the Nile was the fastest way to travel through the land, making both transportation and communication easier. Winds from the north pushed sailboats south, and the current of the Nile carried them north.

Unlike Mesopotamia, which was subject to constant invasion, Egypt had natural barriers that fostered isolation, protected it from invasion, and gave it a sense of security. These barriers included deserts to the west and east; cataracts (rapids) on the southern part of the river, which made defense relatively easy; and the Mediterranean Sea to the north. These barriers, however, were effective only when combined with Egyptian fortifications at strategic locations. Nor did these barriers prevent the development of trade. Indeed, there is evidence of very early trade between Egypt and Mesopotamia.

The regularity of the Nile floods and the relative isolation of the Egyptians created a sense of security and a feeling of changelessness. To the ancient Egyptians, when the Nile flooded each year, "the fields laugh, and people's faces light up." Unlike people in Mesopotamia, Egyptians faced life with a spirit of confidence in the stability of things. Ancient Egyptian civilization was characterized by a remarkable degree of continuity for thousands of years.

The Old and Middle Kingdoms

Modern historians have divided Egyptian history into three major periods, known as the Old Kingdom, the Middle Kingdom, and the New Kingdom. These were periods of long-term stability characterized by strong monarchical authority, competent bureaucracy, freedom from invasion, much construction of temples and pyramids, and considerable intellectual and cultural activity. But between the periods of stability were ages known as the Intermediate Periods, which were characterized by weak political structures and rivalry for leadership,

---

ARTS & IDEAS

The great epic poem of Mesopotamian literature, *The Epic of Gilgamesh*, includes an account by Utnapishtim (a Mesopotamian version of the later biblical Noah), who had built a ship and survived the flood unleashed by the gods to destroy humankind. In this selection, Utnapishtim recounts his story to Gilgamesh, telling how the god Ea advised him to build a boat and how he came to land the boat at the end of the flood.

The Epic of Gilgamesh

In those days the world teemed, the people multiplied, the world bellowed like a wild bull, and the great god was aroused by the clamor. Enlil heard the clamor and he said to the gods in council, "The uproar of mankind is intolerable and sleep is no longer possible by reason of the babel." So the gods agreed to exterminate mankind. Enlil did this, but Ea [Sumerian Enki, god of the waters] because of his oath warned me in a dream, "... Tear down your house and build a boat, abandon possessions and look for life, despise worldly goods and save your soul alive. Tear down your house, I say, and build a boat... then take up into the boat the seed of all living creatures...." [Utnapishtim did as he was told, and then the destruction came.]

For six days and six nights the winds blew, torrent and tempest and flood overwhelmed the world, tempest and flood raged together like warring hosts. When the seventh day dawned the storm from the south subsided, the sea grew calm, the flood was stilled; I looked at the face of the world and there was silence, all mankind was turned to clay. The surface of the sea stretched as flat as a rooftop; I opened a hatch and the light fell on my face. Then I bowed low, I sat down and I wept, the tears streamed down my face, for on every side was the waste of water. I looked for land in vain, but fourteen leagues distant there appeared a mountain, and there the boat grounded; on the mountain of Nisir the boat held fast, she held fast and did not budge.... When the seventh day dawned I loosed a dove and let her go. She flew away, but finding no resting place she returned. Then I loosed a swallow, and she flew away but finding no resting place she returned. I loosed a raven, she saw that the waters had retreated, she ate, she flew around, she cawed, and she did not come back. Then I threw everything open to the four winds, I made a sacrifice and poured out a libation on the mountaintop.

Q *What does this selection from The Epic of Gilgamesh tell you about the relationship between the Mesopotamians and their gods? How might you explain the differences between this account and the biblical flood story in Genesis?*

CENGAGENOW *To read more of The Epic of Gilgamesh, enter the documents area of the World History Resource Center using the access card that is available for World History.*

The Significance of the Nile River and the Pharaoh

RELIGION & PHILOSOPHY

Two of the most important sources of life for the ancient Egyptians were the Nile River and the pharaoh. Egyptians perceived that the Nile made possible the abundant food that was a major source of their well-being. This *Hymn to the Nile*, probably from the nineteenth and twentieth dynasties in the New Kingdom, expresses the gratitude Egyptians felt for the great river.

Hymn to the Nile

Hail to you, O Nile, that issues from the earth
and comes to keep Egypt alive!…
He that waters the meadows which Re created,
in order to keep every kid alive.
He that makes to drink the desert and the place
distant from water: that is his dew coming down
from heaven.…
The lord of fishes, he who makes the marsh-birds to
go upstream.…
He who makes barley and brings emmer [wheat] into
being, that he may make the temples festive.
If he is sluggish, then nostrils are stopped up, and
everybody is poor.…
When he rises, then the land is in jubilation, then
every belly is in joy, every backbone takes on
laughter, and every tooth is exposed.
The bringer of good, rich in provisions, creator of all
good, lord of majesty, sweet of fragrance.…
He who makes every beloved tree to grow, without
lack of them.

The Egyptian king, or pharaoh, was viewed as a god and the absolute ruler of Egypt. His significance and

the gratitude of the Egyptian people for his existence are evident in this hymn from the reign of Sesostris III (c. 1880–1840 B.C.E.).

Hymn to the Pharaoh

He has come unto us that he may carry away Upper
Egypt; the double diadem [crown of Upper and
Lower Egypt] has rested on his head.
He has come unto us and has united the Two Lands;
he has mingled the reed with the bee [symbols of
Lower and Upper Egypt].
He has come unto us and has brought the Black Land
under his sway; he has apportioned to himself the
Red Land.
He has come unto us and has taken the Two Lands
under his protection; he has given peace to the
Two Riverbanks.
He has come unto us and has made Egypt to live;
he has banished its suffering.
He has come unto us and has made the people to live;
he has caused the throat of the subjects to breathe.…
He has come unto us and has done battle for his
boundaries; he has delivered them that were robbed.

Q How do these two hymns underscore the importance of the Nile River and the institution of the pharaoh to Egyptian civilization?

CENGAGENOW *To read more of* Hymn to the Nile, *enter the documents area of the World History Resource Center using the access card that is available for World History.*

---

invasions, a decline in building activity, and a restructuring of society.

The Old Kingdom According to the Egyptians' own tradition, their land consisted initially of numerous populated areas ruled by tribal chieftains. Around 3100 B.C.E., the first Egyptian royal dynasty, under a king called Menes, united Upper and Lower Egypt into a single kingdom. Henceforth, the king would be called "king of Upper and Lower Egypt," and a royal crown, the Double Crown, was created, combining the White Crown of Upper Egypt and the Red Crown of Lower Egypt. Just as the Nile served to unite Upper and Lower Egypt physically, the kingship served to unite the two areas politically.

The Old Kingdom encompassed the third through sixth dynasties of Egyptian kings, lasting from around 2686 to 2180 B.C.E. It was an age of prosperity and splendor, made visible in the construction of the greatest and largest pyramids in Egypt's history. The capital of the Old Kingdom was located at Memphis, south of the delta.

Kingship was a divine institution in ancient Egypt and formed part of a universal cosmic scheme (see the box above): "What is the king of Upper and Lower Egypt? He is a god by whose dealings one lives, the father and mother of all men, alone by himself, without an equal."[6] In obeying their king, subjects helped maintain the cosmic order. A breakdown in royal power could only mean that citizens were offending divinity and weakening the universal structure. Among the various titles of Egyptian kings, that of **pharaoh** (originally meaning "great house" or "palace") eventually came to be the most common.

Although they possessed absolute power, Egyptian kings were supposed to rule not arbitrarily but according to set principles. The chief principle was called *Ma'at*, a spiritual precept that conveyed the ideas of truth and justice and especially right order and harmony. To ancient Egyptians, this fundamental order and harmony

Although theoretically absolute in their power, in practice Egyptian kings did not rule alone. Initially, members of the king's family performed administrative tasks, but by the fourth dynasty, a bureaucracy with regular procedures had developed. Especially important was the office of vizier, "steward of the whole land." Directly responsible to the king, the vizier was in charge of the bureaucracy. For administrative purposes, Egypt was divided into provinces, or *nomes* as they were later called by the Greeks—twenty-two in Upper Egypt and twenty in Lower Egypt. A governor, called by the Greeks a *nomarch,* was head of each nome and was responsible to the king and vizier. Nomarchs, however, tended to build up large holdings of land and power within their nomes, creating a potential rivalry with the pharaohs.

The Middle Kingdom Despite the theory of divine order, the Old Kingdom eventually collapsed, ushering in a period of disarray. Finally, a new royal dynasty managed to pacify all Egypt and inaugurated the Middle Kingdom, a period of stability lasting from around 2055 to 1650 B.C.E. Egyptians later portrayed the Middle Kingdom as a golden age, a clear indication of its stability. Several factors contributed to its vitality. The nome structure was reorganized. The boundaries of each nome were now settled precisely, and the obligations of the nomes to the state were clearly delineated. Nomarchs were confirmed as hereditary officeholders but with the understanding that their duties must be performed faithfully. These included the collection of taxes for the state and the recruitment of labor forces for royal projects, such as stone quarrying.

The Middle Kingdom was characterized by a new concern of the pharaohs for the people. In the Old Kingdom, the pharaoh had been viewed as an inaccessible god-king. Now he was portrayed as the shepherd of his people with the responsibility to build public works and provide for the public welfare. As one pharaoh expressed it, "He [a particular god] created me as one who should do that which he had done, and to carry out that which he commanded should be done. He appointed me as herdsman of this land, for he knew who would keep it in order for him."[7]

Society and Economy in Ancient Egypt

Egyptian society had a simple structure in the Old and Middle Kingdoms; basically, it was organized along hierarchical lines with the god-king at the top. The king was surrounded by an upper class of nobles and priests who participated in the elaborate rituals of life that surrounded the pharaoh. This ruling class ran the government and managed its own landed estates, which provided much of its wealth.

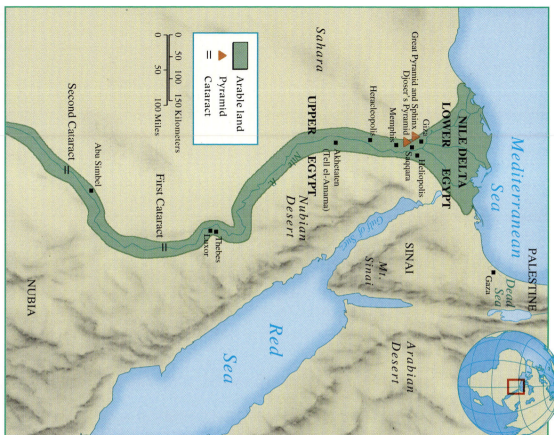

MAP 1.4 **Ancient Egypt.** Egyptian civilization centered on the life-giving water and flood silts of the Nile River, with most of the population living in Lower Egypt, where the river splits to form the Nile delta. Most of the pyramids, built during the Old Kingdom, are clustered south and west of Cairo.

Q How did the lands to the east and west of the river make invasions of Egypt difficult? **View an animated version of this map or related maps at** www.cengage.com/history/Duiker/World6e

had existed throughout the universe since the beginning of time. Pharaohs were the divine instruments who maintained it and were themselves subject to it.

By far the largest number of people in Egypt simply worked the land. In theory, the king owned all the land but granted portions of it to his subjects. Large sections were in the possession of nobles and the temple complexes. Most of the lower classes were serfs, or common people bound to the land, who cultivated the estates. They paid taxes in the form of crops to the king, nobles, and priests; lived in small villages or towns; and provided military service and forced labor for building projects.

The Culture of Egypt

Egypt produced a culture that dazzled and awed its later conquerors. The Egyptians' technical achievements, especially visible in the construction of the pyramids, demonstrated a measure of skill unequaled in the world at that time. To the Egyptians, all of these achievements were part of a cosmic order suffused with the presence of the divine.

Spiritual Life in Egyptian Society The Egyptians had no word for religion because it was an inseparable element of the entire world order to which Egyptian society belonged. The Egyptians were polytheistic and had a remarkable number of gods associated with heavenly bodies and natural forces, hardly unusual in view of the importance to Egypt's well-being of the sun, the river, and the fertile land along its banks. The sun was the source of life and hence worthy of worship. The sun god took on different forms and names, depending on his specific role. He was worshiped as Atum in human form and also as Re, who had a human body but the head of a falcon. The pharaoh took the title of "Son of Re," since he was regarded as the earthly form of Re. Eventually, Re became associated with Amon, an air god of Thebes, as Amon-Re.

River and land deities included Osiris and Isis with their child Horus, who was related to the Nile and to the sun as well. Osiris became especially important as a symbol of resurrection or rebirth. A famous Egyptian myth told of the struggle between Osiris, who brought civilization to Egypt, and his evil brother Seth, who killed him, cut his body into fourteen parts, and tossed them into the Nile River. Osiris' faithful wife Isis found the pieces and, with help from other gods, restored Osiris to life. As a symbol of resurrection and as judge of the dead, Osiris took on an important role for the Egyptians. By identifying with Osiris, one could hope to gain new life just as Osiris had done. The dead, embalmed and mummified, were placed in tombs (in the case of kings, in pyramidal tombs), given the name of Osiris, and by a process of magical identification became Osiris. Like Osiris, they could then be reborn. The flood of the Nile and the new life it brought to Egypt were symbolized by Isis gathering all of Osiris' parts together and were celebrated each spring in the Festival of the New Land.

The Pyramids One of the great achievements of Egyptian civilization, the building of pyramids, occurred

Statue of King Menkaure and His Queen. During the Old Kingdom, kings (eventually called pharaohs) were regarded as gods, divine instruments who maintained the fundamental order and harmony of the universe and wielded absolute power. Seated and standing statues of kings were commonly placed in Egyptian royal tombs. Seen here are the standing portraits of King Menkaure and his queen, Khamerernebty, from the fourth dynasty. By artistic convention, rulers were shown in rigid poses, reflecting their timeless nature. Husband and wife show no emotion but are seen looking out into space.

© Erich Lessing/Art Resource, NY

Below the upper classes were merchants and artisans. Merchants engaged in an active trade up and down the Nile as well as in town and village markets. Some merchants also engaged in international trade; they were sent by the king to Crete and Syria, where they obtained wood and other products. Expeditions traveled into Nubia for ivory and down the Red Sea to Punt for incense and spices. Eventually, trade links were established between ports in the Red Sea and countries as far away as the Indonesian archipelago. Egyptian artisans made an incredible variety of well-built and beautiful goods: stone dishes; painted boxes made of clay; wooden furniture; gold, silver, and copper tools and containers; paper and rope made of papyrus; and linen clothing.

in the time of the Old Kingdom. Pyramids were built as part of a larger complex of buildings dedicated to the dead—in effect, a city of the dead. The area included a large pyramid for the king's burial, smaller pyramids for his family, and *mastabas*, rectangular structures with flat roofs, as tombs for the pharaoh's noble officials.

The tombs were well prepared for their residents, their rooms furnished and stocked with numerous supplies, including chairs, boats, chests, weapons, games, dishes, and a variety of foods. The Egyptians believed that human beings had two bodies, a physical one and a spiritual one they called the *ka*. If the physical body was properly preserved (by mummification) and the tomb was furnished with all the objects of regular life, the *ka* could return, surrounded by earthly comforts, and continue its life despite the death of the physical body.

To preserve the physical body after death, the Egyptians practiced mummification, a process of slowly drying a dead body to prevent it from decomposing. Special workshops, run by priests, performed this procedure, primarily for the wealthy families who could afford it. According to an ancient Greek historian who visited Egypt around 450 B.C.E., "The most refined method is as follows: first of all they draw out the brain through the nostrils with an iron hook.... Then they make an incision in the flank with a sharp Ethiopian stone through which they extract all the internal organs."[8] The liver, lungs, stomach, and intestines were placed in four special jars that were put in the tomb with the mummy. The priests then covered the corpse with a natural salt that absorbed the body's water. Later, they filled the body with spices and wrapped it with layers of linen soaked in resin. At the end of the process, which took about seventy days, a lifelike mask was placed over the head and shoulders of the mummy, which was then sealed in a case and placed in its tomb.

Pyramids were tombs for the mummified bodies of the pharaohs. The largest and most magnificent of all the pyramids was built under King Khufu. Constructed at Giza around 2540 B.C.E., this famous Great Pyramid covers 13 acres, measures 756 feet at each side of its base, and stands 481 feet high (see the comparative illustration in Chapter 6, p. 170). Its four sides are almost precisely oriented to the four points of the compass. The interior included a grand gallery to the burial chamber, which was built of granite with a lidless sarcophagus for the pharaoh's body. The Great Pyramid still stands as a visible symbol of the power of Egyptian kings and the spiritual conviction that underlay Egyptian society. No pyramid built later ever matched its size or splendor. The pyramid was not only the king's tomb; it was also an important symbol of royal power. It could be seen from miles away, a visible reminder of the glory and might of the ruler who was a living god on earth.

Art and Writing Commissioned by kings or nobles for use in temples and tombs, Egyptian art was largely functional. Wall paintings and statues of gods and kings in temples served a strictly spiritual purpose. They were an integral part of the performance of ritual, which was thought necessary to preserve the cosmic order and hence the well-being of Egypt. Likewise, the mural scenes and sculptured figures found in the tombs had a specific function; they were supposed to assist the journey of the deceased into the afterworld.

Egyptian art was also formulaic. Artists and sculptors were expected to observe a strict canon of proportions that determined both form and presentation. This canon gave Egyptian art a distinctive appearance for thousands of years. Especially characteristic was the convention of combining the profile, semiprofile, and frontal views of the human body in relief work and painting in order to represent each part of the body accurately. The result was an art that was highly stylized yet still allowed distinctive features to be displayed.

Writing emerged in Egypt during the first two dynasties. The Greeks later called Egyptian writing **hieroglyphics**, meaning "priest-carvings" or "sacred writings." Hieroglyphs were sacred characters used as picture signs that depicted objects and had a sacred value at the same time. Although hieroglyphs were later simplified into two scripts for writing purposes, they never developed into an alphabet. Egyptian hieroglyphs were initially carved in stone, but later the two simplified scripts were written on papyrus, a paper made from the reeds that grew along the Nile. Most of the ancient Egyptian literature that has come down to us was written on papyrus rolls and wooden tablets.

Disorder and a New Order: The New Kingdom

The Middle Kingdom came to an end around 1650 B.C.E. with the invasion of Egypt by a people from western Asia known to the Egyptians as the Hyksos. The Hyksos used horse-drawn war chariots and overwhelmed the Egyptian soldiers, who fought from donkey carts. For almost a hundred years, the Hyksos ruled much of Egypt, but the conquered took much from their conquerors. From the Hyksos, the Egyptians learned to use bronze in making new farming tools and weapons. They also mastered the military skills of the Hyksos, especially the use of horse-drawn war chariots.

The Egyptian Empire Eventually, a new line of pharaohs—the eighteenth dynasty—made use of the new weapons to throw off Hyksos domination, reunite Egypt, establish the New Kingdom (c. 1550–1070 B.C.E.), and launch the Egyptians along a new militaristic path. During the period of the New Kingdom, Egypt assembled an empire and became the most powerful state in the Middle East.

Massive wealth aided the power of the New Kingdom pharaohs. The Egyptian rulers showed their wealth by building new temples. Queen Hatshepsut (c. 1503–1480 B.C.E.), in particular, one of the first women to become pharaoh in her own right, built a great temple at Deir el Bahri

AKHENATEN'S *HYMN TO ATEN* AND PSALM 104 OF THE HEBREW BIBLE

RELIGION & PHILOSOPHY

Amenhotep IV, more commonly known as Akhenaten, created a religious upheaval in Egypt by introducing the worship of Aten, god of the sun disk, as the chief god. Akhenaten's reverence for Aten is evident in this hymn. Some authorities have noted a similarity in spirit and wording to Psalm 104 of the Old Testament. In fact, some scholars have argued that there might be a connection between the two.

Hymn to Aten

Your rays suckle every meadow.
When you rise, they live, they grow for you.
You make the seasons in order to rear all that you
have made,
The winter to cool them,
And the heat that they may taste you.
You have made the distant sky in order to rise therein,
In order to see all that you do make.
While you were alone,
Rising in your form as the living Aten,
Appearing shining, withdrawing or approaching
You made millions of forms of yourself alone.

Cities, towns, fields, road, and river—
Every eye beholds you over against them,
For you are the Aten of the day over the earth....
The world came into being by your hand,
According as you have made them.
When you have risen they live,
When you set they die.
You are lifetime your own self,
For one lives only through you.
Eyes are fixed on beauty until you set.
All work is laid aside when you set in the west.
But when you rise again,
Everything is made to flourish for the king....
Since you did found the earth
And raise them up for your son,
Who came forth from your body: the King of Upper
and Lower Egypt... Akh-en-Aten.....and the
Chief Wife of the King... Nefert-iti, living and
youthful forever and ever.

Psalm 104:19–25, 27–30

The moon marks off the seasons,
and the sun knows when to go down.

You bring darkness, it becomes night,
and all the beasts of the forest prowl.

The lions roar for their prey
and seek their food from God.

The sun rises, and they steal away;
they return and lie down in their dens.

Then man goes out to his work,
to his labor until evening.

How many are your works, O Lord!
In wisdom you made them all;
the earth is full of your creatures.

There is the sea, vast and spacious,
teeming with creatures beyond number—
living things both large and small....

These all look to you
to give them their food at the proper time.

When you give it to them,
they gather it up;
when you open your hand,
they are satisfied with good things.

When you hide your face,
they are terrified;
when you take away their breath,
they die and return to the dust.

When you send your Spirit,
they are created,
and you renew the face of the earth.

Q What are the similarities between Akhenaten's Hymn to Aten and Psalm 104 of the Hebrew Bible? How would you explain the similarities? What are the significant differences between the two, and what do they tell you about the differences between the religion of the Egyptians and the religion of ancient Israel?

near Thebes. As pharaoh, Hatshepsut sent out military expeditions, encouraged mining, fostered agriculture, and sent a trading expedition up the Nile. Hatshepsut's official statues sometimes show her clothed and bearded like a king. She was referred to as "His Majesty." Hatshepsut was succeeded by her nephew, Thutmosis III (c. 1480–1450 B.C.E.), who led seventeen military campaigns into Syria and Palestine and even reached the Euphrates River. Egyptian forces occupied Palestine and Syria and also moved westward into Libya.

Akhenaten and Religious Change The eighteenth dynasty was not without its troubles, however. Amenhotep IV (c. 1364–1347 B.C.E.) introduced the worship of Aten, god of the sun disk, as the chief god (see the box above) and pursued his worship with great enthusiasm. Changing

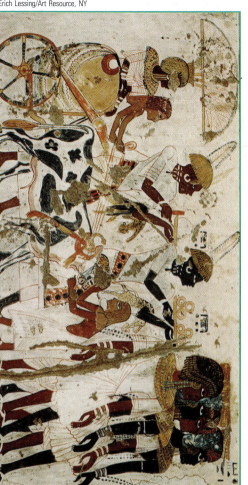

© Erich Lessing/Art Resource, NY

his own name to Akhenaten ("servant of Aten"), the pharaoh closed the temples of other gods and especially endeavored to lessen the power of Amon-Re and his priesthood at Thebes. Akhenaten strove to reduce their influence by replacing Thebes as the capital of Egypt with Akhetaten ("horizon of the Aten"), a new city located at modern Tell el-Amarna, 200 miles north of Thebes.

Akhenaten's attempt at religious change failed. It was too much to ask Egyptians to give up their traditional ways and beliefs, especially since they saw the destruction of the old gods as subversive of the very cosmic order on which Egypt's survival and continuing prosperity depended. Moreover, the priests at Thebes were unalterably opposed to the changes, which had diminished their influence and power. At the same time, Akhenaten's preoccupation with religion caused him to ignore foreign affairs and led to the loss of both Syria and Palestine. Akhenaten's changes were soon undone after his death by those who influenced his successor, the boy-pharaoh Tutankhamun (1347–1338 B.C.E.). Tutankhamun returned the government to Thebes and restored the old gods. The Aten experiment had failed to take hold, and the eighteenth dynasty itself came to an end in 1333.

Decline of the Egyptian Empire

The nineteenth dynasty managed to restore Egyptian power one more time. Under Ramesses II (c. 1279–1213 B.C.E.), the Egyptians regained control of Palestine but were unable to reestablish the borders of their earlier empire. New invasions in the thirteenth century by the "Sea Peoples," as the Egyptians called them, destroyed Egyptian power in Palestine and drove the Egyptians back within their old frontiers. The days of Egyptian empire were ended, and the New Kingdom itself expired with the end of the twentieth dynasty in 1070. For the next thousand years, despite periodical revivals of strength, Egypt was dominated by Libyans, Nubians, Persians, and finally Macedonians, after the conquest of Alexander the Great (see Chapter 4). In the first century B.C.E., Egypt became a province in Rome's mighty empire. Egypt continued, however, to influence its conquerors through the richness of its heritage and the awesome magnificence of its physical remains.

CHRONOLOGY The Egyptians

Early Dynastic Period (Dynasties 1–2)	c. 3100–2686 B.C.E.
Old Kingdom (Dynasties 3–6)	c. 2686–2180 B.C.E.
First Intermediate Period (Dynasties 7–10)	c. 2180–2055 B.C.E.
Middle Kingdom (Dynasties 11–12)	c. 2055–1650 B.C.E.
Second Intermediate Period (Dynasties 13–17)	c. 1650–1550 B.C.E.
New Kingdom (Dynasties 18–20)	c. 1550–1070 B.C.E.
Post-Empire (Dynasties 21–31)	c. 1070–30 B.C.E.

Daily Life in Ancient Egypt: Family and Marriage

Ancient Egyptians had a very positive attitude toward daily life on earth and followed the advice of the wisdom literature, which suggested that people marry young and establish a home and family. Monogamy was the general rule, although a husband was allowed to keep additional wives if his first wife was childless. Pharaohs, of course, were entitled to harems. The queen was acknowledged, however, as the "great wife," with a status higher than that of the other wives. The husband was master in the house, but wives were very much respected and in charge of the household and the education of the children. From a book of wise sayings (which the Egyptians called "instructions") came this advice:

If you are a man of standing, you should found your household and love your wife at home as is fitting. Fill her belly; clothe her back. Ointment is the prescription for her body.

Nubians in Egypt. During the New Kingdom, Egypt expanded to include Palestine and Syria to the north and the kingdom of Nubia to the south. Nubia had emerged as an African kingdom around 2300 B.C.E. Shown here in a fourteenth-century B.C.E. painting from an Egyptian official's tomb in Nubia are Nubians arriving in Egypt with bags and rings of gold. Nubia was a major source of gold for the Egyptians.

Make her heart glad as long as you live. She is a profitable field for her lord. You should not contend with her at law, and keep her far from gaining control....Let her heart be soothed through what may accrue to you; it means keeping her long in your house.[9]

Women's property and inheritance remained in their hands, even in marriage. Although most careers and public offices were closed to women, some women did operate businesses. Peasant women worked long hours in the fields and at numerous domestic tasks. Upper-class women could function as priestesses, and a few queens, such as Hatshepsut, even became pharaohs in their own right.

Marriages were arranged by parents. The primary concerns were family and property, and the chief purpose of marriage was to produce children, especially sons. From the New Kingdom came this piece of wisdom: "Take to yourself a wife while you are [still] a youth, that she may produce a son for you."[10] Daughters were not slighted, however. Numerous tomb paintings show the close and affectionate relationship parents had with both sons and daughters. Although marriages were arranged, some of the surviving love poems from ancient Egypt suggest that some marriages included an element of romance. Here is the lament of a lovesick boy for his "sister" (lovers referred to each other as "brother" and "sister"):

Seven days to yesterday I have not seen the sister,
and a sickness has invaded me;
My body has become heavy,
And I am forgetful of my own self.
If the chief physicians come to me,
My heart is not content with their remedies....
What will revive me is to say to me: "Here she is!"
Her name is what will lift me up....
My health is her coming in from outside:
When I see her, then I am well.[11]

Marriages could and did end in divorce, which was allowed, apparently with compensation for the wife. Adultery, however, was strictly prohibited, with stiff punishments—especially for women, who could have their noses cut off or be burned at the stake.

The Spread of Egyptian Influence: Nubia

The civilization of Egypt had an impact on other peoples in the lands of the eastern Mediterranean. Egyptian products have been found in Crete and Cretan products in Egypt (see Chapter 4). Egyptian influence is also evident in early Greek statues. The Egyptians also had an impact to the south in Nubia (the northern part of modern Sudan). In fact, some archaeologists have recently suggested that the African kingdom of Nubia may have arisen even before the kingdoms of Egypt.

It is clear that contacts between the upper and lower Nile had been established by the late third millennium B.C.E., when Egyptian merchants traveled to Nubia to obtain ivory, ebony, frankincense, and leopard skins. A few centuries later, Nubia had become an Egyptian tributary. At the end of the second millennium B.C.E., Nubia profited from the disintegration of the Egyptian New Kingdom to become the independent state of Kush. Egyptian influence continued, however, as Kushite culture borrowed extensively from Egypt, including religious beliefs, the practice of interring kings in pyramids, and hieroglyphs.

Although its economy was probably founded primarily on agriculture and animal husbandry, Kush developed into a major trading state in Africa that endured for hundreds of years. Its commercial activities were stimulated by the discovery of iron ore in a floodplain near the river at Meroë. Strategically located at the point where a land route across the desert to the south intersected the Nile River, Meroë eventually became the capital of the state. In addition to iron products, Kush supplied goods from Central and East Africa, notably ivory, gold, ebony, and slaves, to the Roman Empire, Arabia, and India. At first, goods were transported by donkey caravans to the point where the river north was navigable. By the last centuries of the first millennium B.C.E., however, the donkeys were being replaced by camels, newly introduced from the Arabian peninsula.

New Centers of Civilization

Focus Questions: What was the significance of the Indo-Europeans? How did Judaism differ from the religions of Mesopotamia and Egypt?

Our story of civilization so far has been dominated by Mesopotamia and Egypt. But significant developments were also taking place on the fringes of these civilizations. Farming had spread into the Balkan peninsula of Europe by 6500 B.C.E., and by 4000 B.C.E., it was well established in southern France, central Europe, and the coastal regions of the Mediterranean. Although migrating farmers from the Anatolian peninsula may have brought some farming techniques into Europe, some historians believe that the Neolithic peoples of Europe domesticated animals and began to farm largely on their own.

One outstanding feature of late Neolithic Europe was the building of megalithic structures. **Megalith** is Greek for "large stone." Radiocarbon dating, a technique

Stonehenge and Other Megalithic Regions in Europe

© Adam Woolfitt/CORBIS

Stonehenge. The Bronze Age in northwestern Europe is known for its megaliths, large standing stones. Between 3200 and 1500 B.C.E., standing stones, placed in circles or lined up in rows, were erected throughout the British Isles and northwestern France. The most famous of these megalithic constructions is Stonehenge in England.

that allows scientists to determine the age of objects, shows that the first megalithic structures were constructed around 4000 B.C.E., more than a thousand years before the great pyramids were built in Egypt. Between 3200 and 1500 B.C.E., standing stones, placed in circles or lined up in rows, were erected throughout the British Isles and northwestern France. Other megalithic constructions have been found as far north as Scandinavia and as far south as the islands of Corsica, Sardinia, and Malta. Archaeologists have demonstrated that the stone circles were used as observatories to detect not only such simple astronomical phenomena as the midwinter and midsummer sunrises but also such sophisticated phenomena as the major and minor standstills of the moon.

Nomadic Peoples: Impact of the Indo-Europeans

On the fringes of civilization lived nomadic peoples who depended on hunting and gathering, herding, and sometimes a bit of farming for their survival. Most important were the pastoral nomads who on occasion overran civilized communities and forged their own empires. Pastoral nomads domesticated animals for both food and clothing and moved along regular migratory routes to provide steady sources of nourishment for their animals.

The Indo-Europeans were among the most important nomadic peoples. These groups spoke languages derived from a single parent tongue. Indo-European languages include Greek, Latin, Persian, Sanskrit, and the Germanic and Slavic tongues (see Table 1.2). The original Indo-European-speaking peoples were probably based in the steppe region north of the Black Sea or in southwestern Asia, in modern Iran or Afghanistan, but around 2000 B.C.E., they began to move into Europe, India, and western Asia. The domestication of horses and the importation of the wheel and wagon from Mesopotamia facilitated the Indo-European migrations to other lands (see Map 1.5).

The Hittites

One group of Indo-Europeans who moved into Asia Minor and Anatolia (modern Turkey) around 1750 B.C.E. coalesced with the native peoples to form the Hittite kingdom, with its capital at Hattusha (Bogazköy in modern Turkey). Between 1600 and 1200 B.C.E., the Hittites formed their own empire in western Asia and even threatened the power of the Egyptians.

The Hittites were the first of the Indo-European peoples to make use of iron, enabling them to construct weapons that were stronger and cheaper to make because of the widespread availability of iron ore. During its height, the Hittite Empire also demonstrated an interesting ability to assimilate other cultures into its own. In borrowed much from Mesopotamia as well as from the native peoples they had subdued. Recent scholarship has stressed the important role of the Hittites in transmitting Mesopotamian culture, as they transformed it, to later civilizations in the Mediterranean area, especially to the Mycenaean Greeks (see Chapter 4).

During its heyday, the Hittite Empire was one of the great powers in western Asia. Constant squabbling over succession to the throne, however, tended to weaken royal authority at times. Especially devastating, however, were attacks by the Sea Peoples from the west and aggressive neighboring tribes. By 1190 B.C.E., Hittite power had come to an end. The destruction of the Hittite kingdom and the weakening of Egypt around 1200 B.C.E.

TABLE 1.2 Some Indo-European Languages

SUBFAMILY	LANGUAGES
Indo-Iranian	*Sanskrit, Persian*
Balto-Slavic	Russian, Serbo-Croatian, Czech, Polish, Lithuanian
Hellenic	Greek
Italic	*Latin,* Romance languages (French, Italian, Spanish, Portuguese, Romanian)
Celtic	Irish, Gaelic
Germanic	Swedish, Danish, Norwegian, German, Dutch, English

NOTE: Languages in italic type are no longer spoken.

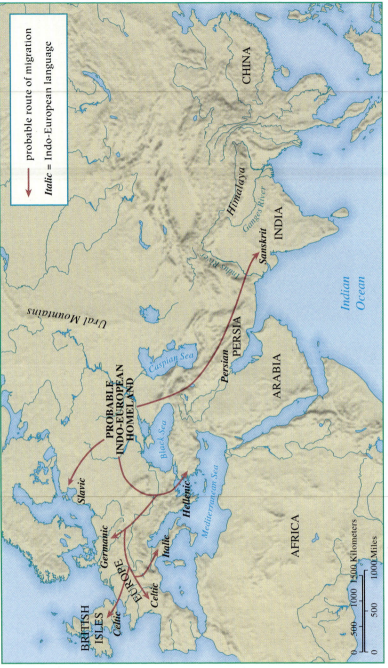

MAP 1.5 **The Spread of the Indo-Europeans.** From their probable homeland in the steppe region north of the Black Sea, Indo-European-speaking peoples moved eventually into Europe, India, and western Asia. The languages shown on the map are all Indo-European languages (see Table 1.2).

Q How do you explain the movements of Indo-European-speaking peoples? ● View an animated version of this map or related maps at www.cengage.com/history/Duiker/Worldce

→ = probable route of migration

Italic = Indo-European language

---

left no dominant powers in western Asia, allowing a patchwork of petty kingdoms and city-states to emerge, especially in the area of Syria and Palestine. The Phoenicians were one of these peoples.

The Phoenicians

A Semitic-speaking people, the Phoenicians lived in the area of Palestine along the Mediterranean coast on a narrow band of land 120 miles long. Their newfound political independence after the demise of Hittite and Egyptian power helped the Phoenicians expand the trade that was already the foundation of their prosperity. The chief cities of Phoenicia—Byblos, Tyre, and Sidon—were ports on the eastern Mediterranean, but they also served as distribution centers for the lands to the east in Mesopotamia. The Phoenicians themselves produced a number of goods for foreign markets, including purple dye, glass, wine, and lumber from the famous cedars of Lebanon. In addition, the Phoenicians improved their ships and became great international sea traders. They charted new routes, not only in the Mediterranean but also in the Atlantic Ocean, where they reached Britain and sailed south along the west coast of Africa. The Phoenicians established a number of colonies in the western

Mediterranean, including settlements in southern Spain, Sicily, and Sardinia. Carthage, the Phoenicians' most famous colony, was located on the north coast of Africa.

Culturally, the Phoenicians are best known as transmitters. Instead of using pictographs or signs to represent whole words and syllables as the Mesopotamians and Egyptians did, the Phoenicians simplified their writing by using twenty-two different signs to represent the sounds of their speech. These twenty-two characters or letters could be used to spell out all the words in the Phoenician language. Although the Phoenicians were not the only people to invent an alphabet, theirs would have special significance because it was eventually passed on to the Greeks. From the Greek alphabet was derived the Roman alphabet that we still use today (Table 1.3 shows the derivation of the letters A to F). The Phoenicians achieved much while independent, but they ultimately fell subject to the Assyrians and Persians.

The Hebrews: The "Children of Israel"

To the south of the Phoenicians lived another group of Semitic-speaking people known as the Hebrews. Although they were a minor factor in the politics of the region, their **monotheism**—belief in but one God—later

TABLE 1.3 The Phoenician, Greek, and Roman Alphabets

Phoenician	Phoenician Name	Modern Symbol	Early Greek	Classical Greek	Greek Name	Early Latin	Classical Latin
𐤀	'aleph	'	A	A	alpha	A	A
𐤁	beth	b	B	B	beta	A	B
𐤂	gimel	g	𐌂	Γ	gamma		C
𐤃	daleth	d	Δ	Δ	delta	D	D
𐤄	he	h	E	E	epsilon	E	E
𐤅	waw	w	F	F	digamma	F	F

SOURCE: Andrew Robinson, *The Story of Writing* (London, 1995), p. 170.

influenced both Christianity and Islam and flourished as a world religion in its own right. The Hebrews had a tradition concerning their origins and history that was eventually written down as part of the Hebrew Bible, known to Christians as the Old Testament. Describing them as a nomadic people, the Hebrews' own tradition states that they were descendants of the patriarch Abraham, who had migrated from Mesopotamia to the land of Canaan, where the Hebrews became identified as the "Children of Israel." Moreover, according to tradition, a drought in Canaan caused many Hebrews to migrate to Egypt, where they lived peacefully until they were enslaved by pharaohs who used them as laborers on building projects. The Hebrews remained in bondage until Moses led his people out of Egypt in the well-known "exodus," which some historians believe occurred in the first half of the thirteenth century B.C.E. According to the biblical account, the Hebrews then wandered for many years in the desert until they entered Canaan. Organized into twelve tribes, the Hebrews became embroiled in conflict with the Philistines, who had settled along the coast of Canaan but were beginning to move inland.

Many scholars today doubt that the biblical account reflects the true history of the early Israelites. They argue that the early books of the Bible, written centuries after the events described, preserve only what the Israelites came to believe about themselves and that recent archaeological evidence often contradicts the details of the biblical account. Some of these scholars have even argued that the Israelites were not nomadic invaders but indigenous peoples in the Canaanite hill country. What is generally agreed, however, is that between 1200 and 1000 B.C.E., the Israelites emerged as a distinct group of people, possibly organized into tribes or a league of tribes, who established a united kingdom known as Israel.

The United Kingdom of Israel The first king of the Israelites was Saul (c. 1020–1000 B.C.E.), who initially achieved some success in the ongoing struggle with the Philistines. But after his death in a disastrous battle with

this enemy, a brief period of anarchy ensued until one of Saul's lieutenants, David (c. 1000–970 B.C.E.), reunited the Israelites, defeated the Philistines, and established control over all of Canaan. Among David's conquests was the city of Jerusalem, which he made into the capital of a united kingdom. David centralized Israel's organization and accelerated the integration of the Israelites into a settled community based on farming and urban life.

David's son Solomon (c. 970–930 B.C.E.) did even more to strengthen royal power. He expanded the political and military establishments and was especially active in extending the trading activities of the Israelites. Solomon is known for his building projects, of which the most famous was the Temple in the city of Jerusalem. The Israelites viewed the Temple as the symbolic center of their religion and hence of the kingdom of Israel itself. The Temple now housed the Ark of the Covenant, a holy chest containing the sacred relics of the Hebrew religion and, symbolically, the throne of the invisible God of Israel. Under Solomon, ancient Israel was at the height of its power, but his efforts to extend royal power throughout his kingdom led to dissatisfaction among some of his subjects.

The Divided Kingdom After Solomon's death, tensions between northern and southern tribes in Israel led to the establishment of two separate kingdoms—the kingdom of Israel, composed of the ten northern tribes, with its capital eventually at Samaria, and the southern kingdom of Judah, consisting of two tribes, with its capital at Jerusalem (see Map 1.6). In 722 or 721 B.C.E., the Assyrians destroyed Samaria, overran the kingdom of Israel, and deported many Hebrews to other parts of the Assyrian Empire. These dispersed Hebrews (the "ten lost tribes") merged with neighboring peoples and gradually lost their identity.

The southern kingdom of Judah was also forced to pay tribute to Assyria but managed to retain its independence as Assyrian power declined. However, a new enemy appeared on the horizon. The Chaldeans defeated

© British Museum, London///The Bridgeman Art Library

CHRONOLOGY The Israelites

Israelites	
Saul (first king)	c. 1020–1000 B.C.E.
King David	c. 1000–970 B.C.E.
King Solomon	c. 970–930 B.C.E.
Northern kingdom of Israel destroyed by Assyria	722 or 721 B.C.E.
Fall of southern kingdom of Judah to Chaldeans; destruction of Jerusalem	586 B.C.E.
Return of exiles to Jerusalem	538 B.C.E.

But the Babylonian captivity of the people of Judah did not last. A new set of conquerors, the Persians, destroyed the Chaldean kingdom and allowed the people of Judah to return to Jerusalem and rebuild their city and Temple. The revived kingdom of Judah remained under Persian control until the conquests of Alexander the Great in the fourth century B.C.E. The people of Judah survived, eventually becoming known as the Jews and giving their name to Judaism, the religion of Yahweh, the Israelite God.

The Spiritual Dimensions of Israel According to the Hebrew conception, there is but one God, called Yahweh, who created the world and everything in it. Yahweh ruled the world and was subject to nothing. This omnipotent creator, however, was not removed from the life he had created but was a just and good God who expected

The King of Israel Pays Tribute to the King of Assyria. By the end of the ninth century B.C.E., the kingdom of Israel had been forced to pay tribute to the Assyrian Empire. The Assyrians overran the kingdom in 722 or 721 B.C.E. and destroyed the capital city of Samaria. In this scene from a black obelisk, King Jehu of Israel is shown paying tribute to King Shalmaneser III of Assyria.

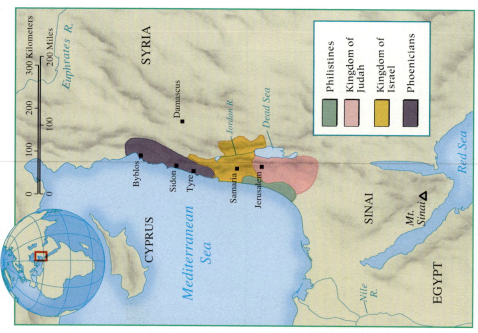

MAP 1.6 The Israelites and Their Neighbors in the First Millennium B.C.E. United under Saul, David, and Solomon, greater Israel split into two states—Israel and Judah—after the death of Solomon. With power divided, the Israelites could not resist invasions that dispersed many of them from Canaan. Some, such as the "ten lost tribes," never returned. Others were sent to Babylon but were later allowed to return under the rule of the Persians.

Q Why was Israel more vulnerable to the Assyrian Empire than Judah was? ☛ View an animated version of this map or related maps at www.cengage.com/history/Duiker/World6e

Assyria, conquered the kingdom of Judah, and completely destroyed Jerusalem in 586 B.C.E. Many upper-class people from Judah were deported to Babylonia; the memory of their exile is still evoked in the stirring words of Psalm 137:

> By the rivers of Babylon, we sat and wept when we
> remembered Zion. . . .
> How can we sing the songs of the Lord while in
> a foreign land?
> If I forget you, O Jerusalem, may my right hand
> forget its skill.
> May my tongue cling to the roof of my mouth if I do
> not remember you,
> If I do not consider Jerusalem my highest joy.[12]

RELIGION & PHILOSOPHY

According to the biblical account, it was during the exodus from Egypt that the Israelites made their covenant with Yahweh. They agreed to obey their God and follow his law. In return, Yahweh promised to take special care of his chosen people. This selection from the biblical book of Exodus describes the making of the covenant and God's commandments to the Israelites.

Exodus 19:1–8

In the third month after the Israelites left Egypt—on the very day—they came to the Desert of Sinai. After they set out from Rephidim, they entered the desert of Sinai, and Israel camped there in the desert in front of the mountain. Then Moses went up to God, and the Lord called to him from the mountain, and said, "This is what you are to say to the house of Jacob and what you are to tell the people of Israel: 'You yourselves have seen what I did to Egypt, and how I carried you on eagles' wings and brought you to myself. Now if you obey me fully and keep my covenant, then out of all nations you will be my treasured possession. Although the whole earth is mine, you will be for me a kingdom of priests and a holy nation.' These are the words you are to speak to the Israelites." So Moses went back and summoned the elders of the people and set before them all the words the Lord had commanded him to speak. The people all responded together, "We will do everything the Lord has said." So Moses brought their answer back to the Lord.

Exodus 20:1–3, 7–17

And God spoke all these words, "I am the Lord your God, who brought you out of Egypt, out of the land of slavery.

You shall have no other gods before me.... You shall not misuse the name of the Lord your God, for the Lord will not hold anyone guiltless who misuses his name. Remember the Sabbath day by keeping it holy. Six days you shall labor and do all your work, but the seventh day is a Sabbath to the Lord your God. On it you shall not do any work, neither you, nor your son or daughter, nor your manservant or maidservant, nor your animals, nor the alien within your gates. For in six days the Lord made the heavens and the earth, the sea, and all that is in them, but he rested on the seventh day. Therefore the Lord blessed the Sabbath day and made it holy. Honor your father and your mother, so that you may live long in the land the Lord your God is giving you. You shall not murder. You shall not commit adultery. You shall not steal. You shall not give false testimony against your neighbor. You shall not covet your neighbor's house. You shall not covet your neighbor's wife, or his manservant or maidservant, his ox or donkey, or anything that belongs to your neighbor."

Q What was the nature of the covenant between Yahweh and the Israelites? What was its moral significance for the Israelites? How might you explain its differences from Hammurabi's code?

CENGAGENOW To read more of the book of Exodus, enter the documents area of the World History Resource Center using the access card that is available for World History.

---

goodness from his people. If they did not obey his will, they would be punished. But he was primarily a God of mercy and love: "The Lord is gracious and compassionate, slow to anger and rich in love. The Lord is good to all; he has compassion on all he has made."13 Each individual could have a personal relationship with this being.

Three aspects of the Hebrew religious tradition had special significance: the covenant, the law, and the prophets. The Israelites believed that during the exodus from Egypt, when Moses, according to biblical tradition, led his people out of bondage and into the Promised Land, God made a covenant or contract with the tribes of Israel, who believed that Yahweh had spoken to them through Moses (see the box above). The Israelites promised to obey Yahweh and follow his law. In return, Yahweh promised to take special care of his chosen people, "a peculiar treasure unto me above all people."

This covenant between Yahweh and his chosen people could be fulfilled, however, only by obedience to the law of God. Most important were the ethical concerns that stood at the center of the law. Sometimes these took the form of specific standards of moral behavior: "You shall not murder. You shall not commit adultery. You shall not steal."14 True freedom consisted of following God's moral standards voluntarily. If people chose to ignore the good, suffering and evil would follow.

The Israelites believed that certain religious teachers, called prophets, were sent by God to serve as his voice to his people (see the box on p. 30). The golden age of prophecy began in the mid-eighth century B.C.E. and continued during the time when the people of Israel and Judah were threatened by Assyrian and Chaldean conquerors. The "men of God" went through the land warning the Israelites that they had failed to keep God's commandments and would be punished for

The Assyrian Military Machine

POLITICS & GOVERNMENT

The Assyrians developed a mighty military machine. They employed a variety of military tactics that met with success whether they were waging guerrilla warfare, fighting set battles, or laying siege to cities. In these three selections, Assyrian kings boast of their military conquests.

King Sennacherib (704–681 B.C.E.) Describes a Battle with the Elamites in 691

At the command of the god Ashur, the great Lord, I rushed upon the enemy like the approach of a hurricane.... I put them to rout and turned them back. I transfixed the troops of the enemy with javelins and arrows.... I cut their throats like sheep.... My prancing steeds, trained to harness, plunged into their welling blood as into a river; the wheels of my battle chariot were bespattered with blood and filth. I filled the plain with the corpses of their warriors like herbage.... As to the sheikhs of the Chaldeans, panic from my onslaught overwhelmed them like a demon. They abandoned their tents and fled for their lives, crushing the corpses of their troops as they went.... In their terror they passed scalding urine and voided their excrement into their chariots.

King Sennacherib Describes His Siege of Jerusalem in 701

As to Hezekiah, the Jew, he did not submit to my yoke. I laid siege to 46 of his strong cities, walled forts, and the countless small villages in their vicinity, and conquered them by means of well-stamped earth-ramps, and battering-rams brought thus near to the walls combined with the attack by foot soldiers, using mines, breaches, as well as sapper work. I drove out of them 200,150 people, young and old, male and female, horses, mules, donkeys, camels, big and small cattle beyond counting, and considered them booty. Himself I made a prisoner in Jerusalem, his royal residence, like a bird in a cage. I surrounded him with earthwork in order to molest those who were leaving his city's gate.

King Ashurbanipal (669–626 B.C.E.) Describes His Treatment of Conquered Babylon

I tore out the tongues of those whose slanderous mouths had uttered blasphemies against my god Ashur and had plotted against me, his god-fearing prince; I defeated them completely. The others, I smashed alive with the very same statues of protective deities with which they had smashed my own grandfather Sennacherib—now finally as a belated burial sacrifice for his soul. I fed their corpses, cut into small pieces, to dogs, pigs,...vultures, the birds of the sky, and also to the fish of the ocean. After I had performed this and thus made quiet again the hearts of the great gods, my lords, I removed the corpses of those whom the pestilence had felled, whose leftovers after the dogs and pigs had fed on them were obstructing the streets, filling the places of Babylon, and of those who had lost their lives through the terrible famine.

Q As seen in their own descriptions, what did Assyrian kings believe was important for military success? Do you think their accounts may be exaggerated? Why?

CENGAGENOW *To read related sources, enter the documents area of the World History Resource Center using the access card that is available for World History.*

Ashurnasirpal recorded this account of his treatment of prisoners:

3000 of their combat troops I felled with weapons.... Many of the captives taken from them I burned in a fire. Many I took alive; from some of these I cut off their hands to the wrist, from others I cut off their noses, ears and fingers; I put out the eyes of many of the soldiers....I burned their young men and women to death.[16]

After conquering another city, the same king wrote, "I fixed up a pile of corpses in front of the city's gate. I flayed the nobles, as many as had rebelled, and spread their skins out on the piles....I flayed many within my land and spread their skins out on the walls."[17] It should be noted that this policy of extreme cruelty to prisoners was not used against all enemies but was primarily reserved for those who were already part of the empire and then rebelled against Assyrian rule.

Assyrian Society Assyrian deportation policies created a polyglot society in which ethnic differences were not very important. What gave identity to the Assyrians themselves was their language, although even that was akin to the language of their southern neighbors in Babylonia, who also spoke a Semitic tongue. Religion was also a cohesive force. Assyria was literally "the land of Ashur," a reference to its chief god. The king, as Ashur's representative on earth, provided a final unifying focus.

Agriculture formed the principal basis of Assyrian life. Assyria was a land of farming villages with relatively few significant cities, especially in comparison to southern Mesopotamia. Unlike the river valleys, where farming required the minute organization of large numbers of people to control irrigation, Assyrian farms received sufficient moisture from regular rainfall.

King Ashurbanipal's Lion Hunt. This relief, sculpted on alabaster as a decoration for the Assyrian northern palace in Nineveh, depicts King Ashurbanipal engaged in a lion hunt. Lion hunts were conducted not in the wild but under controlled circumstances: the king and his retainers faced lions released from cages in an arena. The scene was intended to glorify the king as the conqueror of the king of beasts. Relief sculpture, one of the best-known forms of Assyrian art, reached its zenith under Ashurbanipal just before the Assyrian Empire began its rapid disintegration.

Trade was second to agriculture in economic importance. For internal trade, metals—including gold, silver, copper, and bronze—were used as a medium of exchange. Various agricultural products also served as a form of payment or exchange. Because of their geographical location, the Assyrians served as intermediaries and participated in an international trade in which they imported timber, wine, and precious metals and stones while exporting textiles produced in palaces, temples, and private workshops.

Assyrian Culture The culture of the Assyrian Empire was essentially a hybrid. The Assyrians assimilated much of Mesopotamian civilization and saw themselves as guardians of Sumerian and Babylonian culture. Assyrian kings also tried to maintain old traditions when they rebuilt damaged temples by constructing the new buildings on the original foundations rather than in new locations.

Among the best-known objects of Assyrian art are the relief sculptures found in the royal palaces in three of the Assyrian capital cities, Nimrud, Nineveh, and Khorsabad. These reliefs, which were begun in the ninth century B.C.E. and reached their high point in the reign of Ashurbanipal in the seventh, depicted two different kinds of subject matter: ritual or ceremonial scenes revolving around the king and scenes of hunting and war. The latter show realistic action scenes of the king and his warriors engaged in battle or hunting animals, especially lions. These images depict a strongly masculine world where discipline, brute force, and toughness are the enduring values—indeed, the very values of the Assyrian military monarchy.

The Persian Empire

After the collapse of the Assyrian Empire, the Chaldeans, under their king Nebuchadnezzar II (605–562 B.C.E.), made Babylonia the leading state in western Asia. Nebuchadnezzar rebuilt Babylon as the center of his empire, giving it a reputation as one of the great cities of the ancient world. But the splendor of Chaldean Babylonia proved to be short-lived when Babylon fell to the Persians in 539 B.C.E.

The Persians were an Indo-European-speaking people who lived in southwestern Iran. Primarily nomadic, the Persians were organized into tribes until the Achaemenid dynasty managed to unify them. One of the dynasty's members, Cyrus (559–530 B.C.E.), created a powerful Persian state that rearranged the political map of western Asia.

Cyrus the Great In 550 B.C.E., Cyrus extended Persian control over the Medes, making Media the first Persian **satrapy,** or province. Three years later, Cyrus defeated the prosperous Lydian kingdom in western Asia Minor, and Lydia became another Persian satrapy. Cyrus' forces then went on to conquer the Greek city-states that had been established on the Ionian coast. Cyrus then turned eastward, subduing the eastern part of the Iranian Plateau, Sogdia, and even western India. His eastern frontiers secured, Cyrus entered Mesopotamia in 539 and captured Babylon (see Map 1.7). His treatment of Babylonia showed remarkable restraint and wisdom. Babylonia was made into a Persian province under a Persian **satrap,** or governor, but many government officials were

© Werner Forman/Art Resource, NY

best in their positions. G... took the title "King of All

badly," advised Krishna, "than in doing another man's duty

subcontinent in the ninth or tenth century C.E.), continue

inhabitants, as large as some of the most populous urban centers in Sumerian civilization.

Both Harappa and Mohenjo-Daro were divided into large walled neighborhoods, with narrow lanes separating the rows of houses. Houses varied in size, with some as high as three stories, but all followed the same general plan based on a square courtyard surrounded by rooms. Bathrooms featured an advanced drainage system, which carried wastewater out to drains located under the streets and thence to sewage pits beyond the city walls. But the cities also had the equivalent of the modern slum. At Harappa, tiny dwellings for workers have been found near metal furnaces and the open areas used for pounding grain.

Unfortunately, Harappan writing has not yet been deciphered, so historians know relatively little about the organization of the Harappan state. However, recent archaeological evidence suggests that unlike its contemporaries in Egypt and Sumer, Harappa was not a centralized monarchy with a theocratic base but a collection of over fifteen hundred towns and cities loosely connected by ties of trade and alliance and ruled by a coalition of landlords and rich merchants. There were no royal precincts or imposing burial monuments, and there are few surviving stone or terra-cotta images that might represent kings, priests, or military commanders. It is possible that religion had advanced beyond the stage of spirit worship to belief in a single god or goddess of fertility. Presumably, priests at court prayed to this deity

to maintain the fertility of the soil and guarantee the annual harvest.

As in Mesopotamia and Egypt, the Harappan economy was based primarily on agriculture. Wheat, barley, rice, and peas were apparently the primary crops. The presence of cotton seeds at various sites suggests that the Harappan peoples may have been the first to master the cultivation of this useful crop and possibly introduced it, along with rice, to other societies in the region. But Harappa also developed an extensive trading network that extended to Sumer and other civilizations to the west. Textiles and foodstuffs were apparently imported from Sumer in exchange for metals such as copper, lumber, precious stones, and various types of luxury goods. Much of this trade was conducted by ship via the Persian Gulf, although some undoubtedly went by land.

Harappan Culture   Archaeological remains indicate that the Indus valley peoples possessed a culture as sophisticated in some ways as that of the Sumerians to the west. Although Harappan architecture was purely functional and shows little artistic sensitivity, the aesthetic quality of some of the pottery and sculpture is superb. Harappan painted pottery, wheel-turned and kiln-fired, rivals equivalent work produced elsewhere. Sculpture, however, was the Harappans' highest artistic achievement. Some artifacts possess a wonderful vitality of expression. Fired clay seals show a deft touch in carving animals such as elephants, tigers, rhinoceroses, and antelope, and figures made of copper or terra-cotta show a lively sensitivity and a sense of grace and movement that is almost modern.

Writing was another achievement of Harappan society and dates back at least to the beginning of the third millennium B.C.E. (see the comparative essay "Writing and Civilization" on p. 43). Unfortunately, the only surviving examples of Harappan writing are the pictographic symbols inscribed on clay seals. The script contained more than four hundred characters, but most are too stylized to be identified by their shape, and as noted earlier, scholars have been unable to decipher them. There are no apparent links with Mesopotamian scripts, although, like those, the primary purpose may have been to carry on commercial transactions. Until the script is deciphered, much about the Harappan civilization must remain, as one historian termed it, a fascinating enigma.

The Dancing Girl. Relatively few objects reflecting the creative talents of the Harappan peoples have survived. This bronze figure of a young dancer in repose, 5 inches tall, is a rare metal sculpture from Mohenjo-Daro. The detail and grace of her stance reflect the skill of the artist who molded her some four thousand years ago.

National Museum of India, New Delhi/The Bridgeman Art Library

The origin of the Harappans is still debated, but some scholars have suggested on the basis of ethnographic and linguistic analysis that the language and physical characteristics of the Harappans were similar to those of the Dravidian peoples who live in the Deccan Plateau today. If that is so, Harappa is not a dead civilization, whose culture and peoples have disappeared into the sands of history, but a part of the living culture of the Indian subcontinent.

Political and Social Structures

In several respects, Harappan civilization closely resembled the cultures of Mesopotamia and the Nile valley. Like them, it probably began in tiny farming villages scattered throughout the river valley, some dating back to as early as 6500 or 7000 B.C.E. These villages thrived and grew until by the middle of the third millennium B.C.E. they could support a privileged ruling elite living in walled cities of considerable magnitude and affluence. The center of power was the city of Harappa, which was surrounded by a brick wall over 40 feet thick at its base and more than 3½ miles in circumference. The city was laid out on an essentially rectangular grid, with some streets as wide as 30 feet. Most buildings were constructed of kiln-dried mudbricks and were square in shape, reflecting the grid pattern. At its height, the city may have had as many as eighty thousand

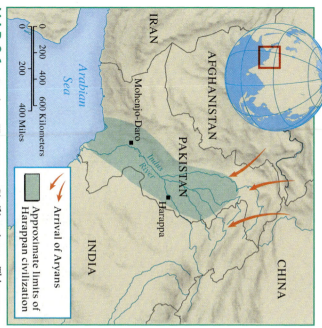

View an animated version of this map or related maps at www.cengage.com/history/Duiker/World6e

MAP 2.1 Ancient Harappan Civilization. This map shows the location of the first civilization that arose in the Indus River valley, which today is located in Pakistan.

Q Based on this map, why do you think Harappan civilization resembled the civilizations of Mesopotamia and Egypt?

Approximate limits of Harappan civilization

Arrival of Aryans

Arabian Sea

IRAN · AFGHANISTAN · PAKISTAN · INDIA · CHINA · Mohenjo-Daro · Harappa · Indus River

0 200 400 600 Kilometers
0 200 400 Miles

© Borromeo/Art Resource, NY

Mohenjo-Daro: Ancient City on the Indus. One of the two major cities of the ancient Indus River civilization was Mohenjo-Daro (below). In addition to rows of residential housing, it had a ceremonial center with a royal palace and a sacred bath that was probably used by the priests to achieve ritual purity. The bath is reminiscent of water tanks in modern Hindu temples, such as the Minakshi Temple in Madurai (right), where the faithful wash their feet prior to religious devotion. Water was an integral part of Hindu temple complexes, where it symbolized Vishnu's cosmic ocean and the concept of ritual purity. Water was a vital necessity in India's arid climate.

© William J. Duiker

inhabitants, as large as some of the most populous urban centers in Sumerian civilization.

Both Harappa and Mohenjo-Daro were divided into large walled neighborhoods, with narrow lanes separating the rows of houses. Houses varied in size, with some as high as three stories, but all followed the same general plan based on a square courtyard surrounded by rooms. Bathrooms featured an advanced drainage system, which carried wastewater out to drains located under the streets and thence to sewage pits beyond the city walls. But the cities also had the equivalent of the modern slum. At Harappa, tiny dwellings for workers have been found near metal furnaces and the open areas used for pounding grain.

Unfortunately, Harappan writing has not yet been deciphered, so historians know relatively little about the organization of the Harappan state. However, recent archaeological evidence suggests that unlike its contemporaries in Egypt and Sumer, Harappa was not a centralized monarchy with a theocratic base but a collection of over fifteen hundred towns and cities loosely connected by ties of trade and alliance and ruled by a coalition of landlords and rich merchants. There were no royal precincts or imposing burial monuments, and there are few surviving stone or terra-cotta images that might represent kings, priests, or military commanders. It is possible that religion had advanced beyond the stage of spirit worship to belief in a single god or goddess of fertility. Presumably, priests at court prayed to this deity

to maintain the fertility of the soil and guarantee the annual harvest.

As in Mesopotamia and Egypt, the Harappan economy was based primarily on agriculture. Wheat, barley, rice, and peas were apparently the primary crops. The presence of cotton seeds at various sites suggests that the Harappan peoples may have been the first to master the cultivation of this useful crop and possibly introduced it, along with rice, to other societies in the region. But Harappa also developed an extensive trading network that extended to Sumer and other civilizations to the west. Textiles and foodstuffs were apparently imported from Sumer in exchange for metals such as copper, lumber, precious stones, and various types of luxury goods. Much of this trade was conducted by ship via the Persian Gulf, although some undoubtedly went by land.

Harappan Culture Archaeological remains indicate that the Indus valley peoples possessed a culture as sophisticated in some ways as that of the Sumerians to the west. Although Harappan architecture was purely functional and shows little artistic sensitivity, the aesthetic quality of some of the pottery and sculpture is superb. Harappan painted pottery, wheel-turned and kiln-fired, rivals equivalent work produced elsewhere. Sculpture, however, was the Harappans' highest artistic achievement. Some artifacts possess a wonderful vitality of expression. Fired clay seals show a deft touch in carving animals such as elephants, tigers, rhinoceroses, and antelope, and figures made of copper or terra-cotta show a lively sensitivity and a sense of grace and movement that is almost modern.

Writing was another achievement of Harappan society and dates back at least to the beginning of the third millennium B.C.E. (see the comparative essay "Writing and Civilization" on p. 43). Unfortunately, the only surviving examples of Harappan writing are the pictographic symbols inscribed on clay seals. The script contained more than four hundred characters, but most are too stylized to be identified by their shape, and as noted earlier, scholars have been unable to decipher them. There are no apparent links with Mesopotamian scripts, although, like those, the primary purpose may have been to carry on commercial transactions. Until the script is deciphered, much about the Harappan civilization must remain, as one historian termed it, a fascinating enigma.

The Dancing Girl. Relatively few objects reflecting the creative talents of the Harappan peoples have survived. This bronze figure of a young dancer in repose, 5 inches tall, is a rare metal sculpture from Mohenjo-Daro. The detail and grace of her stance reflect the skill of the artist who molded her some four thousand years ago.

National Museum of India, New Delhi/The Bridgeman Art Library

COMPARATIVE ESSAY
WRITING AND CIVILIZATION

In the year 3250 B.C.E., King Scorpion of Egypt issued an edict announcing a major victory for his army over rival forces in the region. Inscribed in limestone on a cliff face in the Nile River valley, that edict is perhaps the oldest surviving historical document in the world today.

According to prehistorians, human beings invented the first spoken language about fifty thousand years ago. As human beings spread from Africa to other continents, that first system gradually fragmented and evolved into innumerable separate tongues. By the time the agricultural revolution began about ten thousand years ago, there were perhaps nearly twenty distinct language families in existence around the world.

During the later stages of the agricultural revolution, the first writing systems also began to emerge in various places around the world. The first successful efforts were apparently achieved in Mesopotamia and Egypt, but knowledge of writing soon spread to peoples along the shores of the Mediterranean and in the Indus River valley in South Asia. Wholly independent systems were also invented in China and Mesoamerica. Writing was used for a variety of purposes. King Scorpion's edict suggests that one reason was to enable a ruler to communicate with his subjects on matters of official concern. In other cases, the purpose was to enable human beings to communicate with supernatural forces. In China and Egypt, for example, priests used writing to communicate with the gods. In Mesopotamia and in the Indus River valley, merchants used writing to record commercial and other legal transactions. Finally, writing was also used to present ideas in new ways, giving rise to such early Mesopotamian literature as *The Epic of Gilgamesh*.

How did such early written languages evolve into the complex systems in use today? In almost all cases, the first systems consisted of pictographs, pictorial images of various concrete objects such as trees, water, cattle, body parts, and the heavenly bodies. Eventually, such signs became more stylized to facilitate transcription—much as we often use a cursive script instead of block printing today. Finally,

and most important for their future development, these pictorial images began to take on specific phonetic meaning so that they could represent sounds in the written language. Most sophisticated written systems eventually evolved to a phonetic script, based on an alphabet of symbols to represent all sounds in the spoken language, but others went only part of the way by adding phonetic signs to the individual character to suggest pronunciation while keeping the essence of the original pictograph to indicate meaning. Most of the latter systems, such as hieroglyphics in Egypt and cuneiform in Mesopotamia, eventually became extinct, but the ancient Chinese writing system survives today, in greatly altered form.

The Disk of Phaistos. Discovered on the island of Crete in 1980, this mysterious clay object dating from the eighteenth century B.C.E. contains ideographs in a language that has not yet been deciphered.

The Art Archive/Heraklion Museum/Gianni Dagli Orti

A Lost Civilization?

Until recently, the area north of the Indus River was presumed to be isolated from the emerging river valley civilizations to the south. But archaeologists have now discovered the remnants of a lost culture there that dates back at least to the late third millennium B.C.E. Bronze Age mudbrick settlements surrounded by irrigated fields have been found along a series of oases that stretch several hundred miles from the Caspian Sea into modern-day

Afghanistan. There are also clear indications of the domestication of sheep and goats and of widespread trade with other societies in the region, along with tantalizing hints—in the form of an engraved stone seal found at one site—that the inhabitants of the region were in the process of developing their own form of writing. Although the founders of this mysterious civilization remain unknown, it is now clear that the rudiments of civilization in ancient times were not limited to the great river valleys located on the edges of the African and Asian continents.

found clear signs of social decay, including evidence of trash in the streets, neglect of public services, and overcrowding in urban neighborhoods. Mohenjo-Daro itself may have been destroyed by an epidemic or by natural phenomena such as floods, an earthquake, or a shift in the course of the Indus River. If that was the case, the Aryans arrived in the area after the greatness of Harappan civilization had declined.

© Scala/Art Resource, NY

Harappan Seals. The Harappan peoples, like their contemporaries in Mesopotamia, developed a writing system to record their spoken language. Unfortunately, it has not yet been deciphered. Most extant examples of Harappan writing are found on fired clay seals depicting human figures and animals. These seals have been found in houses and were probably used to identify the owners of goods for sale. Other seals may have been used as amulets or have had other religious significance. Several depict religious figures or ritualistic scenes of sacrifice.

The Arrival of the Aryans

Q Focus Question: What were some of the distinctive features of the class system introduced by the Aryan peoples, and what effects did this system have on Indian civilization?

One of the great mysteries of Harappan civilization is how it came to an end. Archaeologists working at Mohenjo-Daro have discovered signs of first a gradual decay and then a sudden destruction of the city and its inhabitants around 1500 B.C.E. Many of the surviving skeletons have been found in postures of running or hiding, reminiscent of the ruins of the Roman city of Pompeii, destroyed by the eruption of Mount Vesuvius in 79 C.E.

These tantalizing signs of flight before a sudden catastrophe once led scholars to surmise that the city of Mohenjo-Daro (the name was applied by archaeologists and means "city of the dead") and perhaps the remnants of Harappan civilization were destroyed by the Aryans, nomads from the north who arrived in the subcontinent around the middle of the second millennium B.C.E. Although the Aryans were perhaps not as sophisticated culturally as the Harappans, like many nomadic peoples they excelled at the art of war. As in Mesopotamia and the Nile valley, most contacts between pastoral and agricultural peoples proved unstable and often ended in armed conflict. Nevertheless, it is doubtful that the Aryan peoples were directly responsible for the final destruction of Mohenjo-Daro. More likely, Harappan civilization had already fallen on hard times, perhaps as a result of climatic change in the Indus valley. Archaeologists have

The Early Aryans

Historians know relatively little about the origins and culture of the Aryans before they entered India, although they were part of the extensive group of Indo-European-speaking peoples who inhabited vast areas in what is now Siberia and the steppes of Central Asia. Pastoral peoples who migrated from season to season to provide fodder for their herds, the Indo-Europeans are credited by historians with a number of technological achievements, including the invention of horse-drawn chariots and the stirrup, both of which were eventually introduced throughout the region.

Whereas other Indo-European-speaking peoples moved westward and eventually settled in Europe, the Aryans moved south across the Hindu Kush into the plains of northern India. Between 1500 and 1000 B.C.E., they gradually advanced eastward from the Indus valley, across the fertile plain of the Ganges, and later southward into the Deccan Plateau until they had eventually extended their political mastery over the entire subcontinent and its Dravidian inhabitants, although the indigenous culture survived to remain a prominent element in the evolution of traditional Indian civilization.

After they settled in India, the Aryans gradually adapted to the geographical realities of their new homeland and abandoned the pastoral life for agricultural pursuits. They were assisted by the introduction of iron, which probably came from the Middle East, where it had been introduced by the Hittites (see Chapter 1) about 1500 B.C.E. The invention of the iron plow, along with the development of irrigation, allowed the Aryans and their indigenous subjects to clear the dense jungle growth along the Ganges River and transform the Ganges valley into one of the richest agricultural regions in South Asia. The Aryans also developed their first writing system, based on the Aramaic script in the Middle East, and were thus able to transcribe the legends that previously had been passed down from generation to generation by memory (see Map 2.2). Most of what is known about the early Aryans is based on oral traditions passed on in the Rig Veda, an ancient work that was written down after the Aryans arrived in India (it is one of several Vedas, or collections of sacred instructions and rituals).

As in other Indo-European societies, each of the various Aryan tribes was led by a chieftain, called a **raja**, who was assisted by a council of elders composed

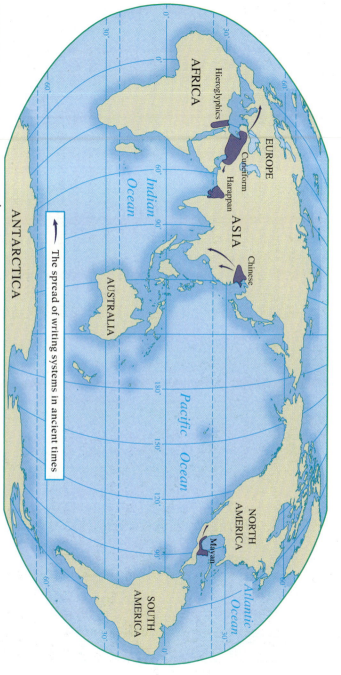

The spread of writing systems in ancient times

MAP 2.2 Writing Systems in the Ancient World. One of the chief characteristics of the first civilizations was the development of a system of written communication. Based on the comparative essay, in what ways were these first writing systems similar, and how were they different? View an animated version of this map or related maps at www.cengage.com/history/Duiker/Worldc

of other leading members of the community; like them, he was normally a member of the warrior class, called the *kshatriya*. The chief derived his power from his ability to protect his people from rival groups, a skill that was crucial in the warring kingdoms and shifting alliances that were typical of early Aryan society. Though the rajas claimed to be representatives of the gods, they were not viewed as gods themselves (see the box on p. 46).

As Aryan society grew in size and complexity, the chieftains began to be transformed into kings, usually called *maharajas* ("great rajas"). Nevertheless, the tradition that the ruler did not possess absolute authority remained strong. Like all human beings, the ruler was required to follow the *dharma*, a set of laws that set behavioral standards for all individuals and classes in Indian society.

The Impact of the Greeks

While competing groups squabbled for precedence in India, powerful new empires were rising to the west. First came the Persian Empire of Cyrus and Darius. Then came the Greeks. After two centuries of sporadic rivalry and warfare, the Greeks achieved a brief period of regional dominance in the late fourth century B.C.E. with the rise of Macedonia under Alexander the Great. Alexander had heard of the riches of India, and in 330 B.C.E., after conquering Persia, he launched an invasion of the east (see Chapter 4). In 326,

his armies arrived in the plains of northwestern India and the Indus River valley. They departed almost as suddenly as they had come, leaving in their wake Greek administrators and a veneer of cultural influence that would affect the area for generations to come.

Alexander the Great's Movements in Asia

The Mauryan Empire

The Alexandrian conquest was a brief interlude in the history of the Indian subcontinent, but it played a formative role, for on the heels of Alexander's departure came the rise of the first dynasty to control much of the region. The founder of the new state, who took the royal title Chandragupta Maurya (324–301 B.C.E.), drove out the Greek administrators whom Alexander had left behind and solidified his control over the northern Indian plain. He established the capital of his new Mauryan Empire at Pataliputra (modern Patna) in

POLITICS & GOVERNMENT

THE ORIGINS OF KINGSHIP

Both India and China had a concept of a golden age in the remote past that provided a model for later governments and peoples to emulate. This passage from the famous Indian epic known as the Mahabharata describes a three-stage process in the evolution of government in human society. Yudhisthira and Bhishma are two of the main characters in the story.

The Mahabharata

Yudhisthira said: "This word 'king' [*raja*] is so very current in this world, O Bharata; how has it originated? Tell me that, O grandfather."

Bhishma said: "Currently, O best among men, do you listen to everything in its entirety—how kingship originated first during the golden age [*krtayuga*]. Neither kingship nor king was there in the beginning, neither scepter [*danda*] nor the bearer of a scepter. All people protected one another by means of righteous conduct, O Bharata, men eventually fell into a state of spiritual lassitude. Then delusion overcame them. Men were thus overpowered by infatuation, O leader of men, on account of the delusion of understanding; their sense of righteous conduct was lost. When understanding was lost, all men, O best of the Bharatas, overpowered by infatuation, became victims of greed. Then they sought to acquire what should not be acquired. Thereby, indeed, O lord, another vice, namely, desire, overcame them. Attachment then attacked them, who had become victims of desire. Attached to objects of sense, they did not discriminate between what should be said and what should not be said, between the edible and inedible and between right and wrong. When this world of men had been submerged in dissipation, all spiritual knowledge [*brahman*] perished; and when spiritual knowledge perished, O king, righteous conduct also perished."

When spiritual knowledge and righteous conduct perished, the gods were overcome with fear, and fearfully sought refuge with Brahma, the creator. Going to the great lord, the ancestor of the worlds, all the gods, afflicted with sorrow, misery, and fear, with folded hands said: "O Lord,

the eternal spiritual knowledge, which had existed in the world of men, has perished because of greed, infatuation, and the like, therefore we have become fearful. Through the loss of spiritual knowledge, righteous conduct also has perished, O God. Therefore, O Lord of the three worlds, mortals have reached a state of indifference. Verily, we showered rain on earth, but mortals showered rain [religious offerings] up to heaven. As a result of the cessation of ritual activity on their part, we faced a serious peril. O grandfather, decide what is most beneficial to use under these circumstances."

Then, the self-born lord said to all those gods: "I will consider what is most beneficial; let your fear depart, O leaders of the gods."

Thereupon he composed a work consisting of a hundred thousand chapters out of his own mind, wherein righteous conduct [*dharma*], as well as material gain [*artha*] and enjoyment of sensual pleasures [*kama*] were described. This group, known as the threefold classification of human objectives, was expounded by the self-born lord; so, too, a fourth objective, spiritual emancipation [*moksha*], which aims at a different goal, and which constitutes a separate group by itself.

Then the gods approached Vishnu, the lord of creatures, and said: "Indicate to us that one person among mortals who alone is worthy of the highest eminence." Then the blessed lord god Narayana reflected, and brought forth an illustrious mind-born son, called Virajas [who, in this version of the origins of the Indian state, became the first king].

 To read more of the Mahabharata, enter the documents area of the World History Resource Center using the access card that is available for World History.

What is the author's purpose here? How does this vision compare with the views then current on the reasons for the emergence of political leadership? How does it compare with the portrayal of kingship in Egypt as described in Hymn to the Pharaoh in Chapter 1?

the Ganges valley (see the map on p. 60). Little is known of his origins, although some sources say he had originally fought on the side of the invading Greek forces but then angered Alexander with his outspoken advice.

Little, too, is known of Chandragupta Maurya's empire. Most accounts of his reign rely on the scattered remnants of a lost work written by Megasthenes, a Greek ambassador to the Mauryan court, in about 302 B.C.E. Chandragupta Maurya was apparently advised by a brilliant court official named Kautilya, whose name has been attached to a treatise on politics called the *Arthasastra*

(see the box on p. 47). The work actually dates from a later time, but it may well reflect Kautilya's ideas.

Although the author of the *Arthasastra* follows Aryan tradition in stating that the happiness of the king lies in the happiness of his subjects, the treatise also asserts that when the sacred law of the dharma and practical politics collide, the latter must take precedence: "Whenever there is disagreement between history and sacred law or between evidence and sacred law, then the matter should be settled in accordance with sacred law. But whenever sacred law is in conflict with rational law, then reason shall be held authoritative."[1] The *Arthasastra* also emphasizes ends rather than means, achieved results rather than methods employed. For this reason, it has often been compared to Machiavelli's famous political treatise of the Italian Renaissance, *The Prince*, written more than a thousand years later (see Chapter 15).

As described in the *Arthasastra*, Chandragupta Maurya's government was highly centralized and even despotic: "It is power and power alone which, only when exercised by the king with impartiality, and in proportion to guilt, over his son or his enemy; maintains both this world and the next."[2] The king possessed a large army and a secret police responsible to his orders (according to the Greek ambassador Megasthenes, Chandragupta Maurya was chronically fearful of assassination, a not unrealistic concern for someone who had allegedly come to power by violence). Reportedly, all food was tasted in his presence, and he made a practice of never sleeping twice in the same bed in his sumptuous palace. To guard against corruption, a board of censors was empowered to investigate cases of possible malfeasance and incompetence within the bureaucracy.

The ruler's authority beyond the confines of the capital may often have been limited, however. The empire was divided into provinces that were ruled by governors. At first, most of these governors were appointed by and reported to the ruler, but later the position became hereditary. The provinces themselves were divided into districts, each under a chief magistrate appointed by the governor. At the base of the government pyramid was the village, where the vast majority of the Indian people lived. The village was governed by a council of elders; membership in the council was normally hereditary and was shared by the wealthiest families in the village.

Caste and Class: Social Structures in Ancient India

When the Aryans arrived in India, they already possessed a social system based on a ruling warrior class and other groupings characteristic of a pastoral society. In India, they encountered peoples living in an agricultural society and initially assigned them a lower position in the community. The result was a set of social institutions and class divisions that have continued to the present day.

The Class System At the crux of the social system that emerged from the clash of cultures was the concept of the superiority of the Aryan peoples over their indigenous subjects. In a sense, it became an issue of color, because the Aryans, a primarily light-skinned people, were contemptuous of their subjects, who were darker. Light skin came to imply high status, whereas dark skin suggested the opposite.

THE DUTIES OF A KING

POLITICS & GOVERNMENT

Kautilya, India's earliest known political philosopher, was an adviser to the Mauryan rulers. The *Arthasastra*, though written down at a later date, very likely reflects his ideas.

This passage sets forth some of the necessary characteristics of a king, including efficiency, diligence, energy, compassion, and concern for the security and welfare of the state. In emphasizing the importance of results rather than motives, Kautilya resembles the Italian Renaissance thinker Machiavelli. But in focusing on winning popular support as the means of becoming an effective ruler, the author echoes the view of the Chinese philosopher Mencius, who declared that the best way to win the empire is to win the people (see Chapter 3).

The *Arthasastra*

Only if a king is himself energetically active do his officers follow him energetically. If he is sluggish, they too remain sluggish. And, besides, they eat up his works. He is thereby easily overpowered by his enemies. Therefore, he should ever dedicate himself energetically to activity....

A king should attend to all urgent business; he should not put it off. For what has been thus put off becomes either difficult or altogether impossible to accomplish.

The vow of the king is energetic activity; his sacrifice is constituted of the discharge of his own administrative duties; his sacrificial fee [to the officiating priests] is his impartiality of attitude toward all; his sacrificial consecration is his anointment as king.

In the happiness of the subjects lies the happiness of the king; in their welfare, his own welfare. The welfare of the king does not lie in the fulfillment of what is dear to him; whatever is dear to the subjects constitutes his welfare.

Therefore, ever energetic, a king should act up to the precepts of the science of material gain. Energetic activity is the source of material gain; its opposite, of downfall.

In the absence of energetic activity, the loss of what has already been obtained and of what still remains to be obtained is certain. The fruit of one's works is achieved through energetic activity—one obtains abundance of material prosperity.

Q To whom was the author of this document directing his advice? How do the ideas expressed here compare with what most people expect of their political leaders in democratic societies of the present day?

CENGAGENOW *To read more of the Arthasastra, enter the documents area of the World History Resource Center using the access card that is available for World History.*

FAMILY & SOCIETY

Social Classes in Ancient India

The *Law of Manu* is a set of behavioral norms allegedly prescribed by India's mythical founding ruler, Manu. The treatise was probably written in the first or second century B.C.E. The following excerpt describes the various social classes in India and their prescribed duties. Many scholars doubt that the social system in India was ever as rigid as it was portrayed here, and some suggest that upper-class Indians may have used the idea of *varna* to enhance their own status in society.

The *Law of Manu*

For the sake of the preservation of this entire creation, the Exceedingly Resplendent One [the Creator of the Universe] assigned separate duties to the classes which had sprung from his mouth, arms, thighs, and feet.

Teaching, studying, performing sacrificial rites, so too making others perform sacrificial rites, and giving away and receiving gifts—these he assigned to the [brahmins].

Protection of the people, giving away of wealth, performance of sacrificial rites, study, and nonattachment to sensual pleasures—these are, in short, the duties of a *kshatriya*.

Tending of cattle, giving away of wealth, trade and commerce, usury, and agriculture—these are the occupations of a *vaisya*.

The Lord has prescribed only one occupation [*karma*] for a *sudra*, namely, service without malice of even these other three classes.

Of created beings, those which are animate are the best; of the animate, those which subsist by means of their intellect; of the intelligent, men are the best; and of men, the [brahmins] are traditionally declared to be the best.

The code of conduct—prescribed by scriptures and ordained by sacred tradition—constitutes the highest *dharma*; hence a twice-born person, conscious of his own Self [seeking spiritual salvation], should be always scrupulous in respect of it.

Q *How might the class system in ancient India, as described here, be compared with social class divisions in other societies in Asia? Why do you think the class system as described here developed in India? What is the difference between the class system (varna) and the jati?*

CENGAGENOW To read more of the Law of Manu, enter the documents area of the World History Resource Center using the access card that is available for World History.

The concept of color, however, was only the physical manifestation of a division that took place in Indian society on the basis of economic functions. Indian classes (called *varna*, literally "color," and commonly but mistakenly known as "castes" in English) did not simply reflect an informal division of labor. Instead, at least in theory, they were a set of rigid social classifications that determined not only one's occupation but also one's status in society and one's hope for ultimate salvation (see "Escaping the Wheel of Life" later in this chapter). There were five major varna in Indian society in ancient times (see the box above). At the top were two classes, collectively viewed as the aristocracy, which represented the ruling elites in Aryan society prior to their arrival in India: the priests and the warriors.

The priestly class, known as the **brahmins,** was usually considered to be at the top of the social scale. Descended from seers who had advised the ruler on religious matters in Aryan tribal society (*brahmin* meant "one possessed of **Brahman,**" a term for the supreme god in the Hindu religion), they were eventually transformed into an official class after their religious role declined in importance. Megasthenes described this class as follows:

From the time of their conception in the womb they are under the care and guardianship of learned men who go to the mother and ... give her prudent hints and counsels, and the women who listen to them most willingly are thought to be the most fortunate in their offspring. After their birth the children are in the care of one person after another, and as they advance in years their masters are men of superior accomplishments. The philosophers reside in a grove in front of the city within a moderate-sized enclosure. They live in a simple style and lie on pallets of straw and [deer] skins. They abstain from animal food and sexual pleasures, and occupy their time in listening to serious discourse and in imparting knowledge to willing ears.[3]

The second class was the *kshatriya,* the warriors. Although often listed below the *brahmins* in social status, many *kshatriyas* were probably descended from the ruling warrior class in Aryan society prior to the conquest of India and thus may have originally ranked socially above the *brahmins,* although they were ranked lower in religious terms. Like the *brahmins,* the *kshatriyas* were originally identified with a single occupation—fighting—but as the character of Aryan society changed, they often switched to other forms of employment. At the same time, new families from other classes were sometimes tacitly accepted into the ranks of the warriors.

The third-ranked class in Indian society was the *vaisya* (literally, "commoner"). The *vaisyas* were usually viewed in economic terms as the merchant class. Some historians have speculated that the *vaisyas* were originally guardians of the tribal herds but that after settling in India,

Harappan civilization	c. 2600–1900 B.C.E.
Arrival of the Aryans	c. 1500 B.C.E.
Life of Gautama Buddha	c. 560–480 B.C.E.
Invasion of India by Alexander the Great	326 B.C.E.
Mauryan dynasty founded	324 B.C.E.
Reign of Chandragupta Maurya	324–301 B.C.E.
Reign of Ashoka	269–232 B.C.E.
Collapse of Mauryan dynasty	183 B.C.E.
Rise of Kushan kingdom	c. first century C.E.

many moved into commercial pursuits. Megasthenes noted that members of this class "alone are permitted to hunt and keep cattle and to sell beasts of burden or to let them out on hire. In return for clearing the land of wild beasts and of birds which infest sown fields, they receive an allowance of corn from the king. They lead a wandering life and dwell in tents."[4] Although this class was ranked below the first two in social status, it shared with them the privilege of being considered **"twice-born,"** a term referring to a ceremony at puberty whereby young males were initiated into adulthood and introduced into Indian society. After the ceremony, male members of the top three classes were allowed to wear the "sacred thread" for the remainder of their lives.

Below the three "twice-born" classes were the **sudras,** who represented the great bulk of the Indian population. The *sudras* were not considered fully Aryan, and the term probably originally referred to the indigenous population. Most *sudras* were peasants or artisans or worked at other forms of manual labor. They had only limited rights in society. In recent years, DNA samples have revealed that most upper-class South Indians share more genetic characteristics with Europeans than their lower-class counterparts do, thus tending to confirm the hypothesis that the Aryans established their political and social dominance over the indigenous population.

At the lowest level of Indian society, and in fact not even considered a legitimate part of the class system itself, were the untouchables (also known as outcastes or **pariahs).** The untouchables probably originated as a slave class consisting of prisoners of war, criminals, ethnic minorities, and other groups considered outside Indian society. Even after slavery was outlawed, the untouchables were given menial and degrading tasks that other Indians would not accept, such as collecting trash, handling dead bodies, or serving as butchers or tanners. According to the estimate of one historian, they may have accounted for a little more than 5 percent of the total population of India in antiquity.

The life of the untouchables was extremely demeaning. They were not considered fully human, and their very presence was considered polluting to members of the other *varna*. No Indian would touch or eat food handled or prepared by an untouchable. Untouchables lived in ghettos and were required to tap two sticks together to announce their approach when they traveled outside their quarters so that others could avoid them.

Technically, these class divisions were absolute. Individuals supposedly were born, lived, and died in the same class. In practice, upward or downward mobility probably took place, and there was undoubtedly some flexibility in economic functions. But throughout most of Indian history, class taboos remained strict. Members were generally not permitted to marry outside their class (although in practice, men were occasionally allowed to marry below their class but not above it). At first, attitudes toward the handling of food were relatively loose, but eventually that taboo grew stronger, and social mores dictated that sharing meals and marrying outside one's class were unacceptable.

The *Jati*

The people of ancient India did not belong to a particular class as individuals but as part of a larger kin group commonly referred to as the **jati** (in Portuguese, *casta*, which evolved into the English term *caste*), a system of extended families that originated in ancient India and still exists in somewhat changed form today. Although the origins of the *jati* system are unknown (there are no indications of strict class distinctions in Harappan society), the *jati* eventually became identified with a specific kinship group living in a specific area and carrying out a specific function in society. Each *jati* was identified with a particular *varna*, and each had its own separate economic function.

Jatis were thus the basic social organization into which traditional Indian society was divided. Each *jati* was itself composed of hundreds or thousands of individual nuclear families and was governed by its own council of elders. Membership in this ruling council was usually hereditary and was based on the wealth or social status of particular families within the community.

In theory, each *jati* was assigned a particular form of economic activity. Obviously, though, not all families in a given *jati* could take part in the same vocation, and as time went on, members of a single *jati* commonly engaged in several different lines of work. Sometimes an entire *jati* would have to move its location in order to continue a particular form of activity. In other cases, a *jati* would adopt an entirely new occupation in order to remain in a certain area. Such changes in habitat or occupation introduced the possibility of movement up or down the social scale. In this way, an entire *jati* could sometimes engage in upward mobility, even though it was not normally possible for individuals, who were tied to their class identity for life.

The class system in ancient India may sound highly constricting, but there were persuasive social and economic reasons why it survived for so many centuries. In the first place, it provided an identity for individuals in a highly hierarchical society. Although an individual might rank lower on the social scale than members of other classes, it was always possible to find others ranked even lower. Class was also a means for new groups, such as mountain tribal people, to achieve a recognizable place in the broader community. Perhaps equally important, the *jati* was a primitive form of welfare system. Each was obliged to provide for any of its members who were poor or destitute. It also provided an element of stability in a society that all too often was in a state of political turmoil.

Daily Life in Ancient India

Beyond these rigid social stratifications was the Indian family. Not only was life centered around the family, but the family, not the individual, was the most basic unit in society.

The Family   The ideal social unit was an extended family, with three generations living under the same roof. It was essentially patriarchal, except along the Malabar coast, near the southwestern tip of the subcontinent, where a matriarchal form of social organization prevailed down to modern times. In the rest of India, the oldest male traditionally possessed legal authority over the entire family unit.

The family was linked together in a religious sense to ancestral members by a series of commemorative rites. Family ceremonies were conducted to honor the departed and to link the living and the dead. The male family head was responsible for leading the ritual. At his death, his eldest son had the duty of conducting the funeral rites.

The importance of the father and the son in family ritual underlined the importance of males in Indian society. Male superiority was expressed in a variety of ways. Women could not serve as priests (although some were accepted as seers), nor were they normally permitted to study the Vedas. In general, males had a monopoly on education, since the primary goal of learning to read was to conduct family rituals. In high-class families, young men, after having been initiated into the sacred thread, began Vedic studies with a **guru** (teacher). Some then went on to higher studies in one of the major cities. The goal of such an education might be either professional or religious. Such young men were not supposed to marry until after twelve years of study.

Marriage   In general, only males could inherit property, except in a few cases where there were no sons. According to law, a woman was always considered a minor. Divorce was prohibited, although it sometimes took place. According to the *Arthasastra*, a wife who had been deserted by her husband could seek a divorce. Polygamy was fairly rare and apparently occurred mainly among the higher classes, but husbands were permitted to take a second wife if the first was barren. Producing children was an important aspect of marriage, both because children provided security for their parents in old age and because they were a physical proof of male potency. Child marriage was common for young girls, whether because of the

desire for children or because daughters represented an economic liability to their parents. But perhaps the most graphic symbol of women's subjection to men was the ritual of **sati** (often written *suttee*), which encouraged the wife to throw herself on her dead husband's funeral pyre. The Greek visitor Megasthenes reported "that he had heard from some persons of wives burning themselves along with their deceased husbands and doing so gladly; and that those women who refused to burn themselves were held in disgrace."[5] All in all, it was undoubtedly a difficult existence. According to the *Law of Manu*, an early treatise on social organization and behavior in ancient India, probably written in the first or second century B.C.E., women were subordinated to men—first to their father, then to their husband, and finally to their sons:

She should do nothing independently
even in her own house.
In childhood subject to her father,
in youth to her husband,
and when her husband is dead to her sons,
she should never enjoy independence....

Though he be uncouth and prone to pleasure,
though he have no good points at all,
the virtuous wife should ever
worship her lord as a god.[6]

The Role of Women   At the root of female subordination to the male was the practical fact that as in most agricultural societies, men did most of the work in the fields. Females were viewed as having little utility outside the home and indeed were considered an economic burden, since parents were obliged to provide a dowry to acquire a husband for a daughter. Female children also appeared to offer little advantage in maintaining the family unit, since they joined the families of their husbands after the wedding ceremony.

Despite all of these indications of female subjection to the male, there are numerous signs that in some ways women often played an influential role in Indian society, and the Hindu code of behavior stressed that they should be treated with respect (see the box on p. 51). Indians appeared to be fascinated by female sexuality, and tradition held that women often used their sexual powers to achieve domination over men. The author of the Mahabharata, a vast epic of early Indian society, complained that "the fire has never too many logs, the ocean never too many rivers, death never too many living souls, and fair-eyed woman never too many men." Despite the legal and social constraints, women often played an important role within the family unit, and many were admired and honored for their talents. It is probably significant that paintings and sculpture from ancient and medieval India frequently show women in a role equal to that of men, and the tradition of the henpecked husband is as prevalent in India as in many Western societies today.

The Economy

The arrival of the Aryans did not drastically change the economic character of Indian society. Not only did most Aryans eventually take up farming, but it is likely that agriculture expanded rapidly under Aryan rule with the invention of the iron plow and the spread of northern Indian culture into the Deccan Plateau. One consequence of this process was to shift the focus of Indian culture from the Indus valley farther eastward to the Ganges River valley, which even today is one of the most densely populated regions on earth. The flatter areas in the Deccan Plateau and in the coastal plains were also turned into cropland.

Indian Farmers

For most Indian farmers, life was harsh. Among the most fortunate were those who owned their own land, although they were required to pay taxes to the state. Many others were subject to the vicissitudes of the market and often paid exorbitant rents to their landlord. Concentration of land in large holdings was limited by the tradition of dividing property among all the sons, but large estates worked by hired laborers or rented out to sharecroppers were not uncommon, particularly in areas where local rajas derived much of their wealth from their property.

Another problem for Indian farmers was the unpredictability of the climate. India is in the monsoon zone. The monsoon is a seasonal wind pattern in southern Asia that blows from the southwest during the summer months and from the northeast during the winter. The southwest monsoon, originating in the Indian Ocean, is commonly marked by heavy rains. When the rains were late, thousands starved, particularly in the drier areas, which were especially dependent on rainfall. Strong governments attempted to deal with such problems by building state-operated granaries and maintaining the irrigation works, but strong governments were rare, and famine was probably all too common. The staple crops in the north were wheat, barley, and millet, with wet rice common in the fertile river valleys. In the south, grain and vegetables were supplemented by various tropical products, cotton, and spices such as pepper, ginger, cinnamon, and saffron.

Trade and Manufacturing

By no means were all Indians farmers. As time passed, India became one of the most advanced trading and manufacturing civilizations in the ancient world. After the rise of the Mauryas, India's role in regional trade began to expand, and the subcontinent became a major transit point in a vast commercial network that extended from the rim of the Pacific Ocean to the Middle East and the Mediterranean Sea. This regional trade went both by sea and by camel caravan. Maritime trade across the Indian Ocean may have begun

---

FAMILY & SOCIETY

THE POSITION OF WOMEN IN ANCIENT INDIA

An indication of the ambivalent attitude toward women in ancient India is displayed in this passage from the *Law of Manu*, which states that respect for women is the responsibility of men. At the same time, it also makes clear that the place of women is in the home.

The *Law of Manu*

Women must be honored and adorned by their father, brothers, husbands, and brother-in-law who desire great good fortune.

Where women, verily, are honored, there the gods rejoice, where, however they are not honored, there all sacred rites prove fruitless.

Where the female relations live in grief—that family soon perishes completely; where, however, they do not suffer from any grievance—that family always prospers. . . .

The father who does not give away his daughter in marriage at the proper time is censurable; censurable is the husband who does not approach his wife in due season; and after the husband is dead, the son, verily is censurable, who does not protect his mother.

Even against the slightest provocations should women be particularly guarded; for unguarded they would bring grief to both the families.

Regarding this as the highest *dharma* of all four classes, husbands though weak, must strive to protect their wives.

His own offspring, character, family, self, and *dharma* does one protect when he protects his wife scrupulously. . . .

The husband should engage his wife in the collections and expenditure of his wealth, in cleanliness, in *dharma*, in cooking food for the family, and in looking after the necessities of the household. . . .

Women destined to bear children, enjoying great good fortune, deserving of worship, the resplendent lights of homes on the one hand and divinities of good luck who reside in the houses on the other—between these there is no difference whatsoever.

Q *How do these attitudes toward women compare with those we have encountered in the Middle East and North Africa?*

CENGAGENOW *To read more of the Law of Manu, enter the documents area of the World History Resource Center using the access card that is available for World History.*

© Atlantide Phototravel (Massimo Borchi)/CORBIS

as early as the fifth century B.C.E. It extended eastward as far as Southeast Asia and China and southward as far as the straits between Africa and the island of Madagascar. Westward to Egypt, on ships carrying up to 1,000 tons in cargo, went spices, teakwood, perfumes, jewels, textiles, precious stones and ivory, and wild animals. In return, India received gold, tin, lead, and wine. The subcontinent had become a major crossroads of trade in the ancient world.

India's expanding role as a manufacturing and commercial hub was undoubtedly a spur to the growth of the state. Under Chandragupta Maurya, the central government became actively involved in commercial and manufacturing activities. It owned mines and land and undoubtedly earned massive profits from its role in regional commerce. Separate government departments were established for trade, agriculture, mining, and the manufacture of weapons, and the movement of private goods was vigorously taxed. Nevertheless, a significant private sector also flourished; it was dominated by great caste guilds, which monopolized key sectors of the economy. A money economy probably came into operation during the second century B.C.E., when copper and gold coins were introduced from the Middle East. This in turn led to the development of banking. But village trade continued to be conducted by means of cowry shells (highly polished shells used as a medium of exchange throughout much of Africa and Asia) or barter throughout the ancient period.

Escaping the Wheel of Life: The Religious World of Ancient India

Q Focus Question: What are the main tenets of Hinduism and Buddhism, and how did each religion influence Indian civilization?

Like Indian politics and society, Indian religion is a blend of Aryan and Dravidian culture. The intermingling of those two civilizations gave rise to an extraordinarily complex set of religious beliefs and practices, filled with diversity and contrast. Out of this cultural mix came two of the world's great religions, Buddhism and **Hinduism,** and several smaller ones, including Jainism and Sikhism.

Hinduism

Evidence about the earliest religious beliefs of the Aryan peoples comes primarily from sacred texts such as the Vedas, four collections of hymns and religious ceremonies transmitted by memory through the centuries by Aryan priests. Many of these religious ideas were probably common to all of the Indo-European peoples before their separation into different groups at least four thousand years ago. Early Aryan beliefs were based on the common concept of a pantheon of gods and goddesses representing

Female Earth Spirit. This earth spirit, sculpted on a gatepost of the Buddhist stupa at Sanchi 2,200 years ago, illustrates how earlier representations of the fertility goddess were incorporated into Buddhist art. Women were revered as powerful fertility symbols and considered dangerous when menstruating or immediately after giving birth. Voluptuous and idealized, the earth spirit could allegedly cause a tree to blossom if she merely touched a branch with her arm or wrapped a leg around the tree's trunk.

great forces of nature similar to the immortals of Greek mythology. The Aryan ancestor of the Greek father-god Zeus, for example, may have been the deity known in early Aryan tradition as Dyaus (see Chapter 4).

The parent god Dyaus was a somewhat distant figure, however, who was eventually overshadowed by other, more functional gods possessing more familiar human traits. For a while, the primary Aryan god was the great warrior god Indra. Indra summoned the Aryan tribal peoples to war and was represented in nature by thunder. Later, Indra declined in importance and was replaced by Varuna, lord of justice. Other gods and goddesses represented various forces of nature or the needs of human beings, such as fire, fertility, and wealth (see the box on p. 53).

The concept of sacrifice was a key element in Aryan religious belief in Vedic times. As in many other ancient cultures, the practice may have begun as human sacrifice, but later animals were used as substitutes. The priestly class, the *brahmins*, played a key role in these ceremonies.

Another element of Indian religious belief in ancient times was the ideal of *asceticism*. Although there is no reference to such practices in the Vedas, by the sixth century B.C.E., self-discipline or subjecting oneself to painful stimuli had begun to replace sacrifice as a means of placating or communicating with the gods. Apparently, the original motive for asceticism was to achieve magical powers, but later, in the Upanishads—a set of commentaries on the Vedas compiled in the sixth century B.C.E.—it was seen as a means of spiritual meditation that would enable the practitioner to reach beyond material reality to a world of truth and bliss beyond earthly joy and sorrow: "Those who practice penance and faith in the forest, the tranquil ones, the knowers of truth, living the life of wandering mendicancy—they depart, freed from passion, through the door of the sun, to where dwells, verily... the imperishable Soul."[7] It is possible that another motive was to permit those with strong religious convictions to communicate directly with metaphysical reality without having to rely on the priestly class at court.

Asceticism, of course, has been practiced in other religions, including Christianity and Islam, but it seems particularly identified with Hinduism, the religion that emerged from the early Indian religious tradition. Eventually, asceticism evolved into the modern practice of body training that we know as *yoga* ("union"), which is accepted today as a meaningful element of Hindu religious practice.

reality called *Brahman*. Today the early form of Hinduism is sometimes called Brahmanism. In the Upanishads—a set of commentaries on the Vedas—the concept began to emerge as an important element of Indian religious belief. It was the duty of the individual self—called the *Atman*—to achieve an understanding of this ultimate reality so that after death the self would merge in spiritual form with *Brahman*. Sometimes *Brahman* was described in more concrete terms as a creator god, eventually known as Vishnu, but more often in terms of a shadowy ultimate reality. In the following passage from the Upanishads, the author speculates on the nature of ultimate reality.

Reincarnation   Another new concept that probably began to appear around the time the Upanishads were written was **reincarnation**. This is the idea that the individual soul is reborn in a different form after death and progresses through several existences on the wheel of life until it reaches its final destination in a union with the Great World Soul, *Brahman*. Because life is harsh, this final release is the objective of all living souls. From this concept comes the term *Brahmanism*, referring to the early Aryan religious tradition.

A key element in this process is the idea of **karma**—that one's rebirth in a next life is determined by one's actions (*karma*) in this life. Hinduism, as it emerged from Brahmanism, placed all living species on a vast scale of existence, including the four classes and the untouchables in human society. The current status of an individual soul, then, is not simply a cosmic accident but the inevitable result of actions that that soul has committed in its past existence.

At the top of the scale are the *brahmins*, who by definition are closest to ultimate release from the law of reincarnation. The *brahmins* are followed in descending order by the other classes in human society and the world of the beasts. Within the animal kingdom, an especially high position is reserved for the cow, which even today is revered by Hindus as a sacred beast. Some scholars have speculated that the unique role played by the cow in Hinduism derives from the value of cattle in Aryan pastoral society. But others have pointed out that

IN THE BEGINNING

RELIGION & PHILOSOPHY

As Indians began to speculate about the nature of the cosmic order, they came to believe in the existence of a single monistic force in the universe, a form of ultimate reality. In the following passage from the Upanishads, the author speculates on the nature of ultimate reality.

The Upanishads

In the beginning..., this world was just being, one only, without a second. Some people, no doubt, say: "In the beginning..., this world was just nonbeing, one only, without a second; from that nonbeing, being was produced."

But how indeed... could it be so? How could being be produced from nonbeing?...

In the beginning this world was being alone, one only, without a second. Being thought to itself: "May I be many, may I procreate." It produced fire. That fire thought to itself: "May I be many, may I procreate." It produced water. Therefore, whenever a person grieves or perspires, then it is from fire [heat] alone that water is produced. That water thought to itself: "May I be many, may I procreate." It produced food; it is from water alone that food for eating is produced.... That divinity [Being] thought to itself: "Well, having entered into these three divinities [fire, water, and food] by means of this living self, let me develop names and forms.

Q How does this concept of the origins of the universe compare with versions proposed in other early civilizations? What, according to this document, is "ultimate reality"?

CENGAGENOW   To read more of the Upanishads, enter the documents area of the World History Resource Center using the access card that is available for World History.

© William J. Duiker

cattle were a source of both money and food and suggest that the cow's sacred position may have descended from the concept of the sacred bull in Harappan culture.

The concept of *karma* is governed by the *dharma*, or the law. A law regulating human behavior, the *dharma* imposes different requirements on different individuals depending on their status in society. Those high on the social scale, such as *brahmins* and *kshatriyas*, are held to a stricter form of behavior than *sudras* are. The *brahmin*, for example, is expected to abstain from eating meat, because that would entail the killing of another living being, thus interrupting its *karma*.

How the concept of reincarnation originated is not known, although it was apparently not unusual for early peoples to believe that the individual soul would be reborn in a different form in a later life. In any case, in India the concept may have had practical causes as well as consequences. In the first place, it tended to provide religious sanction for the rigid class divisions that had begun to emerge in Indian society after the arrival of the Aryans, and it provided moral and political justification for the privileges of those on the higher end of the scale.

At the same time, the concept of reincarnation provided certain compensations for those lower on the ladder of life. For example, it gave hope to the poor that if they behaved properly in this life, they might improve their condition in the next. It also provided a means for unassimilated groups such as ethnic minorities to find a place in Indian society while at the same time permitting them to maintain their distinctive way of life.

The ultimate goal of achieving "good" *karma*, as we have seen, was to escape the cycle of existence. To the sophisticated, the nature of that release was a spiritual union of the individual soul with the Great World Soul, *Brahman*, described in the Upanishads as a form of dreamless sleep, free from earthly desires. Such a concept, however, was undoubtedly too ethereal for the average Indian, who needed a more concrete form of heavenly salvation, a place of beauty and bliss after a life of disease and privation.

Hindu Gods and Goddesses It was probably for this reason that the Hindu religion—in some ways so otherwordly and ascetic—came to be peopled with a multitude of very human gods and goddesses. It has been estimated that the Hindu pantheon contains more than 33,000 deities. Only a small number are primary ones, however, notably the so-called trinity of gods: Brahman the Creator, Vishnu the Preserver, and Shiva (originally the Vedic god Rudra) the Destroyer. Although Brahman (sometimes in his concrete form called Brahma) is considered to be the highest god, Vishnu and Shiva take precedence in the devotional exercises of many Hindus, who can be roughly divided into Vishnuites and Shaivites. In addition to the trinity of gods, all of whom have wives with readily identifiable roles and personalities,

Dancing Shiva. The Hindu deity Shiva is often presented in the form of a bronze statue performing a cosmic dance in which he simultaneously creates and destroys the universe. While his upper right hand creates the cosmos, his upper left hand reduces it in flames, and the lower two hands offer eternal blessing. Shiva's dancing statues visually convey to his followers the message of his power and compassion.

there are countless minor deities, each again with his or her own specific function, such as bringing good fortune, arranging a good marriage, or guaranteeing a son in childbirth.

The rich variety and earthy character of many Hindu deities is somewhat misleading, however, for Hindus regard the multitude of gods as simply different manifestations of one ultimate reality. The various deities also provide a useful means for ordinary Indians to personify their religious feelings. Even though some individuals among the early Aryans attempted to communicate with the gods through animal sacrifice or asceticism, most Indians undoubtedly sought to satisfy their own individual religious needs through devotion, which they expressed through ritual ceremonies and offerings at a Hindu temple. Such offerings were not only a way to seek salvation but also a means of satisfying all the aspirations of daily life.

Over the centuries, then, Hinduism changed radically from its origins in Aryan tribal society and became a religion of the vast majority of the Indian people. Concern with a transcendental union between the individual soul and the Great World Soul contrasted with practical desires for material wealth and happiness; ascetic self-denial contrasted with an earthly emphasis on the pleasures and values of sexual union between marriage partners.

All of these became aspects of Hinduism, the religion of 70 percent of the Indian people.

Buddhism: The Middle Path

In the sixth century B.C.E., a new doctrine appeared in northern India that would eventually begin to rival Hinduism's growing popularity throughout the subcontinent. This new doctrine was called Buddhism.

The Life of Siddhartha Gautama

The historical founder of **Buddhism,** Siddhartha Gautama, was a native of a small kingdom in the foothills of the Himalaya Mountains in what is today southern Nepal. He was born in the mid-sixth century B.C.E., the son of a ruling *kshatriya* family. According to tradition, the young Siddhartha was raised in affluent surroundings and trained, like many other members of his class, in the martial arts. On reaching maturity, he married and began to raise a family. However, at the age of twenty-nine, he suddenly discovered the pain of illness, the sorrow of death, and the degradation caused by old age in the lives of ordinary people and exclaimed, "Would that sickness, age, and death might be forever bound?" From that time on, he decided to dedicate his life to determining the cause and seeking the cure for human suffering.

To find the answers to these questions, Siddhartha abandoned his home and family and traveled widely. At first he tried to follow the model of the ascetics, but he eventually decided that self-mortification did not lead to a greater understanding of life and abandoned the practice. Then one day after a lengthy period of meditation under a tree, he achieved enlightenment as to the meaning of life and spent the remainder of his life preaching it. His conclusions, as embodied in his teachings, became the philosophy (or as some would have it, the religion) of Buddhism. According to legend, the Devil (the Indian term is *Mara*) attempted desperately to tempt him with political power and the company of beautiful girls. But Siddhartha Gautama resisted:

> *Pleasure is brief as a flash of lightning*
> *Or like an autumn shower, only for a moment....*
> *Why should I then covet the pleasures you speak of?*
> *I see your bodies are full of all impurity:*
> *Birth and death, sickness and age are yours.*
> *I seek the highest prize, hard to attain by men—*
> *The true and constant wisdom of the wise.*[8]

How much the modern doctrine of Buddhism resembles the original teachings of Siddhartha Gautama is open to debate, for much time has elapsed since his death and original texts relating his ideas are lacking. Nor is it certain that Siddhartha even intended to found a new religion or doctrine. In some respects, his ideas could be viewed as a reformist form of Hinduism, designed to transfer responsibility from the priests to the individual, much as the sixteenth-century German monk Martin Luther saw his ideas as a reformation of Christianity. Siddhartha accepted much of the belief system of Hinduism, if not all of its practices. For example, he accepted the concept of reincarnation and the role of *karma* as a means of influencing the movement of individual souls up and down the scale of life. He followed Hinduism in praising nonviolence and borrowed the idea of living a life of simplicity and chastity from the ascetics. Moreover, his vision of metaphysical reality—commonly known as **Nirvana**—is closer to the Hindu concept of *Brahman* than it is to the Christian concept of heavenly salvation. Nirvana, which involves an extinction of selfhood and a final reunion with the Great World Soul, is sometimes likened to a dreamless sleep or to a kind of "blowing out" (as of a candle). Buddhists occasionally remark that someone who asks for a description does not understand the concept.

At the same time, the new doctrine differed from existing Hindu practices in a number of key ways. In the first

© Charles & Josette Lenars/CORBIS

The Three Faces of Shiva. In the first centuries C.E., Hindus began to adopt Buddhist rock art. One outstanding example is at the Elephanta Caves, near the modern city of Mumbai (Bombay). Dominating the cave is this 18-foot-high triple-headed statue of Shiva, representing the Hindu deity in all his various aspects. The central figure shows him in total serenity, enveloped in absolute knowledge. The angry profile on the left portrays him as the destroyer, struggling against time, death, and other negative forces. The right-hand profile shows his loving and feminine side in the guise of his beautiful wife, Parvati.

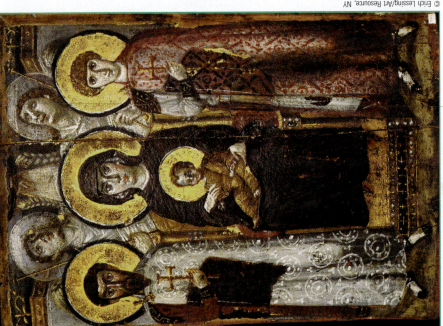

© Erich Lessing/Art Resource, NY

© William J. Duiker

COMPARATIVE ILLUSTRATION

RELIGION & PHILOSOPHY

The Buddha and Jesus. As Buddhism evolved, transforming Siddhartha Gautama, known as the Buddha, from mortal to god, Buddhist art changed as well. Statuary and relief panels began to illustrate the story of his life. In the frieze shown on the left, from the second century C.E., the infant Siddhartha is seen emerging from the hip of his mother, Queen Maya. Although dressed in draperies that reflect Greek influences from Alexander the Great's brief incursion into northwestern India, her sensuous stance and the touching of the tree evoke the female earth spirit of traditional Indian art. On the right is a Byzantine painting depicting the infant Jesus with his mother, the Virgin Mary, dating from the sixth century C.E. Notice that a halo surrounds the head of both the Buddha and Jesus. The halo—a circle of light—is an ancient symbol of divinity. In Hindu, Greek, and Roman art, the heads of gods were depicted as emitting sunlike divine radiances. Early kings adopted crowns made of gold and precious gems to symbolize their own divine authority.

Q In what ways do the mothers of key religious figures shown here share a similar representation? In what ways do they differ?

place, Siddhartha denied the existence of an individual soul. To him, the Hindu concept of *Atman*—the individual soul—meant that the soul was subject to rebirth and thus did not achieve a complete liberation from the cares of this world. In fact, Siddhartha denied the ultimate reality of the material world in its entirety and taught that it was an illusion that had to be transcended. Siddhartha's idea of achieving Nirvana was based on his conviction that the pain, poverty, and sorrow that afflict human beings are caused essentially by their attachment to the things of this

world. Once worldly cares are abandoned, pain and sorrow can be overcome. With this knowledge comes *bodhi*, or wisdom (source of the term *Buddhism* and the familiar name for Gautama the Wise: Gautama Buddha).

Achieving this understanding is a key step on the road to Nirvana, which, as in Hinduism, is a form of release from the wheel of life. According to tradition, Siddhartha transmitted this message in a sermon to his disciples in a deer park at Sarnath, not far from the modern city of Varanasi (Benares). Like so many

HOW TO ACHIEVE ENLIGHTENMENT

One of the most famous passages in Buddhist literature is the sermon at Sarnath, which Siddhartha Gautama delivered to his followers in a deer park outside the holy city of Varanasi (Benares), in the Ganges River valley. Here he set forth the key ideas that would define Buddhist beliefs for centuries to come. During an official visit to Sarnath nearly three centuries later, Emperor Ashoka ordered the construction of a stupa (reliquary) in honor of the Buddha's message.

The Sermon at Benares

Thus have I heard: at one time the Lord dwelt at Benares at Isipatana in the Deer Park. There the Lord addressed the five monks:—

"These two extremes, monks, are not to be practiced by one who has gone forth from the world. What are the two? That conjoined with the passions and luxury, low, vulgar, common, ignoble, and useless; and that conjoined with self-torture, painful, ignoble, and useless. Avoiding these two extremes the Tathagata has gained the enlightenment of the Middle Path, which produces insight and knowledge and tends to calm, to higher knowledge, enlightenment, Nirvana.

"And what, monks, is the Middle Path, of which the Tathagata has gained enlightenment, which produces insight and knowledge, and tends to calm, to higher knowledge, enlightenment, Nirvana? This is the noble Eightfold Way: namely, right view, right intention, right speech, right action, right livelihood, right effort, right mindfulness, right concentration. This, monks, is the Middle Path, of which the Tathagata has gained enlightenment, which produces insight and knowledge, and tends to calm, to higher knowledge, enlightenment, Nirvana.

"1. Now this, monks, is the noble truth of pain: birth is painful, old age is painful, sickness is painful, death is painful, sorrow, lamentation, dejection, and despair are painful. Contact with unpleasant things is painful, not getting what one wishes is painful. In short the five groups of graspings are painful.

"2. Now this, monks, is the noble truth of the cause of pain: the craving, which tends to rebirth, combined with pleasure and lust, finding pleasure here and there; namely, the craving for passion, the craving for existence, the craving for nonexistence.

"3. Now this, monks, is the noble truth of the cessation of pain, the cessation without a remainder of craving, the abandonment, forsaking, release, nonattachment.

"4. Now this, monks, is the noble truth of the way that leads to the cessation of pain: this is the noble Eightfold Way; namely, right view, right intention, right speech, right action, right livelihood, right effort, right mindfulness, right concentration.

"And when, monks, in these four noble truths my due knowledge and insight with its three sections and twelve divisions was well purified, then, monks..., I had attained the highest complete enlightenment. This I recognized. Knowledge and insight arose in me, insight arose that the release of my mind is unshakable; this is my last existence; now there is no rebirth."

Q How did Siddhartha Gautama reach the conclusion that the "four noble truths" was the proper course in living a moral life? How do his ideas compare with the biblical Ten Commandments, discussed in Chapter 1?

CENGAGENOW To read more of Siddhartha Gautama, enter the documents area of the World History Resource Center using the access card that is available for World History.

The Stupa at Sarnath.

© age fotostock/SuperStock

messages, it is deceptively simple and is enclosed in four noble truths: life is suffering, suffering is caused by desire, the way to end suffering is to end desire, and the way to end desire is to avoid the extremes of a life of vulgar materialism and a life of self-torture and to follow the **Middle Path**. Also known as the Eightfold Way, the Middle Path calls for right knowledge, right purpose, right speech, right conduct, right occupation, right effort, right awareness, and right meditation (see the box above).

Buddhism also differed from Hinduism in its relative egalitarianism. Although Siddhartha accepted

© SuperStock

Sanchi Gate and Stupa. Constructed during the reign of Emperor Ashoka in the third century B.C.E., the stupa at Sanchi was enlarged over time, eventually becoming the greatest Buddhist monument on the Indian subcontinent. Originally intended to house a relic of the Buddha, the stupa became a holy place for devotion and a familiar form of Buddhist architecture. Sanchi's four elaborately carved stone gates, each over 40 feet high, tell stories of the Buddha set in joyful scenes of everyday life. Christian churches would later similarly portray events in the life of Jesus to instruct the faithful.

the idea of reincarnation (and hence the idea that human beings differ as a result of *karma* accumulated in a previous existence), he rejected the Hindu division of humanity into rigidly defined classes based on previous reincarnations and taught that all human beings could aspire to Nirvana as a result of their behavior in this life—a message that likely helped Buddhism win support among people at the lower end of the social scale.

In addition, Buddhism was much simpler than Hinduism. Siddhartha rejected the panoply of gods that had become identified with Hinduism and forbade his followers to worship his person or his image after his death. In fact, many Buddhists view Buddhism as a philosophy rather than a religion.

After Siddhartha Gautama's death in 480 B.C.E., dedicated disciples carried his message the length and breadth of India. Buddhist monasteries were established throughout the subcontinent, and temples and **stupas** (stone towers housing relics of the Buddha) sprang up throughout the countryside.

Women were permitted to join the monastic order but only in an inferior position. As Siddhartha had explained, women are "soon angered," "full of passion," and "stupid": "That is the reason...why women have no place in public assemblies...and do not earn their living by any profession." Still, the position of women tended to be better in Buddhist societies than it was elsewhere in ancient India (see the box on p. 59).

Jainism During the next centuries, Buddhism began to compete actively with Hindu beliefs, as well as with another new faith known as **Jainism.** Jainism was founded by Mahavira, a contemporary of Siddhartha Gautama. Resembling Buddhism in its rejection of the reality of the material world, Jainism was more extreme in practice. Where Siddhartha Gautama called for the "middle way" between passion and luxury on one extreme and pain and self-torture on the other, Mahavira preached a doctrine of extreme simplicity to his followers, who kept no possessions and relied on begging for a living. Some even rejected clothing and wandered through the world naked. Perhaps because of its insistence on a life of poverty, Jainism failed to attract enough adherents to become a major doctrine and never received official support. According to tradition, however, Chandragupta Maurya accepted Mahavira's doctrine after abdicating the throne and fasted to death in a Jain monastery.

Ashoka, a Buddhist Monarch Buddhism received an important boost when Ashoka, the grandson of Chandragupta Maurya, converted to Buddhism in the third century B.C.E. Ashoka (269–232 B.C.E.) is widely considered the greatest ruler in the history of India. By his own admission, as noted in rock edicts placed around his kingdom, Ashoka began his reign conquering, pillaging, and killing, but after his conversion to Buddhism, he began to regret his bloodthirsty past and attempted to rule benevolently.

Ashoka directed that banyan trees and shelters be placed along the road to provide shade and rest for weary travelers. He sent Buddhist missionaries throughout India and ordered the erection of stone pillars with official edicts and Buddhist inscriptions to instruct people in the proper way (see Map 2.3 and the illustration on p. 60). According to tradition, his son converted the island of Sri Lanka to Buddhism, and the peoples there accepted a tributary relationship with the Mauryan Empire.

THE VOICES OF SILENCE

FAMILY & SOCIETY

Most of what is known about the lives of women in ancient India comes from the Vedas or other texts written by men. Classical Sanskrit was used exclusively by upper-class males in religious and court functions. Only a few examples of women's writings remain from this period. In the first poem quoted here, a Buddhist nun living in the sixth century B.C.E. reflects on her sense of spiritual salvation and physical release from the drudgery of daily life. The other two poems were produced several hundred years later in southern India by anonymous female authors at a time when strict Hindu traditions had not yet been established in the area. Poetry and song were an essential part of daily life, as women sang while working in the fields, drawing water at the well, or reflecting on the hardships of their daily lives. The second poem quoted here breathes the sensuous joy of sex, while the third expresses the simultaneous grief and pride of a mother as she sends her only son off to war.

"A Woman Well Set Free!"

A woman well set free! How free I am,
How wonderfully free, from kitchen drudgery.
Free from the harsh grip of hunger,
And from empty cooking pots,
Free too of that unscrupulous man,
The weaver of sunshades.
Calm now, and serene I am,
All lust and hatred purged.
To the shade of the spreading trees I go
And contemplate my happiness.

Translated by Uma Chakravarti
and Kumkum Roy

"What She Said to Her Girlfriend"

What she said to her girlfriend:
On beaches washed by seas
older than the earth,
in the groves filled with bird-cries,
on the banks shaded by a punnai
clustered with flowers,
when we made love
my eyes saw him
and my ears heard him;
my arms grow beautiful
in the coupling
and grow lean
as they come away.
What shall I make of this?

Translated by A. K. Ramanujan

"Her Purpose Is Frightening, Her Spirit Cruel"

Her purpose is frightening, her spirit cruel.
That she comes from an ancient house is fitting
surely.
In the battle the day before yesterday,
her father attacked an elephant and died there on
the field.
In the battle yesterday,
her husband faced a row of troops and fell.
And today,
she hears the battle drum,
and, eager beyond reason, gives him a spear in
his hand,
wraps a white garment around him,
smears his dry tuft with oil,
and, having nothing but her one son,
"Go!" she says, sending him to battle.

Translated by George L. Hart III

Q What are the various points of view that are being expressed in these short poems? Can you think of any equivalents from other ancient civilizations at this time?

CENGAGENOW To read related sources, enter the documents area of the World History Resource Center using the access card that is available for World History.

The Rule of the Fishes: India After the Mauryas

Q Focus Question: Why was India unable to maintain a unified empire in the first millennium B.C.E., and how was the Mauryan Empire temporarily able to overcome the tendencies toward disunity?

After Ashoka's death in 232 B.C.E., the Mauryan Empire began to decline. In 183 B.C.E., the last Mauryan ruler was overthrown by one of his military commanders, and India reverted to disunity. A number of new kingdoms, some of them perhaps influenced by the memory of the Alexandrian conquests, arose along the fringes of the subcontinent in Bactria, known today as Afghanistan. In the first century C.E., Indo-European-speaking peoples fleeing from the nomadic Xiongnu warriors in Central Asia seized power in the area and proclaimed the new Kushan kingdom (see Chapter 9). For the next two centuries, the Kushans extended their political sway over northern India as far as the central Ganges valley, while other kingdoms scuffled for predominance elsewhere on the subcontinent. India would not see unity again for another five hundred years.

© Samath, Uttar Pradesh, India/The Bridgeman Art Library

The Lions of Sarnath. Their beauty and Buddhist symbolism make the Lions of Sarnath the most famous of the capitals topping Ashoka's pillars. Sarnath was the holy site where the Buddha first preached, and these roaring lions echo the proclamation of Buddhist teachings to the four corners of the world. The wheel not only represents the Buddha's laws but also proclaims Ashoka's imperial legitimacy as the enlightened Indian ruler.

was not an uneventful period in the history of India, as Indo-Aryan ideas continued to spread southward and both Hinduism and Buddhism evolved in new directions.

The Exuberant World of Indian Culture

Q **Focus Question:** In what ways did the culture of ancient India resemble and differ from the cultural experience of ancient Mesopotamia and Egypt?

Few cultures in the world are as rich and varied as that of India. Most societies excel in some forms of artistic and literary achievement and not in others, but India has produced great works in almost all fields of cultural endeavor—art and sculpture, science, architecture, literature, and music.

Literature

The earliest known Indian literature consists of the four Vedas, which were passed down orally from generation to

---

MAP 2.3 The Empire of Ashoka. Ashoka, the greatest Indian monarch, reigned over the Mauryan dynasty in the third century B.C.E. This map shows the extent of his empire, with the location of the pillar edicts that were erected along major trade routes.

Q Why do you think the pillars and rocks were placed where they were? ➲ **View an animated version of this map or related maps at** www.cengage.com/history/Duiker/World6e

Several reasons for India's failure to maintain a unified empire have been proposed. Some historians suggest that a decline in regional trade during the first millennium C.E. may have contributed to the growth of small land-based kingdoms, which drew their primary income from agriculture. The tenacity of the Aryan tradition, with its emphasis on tribal rivalries, may also have contributed. Although the Mauryan rulers tried to impose a more centralized organization, clan loyalties once again came to the fore after the collapse of the Mauryan dynasty. Furthermore, the behavior of the ruling class was characterized by what Indians call the "rule of the fishes," which glorified warfare as the natural activity of the king and the aristocracy. The *Arthasastra*, which set forth a model of a centralized Indian state, assumed that war was the "sport of kings." Still, this

Legend:
- Pillar edicts
- Rock and minor rock edicts
- Ashoka's Empire, 250 B.C.E.

BACTRIA
HIMALAYAS
GUJARAT
Indus R.
Ganges R.
Pataliputra (Patna)
MAGADHA
Varanasi (Benares)
DECCAN PLATEAU
Godavari R.
Arabian Sea
MALABAR COAST
Indian Ocean
Bay of Bengal
SRI LANKA

0 250 500 750 Kilometers
0 250 500 Miles

60   CHAPTER 2   ANCIENT INDIA

generation until they were finally written down after the Aryan arrived in India. The Rig Veda dates from the second millennium B.C.E. and consists of over a thousand hymns that were used at religious ceremonies. The other three Vedas were written considerably later and contain instructions for performing ritual sacrifices and other ceremonies. The Brahmanas and the Upanishads served as commentaries on the Vedas.

The language of the Vedas was **Sanskrit**, one of the Indo-European family of languages. After the arrival of the Aryans in India, Sanskrit gradually declined as a spoken language and was replaced in northern India by a simpler tongue known as **Prakrit**. Nevertheless, Sanskrit continued to be used as the language of the bureaucracy and of literary expression for many centuries after that and, like Latin in medieval Europe, served as a common language of communication between various regions of India. In the south, a variety of Dravidian languages continued to be spoken.

As early as the fifth century B.C.E., Indian grammarians had codified Sanskrit to preserve the authenticity of the Vedas for the spiritual edification of future generations. A famous grammar written by the scholar Panini in the fourth century B.C.E. set forth four thousand grammatical rules prescribing the correct usage of the spoken and written language. This achievement is particularly impressive in that Europe did not have a science of linguistics until the nineteenth century, when it was developed partly as a result of the discovery of the works of Panini and later Indian linguists.

After the development of a writing system in the first millennium B.C.E., India's holy literature was probably inscribed on palm leaves stitched together into a book somewhat similar to the first books produced on papyrus or parchment in the Mediterranean region. Also written for the first time were India's great historical epics, the Mahabharata and the Ramayana. Both of these epics may have originally been recited at religious ceremonies, but they are essentially histories that recount the martial exploits of great Aryan rulers and warriors.

The Mahabharata, consisting of more than ninety thousand stanzas, was probably written about 100 B.C.E. and describes in great detail a war between cousins for control of the kingdom nine hundred years earlier. Interwoven in the narrative are many fantastic legends of the Hindu gods. Above all, the Mahabharata is a tale of moral confrontations and an elucidation of the ethical precepts of the *dharma*. The most famous section of the book is the so-called Bhagavad Gita, a sermon by the legendary Indian figure Krishna on the eve of a major battle. In this sermon, mentioned at the beginning of this chapter, Krishna sets forth one of the key ethical maxims of Indian society: in taking action, one must be indifferent to success or failure and consider only the moral rightness of the act itself.

The Ramayana, written at about the same time, is much shorter than the Mahabharata. It is an account of a semilegendary ruler named Rama who, as the result of a palace intrigue, is banished from the kingdom and forced to live as a hermit in the forest. Later he fights the demon-king of Sri Lanka, who has kidnapped his beloved wife, Sita. Like the Mahabharata, the Ramayana is strongly imbued with religious and moral significance. Rama himself is portrayed as the ideal Aryan hero, a perfect ruler and an ideal son, while Sita projects the supreme duty of female chastity and wifely loyalty to her husband. The Ramayana is a story of the triumph of good over evil, duty over self-indulgence, and generosity over selfishness. It combines filial and erotic love, conflicts of human passion, character analysis, and poetic descriptions of nature (see the box on p. 62).

The Ramayana also has all the ingredients of an enthralling adventure: giants, wondrous flying chariots, invincible arrows and swords, and magic potions and mantras. One of the real heroes of the story is the monkey-king Hanuman, who flies from India to Sri Lanka to set the great battle in motion. It is no wonder that for millennia the Ramayana has remained a favorite among Indians of all age groups, often performed at festivals today and inspiring a hugely popular TV version produced in recent years.

Architecture and Sculpture

After literature, the greatest achievements of early Indian civilization were in architecture and sculpture. Some of the earliest examples of Indian architecture and sculpture stem from the time of Emperor Ashoka, when Buddhism became the religion of the state. Until the time of the Mauryas, Aryan buildings had been constructed of wood. With the rise of the empire, stone began to be used as artisans arrived in India seeking employment after the destruction of the Persian Empire by Alexander. Many of these stone carvers accepted the patronage of Emperor Ashoka, who used them to spread Buddhist ideas throughout the subcontinent.

There were three main types of religious structures: the pillar, the stupa, and the rock chamber. As noted earlier, during Ashoka's reign, many stone columns were erected alongside roads to commemorate the events in the Buddha's life and mark pilgrim routes to holy places. Weighing up to 50 tons each and rising as high as 32 feet, these polished sandstone pillars were topped with a carved capital, usually depicting lions uttering the Buddha's message. Ten remain standing today (a photograph of one such pillar appears on p. 240).

A stupa was originally meant to house a relic of the Buddha, such as a lock of his hair or a branch of the famous Bodhi tree (the tree beneath which Siddhartha Gautama had first achieved enlightenment), and was constructed in the form of a burial mound (the pyramids in Egypt also derived from burial mounds). Eventually, the stupa became a place for devotion and the most familiar form of Buddhist architecture. Stupas

© William J. Duiker

Symbols of the Buddha. Early Buddhist sculptures referred to the Buddha only through visual symbols that represented his life on the path to enlightenment. In this relief from the stupa at Bharhut, carved in the second century B.C.E., we see four devotees paying homage to the Buddha, who is portrayed as a giant wheel dispensing his "wheel of the law."

that adorned the religious art of ancient India represented salvation and fulfillment for the ordinary Indian.

Science

Our knowledge of Indian science is limited by the paucity of written sources, but it is evident that ancient Indians had amassed an impressive amount of scientific knowledge in a number of areas. Especially notable was their work in mathematics, where they devised the numerical system that we know as Arabic numbers and use today, and in astronomy, where they charted the movements of the heavenly bodies and recognized the spherical nature of the earth at an early date. Their ideas of physics were similar to those of the Greeks; matter was divided into the five elements of earth, air, fire, water, and ether. Many of their technological achievements are impressive, notably the quality of their textiles and the massive stone pillars erected during the reign of Ashoka. As noted, the pillars weighed up to 50 tons each and were transported many miles to their final destination.

CONCLUSION

While the peoples of North Africa and the Middle East were actively building the first civilizations, a similar process was getting under way in the Indus River valley. Much has been learned about the nature of the Indus valley civilization in recent years, but the lack of written records limits our understanding. How did the Harappan people deal with the fundamental human problems mentioned at the close of Chapter 1? The answers remain tantalizingly elusive.

As often happened elsewhere, however, the collapse of Harappan civilization did not lead to the total disappearance of its culture. The new society that eventually emerged throughout the subcontinent after the coming of the Aryans was an amalgam of two highly distinctive cultures, Aryan and Dravidian, each of which made a significant contribution to the politics, social institutions, and creative impulse of ancient Indian civilization.

With the rise of the Mauryan dynasty in the fourth century B.C.E., the distinctive features of a great civilization begin to be clearly visible. It was extensive in its scope, embracing the entire Indian subcontinent and eventually, in the form of Buddhism and Hinduism, spreading to China and Southeast Asia. But the underlying ethnic, linguistic, and cultural diversity of the Indian people posed a constant challenge to the unity of the state. After the collapse of the Mauryas, the subcontinent would not come under a single authority again for several hundred years.

In the meantime, another great experiment was taking place far to the northeast, across the Himalaya Mountains. Like many other civilizations of antiquity, the first Chinese state was concentrated on a major river system. And like them, too, its political and cultural achievements eventually spread far beyond their original habitat. In the next chapter, we turn to the civilization of ancient China.

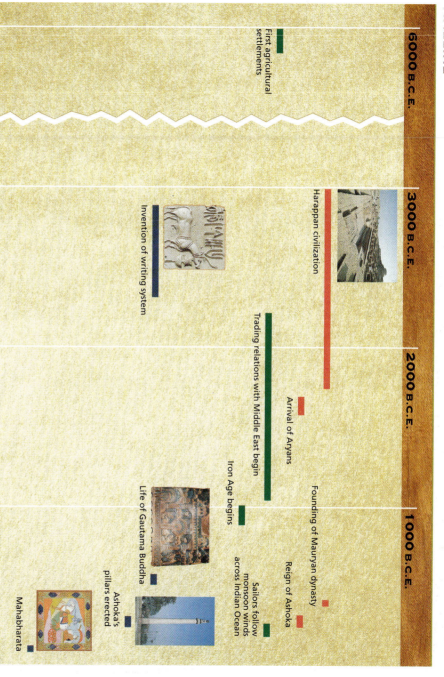

TIMELINE

6000 B.C.E.

First agricultural settlements

3000 B.C.E.

Harappan civilization

Invention of writing system

2000 B.C.E.

Trading relations with Middle East begin

Arrival of Aryans

Founding of Mauryan dynasty

Iron Age begins

Reign of Ashoka

Sailors follow monsoon winds across Indian Ocean

1000 B.C.E.

Life of Gautama Buddha

Ashoka's pillars erected

Mahabharata

CHAPTER NOTES

1. Quoted in R. Lannoy, *The Speaking Tree: A Study of Indian Culture and Society* (London, 1971), p. 318.
2. The quotation is from ibid., p. 319. Note also that the *Law of Manu* says that "punishment alone governs all created beings. . . . The whole world is kept in order by punishment, for a guiltless man is hard to find."
3. Strabo's *Geography*, bk. 15, quoted in M. Edwardes, *A History of India: From the Earliest Times to the Present Day* (London, 1961), p. 55.
4. Ibid., p. 54.
5. Ibid., p. 57.
6. From the *Law of Manu*, quoted in A. L. Basham, *The Wonder That Was India* (London, 1961), pp. 180–181.
7. Mundaka Upanishad 1:2, quoted in W. T. de Bary et al., eds., *Sources of Indian Tradition* (New York, 1966), pp. 28–29.
8. Quoted in A. K. Coomaraswamy, *Buddha and the Gospel of Buddhism* (New York, 1964), p. 34.

SUGGESTED READING

The Emergence of Civilization in India: Harappan Society Several standard histories of India provide a good overview of the ancient period. One of the most readable and reliable is **S. Wolpert, *New History of India*,** 7th ed. (New York, 2003). Also see **B. Metcalf and T. Metcalf, *A Concise History of India*** (Cambridge, 2001).

By far the most informative and readable narrative on the cultural history of India in premodern times is still **A. L. Basham, *The Wonder That Was India*** (London, 1961), which, although somewhat out of date, contains informative sections on prehistory, economy, language, art and literature, society, and everyday life. **R. Thapar, *Early India: From the Origins to AD 1300*** (London, 2002), provides an excellent review of recent scholarship by an Indian historian.

Because of the relative paucity of archaeological exploration in South Asia, evidence for the Harappan period is not as voluminous as for areas such as Mesopotamia and the Nile valley. Some of the best work has been written by scholars who actually worked at the sites. One fine account is **J. M. Kenoyer, *Ancient Cities of the Indus Valley Civilization*** (Karachi, 1998). For a detailed and well-illustrated analysis, see **G. L. Possehl, ed., *The Harappan Civilization: A Contemporary Perspective*** (Amherst, N.Y., 1983). Commercial relations between Harappa and its neighbors are treated in **S. Ratnagar, *Encounters: The Westerly Trade of the Harappan Civilization*** (Oxford, 1981).

For information on the invention of the first writing systems, see **J. T. Hooker, ed., *Reading the Past: Ancient Writing from Cuneiform to the Alphabet*** (London, 1990), and **A. Hurley, *The Alphabet: The History, Evolution, and Design of the Letters We Use Today*** (New York, 1995).

Escaping the Wheel of Life: The Religious World of Ancient India There are a number of good books on the introduction of Buddhism into Indian society. The Buddha's ideals

CONCLUSION   65

are presented in **P. Williams (with A. Tribe)**, *Buddhist Thought: A Complete Introduction to the Indian Tradition* (London, 2000). Also see **J. Strong**, *The Buddha: A Short Biography* (Oxford, 2004). **H. Akira**, *A History of Indian Buddhism: From Sakyamuni to Early Mahayana* (Honolulu, 1990), provides a detailed analysis of early activities by Siddhartha Gautama and his followers. The intimate relationship between Buddhism and commerce is discussed in **Liu Hsin-ju**, *Ancient India and Ancient China: Trades and Religious Exchanges* (Oxford, 1988).

On the early development of Hinduism, see **E. Bryant**, *The Quest for the Origins of Vedic Culture* (Oxford, 2001), and **V. Narayan**, *Hinduism* (Oxford, 2004). For a comparative treatment, see **K. Armstrong**, *The Great Transformation: The Beginning of Our Religious Traditions* (New York, 2006).

The Exuberant World of Indian Culture There are a number of excellent surveys of Indian art, including the comprehensive **S. L. Huntington**, *The Art of Ancient India: Buddhist, Hindu, Jain* (New York, 1985), and the concise *Indian Art*, rev. ed. (London, 1997), by **R. Craven**. See also **V. Dehejia**, *Devi: The Great Goddess* (Washington, D.C., 1999) and *Indian Art* (London, 1997).

Numerous editions of Sanskrit literature are available in English translation. Many are available in the multivolume Harvard Oriental Series. For a shorter annotated anthology of selections from the Indian classics, consult **S. N. Hay, ed.**, *Sources of Indian Tradition*, 2 vols. (New York, 1988), or **J. B. Alphonso-Karkala**, *An Anthology of Indian Literature*, 2d rev. ed. (New Delhi, 1987), put out by the Indian Council for Cultural Relations.

The Mahabharata and Ramayana have been rewritten for 2,500 years. Fortunately, the vibrant versions, retold by William Buck and condensed to four hundred pages each, reproduce the spirit of the originals and enthrall today's imagination. See **W. Buck**, *Mahabharata* (Berkeley, Calif., 1973) and *Ramayana* (Berkeley, Calif., 1976). On the role played by women writers in ancient India, see **S. Tharu and K. Lalita, eds.**, *Women Writing in India: 600 B.C. to the Present*, vol. 1 (New York, 1991).

CENGAGENOW Enter *CengageNOW* using the access card that is available with this text. *CengageNOW* will help you understand the content in this chapter with lesson plans generated for your needs, as well as provide you with a connection to the *Wadsworth World History Resource Center* (see description below for details).

WORLD HISTORY RESOURCE CENTER

Enter the Resource Center using either your *CengageNOW* access card or your separate access card for the *World History Resource Center*. Organized by topic, this Website includes quizzes; images; over 350 primary source documents; interactive simulations, maps, and timelines; movie explorations; and a wealth of other resources. You can read the following documents, and many more, at the *World History Resource Center:*

The *Law of Manu*
The *Rig Veda*

Visit the *World History* Companion Website for chapter quizzes and more:

www.cengage.com/history/Duiker/World6e

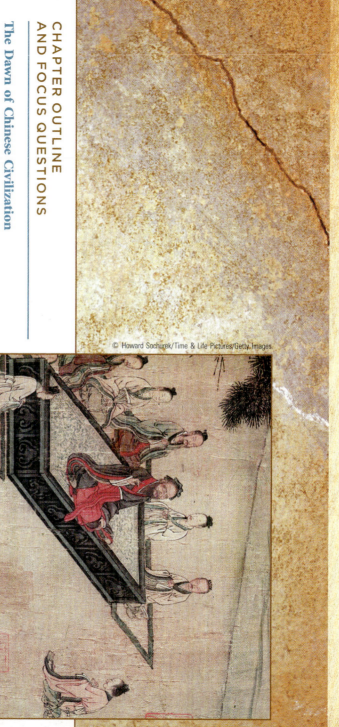

© Howard Sochurek/Time & Life Pictures/Getty Images

Confucius and his disciples

THE MASTER SAID, "If the government seeks to rule by decree, and to maintain order by the use of punishment, the people will seek to evade punishment and have no sense of shame. But if the government leads by virtue and governs through the rules of propriety, the people will feel shame and seek to correct their mistakes."

That statement is from the *Analects*, a collection of remarks attributed to the Chinese philosopher Confucius that were gathered together by his disciples and published after his death in the fifth century B.C.E. Confucius lived at a time when Chinese society was in a state of increasing disarray. The political principles that had governed society since the founding of the Zhou dynasty six centuries earlier were widely ignored, and squabbling principalities scuffled for primacy as the power of the Zhou court steadily declined. The common people groaned under the weight of an oppressive manorial system that left them at the mercy of their aristocratic lords.

In the midst of this turmoil, Confucius traveled the length of the kingdom observing events and seeking employment as a political counselor. In the process, he attracted a number of disciples, to whom he expounded a set of ideas that in later years served as the guiding principles for the Chinese Empire. Some of his ideas are strikingly modern in their thrust. Among them is the revolutionary

67

proposition that government depends on the will of the people.

On the other hand, the principles that Confucius sought to instill into his society had, in his view, all been previously established many centuries in the past—during an alleged "golden age" at the dawn of Chinese history. In that sense, Confucius was a profoundly conservative thinker, seeking to preserve elements in Chinese history that had been neglected by his contemporaries. The dichotomy between tradition and change was thus a key component in Confucian philosophy that would be reflected in many ways over the course of the next 2,500 years.

The civilization that produced Confucius had originated more than fifteen hundred years earlier along the two great river systems of East Asia, the Yellow and the Yangtze. This vibrant new civilization, which we know today as ancient China, expanded gradually into neighboring areas. By the third century B.C.E., it had emerged as a great empire, as well as the dominant cultural and political force in the region.

Like Sumer, Harappa, and Egypt, the civilization of ancient China began as a collection of autonomous villages cultivating food crops along a major river system. Improvements in agricultural techniques led to a food surplus and the growth of an urban civilization characterized by more complex political and social institutions, as well as new forms of artistic and intellectual creativity.

Like its counterparts elsewhere, ancient China faced the challenge posed by the appearance of pastoral peoples on its borders. Unlike Harappa, Sumer, and Egypt, however, ancient China was able to surmount that challenge, and many of its institutions and cultural values survived intact down to the beginning of the twentieth century. For that reason, Chinese civilization is sometimes described as the oldest continuous civilization on earth. ◆

The Dawn of Chinese Civilization

Focus Question: How did geography influence the civilization that arose in China?

According to Chinese legend, Chinese society was founded by a series of rulers who brought the first rudiments of civilization to the region nearly five thousand years ago. The first was Fu Xi (Fu Hsi) (for an explanation regarding the translation of the Chinese written language, see "A Note to Students About Languages and the Dating of Time" on p. xxx), the ox-tamer, who "knotted cords for hunting and fishing," domesticated animals, and introduced the beginnings of family life. The second was Shen Nong (Shen Nung), the divine farmer, who "bent wood for plows and hewed wood for plowshares." He taught the people the techniques of agriculture. Last came Huang Di (Huang Ti), the Yellow Emperor, who "strung a piece of wood for the bow, and whittled little sticks of wood for the arrows." Legend credits Huang Di with creating the Chinese system of writing, as well as with inventing the bow and arrow.[1] Modern historians, of course, do not accept the literal accuracy of such legends but view them instead as part of the process whereby early peoples attempt to make sense of the world and their role in it. Nevertheless, such re-creations of a mythical past often contain an element of truth. Although there is no clear evidence that the "three sovereigns" actually existed, their achievements do symbolize some of the defining characteristics of Chinese civilization: the interaction between nomadic and agricultural peoples, the importance of the family as the basic unit of Chinese life, and the development of a unique system of writing.

The Land and People of China

Although human communities have existed in China for several hundred thousand years, the first *Homo sapiens* arrived in the area sometime after 40,000 B.C.E. as part of the great migration out of Africa. Around the eighth millennium B.C.E., the early peoples living along the riverbanks of northern and central China began to master the cultivation of crops. A number of these early agricultural settlements were in the neighborhood of the Yellow River, where they gave birth to two Neolithic societies known to archaeologists as the **Yangshao** and the **Longshan** cultures (sometimes identified in terms of their pottery as the painted and black pottery cultures, respectively). Similar communities began to appear in the Yangtze valley in central China and along the coast to the south. The southern settlements were based on the cultivation of rice rather than dry crops such as millet, barley, and wheat, but they were as old as those in the north. Thus agriculture, and perhaps other elements of early civilization, may have developed spontaneously in several areas of China rather than radiating outward from one central region.

At first, these simple Neolithic communities were hardly more than villages, but as the inhabitants mastered the rudiments of agriculture, they gradually gave rise to more sophisticated and complex societies. In a pattern that we have already seen elsewhere, civilization gradually spread from these nuclear settlements in the valleys of the Yellow and Yangtze Rivers to other lowland areas of eastern and central China. The two great river valleys, then, can be considered the core regions in the development of Chinese civilization.

Neolithic China

Although these densely cultivated valleys eventually became two of the great food-producing areas of the ancient world, China is more than a land of fertile fields. In fact, only 12 percent of the total land area is arable, compared with 23 percent in the United States. Much of the remainder consists of mountains and deserts that ring the country on its northern and western frontiers.

This often arid and forbidding landscape is a dominant feature of Chinese life and has played a significant role in Chinese history. The geographical barriers served to isolate the Chinese people from advanced agrarian societies in other parts of Asia. The frontier regions in the Gobi Desert, Central Asia, and the Tibetan plateau were sparsely inhabited by peoples of Mongolian, Indo-European, or Turkish extraction. Most were pastoral societies, and like the other river valley civilizations, their contacts with the Chinese were often characterized by mutual distrust and conflict. Although less numerous than the Chinese, many of these peoples possessed impressive skills in war and were sometimes aggressive in seeking wealth or territory in the settled regions south of the Gobi Desert. Over the next two thousand years, the northern frontier became one of the great fault lines of conflict in Asia as Chinese armies

attempted to protect precious farmlands from marauding peoples from beyond the frontier. When China was unified and blessed with capable rulers, it could usually keep the nomadic intruders at bay and even bring them under a loose form of Chinese administration. But in times of internal weakness, China was vulnerable to attack from the north, and on several occasions, nomadic peoples succeeded in overthrowing native Chinese rulers and setting up their own dynastic regimes.

From other directions, China normally had little to fear. To the east lay the China Sea, a lair for pirates and the source of powerful typhoons that occasionally ravaged the Chinese coast but otherwise rarely a source of concern. South of the Yangtze River was a hilly region inhabited by a mixture of peoples of varied linguistic and ethnic stock who lived by farming, fishing, or food gathering. They were gradually absorbed in the inexorable expansion of Chinese civilization.

The Shang Dynasty

Historians of China have traditionally dated the beginning of Chinese civilization to the founding of the Xia

The First Villages in Early China.
Before the invention of writing systems, early humans sought to record events in their lives by means of pictures. Examples are the Neolithic cave paintings in France and Saharan Africa (see Chapters 1 and 8). Shown here to the right is a Neolithic cave painting of a village of stilt houses in Yunnan province in southern China. Stilt houses remain in wide use in parts of southern Asia today as a means of protection against flooding. The smaller photo shows a house in Banpo, an early farming village in central China that was founded perhaps seven thousand years ago. Note that this house is enclosed by walls made of dried mud, a type of dwelling appropriate to a colder climate.

© William J. Duiker

© William J. Duiker

Shell and Bone Writing. The earliest known form of true writing in China dates back to the Shang dynasty and was inscribed on shells or animal bones. Questions for the gods were scratched on bones, which cracked after being exposed to fire. The cracks were then interpreted by sorcerers. The questions often expressed practical concerns: Will it rain? Will the king be victorious in battle? Will he recover from his illness? Originally composed of pictographs and ideographs four thousand years ago, Chinese writing has evolved into an elaborate set of symbols that combine meaning and pronunciation in a single character.

© Werner Forman/Art Resource, NY

(Hsia) dynasty more than four thousand years ago. Although the precise date for the rise of the Xia is in dispute, recent archaeological evidence confirms its existence. Legend maintains that the founder was a ruler named Yu, who is also credited with introducing irrigation and draining the floodwaters that periodically threatened to inundate the northern China plain (see the box on p. 71). The Xia dynasty was replaced by a second dynasty, the Shang, around the sixteenth century B.C.E. The late Shang capital at Anyang, just north of the Yellow River in north-central China, has been excavated by archaeologists. Among the finds were thousands of so-called oracle bones, ox and chicken bones or turtle shells that were used by Shang rulers for divination and to communicate with the gods. The inscriptions on these oracle bones are the earliest known form of Chinese writing and provide much of our information about the beginnings of civilization in China. They describe a culture gradually emerging from the Neolithic to the early Bronze Age.

Political Organization China under the Shang dynasty was a predominantly agricultural society ruled by an aristocratic class whose major occupation was war and control over key resources such as metals and salt. One ancient chronicler complained that "the big affairs of state consist of sacrifice and soldiery."[2] Combat was carried on by means of two-horse chariots. The appearance of chariots in China in the mid-second millennium B.C.E. coincides roughly with similar developments elsewhere, leading some historians to suggest that the Shang

ruling class may originally have invaded China from elsewhere in Asia. But items found in Shang burial mounds are similar to Longshan pottery, implying that the Shang ruling elites were linear descendants of the indigenous Neolithic peoples in the area. If that was the case, the Shang may have acquired their knowledge of horse-drawn chariots through contact with the peoples of neighboring regions.

Some recent support for that assumption has come from evidence unearthed in the sandy wastes of Xinjiang, China's far-northwestern province. There archaeologists have discovered corpses dating back as early as the second millennium B.C.E. with physical characteristics that resemble those of Europeans. They are also clothed in textiles similar to those worn at the time in Europe, suggesting that they may have been members of an Indo-European migration from areas much farther to the west. If that is the case, they were probably familiar with advances in chariot making that occurred a few hundred years earlier in southern Russia and Kazakhstan. By about 2000 B.C.E., spoked wheels were being deposited at grave sites in the Ukraine and also in the Gobi Desert, just north of the great bend of the Yellow River. It is thus likely that the new technology became available to the founders of the Shang dynasty and may have aided their rise to power in northern China.

The Shang king ruled with the assistance of a central bureaucracy in the capital city. His realm was divided into a number of territories governed by aristocratic chieftains, but the king appointed these chieftains and

A TREATISE ON THE YELLOW RIVER AND ITS CANALS

Sima Qian (Szu-ma Ch'ien) was a famous historian of the Han dynasty who lived during the second and first centuries B.C.E. In his most famous work, titled *Historical Records*, he describes the public works projects undertaken during the Xia dynasty to convert the dangerous waters of the Yellow River to human use. Although the identification of irrigation works with Yu may be apocryphal, irrigation works were under way in central China at least as early as the sixth century B.C.E., and China later became one of the foremost hydraulic societies in the ancient world.

Sima Qian, *Historical Records*

The documents on the Hsia dynasty tell us that Emperor Yu spent thirteen years controlling and bringing an end to the floods, and during that period, though he passed by the very gate of his own house, he did not take the time to enter. On land he traveled in a cart and on water in a boat; he rode a sledge to cross the mud and wore cleated shoes in climbing the mountains. In this way he marked out the nine provinces, led the rivers along the bases of the mountains, decided what tribute was appropriate for each region in accordance with the quality of its soil, opened up the nine roads, built embankments around the nine marshes, and made a survey of the nine mountains.

Of all the rivers, the Yellow River caused the greatest damage to China by overflowing its banks and inundating the land, and therefore he turned all his attention to controlling it. Thus he led the Yellow River in a course from Chi-shih past Lung-men and south to the northern side of Mount Hua; from there eastward along the foot of Ti-chu Mountain, past the Meng Ford and the confluence of the Lo River to Ta-p'ei. At this point Emperor Yu decided that, since the river was descending from high ground and the flow of the water was rapid and fierce, it would be difficult to guide it over level ground without danger of frequent disastrous breakthroughs. He therefore divided the flow into two channels, leading it along the higher ground to the north, past the Chiang River and so to Ta-lu. There he spread it out to form the Nine Rivers, brought it together again to make the Backward-Flowing River [tidal river], and thence led it into the Gulf of Pohai. When he had thus opened up the rivers of the nine provinces and fixed the outlets of the nine marshes, peace and order were brought to the lands of the Hsia, and his achievements continued to benefit the Three Dynasties which followed.

Q *For ancient China, controlling the flow of water in the country's major river systems was essential to survival. To what degree was this true of the other major civilizations we have encountered, and how did they deal with the problem?*

CENGAGENOW *To read other works by Sima Qian, enter the documents area of the World History Resource Center using the access card that is available for World History.*

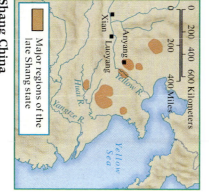

200 0 200 400 600 Kilometers
0 200 400 Miles

Anyang · Luoyang · Xian
Yellow R. · Huai R. · Yangtze R. · Yellow Sea

Major regions of the late Shang state

Shang China

could apparently depose them at will. He was also responsible for the defense of the realm and controlled large armies that often fought on the fringes of the kingdom. The transcendent importance of the ruler was graphically displayed in the ritual sacrifices undertaken at his death, when hundreds of his retainers were buried with him in the royal tomb.

As the inscriptions on the oracle bones make clear, the Chinese ruling elite believed in the existence of supernatural forces and thought that they could communicate with those forces to obtain divine intervention on matters of this world. In fact, the main purpose of the oracle bones was apparently to communicate with the gods. This evidence also suggests that the king was already being viewed as an intermediary between heaven and earth. In fact, an early Chinese character for king consists of three horizontal lines connected by a single vertical line; the middle horizontal line represents the king's place between human society and the divine forces in nature.

The early Chinese also had a clear sense of life in the hereafter. Though some of the human sacrifices discovered in the royal tombs were presumably intended to propitiate the gods, others were meant to accompany the king or members of his family on the journey to the next world (see the comparative illustration on p. 72). From this conviction would come the concept of the **veneration of ancestors** (mistakenly known in the West as "ancestor worship") and the practice, which continues to the present day in many Chinese communities, of burning replicas of physical objects to accompany the departed on their journey to the next world.

Social Structures In the Neolithic period, the farming village was apparently the basic social unit of China, at least in the core region of the Yellow River valley. Villages

© William J. Duiker

© Egyptian National Museum, Cairo, Egypt/The Bridgeman Art Library

© Lowell Georgia/CORBIS

COMPARATIVE ILLUSTRATION

RELIGION & PHILOSOPHY

The Afterlife and Prized Possessions. Like the pharaohs in Egypt, Chinese rulers filled their tombs with prized possessions from daily life. It was believed that if the tombs were furnished and stocked with supplies, including chairs, boats, chests, weapons, games, and dishes, the spiritual body could continue its life despite the death of the physical body. In the photo on the left, we see the remains of a chariot and horses in a burial pit in China's Hebei province that dates from the early Zhou dynasty. The lower photo on the right shows a small boat from the tomb of Tutankhamun in the Valley of the Kings in Egypt. The tradition of providing items of daily use for the departed continues today in Chinese communities throughout Asia. In the upper-right photo, the papier-mâché vehicle will be burned so that it will ascend in smoke to the world of the spirit.

Q How did Chinese tombs compare to the tombs of ancient Egyptian pharaohs? What do the differences tell you about these two societies? What do all of the items shown here have in common?

were organized by clans rather than by nuclear family units, and all residents probably took the common clan name of the entire village. In some cases, a village may have included more than one clan. At Banpo (Pan P'o), an archaeological site near the modern city of Xian that dates back at least seven thousand years, the houses in the village are separated by a ditch, which some scholars think may have served as a divider between two clans. The individual dwellings at Banpo housed nuclear families, but a larger building in the village was apparently used as a clan meeting hall. The clan-based origins of Chinese society may help explain the continued importance of the joint family in traditional China, as well as the relatively small number of family names in Chinese society. Even today there are only about four hundred commonly used family names in a society of more than one billion people, and a colloquial expression for the common people in China today is "the old hundred names."

By Shang times, the classes were becoming increasingly differentiated. It is likely that some poorer peasants did not own their farms but were obliged to work the

land of the chieftain and other elite families in the village. The aristocrats not only made war and served as officials (indeed, the first Chinese character for *official* originally meant "warrior"), but they were also the primary landowners. In addition to the aristocratic elite and the peasants, there were a small number of merchants and artisans, as well as slaves, probably consisting primarily of criminals or prisoners taken in battle.

The Shang are perhaps best known for their mastery of the art of casting bronze. Utensils, weapons, and ritual objects made of bronze (see the comparative essay "The Use of Metals" on p. 73) have been found in royal tombs in urban centers throughout the area known to be under Shang influence. It is also clear that the Shang had achieved a fairly sophisticated writing system that would eventually spread throughout East Asia and evolve into the written language that is still used in China today.

Examples such as these once led observers to assume that Shang China served as a "mother culture," dispensing its technological achievements to its less advanced neighbors. Most scholars today, however, qualify that hypothesis,

COMPARATIVE ESSAY
THE USE OF METALS

Around 6000 B.C.E., people in western Asia discovered how to use metals. They soon realized the advantage in using metal rather than stone to make both tools and weapons. Metal could be shaped more exactly, allowing artisans to make more refined tools and weapons with sharper edges and more precise shapes. Copper, silver, and gold, which were commonly found in their elemental form, were the first metals to be used. These were relatively soft and could be easily pounded into different shapes. But an important step was taken when people discovered that a rock that contained metal could be heated to liquefy the metal (a process called smelting). The liquid metal could then be poured into molds of clay or stone to make precisely shaped tools and weapons.

Copper was the first metal to be used in making tools. The first known copper smelting furnace, dated to 3800 B.C.E., was found in the Sinai. At about the same time, however, artisans in Southeast Asia discovered that tin could be added to copper to make bronze. By 3000 B.C.E., artisans in western Asia were also making bronze. Bronze has a lower melting point that makes it easier to cast, but it is also a harder metal than copper and corrodes less. By 1400 B.C.E., the Chinese were making bronze decorative objects as well as battle-axes and helmets. The widespread use of bronze has led historians to speak of the period from around 3000 to 1200 B.C.E. as the Bronze Age, although this is somewhat misleading in that many peoples continued to use stone tools and weapons even after bronze became available.

But there were limitations to the use of bronze. Tin was not as available as copper, which made bronze tools and weapons expensive. After 1200 B.C.E., bronze was increasingly replaced by iron, which was probably first used around 1500 B.C.E. in western Asia, where the Hittites made new weapons from it. Between 1500 and 600 B.C.E., ironmaking spread across Europe, North Africa, and Asia. Bronze continued to be used, but mostly for jewelry and other domestic purposes. Iron was used to make tools and weapons with sharp edges. Because iron weapons were cheaper than bronze ones, larger numbers of warriors could be armed, and wars could be fought on a larger scale.

Iron was handled differently from bronze: it was heated until it could be beaten into a desired shape. Each hammering made the metal stronger. This wrought iron, as it was called, was typical of iron manufacturing in the West until the late Middle Ages. In China, however, the use of heat-resistant clay in the walls of blast furnaces raised temperatures to 1,537 degrees Celsius, enabling artisans already in the fourth century B.C.E. to liquefy iron so that it too could be cast in molds. Europeans would not develop such blast furnaces until the fifteenth century C.E.

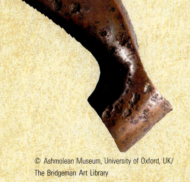

Bronze Axhead. This axhead, manufactured during the second millennium B.C.E., was made by pouring liquid metal into an ax-shaped mold of clay or stone. When it had cooled, artisans would polish the surface to produce a sharp cutting edge.

© Ashmolean Museum, University of Oxford, UK/ The Bridgeman Art Library

---

pointing out that emerging societies elsewhere in China were equally creative in mastering their environment, based on archaeological evidence now being unearthed.

The Zhou Dynasty

Q **Focus Question:** What were the major tenets of Confucianism, Legalism, and Daoism, and what role did each play in political and philosophical debates during the Zhou dynasty?

In the eleventh century B.C.E., the Shang dynasty was overthrown by an aggressive young state located to the west of Anyang, the Shang capital, and near the great bend of the Yellow River as it begins to flow directly eastward to the sea. The new dynasty, which called itself the Zhou (Chou), survived for about eight hundred years and was thus the longest-lived dynasty in the history of China. According to tradition, the last of the Shang rulers was a tyrant who oppressed the people (Chinese sources assert that he was a degenerate who built "ponds of wine" and ordered the composing of lustful music that "ruined the morale of the nation"),[3] leading the ruler of the principality of Zhou to revolt and establish a new dynasty.

The Zhou located their capital in their home territory, near the present-day city of Xian. Later they established a second capital city at modern Luoyang, farther to the east, to administer new territories captured from the Shang. This established a pattern of eastern and western capitals that would endure off and on in China for nearly two thousand years.

Political Structures

The Zhou dynasty (1045–221 B.C.E.) adopted the political system of its predecessors, with some changes. The Shang practice of dividing the kingdom into a number of territories governed by officials appointed by the king was continued under the Zhou. At the apex of the government hierarchy was the Zhou king, who was served by a bureaucracy of growing size and complexity. It now included several ministries responsible for rites, education, law, and public works. Beyond the capital, the Zhou kingdom was divided into a number of principalities, governed by members of the hereditary aristocracy, who were appointed by the king and were at least theoretically subordinated to his authority.

The Mandate of Heaven But the Zhou kings also introduced some innovations. According to the *Rites of Zhou*, one of the oldest surviving documents on statecraft, the Zhou dynasty ruled China because it possessed the **"mandate of Heaven."** According to this concept, Heaven (viewed as an impersonal law of nature rather than as an anthropomorphic deity) maintained order in the universe through the Zhou king, who thus ruled as a representative of Heaven but not as a divine being. The king, who was selected to rule because of his talent and virtue, was then responsible for governing the people with compassion and efficiency. It was his duty to appease the gods in order to protect the people from natural calamities or bad harvests. But if the king failed to rule effectively, he could, theoretically at least, be overthrown and replaced by a new ruler. As noted earlier, this idea was used to justify the Zhou conquest of the Shang. Eventually, the concept of the heavenly mandate would become a cardinal principle of Chinese statecraft.[4] Each founder of a new dynasty would routinely assert that he had earned the mandate of Heaven, and who could disprove it except by overthrowing the king? As a pragmatic Chinese proverb put it, "He who wins is the king; he who loses is the rebel."

In asserting that the ruler had a direct connection with the divine forces presiding over the universe, Chinese tradition reflected a belief that was prevalent in all ancient civilizations. But whereas in some societies, notably in Mesopotamia and Greece (see Chapter 4), the gods were seen as capricious and not subject to human understanding, in China, Heaven was viewed as an essentially benevolent force devoted to universal harmony and order that could be influenced by positive human action. Was this attitude a consequence of the fact that the Chinese environment, though subject to some of the same climatic vicissitudes that plagued other parts of the world, was somewhat more predictable and beneficial than in climatically harsh regions like the Middle East?

Later Chinese would regard the period of the early Zhou dynasty, as portrayed in the *Rites of Zhou* (which, of course, is no more an unbiased source than any modern government document), as a golden age when there was harmony in the world and all was right under Heaven. Whether the system functioned in such an ideal manner, of course, is open to question. In any case, the golden age did not last, whether because it never existed in practice or because of the increasing complexity of Chinese civilization. Perhaps, too, its disappearance was a consequence of the intellectual and moral weakness of the rulers of the Zhou royal house.

By the sixth century B.C.E., the Zhou dynasty began to decline. As the power of the central government disintegrated, bitter internal rivalries arose among the various principalities, where the governing officials had succeeded in making their positions hereditary at the expense of the king. As the power of these officials grew, they began to regulate the local economy and seek reliable sources of revenue for their expanding armies, such as a uniform tax system and government monopolies on key commodities such as salt and iron.

Economy and Society

During the Zhou dynasty, the essential characteristics of Chinese economic and social institutions began to take shape. The Zhou continued the pattern of land ownership that had existed under the Shang: the peasants worked on lands owned by their lord but also had land that they cultivated for their own use. The practice was called the **well field system**, since the Chinese character for well field (井) calls to mind the division of land into nine separate segments. Each peasant family tilled an outer plot for its own use and joined with other families to work the inner one for the hereditary lord (see the box on p. 75). How widely this system was used is unclear, but it represented an ideal described by Confucian scholars of a later day. As the following passage from *The Book of Songs* indicates, life for the average farmer was a difficult one. The "big rat" is probably a reference to the high taxes imposed on the peasants by the government or lord.

Big rat, big rat,
Do not eat my millet!
Three years I have served you,
But you will not care for me.
I am going to leave you
And go to that happy land;
Happy land, happy land,
Where I will find my place.[5]

Trade and manufacturing were carried out by merchants and artisans, who lived in walled towns under the direct control of the local lord. Merchants did not operate independently but were considered the property of the local lord and on occasion could even be bought and sold like chattels. A class of slaves performed a variety of menial tasks and perhaps worked on local irrigation projects. Most of them were probably prisoners of war captured during conflicts with the neighboring principalities.

Scholars do not know how extensive slavery was in ancient times, but slaves probably did not constitute a large portion of the total population.

The period of the later Zhou, from the sixth to the third century B.C.E., was an era of significant economic growth and technological innovation, especially in agriculture. During that time, large-scale water control projects were undertaken to regulate the flow of rivers and distribute water evenly to the fields, as well as to construct canals to facilitate the transport of goods from one region to another (see the box on p. 71). Perhaps the most impressive technological achievement of the period was the construction of the massive water control project on the Min River, a tributary of the Yangtze. This system of canals and spillways, put into operation by the state of Qin a few years prior to the end of the Zhou dynasty, diverted excess water from the river into the local irrigation network and watered an area populated by as many as five million people. The system is still in use today, over two thousand years later.

Food production was also stimulated by a number of advances in farm technology. By the mid-sixth century B.C.E., the introduction of iron had led to the development of iron plowshares, which permitted deep plowing for the first time. Other innovations dating from the later Zhou were the use of natural fertilizer, the collar harness, and the technique of leaving land fallow to preserve or replenish nutrients in the soil (see the box on p. 76). By the late Zhou dynasty, the cultivation of wet rice had become one of the prime sources of food in China. Although rice was difficult and time-consuming to produce, it replaced other grain crops in areas with a warm

FAMILY & SOCIETY

The following passage is from *The Book of Songs*, a classic written during the early Zhou dynasty. This excerpt describes the calendar of peasant life on an estate in ancient China and indicates the various types of service that peasants provided for their lord.

The Book of Songs

In the seventh month the Fire Star passes the meridian;

....

In the ninth month clothes are given out.
In the days of [our] first month, the wind blows cold.
In the days of [our] second, the air is cold.
Without coats, without garments of hair,
How could we get to the end of the year?
In the days of [our] third month we take our plows in hand.
In the days of [our] fourth we make our way to the fields.
Along with wives and children,
We eat in those south-lying acres.
The surveyor of the fields comes and is glad.

In the seventh month the Fire Star passes the meridian;
In the ninth month clothes are given out.
With the spring days the warmth begins,
And the oriole utters its song.
The young women take their deep baskets
And go along the small paths.
Looking for the tender [leaves of the] mulberry trees,
As the spring days lengthen out,
They gather in crowds the white southern wood.
The girl's heart is wounded with sadness,
For she will soon be going with one of the young lords
....

In the eighth month spinning is begun;
We make dark fabrics and yellow,
"With our red dye so bright,
We make robes for our young lords."

....

In the ninth month we prepare the stockyard,
And in the tenth we bring in the harvest.
The millets, the early and the late,
Together with paddy and hemp, beans and wheat.

In the days of [our] second month we cut the ice
with tingling blows;
In the days of [our] third month [it is] stored in the
icehouse.
In the days of [our] fourth month, very early,
A lamb with scallions is offered in sacrifice.
In the ninth month are shrewd frosts;
In the tenth month the stockyard is cleared.
With twin pitchers we hold the feast,
Killed for it is a young lamb.
Up we go into the lord's hall,
Raise the cup of buffalo horn,
"Long life for our lord, may he live forever and ever!"

Now we go up to work in the manor.
"In the day you gather the thatch-reeds;
In the evening twist them into rope;
Go quickly on to the roofs;
Soon you are to sow the grain."

Q Who is the presumed author of this document? Are there suggestions here that men and women had different job responsibilities on the estate? How does this compare with the situation in other ancient civilizations?

ENVIRONMENTAL CONCERNS IN ANCIENT CHINA

Even in antiquity, China possessed a large population that often stretched the limits of the productive potential of the land. In the following excerpt, the Zhou philosopher Mencius appeals to his sovereign to adopt policies that will conserve precious resources and foster the well-being of his subjects. Clearly, Mencius was concerned that environmental needs were being neglected. Unfortunately, his advice has not always been followed, and environmental degradation remains a problem in China today. The destruction of the forests, for example, has deprived China of much of its wood resources, and the present government has launched an extensive program to plant trees.

The *Book of Mencius*

If you do not interfere with the busy season in the fields, then there will be more grain than the people can eat; if you do not allow nets with too fine a mesh to be used in large ponds, then there will be more fish and turtles than they can eat; if hatchets and axes are permitted in the forests on the hills only in the proper seasons, then there will be more timber than they can use. When the people have more grain, more fish and turtles than they can eat, and more timber than they can use, then in the support of their parents when alive and in the mourning of them when dead, they will be able to have no regrets over anything left undone. This is the first step along the Kingly way.

If the mulberry is planted in every homestead of five mu of land, then those who are fifty can wear silk; if chickens, pigs, and dogs do not miss their breeding season, then those who are seventy can eat meat; if each lot of a hundred mu is not deprived of labor during the busy seasons, then families with several mouths to feed will not go hungry. Exercise due care over the education provided by the village schools, and discipline the people by teaching them the duties proper to sons and younger brothers, and those whose heads have turned gray will not be carrying loads on the roads. When those who are seventy wear silk and eat meat and the masses are neither cold nor hungry, it is impossible for their prince not to be a true King.

Now when food meant for human beings is so plentiful as to be thrown to dogs and pigs, you fail to realize that it is time for gathering, and when men drop dead from starvation by the wayside, you fail to realize that it is time for distribution. When people die, you simply say, "It is none of my doing. It is the fault of the harvest." In what way is that different from killing a man by running him through, while saying all the time, "It is none of my doing. It is the fault of the weapon." Stop putting the blame on the harvest and the people of the whole Empire will come to you.

Q *Are these recommendations realistic in terms of what a monarch in ancient China might hope to achieve? Or might farmers resist some of these proposals as likely to harm their own interests?*

CENGAGENOW *To read other selections by Mencius, enter the documents area of the World History Resource Center using the access card that is available for World History.*

---

climate because of its good taste, relative ease of preparation, and high nutritional value.

The advances in agriculture, which enabled the population of China to rise as high as twenty million people during the late Zhou era, were also undoubtedly a major factor in the growth of commerce and manufacturing. During the late Zhou, economic wealth began to replace noble birth as the prime source of power and influence. Utensils made of iron became more common, and trade developed in a variety of useful commodities, including cloth, salt, and manufactured goods.

One of the most important items of trade in ancient China was silk. There is evidence of silkworm raising as early as the Neolithic period. Remains of silk material have been found on Shang bronzes, and a large number of fragments have been recovered in tombs dating from the mid-Zhou era. Silk cloth was used not only for clothing and quilts but also to wrap the bodies of the dead prior to burial. Fragments have been found throughout Central Asia and as far away as Athens, suggesting that the famous Silk Road stretching from central China westward to the Middle East and the Mediterranean Sea was in operation as early as the fifth century B.C.E. (see Map 5.4 on p. 155; see also Chapter 5).

In fact, however, a more important item of trade that initially propelled merchants along the Silk Road was probably jade. Blocks of the precious stone were mined in the mountains of northern Tibet as early as the sixth millennium B.C.E. and began to appear in China during the Shang dynasty. Praised by Confucius as a symbol of purity and virtue, it assumed an almost sacred quality among Chinese during the Zhou dynasty.

With the development of trade and manufacturing, China began to move toward a money economy. The first form of money, as in much of the rest of the world, may have been seashells (the Chinese character for goods or property contains the ideographic symbol for "shell": 貝), but by the Zhou dynasty, pieces of iron shaped like a knife or round coins with a hole in the middle so they could be carried in strings of a thousand were being used. Most ordinary Chinese, however, simply used a system of barter. Taxes, rents, and even the salaries of government officials were normally paid in grain.

The Hundred Schools of Ancient Philosophy

In China, as in other great river valley societies, the birth of civilization was accompanied by the emergence of an organized effort to comprehend the nature of the cosmos and the role of human beings within it. Speculation over such questions began in the very early stages of civilization and culminated at the end of the Zhou era in the "hundred schools" of ancient philosophy, a wide-ranging debate over the nature of human beings, society, and the universe.

Early Beliefs The first hint of religious belief in ancient China comes from relics found in royal tombs of Neolithic times. By then, the Chinese had already developed a religious sense beyond the primitive belief in the existence of spirits in nature. The Shang had begun to believe in the existence of one transcendent god, known as Shang Di, who presided over all the forces of nature. As time went on, the Chinese concept of religion evolved from a vaguely anthropomorphic god to a somewhat more impersonal symbol of universal order known as Heaven (*Tian*, or *T'ien*). There was also much speculation among Chinese intellectuals about the nature of the cosmic order. One of the earliest ideas was that the universe was divided into two primary forces of good and evil, light and dark, male and female, called the *yang* and the *yin*, represented symbolically by the sun (*yang*) and the moon (*yin*). According to this theory, somewhat reminiscent of the religion of Zoroastrianism in Persia, life was a dynamic process of interaction between the forces of *yang* and *yin*. Early Chinese could attempt only to understand the process and perhaps to have some minimal effect on its operation. They could not hope to reverse it. It is sometimes asserted that this belief has contributed to the heavy element of fatalism in Chinese popular wisdom. The Chinese have traditionally believed that bad times will be followed by good times and vice versa.

The belief that there was some mysterious "law of nature" that could be interpreted by human beings led to various attempts to predict the future, such as the Shang oracle bones and other methods of divination. Philosophers invented ways to interpret the will of nature, while shamans, playing a role similar to the *brahmins* in India, were employed at court to assist the emperor in his policy deliberations until at least the fifth century C.E. One of the most famous manuals used for this purpose was the *Yi Jing* (*I Ching*), known in English as the *Book of Changes*.

Confucianism Efforts to divine the mysterious purposes of Heaven notwithstanding, Chinese thinking about metaphysical reality also contained a strain of pragmatism, readily apparent in the ideas of the great philosopher Confucius. Confucius (the name is the Latin form of his honorific title, *Kung Fuci*, or *K'ung Fu-tzu*, meaning Master Kung) was born in the state of Lu (in the modern province of Shandong) in 551 B.C.E. After reaching maturity, he apparently hoped to find employment as a political adviser in one of the principalities into which China was divided at that time, but he had little success in finding a patron. Nevertheless, he made an indelible mark on history as an independent (and somewhat disgruntled) political and social philosopher.

In conversations with his disciples contained in the *Analects*, Confucius often adopted a detached and almost skeptical view of Heaven. "You are unable to serve man," he commented on one occasion; "how then can you hope to serve the spirits? While you do not know life, how can you know about death?" In many instances, he appeared to advise his followers to revere the deities and the ancestral spirits but to keep them at a distance. Confucius believed it was useless to speculate too much about metaphysical questions. Better by far to assume that there was a rational order to the universe and then concentrate on ordering the affairs of this world.[6]

Confucius' interest in philosophy, then, was essentially political and ethical. The universe was constructed in such a way that if human beings could act harmoniously in accordance with its purposes, their own affairs would prosper. Much of his concern was with human behavior. The key to proper behavior was to behave in accordance with the **Dao** (Way). Confucius assumed that all human beings had their own *Dao*, depending on their individual role in life, and it was their duty to follow it. Even the ruler had his own *Dao*, and he ignored it at his peril, for to do so could mean the loss of the mandate of Heaven. The idea of the *Dao* is reminiscent of the concept of *dharma* in ancient India and played a similar role in governing the affairs of society.

Two elements in the Confucian interpretation of the *Dao* are particularly worthy of mention. The first is the concept of duty. It was the responsibility of all individuals to subordinate their own interests and aspirations to the broader need of the family and the community. Confucius assumed that if each individual worked hard to fulfill his or her assigned destiny, the affairs of society as a whole would prosper as well. In this respect, it was important for the ruler to set a good example. If he followed his "kingly way," the beneficial effects would radiate throughout society (see the box on p. 78).

The second key element is the idea of humanity, sometimes translated as "human-heartedness." This concept involves a sense of compassion and empathy for others. It is similar in some ways to Christian concepts, but with a subtle twist. Where Christian teachings call on human beings to "behave toward others as you would have them behave toward you," the Confucian maxim is put in a different way: "Do not do unto others what you would not wish done to yourself." To many Chinese, this attitude symbolizes an element of tolerance in the Chinese

THE WAY OF THE GREAT LEARNING

POLITICS & GOVERNMENT

Few texts exist today that were written by Confucius himself. Most were written or edited by his disciples. The following text, titled *The Great Learning*, was probably written two centuries after Confucius' death, but it illustrates his view that good government begins with the cultivation of individual morality and proper human relationships at the basic level. This conviction that to bring peace to the world, you must cultivate your own person continued to win general approval down to modern times. There are interesting similarities between such ideas and the views expressed in the Indian treatise *Arthasastra*, discussed in Chapter 2.

The Great Learning

The Way of the Great Learning consists in clearly exemplifying illustrious virtue, in loving the people, and in resting in the highest good.

Only when one knows where one is to rest can one have a fixed purpose. Only with a fixed purpose can one achieve calmness of mind. Only with calmness of mind can one attain serene repose. Only in serene repose can one carry on careful deliberation. Only through careful deliberation can one have achievement. Things have their roots and branches; affairs have their beginning and end. He who knows what comes first and what comes last comes himself near the Way.

The ancients who wished clearly to exemplify illustrious virtue throughout the world would first set up good government in their states. Wishing to govern well their states, they would first regulate their families. Wishing to regulate their families, they would first cultivate their persons. Wishing to cultivate their persons, they would first rectify their minds. Wishing to rectify their minds, they would first seek sincerity in their thoughts. Wishing for sincerity in their thoughts, they would first extend their knowledge. The extension of knowledge lay in the investigation of things. For only when things are investigated is knowledge extended; only when knowledge is extended are thoughts sincere; only when thoughts are sincere are minds rectified; only when minds are rectified are our persons cultivated; only when our persons are cultivated are our families regulated; only when families are regulated are states well governed; and only when states are well governed is there peace in the world.

From the emperor down to the common people, all, without exception, must consider cultivation of the individual character as the root. If the root is in disorder, it is impossible for the branches to be in order. To treat the important as unimportant and to treat the unimportant as important—this should never be. This is called knowing the root; this is called the perfection of knowledge.

Q *Compare these views, which reflect one of the most basic elements in Confucian thought—that proper moral behavior must begin at the level of the individual if it is to succeed within the framework of the larger community—with moral teachings expressed in other ancient civilizations. Would the Indian political adviser Kautilya, for example, agree with such views?*

---

character that has not always been practiced in other societies.[7]

Confucius may have considered himself a failure because he never attained the position he wanted, but many of his contemporaries found his ideas appealing, and in the generations after his death, his message spread widely throughout China. Confucius was an outspoken critic of his times and lamented the disappearance of what he regarded as the golden age of the early Zhou. One classical source quoted him as follows:

The practice of the Great Way, the illustrious men of the Three Dynasties—these I shall never know in person. And yet they inspire my ambition. When the Great Way was practiced, the world was shared by all alike. The worthy and the able were promoted to office and practiced good faith and lived in affection. There they did not regard as parents only their own parents, or as sons only their own sons. The aged found a fitting close to their lives, the robust their proper employment; the young were provided with an upbringing and the widow and widower, the orphaned and the sick, with proper care. Men had their talks and women their hearths. They hated to see goods lying about in waste, yet they did not hoard them for themselves; they disliked the thought that their energies were not fully used, yet they used them not for private ends. Therefore all evil plotting was prevented and thieves and rebels did not arise, so that people could leave their outer gates unbolted. This was the age of Grand Unity.[8]

In fact, however, Confucius was not just another disgruntled Chinese conservative mourning the passing of the good old days; rather, he was a revolutionary thinker, many of whose key ideas looked forward rather than backward. Perhaps his most striking political idea was that the government should be open to all men of superior quality, not limited to those of noble birth. As one of his disciples reports in the *Analects*: "The Master said, by nature, men are nearly alike; by practice, they get to be wide apart."[9] Confucius undoubtedly had himself in mind as one of those "superior" men, but the capacity of the hereditary lords must have added strength to his convictions.

The concept of rule by merit was, of course, not an unfamiliar idea in the China of his day; the *Rites of Zhou*

© Topham/The Image Works

had clearly stated that the king himself deserved to rule because of his talent and virtue, rather than as the result of noble birth. In practice, however, aristocratic privilege must often have opened the doors to political influence, and many of Confucius' contemporaries must have regarded his appeal for government by talent as both exciting and dangerous. Confucius did not explicitly question the right of the hereditary aristocracy to play a leading role in the political process, nor did his ideas have much effect in his lifetime. Still, they introduced a new concept that was later implemented in the form of a bureaucracy selected through a civil service examination (see "Confucianism and the State" later in this chapter).

Confucius' ideas, passed on to later generations through the *Analects* as well as through writings attributed to him, had a strong impact on Chinese political thinkers of the late Zhou period, a time when the existing system was in disarray and open to serious question. But as with most great thinkers, Confucius' ideas were sufficiently ambiguous to be interpreted in contradictory ways. Some, like the philosopher Mencius (370–290 B.C.E.), stressed the humanistic side of Confucian ideas, arguing that human beings were by nature good and hence could be taught their civic responsibilities by example. He also stressed that the ruler had a duty to govern with compassion:

It was because Chieh and Chou lost the people that they lost the empire, and it was because they lost the hearts of the people that they lost the people. Here is the way to win the empire: win the people and you win the empire. Here is the way to win the people: win their hearts and you win the people. Here is the way to win their hearts: give them and share with them what they like, and do not do to them what they do not like. The people turn to a human ruler as water flows downward or beasts take to wilderness.[10]

Here is a prescription for political behavior that could win wide support in our own day. Other thinkers, however, rejected Mencius' rosy view of human nature and argued for a different approach.

Legalism One school of thought that became quite popular during the "hundred schools" era in ancient China was the philosophy of Legalism. Taking issue with the view of Mencius and other disciples of Confucius that human nature was essentially good, the Legalists argued that human beings were by nature evil and would follow the correct path only if coerced by harsh laws and stiff punishments. These thinkers were referred to as the School of Law because they rejected the Confucian view that government by "superior men" could solve society's problems and argued instead for a system of impersonal laws.

The Legalists also disagreed with the Confucian belief that the universe has a moral core. They therefore believed that only firm action by the state could bring about social order. Fear of harsh punishment, more than the promise of material reward, could best motivate the common people to serve the interests of the ruler. Because human nature was essentially corrupt, officials could not be trusted to carry out their duties in a fair and evenhanded manner, and only a strong ruler could create an orderly society. All human actions should be subordinated to the effort to create a strong and prosperous state subject to his will.

Daoism One of the most popular alternatives to **Confucianism** was the philosophy of **Daoism** (frequently spelled Taoism). According to Chinese tradition, the Daoist school was founded by a contemporary of Confucius popularly known as Lao Tzu (Lao Zi), or the Old Master. Many modern scholars, however, are skeptical that Lao Tzu actually existed.

Obtaining a clear understanding of the original concepts of Daoism is difficult because its primary document, a short treatise known as the *Dao De Jing* (sometimes translated as *The Way of the Tao*), is an enigmatic book whose interpretation has baffled scholars for centuries. The opening line, for example, explains less what the *Dao* is than what it is not: "The Tao [Way] that can be told of is

Confucius and Lao Tzu. It is not likely that the two ancient Chinese philosophers ever met, for little is known about the life of Lao Tzu (shown on the left in the illustration), but according to tradition, the two allegedly held a face-to-face meeting. The discussion must have been interesting, for their points of view about the nature of reality were diametrically opposed. Nevertheless, the Chinese have managed to preserve both traditions, perhaps a reflection of the dualities represented in the Chinese approach to life. A similar duality existed among Platonists and Aristotelians in ancient Greece (see Chapter 4).

THE DAOIST ANSWER TO CONFUCIANISM

RELIGION & PHILOSOPHY

The *Dao De Jing* (*The Way of the Tao*) is the great classic of philosophical Daoism (Taoism). Traditionally attributed to the legendary Chinese philosopher Lao Tzu (Old Master), it was probably written during the era of Confucius. This opening passage illustrates two of the key ideas that characterize Daoist belief: it is impossible to define the nature of the universe, and inaction (not Confucian action) is the key to ordering the affairs of human beings.

The Way of the Tao

The Tao that can be told of is not the eternal Tao;
The name that can be named is not the eternal name.
The Nameless is the origin of Heaven and Earth;
The Named is the mother of all things.

Therefore let there always be nonbeing so we may
   see their subtlety;
And let there always be being so we may see their
   outcome.

The two are the same,
But after they are produced, they have different
   names.
They both may be called deep and profound.
Deeper and more profound,
The door of all subtleties!

When the people of the world all know beauty as
   beauty,
There arises the recognition of ugliness.
When they all know the good as good,

There arises the recognition of evil.
Therefore:
Being and nonbeing produce each other;
Difficult and easy complete each other;
Long and short contrast each other;
High and low distinguish each other;
Sound and voice harmonize each other;
Front and behind accompany each other.

Therefore the sage manages affairs without action
And spreads doctrines without words.
All things arise, and he does not turn away from
   them.

He produces them but does not take possession
   of them.
He acts but does not rely on his own ability.
He accomplishes his task but does not claim credit for it.
It is precisely because he does not claim credit that
   his accomplishment remains with him.

Q What is Lao Tzu, the presumed author of this document, trying to express about the basic nature of the universe? Based on The Great Learning and The Way of the Tao, how do you think the Chinese attempted to understand the order of nature through their philosophies?

CENGAGENOW. To read more selections from the Dao De Jing, enter the documents area of the World History Resource Center using the access card that is available for World History.

---

not the eternal Tao. The name that can be named is not the eternal name."[11]

Nevertheless, the basic concepts of Daoism are not especially difficult to understand. Like Confucianism, Daoism does not anguish over the underlying meaning of the cosmos. Rather, it attempts to set forth proper forms of behavior for human beings here on earth. In most other respects, however, Daoism presents a view of life and its ultimate meaning that is almost diametrically opposed to that of Confucianism. Where Confucian doctrine asserts that it is the duty of human beings to improve life here on earth, Daoists contend that the true way to interpret the will of Heaven is not action but inaction (*wu wei*). The best way to act in harmony with the universal order is to act spontaneously and let nature take its course (see the box above).

Such a message could be very appealing to people who were uncomfortable with the somewhat rigid flavor of the Confucian work ethic and preferred a more individualistic approach. This image would eventually find graphic expression in Chinese landscape painting, which

in its classical form would depict naturalistic scenes of mountains, water, and clouds and underscore the fragility and smallness of individual human beings.

Daoism achieved considerable popularity in the waning years of the Zhou dynasty. It was especially popular among intellectuals, who may have found it appealing as an escapist antidote in a world characterized by growing disorder.

Popular Beliefs Daoism also played a second role as a framework for popular spiritualistic and animistic beliefs among the common people. Popular Daoism was less a philosophy than a religion; it comprised a variety of rituals and behaviors that were regarded as a means of achieving heavenly salvation or even a state of immortality on earth. Daoist sorcerers practiced various types of mind- or body-training exercises in the hope of achieving power, sexual prowess, and long life. It was primarily this form of Daoism that survived into a later age.

The philosophical forms of Confucianism and Daoism did not provide much meaning to the mass of the

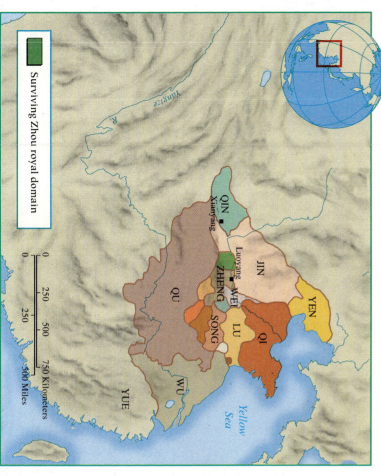

Surviving Zhou royal domain

0 250 500 750 Kilometers
0 250 500 Miles

MAP 3.1 China During the Period of the Warring States. From the fifth to the third centuries B.C.E., China was locked in a time of civil strife known as the Period of the Warring States. This map shows the Zhou dynasty capital at Luoyang, along with the major states that were squabbling for precedence in the region. The state of Qin would eventually suppress its rivals and form the first unified Chinese empire, with its capital at Xianyang (near modern Xian).

Q Why did most of the early states emerge in areas adjacent to China's two major river systems, the Yellow and the Yangtze? **View an animated version of this map or related maps at www.cengage.com/history/Duiker/World6e**

population, for whom philosophical debate over the ultimate meaning of life was not as important as the daily struggle for survival. Even among the elites, interest in the occult and in astrology was high, and magicoreligious ideas coexisted with the interest in natural science and humanistic philosophy throughout the ancient period.

For most Chinese, Heaven was not a vague, impersonal law of nature, as it was for many Confucian and Daoist intellectuals, but was instead a terrain peopled with innumerable gods and spirits of nature, both good and evil, who existed in trees, mountains, and streams as well as in heavenly bodies. As human beings mastered the techniques of farming, they called on divine intervention to guarantee a good harvest. Other gods were responsible for the safety of fishers, transportation workers, or prospective mothers.

Another aspect of popular religion was the belief that the spirits of deceased human beings lived in the atmosphere for a time before ascending to heaven or descending to hell. During that period, surviving family members had to care for the spirits through proper ritual, or they would become evil spirits and haunt the survivors.

Thus in ancient China, human beings were offered a variety of interpretations of the nature of the universe. Confucianism satisfied the need for a rational doctrine of nation building and social organization at a time when the existing political and social structure was beginning to disintegrate. Philosophical Daoism provided a more sensitive approach to the vicissitudes of fate and nature and a framework for a set of diverse animistic beliefs at the popular level. But neither could satisfy the deeper emotional needs that sometimes inspire the human spirit. Neither could effectively provide solace in a time of sorrow or the hope of a better life in the hereafter. Something else would be needed to fill the gap.

The First Chinese Empire: The Qin Dynasty

Q Focus Question: How did the first emperor of the Qin dynasty transform the political, social, and economic institutions of early China?

During the last two centuries of the Zhou dynasty (the fourth and third centuries B.C.E.), the authority of the king became increasingly nominal, and several of the small principalities into which the Zhou kingdom had been divided began to evolve into powerful states that presented a potential challenge to the Zhou ruler himself. Chief among these were Qu (Ch'u) in the central Yangtze valley, Wu in the Yangtze delta, and Yue (Yueh) along the southeastern coast. At first, their mutual rivalries were in check, but by the late fifth century B.C.E., competition intensified into civil war, giving birth to the so-called Period of the Warring States (see the box on p. 82). Powerful principalities vied with each other for preeminence and largely ignored the now purely titular authority of the Zhou court (see Map 3.1). New forms of warfare also emerged with the invention of iron weapons and the introduction of the foot soldier. Cavalry, too, made its first appearance, armed with the powerful crossbow.

THE ART OF WAR

POLITICS & GOVERNMENT

With the possible exception of the nineteenth-century German military strategist Karl von Clausewitz, there is probably no more famous or respected writer on the art of war than the ancient Chinese thinker Sun Tzu. Yet surprisingly little is known about him. Recently discovered evidence suggests that he lived in the fifth century B.C.E., during the chronic conflict of the Period of Warring States, and that he was an early member of an illustrious family of military strategists who advised Zhou rulers for more than two hundred years. But despite the mystery surrounding his life, there is no doubt of his influence on later generations of military planners. Among his most avid followers in our day have been the revolutionary leaders Mao Zedong and Ho Chi Minh, as well as the Japanese military strategists who planned the attacks on Port Arthur and Pearl Harbor.

The following brief excerpt from his classic, *The Art of War*, provides a glimmer into the nature of his advice, still so timely today.

Selections from Sun Tzu

Sun Tzu said:

"In general, the method for employing the military is this:... Attaining one hundred victories in one hundred battles is not the pinnacle of excellence. Subjugating the enemy's army without fighting is the true pinnacle of excellence....

"Thus the highest realization of warfare is to attack the enemy's plans; next is to attack their alliances; next to attack their army; and the lowest is to attack their fortified cities.

"This tactic of attacking fortified cities is adopted only when unavoidable. Preparing large movable protective shields, armored assault wagons, and other equipment and devices will require three months. Building earthworks will require another three months to complete. If the general cannot overcome his impatience but instead launches an assault wherein his men swarm over the walls like ants, he will kill one-third of his officers and troops, and the city will still not be taken. This is the disaster that results from attacking [fortified cities].

"Thus one who excels at employing the military subjugates other people's armies without engaging in battle, captures other people's fortified cities without attacking them, and destroys others people's states without prolonged fighting. He must fight under Heaven with the paramount aim of 'preservation.'...

"In general, the strategy of employing the military is this: If your strength is ten times theirs, surround them; if five, then attack them; if double, then divide your forces. If you are equal in strength to the enemy, you can engage him. If fewer, you can circumvent him. If outmatched, you can avoid him....

"Thus there are five factors from which victory can be known:

"*One who knows when he can fight, and when he cannot fight, will be victorious.*

"*One who recognizes how to employ large and small numbers will be victorious.*

"*One whose upper and lower ranks have the same desires will be victorious.*

"*One who, fully prepared, awaits the unprepared will be victorious.*

"*One whose general is capable and not interfered with by the ruler will be victorious.*

"These five are the Way (Tao) to know victory....

"Thus it is said that one who knows the enemy and knows himself will not be endangered in a hundred engagements. One who does not know the enemy but knows himself will sometimes be victorious, sometimes meet with defeat. One who knows neither the enemy nor himself will invariably be defeated in every engagement."

Q *Why are the ideas of Sun Tzu about the art of war still so popular among military strategists after 2,500 years? How might he advise U.S. and other statesmen to deal with the problem of international terrorism today?*

CENGAGENOW *To read more of* The Art of War, *enter the documents area of the* World History *Resource Center using the access card that is available for World History.*

The Qin Dynasty (221–206 B.C.E.)

One of the primary reasons for the triumph of the Qin was probably the character of the Qin ruler, known to history as Qin Shi Huangdi (Ch'in Shih Huang Ti), or the First Emperor of Qin. A man of forceful personality and immense ambition, Qin Shi Huangdi had ascended to the throne of Qin in 246 B.C.E. at the age of thirteen. Described by the famous Han dynasty historian Sima Qian

Eventually, the relatively young state of Qin, located in the original homeland of the Zhou, became a key player in these conflicts. Benefiting from a strong defensive position in the mountains to the west of the great bend of the Yellow River, as well as from their control of the rich Sichuan plains, the Qin gradually subdued their main rivals through conquest or diplomatic maneuvering. In 221 B.C.E., the Qin ruler declared the establishment of a new dynasty, the first truly unified government in Chinese history.

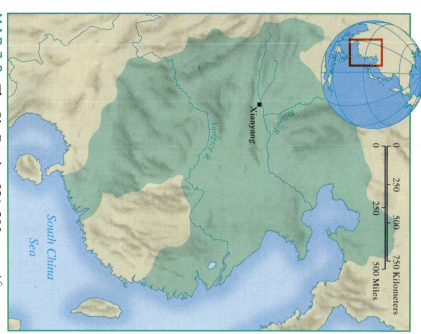

MAP 3.2 **The Qin Empire, 221–206 B.C.E.** After a struggle of several decades, the state of Qin was finally able to subdue its rivals and create the first united empire in the history of China. The capital was located at Xianyang, near the modern city of Xian.

Q What factors may have aided Qin in its effort to dominate the region? View an animated version of this map or related maps at **www.cengage.com/history/Duiker/World6e**

as having "the chest of a bird of prey, the voice of a jackal, and the heart of a tiger," the new king found the Legalist views of his adviser Li Su (Li Ssu) only too appealing. In 221 B.C.E., Qin Shi Huangdi defeated the last of his rivals and founded a new dynasty with himself as emperor (see Map 3.2).

Political Structures The Qin dynasty transformed Chinese politics. Philosophical doctrines that had proliferated during the late Zhou period were prohibited, and Legalism was adopted as the official ideology. Those who opposed the policies of the new regime were punished and sometimes executed, while books presenting ideas contrary to the official orthodoxy were publicly put to the torch, perhaps the first example of book burning in history (see the box on p. 84).

Legalistic theory gave birth to a number of fundamental administrative and political developments, some of which would survive the Qin and serve as a model for future dynasties. In the first place, unlike the Zhou, the Qin was a highly centralized state. The central bureaucracy was divided into three primary ministries: a civil authority, a military authority, and a censorate, whose inspectors surveyed the efficiency of officials throughout the system. This would later become standard administrative procedure for future Chinese dynasties.

Below the central government were two levels of administration: provinces and counties. Unlike the Zhou system, officials at these levels did not inherit their positions but were appointed by the court and were subject to dismissal at the emperor's whim. Apparently, some form of merit system was used, although there is no evidence that selection was based on performance in an examination. The civil servants may have been chosen on the recommendation of other government officials. A penal code provided for harsh punishments for all wrongdoers. Officials were watched by the censors, who reported directly to the throne. Those guilty of malfeasance in office were executed.

Society and the Economy Qin Shi Huangdi, who had a passion for centralization, unified the system of weights and measures, standardized the monetary system and the written forms of Chinese characters, and ordered the construction of a system of roads extending throughout the empire. He also attempted to eliminate the remaining powers of the landed aristocrats and divided their estates among the peasants, who were now taxed directly by the state. He thus eliminated potential rivals and secured tax revenues for the central government. Members of the aristocratic clans were required to live in the capital city at Xianyang (Hsien-yang), just north of modern Xian, so that the court could monitor their activities. Such a system may not have been advantageous to the peasants in all respects, however, since the central government could now collect taxes more effectively and mobilize the peasants for military service and for various public works projects.

The Qin dynasty was equally unsympathetic to the merchants, whom it viewed as parasites. Private commercial activities were severely restricted and heavily taxed, and many vital forms of commerce and manufacturing, including mining, wine making, and the distribution of salt, were placed under a government monopoly.

Qin Shi Huangdi was equally aggressive in foreign affairs. His armies continued the gradual advance to the south that had taken place during the final years of the Zhou dynasty, extending the border of China to the edge of the Red River in modern Vietnam. To supply the Qin armies operating in the area, a canal was dug that provided direct inland navigation from the Yangtze River in central China to what is now the modern city of Guangzhou (Canton) in the south.

Beyond the Frontier: The Nomadic Peoples and the Great Wall The main area of concern for the Qin emperor, however, was in the north, where a nomadic people,

MEMORANDUM ON THE BURNING OF BOOKS

Li Su, who is quoted in the following passage, was a chief minister of the First Emperor of Qin. An exponent of Legalism, Li Su hoped to eliminate all rival theories on government. His recommendation to the emperor on the subject was recorded by the Han dynasty historian Sima Qian. The emperor approved the proposal and ordered all books contrary to the spirit of Legalist ideology to be destroyed on pain of death. Fortunately, some texts were preserved by being hidden or even memorized by their owners and were thus available to later generations. For centuries afterward, the First Emperor of Qin and his minister were singled out for criticism because of their intolerance and their effort to control the minds of their subjects. Totalitarianism, it seems, is not a modern concept.

Sima Qian, *Historical Records*

In earlier times the empire disintegrated and fell into disorder, and no one was capable of unifying it. Thereupon the various feudal lords rose to power. In their discourses they all praised the past in order to disparage the present and embellished empty words to confuse the truth. Everyone cherished his own favorite school of learning and criticized what had been instituted by the authorities. But at present Your Majesty possesses a unified empire, has regulated the distinctions of black and white, and has firmly established for yourself a position of sole supremacy. And yet these independent schools, joining with each other, criticize the codes of laws and instructions. Hearing of the promulgation of a decree, they criticize it, each from the standpoint of his own school. At home they disapprove of it in their

hearts; going out they criticize it in the thoroughfare. They seek a reputation by discrediting their sovereign; they appear superior by expressing contrary views, and they lead the lowly multitude in the spreading of slander. If such license is not prohibited, the sovereign power will decline above and partisan factions will form below. It would be well to prohibit this.

Your servant suggests that all books in the imperial archives, save the memoirs of Ch'in, be burned. All persons in the empire, except members of the Academy of Learned Scholars, in possession of the *Book of Odes*, the *Book of History*, and discourses of the hundred philosophers should take them to the local governors and have them indiscriminately burned. Those who dare to talk to each other about the *Book of Odes* and the *Book of History* should be executed and their bodies exposed in the marketplace. Anyone referring to the past to criticize the present should, together with all members of his family, be put to death. Officials who fail to report cases that have come under their attention are equally guilty. After thirty days from the time of issuing the decree, those who have not destroyed their books are to be branded and sent to build the Great Wall. Books not to be destroyed will be those on medicine and pharmacy, divination by the tortoise and milfoil, and agriculture and arboriculture. People wishing to pursue learning should take the officials as their teachers.

Q *Why does the Legalist thinker Li Su feel that his proposal to destroy dangerous ideas is justified? Are there examples of similar thinking in our own time? Are there occasions when it might be permissible to outlaw unpopular ideas?*

known to the Chinese as the Xiongnu (Hsiung-nu) and possibly related to the Huns (see Chapter 5), had become increasingly active in the area of the Gobi Desert. The area north of the Yellow River had been sparsely inhabited since prehistoric times. During the Qin period, the climate of northern China was somewhat milder and moister than it is today, and parts of the region were heavily forested. The local population probably lived by hunting and fishing, practicing limited forms of agriculture, or herding animals such as cattle or sheep.

As the climate gradually became drier, people were forced to rely increasingly on animal husbandry as a means of livelihood. Their response was to master the art of riding on horseback and to adopt the nomadic life. Organized loosely into communities consisting of a number of kinship groups, they ranged far and wide in search of pasture for their herds of cattle, goats, or sheep. As they moved seasonally from one pasture to

another, they often traveled several hundred miles carrying their goods and their circular felt tents, called *yurts*.

But the new way of life presented its own challenges. Increased food production led to a growing population, which in times of drought outstripped the available resources. Rival groups then competed for the best pastures. After they mastered the art of fighting on horseback in the middle of the first millennium B.C.E., territorial warfare became commonplace throughout the entire frontier region, from the Pacific Ocean to Central Asia.

By the end of the Zhou dynasty in the third century B.C.E., the nomadic Xiongnu posed a serious threat to the security of China's northern frontier, and a number of Chinese principalities in the area began to build walls and fortifications to keep them out. But warriors on horseback possessed significant advantages over the infantry of the Chinese.

Qin Shi Huangdi's answer to the problem was to strengthen the walls to keep the marauders out. In Sima Qian's words:

First Emperor of the Ch'in dispatched Meng T'ien to lead a force of a hundred thousand men north to attack the barbarians. He seized control of all the lands south of the Yellow River and established border defenses along the river, constructing forty-four walled district cities overlooking the river and manning them with convict laborers transported to the border for garrison duty. Thus he utilized the natural mountain barriers to establish the border defenses, scooping out the valleys and constructing ramparts and building installations at other points where they were needed. The whole line of defenses stretched over ten thousand li [a li is one-third of a mile] from Lin-t'ao to Liao-tung and even extended across the Yellow River and through Yang-shan and Pei-chia.[12]

Today, of course, we know Qin Shi Huangdi's project as the Great Wall, which extends nearly 4,000 miles from the sandy wastes of Central Asia to the sea. It is constructed of massive granite blocks, and its top is wide enough to serve as a roadway for horse-drawn chariots. Although the wall that appears in most photographs today was built 1,500 years after the Qin, during the Ming dynasty, some of the walls built by the Qin remain standing. Their construction was a massive project that required the efforts of thousands of laborers, many of whom met their deaths there and, according to legend, are buried within the wall.

The Fall of the Qin

The Legalist system put in place by the First Emperor of Qin was designed to achieve maximum efficiency as well as total security for the state. It did neither. Qin Shi Huangdi was apparently aware of the dangers of factions within the imperial family and established a class of **eunuchs** (castrated males) who served as personal attendants for himself and female members of the royal family. The original idea may have been to restrict the influence of male courtiers, and the eunuch system later became a standard feature of the Chinese imperial system. But as confidential advisers to the royal family, eunuchs were in a position of influence. The rivalry between the "inner" imperial court and the "outer" court of bureaucratic officials led to tensions that persisted until the end of the imperial system.

By ruthlessly gathering control over the empire into his own hands, Qin Shi Huangdi had hoped to establish a rule that, in the words of Sima Qian, "would be enjoyed by his sons for ten thousand generations." In fact, his centralizing zeal alienated many key groups. Landed aristocrats and Confucian intellectuals, as well as the common people, groaned under the censorship of thought and speech, harsh taxes, and forced labor projects. "He killed men," recounted the historian, "as though he thought he could never finish, he punished men as though he was afraid he would never get around to them all, and the whole world revolted against him."[13]

Shortly after the emperor died in 210 B.C.E., the dynasty descended into factional rivalry, and four years later it was overthrown.

The disappearance of the Qin brought an end to an experiment in absolute rule that later Chinese historians would view as a betrayal of humanistic Confucian principles. But in another sense, the Qin system was a response—though somewhat extreme—to the problems of administering a large and increasingly complex society. Although later rulers would denounce Legalism and enthrone Confucianism as the new state orthodoxy, in practice they would make use of a number of the key tenets of Legalism to administer the empire and control the behavior of their subjects.

CHRONOLOGY Ancient China

Xia (Hsia) dynasty	?–c. 1570 B.C.E.
Shang dynasty	c. 1570–c. 1045 B.C.E.
Zhou (Chou) dynasty	c. 1045–221 B.C.E.
Life of Confucius	551–479 B.C.E.
Period of the Warring States	403–221 B.C.E.
Life of Mencius	370–290 B.C.E.
Qin (Ch'in) dynasty	221–206 B.C.E.
Life of the First Emperor of Qin	259–210 B.C.E.

Daily Life in Ancient China

Q Focus Question: What were the key aspects of social and economic life in early China?

Few social institutions have been as closely identified with China as the family. As in most agricultural civilizations, the family served as the basic economic and social unit in society. In traditional China, however, it took on an almost sacred quality as a microcosm of the entire social order.

The Role of the Family

In Neolithic times, the farm village, organized around the clan, was the basic social unit in China, at least in the core region of the Yellow River valley. Even then, however, the smaller family unit was becoming more important, at least among the nobility, who attached considerable significance to the veneration of their ancestors.

During the Zhou dynasty, the family took on increasing importance, in part because of the need for cooperation in agriculture. The cultivation of rice, which had become the primary crop along the Yangtze River and in the provinces to the south, is highly labor-intensive. The seedlings must be planted in several inches of water in a nursery bed and then transferred individually to the paddy beds, which must be irrigated

© William J. Duiker

Flooded Rice Fields. Rice, first cultivated in China seven or eight thousand years ago, is a labor-intensive crop that requires many workers to plant the seedlings and organize the distribution of water. Initially, the fields are flooded to facilitate the rooting of the rice seedlings and to add nutrients to the soil. Fish breeding in the flooded fields help keep mosquitoes and other insects in check. As the plants mature, the fields are drained, and the plants complete their four-month growing cycle in dry soil. Shown here is an example of terracing on a hillside to preserve water for the nourishment of young seedlings. The photo below illustrates the backbreaking task of transplanting rice seedlings in a flooded field in Vietnam today.

© William J. Duiker

constantly. During the harvest, the stalks must be cut and the kernels carefully separated from the stalks and husks. As a result, children—and the labor they supplied—were considered essential to the survival of the family, not only during their youthful years but also later, when sons were expected to provide for their parents. Loyalty to family members came to be considered even more important than loyalty to the broader community or the state. Confucius commented that it is the mark of a civilized society that a son should protect his father even if the latter has committed a crime against the community.

At the crux of the concept of family was the idea of **filial piety,** which called on all members of the family to subordinate their personal needs and desires to the patriarchal head of the family. More broadly, it created a hierarchical system in which every family member had a place. All Chinese learned the **five relationships** that were the key to a proper social order. The son was subordinate to the father, the wife to her husband, the younger brother to the older brother, and all were subject to their king. The final relationship was the proper one between friend and friend. Only if all members of the family and the community as a whole behaved in a properly filial manner would society function effectively.

A stable family system based on obedient and hard-working members can serve as a bulwark for an efficient government, but putting loyalty to the family and the clan over loyalty to the state can also present a threat to a centralizing monarch. For that reason, the Qin dynasty attempted to destroy the clan system in China and assert the primacy of the state. Legalists even imposed heavy taxes on any family with more than two adult sons in order to break down the family concept. The Qin reportedly also originated the practice of organizing several family units into larger groups of five and ten families that would exercise mutual control and surveillance. Later dynasties continued the practice under the name of the **Bao-jia (Pao-chia) system.**

But the efforts of the Qin to eradicate or at least reduce the importance of the family system ran against

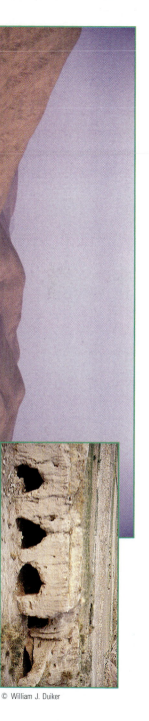

© William J. Duiker

© William J. Duiker

Heartland of Ancient China. The Yellow River valley and its neighboring regions have always been viewed as the heartland of ancient Chinese civilization. Rich clay soils, known by geologists as loess and carried southward by the winds from the vast Gobi Desert, created a thick blanket of rich loam in which to plant the grain crops that sustained the Chinese people. In the larger photograph, even the walls of the village are constructed of this rich yellow earth. The hills in the background are pockmarked with cave dwellings (smaller photo) that have housed the local inhabitants since prehistoric times.

Lifestyles

We know much more about the lifestyle of the elites than that of the common people in ancient China. The first houses were probably constructed of wooden planks, but later Chinese mastered the art of building in tile and brick. By the first millennium B.C.E., most public buildings and the houses of the wealthy were probably constructed in this manner. By the second century B.C.E., most Chinese probably lived in simple houses of mud, wooden planks, or brick with thatch or occasionally tile roofs. But in some areas, especially the loess (pronounced "less," a type of soil common in North China) regions of northern China, cave dwelling remained common down to modern times. The most famous cave dweller of modern times was Mao Zedong, who lived in a cave in Yan'an during his long struggle against Chiang Kai-shek.

Chinese houses usually had little furniture; most people squatted or sat with their legs spread out on the packed-mud floor. Chairs were apparently not introduced until the sixth or seventh century C.E. Clothing was simple, consisting of cotton trousers and shirts in the summer and wool or burlap in the winter.

The staple foods were millet in the north and rice in the south. Other common foods were wheat, barley, soybeans, mustard greens, and bamboo shoots. In early times, such foods were often consumed in the form of porridge, but by the Zhou dynasty, stir-frying in a wok was becoming common. When possible, the Chinese family would vary its diet of grain foods with vegetables, fruit (including pears, peaches, apricots, and plums), and fish or meat; but for most, such additions to the daily plate of rice, millet, or soybeans were a rare luxury.

Alcohol in the form of ale was drunk at least by the higher classes and by the early Zhou era had already begun to inspire official concern. According to the *Book of History,* "King Wen admonished... the young nobles... that they should not ordinarily use spirits; and throughout all the states he required that they should be drunk only on occasion of sacrifices, and that then virtue should preside so that there might be no drunkenness."[14] For the poorer classes, alcohol in any form was probably a rare luxury. Chinese legend hints that tea—a plant originally found in upland regions in southern China and Southeast Asia—was introduced by the mythical emperor Shen Nong. In fact, however, tea drinking did not become widespread in China until around 500 C.E. By then it was lauded for its medicinal qualities and its capacity to soothe the spirit.

tradition and the dynamics of the Chinese economy, and under the Han dynasty, which followed the Qin, the family revived and increased in importance. With official encouragement, the family system began to take on the character that it would possess until our own day. The family was not only the basic economic unit; it was also the basic social unit for education, religious observances, and training in ethical principles.

Cities

Most Chinese, then as now, lived in the countryside. But as time went on, cities began to play a larger role in Chinese society. The first towns were little more than forts for the local aristocracy; they were small in size and limited in population. By the Zhou era, however, larger towns, usually located on the major trade routes, began to combine administrative and economic functions, serving as regional markets or manufacturing centers. Such cities were usually surrounded by a wall and a moat, and a raised platform might be built within the walls to provide a place for ritual ceremonies and housing for the ruler's family.

The Humble Estate: Women in Ancient China

Male dominance was a key element in the social system of ancient China. As in many traditional societies, the male was considered of transcendent importance because of his role as food procurer or, in the case of farming communities, food producer. In ancient China, men worked in the fields and women raised children and served in the home. This differential in sexual roles goes back to prehistoric times and is embedded in Chinese creation myths. According to legend, Fu Xi's wife Nu Wa assisted her husband in organizing society by establishing the institution of marriage and the family. Yet Nu Wa was not just a household drudge. After Fu Xi's death, she became China's first female sovereign.

During ancient times, women apparently did not normally occupy formal positions of authority, but they often became a force in politics, especially at court, where wives of the ruler or other female members of the royal family were often influential in palace intrigues. Such activities were frowned on, however, as the following passage from *The Book of Songs* attests:

A clever man builds a city,
A clever woman lays one low;
With all her qualifications, that clever woman
Is but an ill-omened bird.
A woman with a long tongue
Is a flight of steps leading to calamity;
For disorder does not come from heaven,
But is brought about by women.
Among those who cannot be trained or taught
Are women and eunuchs.[15]

Confucian thought, while not denigrating the importance of women as mothers and homemakers, accepted the dual roles of men and women in Chinese society. Men governed society. They carried on family ritual through the veneration of ancestors. They were the warriors, scholars, and ministers. Their dominant role was firmly enshrined in the legal system. Men were permitted to have more than one wife and to divorce a spouse who did not produce a male child. Women were denied the right to own property, and there was no dowry system in ancient China that would have provided the wife with a degree of financial security from her husband and his family. As the third-century C.E. woman poet Fu Xuan lamented:

How sad it is to be a woman
Nothing on earth is held so cheap.
No one is glad when a girl is born.
By her the family sets no store.
No one cries when she leaves her home
Sudden as clouds when the rain stops.[16]

Chinese Culture

Q Focus Question: What were the chief characteristics of the Chinese arts and writing system? How did they differ from those in Egypt and Mesopotamia?

Modern knowledge about artistic achievements in ancient civilizations is limited because often little has survived the ravages of time. Fortunately, many ancient civilizations, such as Egypt and Mesopotamia, were located in relatively arid areas where many artifacts were preserved, even over thousands of years. In more humid regions, such as China and South Asia, the cultural residue left by the civilizations of antiquity has been adversely affected by climate.

As a result, relatively little remains of the cultural achievements of the prehistoric Chinese aside from Neolithic pottery and the relics found at the site of the Shang dynasty capital at Anyang. In recent years, a rich trove from the time of the Qin Empire has been unearthed near the tomb of Qin Shi Huangdi near Xian and at Han tombs nearby. But little remains of the literature of ancient China and almost none of the painting, architecture, and music.

Metalwork and Sculpture

Discoveries at archaeological sites indicate that ancient China was a society rich in cultural achievement. The pottery found at Neolithic sites such as Longshan and Yangshao exhibits a freshness and vitality of form and design, and the ornaments, such as rings and beads, show a strong aesthetic sense.

The nature of gender relationships was also graphically demonstrated in the Chinese written language. The character for man (男) combines the symbols for strength and rice field, while the character for woman (女) represents a person in a posture of deference and respect. The character for peace (安) is a woman under a roof. A wife is symbolized by a woman with a broom. Male chauvinism has deep linguistic roots in China.

© William J. Duiker

A Shang Wine Vessel. Used initially as food containers in royal ceremonial rites during the Shang dynasty, Chinese bronzes were the product of an advanced technology unmatched by any contemporary civilization. This wine vessel displays a deep green patina as well as a monster motif, complete with large globular eyes, nostrils, and fangs, typical of many Shang bronzes. Known as the *taotie*, this fanciful beast is normally presented in silhouette as two dragons face to face so that each side forms half of the mask. Although the *taotie* presumably served as a guardian force against evil spirits, scholars are still not aware of its exact significance for early Chinese peoples.

Bronze Casting

The pace of Chinese cultural development began to quicken during the Shang dynasty, which ruled in northern China from the sixteenth to the eleventh century B.C.E. At that time, objects cast in bronze began to appear. Various bronze vessels were produced for use in preparing and serving food and drink in the ancestral rites. Later vessels were used for decoration or for dining at court.

The method of casting used was one reason for the extraordinary quality of Shang bronze work. Bronze workers in most ancient civilizations used the lost-wax method, for which a model was first made in wax. After a clay mold had been formed around it, the model was heated so that the wax would melt away, and the empty space was filled with molten metal. In China, clay molds composed of several sections were tightly fitted together prior to the introduction of the liquid bronze. This technique, which had evolved from ceramic techniques used during the Neolithic period, enabled the artisans to apply the design directly to the mold and thus contributed to the clarity of line and rich surface decoration of the Shang bronzes.

Bronze casting became a large-scale business, and more than ten thousand vessels of an incredible variety of form and design survive today. Factories were located not only in the Yellow River valley but also in Sichuan province, in southern China. The art of bronze working continued into the Zhou dynasty, but the quality and originality declined. The Shang bronzes remain the pinnacle of creative art in ancient China.

One reason for the decline of bronze casting in China was the rise in popularity of iron. Ironmaking developed in China around the ninth or eighth century B.C.E., much later than in the Middle East, where it had been mastered almost a thousand years earlier. Once familiar with the process, however, the Chinese quickly moved to the forefront. Ironworkers in Europe and the Middle East, lacking the technology to achieve the high temperatures necessary to melt iron ore for casting, were forced to work with wrought iron, a cumbersome and expensive process. By the fourth century B.C.E., the Chinese had invented the technique of the blast furnace, powered by a person operating a bellows. They were therefore able to manufacture cast-iron ritual vessels and agricultural tools centuries before an equivalent technology appeared in the West.

Another reason for the deterioration of the bronze-casting tradition was the development of cheaper materials such as lacquerware and ceramics. Lacquer, made from resins obtained from the juices of sumac trees native to the region, had been produced since Neolithic times, and by the second century B.C.E. it had become a popular method of applying a hard coating to objects made of wood or fabric. Pottery, too, had existed since early times, but technological advances led to the production of a high-quality form of pottery covered with a brown or gray-green glaze, the latter known popularly as celadon. By the end of the first millennium B.C.E., both lacquerware and pottery replaced bronze in popularity, much as plastic goods have replaced more expensive materials in our own time.

The First Emperor's Tomb

In 1974, in a remarkable discovery, farmers digging a well about 35 miles east of Xian unearthed a number of terra-cotta figures in an underground pit about one mile east of the burial mound of the First Emperor of Qin. Chinese archaeologists sent to work at the site discovered a vast terra-cotta army that they believed was a re-creation of Qin Shi Huangdi's imperial guard, which was to accompany the emperor on his journey to the next world.

© Martin Puddy/Getty Images

© William J. Duiker

The Tomb of Qin Shi Huangdi. The First Emperor of Qin ordered the construction of an elaborate mausoleum, an underground palace complex protected by an army of terra-cotta soldiers and horses to accompany him on his journey to the afterlife. This massive formation of six thousand life-size armed soldiers, discovered accidentally by farmers in 1974, reflects Qin Shi Huangdi's grandeur and power.

One of the astounding features of the terra-cotta army is its size. The army is enclosed in four pits that were originally encased in a wooden framework, which has disintegrated. More than a thousand figures have been unearthed in the first pit, along with horses, wooden chariots, and seven thousand bronze weapons. Archaeologists estimate that there are more than six thousand figures in that pit alone.

Equally impressive is the quality of the work. Slightly larger than life-size, the figures were molded of finely textured clay and then fired and painted. The detail on the uniforms is realistic and sophisticated, but the most striking feature is the individuality of the facial features of the soldiers. Apparently, ten different head shapes were used and were then modeled further by hand to reflect the variety of ethnic groups and personality types in the army.

The discovery of the terra-cotta army also shows that the Chinese had come a long way from the human sacrifices that had taken place at the death of Shang sovereigns more than a thousand years earlier. But the project must have been ruinously expensive and is additional evidence of the burden the Qin ruler imposed on his subjects. One historian has estimated that one-third of the national income in Qin times may have been spent on preparations for the ruler's afterlife. The emperor's mausoleum has not yet been unearthed, but it is enclosed in a mound nearly 250 feet high and is surrounded by a rectangular wall nearly 4 miles around. According to the Han historian Sima Qian, the ceiling is a replica of the heavens, while the floor contains a relief model of the entire Qin kingdom, with rivers flowing in mercury. According to tradition, traps were set within the mausoleum to prevent intruders, and the workers applying the final touches were buried alive in the tomb with its secrets.

Language and Literature

Precisely when writing developed in China cannot be determined, but certainly by Shang times, as the oracle bones demonstrate, the Chinese had developed a simple but functional script. Like many other languages of antiquity, it was primarily ideographic and pictographic in form. Symbols, usually called "characters," were created to represent an idea or to form a picture of the object to be represented. For example, the Chinese characters for mountain (山), the sun (日), and the moon (月) were meant to represent the objects themselves. Other characters, such as "big" (大) (a man with his arms outstretched), represent an idea. The character for "east" (東) symbolizes the sun coming up behind the trees.

Each character, of course, would be given a sound by the speaker when pronounced. In other cultures, this

Smithsonian Institution, Washington, DC//Photo © William J. Duiker

	sun	hill	water	man	woman
Mesopotamian Cuneiform					
Egyptian Hieroglyphics					
Oracle Bone Script					
Modern Chinese	日	山	水	男	女

Pictographs in Ancient Cultures. Virtually all written language evolved from pictographs—representations of physical objects that were eventually stylized and tied to sounds in the spoken language. This chart shows pictographs that originated independently in three ancient cultures and the stylized modern characters into which the Chinese oracle pictographs evolved.

process led to the abandonment of the system of ideographs and the adoption of a written language based on phonetic symbols. The Chinese language, however, has never entirely abandoned its original ideographic format, although the phonetic element has developed into a significant part of the individual character. In that sense, the Chinese written language is virtually unique in the world today.

One reason the language retained its ideographic quality may have been the aesthetics of the written characters. By the time of the Qin dynasty, if not earlier, the written language came to be seen as an art form as well as a means of communication, and calligraphy became one of the most prized forms of painting in China.

Even more important, if the written language had developed in the direction of a phonetic alphabet, it could no longer have served as the written system for all the peoples of the expanding Chinese civilization. Although the vast majority spoke a tongue derived from a parent Sinitic language (a system distinguished by variations in pitch, a characteristic that gives Chinese its lilting quality even today), the languages spoken in various regions of the country differed from each other in pronunciation and to a lesser degree in vocabulary and syntax; for the most part, they were (and are today) mutually unintelligible.

The Chinese answer to this problem was to give all the spoken languages the same writing system. Although any character might be pronounced differently in different regions of China, that character would be written the same way (after the standardization undertaken under the Qin). Written characters could therefore be read by educated Chinese from one end of the country to the other. This became the language of the bureaucracy and the vehicle for the transmission of Chinese culture from the Great Wall to the southern border and beyond. However, the written language was not identical to the spoken form; it eventually evolved its own vocabulary and grammatical structure, and as a result, users of written Chinese required special training.

The earliest extant form of Chinese literature dates from the Zhou dynasty. It was written on silk or strips of bamboo and consisted primarily of historical records such as the *Rites of Zhou*, philosophical treatises such as the *Analects* and *The Way of the Tao*, and poetry, as recorded in *The Book of Songs* and the *Song of the South* (see the box on p. 92). In later years, when Confucian principles had been elevated to a state ideology, the key works identified with the Confucian school were integrated into a set of so-called Confucian Classics. These works became required reading for generations of Chinese schoolchildren and introduced them to the forms of behavior that would be required of them as adults.

Music

From early times in China, music was viewed not just as an aesthetic pleasure but also as a means of achieving political order and refining the human character. In fact, music may have originated as an accompaniment to sacred rituals at the royal court. According to the *Historical Records*, written during the Han dynasty, "When our sage-kings of the past instituted rites and music, their objective was far from making people indulge in the . . . amusements of singing and dancing. . . . Music is produced to purify the heart, and rites introduced to rectify the behavior."[17] Eventually, however, music began to be appreciated for its own sake as well as to accompany singing and dancing.

A wide variety of musical instruments were used, including flutes, various stringed instruments, bells and chimes, drums, and gourds. Bells cast in bronze were first used as musical instruments in the Shang period; they were hung in rows and struck with a wooden mallet. The finest were produced during the

LOVE SPURNED IN ANCIENT CHINA

ARTS & IDEAS

The Book of Songs is an anthology of about three hundred poems written during the early Zhou dynasty. According to tradition, they were selected by Confucius from a much larger collection. In later years, many were given political interpretations. The poem reprinted here, however, expresses a very human cry of love spurned.

The Book of Songs: The Odes

You seemed a guileless youth enough,
Offering for silk your woven stuff;
But silk was not required by you:
I was the silk you had in view.
With you I crossed the ford, and while
We wandered on for many a mile
I said, "I do not wish delay,
But friends must fix our wedding-day.....
Oh, do not let my words give pain,
But with the autumn come again."

And then I used to watch and wait
To see you passing through the gate;
And sometimes, when I watched in vain,
My tears would flow like falling rain;
But when I saw my darling boy,
I laughed and cried aloud for joy.
The fortune-tellers, you declared,
Had all pronounced us duly paired;
"Then bring a carriage," I replied,
"And I'll away to be your bride."

The mulberry tree upon the ground,
Now sheds its yellow leaves around.
Three years have slipped away from me
Since first I shared your poverty;

And now again, alas the day!
Back through the ford I take my way.

My heart is still unchanged, but you
Have uttered words now proved untrue;
And you have left me to deplore
A love that can be mine no more.

For three long years I was your wife,
And led in truth a toilsome life;
Early to rise and late to bed,
Each day alike passed o'er my head.
I honestly fulfilled my part,
And you—well, you have broke my heart.
The truth my brothers will not know,
So all the more their gibes will flow.
I grieve in silence and repine
That such a wretched fate is mine.

Ah, hand in hand to face old age!—
Instead, I turn a bitter page.
O for the riverbanks of yore;
O for the much-loved marshy shore;
The hours of girlhood, with my hair
Ungathered, as we lingered there.
The words we spoke, that seemed so true,
I little thought that I should rue;
I little thought the vows we swore
Would some day bind us two no more.

Q *It has been said that traditional Chinese thought lacked a sense of tragedy similar to the great dramatic tragedies composed in ancient Greece. Does this passage qualify as tragedy? If not, why not?*

mid-Zhou era and are considered among the best examples of early bronze work in China. Some weighed over two tons and, in combination as shown in the photo on p. 93, covered a range of several octaves. Bronze bells have not been found in any other contemporary civilization and are considered one of the great cultural achievements of ancient China. The largest known bell dating from the Roman Empire, for example, is only 6 centimeters high.

By the late Zhou era, bells had begun to give way as the instrument of choice to strings and wind instruments, and the purpose of music shifted from ceremony to entertainment. This led conservative critics to rail against the onset of an age of debauchery.

Ancient historians stressed the relationship between music and court life, but it is highly probable that music, singing, and dancing were equally popular among the common people. The *Book of History*, purporting to describe conditions in the late third millennium B.C.E., suggests that ballads emanating from the popular culture were welcomed at court. Nevertheless, court music and popular music differed in several respects. Among other things, popular music was more likely to be motivated by the desire for pleasure than for the purpose of law and order and moral uplift. Those differences continued to be reflected in the evolution of music in China down to modern times.

92 CHAPTER 3 CHINA IN ANTIQUITY

© William J. Duiker

Music in the Confucian Era. According to Confucius, "If a man lack benevolence, what has he to do with music?" The purpose of music, to followers of the Master, was to instill in the listener a proper respect for ethical conduct. Foremost among the instruments in the Confucian era were bronze bells. Shown here is a collection of bells dating from the Zhou dynasty. The photo on the right highlights the stylized face of a dragon on this bell from the ninth century B.C.E. The monster motif, known as the *taotie*, with its globular eyes, nostrils, and fangs, is characteristic of both Shang and Zhou bronze objects.

© William J. Duiker

CONCLUSION

Of the great classical civilizations discussed in Part I of this book, China was the last to come into full flower. By the time the Shang began to emerge as an organized state, the societies in Mesopotamia and the Nile valley had already reached an advanced level of civilization. Unfortunately, not enough is known about the early stages of these civilizations to allow us to determine why some developed earlier than others, but one likely reason for China's late arrival was that it was virtually isolated from other emerging centers of culture elsewhere in the world and thus was compelled to develop essentially on its own. Only at the end of the first millennium B.C.E. did China come into regular contact with other civilizations in South Asia, the Middle East, and the Mediterranean.

Once embarked on its own path toward the creation of a complex society, however, China achieved results that were in all respects the equal of its counterparts elsewhere. By the rise of the first unified empire in the late third century B.C.E., the state extended from the edge of the Gobi Desert in the north to the subtropical regions near the borders of modern Vietnam in the south. Chinese philosophers had engaged in debate over intricate questions relating to human nature and the state of the universe, and China's artistic and technological achievements—especially in terms of bronze casting and the terra-cotta figures entombed in Qin Shi

Huangdi's mausoleum—were unsurpassed throughout the world.

In its single-minded effort to bring about the total regimentation of Chinese society, however, the Qin dynasty left a mixed legacy for later generations. Some observers, notably the China scholar Karl Wittfogel, have speculated that the need to establish and regulate a vast public irrigation network, as had been created in China under the Zhou dynasty, led naturally to the emergence of a form of **Oriental despotism** that would henceforth be applied in all such **hydraulic societies.** Recent evidence, however, disputes this view, suggesting that the emergence of strong central government followed, rather than preceded, the establishment of a large irrigation system. The preference for autocratic rule is probably better explained by the desire to limit the emergence of powerful regional landed interests and maintain control over a vast empire.

One reason for China's striking success was undoubtedly that unlike its contemporary civilizations, it long was able to fend off the danger from nomadic peoples along its northern frontier. By the end of the second century B.C.E., however, the Xiongnu were looming ominously, and tribal warriors began to nip at the borders of the empire. While the dynasty was strong, the problem was manageable, but when internal difficulties began to corrode the unity of the state, China became increasingly vulnerable to the threat from the north and entered its own time of troubles.

Meanwhile, another great civilization was beginning to take form on the northern shores of the Mediterranean Sea. Unlike China and the other ancient societies discussed thus far, this new civilization in Europe was based as much on trade as on agriculture. Yet the political and cultural achievements of ancient Greece were the equal of any of the great human experiments that had preceded it and soon began to exert a significant impact on the rest of the ancient world.

TIMELINE

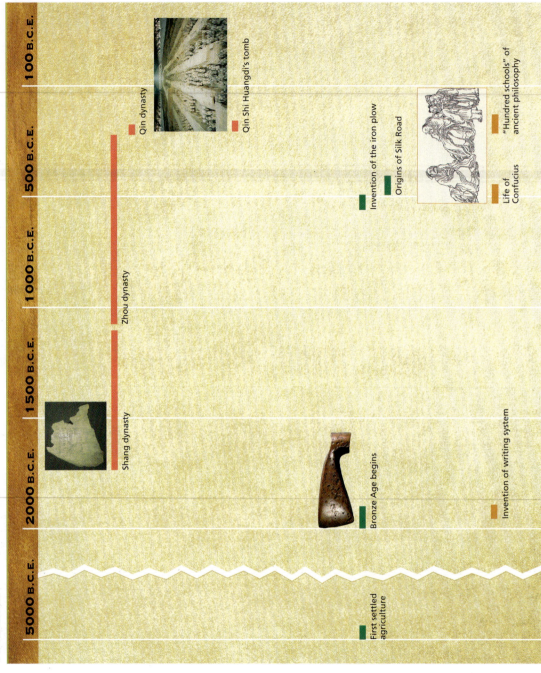

CHAPTER NOTES

1. *Book of Changes*, quoted in Chang Chi-yun, *Chinese History of Fifty Centuries*, vol. 1, *Ancient Times* (Taipei, 1962), pp. 15, 31, and 65.

2. Ibid., p. 381.

3. Quoted in E. N. Anderson, *The Food of China* (New Haven, Conn., 1988), p. 21.

4. According to Chinese tradition, the *Rites of Zhou* was written by the duke of Zhou himself near the time of the founding of the Zhou dynasty. However, modern historians believe that it was written much later, perhaps as late as the fourth century B.C.E.

5. From *The Book of Songs*, quoted in S. de Grazia, ed., *Masters of Chinese Political Thought: From the Beginnings to the Han Dynasty* (New York, 1973), pp. 40–41.

6. *Confucian Analects* (Lun Yu), ed. J. Legge (Taipei, 1963), 11:11 and 6:20.

7. Ibid, 15:23.

8. *Book of Rites*, sec. 9, quoted in W. T. de Bary et al, eds, *Sources of Chinese Tradition* (New York, 1960), p. 192.

9. *Confucian Analects*, 17:2.
10. *Book of Mencius* (Meng Zi), 4A:9, quoted in de Bary, *Sources of Chinese Tradition*, p. 107.
11. Quoted in ibid., p. 53.
12. B. Watson, *Records of the Grand Historian of China* (New York, 1961), vol. 2, pp. 155, 160.
13. Ibid., pp. 32, 53.
14. C. Waltham, *Shu Ching: Book of History* (Chicago, 1971), p. 154.
15. Quoted in H. A. Giles, *A History of Chinese Literature* (New York, 1923), p. 19.
16. A. Waley, ed., *Chinese Poems* (London, 1983), p. xx.
17. Chang Chi-yun, *Chinese History*, vol. 1, p. 183.

SUGGESTED READING

The Dawn of Chinese Civilization   Several general histories of China provide a useful overview of the period of antiquity. Perhaps the best known is the classic *East Asia: Tradition and Transformation* (Boston, 1973), by **J. K. Fairbank, E. O. Reischauer, and A. M. Craig**. For an authoritative overview of the ancient period, see **M. Loewe and E. L. Shaughnessy**, *The Cambridge History of Ancient China from the Origins of Civilization to 221 B.C.* (Cambridge, 1999). Political and social maps of China can be found in **A. Herrmann**, *A Historical Atlas of China* (Chicago, 1966).

The period of the Neolithic era and the Shang dynasty has received increasing attention in recent years. For an impressively documented and annotated overview, see **K. C. Chang et al.**, *The Formation of Chinese Civilization: An Archaeological Perspective* (New Haven, Conn., 2005), and **R. Thorp**, *China in the Early Bronze Age* (Philadelphia, 2005). **D. Keightley**, *The Origins of Chinese Civilization* (Berkeley, Calif., 1983), presents a number of interesting articles on selected aspects of the period.

The Zhou and Qin Dynasties   The Zhou and Qin dynasties have also received considerable attention. The former is exhaustively analyzed in **Cho-Yun Hsu** and **J. M. Linduff**, *Western Zhou Civilization* (New Haven, Conn., 1988), and **Li Xueqin**, *Eastern Zhou and Qin Civilizations* (New Haven, Conn., 1985). The latter is a translation of an original work by a mainland Chinese scholar and is especially interesting for its treatment of the development of the silk industry and the money economy in ancient China. On bronze casting, see **E. L. Shaughnessy**, *Sources of Eastern Zhou History* (Berkeley, Calif., 1991). For recent treatments of the tumultuous Qin dynasty, see **M. Lewis**, *The Early Chinese Empires: Qin and Han* (Cambridge, Mass., 2007), and **C. Holcombe**, *The Genesis of East Asia, 221 B.C.–A.D. 907* (Honolulu, 2001).

The philosophy of ancient China has attracted considerable attention from Western scholars. For excerpts from all the major works of the "hundred schools," consult **W. T. de Bary and I. Bloom**, eds., *Sources of Chinese Tradition*, vol. 1 (New York, 1999). On Confucius, see **B. W. Van Norden**, ed., *Confucius and the Analects: New Essays* (Oxford, 2002). Also see **F. Mote**, *Intellectual Foundations of China*, 2d ed. (New York, 1989).

Daily Life in Ancient China   For works on general culture and science, consult the illustrated work by **R. Temple**, *The Genius of China: 3000 Years of Science, Discovery, and Invention* (New York, 1986), and **J. Needham**, *Science in Traditional China: A Comparative Perspective* (Boston, 1981). See also **E. N. Anderson**, *The Food of China* (New Haven, Conn., 1988). Environmental issues are explored in **M. Elvin**, *The Retreat of the Elephants: An Environmental History of China* (New Haven, Conn., 2004).

Chinese Culture   For an introduction to classical Chinese literature, consult the three standard anthologies: **Liu Wu-Chi**, *An Introduction to Chinese Literature* (New York, 1961); **V. H. Mair**, ed., *The Columbia Anthology of Traditional Chinese Literature* (New York, 1994); and **S. Owen**, ed., *An Anthology of Chinese Literature: Beginnings to 1911* (New York, 1996). For a comprehensive introduction to Chinese art, consult **M. Sullivan**, *The Arts of China*, 4th ed. (Berkeley, Calif., 1999), with good illustrations in color. Also see **M. Tregear**, *Chinese Art*, rev. ed. (London, 1997), and *Art Treasures in China* (New York, 1994). Also of interest is **P. B. Ebrey**, *The Cambridge Illustrated History of China* (Cambridge, 1999). On some recent finds, consult **J. Rowson**, *Mysteries of Ancient China: New Discoveries from the Early Dynasties* (New York, 1996). On Chinese music, see **J. F. So**, ed., *Music in the Age of Confucius* (Washington, D.C., 2000).

WORLD HISTORY RESOURCE CENTER

Enter the Resource Center using either your CengageNOW access card or your separate access card for the World History Resource Center. Organized by topic, this Website includes quizzes; images; over 350 primary source documents; interactive simulations, maps, and timelines; movie explorations; and a wealth of other resources. You can read the following documents, and many more, at the *World History Resource Center*:

I Ching

Confucius, *Analects*

Visit the *World History* Companion Website for chapter quizzes and more:

www.cengage.com/history/Duiker/World6e

CENGAGENOW   Enter CengageNOW using the access card that is available with this text. *CengageNOW* will help you understand the content in this chapter with lesson plans generated for your needs, as well as provide you with a connection to the *Wadsworth World History Resource Center* (see description below for details).

CHAPTER 4

THE CIVILIZATION OF THE GREEKS

© British Museum, London, UK/The Bridgeman Art Library

A bust of Pericles

CHAPTER OUTLINE AND FOCUS QUESTIONS

Early Greece

Q How did the geography of Greece affect Greek history? Who was Homer, and why was his work used as the basis for Greek education?

The Greek City-States (c. 750–c. 500 B.C.E.)

Q What were the chief features of the *polis*, or city-state, and how did the city-states of Athens and Sparta differ?

The High Point of Greek Civilization: Classical Greece

Q What did the Greeks mean by democracy, and in what ways was the Athenian political system a democracy? What effect did the two great conflicts of the fifth century—the Persian Wars and the Peloponnesian War—have on Greek civilization?

The Rise of Macedonia and the Conquests of Alexander

Q How was Alexander the Great able to amass his empire, and what was his legacy?

The World of the Hellenistic Kingdoms

Q How did the political, economic, and social institutions of the Hellenistic world differ from those of Classical Greece?

CRITICAL THINKING

Q In what ways did the culture of the Hellenistic period differ from that of the Classical period, and what do those differences suggest about society in the two periods?

DURING THE ERA OF CIVIL WAR in China known as the Period of the Warring States, a civil war also erupted on the northern shores of the Mediterranean Sea. In 431 B.C.E., two very different Greek city-states—Athens and Sparta—fought for domination of the Greek world. The people of Athens felt secure behind their walls and in the first winter of the war held a public funeral to honor those who had died in battle. On the day of the ceremony, the citizens of Athens joined in a procession, with the relatives of the dead wailing for their loved ones. As was the custom in Athens, one leading citizen was asked to address the crowd, and on this day it was Pericles who spoke to the people. He talked about the greatness of Athens and reminded the Athenians of the strength of their political system: "Our constitution," he said, "is called a democracy because power is in the hands not of a minority but of the whole people. When it is a question of settling private disputes, everyone is equal before the law.… Just as our political life is free and open, so is our day-to-day life in our relations with each other.… Here each individual is interested not only in his own affairs but in the affairs of the state as well."

In this famous funeral oration, Pericles gave voice to the ideals of democracy and the importance of the

Early Greece

Focus Questions: How did the geography of Greece affect Greek history? Who was Homer, and why was his work used as the basis for Greek education?

individual, ideals that were quite different from those of some other ancient societies, in which the individual was subordinated to a larger order based on obedience to an exalted emperor. The Greeks asked some basic questions about human life: What is the nature of the universe? What is the purpose of human existence? What is our relationship to divine forces? What constitutes a community? What are the true sources of law? What is truth itself, and how do we realize it? Not only did the Greeks answer these questions, but they also created a system of logical, analytical thought to examine them. Their answers and their system of rational thought laid the intellectual foundation for Western civilization's understanding of the human condition.

The remarkable story of ancient Greek civilization begins with the arrival of the Greeks around 1900 B.C.E. By the eighth century B.C.E., the characteristic institution of ancient Greek life, the *polis*, or city-state, had emerged. Greek civilization flourished and reached its height in the Classical era of the fifth century B.C.E., but the inability of the Greek city-states to end their fratricidal warfare eventually left them vulnerable to the Macedonian king Philip II and helped bring an end to the era of independent Greek city-states.

Although the city-states were never the same after their defeat by the Macedonian monarch, this defeat did not end the influence of the Greeks. Philip's son Alexander led the Macedonians and Greeks on a spectacular conquest of the Persian Empire and opened the door to the spread of Greek culture throughout the Middle East. ◆

Geography played an important role in Greek history. Compared to Mesopotamia and Egypt, Greece occupied a small area, a mountainous peninsula that encompassed only 45,000 square miles of territory, about the size of the state of Louisiana. The mountains and the sea were especially significant. Much of Greece consists of small plains and river valleys surrounded by mountain ranges 8,000 to 10,000 feet high. The mountains isolated Greeks from one another, causing Greek communities to follow their own separate paths and develop their own ways of life. Over a period of time, these communities became so fiercely attached to their independence that they were willing to fight one another to gain advantage. No doubt the small size of these independent Greek communities fostered participation in political affairs and unique cultural expressions, but the rivalry among them also led to the internecine warfare that ultimately devastated Greek society.

The sea also influenced Greek society. Greece had a long seacoast, dotted by bays and inlets that provided numerous harbors. The Greeks also inhabited a number of islands to the west, south, and east of the Greek mainland. It is no accident that the Greeks became seafarers who sailed out into the Aegean and Mediterranean Seas to make contact with the outside world and later to establish colonies that would spread Greek civilization throughout the Mediterranean region.

Greek topography helped determine the major territories into which Greece was ultimately divided (see Map 4.1). South of the Gulf of Corinth was the Peloponnesus, virtually an island attached by a tiny isthmus to the mainland. Consisting mostly of hills, mountains, and small valleys, the Peloponnesus was the location of Sparta, as well as the site of Olympia, where athletic games were held. Northeast of the Peloponnesus was the Attic peninsula (or Attica), the home of Athens, hemmed in by mountains to the north and west and surrounded by the sea to the south and east. Northwest of Attica was Boeotia in central Greece, with its chief city of Thebes. To the north of Boeotia was Thessaly, which contained the largest plains and became a great producer of grain and horses. To the north of Thessaly lay Macedonia, which was not of much importance in Greek history until 338 B.C.E., when the Macedonian king Philip II conquered the Greeks.

Minoan Crete

The earliest civilization in the Aegean region emerged on the large island of Crete, southeast of the Greek mainland. A Bronze Age civilization that used metals, especially bronze, in making weapons had been established there by 2800 B.C.E. This civilization was discovered at the turn of the twentieth century by the English archaeologist Arthur Evans, who named it "Minoan" after Minos, a legendary king of Crete. In language and religion, the Minoans were not Greek, although they did have some influence on the peoples of the Greek mainland.

Evans's excavations on Crete unearthed an enormous palace complex at Knossus, near modern Iráklion (Heraclion). The remains revealed a rich and prosperous culture, with Knossus as the apparent center of a far-ranging "sea empire," probably largely commercial in nature. We know from the archaeological remains that the people of Minoan Crete were accustomed to sea travel and had made contact with the more advanced civilization of Egypt. Egyptian products have been found in Crete and Cretan products in Egypt. Minoan Cretans also had contacts with and exerted influence on the Greek-speaking inhabitants of the Greek mainland.

The Minoan civilization reached its height between 2000 and 1450 B.C.E. The palace at Knossus, the royal seat of the kings, was an elaborate structure that included

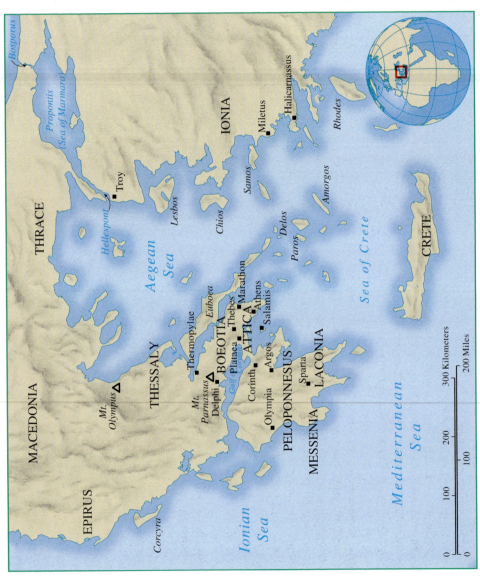

MAP 4.1 **Ancient Greece (c. 750–338 B.C.E.).** Between 750 and 500 B.C.E., Greek civilization witnessed the emergence of the city-state as the central institution in Greek life and the Greeks' colonization of the Mediterranean and Black Seas. Classical Greece lasted from about 500 to 338 B.C.E. and encompassed the high points of Greek civilization in arts, science, philosophy, and politics, as well as the Persian Wars and the Peloponnesian War.

Q How does the geography of Greece help explain the rise and development of the Greek city-state? View an animated version of this map or related maps at www.cengage.com/history/Duiker/World6e

numerous private living rooms for the royal family and workshops for making decorated vases, ivory figurines, and jewelry. Even bathrooms, with elaborate drains, like those found at Mohenjo-Daro in India, formed part of the complex. The rooms were decorated with brightly colored frescoes showing sporting events and nature scenes. Storerooms in the palace held enormous jars of oil, wine, and grain, paid as taxes in kind to the king.

The centers of Minoan civilization on Crete suffered a sudden and catastrophic collapse around 1450 B.C.E. Some historians believe that a tsunami triggered by a powerful volcanic eruption on the island of Thera was responsible for the devastation. That explosion, however, had taken place almost two hundred years earlier, and most historians today maintain that the destruction was the result of invasion and pillage of a weakened Cretan society by mainland Greeks known as the Mycenaeans.

The First Greek State: Mycenae

The term *Mycenaean* is derived from Mycenae, a remarkable fortified site excavated by the amateur German archaeologist Heinrich Schliemann starting in 1870. Mycenae was one center in a Mycenaean Greek civilization that flourished between 1600 and 1100 B.C.E. The Mycenaean Greeks were part of the Indo-European family of peoples (see Chapter 1) who spread from their original location into southern and

Minoan Crete and Mycenaean Greece

© Erich Lessing/Art Resource, NY

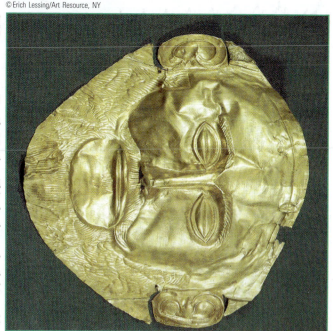

A Mycenaean Death Mask. This death mask of thin gold was one of several found by Heinrich Schliemann in his excavation of Grave Circle A at Mycenae. These masks are similar to the gold mummy masks used in Egyptian royal tombs. Schliemann claimed—incorrectly—that he had found the mask of Agamemnon, king of Mycenae in Homer's *Iliad*.

western Europe, India, and Persia. One group entered the territory of Greece from the north around 1900 B.C.E. and eventually managed to gain control of the Greek mainland and develop a civilization.

Mycenaean civilization, which reached its high point between 1400 and 1200 B.C.E., consisted of a number of powerful monarchies based in fortified palace complexes, which were built on hills and surrounded by gigantic stone walls, such as those found at Mycenae, Tiryns, Pylos, Thebes, and Orchomenos. These various centers of power probably formed a loose confederacy of independent states, with Mycenae the strongest.

The Mycenaeans were above all a warrior people who prided themselves on their heroic deeds in battle. Archaeological evidence indicates that the Mycenaean monarchies also developed an extensive commercial network. Mycenaean pottery has been found throughout the Mediterranean basin, in Syria and Egypt to the east and Sicily and southern Italy to the west. But some scholars also believe that the Mycenaeans, led by Mycenae itself, spread outward militarily, conquering Crete and making it part of the Mycenaean world. The most famous of all their supposed military adventures has come down to us in the epic poetry of Homer (discussed later in this chapter). Did the Mycenaean Greeks, led by Agamemnon, king of Mycenae, sack the city of Troy on the northwestern coast of Asia Minor around 1250 B.C.E.? Scholars have been debating this question since Schliemann's excavations began. Many believe in the Homeric legend, even if the details

have become shrouded in mystery. Many historians today believe that the city of Troy was a vassal of the Hittite Empire and guarded the southern entrance to the Hellespont (today known as the Dardanelles). If so, the Greeks may have had an economic motive for seizing Troy and opening a trade route to the Black Sea.

By the late thirteenth century, Mycenaean Greece was showing signs of serious trouble. Mycenae itself was burned around 1190 B.C.E., and other Mycenaean centers show a similar pattern of destruction as new waves of Greek-speaking invaders moved into Greece from the north. By 1100 B.C.E., the Mycenaean culture was coming to an end, and the Greek world was entering a new period of considerable insecurity.

The Greeks in a Dark Age (c. 1100–c. 750 B.C.E.)

After the collapse of Mycenaean civilization, Greece entered a difficult era of declining population and falling food production; not until 850 B.C.E. did farming—and Greece itself—revive. Because of both the difficult conditions and the fact that we have few records to help us reconstruct what happened in this period, historians refer to it as the Dark Age.

During the Dark Age, large numbers of Greeks left the mainland and migrated across the Aegean Sea to various islands and especially to the southwestern shore of Asia Minor, a strip of territory that came to be called Ionia. Two other major groups of Greeks settled in established parts of Greece. The Aeolian Greeks of northern and central Greece colonized the large island of Lesbos and the adjacent territory of the mainland. The Dorians established themselves in southwestern Greece, especially in the Peloponnesus, as well as on some of the south Aegean islands, including Crete.

As trade and economic activity began to recover, iron replaced bronze in the construction of weapons, making them affordable for more people. At some point in the eighth century B.C.E., the Greeks adopted the Phoenician alphabet to give themselves a new system of writing. And near the very end of the Dark Age appeared the work of Homer, who has come to be viewed as one of the greatest poets of all time.

Homer and Homeric Greece

The *Iliad* and the *Odyssey*, the first great epic poems of early Greece, were based on stories that had been passed down from generation to generation. It is generally assumed that Homer made use of these oral traditions to compose the *Iliad*, his epic poem of the Trojan War. The war was caused when Paris, a prince of Troy, kidnapped Helen, wife of the king of the Greek state of Sparta, outraging all the Greeks. Under the leadership of the Spartan king's brother, Agamemnon of Mycenae, the Greeks attacked Troy. After ten years of combat, the Greeks finally sacked the city. The *Iliad* is not so much the story of the war itself, however, as it is the tale of the Greek hero Achilles and how the "wrath of Achilles" led to disaster.

The Slaying of Hector. This scene, painted on a Corinthian Greek vase, depicts the final battle between Achilles and the Trojan hero Hector, as recounted in Homer's *Iliad*. The *Iliad* is Homer's epic masterpiece and was used by later Greeks to teach the aristocratic values of courage and honor.

© AAAC/Topham/The Image Works

The *Odyssey*, Homer's other masterpiece, is an epic romance that recounts the journeys of one of the Greek heroes, Odysseus, from the fall of Troy until his eventual return to his wife, Penelope, twenty years later. But there is a larger vision here as well: the testing of the heroic stature of Odysseus until, by both cunning and patience, he prevails. In the course of this testing, the underlying moral message is "that virtue is a better policy than vice."[1]

Although the *Iliad* and the *Odyssey* supposedly deal with the heroes of the Mycenaean age of the thirteenth century B.C.E., many scholars believe that they really describe the social conditions of the Dark Age. According to the Homeric view, Greece was a society based on agriculture in which a landed warrior-aristocracy controlled much wealth and exercised considerable power. Homer's world reflects the values of aristocratic heroes.

Homer's Enduring Importance This, of course, explains the importance of Homer to later generations of Greeks. Homer did not so much record history as make it. The Greeks regarded the *Iliad* and the *Odyssey* as authentic history. They gave the Greeks an idealized past, somewhat like the concept of the Golden Age in ancient China, with a legendary age of heroes and came to be used as standard texts for the education of generations of Greek males. As one Athenian stated, "My father was anxious to see me develop into a good man . . . and as a means to this end he compelled me to memorize all of Homer."[2] The values Homer inculcated were essentially the aristocratic values of courage and honor (see the box on p. 101). It was important to strive for the excellence befitting a hero, which the Greeks called *arete*. In the warrior-aristocratic world of Homer, *arete* is won in struggle or contest. Through his willingness to fight, the hero protects his family and friends, preserves his own honor and his family's, and earns his reputation. In the Homeric world, aristocratic

women, too, were expected to pursue excellence. Penelope, for example, the wife of Odysseus, the hero of the *Odyssey*, remains faithful to her husband and displays great courage and intelligence in preserving their household during her husband's long absence. Upon his return, Odysseus praises her for her excellence: "Madame, there is not a man in the wide world who could find fault with you. For your fame has reached heaven itself, like that of some perfect king, ruling a populous and mighty state with the fear of god in his heart, and upholding the right."[3]

To later generations of Greeks, these heroic values formed the core of aristocratic virtue, a fact that explains the tremendous popularity of Homer as an educational tool. Homer gave to the Greeks a single universally accepted model of heroism, honor, and nobility. But in time, as a new world of city-states emerged in Greece, new values of cooperation and community also transformed what the Greeks learned from Homer.

The Greek City-States (c. 750–c. 500 B.C.E.)

Q Focus Question: What were the chief features of the *polis*, or city-state, and how did the city-states of Athens and Sparta differ?

During the Dark Age, Greek villages gradually expanded and evolved into independent city-states. In the eighth century B.C.E., Greek civilization burst forth with new energies, beginning the period that historians have called the Archaic Age of Greece. Two major developments stand out in this era: the evolution of the city-state, or what the Greeks called a *polis* (plural, *poleis*), as the central institution in Greek life and the Greeks' colonization of the Mediterranean and Black Seas.

FAMILY & SOCIETY

The *Iliad* and the *Odyssey*, which the Greeks believed were both written by Homer, were used as basic texts for the education of Greeks for hundreds of years during antiquity. This passage from the *Iliad*, describing the encounter between Hector, prince of Troy, and his wife, Andromache, illustrates the Greek ideal of gaining honor through combat. At the end of the passage, Homer also reveals what became the Greek attitude toward women: they are supposed to spin and weave and take care of their households and children.

Homer, *Iliad*

Hector looked at his son and smiled, but said nothing. Andromache, bursting into tears, went up to him and put her hand in his. "Hector," she said, "you are possessed. This bravery of yours will be your end. You do not think of your little boy or your unhappy wife, whom you will make a widow soon. Some day the Achaeans [Greeks] are bound to kill you in a massed attack. And when I lose you I might as well be dead.... I have no father, no mother, now.... I had seven brothers too at home. In one day all of them went down to Hades' House. The great Achilles of the swift feet killed them all....

"So you, Hector, are father and mother and brother to me, as well as my beloved husband. Have pity on me now; stay here on the tower; and do not make your wife a widow an orphan and your wife a widow...."

"All that, my dear," said the great Hector of the glittering helmet, "is surely my concern. But if I hid myself like a coward and refused to fight, I could never face the Trojans and the Trojan ladies in their trailing gowns. Besides, it would go against the grain, for I have trained myself always, like a good soldier, to take my place in the front line and win glory for my father and myself...."

As he finished, glorious Hector held out his arms to take his boy. But the child shrank back with a cry to the bosom of his girdled nurse, alarmed by his father's appearance. He was frightened by the bronze of the helmet and the horsehair plume that he saw nodding grimly down at him. His father and his lady mother had to laugh. But noble Hector quickly took his helmet off and put the dazzling thing on the ground. Then he kissed his son, dandled him in his arms, and prayed to Zeus and the other gods:

"Zeus, and you other gods, grant that this boy of mine may be, like me, preeminent in Troy; as strong and brave as I; a mighty king of Ilium. May people say, when he comes back from battle, 'Here is a better man than his father.' Let him bring home the bloodstained armor of the enemy he has killed, and make his mother happy."

Hector handed the boy to his wife, who took him to her fragrant breast. She was smiling through her tears, and when her husband saw this he was moved. He stroked her with his hand and said, "My dear, I beg you not to be too much distressed. No one is going to send me down to Hades before my proper time. But Fate is a thing that no man born of woman, coward, or hero can escape. Go home now, and attend to your own work, the loom and the spindle, and see that the maidservants get on with theirs. War is men's business; and this war is the business of every man in Ilium, myself above all."

Q *What important ideals for Greek men and women are revealed in this passage from the* Iliad? *How do the women's ideals compare with those for ancient Indian and Chinese women?*

CENGAGENOW *To read Book 1 of the* Iliad, *enter the documents area of the World History Resource Center using the access card that is available for World History.*

The *Polis*

In the most basic sense, a *polis* could be defined as a small but autonomous political unit in which all major political, social, and religious activities were carried out at one central location. The *polis* consisted of a city, town, or village and its surrounding countryside. The city, town, or village was the focus, a central point where the citizens of the *polis* could assemble for political, social, and religious activities. In some *poleis*, this central meeting point was a hill, like the Acropolis in Athens, which could serve as a place of refuge during an attack and later at some sites came to be the religious center on which temples and public monuments were erected. Below the acropolis would be an *agora*, an open place that served both as a market and as a place where citizens could assemble.

Poleis varied greatly in size, from a few square miles to a few hundred square miles. They also varied in population.

Athens had a population of about 250,000 by the fifth century B.C.E. But most *poleis* were much smaller, consisting of only a few hundred to several thousand people.

Although our word *politics* is derived from the Greek term *polis*, the *polis* itself was much more than a political institution. It was a community of citizens in which all political, economic, social, cultural, and religious activities were focused. As a community, the *polis* consisted of citizens with political rights (adult males), citizens with no political rights (women and children), and noncitizens (slaves and resident aliens). All citizens of a *polis* possessed fundamental rights, but these rights were coupled with responsibilities. The Greek philosopher Aristotle argued that the citizen did not just belong to himself: "We must rather regard every citizen as belonging to the state." However, the loyalty that citizens had to their city-states also had a negative side.

© Scala/Art Resource, NY

The Hoplite Forces. The Greek hoplites were infantrymen equipped with large round shields and long thrusting spears. In battle, they advanced in tight phalanx formation and were dangerous opponents as long as this formation remained unbroken. This vase painting from the seventh century B.C.E. shows two groups of hoplite warriors engaged in battle. The piper on the left is leading another line of soldiers preparing to enter the fray.

City-states distrusted one another, and the division of Greece into fiercely patriotic independent units helped bring about its ruin.

A New Military System: The Greek Way of War The development of the *polis* was paralleled by the emergence of a new military system. Greek fighting had previously been dominated by aristocratic cavalrymen, who reveled in individual duels with enemy soldiers. But by the end of the eighth century B.C.E., a new military order came into being that was based on **hoplites,** heavily armed infantrymen who wore bronze or leather helmets, breastplates, and greaves (shin guards). Each carried a round shield, a short sword, and a thrusting spear about 9 feet long. Hoplites advanced into battle as a unit, forming a **phalanx** (a rectangular formation) in tight order, usually eight ranks deep. As long as the hoplites kept their order, were not outflanked, and did not break, they either secured victory or, at the very least, suffered no harm. The phalanx was easily routed, however, if it broke its order. Thus the safety of the phalanx depended above all on the solidarity and discipline of its members. As one seventh-century B.C.E. poet noted, a good hoplite was "a short man firmly placed upon his legs, with a courageous heart, not to be uprooted from the spot where he plants his legs."[4]

The hoplite force had political as well as military repercussions. The aristocratic cavalry was now outdated. Since each hoplite provided his own armor, men of property, both aristocrats and small farmers, made up the new phalanx. Those who could become hoplites and fight for the state could also challenge aristocratic control.

In the world of the Greek city-states, war became an integral part of the Greek way of life. The Greek philosopher Plato described war as "always existing by nature between every Greek city-state."[5] The Greeks adopted a tradition of warfare that became a prominent element of Western civilization. The Greek way of war exhibited a number of prominent features. The Greeks possessed excellent weapons and body armor, making effective use of technological improvements. Greeks armies included a wide number of citizen-soldiers, who gladly accepted the need for training and discipline, giving them an edge over the often far larger armies of mercenaries. Moreover, the Greeks displayed a willingness to engage the enemy head-on, thus deciding a battle quickly and with as few casualties as possible. Finally, the Greeks demonstrated the effectiveness of heavy infantry in determining the outcome of battle. All these features of Greek warfare remained part of Western warfare for centuries.

Colonization and the Growth of Trade

Between 750 and 550 B.C.E., large numbers of Greeks left their homeland to settle in distant lands. The growing gulf between rich and poor, overpopulation, and the development of trade were all factors that spurred the establishment of colonies. Invariably, each colony saw itself as an independent *polis* whose links to the mother *polis* (the *metropolis*) were not political but based on sharing common social, economic, and especially religious practices.

In the western Mediterranean, new Greek settlements were established along the coastline of southern Italy, southern France, eastern Spain, and northern Africa west of Egypt. To the north, the Greeks set up colonies in Thrace, where they sought good agricultural lands to grow grains. Greeks also settled along the shores of the Black Sea and secured the approaches to it with cities on the Hellespont and Bosporus, most notably Byzantium, site of the later Constantinople (Istanbul). In establishing these settlements, the Greeks spread their culture throughout the Mediterranean basin. Moreover, colonization helped the Greeks foster a greater sense of Greek identity. Before the eighth century, Greek communities were mostly isolated from one another, leaving many neighboring states on unfriendly terms. Once colonization began, communities went abroad and found peoples with different languages and customs, they became more aware of their own linguistic and cultural similarities.

Colonization also led to increased trade and industry. The Greeks on the mainland sent their pottery, wine, and olive oil to these areas; in return, they received grains and metals from the west and fish, timber, wheat, metals, and slaves from the Black Sea region. In many *poleis*, the expansion of trade and industry created a new group of rich men who desired political privileges commensurate with their wealth but found such privileges impossible to gain because of the power of the ruling aristocrats.

Tyranny in the Greek Polis

The aspirations of the new industrial and commercial groups laid the groundwork for the rise of **tyrants** in the seventh and sixth centuries B.C.E. They were not necessarily oppressive or wicked, as the modern English word *tyrant* connotes. Greek tyrants were rulers who came to power in an unconstitutional way; a tyrant was not subject to the law. Many tyrants were actually aristocrats who opposed the control of the ruling aristocratic faction in their cities. The support for the tyrants, however, came from the new rich who made their money in trade and industry, as well as from poor peasants who were becoming increasingly indebted to landholding aristocrats. Both groups were opposed to the domination of political power by aristocratic **oligarchies** (*oligarchy* means "rule by the few").

Once in power, the tyrants built new marketplaces, temples, and walls that not only glorified the city but also enhanced their own popularity. Tyrants also favored the interests of merchants and traders. Despite these achievements, however, **tyranny** was largely extinguished by the end of the sixth century B.C.E. Greeks believed in the rule of law, and tyranny made a mockery of that ideal.

Although tyranny did not last, it played a significant role in the evolution of Greek history by ending the rule of narrow aristocratic oligarchies. Once the tyrants were eliminated, the door was opened to the participation of new and more people in governing the affairs of the community. Although this trend culminated in the development of democracy in some communities, in other states expanded oligarchies of one kind or another managed to remain in power. Greek states exhibited considerable variety in their governmental structures; this can perhaps best be seen by examining the two most famous and most powerful Greek city-states, Sparta and Athens.

Sparta

Located in the southwestern Peloponnesus, Sparta, like other Greek states, faced the need for more land. Instead of sending its people out to found new colonies, the Spartans conquered the neighboring Laconians and later, beginning around 730 B.C.E., undertook the conquest of neighboring Messenia despite its larger size and population. Messenia possessed a large, fertile plain ideal for growing grain. After its conquest in the seventh century B.C.E., the Messenians, like the Laconians earlier, were reduced to serfdom (they were known as **helots**, a name derived from a Greek word for "capture") and made to work for the Spartans. To ensure control over their conquered Laconian and Messenian helots, the Spartans made a conscious decision to create a military state.

The New Sparta

Between 800 and 600 B.C.E., the Spartans instituted a series of reforms that are associated with the name of the lawgiver Lycurgus (see the box on p. 104). Although historians are not sure that Lycurgus ever existed, there is no doubt about the result of the reforms that were made: the lives of Spartans were now rigidly organized and tightly controlled (to this day, the word *spartan* means "highly self-disciplined"). Boys were taken from their mothers at the age of seven and put under control of the state. They lived in military-style barracks, where they were subjected to harsh discipline to make them tough and given an education that stressed military training and obedience to authority. At twenty, Spartan males were enrolled in the army for regular military service. Although allowed to marry, they continued to live in the barracks and ate all their meals in public dining halls with their fellow soldiers. Meals were simple; the famous Spartan black broth consisted of a piece of pork boiled in blood, salt, and vinegar, causing a visitor who ate in a public mess to remark that he now understood why Spartans were not afraid to die. At thirty, Spartan males were recognized as mature and allowed to vote in the assembly and live at home, but they remained in military service until the age of sixty.

THE LYCURGAN REFORMS

FAMILY & SOCIETY

To maintain their control over the conquered Messenians, the Spartans instituted the reforms that created their military state. In this account of the lawgiver Lycurgus, the Greek historian Plutarch discusses the effect of these reforms on the treatment and education of boys.

Plutarch, *Lycurgus*

Lycurgus was of another mind; he would not have masters bought out of the market for his young Spartans,...nor was it lawful, indeed, for the father himself to breed up the children after his own fancy; but as soon as they were seven years old they were to be enrolled in certain companies and classes, where they all lived under the same order and discipline, doing their exercises and taking their play together. Of these, he who showed the most conduct and courage was made captain; they had their eyes always upon him, obeyed his orders, and underwent patiently whatsoever punishment he inflicted; so that the whole course of their education was one continued exercise of a ready and perfect obedience. The old men, too, were spectators of their performances, and often raised quarrels and disputes among them, to have a good opportunity of finding out their different characters, and of seeing which would be valiant, which a coward, when they should come to more dangerous encounters. Reading and writing they gave them, just enough to serve their turn; their chief care was to make them good subjects, and to teach them to endure pain and conquer in battle. To this end, as they grew in years, their discipline was proportionately increased; their heads were close-clipped, they were accustomed to go barefoot, and for the most part to play naked.

After they were twelve years old, they were no longer allowed to wear any undergarments; they had one coat to serve them a year; their bodies were hard and dry, with but little acquaintance of baths and unguents; these

human indulgences they were allowed only on some few particular days in the year. They lodged together in little bands upon beds made of the rushes which grew by the banks of the river Eurotas, which they were to break off with their hands with a knife; if it were winter, they mingled some thistledown with their rushes, which it was thought had the property of giving warmth. By the time they were come to this age there was not any of the more hopeful boys who had not a lover to bear him company. The old men, too, had an eye upon them, coming often to the grounds to hear and see them contend either in wit or strength with one another, and this as seriously...as if they were their fathers, their tutors, or their magistrates; so that there scarcely was any time or place without someone present to put them in mind of their duty, and punish them if they had neglected it.

[Spartan boys were also encouraged to steal their food.] They stole, too, all other meat they could lay their hands on, looking out and watching all opportunities, when people were asleep or more careless than usual. If they were caught, they were not only punished with whipping, but hunger, too, being reduced to their ordinary allowance, which was but very slender, and so contrived on purpose, that they might set about to help themselves, and be forced to exercise their energy and address. This was the principal design of their hard fare.

Q *What does this passage from Plutarch's account of Lycurgus reveal about the nature of the Spartan state? Why would this whole program have been distasteful to the Athenians?*

CENGAGENOW *To read more of Plutarch's* Life of Lycurgus, *enter the documents area of the World History Resource Center using the access card that is available for World History.*

While their husbands remained in military barracks until age thirty, Spartan women lived at home. Because of this separation, Spartan women had greater freedom of movement and greater power in the household than was common for women elsewhere in Greece. Spartan women were encouraged to exercise and remain fit to bear and raise healthy children. Like the men, Spartan women engaged in athletic exercises in the nude. Many Spartan women upheld the strict Spartan values, expecting their husbands and sons to be brave in war. The story is told that as a Spartan mother was burying her son, an old woman came up to her and said, "You poor woman, what a misfortune." "No," replied the mother, "because I bore him so that he might die for Sparta, and that is what has happened, as I wished."[6]

The Spartan State The so-called Lycurgan reforms also reorganized the Spartan government, creating an oligarchy. Two kings were primarily responsible for military affairs and served as the leaders of the Spartan army on its campaigns. The two kings shared power with a body called the *gerousia*, a council of elders. It consisted of twenty-eight citizens over the age of sixty, who were elected for life, and the two kings. The primary task of the *gerousia* was to prepare proposals that would be presented to the *apella*, an assembly of all male citizens. The assembly did not debate but only voted on the proposals put before it by the *gerousia*; rarely did the assembly reject these proposals. The assembly also elected the *gerousia* and another body known as the *ephors*, a group of five men who were responsible for supervising the education of youth and the conduct of all citizens.

To make their new military state secure, the Spartans deliberately turned their backs on the outside world. Foreigners, who might bring in new ideas, were discouraged from visiting Sparta. Nor were Spartans, except for military reasons, allowed to travel abroad, where they might pick up new ideas dangerous to the stability of the state. Likewise, Spartan citizens were discouraged from studying philosophy, literature, or the arts—subjects that might encourage new thoughts. The art of war was the Spartan ideal, and all other arts were frowned on.

In the sixth century, Sparta used its military might and the fear it inspired to gain greater control of the Peloponnesus by organizing an alliance of almost all the Peloponnesian states. Sparta's strength enabled it to dominate this Peloponnesian League and determine its policies. By 500 B.C.E., the Spartans had organized a powerful military state that maintained order and stability in the Peloponnesus. Raised from early childhood to believe that total loyalty to the Spartan state was the basic reason for existence, the Spartans viewed their strength as justification for their militaristic ideals and regimented society,

Athens

By 700 B.C.E., Athens had established a unified *polis* on the peninsula of Attica. Although early Athens had been ruled by a monarchy, by the seventh century B.C.E. it had fallen under the control of its aristocrats. They possessed the best land and controlled political and religious life by means of a council of nobles, assisted by a board of nine officials called *archons*. Although there was an assembly of full citizens, it possessed few powers.

Near the end of the seventh century B.C.E., Athens faced political turmoil because of serious economic problems. Increasing numbers of Athenian farmers found themselves sold into slavery when they were unable to repay loans they had obtained from their aristocratic neighbors, pledging themselves as collateral. Repeatedly, there were cries to cancel the debts and give land to the poor.

The Reforms of Solon   The ruling Athenian aristocrats responded to this crisis by choosing Solon, a reform-minded aristocrat, as sole archon in 594 B.C.E. and giving him full power to make changes. Solon canceled all land debts, outlawed new loans based on humans as collateral, and freed people who had fallen into slavery for debts. He refused, however, to carry out land redistribution and hence failed to deal with the basic cause of the economic crisis. This failure, however, was overshadowed by the commercial and industrial prosperity that Athens began to experience in the following decades.

Like his economic reforms, Solon's political measures were also a compromise. Though by no means eliminating the power of the aristocracy, they opened the door to the participation of new people, especially the non-aristocratic wealthy, in the government. But Solon's reforms, though popular, did not solve Athens's problems.

Aristocratic factions continued to vie for power, and the poorer peasants resented Solon's failure to institute land redistribution. Internal strife finally led to the very institution Solon had hoped to avoid—tyranny. Pisistratus, an aristocrat, seized power in 560 B.C.E. Pursuing a foreign policy that aided Athenian trade, Pisistratus remained popular with the mercantile and industrial classes. But the Athenians rebelled against his son and ended the tyranny in 510 B.C.E. Although the aristocrats attempted to reestablish an aristocratic oligarchy, Cleisthenes, another aristocratic reformer, opposed this plan and, with the backing of the Athenian people, gained the upper hand in 508 B.C.E.

The Reforms of Cleisthenes   Cleisthenes created the Council of Five Hundred, chosen by lot by the ten tribes in which all citizens had been enrolled. The council was responsible for the administration of both foreign and financial affairs and prepared the business that would be handled by the assembly. This assembly of all male citizens had final authority in the passing of laws after free and open debate; thus Cleisthenes' reforms had reinforced the central role of the assembly of citizens in the Athenian political system.

The reforms of Cleisthenes created the foundations for Athenian democracy. More changes would come in the fifth century, when the Athenians themselves would begin to use the word *democracy* to describe their system (from the Greek words *demos*, "people," and *kratia*, "power"). By 500 B.C.E., Athens was more united than it had been and was on the verge of playing a more important role in Greek affairs.

Foreign Influence on Early Greek Culture

As the Greeks moved out into the eastern Mediterranean, they came into increased contacts with the older civilizations of the Near East and Egypt, which had a strong impact on early Greek culture. The Greeks adopted new gods and goddesses as well as new myths—such as the story of the flood—from Mesopotamian traditions. Greek pottery in the eighth and seventh centuries began to use new motifs—such as floral designs—borrowed from the Near East. Greek sculpture, particularly that of the Ionian Greek settlements in southwestern Asia Minor, demonstrates the impact of the considerably older Egyptian civilization. There we first see the life-size stone statues of young male nudes known as *kouros* figures. The *kouros* bears a strong resemblance to Egyptian statues of the New Kingdom. The figures are not realistic but stiff, the face bearing the hint of a smile; one leg is advanced ahead of the other, and the arms are held rigidly at the sides of the body.

Greek literature was also the beneficiary of a Greek alphabet that owed much to the Phoenicians (see Chapter 1). The Greeks adopted some of the twenty-two Phoenician consonants as Greek consonants and used other symbols to represent vowel sounds, which the Greeks had. In the process, the Greeks

by the Macedonian king Philip II in 338 B.C.E. Many of the cultural contributions of the Greeks occurred during this period. The age began with a mighty confrontation between the Greek states and the mammoth Persian Empire.

The Challenge of Persia

As the Greeks spread throughout the Mediterranean, they came into contact with the Persian Empire to the east (see Chapter 1). The Ionian Greek cities in western Asia Minor had already fallen subject to the Persian Empire by the mid-sixth century B.C.E. An unsuccessful revolt by the Ionian cities in 499 B.C.E.—assisted by the Athenian navy—led the Persian ruler Darius to seek revenge by attacking the mainland Greeks. In 490 B.C.E., the Persians landed an army on the plain of Marathon, only 26 miles from Athens. The Athenians and their allies were clearly outnumbered, but led by Miltiades, one of the Athenian leaders who insisted on attacking, the Greek hoplites charged across the plain of Marathon and crushed the Persian forces.

Xerxes, the new Persian monarch after the death of Darius in 486 B.C.E., vowed revenge and planned to invade. In preparation for the attack, some of the Greek states formed a defensive league under Spartan leadership, while the Athenians pursued a new military policy by developing a navy. By the time of the Persian invasion in 480 B.C.E., the Athenians had produced a fleet of about two hundred vessels.

Xerxes led a massive invasion force into Greece: close to 150,000 troops, almost seven hundred naval ships, and hundreds of supply ships to keep the large army fed. The Greeks tried to delay the Persians at the pass of Thermopylae, along the main road into central Greece. A Greek force numbering close to nine thousand, under the leadership of the Spartan king, Leonidas, and his contingent of three hundred Spartans, held off the Persian army for two days. The Spartan troops were especially brave. When told that Persian arrows would darken the sky in battle, one Spartan warrior supposedly responded, "That is good news. We will fight in the shade!" Unfortunately for the Greeks, a traitor told the Persians how to use a mountain path to outflank the Greek force. The Spartans fought to the last man.

The Athenians, now threatened by the onslaught of the Persian forces, abandoned their city. While the Persians sacked and burned Athens, the Greek fleet remained offshore near the island of Salamis and challenged the Persian navy to fight. Although the Greeks were outnumbered, they managed to outmaneuver the Persian fleet and utterly defeated it. A few months later, early in 479 B.C.E., the Greeks formed the largest Greek army seen up to that time and decisively defeated the Persian army at Plataea, northwest of Attica. The Greeks had won the war and were now free to pursue their own destiny.

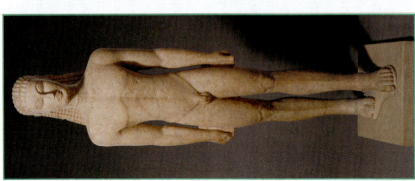

©Scala/Art Resource, NY

Image copyright © The Metropolitan Museum of Art/Art Resource, NY

Kouros. On the left is a statue of a young male nude from around 600 B.C.E., making it an early example of Greek *kouros* sculpture. Such statues, which were placed in temples along with companion figures of clothed young women, known as *korai*, were meant to be representations of the faithful dedicated to the gods. At the right is an early-seventh-century B.C.E. statue of an Egyptian nobleman. The strong influence of Egyptian sculpture on Greek art is clear; unlike the Egyptians, however, Greek sculptors preferred depicting male figures in the nude.

created a truly phonetic alphabet, probably between 800 and 750 B.C.E., thus making the Greek language easier to read and write than Egyptian hieroglyphics and Mesopotamian cuneiform. Greek could be used to record laws and commercial transactions and to write the poetry, philosophical treatises, and other literary works that distinguish Greek culture.

The High Point of Greek Civilization: Classical Greece

Q Focus Questions: What did the Greeks mean by democracy, and in what ways was the Athenian political system a democracy? What effect did the two great conflicts of the fifth century—the Persian Wars and the Peloponnesian War—have on Greek civilization?

Classical Greece is the name given to the period of Greek history from around 500 B.C.E. to the conquest of Greece

The Art Archive/Acropolis Museum, Athens, Greece/Gianni Dagli Orti

© AAAC/Topham/The Image Works

CHRONOLOGY The Persian Wars

Rebellion of Greek cities in Asia Minor	499–494 B.C.E.
Battle of Marathon	490 B.C.E.
Xerxes invades Greece	480–479 B.C.E.
Battles of Thermopylae and Salamis	480 B.C.E.
Battle of Plataea	479 B.C.E.

The Growth of an Athenian Empire in the Age of Pericles

After the defeat of the Persians, Athens took over the leadership of the Greek world by forming a defensive alliance against the Persians called the Delian League in the winter of 478–477 B.C.E. Its main headquarters was on the island of Delos, but its chief officials, including the treasurers and commanders of the fleet, were Athenian. Under the leadership of the Athenians, the Delian League pursued the attack against the Persian Empire. Virtually all of the Greek states in the Aegean were liberated from Persian control. Arguing that the Persian threat was now over, some members of the Delian League wished to withdraw. But the Athenians forced them to remain in the league and to pay tribute. In 454 B.C.E., the Athenians moved the treasury of the league from Delos to Athens. By controlling the Delian League, Athens had created an empire.

At home, Athenians favored the new imperial policy, especially after 461 B.C.E., when a political faction, led by a young aristocrat named Pericles, triumphed. Under Pericles, who remained a dominant figure in Athenian politics for more than three decades, Athens embarked on a policy of expanding democracy at home and its new empire abroad. This period of Athenian and Greek history, which historians have subsequently labeled the Age of Pericles, witnessed the height of Athenian power and the culmination of its brilliance as a civilization.

In the Age of Pericles, the Athenians became deeply attached to their democratic system. The sovereignty of the people was embodied in the assembly, which consisted of all male citizens over eighteen years of age. In the 440s, that was probably a group of about 43,000. Not all attended, however, and the number present at the meetings, which were held every ten days on a hillside east of the Acropolis, seldom reached 6,000. The assembly passed all laws and made final decisions on war and foreign policy.

Routine administration of public affairs was handled by a large body of city magistrates, usually chosen by lot without regard to class and usually serving only one-year terms. This meant that many male citizens held public office at some time in their lives. A board of ten officials known as generals (strategoi) were elected by public vote to guide affairs of state, although their power depended on the respect they had earned. Generals were usually wealthy aristocrats, even though the people were free to select otherwise. The generals could be reelected, enabling individual leaders to play an important political role. Pericles' frequent reelection (fifteen times) as one of the ten generals made him one of the leading politicians between 461 and 429 B.C.E.

Pericles expanded the Athenians' involvement in democracy, which is what by now the Athenians had come to call their form of government (see the box on p. 108). Power was in the hands of the people; male citizens voted in the assemblies and served as jurors in the courts. Lower-class citizens were now eligible for public offices formerly closed to them. Pericles also introduced state pay for

The Greek Trireme. The trireme became the standard warship of ancient Greece. Highly maneuverable, fast, and outfitted with metal prows, Greek triremes were especially effective at ramming enemy ships. The bas-relief shows a fifth-century B.C.E. Athenian trireme. The photo shows the *Olympias,* a trireme reconstructed by the Greek navy.

ATHENIAN DEMOCRACY: THE FUNERAL ORATION OF PERICLES

POLITICS & GOVERNMENT

In his *History of the Peloponnesian War*, the Greek historian Thucydides presented his reconstruction of the eulogy given by Pericles in the winter of 431–430 B.C.E. to honor the Athenians killed in the first campaigns of the Great Peloponnesian War. It is a magnificent, idealized description of Athenian democracy at its height.

Thucydides, *History of the Peloponnesian War*

Our constitution is called a democracy because power is in the hands not of a minority but of the whole people. When it is a question of settling private disputes, everyone is equal before the law; when it is a question of putting one person before another in positions of public responsibility, what counts is not membership of a particular class, but the actual ability which the man possesses. No one, so long as he has it in him to be of service to the state, is kept in political obscurity because of poverty. And, just as our political life is free and open, so is our day-to-day life in our relations with each other. We do not get into a state with our next-door neighbor if he enjoys himself in his own way, nor do we give him the kind of black looks which, though they do no real harm, still do hurt people's feelings. We are free and tolerant in our private lives; but in public affairs we keep to the law. This is because it commands our deep respect.

We give our obedience to those whom we put in positions of authority, and we obey the laws themselves, especially those which are for the protection of the oppressed, and those unwritten laws which it is an acknowledged shame to break.... Here each individual is interested not only in his own affairs but in the affairs of the state as

well: even those who are mostly occupied with their own business are extremely well-informed on general politics—this is a peculiarity of ours: we do not say that a man who takes no interest in politics is a man who minds his own business; we say that he has no business here at all. We Athenians, in our own persons, take our decisions on policy or submit them to proper discussions: for we do not think that there is an incompatibility between words and deeds; the worst thing is to rush into action before the consequences have been properly debated.... Taking everything together then, I declare that our city is an education to Greece, and I declare that in my opinion each single one of our citizens, in all the manifold aspects of life, is able to show himself the rightful lord and owner of his own person, and do this, moreover, with exceptional grace and exceptional versatility. And to show that this is no empty boasting for the present occasion, but real tangible fact, you have only to consider the power which our city possesses and which has been won by those very qualities which I have mentioned.

Q *In the eyes of Pericles, what are the ideals of Athenian democracy? In what ways does Pericles exaggerate his claims? Why would the Athenian passion for debate described by Pericles have been distasteful to the Spartans? On the other hand, how does eagerness for discussion perfectly suit democracy?*

CENGAGENOW *To read more of Thucydides' History, enter the documents area of the World History Resource Center using the access card that is available for World History.*

---

officeholders, including the widely held jury duty. This meant that even poor citizens could hold public office and afford to participate in public affairs. Nevertheless, although the Athenians developed a system of government that was unique in its time in which citizens had equal rights and the people were the government, aristocrats continued to hold the most important offices, and many people, including women, slaves, and foreigners residing in Athens, were not given the same political rights.

Under Pericles, Athens became the leading center of Greek culture. The Persians had destroyed much of the city during the Persian Wars, but Pericles used the treasury money of the Delian League to set in motion a massive rebuilding program. New temples and statues soon made the greatness of Athens more visible. Art, architecture, and philosophy flourished, and Pericles broadly boasted that Athens had become the "school of Greece." But the achievements of Athens alarmed the other Greek states, especially Sparta, and soon all Greece was confronting a new war.

The Great Peloponnesian War and the Decline of the Greek States

During the forty years after the defeat of the Persians, the Greek world came to be divided into two major camps: Sparta and its supporters and the Athenian maritime empire. Sparta and its allies feared the growing Athenian empire. Then, too, Athens and Sparta had created two very different kinds of societies, and neither state was able to tolerate the other's system. A series of disputes finally led to the outbreak of war in 431 B.C.E.

At the beginning of the war, both sides believed they had winning strategies. The Athenians planned to remain behind the protective walls of Athens while the overseas empire and the navy would keep them supplied. Pericles knew that the Spartans and their allies could beat the Athenians in open battles, which was the chief aim of the Spartan strategy. The Spartans and their allies invaded Attica and ravaged the fields and orchards, hoping that the Athenians would send out their army to fight beyond the walls. But Pericles was convinced that Athens was secure behind its walls and stayed put.

In the second year of the war, however, plague devastated the crowded city of Athens and wiped out possibly one-third of the population. Pericles himself died the following year (429 B.C.E.), a severe loss to Athens. Despite the losses from the plague, the Athenians fought on in a struggle that dragged on for another twenty-seven years. A final crushing blow came in 405 B.C.E., when the Athenian fleet was destroyed at Aegospotami on the Hellespont. Athens was besieged and surrendered in 404. Its walls were torn down, the navy was disbanded, and the Athenian empire was no more. The great war was finally over.

The Great Peloponnesian War weakened the major Greek states and destroyed any possibility of cooperation among the states. The next seventy years of Greek history are a sorry tale of efforts by Sparta, Athens, and Thebes, a new Greek power, to dominate Greek affairs. Focused on their petty wars, the Greek states remained oblivious to the growing power of Macedonia to their north.

The Culture of Classical Greece

Classical Greece was a period of remarkable intellectual and cultural growth throughout the Greek world, and Periclean Athens was the most important center of Classical Greek culture.

The Writing of History

History as we know it, as the systematic analysis of past events, was introduced to the Western world by the Greeks. Herodotus (c. 484–c. 425 B.C.E.) wrote *History of the Persian Wars*, a work commonly regarded as the first real history in Western civilization. The central theme of Herodotus' work is the conflict between the Greeks and the Persians, which he viewed as a struggle between freedom and despotism. Herodotus traveled extensively and questioned many people to obtain his information. He was a master storyteller and sometimes included considerable fanciful material, but he was also capable of exhibiting a critical attitude toward the materials he used.

Thucydides (c. 460–c. 400 B.C.E.) was a better historian by far; indeed, he is considered the greatest historian of the ancient world. Thucydides was an Athenian and a participant in the Peloponnesian War. He had been elected a general, but a defeat in battle led the fickle Athenian assembly to send him into exile, which gave him the opportunity to write his *History of the Peloponnesian War*.

Unlike Herodotus, Thucydides was not concerned with underlying divine forces or gods as explanatory causal factors in history. He saw war and politics in purely rational terms, as the activities of human beings. He examined the causes of the Peloponnesian War in a clear, methodical, objective fashion, placing much emphasis on accuracy and the precision of his facts. As he stated:

> With regard to my factual reporting of the events of the war I have made it a principle not to write down the first story that came my way, and not even to be guided by my own

general impressions; either I was present myself at the events which I have described or else I heard of them from eyewitnesses whose reports I have checked with as much thoroughness as possible.[7]

Thucydides also provided remarkable insight into the human condition. He believed that political situations recur in similar fashion and that the study of history is therefore of great value in understanding the present.

Greek Drama

Drama as we know it in Western culture was originated by the Greeks. Plays were presented in outdoor theaters as part of religious festivals. The form of Greek plays remained fairly stable. Three male actors who wore masks acted all the parts. A chorus, also male, spoke lines that explained what was going on. Action was very limited because the emphasis was on the story and its meaning.

The first Greek dramas were tragedies, plays based on the suffering of a hero and usually ending in disaster. Aeschylus (525–456 B.C.E.) is the first tragedian whose plays are known to us. As was customary in Greek tragedy, his plots are simple, and the entire drama focuses on a single tragic event and its meaning. Greek tragedies were sometimes presented in a trilogy (a set of three plays) built around a common theme. The only complete trilogy we possess, called the *Oresteia*, was composed by Aeschylus. The theme of this trilogy is derived from Homer. Agamemnon, the king of Mycenae, returns a hero from the defeat of Troy. His wife, Clytemnestra, avenges the sacrificial death of her daughter Iphigenia by murdering Agamemnon, who had been responsible for Iphigenia's death. In the second play of the trilogy, Agamemnon's son Orestes avenges his father by killing his mother. Orestes is then pursued by the avenging Furies, who torment him for killing his mother. Evil acts breed evil acts, and suffering is one's lot, suggests Aeschylus. But Orestes is put on trial and acquitted by Athena, the patron goddess of Athens. Personal vendetta has been eliminated, and law has prevailed.

Another great Athenian playwright was Sophocles (c. 496–406 B.C.E.), whose most famous creation was *Oedipus the King*. In this play, the oracle of Apollo foretells that a man (Oedipus) will kill his own father and marry his mother. Despite all attempts at prevention, the tragic events occur. Although it appears that Oedipus suffered the fate determined by the gods, Oedipus also accepts that he himself as a free man must bear responsibility for his actions: "It was Apollo, friends, Apollo, that brought this bitter bitterness, my sorrows to completion. But the hand that struck me was none but my own."[8]

The third outstanding Athenian tragedian, Euripides (c. 485–406 B.C.E.), moved beyond his predecessors by creating more realistic characters. His plots also became more complex, with a greater interest in real-life situations. Euripides was controversial; he questioned traditional moral and religious values. For example, he was critical of the traditional view that war was glorious. He portrayed war as brutal and barbaric.

ATHENIAN COMEDY: SEX AS AN ANTIWAR INSTRUMENT

Greek comedy became a regular feature of the dramatic presentations at the festival of Dionysus in Athens beginning in 488–487 B.C.E. Aristophanes used his comedies to present political messages, especially to express his antiwar sentiments. The plot of *Lysistrata* centers on a sex strike by wives in order to get their husbands to end the Peloponnesian War. In this scene from the play, Lysistrata (whose name means "she who dissolves the armies") has the women swear a special oath. The oath involves a bowl of wine offered as a libation to the gods.

Aristophanes, *Lysistrata*

LYSISTRATA: All of you women: come, touch the bowl, and repeat after me: I WILL HAVE NOTHING TO DO WITH MY HUSBAND OR MY LOVER

KALONIKE: I will have nothing to do with my husband or my lover

LYSISTRATA: THOUGH HE COME TO ME IN PITIABLE CONDITION

KALONIKE: Though he come to me in pitiable condition
(Oh, Lysistrata! This is killing me!)

LYSISTRATA: I WILL STAY IN MY HOUSE UNTOUCHABLE

KALONIKE: I will stay in my house untouchable

LYSISTRATA: IN MY THINNEST SAFFRON SILK

KALONIKE: In my thinnest saffron silk

LYSISTRATA: AND MAKE HIM LONG FOR ME.

KALONIKE: And make him long for me.

LYSISTRATA: I WILL NOT GIVE MYSELF

KALONIKE: I will not give myself

LYSISTRATA: AND IF HE CONSTRAINS ME

KALONIKE: And if he constrains me

LYSISTRATA: I WILL BE AS COLD AS ICE AND NEVER MOVE

KALONIKE: I will be as cold as ice and never move

LYSISTRATA: I WILL NOT LIFT MY SLIPPERS TOWARD THE CEILING

KALONIKE: I will not lift my slippers toward the ceiling

LYSISTRATA: OR CROUCH ON ALL FOURS LIKE THE LIONESS IN THE CARVING

KALONIKE: Or crouch on all fours like the lioness in the carving

LYSISTRATA: AND IF I KEEP THIS OATH LET ME DRINK FROM THIS BOWL

KALONIKE: And if I keep this oath let me drink from this bowl

LYSISTRATA: IF NOT, LET MY OWN BOWL BE FILLED WITH WATER.

KALONIKE: If not, let my own bowl be filled with water.

LYSISTRATA: You have all sworn?

MYRRHINE: We have

Q *How does this selection from Aristophanes illustrate the political use of comedy?*

Greek tragedies dealt with universal themes still relevant to our day. They probed such problems as the nature of good and evil, the rights of the individual, the nature of divine forces, and the nature of human beings. Over and over, the tragic lesson was repeated: humans were free and yet could operate only within limitations imposed by the gods. To strive to do the best may not always gain a person success in human terms but is nevertheless worthy of the endeavor. Greek pride in human accomplishment and independence is real. As the chorus chants in Sophocles' *Antigone:* "Is there anything more wonderful on earth, our marvelous planet, than the miracle of man?"[9]

Greek comedy developed later than tragedy. The plays of Aristophanes (c. 450–c. 385 B.C.E.), who used both grotesque masks and obscene jokes to entertain the Athenian audience, are examples of Old Comedy. But comedy in Athens was also more clearly political than tragedy. It was used to attack or savagely satirize both politicians and intellectuals. Of special importance to Aristophanes was his opposition to the Peloponnesian War. *Lysistrata,* performed in 411 B.C.E., when Athens was in serious danger of losing the war, had a comic but effective message against the war (see the box above).

The Arts: The Classical Ideal The artistic standards established by the Greeks of the Classical period have largely dominated the arts of the Western world. Greek art was concerned with expressing eternally true ideals. Its subject matter was basically the human being, expressed harmoniously as an object of great beauty. The Classical style, based on the ideals of reason, moderation, symmetry, balance, and harmony in all things, was meant to civilize the emotions.

In architecture, the most important form was the temple dedicated to a god or goddess. At the center of Greek temples were walled rooms that housed the statues of deities and treasuries in which gifts to the gods and goddesses were safeguarded. These central rooms were surrounded by a screen of columns that made Greek temples open structures rather than closed ones. The columns were originally made of wood but were changed to marble in the fifth century B.C.E.

Some of the finest examples of Greek Classical architecture were built in fifth-century Athens. The most famous building, regarded as the finest example of the Classical Greek temple, was the Parthenon, built between 447 and 432 B.C.E. Consecrated to Athena, the patron goddess of Athens, the Parthenon was also dedicated to the glory of the city-state and its inhabitants. The Parthenon typifies the principles of Classical architecture: calmness, clarity, and the avoidance of superfluous detail.

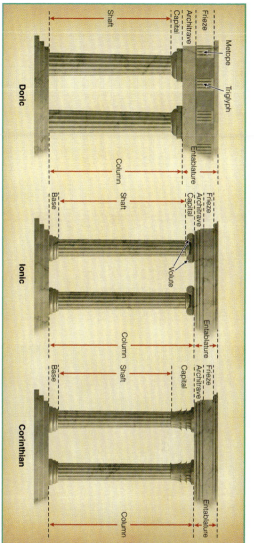

© Art Resource, NY

Doric — Shaft, Capital, Architrave, Frieze, Metope, Triglyph, Entablature, Column

Ionic — Frieze, Architrave, Capital, Shaft, Base, Volute, Entablature, Column, Shaft, Base, Capital, Architrave, Frieze, Entablature

Corinthian — Column

Doric, Ionic, and Corinthian Orders. The Greeks used different shapes and sizes in the columns of their temples. The Doric order, evolved first in the Dorian Peloponnesus, consisted of thick, fluted columns with simple capitals (the decorated tops of the columns). The Greeks considered the Doric order grave, dignified, and masculine. The Ionic style was first developed in western Asia Minor and consisted of slender columns with spiral-shaped capitals. The Greeks characterized the Ionic order as slender, elegant, and feminine. Corinthian columns, with their more detailed capitals modeled after acanthus leaves, came later, near the end of the fifth century B.C.E.

Greek sculpture also developed a style that differed significantly from the artificial stiffness of the figures of earlier times, which had been influenced by Egyptian sculpture. Statues of the male nude, the favorite subject of Greek sculptors, now exhibited more relaxed attitudes; their faces were self-assured, their bodies flexible and smooth-muscled. Although the figures possessed natural features that made them lifelike, Greek sculptors sought to achieve not realism but a standard of ideal beauty. Polyclitus, a fifth-century sculptor, wrote a treatise (now lost) on a canon of proportions that he illustrated in a work known as the *Doryphoros*. His theory maintained that the use of ideal proportions, based on mathematical ratios found in nature, could produce an ideal human form, beautiful in its perfected and refined features. This search for ideal beauty was the dominant feature of the classical standard in sculpture.

© Photodisc (Adam Crowley)/GettyImages

The Parthenon. The arts in Classical Greece were designed to express the eternal ideals of reason, moderation, symmetry, balance, and harmony. In architecture, the most important form was the temple, and the classic example of this kind of architecture is the Parthenon, built between 447 and 432 B.C.E. Located on the Acropolis in Athens, the Parthenon was dedicated to Athena, the patron goddess of the city, but it also served as a shining example of the power and wealth of the Athenian empire.

The Greek Love of Wisdom

Philosophy is a Greek word that originally meant "love of wisdom." Early Greek philosophers were concerned with the development of critical or rational thought about the nature of the universe and the place of divine forces and souls in it.

Much of early Greek philosophy focused on the attempt to explain the universe on the basis of unifying principles. Thales of Miletus, an Ionian Greek who lived around 600 B.C.E., postulated the unity of the universe. All things were linked by water as the basic substance. Another Ionian Greek, Pythagoras (c. 580–c. 490 B.C.E.), taught that the essence of the universe could be found in music and numbers. These early Greek philosophers may have eliminated the role of the gods as they were portrayed in Greek myths, but they did not eliminate divinity itself from the world, tending instead to identify it with the underlying, unchanging forces that govern the universe.

Many Greeks, however, were simply not interested in such speculations. The **Sophists** were a group of philosophical teachers in the fifth century B.C.E. who rejected such speculation as foolish. Like their near contemporary Confucius in China (see Chapter 3), they argued that

to be skeptics who questioned the traditional values of their societies. To the Sophists, there was no absolute right or wrong. True wisdom consisted of being able to perceive and pursue one's own good. Because of these ideas, many people viewed the Sophists as harmful to society and especially dangerous to the values of young people.

In Classical Greece, Athens became the foremost intellectual and artistic center. Its reputation is perhaps strongest of all in philosophy. Socrates, Plato, and Aristotle raised basic questions that have been debated for two thousand years, for the most part the very same philosophical questions we wrestle with today.

Socrates (469–399 B.C.E.) left no writing behind, but we know about him from his pupils. Socrates was a stonemason whose true love was philosophy. He taught a number of pupils, although not for pay, because he believed that the goal of education was to improve the individual. His approach, still known as the **Socratic method,** employs a question-and-answer technique to lead pupils to see things for themselves using their own reason. Socrates believed that all knowledge is within each person; only critical examination was needed to call it forth. This was the real task of philosophy, since "the unexamined life is not worth living."

Socrates questioned authority and criticized some traditional Athenian values, and this soon led him into trouble. Athens had had a tradition of free thought and inquiry, but defeat in the Peloponnesian War had created an environment intolerant of open debate and soul-searching. Socrates was accused and convicted of corrupting the youth of Athens by his teaching. An Athenian jury sentenced him to death.

One of Socrates' disciples was Plato (c. 429–347 B.C.E.), considered by many the greatest philosopher of Western civilization. Unlike his master Socrates, who wrote nothing, Plato wrote a great deal. He was fascinated with the question of reality: How do we know what is real? According to Plato, a higher world of eternal, unchanging Ideas or Forms has always existed. To know these Forms is to know truth. These ideal Forms constitute reality and can only be apprehended by a trained mind—which, of course, is the goal of philosophy. The objects that we perceive with our senses are simply reflections of the ideal Forms. They are shadows; reality is in the Forms themselves.

Plato's ideas of government were set out in his dialogue titled *The Republic.* Based on his experience in Athens, Plato had come to distrust the workings of democracy. It was obvious to him that individuals could not attain an ethical life unless they lived in a just and rational state. Plato's search for the just state led him to construct an ideal state in *The Republic,* in which the population was divided into three basic groups. At the top was an upper class, a ruling elite, the philosopher-kings: "Unless...political power and philosophy meet together..., there can be no rest from troubles...for states, nor yet, as I believe, for all mankind."[10] The second group were those who showed courage; they would be the

© Scala/Art Resource, NY

Doryphoros. This statue, known as the *Doryphoros,* or spear carrier, is by the fifth-century B.C.E. sculptor Polyclitus, who believed it illustrated the ideal proportions of the human figure. Classical Greek sculpture moved away from the stiffness of earlier figures but retained the young male nude as the favorite subject. The statues became more lifelike, with relaxed poses and flexible, smooth-muscled bodies. The aim of sculpture, however, was not simply realism but rather the expression of ideal beauty.

understanding the universe was beyond the reach of the human mind (see the comparative essay "The Axial Age" on p. 113). It was more important for individuals to improve themselves, so the only worthwhile object of study was human behavior. The Sophists were wandering scholars who sold their services as professional teachers to the young men of Greece, especially those of Athens. The Sophists stressed the importance of **rhetoric** (the art of persuasive oratory) in winning debates and swaying an audience, a skill that was especially valuable in democratic Athens. Unlike Confucius, however, the Sophists tended

COMPARATIVE ESSAY
THE AXIAL AGE

By the fourth century B.C.E., important regional civilizations existed in China, India, Southwest Asia, and the Mediterranean. During their formative periods between 700 and 300 B.C.E., all were characterized by the emergence of religious and philosophical thinkers who established ideas—or "axes"—that became the basis for religions and philosophical thought in those societies for hundreds of years. Ever since, some historians have used the term "the Axial Age" to refer to the period when these ideas developed.

During the fifth and fourth centuries in Greece, the philosophers Socrates, Plato, and Aristotle not only proclaimed philosophical and political ideas crucial to the Greek world and later Western civilization but also conceived of a rational method of inquiry that became important to modern science. By the seventh century B.C.E., concepts of monotheism had developed in Persia through the teachings of Zoroaster and in Canaan through the Hebrew prophets. In Judaism, the Hebrews developed a world religion that influenced the later religions of Christianity and Islam.

During the sixth century, two major schools of thought—Confucianism and Daoism—emerged in China. Both sought to spell out the principles that would create a stable order in society. And although each presented a view of reality that was diametrically opposite to the other, both came to have an impact on Chinese civilization that lasted into the twentieth century.

Two of the world's greatest religions, Hinduism and Buddhism, began in India during the Axial Age. Hinduism was an outgrowth of the religious beliefs of the Aryan peoples who settled India. The ideas of Hinduism were expressed in the sacred texts known as the Vedas and in the Upanishads, which were commentaries on the Vedas compiled in the sixth century B.C.E. With its belief in reincarnation, Hinduism provided justification for the rigid caste system of India. Buddhism was the product of one man, Siddhartha Gautama, known as the Buddha, who lived in the sixth century B.C.E. The Buddha's simple message of achieving wisdom created a new spiritual philosophy that came to rival Hinduism. Although a product of India, Buddhism also spread to other parts of the world.

Philosophers in the Axial Age. This mosaic from Pompeii re-creates a gathering of Greek philosophers at the school of Plato.

© Erich Lessing/Art Resource, NY

Although these philosophies and religions developed in different areas of the world, they had some features in common. Like the Chinese philosophers Plato and Aristotle had different points of view about the nature of reality. Thinkers in India and China also developed rational methods of inquiry similar to those of Plato and Aristotle. And regardless of their origins, when we speak of Judaism, Hinduism, Buddhism, Confucianism, Daoism, or Greek philosophical thought, we realize that the ideas of the Axial Age not only spread around the world at different times but are also still an integral part of our world today.

Q *What do historians mean when they speak of the Axial Age? What do you think would explain the emergence of similar ideas in different parts of the world during this period?*

years, was Aristotle (384–322 B.C.E.), who later became a tutor to Alexander the Great. Aristotle did not accept Plato's theory of ideal Forms. Instead he believed that by examining individual objects, we can perceive their form and arrive at universal principles, but that these principles do not exist as a separate higher world of reality beyond material things but are a part of things themselves. Aristotle's interests, then, lay in analyzing and classifying things based on thorough research and investigation.

warriors who protected the society. All the rest made up the masses, essentially people driven not by wisdom or courage but by desire. They would be the producers of society—the artisans, tradespeople, and farmers. Contrary to common Greek custom, Plato also believed that men and women should have the same education and equal access to all positions.

Plato established a school at Athens known as the Academy. One of his pupils, who studied there for twenty

His interests were wide-ranging, and he wrote treatises on an enormous number of subjects: ethics, logic, politics, poetry, astronomy, geology, biology, and physics.

Like Plato, Aristotle wished for an effective form of government that would rationally direct human affairs. Unlike Plato, he did not seek an ideal state based on the embodiment of an ideal Form of justice but tried to find the best form of government by a rational examination of existing governments. For his *Politics*, Aristotle examined the constitutions of 158 states and arrived at general categories for organizing governments. He identified three good forms of government: monarchy, aristocracy, and constitutional government. But based on his examination, he warned that monarchy can easily turn into tyranny, aristocracy into oligarchy, and constitutional government into radical democracy or anarchy. He favored constitutional government as the best form for most people.

Aristotle's philosophical and political ideas played an enormous role in the development of Western thought during the Middle Ages (see Chapter 12). So did his ideas on women. Aristotle maintained that women were biologically inferior to men: "A woman is, as it were, an infertile male. She is female in fact on account of a kind of inadequacy." Therefore, according to Aristotle, women must be subordinated to men, not only in the community but also in marriage: "The association between husband and wife is clearly an aristocracy. The man rules by virtue of merit, and in the sphere that is his by right; but he hands over to his wife such matters as are suitable for her."[11]

Greek Religion

As was the case throughout the ancient world, religion played an important role in Greek society and was intricately connected to every aspect of daily life; it was both social and practical. Public festivals, which originated from religious practices, served specific functions: boys were prepared to be warriors, girls to be mothers. Because religion was related to every aspect of life, citizens had to have a proper attitude toward the gods. Religion was a civic cult necessary for the well-being of the state. Temples dedicated to a god or goddess were the major buildings in Greek cities.

The poetry of Homer gave an account of the gods that provided Greek religion with a definite structure. Over a period of time, all Greeks came to accept a common religion. There were twelve chief gods who supposedly lived on Mount Olympus, the highest mountain in Greece. Among the twelve were Zeus, the chief deity and father of the gods; Athena, goddess of wisdom and crafts; Apollo, god of the sun and poetry; Aphrodite, goddess of love; and Poseidon, brother of Zeus and god of the seas and earthquakes. Although the twelve Olympian gods were common to all Greeks, each *polis* usually singled out one of the twelve Olympians as a guardian deity for the community. Athena was the patron goddess of Athens, for example.

Greek religion did not have a body of doctrine, nor did it focus on morality. It gave little or no hope of life after death for most people. Because the Greeks wanted the gods to look favorably on their activities, ritual assumed enormous proportions in Greek religion. Prayers were often combined with gifts to the gods based on the principle "I give so that you, the gods, will give in return." Yet the Greeks were well aware of the capricious nature of the gods, who were assigned recognizably human qualities and often engaged in fickle or even vengeful behavior toward other deities or human beings.

Festivals also developed as a way to honor the gods and goddesses. Some of these (the Panhellenic celebrations) came to have international significance and were held at special locations, such as those dedicated to the worship of Zeus at Olympia or to Apollo at Delphi. Numerous events were held in honor of the gods at the great festivals, including athletic competitions to which all Greeks were invited. The first such games were held at the Olympic festival in 776 B.C.E. and were then held every four years thereafter to honor Zeus. Initially, the Olympic contests consisted of footraces and wrestling, but later boxing, javelin throwing, and various other contests were added.

As another practical side of Greek religion, Greeks wanted to know the will of the gods. To do so, they made use of the *oracle*, a sacred shrine dedicated to a god or goddess who revealed the future. The most famous was the oracle of Apollo at Delphi, located on the side of Mount Parnassus, overlooking the Gulf of Corinth. At Delphi, a priestess listened to questions while in a state of ecstasy that was believed to be induced by Apollo. Her responses were interpreted by the priests and given in verse form to the person asking questions. Representatives of states and individuals traveled to Delphi to consult the oracle of Apollo. States might inquire whether they should undertake a military expedition; individuals might raise such questions as "Heracleidas asks whether he will have offspring from the wife he has now." Responses were often enigmatic and at times even politically motivated. Croesus, the king of Lydia in Asia Minor who was known for his incredible wealth, sent messengers to the oracle at Delphi, asking whether he should go to war with the Persians. The oracle replied that if Croesus attacked the Persians, he would destroy a mighty empire. Overjoyed to hear these words, Croesus made war on the Persians but was crushed. A mighty empire was indeed destroyed—his own.

Daily Life in Classical Athens

The *polis* was above all a male community: only adult male citizens took part in public life. In Athens, this meant the exclusion of women, slaves, and foreign residents, or roughly 85 percent of the total population in Attica. There were probably 150,000 citizens in Athens, of whom about 43,000 were adult males who exercised political power. Resident foreigners, who numbered about 35,000, received the protection of the laws but were also subject to some of the responsibilities of citizens, namely, military service and the funding of festivals. The remaining social group, the slaves, numbered around 100,000. Most slaves in Athens worked in the home as cooks and maids or toiled in the fields. Some were owned by the state and worked on public construction projects.

Economy and Lifestyle

The Athenian economy was based largely on agriculture and trade. Athenians grew grains, vegetables, and fruit for local consumption. Grapes and olives were cultivated for wine and olive oil, which were used locally and also exported. The Athenians raised sheep and goats for wool and dairy products. Because of the size of the population in Attica and the lack of abundant fertile land, Athens had to import 50 to 80 percent of its grain, a staple in the Athenian diet. Trade was thus very important to the Athenian economy. Perhaps that is one reason why the Greeks were among the first to mint silver coins, a practice that caused environmental problems by releasing toxic lead into the atmosphere.

The Athenian lifestyle was basically simple. Athenian houses were furnished with necessities bought from artisans, such as beds, couches, tables, chests, pottery, stools, baskets, and cooking utensils. Wives and slaves made clothes and blankets at home. The Athenian diet was rather plain and relied on such basic foods as barley, wheat, millet, lentils, grapes, figs, olives, almonds, bread made at home, vegetables, eggs, fish, cheese, and chicken. Olive oil was widely used, not only for eating but also for burning in lamps and rubbing on the body after washing and exercise. Although country houses kept animals, they were used for reasons other than their flesh: oxen for plowing, sheep for wool, and goats for milk and cheese.

Family and Relationships

The family was a central institution in ancient Athens. It was composed of husband, wife, and children (a nuclear family), although other dependent relatives and slaves were regarded as part of the family economic unit. The family's primary social function was to produce new citizens. Strict laws of the fifth century had stipulated that a citizen must be the offspring of a legally acknowledged marriage between two Athenian citizens whose parents were also citizens.

Adult female citizens could participate in most religious cults and festivals but were otherwise excluded from public life. They could not own property beyond personal items and always had a male guardian. An Athenian woman was expected to be a good wife. Her foremost obligation was to bear children, especially male children who would preserve the family line. A wife was also to take care of her family and her house, either doing the household work herself or supervising the slaves who did the actual work (see the box on p. 116).

Women were kept under strict control. Because they were married at fourteen or fifteen, they were taught about their responsibilities early. Although many managed

Image copyright © The Metropolitan Museum of Art/Art Resource, NY

Women in the Loom Room. In Athens, women were citizens and could participate in religious cults and festivals, but they had no rights and were barred from political activity. Women were thought to belong in the house, caring for the children and the needs of the household. A principal activity of Greek women was the making of clothes. This vase shows two women working on a warp-weighted loom.

to learn and play musical instruments, they were not given any formal education. And women were expected to remain at home out of sight unless attending funerals or festivals. If they left the house, they were to be accompanied. A woman working alone in public was either poverty-stricken or not a citizen.

Male homosexuality was also a prominent feature of Athenian life. The Greek homosexual ideal was a relationship between a mature man and a young male. It is most likely that this was an aristocratic ideal and not one practiced by the common people. While the relationship was frequently physical, the Greeks also viewed it as educational. The older male (the "lover") won the love of his "beloved" through his value as a teacher and the devotion he demonstrated in training his charge. In a sense, this love relationship was seen as a way of initiating young males into the male world of political and military dominance. The Greeks did not feel that the coexistence of homosexual and heterosexual predilections created any special problems for individuals or their society.

OPPOSING VIEWPOINTS
WOMEN IN ATHENS AND SPARTA

FAMILY & SOCIETY

In Classical Athens, a woman's place was in the home. She had two major responsibilities as a wife—bearing and raising children and managing the household. In the first selection, Xenophon relates the instructions of an Athenian to his new wife. Although women in Sparta had the same responsibilities as women in Athens, they assumed somewhat different roles as a result of the Spartan lifestyle. The second, third, and fourth selections demonstrate these differences as seen in the accounts of three ancient Greek writers.

Xenophon, *Oeconomicus*

[Ischomachus addresses his new wife:] For it seems to me, dear, that the gods with great discernment have coupled together male and female, as they are called, chiefly in order that they may form a perfect partnership in mutual service. For, in the first place that the various species of living creatures may not fail, they are joined in wedlock for the production of children. Secondly, offspring to support them in old age is provided by this union, to human beings, at any rate. Thirdly, human beings live not in the open air, like beasts, but obviously need shelter. Nevertheless, those who mean to win stores to fill the covered place, have need of someone to work at the open-air occupations; since plowing, sowing, planting and grazing are all such open-air employments; and these supply the needful food. For he made the man's body and mind more capable of enduring cold and heat, and journeys and campaigns; and therefore imposed on him the outdoor tasks. To the woman, since he had made her body less capable of such endurance, I take it that God has assigned the indoor tasks. And knowing that he had created in the woman and had imposed on her the nourishment of the infants, he meted out to her a larger portion of affection for newborn babes than to the man. . . .

Your duty will be to remain indoors and send out those servants whose work is outside, and superintend those who are to work indoors, and to receive the incomings, and distribute so much of them as must be spent, and watch over so much as is to be kept in store, and take care that the sum laid by for a year be not spent in a month. And when wool is brought to you, you must see that cloaks are made for those that want them. You must see too that the dry corn is in good condition for making food. One of the duties that fall to you, however, will perhaps seem rather thankless: you will have to see that any servant who is ill is cared for.

Xenophon, *Constitution of the Spartans*

First, to begin at the beginning, I will start with the begetting of children. Elsewhere those girls who are going to have children and are considered to have been well

brought up are nourished with the plainest diet which is practicable and the smallest amount of luxury good possible; wine is certainly not allowed them at all, or only if well diluted. Just as the majority of craftsmen are sedentary, the other Greeks expect their girls to sit quietly and work wool. But how can one expect girls brought up like this to give birth to healthy babies? Lycurgus considered slave girls quite adequate to produce clothing, and thought that for free women the most important job was to bear children. In the first place, therefore, he prescribed physical training for the female sex no less than for the male; and next, just as for men, he arranged competitions of racing and strength for women also, thinking that if both parents were strong their children would be more robust.

Aristotle, *Politics*

Now, this license of the [Spartan] women, from the earliest times, was to be expected. For the men were absent from home for long periods of time on military expeditions, fighting the war against the Argives and again against the Arkadians and Messenians. . . . And nearly two-fifths of the whole country is in the hands of women, both because there have been numerous heiresses, and because large dowries are customary. And yet it would have been better to have regulated them, and given none at all or small or even moderate ones. But at present it is possible for a man to give an inheritance to whomever he chooses.

Plutarch, *Lycurgus*

Since Lycurgus regarded education as the most important and finest duty of the legislator, he began at the earliest stage by looking at matters relating to marriages and births. For he exercised the girls' bodies with races and wrestling and discus and javelin throwing, so that the embryos formed in them would have a strong start in strong bodies and develop better, and they would undergo their pregnancies with vigor and would cope well and easily with childbirth. He got rid of daintiness and sheltered upbringing and effeminacy of all kinds, by accustoming the girls no less than the young men to walking naked in processions and dancing and singing at certain festivals, when young men were present and watching. The nudity of the girls had nothing disgraceful in it for modesty was present and immorality absent, but rather it made them accustomed to simplicity and enthusiastic as to physical fitness, and gave the female sex a taste of noble spirit, in as much as they too had a share in valor and ambition.

Q *In what ways were the lifestyles of Athenian and Spartan women the same? In what ways were they different? How did the Athenian and Spartan views of the world shape their conceptions of gender and gender roles, and why were those conceptions different?*

The Rise of Macedonia and the Conquests of Alexander

Q Focus Question: How was Alexander the Great able to amass his empire, and what was his legacy?

While the Greek city-states were continuing to fight each other, to their north a new and ultimately powerful kingdom was emerging in its own right. Its people, the Macedonians, were viewed as barbarians by their southern neighbors, the Greeks. The Macedonians were mostly rural folk, organized in tribes, not city-states, and not until the end of the fifth century B.C.E. did Macedonia emerge as an important kingdom. But when Philip II (359–336 B.C.E.) came to the throne, he built an efficient army and turned Macedonia into the strongest power of the Greek world—one that was soon drawn into the conflicts among the Greeks.

The Athenians at last took notice of the new contender. Fear of Philip led them to ally with a number of other Greek states and confront the Macedonians at the Battle of Chaeronea, near Thebes, in 338 B.C.E. The Macedonian army crushed the Greeks, and Philip was now free to consolidate his control over the Greek peninsula. The Greek states were joined together in an alliance that we call the Corinthian League because they met at Corinth. All members took an oath of loyalty: "I swear by Zeus, Earth, Sun, Poseidon, Athena, Ares, and all the gods and goddesses. I will abide by the peace, and I will not break the agreements with Philip the Macedonian, nor will I take up arms with hostile intent against any one of those who abide by the oaths either by land or by sea."[12] Philip insisted that the Greek states end their bitter rivalries and cooperate with him in a war against Persia. Before Philip could undertake his invasion of Asia, however, he was assassinated, leaving the task to his son Alexander.

Alexander the Great

Alexander was only twenty when he became king of Macedonia. He was in many ways prepared to rule by his father, who had taken Alexander along on military campaigns and had given him control of the cavalry at the important battle of Chaeronea. After his father's assassination, Alexander moved quickly to assert his authority, securing the Macedonian frontiers and smothering a rebellion in Greece. He then turned to his father's dream, the invasion of the Persian Empire.

Alexander's Conquests
There is no doubt that Alexander was taking a chance in attacking the Persian Empire, which was still a strong state. In the spring of 334 B.C.E., Alexander entered Asia Minor with an army of 37,000 men. About half were Macedonians, the rest Greeks and other allies. The cavalry, which would play an important role as a striking force, numbered about 5,000.

Alexander's first confrontation with the Persians, at a battle at the Granicus River in 334 B.C.E., almost cost him his life but resulted in a major victory. By the following spring, the entire western half of Asia Minor was in Alexander's hands (see Map 4.2). Meanwhile, the Persian king, Darius III, mobilized his forces to stop Alexander's army. Although the Persian troops outnumbered Alexander's, the Battle of Issus was fought on a narrow field that canceled the advantage of superior numbers and resulted in another Macedonian success. After his victory at Issus in 333 B.C.E., Alexander turned south, and by the winter of 332, Syria, Palestine, and Egypt were under his domination. He took the traditional title of pharaoh of Egypt and founded the first of a series of cities named after him (Alexandria) as the Greek administrative capital of Egypt. It became (and remains today) one of Egypt's and the Mediterranean world's most important cities.

In 331 B.C.E., Alexander renewed his offensive, moved into the territory of the ancient Mesopotamian kingdoms, and fought a decisive battle with the Persians at Gaugamela, northwest of Babylon. After his victory,

Alexander the Great. This marble head of Alexander the Great was made in the second or first century B.C.E. The long hair and tilt of his head reflect the description of Alexander in the literary sources of the time. Alexander claimed to be descended from Heracles, a Greek hero worshiped as a god, and when he proclaimed himself pharaoh of Egypt, he gained recognition as a living deity. It is reported that one statue, now lost, showed Alexander gazing at Zeus. At the base of the statue were the words "I place the earth under my sway; you, O Zeus, keep Olympus."

© British Museum, London/HIP/Art Resource, NY

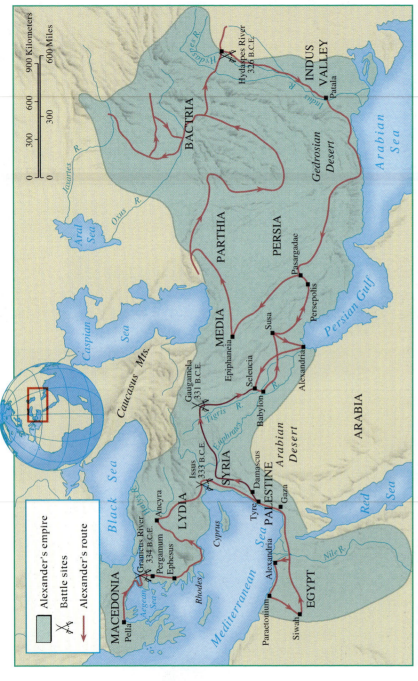

MAP 4.2 The Conquests of Alexander the Great. In just twelve years, Alexander the Great conquered vast territories. Dominating lands from west of the Nile to east of the Indus, he brought the Persian Empire, Egypt, and much of the Middle East under his control. **Q** Approximately how far did he and his troops travel during those twelve years?

Alexander entered Babylon and then proceeded to the Persian capitals at Susa and Persepolis, where he acquired the Persian treasuries and took possession of vast quantities of gold and silver. By 330, Alexander was again on the march, pursuing Darius. After Darius was killed by one of his own men, Alexander took the title and office of Great King of the Persians.

But Alexander was not content to rest with the spoils of the Persian Empire. Over the next three years, he moved east and northeast, as far as modern Pakistan. By the summer of 327 B.C.E., he had entered India, which at that time was divided into a number of warring states. In 326 B.C.E., Alexander and his armies arrived in the plains of northwestern India. At the Battle of the Hydaspes River, Alexander won a brutally fought battle (see the box on p. 120). When Alexander made clear his determination to march east to conquer more of India, his soldiers, weary of campaigning year after year, mutinied and refused to go on. Reluctantly, Alexander turned back, leading his men across the arid lands of southern Persia. Conditions in the desert were appalling; the blazing sun and lack of water led to thousands of deaths before Alexander and his remaining troops reached Babylon. Alexander planned still more campaigns, but in June 323 B.C.E., weakened from wounds, fever, and probably excessive alcohol consumption, he died at the age of thirty-two.

The Legacy of Alexander Alexander is one of the most puzzling great figures in history. Historians relying on the same sources draw vastly different pictures of him. Some portray him as an idealistic visionary and others as a ruthless Machiavellian. How did Alexander the Great view himself? We know that he sought to imitate Achilles, the warrior-hero of Homer's *Iliad*. Alexander kept a copy of the *Iliad*—and a dagger—under his pillow. He also claimed to be descended from Heracles, the Greek hero who came to be worshiped as a god.

Regardless of his ideals, motives, or views about himself, one fact stands out: Alexander ushered in a completely new age, the Hellenistic era. The word *Hellenistic* is derived from a Greek word meaning "to imitate Greeks." It is an appropriate way, then, to describe an age that saw the extension of the Greek language and ideas to the non-Greek world of the Middle East. Alexander's destruction of the Persian monarchy created opportunities for Greek engineers, intellectuals, merchants, soldiers, and administrators. Those who followed Alexander and his successors participated in a new political unity based on the principle of monarchy. His successors used force to establish military

Reign of Philip II	359–336 B.C.E.
Battle of Chaeronea; Philip II conquers Greece	338 B.C.E.
Reign of Alexander the Great	336–323 B.C.E.
Alexander invades Asia; Battle of Granicus River	334 B.C.E.
Battle of Issus	333 B.C.E.
Battle of Gaugamela	331 B.C.E.
Fall of Persepolis, the Persian capital	330 B.C.E.
Alexander enters India	327 B.C.E.
Battle of Hydaspes River	326 B.C.E.
Death of Alexander	323 B.C.E.

The World of the Hellenistic Kingdoms

Q **Focus Question:** How did the political, economic, and social institutions of the Hellenistic world differ from those of Classical Greece?

The united empire that Alexander created by his conquests disintegrated after his death. All too soon, Macedonian military leaders were engaged in a struggle for power, and by 301 B.C.E., all hope of unity was dead.

But Alexander also left a cultural legacy. As a result of his conquests, Greek language, art, architecture, and literature spread throughout the Middle East. The urban centers of the Hellenistic age, many founded by Alexander and his successors, became springboards for the diffusion of Greek culture. While the Greeks spread their culture in the east, they were also inevitably influenced by eastern ways. Thus Alexander's legacy created one of the basic characteristics of the Hellenistic world: the clash and fusion of different cultures.

monarchies that dominated the Hellenistic world after his death. Autocratic power became a regular feature of those Hellenistic monarchies and was part of Alexander's political legacy to the Hellenistic world. His vision of empire no doubt inspired the Romans, who were, of course, the real heirs of Alexander's legacy.

Hellenistic Monarchies

Eventually, four Hellenistic kingdoms emerged as the successors to Alexander (see Map 4.3 on p. 122). In Macedonia, the struggle for power led to the extermination of Alexander the Great's dynasty. Not until 276 B.C.E. did Antigonus Gonatas, the grandson of one of Alexander's generals, succeed in establishing the Antigonid dynasty as rulers of Macedonia and Greece. Another

Hellenistic kingdom emerged in Egypt, where a Macedonian general named Ptolemy established himself as king in 305 B.C.E., initiating the Ptolemaic dynasty of pharaohs. A third Hellenistic kingdom came into being in 230 B.C.E., when Attalus I declared himself king of Pergamum in Asia Minor and established the Attalid dynasty.

The Seleucid Kingdom and India
By far the largest of the Hellenistic kingdoms was founded by the general Seleucus, who established the Seleucid dynasty of Syria, which controlled much of the old Persian Empire from Turkey in the west to India in the east. The Seleucids, however, found it increasingly difficult to maintain control of the eastern territories. In fact, the Indian ruler Chandragupta Maurya created a new Indian state, the Mauryan Empire, in 324 B.C.E. (see Chapter 2) and drove out the Seleucid forces. His grandson Ashoka extended the empire to include most of India. A pious Buddhist, Ashoka sought to convert the remaining Greek communities in northwestern India to his religion.

The Seleucid rulers maintained relations with the Mauryan Empire. Trade was fostered, especially in such luxuries as spices and jewels. Seleucus also sent Greek and Macedonian ambassadors to the Mauryan court. Best known of these was Megasthenes, whose report on the people of India remained one of the West's best sources of information until the Middle Ages.

Political Institutions

The Hellenistic monarchies created a semblance of stability for several centuries, even though Hellenistic kings refused to accept the status quo and periodically engaged in wars to alter it. At the same time, an underlying strain always existed between the new Greco-Macedonian ruling class and the native populations. Together these factors created a certain degree of tension that was never truly ended until the Roman state stepped in and imposed a new order.

Although Alexander the Great had apparently planned to fuse Greeks and easterners—he used Persians as administrators, encouraged his soldiers to marry easterners, and did so himself—Hellenistic monarchs who succeeded him relied primarily on Greeks and Macedonians to form the new ruling class. Even those easterners who did advance to important administrative posts had learned Greek (all government business was transacted in Greek) and had become Hellenized in a cultural sense. The Greek ruling class was determined to maintain its privileged position.

Hellenistic Cities

Cities played an especially important role in the Hellenistic kingdoms. Throughout his conquests, Alexander had founded new cities and military settlements, and Hellenistic kings did likewise. The new population centers varied considerably in size and importance. Military settlements were meant to maintain order and might consist of only a few hundred men strongly dependent on

Alexander Meets an Indian King

POLITICS & GOVERNMENT

In his campaigns in India, Alexander fought a number of difficult battles. At the Battle of the Hydaspes River, he faced a strong opponent in the Indian king Porus. After defeating Porus, Alexander treated him with respect, according to Arrian, Alexander's ancient biographer.

Arrian, *The Campaigns of Alexander*

Throughout the action Porus had proved himself a man indeed, not only as a commander but as a soldier of the truest courage. When he saw his cavalry cut to pieces, most of his infantry dead, and his elephants killed or roaming riderless and bewildered about the field, his behaviour was very different from that of the Persian King Darius: unlike Darius, he did not lead the scramble to save his own skin, but so long as a single unit of his men held together, fought bravely on. It was only when he was himself wounded that he turned the elephant on which he rode and began to withdraw…. Alexander, anxious to save the life of this great soldier, sent … [to him] an Indian named Meroes, a man he had been told had long been Porus's friend. Porus listened to Meroes's message, stopped his elephant, and dismounted; he was much distressed by thirst, so when he had revived himself by drinking, he told Meroes to conduct him with all speed to Alexander.

Alexander, informed of his approach, rode out to meet him…. When they met, he reined in his horse, and looked at his adversary with admiration: he was a magnificent figure of a man, over seven feet high and of great personal beauty; his bearing had lost none of its pride; his air was of one brave man meeting another, of a king in the presence of a king, with whom he had fought honourably for his kingdom.

Alexander was the first to speak. "What," he said, "do you wish that I should do with you?" "Treat me as a king ought," Porus is said to have replied. "For my part," said Alexander, pleased by his answer, "your request shall be granted. But is there not something you would wish for yourself? Ask it." "Everything," said Porus, "is contained in this one request."

The dignity of these words gave Alexander even more pleasure, and he restored to Porus his sovereignty over his subjects, adding to his realm other territory of even greater extent. Thus he did indeed use a brave man as a king ought, and from that time forward found him in every way a loyal friend.

Q *What do we learn from Arrian's account about Alexander's military skills and Indian methods of fighting?*

---

the king. But there were also new independent cities with thousands of inhabitants. Alexandria in Egypt was the largest city in the Mediterranean region by the first century B.C.E. Seleucus was especially active in founding new cities, according to one ancient writer:

The other kings have exulted in destroying existing cities; he, on the other hand, arranged to build cities which did not yet exist. He established so many … that they were enough to carry the names of towns in Macedonia as well as the names of those in his family…. One can go to Phoenicia to see his cities; one can go to Syria and see even more.[13]

Hellenistic rulers encouraged a massive spread of Greek colonists to the Middle East because of their intrinsic value to the new monarchies. Greeks (and Macedonians) provided not only recruits for the army but also a pool of civilian administrators and workers who contributed to economic development. Even architects, engineers, dramatists, and actors were in demand in the new Greek cities. Many Greeks and Macedonians were quick to see the advantages of moving to the new urban centers and gladly sought their fortunes in the Middle East. The Greek cities of the Hellenistic era were the chief agents in the spread of Greek culture in the Middle East—as far, in fact, as modern Afghanistan and India.

The Greeks' belief in their own cultural superiority provided an easy rationalization for their political dominance of the eastern cities. But Greek control of the new

cities was also necessary because the kings frequently used the cities as instruments of government, enabling them to rule considerable territory without an extensive bureaucracy. At the same time, for security reasons, the Greeks needed the support of the kings. After all, the Hellenistic cities were islands of Greek culture in a sea of non-Greeks.

The Importance of Trade

Agriculture was still of primary importance to both the native populations and the new Greek cities of the Hellenistic world. The Greek cities continued their old agrarian patterns. A well-defined citizen body owned land and worked it with the assistance of slaves. But these farms were isolated units in a vast area of land ultimately owned by the king or assigned to large estate owners and worked by native peasants dwelling in villages.

Commerce experienced considerable expansion in the Hellenistic era. Indeed, trading contacts linked much of the Hellenistic world. The decline in the number of political barriers encouraged more commercial traffic. Although Hellenistic monarchs still fought wars, the conquests of Alexander and the policies of his successors made possible greater trade between east and west. Two major trade routes connected the east with the Mediterranean. The central route was the major one and led by sea from India to the Persian Gulf, up the Tigris River to Seleucia on the Tigris. Overland routes from Seleucia then led to Antioch and

Alexander is a product of director Oliver Stone's lifelong fascination with Alexander, the king of Macedonia who conquered the Persian Empire in the fourth century B.C.E. and launched the Hellenistic era. Stone's epic film cost $150 million, which resulted in an elaborate and in places visually beautiful film that attempts to tell the story of Alexander's short life in a variety of scenes. Narrated by the aging Ptolemy (Anthony Hopkins), one of Alexander's Macedonian generals who took control of Egypt after his death, the film tells the life of Alexander (Colin Farrell) through an intermix of battle scenes, scenes showing the progress of Alexander and his army through the Middle East and India, and flashbacks from his early years. Stone portrays Alexander's relationship with his mother, Olympias (Angelina Jolie), as instrumental in his early development while also focusing on his rocky relationship with his father, King Philip II (Val Kilmer). The movie elaborates on the major battle at Gaugamela in 331 B.C.E., where the Persian leader Darius is forced to flee, and then follows Alexander as he conquers the rest of the Persian Empire and continues east into India. After his troops begin to mutiny, Alexander returns to the Persian capital of Babylon, where he dies on June 10, 323 B.C.E.

The enormous amount of money spent on the film enabled Stone to achieve a stunning visual spectacle, but as history, the film leaves much to be desired. The character of Alexander is never developed in depth. He is shown at times as a weak character who is plagued by doubts over his own decisions and often seems obsessed with his desire for glory. Alexander is also portrayed as an idealistic leader who believed that the people he conquered wanted change, that he was "freeing the people of the world," and that Asia and Europe would grow together into a single entity. But was Alexander an idealistic dreamer, as Stone apparently believes, or was he a military leader who, following the dictum that "fortune favors the bold," ran roughshod over the wishes of his soldiers in order to follow his dream and was responsible for mass slaughter in the process? The latter is a perspective that Stone glosses over, but Ptolemy, at least, probably expresses the more

realistic notion that "none of us believed in his dream." The movie also does not elaborate on Alexander's wish to be a god. Certainly, Alexander aspired to divine honors; at one point he sent instructions to the Greek cities to "vote him a god." Stone's portrayal of Alexander is perhaps most realistic in presenting Alexander's drinking binges and his bisexuality, which was common in the Greco-Roman world. His marriage to Roxane (Rosario Dawson), daughter of a Bactrian noble, is shown, as well as his love for his lifelong companion, Hephaestion (Jared Leto), and his sexual relationship with the Persian male slave Bagoas (Francisco Bosch).

The film contains a number of inaccurate historical details. Alexander's first encounters with the Persian royal princesses and Bagoas did not occur when he entered Babylon for the first time. Alexander did not kill Cleitas in India, and he was not wounded in India at the Battle of Hydaspes but at the siege of Malli. Specialists in Persian history have also argued that Persian military forces were much more disciplined than they are shown in the film.

Alexander (Colin Farrell) reviewing his troops before the Battle of Gaugamela.

Warner Bros./The Kobal Collection/Jaap Buitendijk

Ephesus. A southern route wound its ways from India by sea but went around Arabia and up the Red Sea to Petra and later Berenice. Caravan routes then led overland to Coptos on the Nile, thence to Alexandria and the Mediterranean.

An incredible variety of products were traded: gold and silver from Spain; salt from Asia Minor; timber from Macedonia; ebony, gems, ivory, and spices from India; frankincense (used on altars) from Arabia; slaves from Thrace, Syria, and Asia Minor; fine wines from Syria and western Asia Minor; olive oil from Athens; and numerous exquisite foodstuffs, such as the famous prunes of Damascus. The greatest trade, however, was in the basic staple of life—grain.

Social Life: New Opportunities for Women

One of the noticeable features of social life in the Hellenistic world was the emergence of new opportunities for women—at least, for upper-class women—especially in the economic realm. Documents show increasing numbers of women involved in managing slaves, selling property, and

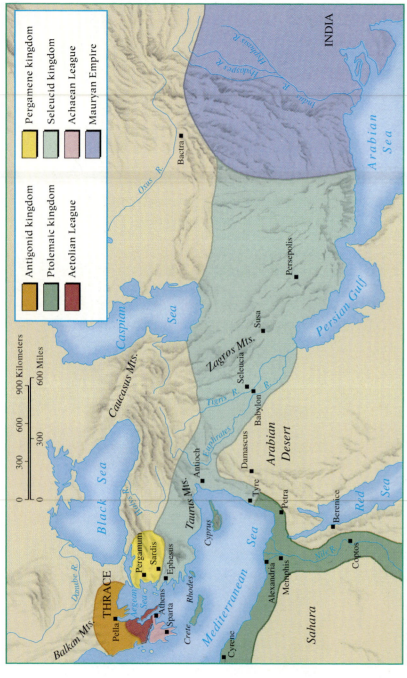

MAP 4.3 **The World of the Hellenistic Kingdoms.** Alexander died unexpectedly at the age of thirty-two and did not designate a successor. Upon his death, his generals struggled for power, eventually establishing four monarchies that spread Hellenistic culture and fostered trade and economic development.

Q Which kingdom encompassed most of the old Persian Empire?

making loans. Even then, legal contracts in which women were involved had to include their official male guardians. Only in Sparta were women free to control their own economic affairs. Many Spartan women were noticeably wealthy; females owned 40 percent of Spartan land.

Spartan women, however, were an exception, especially on the Greek mainland. Women in Athens, for example, still remained highly restricted and supervised. Although a few philosophers welcomed female participation in men's affairs, many philosophers rejected equality between men and women and asserted that the traditional roles of wives and mothers were most satisfying for women.

But the opinions of philosophers did not prevent upper-class women from making gains in areas other than the economic sphere (see the box on p. 123). New possibilities for females arose when women in some areas of the Hellenistic world were allowed to pursue education in the traditional fields of literature, music, and even athletics. Education, then, provided new opportunities for women: female poets appeared in the third century B.C.E., and there are instances of women involved in both scholarly and artistic activities.

The creation of the Hellenistic monarchies, which represented a considerable departure from the world of the city-state, also gave new scope to the role played by the monarchs' wives, the Hellenistic queens. In Macedonia, a

pattern of alliances between mothers and sons provided openings for women to take an active role in politics, especially in political intrigue. In Egypt, opportunities for royal women were even greater because the Ptolemaic rulers reverted to an Egyptian custom of kings marrying their own sisters. Of the first eight Ptolemaic rulers, four wed their sisters. Ptolemy II and his sister-wife Arsinoë II were both worshiped as gods in their lifetimes. Arsinoë played an energetic role in government and was involved in the expansion of the Egyptian navy. She was also the first Egyptian queen whose portrait appeared on coins with that of her husband.

Culture in the Hellenistic World

Although the Hellenistic kingdoms encompassed vast territories and many diverse peoples, a sense of unity resulted from the diffusion of Greek culture. The Hellenistic era was a period of considerable accomplishment in many areas—literature, art, science, and philosophy. Although these achievements occurred throughout the Hellenistic world, certain centers, especially the great cities of Alexandria and Pergamum, stood out. In both cities, cultural developments were encouraged by the rulers themselves. Rich Hellenistic monarchs had considerable resources with which to patronize culture.

FAMILY & SOCIETY

Upper-class women in Hellenistic society enjoyed noticeable gains, and even in the lives of ordinary women, a new assertiveness came to the fore despite the continuing domination of society by men. The first selection is taken from the letter of a wife to her husband, complaining about his failure to return home. In the second selection, a father complains that his daughter has abandoned him, contrary to an Egyptian law providing that children who have been properly raised should support their parents.

Letter from Isias to Hephaistion, 168 B.C.E.

If you are well and other things are going right, it would accord with the prayer that I make continually to the gods. I myself and the child and all the household are in good health and think of you always. When I received your letter from Horos, in which you announce that you are in detention in the Serapeum at Memphis, for the news that you are well I straightway thanked the gods, but about your not coming home, when all the others who had been secluded there have come, I am ill-pleased, because after having piloted myself and your child through such bad times and been driven to every extremity owing to the price of wheat, I thought that now at least, with you at home, I should enjoy some respite, whereas you have not even thought of coming home nor given any regard to our circumstances, remembering how I was in want of everything while you were still here, not to mention this long lapse of time and these critical days, during which you have sent us nothing. As, moreover, Horos who delivered the letter has brought news of your having been released from detention, I am thoroughly ill-pleased. Notwithstanding, as your mother also is annoyed, for her sake as well as for mine please return to the city, if nothing more pressing holds you back. You will do me a favor by taking care of your bodily health. Farewell.

Letter from Kiesikles to King Ptolemy, 220 B.C.E.

I am wronged by Dionysios and by Nike my daughter. For though I raised her, my own daughter, and educated her and brought her to maturity, when I was stricken with bodily ill-health and was losing my eyesight, she was not minded to furnish me with any of the necessities of life. When I sought to obtain justice from her in Alexandria, she begged my pardon, and in the eighteenth year she swore me a written royal oath to give me each month twenty drachmas, which she was to earn by her own bodily labor.... But now corrupted by Dionysios, who is a comic actor, she does not do for me anything of what was in the written oath, despising my weakness and ill-health. I beg you, therefore, O king, not to allow me to be wronged by my daughter and by Dionysios the actor who corrupted her, but to order Diophanes the strategus [a provincial administrator] to summon them and hear us out; and if I am speaking the truth, let Diophanes deal with her corrupter as seems good to him and compel my daughter Nike to do justice to me. If this is done I shall no longer be wronged but by fleeing to you, O king, I shall obtain justice.

Q *What specific complaints are contained in each letter? What do these complaints reveal about some women in the Hellenistic world? Judging by the content of these letters, what freedoms did Hellenistic women enjoy? How autonomous were they? Based on your knowledge of gender and gender roles in shaping earlier cultures, how did Hellenistic civilization differ in its conceptions of what was "proper" for men and women?*

New Directions in Literature and Art

The Hellenistic age produced an enormous quantity of literature, most of which has not survived. Hellenistic monarchs, who held literary talent in high esteem, subsidized writers on a grand scale. The Ptolemaic rulers of Egypt were particularly lavish. The combination of their largesse and a famous library with over 500,000 scrolls drew a host of scholars and authors to Alexandria, including a circle of poets. Theocritus (c. 315–250 B.C.E.), originally a native of the island of Sicily, wrote "little poems" known as *idylls* dealing with erotic subjects, lovers' complaints, and pastoral themes expressing love of nature and appreciation of nature's beauties.

In the Hellenistic era, Athens remained the theatrical center of the Greek world. Tragedy had fallen by the wayside, but a new style of comedy came to the fore. New Comedy completely rejected political themes and sought only to entertain and amuse. The Athenian playwright Menander (c. 342–291 B.C.E.) was perhaps the best representative of New Comedy. Plots were simple: typically, a hero falls in love with a not-really-so-bad prostitute, who turns out eventually to be the long-lost daughter of a rich neighbor. The hero marries her, and they live happily ever after.

In addition to being patrons of literary talent, the Hellenistic monarchs were eager to beautify and adorn the cities within their states. The founding of new cities and the rebuilding of old ones provided numerous opportunities for Greek architects and sculptors. The buildings of the Greek homeland—gymnasia, baths, theaters, and of course temples—lined the streets of these cities.

Both Hellenistic monarchs and rich citizens patronized sculptors. Thousands of statues, many paid for by the people honored, were erected in towns and cities all over the Hellenistic world. Sculptors traveled throughout this world, attracted by the material rewards offered by wealthy patrons. As a result, Hellenistic sculpture was characterized by a considerable degree of uniformity. Hellenistic artistic

the earth was at the center of the universe. Another astronomer, Eratosthenes (c. 275–194 B.C.E.), determined that the earth was round and calculated its circumference at 24,675 miles—within 200 miles of the actual figure.

A third Alexandrian scholar was Euclid, who lived around 300 B.C.E. He established a school in Alexandria but is primarily known for his work titled *Elements*. This was a systematic organization of the fundamental elements of geometry as they had already been worked out; it became the standard textbook of plane geometry and was used up to modern times.

By far the most famous scientist of the period was Archimedes (287–212 B.C.E.) of Syracuse. Archimedes was especially important for his work on the geometry of spheres and cylinders and for establishing the value of the mathematical constant pi. Archimedes was also a practical inventor. He may have devised the so-called Archimedean screw, used to pump water out of mines and to lift irrigation water, as well as a compound pulley for transporting heavy weights. During the Roman siege of Syracuse, he constructed a number of devices to thwart the attackers. According to Plutarch's account, the Romans became so frightened "that if they did but see a little rope or a piece of wood from the wall, instantly crying out, that there it was again, Archimedes was about to let fly some engine at them, they turned their backs and fled."[14] Archimedes' accomplishments inspired a wealth of semilegendary stories. Supposedly, he discovered specific gravity by observing the water he displaced in his bath and became so excited by his realization that he jumped out of the water and ran home naked, shouting, "*Eureka!*" ("I have found it!"). He is said to have emphasized the importance of levers by proclaiming to the king of Syracuse, "Give me a lever and a place to stand, and I will move the earth." The king was so impressed that he encouraged Archimedes to lower his sights and build defensive weapons instead.

Philosophy: New Schools of Thought   While Alexandria and Pergamum became the renowned cultural centers of the Hellenistic world, Athens remained the prime center for philosophy. After Alexander the Great, the home of Socrates, Plato, and Aristotle continued to attract the most illustrious philosophers from the Greek world, who chose to establish their schools there. New schools of philosophical thought reinforced Athens's reputation as a philosophical center.

Epicurus (341–270 B.C.E.), the founder of **Epicureanism,** established a school in Athens near the end of the fourth century B.C.E. Epicurus believed that human beings were free to follow self-interest as a basic motivating force. Happiness was the goal of life, and the means to achieve it was the pursuit of pleasure, the only true good. But the pursuit of pleasure was not meant in a physical, hedonistic sense (which is what our word *epicurean* has come to mean). Pleasure was not satisfying one's desire in an active, gluttonous fashion but rather freedom from emotional turmoil, freedom from worry—the freedom that came from a mind at rest. To achieve this kind of pleasure, one had to free oneself from public

Old Market Woman. No longer interested in capturing ideal beauty in their work as they had in Classical Greek times, sculptors in the Hellenistic era moved toward a more emotional and realistic art. This statue of an old market woman is typical of this trend. She is seen carrying chickens and a basket of fruit. Haggard and mired in poverty, she struggles just to go on living.

Image copyright © The Metropolitan Museum of Art/Art Resource, NY

styles even affected artists in India (see the comparative illustration on p. 125). While maintaining the technical skill of the Classical period, Hellenistic sculptors moved away from the idealism of fifth-century classicism to a more emotional and realistic art, seen in numerous statues of old women, drunks, and little children at play.

A Golden Age of Science   The Hellenistic era witnessed a more conscious separation of science from philosophy. In Classical Greece, what we would call the physical and life sciences had been divisions of philosophical inquiry. Nevertheless, by the time of Aristotle, the Greeks had already established an important principle of scientific investigation: empirical research, or systematic observation as the basis for generalization. In the Hellenistic age, the sciences tended to be studied in their own right.

One of the traditional areas of Greek science was astronomy, and two Alexandrian scholars continued this exploration. Aristarchus of Samos (c. 310–230 B.C.E.) developed a *heliocentric* view of the universe, contending that the sun and the fixed stars remain stationary while the earth rotates around the sun in a circular orbit. He also argued that the earth rotates around its own axis. This view was not widely accepted, and most scholars clung to the earlier *geocentric* view of the Greeks, which held that

The Art Archive/Gianni Dagli Orti

Hellenistic Sculpture and a Greek-Style Buddha. Greek architects and sculptors were highly valued throughout the Hellenistic world. Shown on the left is a terra-cotta statuette of a draped young woman, made as a tomb offering near Thebes, probably around 300 B.C.E. The incursion of Alexander into the western part of India resulted in some Greek cultural influences there, especially during the Hellenistic era. During the first century B.C.E., Indian sculptors in Gandhara, which is today part of Pakistan, began to make statues of the Buddha. The Buddhist Gandharan style combined Indian and Hellenistic artistic traditions, which is evident in the stone sculpture of the Buddha on the right. Note the wavy hair topped by a bun tied with a ribbon, also a feature of earlier statues of Greek deities. This Buddha is also seen wearing a Greek-style toga.

Q How would you explain the impact of Hellenistic sculpture on India? What would you conclude from this example about the influence of conquerors on conquered people?

© Borromeo/Art Resource, NY

affairs and politics. But this was not a renunciation of all social life, for to Epicurus, a life could be complete only when it was based on friendship. Epicurus' own life in Athens was an embodiment of his teachings. He and his friends created their own private community where they could pursue their ideal of true happiness.

Another school of thought was **Stoicism**, which became the most popular philosophy of the Hellenistic world and later flourished in the Roman Empire as well. It was the product of a teacher named Zeno (335–263 B.C.E.), who came to Athens and began to teach in a public colonnade known as the Painted Portico (the *Stoa Poikile*—hence the name Stoicism.). Like Epicureanism, Stoicism was concerned with how individuals find happiness. But

Stoics took a radically different approach to the problem. To them, happiness, the supreme good, could be found only by living in harmony with the divine will, by which people gained inner peace (see the box on p. 126). Life's problems could not disturb these people, and they could bear whatever life offered (hence our word *stoic*). Unlike Epicureans, Stoics did not believe in the need to separate oneself from the world and politics. Public service was regarded as noble, and the real Stoic was a good citizen and could even be a good government official.

Both Epicureanism and Stoicism focused primarily on human happiness, and their popularity would suggest a fundamental change in the Greek lifestyle. In the Classical Greek world, the happiness of individuals and the meaning of life were closely associated with the life of the *polis*. One found fulfillment in the community. In the Hellenistic kingdoms, the sense that one could find satisfaction and fulfillment through life in the *polis* had weakened. People sought new philosophies that offered personal happiness, and in the cosmopolitan world of the Hellenistic states, with their mixture of peoples, a new openness to thoughts of universality could also emerge. For some people, Stoicism embodied this larger sense of community. The appeal of new philosophies in the Hellenistic era can also be explained by the apparent decline in certain aspects of traditional religion.

Religion in the Hellenistic World When the Greeks spread throughout the Hellenistic kingdoms, they took their gods with them. But over a period of time, there was a noticeable decline in the vitality of the traditional Greek religion, which left Greeks receptive to the numerous reli-

gious cults of the eastern world. The eastern religions that appealed most to Greeks, however, were the **mystery religions**. What was the source of their attraction?

Mystery cults, with their secret initiations and promises of individual salvation, were not new to the Greek world. But the Greeks of the Hellenistic era were also strongly influenced by eastern mystery cults, such as those of Egypt, which offered a distinct advantage over the Greek mystery religions. The latter had usually been connected to specific locations (such as Eleusis), which meant that a would-be initiate had to undertake a pilgrimage in order to participate in the rites. In contrast, the eastern mystery religions were readily available since temples to their gods and goddesses were located

RELIGION & PHILOSOPHY

The Stoic Ideal of Harmony with God

The Stoic Cleanthes (331–232 B.C.E.) succeeded Zeno as head of this school of philosophy. One historian of Hellenistic civilization has called this work by Cleanthes the greatest religious hymn in Greece. Certainly, it demonstrates that Stoicism, unlike Epicureanism, did have an underlying spiritual foundation. This poem has been compared to the great psalms of the Hebrews.

Cleanthes, *Hymn to Zeus*

Nothing occurs on the earth apart from you, O God,
nor in the heavenly regions nor on the sea, except
what bad men do in their folly; but you know
how to make the odd even, and to harmonize
what is dissonant; to you the alien is akin.
And so you have wrought together into one all
things that are good and bad.
So that there arises one eternal logos [rationale] of
all things,
Which all bad mortals shun and ignore,
Unhappy wretches, ever seeking the possession of
good things
They neither see nor hear the universal law of God,
By obeying which they might enjoy a happy life.

Q *Based on Cleanthes' poem, what are some of the beliefs of the Stoics? How do they differ from Epicureanism?*

---

throughout the Greek cities of the east. All of the mystery religions were based on the same fundamental premises. Individuals could pursue a path to salvation and achieve eternal life by being initiated into a union with a savior god or goddess who had died and risen again.

The Egyptian cult of Isis was one of the most popular of the mystery religions. Isis was the goddess of women, marriage, and children; as one of her hymns states, "I am she whom women call goddess. I ordained that women should be loved by men: I brought wife and husband together, and invented the marriage contract. I ordained that women should bear children."[15] Isis was also portrayed as the giver of civilization, who had brought laws and letters to all humankind. The cult of Isis offered a precious commodity to its initiates—the promise of eternal life. In many ways, the cult of Isis and the other mystery religions of the Hellenistic era helped pave the way for Christianity.

CONCLUSION

Unlike the great centralized empires of the Persians and the Chinese, ancient Greece consisted of a large number of small, independent city-states, most of which had populations of only a few thousand. Despite the small size of their city-states, these ancient Greeks created a civilization that was the fountainhead of Western culture. Socrates, Plato, and Aristotle established the foundations of Western philosophy. Western literary forms are largely derived from Greek poetry and drama. Greek notions of harmony, proportion, and beauty have remained the touchstones for all subsequent Western art. A rational method of inquiry, so important to modern science, was conceived in ancient Greece. Many political terms are Greek in origin, and so are concepts of the rights and duties of citizenship, especially as they were conceived in Athens, the first great democracy. Especially during the Classical period, the Greeks raised and debated the fundamental questions about the purpose of human existence, the structure of human society, and the nature of the universe that have concerned thinkers ever since.

All of these achievements came from a group of small city-states in ancient Greece. And yet there remains an element of tragedy about Greek civilization. For all of their brilliant accomplishments, the Greeks were unable to rise above the divisions and rivalries that caused them to fight each other and undermine their own civilization. Of course, their cultural contributions have outlived their political struggles. And the Hellenistic era, which emerged after the Greek city-states had lost their independence, made possible the spread of Greek ideas to larger areas.

The Hellenistic period was a vibrant one. New cities arose and flourished. New philosophical ideas captured the minds of many. Significant achievements were made in art, literature, and science. Greek culture spread throughout the Middle East and made an impact wherever it was carried. But serious problems remained. Hellenistic rulers continued to engage in inconclusive wars. Much of the formal culture was the special preserve of the Greek conquerors, whose attitude of superiority kept them largely separated from the native masses of the Hellenistic kingdoms. Although the Hellenistic world achieved a degree of political stability, by the late third century B.C.E., signs of decline were beginning to multiply. Some of the more farsighted leaders perhaps realized the danger the growing power of Rome presented to the Hellenistic world. The Romans would ultimately inherit Alexander's empire and Greek culture, and we now turn to them to try to understand what made them such successful conquerors.

TIMELINE

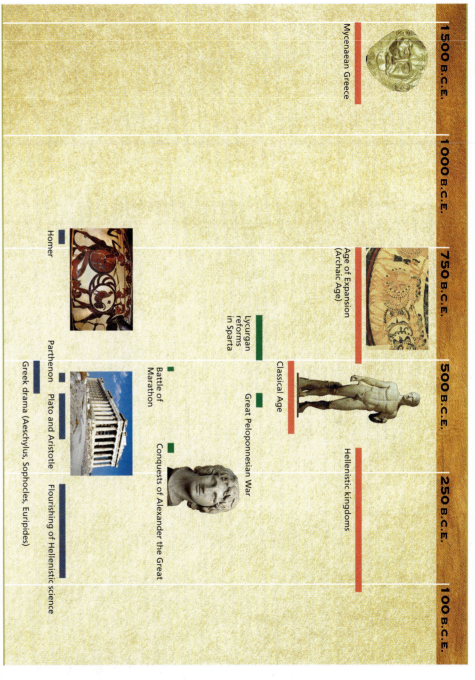

| 1500 B.C.E. | 1000 B.C.E. | 750 B.C.E. | 500 B.C.E. | 250 B.C.E. | 100 B.C.E. |

Mycenaean Greece

Age of Expansion (Archaic Age)

Homer

Lycurgan reforms in Sparta

Classical Age

Battle of Marathon

Great Peloponnesian War

Hellenistic kingdoms

Conquests of Alexander the Great

Parthenon

Plato and Aristotle

Flourishing of Hellenistic science

Greek drama (Aeschylus, Sophocles, Euripides)

CHAPTER NOTES

1. Homer, *Odyssey*, trans. E. V. Rieu (New York, 1959), p. 337.
2. Xenophon, *Symposium*, trans. O. J. Todd (New York, 1946), III, 5.
3. Homer, *Odyssey*, pp. 290–291.
4. Quoted in T. R. Martin, *Ancient Greece* (New Haven, Conn., 1996), p. 62.
5. Quoted in V. D. Hanson, *The Wars of the Ancient Greeks*, rev. ed. (London, 2006), p. 14.
6. These words from Plutarch are quoted in E. Fantham et al., *Women in the Classical World* (New York, 1994), p. 64.
7. Thucydides, *The Peloponnesian War*, trans. R. Warner (New York, 1954), p. 24.
8. Sophocles, *Oedipus the King*, trans. D. Grene (Chicago, 1959), pp. 68–69.
9. Sophocles, *Antigone*, trans. D. Taylor (London, 1986), p. 146.
10. Plato, *The Republic*, trans. F. M. Cornford (New York, 1945), pp. 178–179.
11. Quotations from Aristotle are in S. Blundell, *Women in Ancient Greece* (Cambridge, Mass., 1995), pp. 106, 186.
12. Quoted in S. B. Pomeroy et al., *Ancient Greece: A Political, Social, and Cultural History* (Oxford, 1999), p. 390.
13. Quoted in G. Shipley, *The Greek World After Alexander, 323–30 B.C.* (London, 2000), p. 304.
14. Plutarch, *Life of Marcellus*, trans. J. Dryden (New York, n.d.), p. 378.
15. Quoted in W. W. Tarn, *Hellenistic Civilization* (London, 1930), p. 324.

SUGGESTED READING

General Works

For a brief illustrated introduction to Greek history, see **J. Camp and E. Fisher, The World of the Ancient Greeks** (London, 2002). Good general introductions to Greek history include *The Oxford History of the Classical World*, ed. **J. Boardman, J. Griffin, and O. Murray** (Oxford, 1986), pp. 19–314; **T. R. Martin,** *Ancient Greece* (New Haven, Conn., 1996); **P. Cartledge,** *The Cambridge Illustrated History of Ancient Greece* (Cambridge, 1998); and **S. B. Pomeroy et al.,** *Ancient Greece: A Political, Social, and Cultural History* (New York, 1998). On the Greek way of war, see **V. D. Hanson, The Wars of the Ancient Greeks,** rev. ed. (London, 2006).

Early Greek History

Early Greek history is examined in **O. Murray, Early Greece,** 2d ed. (Cambridge, Mass., 1993); **J. L. Fitton, The Discovery of the Greek Bronze Age** (Cambridge, 1995); and **J. Hall, History of the Archaic Greek World, c. 1200–479 B.C.** (London, 2006). On colonization, see **J. Boardman, The Greeks Overseas,** rev. ed. (Baltimore, 1980). On tyranny, see **J. F. McGlew,**

CONCLUSION 127

Tyranny and Political Culture in Ancient Greece (Ithaca, N.Y., 1993). On Sparta, see P. Cartledge, *Spartan Reflections* (Berkeley, Calif., 2001) and *The Spartans* (New York, 2003). On early Athens, see the still valuable A. Jones, *Athenian Democracy* (London, 1957), and R. Osborne, *Demos* (Oxford, 1985). The Persian Wars are examined in P. Green, *The Greco-Persian Wars* (Berkeley, Calif., 1996).

Classical Greece A general history of Classical Greece can be found in P. J. Rhodes, *A History of the Greek Classical World, 478–323 B.C.* (London, 2006). Important works on Athens include C. W. Fornara and L. J. Samons II, *Athens from Cleisthenes to Pericles* (Berkeley, Calif., 1991); D. Stockton, *The Classical Athenian Democracy* (Oxford, 1990); and D. Kagan, *Pericles of Athens and the Birth of Democracy* (New York, 1991). There is also a good collection of essays in P. J. Rhodes, ed., *Athenian Democracy* (New York, 2004). On the development of the Athenian empire, see M. F. McGregor, *The Athenians and Their Empire* (Vancouver, 1987). The best way to examine the Great Peloponnesian War is to read the work of Thucydides, *History of the Peloponnesian War*, trans. R. Warner (Harmondsworth, England, 1954). Recent accounts include J. F. F. Lazenby, *The Peloponnesian War* (New York, 2004), and D. Kagan, *The Peloponnesian War* (New York, 2003).

Greek Culture For a history of Greek art, see M. Fullerton, *Greek Art* (Cambridge, 2000). On sculpture, see A. Stewart, *Greek Sculpture: An Exploration* (New Haven, Conn., 1990). On Greek drama, see the general work by J. De Romilly, *A Short History of Greek Literature* (Chicago, 1985). On Greek philosophy, a detailed study is available in W. K. C. Guthrie, *A History of Greek Philosophy*, 6 vols. (Cambridge, 1962–1981). On Greek religion, see J. N. Bremmer, *Greek Religion* (Oxford, 1994). On athletic competitions, see S. G. Miller, *Ancient Greek Athletics* (New Haven, Conn., 2004).

Family and Women On the family and women, see C. B. Patterson, *The Family in Greek History* (New York, 1998); P. Brule, *Women of Ancient Greece*, trans. A. Nevill (Edinburgh, 2004); and S. Blundell, *Women in Ancient Greece* (Cambridge, Mass., 1995).

General Works on the Hellenistic Era For a general introduction, see P. Green, *The Hellenistic Age: A Short History* (New York, 2007). The best general surveys of the Hellenistic era are F. W. Walbank, *The Hellenistic World*, rev. ed. (Cambridge, Mass., 2006), and G. Shipley, *The Greek World After Alexander, 323–30 B.C.* (New York, 2000). For a good introduction to the early history of Macedonia, see E. N. Borza, *In the Shadow of Olympus: The Emergence of Macedon* (Princeton, N.J., 1990). There are considerable differences of opinion about Alexander the Great. Good biographies include R. L. Fox, *Alexander the Great* (London, 1973); P. Cartledge, *Alexander the Great* (New York, 2004); N. G. L. Hammond, *The Genius of Alexander the Great* (Chapel Hill, N.C., 1997); G. M. Rogers, *Alexander* (New York, 2004); and P. Green, *Alexander of Macedon* (Berkeley, Calif., 1991).

Hellenistic Monarchies The various Hellenistic monarchies can be examined in N. G. L. Hammond and F. W. Walbank, *A History of Macedonia*, vol. 3, *336–167 B.C.* (Oxford, 1988); S. Sherwin-White and A. Kuhrt, *From Samarkand to Sardis: A New Approach to the Seleucid Empire* (Berkeley, Calif., 1993); and N. Lewis, *Greeks in Ptolemaic Egypt* (Oxford, 1986). See also the collection of essays in C. Habicht, *Hellenistic Monarchies* (Ann Arbor, Mich., 2006). On economic and social trends, see the classic and still indispensable M. I. Rostovtzeff, *Social and Economic History of the Hellenistic World*, 3 vols, 2d ed. (Oxford, 1953). Hellenistic women are examined in two works by S. B. Pomeroy, *Goddesses, Whores, Wives, and Slaves: Women in Classical Antiquity* (New York, 1975) and *Women in Hellenistic Egypt* (New York, 1984).

Hellenistic Culture For a general introduction to Hellenistic culture, see J. Onians, *Art and Thought in the Hellenistic Age* (London, 1979). The best general survey of Hellenistic philosophy is A. A. Long, *Hellenistic Philosophy: Stoics, Epicureans, Skeptics*, 2d ed. (London, 1986). A superb work on Hellenistic science is G. E. R. Lloyd, *Greek Science After Aristotle* (London, 1973). On various facets of Hellenistic religion see A. Tripolitis, *Religions of the Hellenistic-Roman Age* (Ann Arbor, Mich., 2001).

CENGAGENOW Enter *CengageNOW* using the access card that is available with this text. *CengageNOW* will help you understand the content in this chapter with lesson plans generated for your needs, as well as provide you with a connection to the *Wadsworth World History Resource Center* (see description below for details).

WORLD HISTORY RESOURCE CENTER

Enter the Resource Center using either your *CengageNOW* access card or your separate access card for the *World History Resource Center*. Organized by topic, this Website includes quizzes; images; over 350 primary source documents; interactive simulations, maps, and timelines; movie explorations; and a wealth of other resources. You can read the following documents, and many more, at the *World History Resource Center*:

Homer, *Odyssey*, book 1
Plato, *Republic*, books 5 and 6

Visit the *World History* Companion Website for chapter quizzes and more:

www.cengage.com/history/Duiker/World6e

CHAPTER 5

THE FIRST WORLD CIVILIZATION: ROME, CHINA, AND THE EMERGENCE OF THE SILK ROAD

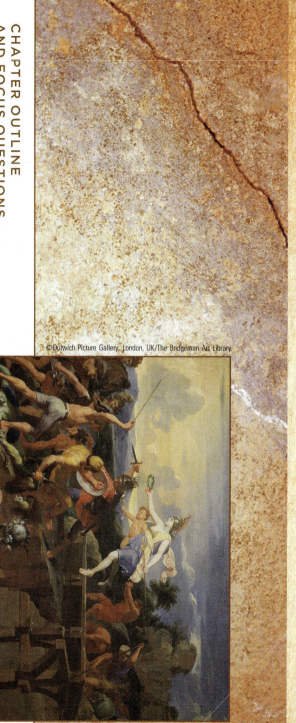

© Dulwich Picture Gallery, London, UK/The Bridgeman Art Library

Horatius defending the bridge, as envisioned by Charles Le Brun, a seventeenth-century French painter

CHAPTER OUTLINE AND FOCUS QUESTIONS

Early Rome and the Republic

Q What policies and institutions help explain the Romans' success in conquering Italy? How did Rome achieve its empire from 264 to 133 B.C.E., and what problems did Rome face as a result of its growing empire?

The Roman Empire at Its Height

Q What were the chief features of the Roman Empire at its height in the second century C.E.?

Crisis and the Late Empire

Q What reforms did Diocletian and Constantine institute, and to what extent were the reforms successful?

Transformation of the Roman World: The Development of Christianity

Q What characteristics of Christianity enabled it to grow and ultimately to triumph?

The Glorious Han Empire (202 B.C.E.–221 C.E.)

Q What were the chief features of the Han Empire?

CRITICAL THINKING

Q In what ways were the Roman Empire and the Han Chinese Empire similar, and in what ways were they different?

ALTHOUGH THE ASSYRIANS, Persians, and Indians under the Mauryan dynasty had created empires, they were neither as large nor as well controlled as the Han and Roman Empires that flourished at the beginning of the first millennium C.E. They were the largest political entities the world had yet seen. The Han Empire extended from Central Asia to the Pacific Ocean; the Roman Empire encompassed the lands around the Mediterranean, parts of the Middle East, and western and central Europe. Although there were no diplomatic contacts between the two civilizations, the Silk Road linked the two great empires commercially.

Roman history is the remarkable story of how a group of Latin-speaking people, who established a small community on a plain called Latium in central Italy, went on to conquer all of Italy and then the entire Mediterranean world. Why were the Romans able to do this? Scholars do not really know all the answers, but the Romans had their own explanation. Early Roman history is filled with legendary tales of the heroes who made Rome great. One of the best known is the story of Horatius at the bridge. Threatened by attack from the neighboring Etruscans, Roman farmers abandoned their fields and moved into the city, where they would be protected by the walls.

One weak point in the Roman defenses, however, was a wooden bridge over the Tiber River. Horatius was on guard at the bridge when a sudden assault by the Etruscans caused many Roman troops to throw down their weapons and flee. Horatius urged them to make a stand at the bridge; when they hesitated, he told them to destroy the bridge behind him while he held the Etruscans back. Astonished at the sight of a single defender, the confused Etruscans threw their spears at Horatius, who caught them on his shield and barred the way. By the time the Etruscans were about to overwhelm the lone defender, the Roman soldiers had brought down the bridge. Horatius then dived fully armed into the water and swam safely to the other side through a hail of arrows. Rome had been saved by the courageous act of a Roman who knew his duty and was determined to carry it out. Courage, duty, determination—these qualities would serve the many Romans who believed that it was their divine mission to rule nations and peoples. As one orator proclaimed, "By heaven's will my Rome shall be capital of the world."[1] ◆

Early Rome and the Republic

Q **Focus Questions:** What policies and institutions help explain the Romans' success in conquering Italy? How did Rome achieve its empire from 264 to 133 B.C.E., and what problems did Rome face as a result of its growing empire?

Italy is a peninsula extending about 750 miles from north to south (see Map 5.1). It is not very wide, however, averaging about 120 miles across. The Apennines form a ridge down the middle of Italy that divides west from east. Nevertheless, Italy has some fairly large fertile plains that are ideal for farming. Most important are the Po River valley in the north; the plain of Latium, on which Rome was located; and Campania to the south of Latium. To the east of the Italian peninsula is the Adriatic Sea and to the west the Tyrrhenian Sea, bounded by the large islands of Corsica and Sardinia. Sicily lies just west of the "toe" of the boot-shaped Italian peninsula.

Geography had an impact on Roman history. Although the Apennines bisected Italy, they were less rugged than the mountain ranges of Greece and did not divide the peninsula into small isolated communities. Italy also possessed considerably more productive agricultural land than Greece, enabling it to support a large population. Rome's location was favorable from a geographical point of view. Located 18 miles inland on the Tiber River, Rome had access to the sea and yet was far enough inland to be safe from pirates. Built on seven hills, it was easily defended.

Moreover, the Italian peninsula juts into the Mediterranean, making Italy an important crossroads between the western and eastern ends of the sea. Once Rome had unified Italy, involvement in Mediterranean affairs

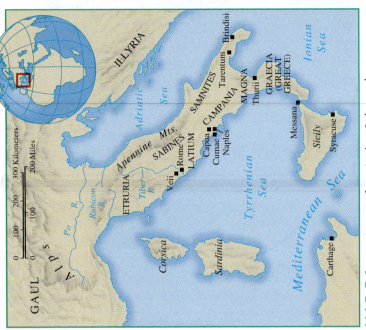

MAP 5.1 **Ancient Italy.** Ancient Italy was home to several groups. Both the Etruscans in the north and the Greeks in the south had a major influence on the development of Rome. Once Rome conquered the Etruscans, Sabines, Samnites, and other local groups, what aspects of the Italian peninsula helped make it defensible against outside enemies? ◆ **View an animated version of this map or related maps at** www.cengage.com/history/Duiker/World6e

was natural. And after the Romans had conquered their Mediterranean empire, governing it was made easier by Italy's central location.

Early Rome

According to Roman legend, Rome was founded by twin brothers, Romulus and Remus, in 753 B.C.E., and archaeologists have found that by around that time, a village of huts had been built on the tops of Rome's hills. The early Romans, basically a pastoral people, spoke Latin, which, like Greek, belongs to the Indo-European family of languages (see Table 1.2 in Chapter 1). The Roman historical tradition also maintained that early Rome (753–509 B.C.E.) had been under the control of seven kings and that two of the last three had been Etruscans, people who lived north of Rome in Etruria. Historians believe that the king list may have some historical accuracy. What is certain is that Rome did fall under the influence of the Etruscans for about a hundred years during the period of the kings and that by the beginning of the sixth century, under Etruscan influence, Rome began to emerge as a city. The Etruscans were responsible for an outstanding building program. They

The City of Rome

constructed the first roadbed of the chief street through Rome, the Sacred Way, before 575 B.C.E. and oversaw the development of temples, markets, shops, streets, and houses. By 509 B.C.E., supposedly when the monarchy was overthrown and a republican form of government was established, a new Rome had emerged, essentially a result of the fusion of Etruscan and native Roman elements. After Rome had expanded over its seven hills and the valleys in between, the Servian Wall was built in the fourth century B.C.E. to surround the city.

The Roman Republic

The transition from monarchy to a republican government was not easy. Rome felt threatened by enemies from every direction and, in the process of meeting these threats, embarked on a military course that led to the conquest of the entire Italian peninsula.

The Roman Conquest of Italy At the beginning of the Republic, Rome was surrounded by enemies, including the Latin communities on the plain of Latium. If we are to believe Livy, one of the chief ancient sources for the history of the early Roman Republic, Rome was engaged in almost continuous warfare with these enemies for the next hundred years. In his account, Livy provided a detailed narrative of Roman efforts. Many of his stories were legendary in character; writing in the first century B.C.E., he used his stories to teach Romans the moral values and virtues that had made Rome great. These included tenacity, duty, courage, and especially discipline (see the box on p. 132).

By 340 B.C.E., Rome had crushed the Latin states in Latium. During the next fifty years, the Romans waged a successful struggle with hill peoples from central Italy and then came into direct contact with the Greek communities. The Greeks had arrived on the Italian peninsula in large numbers during the age of Greek colonization (750–550 B.C.E.; see Chapter 4). Initially, the Greeks settled in southern Italy and then crept around the coast and up the peninsula. The Greeks had much influence on Rome. They cultivated olives and grapes, passed on their alphabet, and provided artistic and cultural models through their sculpture, architecture, and literature. By 267 B.C.E., the Romans had completed the conquest of southern Italy by defeating the Greek cities. After crushing the remaining Etruscan states to the north in 264 B.C.E., Rome had conquered most of Italy.

To rule Italy, the Romans devised the Roman Confederation. Under this system, Rome allowed some peoples—especially the Latins—to have full Roman citizenship. Most of the remaining communities were made allies. They remained free to run their own local affairs but were required to provide soldiers for Rome. Moreover, the Romans made it clear that loyal allies could improve their status and even have hope of becoming Roman citizens. The Romans had found a way to give conquered peoples a stake in Rome's success.

In the course of their expansion throughout Italy, the Romans had pursued consistent policies that help explain their success. The Romans were superb diplomats who excelled in making the correct diplomatic decisions. In addition, the Romans were not only good soldiers but also persistent ones. The loss of an army or a fleet did not cause them to quit but spurred them on to build new armies and new fleets. Finally, the Romans had a practical sense of strategy. As they conquered, the Romans established colonies—fortified towns—at strategic locations throughout Italy. By building roads to these settlements and connecting them, the Romans created an impressive communications and military network that enabled them to rule effectively and efficiently (see the comparative illustration "Roman and Chinese Roads" on p. 133). By insisting on military service from the allies in the Roman Confederation, Rome essentially mobilized the entire military manpower of all Italy for its wars.

The Roman State After the overthrow of the monarchy, Roman nobles, eager to maintain their position of power, established a republican form of government. The chief executive officers of the Roman Republic were the **consuls** and **praetors.** Two consuls, chosen annually, administered the government and led the Roman army into battle. In 366 B.C.E., the office of praetor was created. The praetor was in charge of civil law (law as it applied to Roman citizens), but he could also lead armies and govern Rome when the consuls were away from the city. As the Romans' territory expanded, they added another praetor to judge cases in which one or both people were noncitizens. The Roman state also had a number of administrative officials who handled specialized duties, such as the administration of financial affairs and supervision of the public games of Rome.

The Roman **senate** came to hold an especially important position in the Roman Republic. The senate or council of elders was a select group of about three hundred men who served for life. The senate could only advise the magistrates, but this advice was not taken lightly and by the third century B.C.E. had virtually the force of law.

The Roman Republic had a number of popular assemblies. By far the most important was the **centuriate assembly.** Organized by classes based on wealth, it was structured in such a way that the wealthiest citizens always had a majority. This assembly elected the chief

CINCINNATUS SAVES ROME: A ROMAN MORALITY TALE

POLITICS & GOVERNMENT

There is perhaps no better account of how the virtues of duty and simplicity enabled good Roman citizens to prevail during the travails of the fifth century B.C.E. than Livy's account of Cincinnatus. He was chosen dictator, supposedly in 457 B.C.E., to defend Rome against the attacks of the Aequi. The position of dictator was a temporary expedient used only in emergencies; the consuls would resign, and a leader with unlimited power would be appointed for a specified period (usually six months). In this account, Cincinnatus did his duty, defeated the Aequi, and returned to his simple farm in just fifteen days.

Livy, *The Early History of Rome*

The city was thrown into a state of turmoil, and the general alarm was as great as if Rome herself were surrounded. Nautius was sent for, but it was quickly decided that he was not the man to inspire full confidence; the situation evidently called for a dictator, and, with no dissentient voice, Lucius Quinctius Cincinnatus was named for the post.

Now I would solicit the particular attention of those numerous people who imagine that money is everything in this world, and that rank and ability are inseparable from wealth: let them observe that Cincinnatus, the one man in whom Rome reposed all her hope of survival, was at that moment working a little three-acre farm . . . west of the Tiber, just opposite the spot where the shipyards are today. A mission from the city found him at work on his land—digging a ditch, maybe, or plowing. Greetings were exchanged, and he was asked—with a prayer for divine blessing on himself and his country—to put on his toga and hear the Senate's instructions. This naturally surprised him, and, asking if all were well, he told his wife Racilia to run

to their cottage and fetch his toga. The toga was brought, and wiping the grimy sweat from his hands and face he put it on; at once the envoys from the city saluted him, with congratulations, as Dictator, invited him to enter Rome, and informed him of the terrible danger of Muni-cius' army. A state vessel was waiting for him on the river, and on the city bank he was welcomed by his three sons who had come to meet him, then by other kinsmen and friends, and finally by nearly the whole body of senators. Closely attended by all these people and preceded by his lictors he was then escorted to his residence through streets lined with great crowds of common folk who, be it said, were by no means so pleased to see the new Dictator, as they thought his power excessive and dreaded the way in which he was likely to use it. . . .

[Cincinnatus proceeds to raise an army, march out, and defeat the Aequi.]

In Rome the Senate was convened by Quintus Fabius the City Prefect, and a decree was passed inviting Cincinnatus to enter in triumph with his troops. The chariot he rode in was preceded by the enemy commanders and the military standards, and followed by his army loaded with its spoils. . . . Cincinnatus finally resigned after holding office for fifteen days, having originally accepted it for a period of six months.

Q *What values did Livy emphasize in his account of Cincinnatus? How important were those values to Rome's success? Why did Livy say he wrote his history? As a writer in the Augustan Age, would he have pleased or displeased Augustus with such a purpose?*

CENGAGENOW *To read more of Livy's writings, enter the documents area of the World History Resource Center using the access card that is available for World History.*

---

magistrates and passed laws. Another assembly, the **council of the plebs,** came into being as a result of the struggle of the orders.

This struggle arose as a result of the division of early Rome into two groups, the patricians and the plebeians. The **patricians** were great landowners, who constituted an aristocratic governing class. Only they could be consuls, magistrates, and senators. The **plebeians** constituted the considerably larger group of nonpatrician large landowners, less wealthy landholders, artisans, merchants, and small farmers. Although they, too, were citizens, they did not have the same rights as the patricians. Both patricians and plebeians could vote, but only the patricians could be elected to governmental offices. Both had the right to make legal contracts and marriages, but intermarriage between patricians and plebeians was forbidden. At the beginning of the fifth century B.C.E., the

plebeians began a struggle to seek both political and social equality with the patricians.

The struggle between the patricians and plebeians dragged on for hundreds of years, but it led to success for the plebeians. The council of the plebs, a popular assembly for plebeians only, was created in 471 B.C.E., and new officials, known as **tribunes of the plebs,** were given the power to protect plebeians against arrest by patrician magistrates. A new law allowed marriages between patricians and plebeians, and in the fourth century B.C.E., plebeians were permitted to become consuls. Finally, in 287 B.C.E, the council of the plebs received the right to pass laws for all Romans.

The struggle between the patricians and plebeians, then, had a significant impact on the development of the Roman state. Theoretically, by 287 B.C.E., all Roman citizens were equal under the law, and all could strive for

---

132 C H A P T E R 5 THE FIRST WORLD CIVILIZATION: ROME, CHINA, AND THE EMERGENCE OF THE SILK ROAD

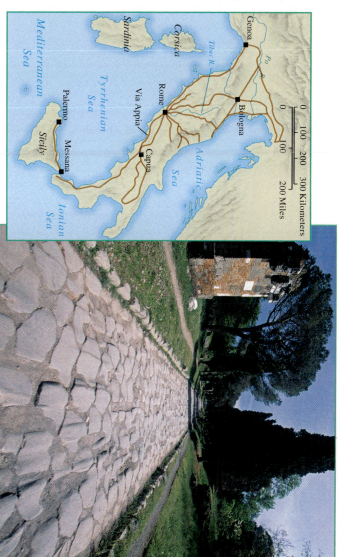

© Jon Arnold Images (Walter Bibikow)/Alamy

China Tourism Press/Getty Images

COMPARATIVE ILLUSTRATION

Roman and Chinese Roads. The Romans built a remarkable system of roads. After laying a foundation of gravel, which allowed for drainage, the Roman builders topped it with flagstones, closely fitted together. Unlike other peoples who built similar kinds of roads, the Romans did not follow the contours of the land but made their roads as straight as possible to facilitate communications and transportation, especially for military purposes. Seen here is a view of the Via Appia (Appian Way), built in 312 B.C.E., under the leadership of the censor and consul Appius Claudius (Roman roads were often named after the great Roman families who encouraged their construction). The Via Appia (shown on the map) was meant to make it easy for Roman armies to march from Rome to the newly conquered city of Capua, a distance of 152 miles. Under the Empire, roads were extended to provinces throughout the Mediterranean, parts of western and eastern Europe, and into western Asia. By the beginning of the fourth century C.E., the Roman Empire contained 372 major roads covering 50,000 miles.

Like the Roman Empire, the Han Empire relied on roads constructed with stone slabs for the movement of military forces. The First Emperor of Qin was responsible for the construction of 4,350 miles of roads, and by the end of the second century C.E., China had almost 22,000 miles of roads. Although roads in both the Roman and Chinese Empires were originally constructed for military purposes, they came to be used to facilitate communications and commercial traffic.

Q What was the importance of roads to both the Roman and Han Empires?

The Roman Conquest of the Mediterranean (264–133 B.C.E.)

After their conquest of the Italian peninsula, the Romans found themselves face to face with a formidable Mediterranean power—Carthage. Founded around

political office. But in reality, as a result of the right of intermarriage, a select number of patrician and plebeian families formed a new senatorial aristocracy that came to dominate the political offices. The Roman Republic had not become a democracy.

INTERACTION & EXCHANGE

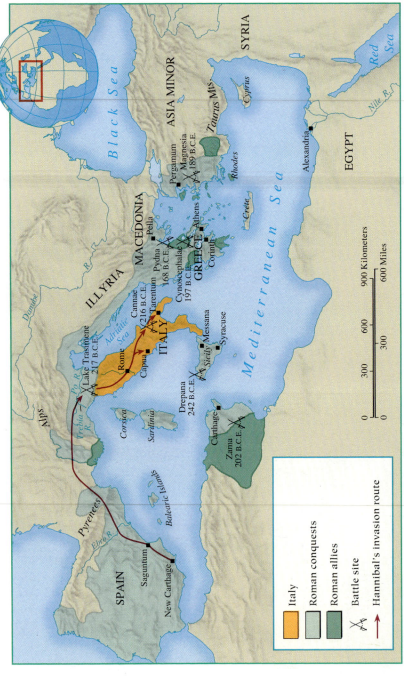

MAP 5.2 **Roman Conquests in the Mediterranean, 264–133 B.C.E.** Beginning with the Punic Wars, Rome expanded its holdings, first in the western Mediterranean at the expense of Carthage and later in Greece and western Asia Minor.

Q What aspects of Mediterranean geography, combined with the territorial holdings and aspirations of Rome and the Carthaginians, made the Punic Wars more likely?

800 B.C.E. on the coast of North Africa by Phoenicians, Carthage had flourished and assembled an enormous empire in the western Mediterranean. By the third century B.C.E., the Carthaginian Empire included the coast of northern Africa, southern Spain, Sardinia, Corsica, and western Sicily. The presence of Carthaginians in Sicily, so close to the Italian coast, made the Romans apprehensive. In 264 B.C.E., the two powers began a lengthy struggle for control of the western Mediterranean (see Map 5.2).

In the First Punic War (the Latin word for Phoenician was *Punicus*), the Romans resolved to conquer Sicily. The Romans—a land power—realized that they could not win the war without a navy and promptly developed a substantial naval fleet. After a long struggle, a Roman fleet defeated the Carthaginian navy off Sicily, and the war quickly came to an end. In 241 B.C.E., Carthage gave up all rights to Sicily and had to pay an indemnity. Sicily became the first Roman province.

Carthage vowed revenge and extended its domains in Spain to compensate for the territory lost to Rome. When the Romans encouraged one of Carthage's Spanish allies to revolt against Carthage, Hannibal, the greatest of the Carthaginian generals, struck back, beginning the Second Punic War (218–201 B.C.E.).

This time, the Carthaginian strategy aimed at bringing the war home to the Romans and defeating them in their own backyard. Hannibal crossed the Alps with an army of thirty to forty thousand men and inflicted a series of defeats on the Romans. At Cannae in 216 B.C.E., the Romans lost an army of almost forty thousand men. Rome seemed on the brink of disaster but refused to give up, raised yet another army, and began to reconquer some of the Italian cities that had gone over to Hannibal's side. They also sent troops to Spain, and by 206 B.C.E., Spain was freed of the Carthaginians.

The Romans then took the war directly to Carthage, forcing the Carthaginians to recall Hannibal from Italy. At the Battle of Zama in 202 B.C.E., the Romans crushed Hannibal's forces, and the war was over. By the peace treaty signed in 201 B.C.E., Carthage lost Spain, which became another Roman province. Rome had become the dominant power in the western Mediterranean.

Fifty years later, the Romans fought their third and final struggle with Carthage. In 146 B.C.E., Carthage was destroyed. For ten days, Roman soldiers burned and pulled down all of the city's buildings (see the box on p. 135). The inhabitants—fifty thousand men, women, and children—were sold into slavery. The territory of Carthage became a Roman province called Africa.

THE DESTRUCTION OF CARTHAGE

The Romans used a technical breach of Carthage's peace treaty with Rome to undertake a third and final war with Carthage (149–146 B.C.E.). Although Carthage posed no real threat to Rome's security, the Romans still remembered the traumatic experiences of the Second Punic War, when Hannibal had ravaged much of their homeland. The hard-liners gained the upper hand in the senate and called for the complete destruction of Carthage. The city was razed, the survivors sold into slavery, and the land turned into a province. In this passage, the historian Appian of Alexandria describes the final destruction of Carthage by the Romans under the command of Scipio Aemilianus.

Appian, *Roman History*

Then came new scenes of horror. The fire spread and carried everything down, and the soldiers did not wait to destroy the buildings little by little, but pulled them all down together. So the crashing grew louder, and many fell with the stones into the midst dead. Others were seen still living, especially old men, women, and young children who had hidden in the inmost nooks of the houses, some of them wounded, some more or less burned, and uttering horrible cries. Still others, thrust out and falling from such a height with the stones, timbers, and fire, were torn asunder into all kinds of horrible shapes, crushed and mangled. Nor was this the end of their miseries, for the street cleaners, who were removing the rubbish with axes, mattocks, and boat hooks, and making the roads passable, tossed with these instruments the dead and the living together into holes in the ground, sweeping them along like sticks and stones or turning them over with their iron tools, and man was used for filling up a ditch. Some were thrown in head foremost, while their legs, sticking out of the ground, writhed a long time. Others fell with their feet downward and their heads above ground. Horses ran over them, crushing their faces and skulls, not purposely on the part of the riders, but in their headlong haste. Nor did the street cleaners either do these things on purpose; but the press of war, the glory of approaching victory, the rush of the soldiers, the confused noise of heralds and trumpeters all round, the tribunes and centurions changing guard and marching the cohorts hither and thither—all together made everybody frantic and heedless of the spectacle before their eyes.

Six days and nights were consumed in this kind of turmoil, the soldiers being changed so that they might not be worn out with toil, slaughter, want of sleep, and these horrid sights....

Scipio, beholding this city, which had flourished 700 years from its foundation and had ruled over so many lands, islands, and seas, as rich in arms and fleets, elephants, and money as the mightiest empires, but far surpassing them in hardihood and high spirit ... now come to its end in total destruction—Scipio, beholding this spectacle, is said to have shed tears and publicly lamented the fortune of the enemy. After meditating by himself a long time and reflecting on the inevitable fall of cities, nations, and empires, as well as of individuals, upon the fate of Troy, that once proud city, upon the fate of the Assyrian, the Median, and afterwards of the great Persian empire, and, most recently of all, of the splendid empire of Macedon, either voluntarily or otherwise the words of the poet [Homer, *Iliad*] escaped his lips:

The day shall come in which our sacred Troy
And Priam, and the people over whom
Spear-bearing Priam rules, shall perish all.

Being asked by Polybius in familiar conversation (for Polybius had been his tutor) what he meant by using these words, Polybius says that he did not hesitate frankly to name his own country, for whose fate he feared when he considered the mutability of human affairs. And Polybius wrote this down just as he heard it.

Q *What does the description of Rome's destruction of Carthage reveal about the nature of Roman imperialism? What features seem more rhetorical than realistic? Why?*

During its struggle with Carthage, Rome also had problems with the Hellenistic states in the eastern Mediterranean, and after the defeat of Carthage, Rome turned its attention there. In 148 B.C.E., Macedonia was made a Roman province, and two years later, Greece was placed under the control of the Roman governor of Macedonia. In 133 B.C.E., the king of Pergamum deeded his kingdom to Rome, giving Rome its first province in Asia. Rome was now master of the Mediterranean Sea.

Evolution of the Roman Army By the fourth century B.C.E., the Roman army consisted of four legions, each made up of four thousand to five thousand men; each legion had about three hundred cavalry and the rest infantry. The infantry consisted of three lines of battle. The *hastati* (spearmen), consisting of the youngest recruits, formed the front line; they were armed with heavy spears and short swords and protected by a large oval shield, helmet, breastplate, and greaves (shin guards). The *principes* (chief men), armed and protected like the *hastati*, formed the second line. The third line of battle was formed by the *triarii* (third-rank men), who knelt behind the first two lines, ready to move up and fill any gaps. A fourth group of troops, poor citizens who wore cloaks

armies, and the number of legions rose to twenty-five. Major changes in recruitment would not come until the first century B.C.E. with the military reforms of Marius (see "Growing Unrest and a New Role for the Roman Army" in the next section).

CHRONOLOGY The Roman Conquest of Italy and the Mediterranean	
End of Latin revolts	340 B.C.E.
Creation of the Roman Confederation	338 B.C.E.
First Punic War	264–241 B.C.E.
Second Punic War	218–201 B.C.E.
Battle of Cannae	216 B.C.E.
Roman seizure of Spain	206 B.C.E.
Battle of Zama	202 B.C.E.
Third Punic War	149–146 B.C.E.
Macedonia made a Roman province	148 B.C.E.
Destruction of Carthage	146 B.C.E.
Kingdom of Pergamum to Rome	133 B.C.E.

but no armor and were lightly armed, functioned as skirmishers who usually returned to the rear lines after their initial contact with the enemy to form backup reserves.

In the early Republic, the army was recruited from citizens between the ages of eighteen and forty-six who had the resources to equip themselves for battle. Since most of them were farmers, they enrolled only for a year, campaigned during the summer months, and returned home in time for the fall harvest. Later, during the Punic Wars of the third century B.C.E., the period of service had to be extended, although this was resisted by farmers whose livelihoods could be severely harmed by a long absence. Nevertheless, after the disastrous battle of Cannae in 216 B.C.E., the Romans were forced to recruit larger

The Decline and Fall of the Roman Republic (133–31 B.C.E.)

By the middle of the second century B.C.E., Roman domination of the Mediterranean Sea was complete. Yet the process of creating an empire had weakened the internal stability of Rome, leading to a series of crises that plagued the empire for the next hundred years.

Growing Unrest and a New Role for the Roman Army

By the second century B.C.E., the senate had become the effective governing body of the Roman state. It comprised three hundred men, drawn primarily from the landed aristocracy; they remained senators for life and held the chief magistracies of the Republic. The senate directed the wars of the third and second centuries and took control of both foreign and domestic policy, including financial affairs.

Of course, these aristocrats formed only a tiny minority of the Roman people. The backbone of the Roman state had traditionally been the small farmers. But over time, many small farmers had found themselves unable to compete with large, wealthy landowners and had lost their lands. By taking over state-owned land and by buying out small peasant owners, these landed aristocrats had amassed large estates (called **latifundia**) that used slave labor. Thus, the rise of the *latifundia* contributed to a decline in the number of small citizen farmers who were available for military service. Moreover, many of these small farmers drifted to the cities, especially Rome, forming a large class of landless poor.

Some aristocrats tried to remedy this growing economic and social crisis. Two brothers, Tiberius and Gaius Gracchus, came to believe that the underlying cause of Rome's problems was the decline of the small farmer. To help the landless poor, they bypassed the senate by having the council of the plebs pass land-reform bills that called for the government to reclaim public land held by large landowners and to distribute it to landless Romans. Many senators, themselves large landowners whose estates included broad tracts of public land, were furious. A group of senators took the law into their own hands and murdered Tiberius in 133 B.C.E. Gaius later suffered the same fate. The attempts of the Gracchus brothers to bring reforms had opened the door to further violence. Changes in the Roman army soon brought even worse problems.

In the closing years of the second century B.C.E., a Roman general named Marius began to recruit his armies in a new way. The Roman army had traditionally been a conscript army of small farmers who were

Roman Legionaries. The Roman legionaries, famed for their courage and tenacity, made Roman domination of the Mediterranean Sea possible. At the time of the Punic Wars, the Roman legionaries wore chain-mail armor and plumed helmets and carried oval shields, as seen in this portrait of legionaries on the relief on the sarcophagus of Domitius Ahenobarbus, about 100 C.E. Heavy javelins and swords were their major weapons. This equipment remained standard until the time of Julius Caesar.

© Erich Lessing/Art Resource, NY

landholders. Marius recruited volunteers from both the urban and rural poor who possessed no property. These volunteers swore an oath of loyalty to the general, not the senate, and thus constituted a professional-type army no longer subject to the state. Moreover, to recruit these men, the generals would promise them land, forcing the generals to play politics in order to get laws passed that would provide the land promised to their veterans. Marius had created a new system of military recruitment that placed much power in the hands of the individual generals.

The Collapse of the Republic

The first century B.C.E. was characterized by two important features: the jostling for dominance of a number of powerful individuals and the civil wars generated by their conflicts. Three individuals came to hold enormous military and political power—Crassus, Pompey, and Julius Caesar. Crassus was known as the richest man in Rome and led a successful military command against a major slave rebellion. Pompey had returned from a successful military command in Spain in 71 B.C.E. and had been hailed as a military hero. Julius Caesar also had a military command in Spain. In 60 B.C.E., Caesar joined with Crassus and Pompey to form a coalition that historians call the First Triumvirate (*triumvirate* means "three-man rule").

The combined wealth and influence of these three men was enormous, enabling them to dominate the political scene and achieve their basic aims: Pompey received a command in Spain, Crassus a command in Syria, and Caesar a special military command in Gaul (modern France). When Crassus was killed in battle in 53 B.C.E., it left two powerful men with armies in direct competition. Caesar had conquered all of Gaul and gained fame, wealth, and military experience as well as an army of seasoned veterans who were loyal to him. When leading senators endorsed Pompey as the less harmful to their cause and voted for Caesar to lay down his command and return as a private citizen to Rome, Caesar refused. He chose to keep his army and moved into Italy illegally by crossing the Rubicon, the river that formed the southern boundary of his province. Caesar marched on Rome and defeated the forces of Pompey and his allies, leaving Caesar in complete control of the Roman government.

Caesar was officially made **dictator** in 47 B.C.E. and three years later was named dictator for life. Realizing the need for reforms, he gave land to the poor and increased the senate to nine hundred members. He also reformed the calendar by introducing the Egyptian solar year of 365 days (with later changes in 1582, it became the basis of our own calendar). Caesar planned much more in the way of building projects and military adventures in the East, but in 44 B.C.E., a group of leading senators assassinated him.

Within a few years after Caesar's death, two men had divided the Roman world between them—Octavian, Caesar's grandnephew and heir, taking the western

Caesar. Conqueror of Gaul and member of the First Triumvirate, Julius Caesar is perhaps the best-known figure of the late Republic. Caesar became dictator of Rome in 47 B.C.E. and after his victories in the civil war was made dictator for life. Some members of the senate who resented his power assassinated him in 44 B.C.E. Pictured is a marble copy of a bust of Caesar.

© Scala/Art Resource, NY

portion and Antony, Caesar's ally and assistant, the eastern half. But the empire of the Romans, large as it was, was still too small for two masters, and Octavian and Antony eventually came into conflict. Antony allied himself closely with the Egyptian queen, Cleopatra VII. At the Battle of Actium in Greece in 31 B.C.E., Octavian's forces smashed the army and navy of Antony and Cleopatra, who both fled to Egypt, where they committed suicide a year later. Octavian, at the age of thirty-two, stood supreme over the Roman world. The civil wars were ended. And so was the Republic.

The Roman Empire at Its Height

> **Focus Question:** What were the chief features of the Roman Empire at its height in the second century C.E.?

With the victories of Octavian, peace finally settled on the Roman world. Although civil conflict still erupted occasionally, the new imperial state constructed by Octavian experienced remarkable stability for the next two hundred years. The Romans imposed their peace on the largest empire established in antiquity.

The Age of Augustus (31 B.C.E.–14 C.E.)

In 27 B.C.E., Octavian proclaimed the "restoration of the Republic." He understood that only traditional republican forms would satisfy the senatorial aristocracy. At the same time, Octavian was aware that the Republic could not be fully restored. Although he gave some power to the senate, Octavian in reality became the first Roman emperor. The senate awarded him the title of Augustus, "the revered one"–a fitting title, in view of his power, that had previously been reserved for gods. Augustus proved highly popular, but the chief source of his power was his continuing control of the army. The senate gave Augustus the title of *imperator* (our word *emperor*), or commander in chief.

Augustus maintained a standing army of twenty-eight legions, or about 150,000 men (a legion was a military unit of about 5,000 troops). Only Roman citizens could be legionaries, while subject peoples could serve as auxiliary forces, which numbered around 130,000 under Augustus. Augustus was also responsible for setting up a **praetorian guard** of roughly 9,000 men who had the important task of guarding the emperor.

While claiming to have restored the Republic, Augustus inaugurated a new system for governing the provinces. Under the Republic, the senate had appointed the governors of the provinces. Now certain provinces were given to the emperor, who assigned deputies known as *legates* to govern them. The senate continued to name the governors of the remaining provinces, but the authority of Augustus enabled him to overrule the senatorial governors and establish a uniform imperial policy.

Augustus also stabilized the frontiers of the Roman Empire. He conquered the central and maritime Alps and then expanded Roman control of the Balkan peninsula up to the Danube River. His attempt to conquer Germany failed when three Roman legions, led by a general named Varus, were massacred in 9 C.E. by a coalition of German tribes. His defeats in Germany taught Augustus that Rome's power was not unlimited and also devastated him; for months, he would beat his head on a door, shouting, "Varus, give me back my legions!"

Augustus died in 14 C.E. after dominating the Roman world for forty-five years. He had created a new order while placating the old by restoring traditional values. By the time of his death, his new order was so well established that few agitated for an alternative. Indeed, as the Roman historian Tacitus pointed out, "Practically no one had ever seen truly Republican government.... Political equality was a thing of the past; all eyes watched for imperial commands."[2]

The Early Empire (14–180)

There was no serious opposition to Augustus' choice of his stepson Tiberius as his successor. By his actions, Augustus established the Julio-Claudian dynasty; the next

© Scala/Art Resource, NY

Augustus. Octavian, Caesar's adopted son, emerged victorious from the civil conflict that rocked the Republic after Caesar's assassination. The senate awarded him the title Augustus. This marble statue from Prima Porta, an idealized portrait, is based on Greek rather than Roman models. The statue was meant to be a propaganda piece, depicting a youthful general addressing his troops. At the bottom stands Cupid, the son of Venus, goddess of love, meant to be a reminder that the Julians, Caesar's family, claimed descent from Venus, thus emphasizing the ruler's divine background.

four successors of Augustus were related to the family of Augustus or that of his wife, Livia.

Several major tendencies emerged during the reigns of the Julio-Claudians (14–68 C.E.) In general, more and more of the responsibilities that Augustus had given to the senate tended to be taken over by the emperors, who also instituted an imperial bureaucracy, staffed by talented freedmen, to run the government on a daily basis. As the Julio-Claudian successors of Augustus acted more openly as rulers rather than "first citizens of the state," the opportunity for arbitrary and corrupt acts also increased. Nero (54–68), for example, freely eliminated people he wanted out of the way, including his own mother, whose murder he arranged. Without troops, the senators proved unable to oppose these excesses, but the Roman legions finally revolted. Abandoned by his guards, Nero chose to commit suicide by stabbing himself in the throat after uttering his final words, "What an artist the world is losing in me!"

The Five Good Emperors (96–180)

Many historians regard the **Pax Romana** (the "Roman peace") and the prosperity it engendered as the chief benefits of Roman rule during the first and second centuries C.E. These benefits were especially noticeable during the reigns of the five so-called **good emperors.** These rulers treated the ruling classes with respect, maintained peace in the empire, and supported generally beneficial domestic policies. Though absolute monarchs, they were known for their tolerance and diplomacy. By adopting capable men as their sons and successors, the first four of these emperors reduced the chances of succession problems.

Under the five good emperors, the powers of the emperor continued to expand at the expense of the senate. Increasingly, imperial officials appointed and directed by the emperor took over the running of the government. The good emperors also extended the scope of imperial administration to areas previously untouched by the imperial government. Trajan (98–117) implemented an alimentary program that provided state funds to assist poor parents in raising and educating their children. The good emperors were widely praised for their extensive building programs. Trajan and Hadrian (117–138) were especially active in constructing public works—aqueducts, bridges, roads, and harbor facilities—throughout the empire.

Frontiers and the Provinces

Although Trajan extended Roman rule into Dacia (modern Romania), Mesopotamia, and the Sinai peninsula (see Map 5.3), his successors recognized that the empire was overextended and returned to Augustus' policy of defensive imperialism. Hadrian withdrew Roman forces from much of Mesopotamia. Although he retained Dacia and Arabia, he went on the defensive in his frontier policy by reinforcing the fortifications along a line connecting the Rhine and Danube Rivers and building a defensive wall 80 miles long across northern Britain to keep the Scots out of Roman Britain. By the end of the second century, the Roman forces were established in permanent bases behind the frontiers.

At its height in the second century C.E., the Roman Empire was one of the greatest states the world had seen. It covered about 3.5 million square miles and had a population, like that of Han China, estimated at more than fifty million. While the emperors and the imperial administration provided a degree of unity, considerable leeway was given to local customs, and the privileges of Roman citizenship were extended to many people throughout the empire. In 212, the emperor Caracalla completed the process by giving Roman citizenship to every free inhabitant of the empire. Latin was the language of the western part of the empire, while Greek was used in the east. Roman culture spread to all parts of the empire and freely mixed with Greek culture, creating what has been called Greco-Roman civilization.

The administration and cultural life of the Roman Empire depended greatly on cities and towns. A provincial governor's staff was not large, so it was left to local city officials to act as Roman agents in carrying out many government functions, especially those related to taxes. Cities were important in the spread of Roman culture, law, and the Latin language, and they resembled one another with their temples, markets, amphitheaters, and other public buildings.

Most towns and cities were not large by modern standards. The largest was Rome, but there were also some large cities in the east: Alexandria in Egypt numbered more than 300,000 inhabitants. In the west, cities were usually small, with only a few thousand inhabitants.

Prosperity in the Early Empire

The Early Empire was a period of considerable prosperity. Internal peace resulted in unprecedented levels of trade. Merchants from all over the empire came to the chief Italian ports of Puteoli on the Bay of Naples and Ostia at the mouth of the Tiber River. Long-distance trade beyond the Roman frontiers also developed during the Early Empire. Economic expansion in both the Roman and Chinese Empires helped foster the growth of this trade. Although both empires built roads chiefly for military purposes, the roads also came to be used to facilitate trade. Moreover, by creating large empires, the Romans and Chinese not only established internal stability but also pacified bordering territories, thus reducing the threat that bandits posed to traders. As a result, merchants developed a network of trade routes that brought these two great empires into commercial contact. Most important was the overland Silk Road, a regular caravan route between West and East (see "Imperial Expansion and the Origins of the Silk Road" later in this chapter).

Despite the profits from trade and commerce, agriculture remained the chief pursuit of most people and the underlying basis of Roman prosperity. Although the large *latifundia* still dominated agriculture, especially in southern and central Italy, small peasant farms continued to flourish, particularly in Etruria and the Po valley. Although large estates depended on slaves for the raising of sheep and cattle, the lands of some *latifundia* were also

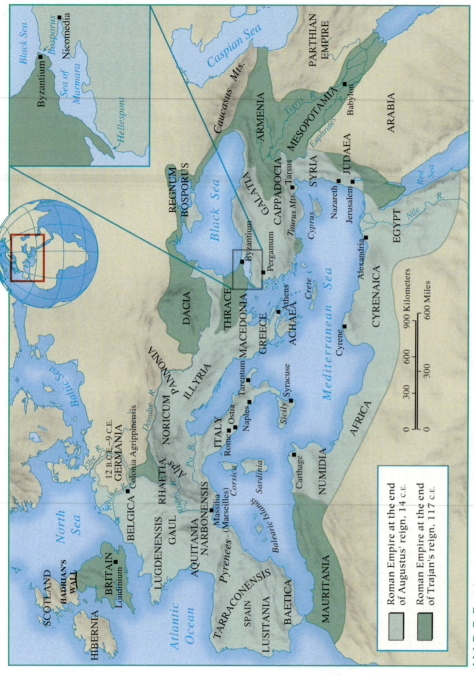

MAP 5.3   The Roman Empire from Augustus to Trajan (14–117).   Augustus and later emperors continued the expansion of the Roman Empire, adding more resources but also increasing the tasks of administration and keeping the peace. Compare this map with Map 5.2. **Q** Which of Trajan's acquisitions were relinquished during Hadrian's reign?

Roman Empire at the end of Augustus' reign, 14 C.E.

Roman Empire at the end of Trajan's reign, 117 C.E.

worked by free tenant farmers who paid rent in labor, produce, or sometimes cash.

The prosperity of the Roman world left an enormous gulf between rich and poor. The development of towns and cities, so important to the creation of any civilization, is based largely on the agricultural surpluses of the countryside. In ancient times, the margin of surplus produced by each farmer was relatively small. Therefore, the upper classes and urban populations had to be supported by the labor of a large number of agricultural producers, who never found it easy to produce much more than for themselves.

Culture and Society in the Roman World

One of the notable characteristics of Roman culture and society is the impact of the Greeks. Greek ambassadors, merchants, and artists traveled to Rome and spread Greek thought and practices. After their conquest of the Hellenistic kingdoms, Roman generals shipped Greek manuscripts and artworks back to Rome. Multitudes of

educated Greek slaves labored in Roman households. Rich Romans hired Greek tutors and sent their sons to Athens to study. As the Roman poet Horace said, "Captive Greece took captive her rude conqueror." Greek thought captivated the less sophisticated Roman minds, and the Romans became willing transmitters of Greek culture.

Roman Literature   The Latin literature that first emerged in the third century B.C.E. was strongly influenced by Greek models. It was not until the last century of the Republic that the Romans began to produce a new poetry in which Latin poets were able to use various Greek forms to express their own feelings about people, social and political life, and love.

The high point of Latin literature was reached in the age of Augustus, often called the golden age of Latin literature. The most distinguished poet of the Augustan Age was Virgil (70–19 B.C.E.). The son of a small landholder in northern Italy, he welcomed the rule of Augustus and wrote his greatest work in the emperor's honor. Virgil's masterpiece was the *Aeneid*, an epic poem

The Art Archive/Bardo Museum, Tunis, Tunisia/Gianni Dagli Orti

Trade in the Roman Empire. Trade was an important ingredient in the prosperity of the Early Roman Empire. Although Roman roads were excellent, most goods traveled by boat throughout the Mediterranean and beyond. This third-century C.E. Roman mosaic from Sousse, Tunisia, shows workers unloading a cargo of iron ore from a ship.

clearly intended to rival the work of Homer. The connection between Troy and Rome is made in the poem when Aeneas, a hero of Troy, survives the destruction of that city and eventually settles in Latium—establishing a link between Roman civilization and Greek history. Aeneas is portrayed as the ideal Roman—his virtues are duty, piety, and faithfulness. Virgil's overall purpose was to show that Aeneas had fulfilled his mission to establish the Romans in Italy and thereby start Rome on its divine mission to rule the world.

As Virgil expressed it, ruling was Rome's gift.

Let others fashion from bronze more lifelike,
breathing images—
For so they shall—and evoke living faces from marble;
Others excel as orators, others track with their
instruments
The planets circling in heaven and predict when
stars will appear.
But, Romans, never forget that government is your
medium!
Be this your art—to practise men in the habit of peace,
Generosity to the conquered, and firmness against
aggressors.[3]

Roman Art The Romans were also dependent on the Greeks for artistic inspiration. The Romans developed a taste for Greek statues, which they placed not only in public buildings but also in their private houses. The Romans' own portrait sculpture was characterized by an intense realism that included even unpleasant physical details. Wall paintings and frescoes in the homes of the rich realistically depicted landscapes, portraits, and scenes from mythological stories.

The Romans excelled in architecture, a highly practical art. Although they continued to adapt Greek styles and made use of colonnades and rectangular structures, the Romans were also innovative. They made considerable use of curvilinear forms: the arch, vault, and dome. The Romans were also the first people in antiquity to use concrete on a massive scale. They constructed huge buildings—public baths, such as those of Caracalla, and amphitheaters capable of seating fifty thousand spectators. These large buildings were made possible by Roman engineering skills. These same skills were put to use in constructing roads, aqueducts, and bridges; a network of 50,000 miles of roads linked all parts of the empire, and in Rome, almost a dozen aqueducts kept the population of one million supplied with water.

Roman Law One of Rome's chief gifts to the Mediterranean world of its day and to later generations was its system of law. Rome's first code of laws was the Twelve Tables of 450 B.C.E., but that was designed for a simple farming society and proved inadequate for later needs. So from the Twelve Tables the Romans developed a system of civil law that applied to all Roman citizens. As Rome expanded, problems arose between citizens and noncitizens and also among noncitizen residents of the empire. Although some of the rules of civil law could be used in these cases, special rules were often needed. These rules gave rise to a body of law known as the *law of nations*, defined as the part of the law that applied to both Romans and foreigners. Under the influence of Stoicism, the Romans came to identify their law of nations with **natural law**, a set of universal laws based on reason. This enabled them to establish standards of justice that applied to all people.

These standards of justice included principles that we would immediately recognize. A person was regarded as innocent until proved otherwise. People accused of wrongdoing were allowed to defend themselves before a judge. A judge, in turn, was expected to weigh evidence carefully before arriving at a decision. These principles lived on long after the fall of the Roman Empire.

The Roman Family At the heart of the Roman social structure stood the family, headed by the *paterfamilias*—the dominant male. The household also included the wife, sons with their wives and children, unmarried daughters, and slaves. Like the Greeks, Roman males believed that females needed male guardians (see the box on p. 143). The *paterfamilias* exercised that authority; upon his death, sons or nearest male relatives assumed the role of guardians.

© Photodisc (David Buffington)/Getty Images

© PictureNet/CORBIS

The Pantheon. Shown here is the Pantheon, one of Rome's greatest buildings. Constructed of brick, six kinds of concrete, and marble, it is a stunning example of the Romans' engineering skills. The outside porch of the Pantheon contains eighteen Corinthian columns made of granite, but it is the inside of the temple that amazes onlookers. The interior is a large circular space topped by a huge dome. A hole in the center of the roof is the only source of light. The dome, built up layer by layer, was made of concrete, weighing 10 million pounds. The walls holding the dome are almost 20 feet thick.

Fathers arranged the marriages of daughters. In the Republic, women married "with legal control" passing from father to husband. By the mid-first century B.C.E., the dominant practice had changed to "without legal control," which meant that married daughters officially remained within the father's legal power. Since the fathers of most married women died sooner or later, not being in the "legal control" of a husband entailed independent property rights that forceful women could translate into considerable power within the household and outside it.

Some parents in upper-class families provided education for their daughters by hiring private tutors or sending them to primary schools. At the age when boys were entering secondary schools, however, girls were pushed into marriage. The legal minimum age for marriage was twelve, although fourteen was a more common age in practice (for males, the legal minimum age was fourteen, and most men married later). Although some Roman doctors warned that early pregnancies could be dangerous for young girls, early marriages persisted because women died at a relatively young age. A good example is Tullia, Cicero's beloved daughter. She was married at sixteen, widowed at twenty-two, remarried

one year later, divorced at twenty-eight, remarried at twenty-nine, and divorced at thirty-four. She died at thirty-four, which was not unusually young for women in Roman society.

By the second century C.E., significant changes were occurring in the Roman family. The *paterfamilias* no longer had absolute authority over his children; he could no longer sell his children into slavery or have them put to death. Moreover, the husband's absolute authority over his wife had also disappeared, and by the late second century, upper-class Roman women had considerable freedom and independence.

Slaves and Their Masters Although slavery was a common institution throughout the ancient world, no people possessed more slaves or relied so much on slave labor as the Romans eventually did. Slaves were used in many ways in Roman society. The rich owned the most and the best. In the late Roman Republic, it became a badge of prestige to be attended by many slaves. Greek slaves were in much demand as tutors, musicians, doctors, and artists. Roman businessmen would employ them as shop assistants or craftspeople. Slaves were also used as farm laborers; in fact, huge gangs of slaves worked

©Erich Lessing/Art Resource, NY

FAMILY & SOCIETY

CATO THE ELDER ON WOMEN

During the Second Punic War, the Romans enacted the Oppian Law, which limited the amount of gold women could possess and restricted their dress and use of carriages. In 195 B.C.E., an attempt to repeal the law was made, and women demonstrated in the streets on behalf of this effort. According to the Roman historian Livy, the conservative Roman official Cato the Elder spoke against repeal and against the women favoring it. Although the words are probably not Cato's own, they do reflect a traditional male Roman attitude toward women.

Livy, *History of Rome*

"If each of us, citizens, had determined to assert his rights and dignity as a husband with respect to his own spouse, we should have less trouble with the sex as a whole; as it is, our liberty, destroyed at home by female violence, even here in the Forum is crushed and trodden underfoot, and because we have not kept them individually under control, we dread them collectively.... But from no class is there not the greatest danger if you permit them meetings and gatherings and secret consultations....

"Our ancestors permitted no women to conduct even personal business without a guardian to intervene in her behalf; they wished them to be under the control of fathers, brothers, husbands; we (Heaven help us!) allow them now even to interfere in public affairs, yes, and to visit the Forum and our informal and formal sessions. What else are they doing now on the streets and at the corners except urging the bill of the tribunes and voting for the repeal of the law? Give loose rein to their uncontrollable nature and to this untamed creature and expect that they will themselves set bounds to their license; unless you act, this is the least of the things enjoyed upon women by custom or law and to which they submit with a feeling of injustice. It is complete liberty or, rather, if we wish to speak the truth, complete license that they desire.

"If they win in this, what will they not attempt? Review all the laws with which your forefathers restrained their license and made them subject to their husbands; even with all these bonds you can scarcely control them. What of this? If you suffer them to seize these bonds one by one and wrench themselves free and finally to be placed on a parity with their husbands, do you think that you will be able to endure them? The moment they begin to be your equals, they will be your superiors....

"Now they publicly address other women's husbands, and, what is more serious, they beg for a law and votes, and from sundry men they get what they ask. In matters affecting yourself, your property, your children, you, Sir, can be importuned; once the law has ceased to set a limit to your wife's expenditures you will never set it yourself. Do not think, citizens, that the situation which existed before the law was passed will ever return."

Q What particular actions on the part of the women protesting this law have angered Cato? What more general concerns does he have about Roman women? What does he believe is women's ultimate goal in regard to men?

the large landed estates under pitiful conditions. Many slaves of all nationalities were used as menial household workers, such as cooks, waiters, cleaners, and gardeners. Contractors used slave labor to build roads, aqueducts, and other public structures.

The treatment of Roman slaves varied. There are numerous instances of humane treatment by masters and situations where slaves even protected their owners from danger out of gratitude and esteem. Slaves were also

Roman Women. Roman women, especially those of the upper class, developed comparatively more freedom than women in Classical Athens despite the persistent male belief that women required guardianship. This mural decoration, found in the remains of a villa destroyed by the eruption of Mount Vesuvius, shows a group of Pompeian ladies with their slave hairdresser.

THE ROMAN FEAR OF SLAVES

FAMILY & SOCIETY

The lowest stratum of the Roman population consisted of slaves. They were used extensively in households, at the court, as artisans in industrial enterprises, as business managers, and in numerous other ways. Although some historians have argued that slaves were treated more humanely during the Early Empire, these selections by the Roman historian Tacitus and the Roman statesman Pliny indicate that slaves still rebelled against their masters because of mistreatment. Many masters continued to live in fear of their slaves, as witnessed by the saying "As many enemies as you have slaves."

Tacitus, *The Annals of Imperial Rome*

Soon afterwards the City Prefect, Lucius Pedanius Secundus, was murdered by one of his slaves [in 61 C.E.]. Either Pedanius had refused to free the murderer after agreeing to a price, or the slave, in a homosexual infatuation, found competition from his master intolerable. After the murder, ancient custom required that every slave residing under the same roof must be executed. But a crowd gathered, eager to save so many innocent lives; and rioting began. The senatehouse was besieged. Inside, there was feeling against excessive severity, but the majority opposed any change. Among the latter was Gaius Cassius Longinus, who when his turn came spoke as follows....

"An ex-consul has been deliberately murdered by a slave in his own home. None of his fellow-slaves prevented or betrayed the murderer, though the senatorial decree threatening the whole household with execution still stands. Exempt them from the penalty if you like. But then, if the City Prefect was not important enough to be immune; who will be? Who will have enough slaves to protect him if Pedanius' four hundred were too few? Who can rely on his household's help if even fear for their own lives does not make them shield us?"

[The sentence of death was carried out.]

Pliny the Younger to Acilius

This horrible affair demands more publicity than a letter—Larcius Macedo, a senator and ex-praetor, has fallen a victim to his own slaves. Admittedly he was a cruel and overbearing master, too ready to forget that his father had been a slave, or perhaps too keenly conscious of it. He was taking a bath in his house at Formiae when suddenly he found himself surrounded; one slave seized him by the throat while the others struck his face and hit him in the chest and stomach and—shocking to say—in his private parts. When they thought he was dead they threw him onto the hot pavement, to make sure he was not still alive. Whether unconscious or feigning to be so, he lay there motionless, thus making them believe that he was quite dead. Only then was he carried out, as if he had fainted with the heat, and received by his slaves who had remained faithful, while his concubines ran up, screaming frantically. Roused by their cries and revived by the cooler air he opened his eyes and made some movement to show that he was alive, it being now safe to do so. The guilty slaves fled, but most of them have been arrested and a search is being made for the others. Macedo was brought back to life with difficulty, but only for a few days; at least he died with the satisfaction of having revenged himself, for he lived to see the same punishment meted out as for murder. There you see the dangers, outrages, and insults to which we are exposed. No master can feel safe because he is kind and considerate; for it is their brutality, not their reasoning capacity, which leads slaves to murder masters.

Q *What do these texts reveal about the practice of slavery in the Roman Empire? What were Roman attitudes toward the events discussed in them?*

CENGAGENOW *To read other works by Tacitus and Pliny, enter the documents area of the World History Resource Center using the access card that is available for World History.*

---

subject to severe punishments, torture, abuse, and hard labor that drove some to run away, despite the stringent laws Romans had against aiding a runaway slave. Some slaves revolted against their owners and even murdered them, causing some Romans to live in unspoken fear of their slaves (see the box above).

Near the end of the second century B.C.E., large-scale slave revolts occurred in Sicily, where enormous gangs of slaves were subjected to horrible working conditions on large landed estates. The most famous uprising on the Italian peninsula occurred in 73 B.C.E. Led by a gladiator named Spartacus, the revolt broke out in southern Italy and involved seventy thousand slaves. Spartacus managed to defeat several Roman armies before being trapped and killed in southern Italy in 71 B.C.E. Six thousand of his followers were crucified, the traditional form of execution for slaves.

Imperial Rome At the center of the colossal Roman Empire was the ancient city of Rome. A true capital city, Rome had the largest population of any city in the empire, close to one million by the time of Augustus. Only Chang'an, the imperial capital of the Han Empire in China, had a comparable population during this time.

Both food and entertainment were provided on a grand scale for the inhabitants of Rome. The poet Juvenal said of the Roman masses, "But nowadays, with no vote to sell, their motto is 'Couldn't care less.' Time was when their plebiscite elected generals, heads of state,

Spartacus, directed by Stanley Kubrick, is based on *Spartacus*, a novel written by Howard Fast, and focuses for the most part on the major events in the life of the gladiator who led a major rebellion against the Romans. Kirk Douglas stars as a Thracian slave who was bought and trained as a gladiator by Batiatus, a role played by Peter Ustinov, who won an Oscar for Best Supporting Actor for his performance. Spartacus leads a revolt in the gladiatorial camp in Capua run by Batiatus, flees with the other gladiators, and then brings together a large number of escaped slaves as they move through southern Italy. The gladiators among them are able to create the semblance of a trained army, and they are initially successful in conquering a force sent from the city of Rome. Eventually, however, they are defeated by the army of Crassus (Laurence Olivier), who is aided by the unexpected arrival of the forces of two other Roman generals. Many of the leaders of the revolt, including Spartacus, are crucified as punishment for their rebellion. Nevertheless, the movie has a typical happy Hollywood ending, which is entirely fictional. Varinia, a slave woman (Jean Simmons) who has married Spartacus and given birth to his son, bids a final farewell to the crucified Spartacus, who sees his son and is assured by Varinia that he will live as a free man.

Freedom is the key word for this entire movie. Spartacus is portrayed as a man who dreamed of the death of slavery, thousands of years before its death (although he would be disappointed to know that it still survives in some corners of the world today). The film rings with the words of freedom: "We only want our freedom," "We must stay true to ourselves; we are brothers and we are free," and "I pray for a son who must be born free." Indeed, freedom was also on the minds of the film's creators. The film appeared in 1960, only a few years after Senator Joseph McCarthy's anti-Communist crusade in the 1950s had led to an exaggerated fear of Communists. Both Howard Fast, the author of the novel, and Dalton Trumbo, the screenwriter for the film, had been blacklisted from working in Hollywood as a result of McCarthy's charges that they were Communists or Communist sympathizers. The film was a statement of Hollywood's determination to allow both men to work freely and openly. The speeches about freedom also evoke the rhetoric of free world versus communism that was heard frequently during the height of the Cold War in the 1950s.

commanders of legions; but now they've pulled in their horns, there's only two things that concern them: Bread and Circuses."[4] Public spectacles were provided by the emperor as part of the great religious festivals celebrated by the state. Most famous were the gladiatorial shows, which took place in amphitheaters. Perhaps the most famous was the amphitheater known as the Colosseum,

constructed in Rome to seat fifty thousand spectators. In most cities and towns, amphitheaters were the biggest buildings, rivaled only by the circuses (arenas) for races and the public baths.

Gladiatorial games were held from dawn to dusk. Contests to the death between trained fighters formed the central focus of these games, but the games

Spartacus (Kirk Douglas) collects booty and followers as he leads his army south.

Although the general outlines of the film are historically accurate (there was a slave rebellion in southern Italy from 73 to 71 B.C.E. led by a slave rebellion in southern Italy Roman troops commanded by Crassus), it also contains a number of historical inaccuracies. Although many slave leaders were crucified, Spartacus was not one of them. He was killed in the final battle, and his body was never found. Crassus, the general who crushed the slave rebellion, was not seeking dictatorial power as the film insists. The character of Gracchus is depicted as a mob-loving popular senatorial leader, although the Gracchus brothers had died some fifty years before the revolt. Julius Caesar had nothing to do with Spartacus, nor was he made prefect of the city, a position that did not yet exist.

Bryna/Universal/The Kobal Collection

included other forms of entertainment as well. Criminals of all ages and both genders were sent into the arena without weapons to face certain death from wild animals who would tear them to pieces. Numerous types of animal contests were also held: wild beasts against each other, such as bears against buffaloes; staged hunts with men shooting safely from behind iron bars; and gladiators in the arena with bulls, tigers, and lions. It is recorded that five thousand beasts were killed in one day of games when Emperor Titus inaugurated the Colosseum in 80 C.E.

Disaster in Southern Italy   Gladiatorial spectacles were contrived by humans, but the Roman Empire also experienced some spectacular natural disasters. One of the greatest was the eruption of Mount Vesuvius on August 24, 79 C.E. Although known to be a volcano, Vesuvius was thought to be extinct, its hillsides green with flourishing vineyards. Its eruption threw up thousands of tons of lava and ash. Toxic fumes killed many people, and the nearby city of Pompeii was quickly buried under volcanic ash. To the west, Herculaneum and other communities around the Bay of Naples were submerged beneath a mud flow (see the box on p. 147). Not for another 1,700 years were systematic excavations begun on the buried towns. The examination of their preserved remains have enabled archaeologists to reconstruct the everyday life and art of these Roman towns. Their discovery in the eighteenth century was an important force in stimulating both scholarly and public interest in classical antiquity and helped give rise to the Neoclassical style of that century.

Crisis and the Late Empire

Q Focus Question: What reforms did Diocletian and Constantine institute, and to what extent were the reforms successful?

During the reign of Marcus Aurelius, the last of the five good emperors, a number of natural catastrophes struck Rome. To many Romans, these natural disasters seemed to portend an ominous future for Rome. New problems arose soon after the death of Marcus Aurelius in 180.

Crises in the Third Century

In the course of the third century, the Roman Empire came near to collapse. Military monarchy under the Severan rulers (193–235), which restored order after a series of civil wars, was followed by military anarchy. For the next forty-nine years, the Roman imperial throne was occupied by anyone who had the military strength to seize it—a total of twenty-two emperors, only two of whom did not meet a violent death. At the same time, the empire was beset by a series of invasions, no doubt exacerbated by the civil wars. In the east, the

Sassanid Persians made inroads into Roman territory. Germanic tribes also poured into the empire. Not until the end of the third century were most of the boundaries restored.

Invasions, civil wars, and plague came close to causing an economic collapse of the Roman Empire in the third century. There was a noticeable decline in trade and small industry, and the labor shortage caused by the plague affected both military recruiting and the economy. Farm production deteriorated significantly as fields were ravaged by invaders or, even more often, by the defending Roman armies. The monetary system began to collapse as a result of debased coinage and inflation. Armies were needed more than ever, but financial strains made it difficult to pay and enlist more soldiers. By the mid-third century, the state had to hire Germans to fight under Roman commanders.

The Late Roman Empire

At the end of the third and beginning of the fourth centuries, the Roman Empire gained a new lease on life through the efforts of two strong emperors, Diocletian and Constantine. Under their rule, the empire was transformed into a new state, the so-called Late Empire, distinguished by a new governmental structure, a rigid economic and social system, and a new state religion—Christianity (see "Transformation of the Roman World: The Development of Christianity" later in this chapter).

The Reforms of Diocletian and Constantine   Both Diocletian (284–305) and Constantine (306–337) expanded imperial control by strengthening and expanding the administrative bureaucracies of the Roman Empire. A hierarchy of officials exercised control at the various levels of government. The army was enlarged, and mobile units were set up that could be quickly moved to support frontier troops when the borders were threatened.

Constantine's biggest project was the construction of a new capital city in the east, on the site of the Greek city of Byzantium on the shores of the Bosporus. Eventually renamed Constantinople (modern Istanbul), the city was developed for defensive reasons and had an excellent strategic location. Calling it his "New Rome," Constantine endowed the city with a forum, large palaces, and a vast amphitheater.

The political and military reforms of Diocletian and Constantine greatly increased two institutions—the army

Location of Constantinople, the "New Rome"

FAMILY & SOCIETY

Pliny the Younger, an upper-class Roman who rose to the position of governor of Bithynia in Asia Minor, wrote a letter to the Roman historian Tacitus, describing the death of his uncle, Pliny the Elder, as a result of the eruption of Mount Vesuvius. Pliny the Elder was the commander of a fleet at Misenum. When the eruption occurred, his curiosity led him to take a detachment of his fleet to the scene. He landed at Stabiae, where he died from toxic fumes.

Pliny, Letter to Cornelius Tacitus

Thank you for asking me to send you a description of my uncle's death so that you can leave an accurate account of it for posterity.... It is true that he perished in a catastrophe which destroyed the loveliest regions of the earth, a fate shared by whole cities and their people, and one so memorable that it is likely to make his name live for ever....

My uncle was stationed at Misenum, in active command of the fleet. On 24 August, in the early afternoon, my mother drew his attention to a cloud of unusual size and appearance.... He called for his shoes and climbed up to a place which would give him the best view of the phenomenon. It was not clear at that distance from which mountain the cloud was rising (it was afterwards known to be Vesuvius); its general appearance can best be expressed as being like an umbrella pine, for it rose to a great height on a sort of trunk and then split off into branches, I imagine because it was thrust upwards by the first blast and then left unsupported as the pressure subsided, or else it was borne down by its own weight so that it spread out and gradually dispersed. In places it looked white, elsewhere blotched and dirty, according to the amount of soil and ashes it carried with it. My uncle's scholarly acumen saw at once that it was important enough for a closer inspection, and he ordered a boat to be made ready....

[Unable to go farther by sea, he lands at Stabiae.]

Meanwhile on Mount Vesuvius broad sheets of fire and leaping flames blazed at several points, their bright glare emphasized by the darkness of night. My uncle tried to allay the fears of his companions by repeatedly declaring that these were nothing but bonfires left by the peasants in their terror, or else empty houses on fire in the districts they had abandoned....

They debated whether to stay indoors or take their chance in the open, for the buildings were now shaking with violent shocks, and seemed to be swaying to and fro as if they were torn from their foundations. Outside on the other hand, there was the danger of falling pumice-stones, even though these were light and porous; however, after comparing the risks they chose the latter. In my uncle's case one reason outweighed the other, but for the others it was a choice of fears. As a protection against falling objects they put pillows on their heads tied down with cloths.

Elsewhere there was daylight by this time, but they were still in darkness, blacker and denser than any ordinary night, which they relieved by lighting torches and various kinds of lamp. My uncle decided to go down to the shore and investigate on the spot the possibility of any escape by sea, but he found the waves still wild and dangerous. A sheet was spread on the ground for him to lie down, and he repeatedly asked for cold water to drink. Then the flames and smell of sulphur which gave warning of the approaching fire drove the others to take flight and roused him to stand up. He stood leaning on two slaves and then suddenly collapsed, I imagine because the dense fumes choked his breathing by blocking his windpipe which was constitutionally weak and narrow and often inflamed. When daylight returned on the 26th—two days after the last day he had seen—his body was found intact and uninjured, still fully clothed and looking more like sleep than death.

Q *What do you think were the reactions of upper-class Romans to this event? What do you think was the reaction of lower-class Romans?*

CENGAGENOW™ *To read other works by Pliny, enter the documents area of the World History Resource Center using the access card that is available for World History.*

---

and the civil service—that drained most of the public funds. Though more revenues were needed to pay for the army and the bureaucracy, the population was not growing, so the tax base could not be expanded. To ensure the tax base and keep the empire going despite the shortage of labor, the emperors issued edicts that forced people to remain in their designated vocations. Basic jobs, such as baker or shipper, became hereditary. The fortunes of free tenant farmers also declined. Soon they found themselves bound to the land by large landowners who took advantage of depressed agricultural conditions to enlarge their landed estates.

The End of the Western Empire Constantine had reunited the Roman Empire and restored a semblance of order. After his death, however, the empire continued to divide into western and eastern parts, which had become two virtually independent states by 395. In the course of the fifth century, while the empire in the east remained intact under the Roman emperor in Constantinople, the administrative structure of the empire in the west collapsed and was replaced by an assortment of Germanic kingdoms. The process was a gradual one, beginning with the movement of Germans into the empire.

Although the Romans had established a series of political frontiers along the Rhine and Danube Rivers, Romans and Germans often came into contact across these boundaries. Until the fourth century, the empire had proved capable of absorbing these people without harm to its political structure. In the late fourth century, however, the Germanic tribes came under new pressure when the Huns, a fierce tribe of nomads from the steppes of Asia who may have been related to the Xiongnu, the invaders of the Han Empire in China, moved into the Black Sea region, possibly attracted by the riches of the empire to its south. One of the groups displaced by the Huns was the Visigoths, who moved south and west, crossed the Danube into Roman territory, and settled down as Roman allies. But the Visigoths soon revolted, and the Roman attempt to stop them at Adrianople in 378 led to a crushing defeat for Rome.

Increasing numbers of Germans now crossed the frontiers. In 410, the Visigoths sacked Rome. Vandals poured into southern Spain and Africa, Visigoths into Spain and Gaul. The Vandals crossed into Italy from North Africa and ravaged Rome again in 455. By the middle of the fifth century, the western provinces of the Roman Empire had been taken over by Germanic peoples who set up their own independent kingdoms. At the same time, a semblance of imperial authority remained in Rome, although the real power behind the throne tended to rest in the hands of important military officials known as masters of the soldiers. These military commanders controlled the government and dominated the imperial court. In 476, Odoacer, a new master of the soldiers, himself of German origin, deposed the Roman emperor, the boy Romulus Augustulus. To many historians, the deposition of Romulus signaled the end of the Roman Empire in the west. Of course, this is only a symbolic date, as much of direct imperial rule had already been lost in the course of the fifth century.

Transformation of the Roman World: The Development of Christianity

Q Focus Question: What characteristics of Christianity enabled it to grow and ultimately to triumph?

The rise of Christianity marked a fundamental break with the dominant values of the Greco-Roman world. To understand the rise of Christianity, we must first examine both the religious environment of the Roman world and the Jewish background from which Christianity emerged.

The Roman state religion focused on the worship of a pantheon of Greco-Roman gods and goddesses, including Juno, the patron goddess of women; Minerva, the goddess of craftspeople; Mars, the god of war; and Jupiter Optimus Maximus ("best and greatest"), who became the patron deity of Rome and assumed a central place in the religious life of the city. The Romans believed that the observance of proper ritual by state priests brought them into a right relationship with the gods, thereby guaranteeing security, peace, and prosperity, and that their success in creating an empire confirmed the favor of the gods. As the first-century B.C.E. politician Cicero claimed, "We have overcome all the nations of the world because we have realized that the world is directed and governed by the gods."[5]

The polytheistic Romans were extremely tolerant of other religions. They allowed the worship of native gods and goddesses throughout their provinces and even adopted some of the local deities. In addition, beginning with Augustus, emperors were often officially made gods by the Roman senate, thus bolstering support for the emperors (see the comparative essay "Rulers and Gods" on p. 149).

The desire for a more emotional spiritual experience led many people to the mystery religions of the Hellenistic east, which flooded into the western Roman world during the Early Empire. The mystery religions offered their followers entry into a higher world of reality and the promise of a future life superior to the present one.

In addition to the mystery religions, the Romans' expansion into the eastern Mediterranean also brought them into contact with the Jews. Roman involvement with the Jews began in 63 B.C.E., and by 6 C.E., Judaea (which embraced the old Jewish kingdom of Judah) had been made a province and placed under the direction of a Roman procurator. But unrest continued, augmented by divisions among the Jews themselves. One group, the Essenes, awaited a Messiah who would save Israel from oppression, usher in the kingdom of God, and establish paradise on earth. Another group, the Zealots, were militant extremists who advocated the violent overthrow of Roman rule. A Jewish revolt in 66 C.E. was crushed by the Romans four years later. The Jewish Temple in Jerusalem was destroyed, and Roman power once more stood supreme in Judaea.

The Origins of Christianity

Jesus of Nazareth (c. 6 B.C.E.–c. 29 C.E.) was a Palestinian Jew who grew up in Galilee, an important center of the militant Zealots. Jesus' message was simple. He reassured his fellow Jews that he did not plan to undermine their traditional religion. What was important was not strict adherence to the letter of the law but the transformation of the inner person: "So in everything, do to others what you would have them do to you, for this

COMPARATIVE ESSAY
RULERS AND GODS

All of the world's earliest civilizations believed that there was a close relationship between rulers and gods. In Egypt, pharaohs were considered gods whose role was to maintain the order and harmony of the universe in their own kingdom. In the words of an Egyptian hymn, "What is the king of Upper and Lower Egypt? He is a god by whose dealings one lives, the father and mother of all men, alone by himself, without an equal." In Mesopotamia, India, and China, rulers were thought to rule with divine assistance. Kings were often seen as rulers who derived their power from the gods and who were the agents or representatives of the gods. In ancient India, rulers claimed to be representatives of the gods because they were descended from Manu, the first man who had been made a king by Brahman, the chief god. Many Romans believed that their success in creating an empire was a visible sign of divine favor.

Their supposed connection to the gods also caused rulers to seek divine aid in the affairs of the world. This led to the art of divination, an organized method to discover the intentions of the gods. In Mesopotamian and Roman society, one form of divination involved the examination of the livers of sacrificed animals; features seen in the livers were interpreted to foretell events to come. The Chinese used oracle bones to receive advice from supernatural forces that were beyond the power of human beings. Questions to the gods were scratched on turtle shells or animal bones, which were then exposed to fire. Shamans examined the resulting cracks on the surface of the shells or bones and interpreted their meaning as messages from supernatural forces. The Greeks divined the will of the gods by use of the oracle, a sacred shrine dedicated to a god or goddess who revealed the future in response to a question.

Underlying all of these divinatory practices was a belief in a supernatural universe, that is, a world in which divine forces were in charge and in which humans were dependent for their own well-being on those divine forces. It was not until the Scientific Revolution of the modern world that many people began to believe in a natural world that was not governed by spiritual forces.

Q *What role did spiritual forces play in early civilizations?*

©Fitzwilliam Museum, University of Cambridge, UK/The Bridgeman Art Library

Vishnu. Brahma the Creator, Shiva the Destroyer, and Vishnu the Preserver are the three chief Hindu gods of India. Vishnu is known as the Preserver because he mediates between Brahma and Shiva and thus maintains the stability of the universe.

---

sums up the Law and the Prophets."[6] God's command was simple—to love God and one another: "Love the Lord your God with all your heart and with all your soul and with all your mind and with all your strength." The second is this: Love your neighbor as yourself."[7] In the Sermon on the Mount (see the box on p. 150), Jesus presented the ethical concepts—humility, charity, and brotherly love—that would form the basis of the value system of medieval Western civilization.

To the Roman authorities of Palestine, however, Jesus was a potential revolutionary who might transform Jewish expectations of a messianic kingdom into a revolt against Rome. Therefore, Jesus found himself denounced on many sides, and the procurator Pontius Pilate ordered his crucifixion. But that did not solve the problem. A few loyal followers of Jesus spread the story that Jesus had overcome death, had been resurrected, and had then ascended into heaven. The belief in Jesus' resurrection became an important tenet of Christian doctrine. Jesus was now hailed as "the anointed one" (*Christus* in Greek), the Messiah who would return and usher in the kingdom of God on earth.

Christianity began, then, as a religious movement within Judaism and was viewed that way by Roman authorities for many decades. One of the prominent figures in early Christianity, however, Paul of Tarsus (c. 5–c. 67), believed that the message of Jesus should be preached not only to Jews but to Gentiles (non-Jews) as well. Paul taught that Jesus was the Savior, the son of God, who had come to earth to save all humans, who were all sinners as a result of Adam's sin of disobedience against God. By his death, Jesus had atoned for the sins of all humans and made possible their reconciliation with God and hence their salvation. By accepting Jesus as their Savior, they too could be saved.

The Spread of Christianity

Christianity spread slowly at first. Although the teachings of early Christianity were mostly disseminated by the preaching of convinced Christians, written materials also appeared. Among them were a series of epistles (letters) written by Paul outlining Christian beliefs for different Christian communities. Some of Jesus'

RELIGION & PHILOSOPHY

CHRISTIAN IDEALS: THE SERMON ON THE MOUNT

Christianity was one of many religions competing for attention in the Roman Empire during the first and second centuries. The rise of Christianity marked a fundamental break with the value system of the upper-class elites who dominated the world of classical antiquity. As these excerpts from the Sermon on the Mount in the New Testament gospel of Saint Matthew illustrate, Christians emphasized humility, charity, brotherly love, and a belief in the inner being and a spiritual kingdom superior to this material world. These values and principles were not those of classical Greco-Roman civilization as exemplified in the words and deeds of its leaders.

The Gospel According to Saint Matthew

Now when he saw the crowds, he went up on a mountainside and sat down. His disciples came to him, and he began to teach them, saying:

Blessed are the poor in spirit: for theirs is the kingdom of heaven.

Blessed are those who mourn: for they will be comforted.

Blessed are the meek: for they will inherit the Earth.

Blessed are those who hunger and thirst for righteousness: for they will be filled.

Blessed are the merciful: for they will be shown mercy.

Blessed are the pure in heart: for they will see God.

Blessed are the peacemakers: for they will be called sons of God.

Blessed are those who are persecuted because of righteousness: for theirs is the kingdom of heaven....

You have heard that it was said, "Eye for eye, and tooth for tooth." But I tell you, Do not resist an evil person. If someone strikes you on the right cheek, turn to him the other also....

You have heard that it was said, "Love your neighbor, and hate your enemy." But I tell you, Love your enemies and pray for those who persecute you....

Do not store up for yourselves treasures on Earth, where moth and rust destroy, and where thieves break in and steal. But store up for yourselves treasures in heaven, where moth and rust do not destroy, and where thieves do not break in and steal. For where your treasure is, there your heart will be also....

No one can serve two masters. Either he will hate the one and love the other, or he will be devoted to the one and despise the other. You cannot serve both God and Money.

Therefore I tell you, do not worry about your life, what you will eat or drink; or about your body, what you will wear. Is not life more important than food, and the body more important than clothes? Look at the birds of the air; they do not sow or reap or store away in barns, and yet your heavenly Father feeds them. Are you not much more valuable than they?...So do not worry, saying, What shall we eat? or What shall we drink? or What shall we wear? For the pagans run after all these things, and your heavenly Father knows that you need them. But seek first his kingdom and his righteousness, and all these things will be given to you as well.

Q *What were the ideals of early Christianity? How do they differ from the values and principles of classical Greco-Roman civilization? Compare this sermon to the Buddha's sermon on the Four Noble Truths in Chapter 2. How are they different? How are they similar?*

CENGAGENOW *To read more of the Sermon on the Mount, enter the documents area of the World History Resource Center using the access card that is available for World History.*

disciples may also have preserved some of the sayings of the master in writing and would have passed on personal memories that became the basis of the written gospels—the "good news" concerning Jesus—of Matthew, Mark, Luke, and John, which by the end of the first century C.E. had become the authoritative record of Jesus' life and teachings and formed the core of the New Testament. Recently, some scholars have argued that other gospels, such as that of Thomas, were rejected because they deviated from the beliefs about Jesus held by the emerging church leaders.

Although Jerusalem was the first center of Christianity, its destruction by the Romans in 70 C.E. dispersed the Christians and left individual Christian churches with considerable independence. By 100,

Christian churches had been established in most of the major cities of the east and in some places in the western part of the empire. Many early Christians came from the ranks of Hellenized Jews and the Greek-speaking populations of the east. But in the second and third centuries, an increasing number of followers came from Latin-speaking peoples.

Initially, the Romans did not pay much attention to the Christians, whom they regarded as simply another Jewish sect. As time passed, however, the Roman attitude toward Christianity began to change. The Romans tolerated other religions as long as they did not threaten public order or public morals. Many Romans came to view Christians as harmful to the Roman state because they refused to worship the state gods and emperors.

© Scala/Art Resource, NY

Nevertheless, Roman persecution of Christians in the first and second centuries was only sporadic and local, never systematic. In the second century, Christians were largely ignored as harmless (see the box on p. 152). By the end of the reigns of the five good emperors, Christians still represented a small minority within the empire, but one of considerable strength.

The Triumph of Christianity

Christianity grew slowly in the first century, took root in the second, and by the third had spread widely. Why was the new faith able to attract so many followers? First, the Christian message had much to offer the Roman world. The promise of salvation, made possible by Jesus' death and resurrection, made a resounding impact on a world full of suffering and injustice. Christianity seemed to imbue life with a meaning and purpose beyond the simple material things of everyday reality. Second, Christianity seemed familiar. It was regarded as simply another mystery religion, offering immortality as the result of the sacrificial death of a savior-god. At the same time, it offered more than the other mystery religions did. Jesus had been a human figure who was easy to relate to.

Moreover, the sporadic persecution of Christians by the Romans in the first and second centuries, which did little to stop the growth of Christianity, in fact served to strengthen Christianity as an institution in the second and third centuries by causing it to become more organized. Crucial to this change was the emerging role of the bishops, who began to assume more control over church communities. The Christian church was creating a well-defined hierarchical structure in which the bishops and clergy were salaried officers separate from the laity or regular church members.

As the Christian church became more organized, some emperors in the third century responded with more

systematic persecutions, but their schemes failed. The last great persecution was at the beginning of the fourth century, but by that time, Christianity had become too strong to be eradicated by force. After Constantine became the first Christian emperor, Christianity flourished. Although Constantine was not baptized until the end of his life, in 313 he issued the Edict of Milan officially tolerating Christianity. Under Theodosius the Great (378–395), it was made the official religion of the Roman Empire. In less than four centuries, Christianity had triumphed.

Jesus and His Apostles. Pictured is a fourth-century C.E. fresco from a Roman catacomb depicting Jesus and his apostles. Catacombs were underground cemeteries where early Christians buried their dead. Christian tradition holds that in times of imperial repression, Christians withdrew to the catacombs to pray and hide.

The Glorious Han Empire (202 B.C.E.–221 C.E.)

Q **Focus Question:** What were the chief features of the Han Empire?

During the same centuries that Roman civilization was flourishing in the West, China was the home of its own great empire. The fall of the Qin dynasty in 206 B.C.E. had been followed by a brief period of civil strife as aspiring successors competed for hegemony. Out of this strife emerged one of the greatest and most durable dynasties in Chinese history—the Han. The Han dynasty would later become so closely identified with the advance of Chinese civilization that even today the Chinese sometimes refer to themselves as "people of Han" and to their language as the "language of Han."

The founder of the Han dynasty was Liu Bang (Liu Pang), a commoner of peasant origin who would be known historically by his title of Han Gaozu (Han Kao Tsu, or Exalted Emperor of Han). Under his strong rule and that of his successors, the new dynasty quickly moved to consolidate its control over the empire and promote the welfare of its subjects. Efficient and benevolent, at least

OPPOSING VIEWPOINTS

ROMAN AUTHORITIES AND A CHRISTIAN ON CHRISTIANITY

At first, Roman authorities were uncertain how to deal with the Christians. In the second century, as seen in the following exchange between Pliny the Younger and the emperor Trajan, Christians were often viewed as harmless and yet were subject to persecution if they persisted in their beliefs. Pliny was governor of the province of Bithynia in northwestern Asia Minor (present-day Turkey). He wrote to the emperor for advice about how to handle people accused of being Christians. Trajan's response reflects the general approach toward Christians by the emperors of the second century. The final selection is taken from *Against Celsus*, written about 246 by Origen of Alexandria. In it, Origen defended the value of Christianity against Celsus, a philosopher who had launched an attack on Christians and their teachings.

An Exchange Between Pliny and Trajan

Pliny to Trajan

It is my custom to refer all my difficulties to you, Sir, for no one is better able to resolve my doubts and to inform my ignorance.

I have never been present at an examination of Christians. Consequently, I do not know the nature of the extent of the punishments usually meted out to them, nor the grounds for starting an investigation and how far it should be pressed....

For the moment this is the line I have taken with all persons brought before me on the charge of being Christians. I have asked them in person if they are Christians, and if they admit it, I repeat the question a second and third time, with a warning of the punishment awaiting them. If they persist, I order them to be led away for execution; for, whatever the nature of their admission, I am convinced that their stubbornness and unshakable obstinacy ought not to go unpunished. There have been others similarly fanatical who are Roman citizens. I have entered them on the list of persons to be sent to Rome for trial.

Now that I have begun to deal with this problem, as so often happens, the charges are becoming more widespread and increasing in variety. An anonymous pamphlet has been circulated which contains the names of a number of accused persons....

I have therefore postponed any further examination and hastened to consult you. The question seems to me to be worthy of your consideration, especially in view of the number of persons endangered; for a great many individuals of every age and class, both men and women, are being brought to trial, and this is likely to continue. It is not only the towns, but villages and rural districts too which are infected through contact with this wretched cult. I think though that it is still possible for it to be checked and directed to better ends, for there is no doubt that people have begun to throng the temples which had been almost entirely deserted for a long time; the sacred rites which had been allowed to lapse are being performed again, and flesh of sacrificial victims is on sale everywhere, though up till recently scarcely anyone could be found to buy it. It is easy to infer from this that a great many people could be reformed if they were given an opportunity to repent.

Trajan to Pliny

You have followed the right course of procedure, my dear Pliny, in your examination of the cases of persons charged with being Christians, for it is impossible to lay down a general rule to a fixed formula. These people must not be hunted out; if they are brought before you and the charge against them is proved, they must be punished, but in the case of anyone who denies that he is a Christian, and makes it clear that he is not by offering prayers to our gods, he is to be pardoned as a result of his repentance however suspect his past conduct may be. But pamphlets circulated anonymously must play no part in any accusation. They create the worst sort of precedent and are quite out of keeping with the spirit of our age.

Origen, *Against Celsus*

[Celsus] says that Christians perform their rites and teach their doctrines in secret, and they do this with good reason to escape the death penalty that hangs over them. He compares the danger to the risks encountered for the sake of philosophy as by Socrates.... I reply to this that in Socrates' cases the Athenians at once regretted what they had done, and cherished no grievance against him.... But in the case of the Christians the Roman Senate, the contemporary emperors, the army,... and the relatives of believers fought against the gospel and would have hindered it; and it would have been defeated by the combined force of so many unless it had overcome and risen above the opposition by divine power, so that it has conquered the whole world that was conspiring against it....

He [also] ridicules our teachers of the gospel who try to elevate the soul in every way to the Creator of the universe.... He compares them [Christians] to wool-workers in houses, cobblers, laundry-workers, and the most obtuse yokels, as if they called children quite in infancy and women to evil practices, telling them to leave their father and teachers and to follow them. But let Celsus...tell us how we make women and children leave noble and sound teaching, and call them to wicked practices. But he will not

(continued)

by the standards of the time, Gaozu maintained the centralized political institutions of the Qin but abandoned its harsh Legalistic approach to law enforcement. Han rulers discovered in Confucian principles a useful foundation for the creation of a new state philosophy. Under the Han, Confucianism began to take on the character of an official ideology.

Confucianism and the State

The integration of Confucian doctrine with Legalist institutions, creating a system generally known as **State Confucianism**, did not take long to accomplish. In doing this, the Han rulers retained many of the Qin institutions. For example, they borrowed the tripartite division of the central government into civilian and military authorities and a censorate. The government was headed by a "grand council" including representatives from all three segments of government. The Han also retained the system of local government, dividing the empire into provinces and districts.

Finally, the Han continued the Qin system of selecting government officials on the basis of merit rather than birth. Shortly after founding the new dynasty, Han Gaozu decreed that local officials would be asked to recommend promising candidates for public service. Thirty years later, in 165 B.C.E., the first known **civil service examination** was established to candidates for positions in the bureaucracy. Shortly after that, an academy was established to train candidates. The first candidates were almost all from aristocratic or other wealthy families, and the Han bureaucracy itself was still dominated by the traditional hereditary elite. Still, the principle of selecting officials on the basis of talent had been established and would eventually become standard practice.

Under the Han dynasty, the population increased rapidly—by some estimates rising from about twenty million to over sixty million at the height of the dynasty—creating a growing need for a large and efficient bureaucracy to maintain the state in proper working order. Unfortunately, the Han were unable to resolve all of the problems left over from the past. Factionalism at court remained a serious problem and undermined the efficiency of the central government. Equally important, despite their efforts, the Han rulers were never able to restrain the great aristocratic families, who continued to play a dominant role in political and economic affairs. The failure to curb the power of the wealthy clans eventually became a major factor in the collapse of the dynasty.

The Economy

Han rulers also retained some of the economic and social policies of their predecessors. In rural areas, they saw that a free peasantry paying taxes directly to the state would both limit the wealth and power of the great noble families and increase the state's revenues. The Han had difficulty preventing the recurrence of the economic inequities that had characterized the last years of the Zhou, however (see the box on p. 154). The land taxes were relatively light, but the peasants also faced a number of other exactions, including military service and forced labor of up to one month annually. Although the use of iron tools brought new lands under the plow and food production increased steadily, the trebling of the population under the Han eventually reduced the average size of the individual farm plot to about one acre per capita, barely enough for survival. As time went on, many poor peasants were forced to sell their land and become tenant farmers, paying rents of up to half the annual harvest. Thus land once again came to be concentrated in the hands of the powerful clans, which often owned thousands of acres worked by tenants.

Although such economic problems contributed to the eventual downfall of the dynasty, in general the Han era was one of unparalleled productivity and prosperity. The period was marked by a major expansion of trade, both domestic and foreign. This was not necessarily due to official encouragement. In fact, the Han were as suspicious of private merchants as their predecessors had been and levied stiff taxes on trade in an effort to limit commercial activities. Merchants were also subject to severe social constraints. They were disqualified from seeking office, restricted in their place of residence, and

(continued)

be able to prove anything of any kind against us. On the contrary, we deliver women from licentiousness and from perversion caused by their associates, and from all mania for theaters and dancing, and from superstition, while we make boys self-controlled when they come to the age of puberty and burn with desires for sexual pleasure, showing them not only the disgrace of their sins, but also what a state these pleasures produce in the souls of bad men, and what penalties they will suffer and how they will be punished.

Q What were Pliny's personal opinions of Christians? Why was he willing to execute them? What was Trajan's response, and what were its consequences for the Christians? What major points did Origen make about the benefits of the Christian religion? Why did the Roman authorities consider these ideas dangerous to the Roman state?

AN EDICT FROM THE EMPEROR

EARTH & ENVIRONMENT

According to Confucian doctrine, Chinese monarchs ruled with the mandate of Heaven so long as they properly looked after the welfare of their subjects. One of their most important responsibilities was to maintain food production at a level sufficient to feed their people. Natural calamities such as floods, droughts, and earthquakes were interpreted as demonstrations of displeasure with the "Son of Heaven" on earth. In this edict, Emperor Wendi (r. 180–157 B.C.E.) wonders whether he has failed in his duty to carry out his imperial Dao (Way), thus incurring the wrath of Heaven. After the edict was issued in 163 B.C.E., the government took steps to increase the grain harvest, bringing an end to the food shortages.

Han Shu (History of the Han Dynasty)

For the past years there have been no good harvests, and our people have suffered the calamities of flood, drought, and pestilence. We are deeply grieved by this, but being ignorant and unenlightened, we have been unable to discover where the blame lies. We have considered whether our administration has been guilty of some error or our actions of some fault. Have we failed to follow the Way of Heaven or to obtain the benefits of Earth? Have we caused disharmony in human affairs or neglected the gods that they do not accept our offerings? What has

brought on these things? Have the provisions for our officials been too lavish or have we indulged in too many unprofitable affairs? Why is the food of the people so scarce? When the fields are surveyed, they have not decreased, and when the people are counted they have not grown in number, so that the amount of land for each person is the same as before or even greater. And yet there is a drastic shortage of food. Where does the blame lie? Is it that too many people pursue secondary activities to the detriment of agriculture? Is it that too much grain is used to make wine or too many domestic animals are being raised? I have been unable to attain a proper balance between important and unimportant affairs. Let this matter be debated by the chancellor, the nobles, the high officials, and learned doctors. Let all exhaust their efforts and ponder deeply whether there is some way to aid the people. Let nothing be concealed from us!

Q *What reasons does Emperor Wendi advance to explain the decline in grain production in China? What are the possible solutions that he proposes? Does his approach meet the requirements for official behavior raised by Chinese philosophers such as Mencius?*

CENGAGENOW · *To read more of the Han Shu, enter the documents area of the World History Resource Center using the access card that is available for World History.*

Imperial Expansion and the Origins of the Silk Road

The Han emperors continued the process of territorial expansion and consolidation that had begun under the Zhou and the Qin. Han rulers, notably Han Wudi (Han Wu Ti, or Martial Emperor of Han), successfully completed the assimilation into the empire of the regions south of the Yangtze River, including the Red River delta in what is today northern Vietnam. Han armies also marched westward as far as the Caspian Sea, pacifying nomadic tribal peoples and extending China's boundary far into Central Asia (see Map 5.5 on p. 156).

The latter project apparently was originally planned as a means to fend off pressure from the nomadic Xiongnu peoples, who periodically threatened Chinese lands from their base area north of the Great Wall. In 138 B.C.E., Han Wudi dispatched the courtier Zhang Qian (Chang Ch'ien) on a mission westward into Central Asia to seek alliances with peoples living in the area against the common Xiongnu menace. Zhang Qian returned home with ample information about political and economic conditions in Central Asia. The new knowledge provoked the Han court to establish the first

viewed in general as parasites providing little true value to Chinese society.

The state itself directed much trade and manufacturing; it manufactured weapons, for example, and operated shipyards, granaries, and mines. The government also moved cautiously into foreign trade, mostly with neighboring areas in Central and Southeast Asia, although trade relations were established with countries as far away as India and the Mediterranean, where active contacts were maintained with the Roman Empire (see Map 5.4). Some of this long-distance trade was carried by sea through southern ports like Guangzhou, but more was transported by overland caravans on the Silk Road (see Chapter 10) and other routes that led westward into Central Asia.

New technology contributed to the economic prosperity of the Han era. Significant progress was achieved in such areas as textile manufacturing, water mills, and iron casting; skill at ironworking led to the production of steel a few centuries later. Paper was invented under the Han, and the development of the rudder and fore-and-aft rigging permitted ships to sail into the wind for the first time. Thus equipped, Chinese merchant ships carrying heavy cargoes could sail throughout the islands of Southeast Asia and into the Indian Ocean.

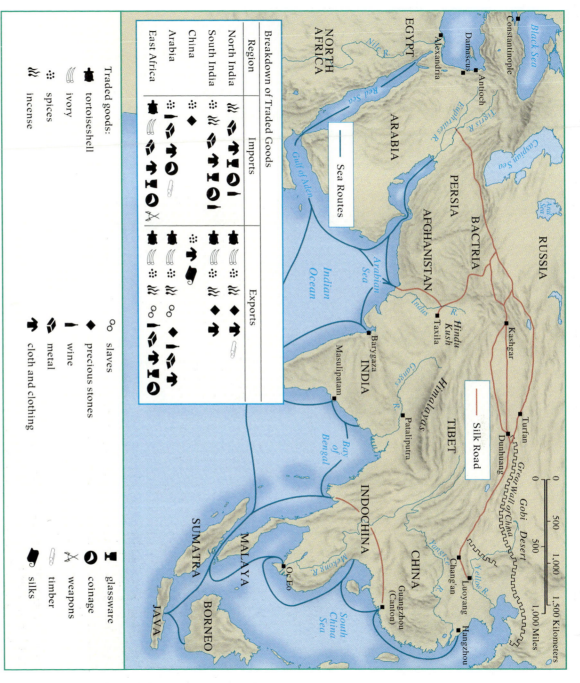

MAP 5.4 **Trade Routes of the Ancient World.** This map shows the various land and maritime routes that extended from China toward other civilizations that were located to the south and west of the Han Empire. The various goods that were exchanged are identified at the bottom of the map.

Q What were the major goods exported from China?

Sea Routes

Silk Road

Traded goods:
- 🐢 tortoiseshell
- ivory
- spices
- incense
- slaves
- precious stones
- wine
- metal
- cloth and clothing
- glassware
- coinage
- weapons
- timber
- silks

Breakdown of Traded Goods

Region	Imports	Exports
North India		
South India		
China		
Arabia		
East Africa		

Chinese military presence in the area of the Taklamakan Desert and the Tian Shan (Heavenly Mountains). Eventually, this area would become known to the Chinese people as Xinjiang, or "New Region."

Chinese commercial exchanges with peoples in Central Asia now began to expand dramatically. Eastward into China came grapes, precious metals, glass objects, and horses from Persia and Central Asia. Horses were of particular significance because Chinese military strategists had learned of the importance of cavalry in their battles against the Xiongnu and sought the sturdy Ferghana horses of Bactria to increase their own military effectiveness. In return, China exported goods, especially silk, to countries to the west.

Silk, a filament recovered from the cocoons of silkworms, had been produced in China since the fourth millennium B.C.E. Eventually, knowledge of the wonder product reached the outside world, and Chinese silk exports began to rise dramatically. By the second century B.C.E., the first items made from silk reached the Mediterranean Sea, stimulating the first significant contacts between China and Rome, its great counterpart in the west. The bulk of the trade went overland through Central Asia (thus earning this route its name, the Silk Road), although significant exchanges also took place via the maritime route (see Chapter 9). Silk became a craze among Roman elites, leading to a vast outflow of silver from Rome to China and provoking

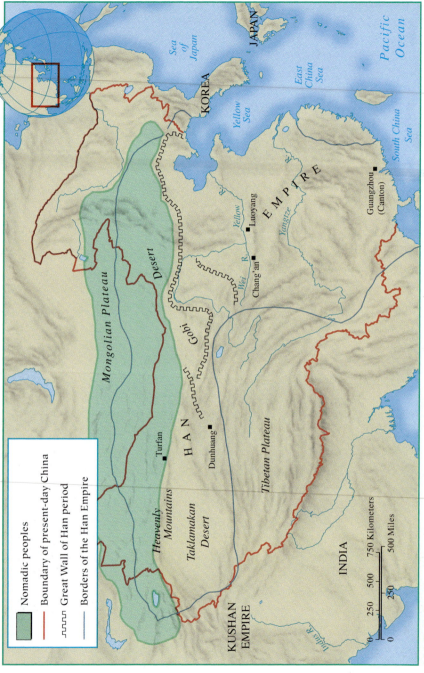

MAP 5.5   The Han Empire. This map shows the territory under the control of the Han Empire at its greatest extent during the first century B.C.E. Note the Great Wall's placement relative to nomadic peoples.

Q How did the expansion of Han rule to the west parallel the Silk Road?

the Roman emperor Tiberius to grumble that "the ladies and their baubles are transferring our money to the foreigners."

The silk trade also stimulated a degree of mutual curiosity between the two great civilizations but not much mutual knowledge or understanding. Roman authors like Pliny and the geographer Strabo (who speculated that silk was produced from the leaves of a "silk tree") wrote of a strange land called "Seres" far to the east, while Chinese sources mentioned the empire of "Great Qin" at the far end of the Silk Route to the west. So far as is known, no personal or diplomatic contacts between the two civilizations ever took place. But two great empires at either extreme of the Eurasian supercontinent had for the first time been linked in a commercial relationship.

family—the linear descendant of the clan system in the Zhou dynasty—continued to hold sway in much of the countryside.

Under the Han, women continued to play a secondary role in society. Ban Zhao, a prominent female historian of the Han dynasty whose own career was an exception to the rule, described that role as follows:

> To be humble, yielding, respectful and reverential; to put herself after others—these qualities are those exemplifying woman's low and humble estate. To retire late and rise early; not to shirk exertion from dawn to dark—this is called being diligent. To behave properly and decorously in serving her husband; to be serene and self-possessed, shunning jests and laughter—this is called being worthy of continuing the husband's lineage. If a woman possesses the above-mentioned three qualities, then her reputation shall be excellent.[8]

The vast majority of Chinese continued to live in rural areas, but the number of cities, mainly at the junction of rivers and trade routes, was on the increase. The largest was the imperial capital of Chang'an, which was one of the great cities of the ancient world and rivaled Rome in magnificence. The city covered a total

Social Changes

Under the Han dynasty, Chinese social institutions evolved into more complex forms than had been the case in past eras. The emergence of a free peasantry resulted in a strengthening of the nuclear family, although the joint

area of nearly 16 square miles and was enclosed by a 12-foot earthen wall surrounded by a moat. Twelve gates provided entry into the city, and eight major avenues ran east-west or north-south. Each avenue was nearly 150 feet wide; a center strip in each avenue was reserved for the emperor, whose palace and gardens occupied nearly half of the southern and central parts of the city.

Religion and Culture

The Han dynasty's adoption of Confucianism as the official philosophy of the state did not have much direct impact on the religious beliefs of the Chinese people. Although official sources sought to flesh out the scattered metaphysical references in the Confucian canon with a more coherent cosmology, the pantheon of popular religion was still peopled by local deities and spirits of nature, some connected with popular Daoism. Sometime in the first century C.E., however, a new salvationist faith appeared on the horizon. Merchants from Central Asia carrying their wares over the Silk Road brought the Buddhist faith to China for the first time. At first, its influence was limited, as no Buddhist text was translated into Chinese from the original Sanskrit until the fifth century C.E. But the terrain was ripe for the introduction of a new religion into China, and the first Chinese monks departed for India shortly after the end of the Han dynasty.

Cultural attainments under the Han tended in general to reflect traditional forms, although there was considerable experimentation with new forms of expression. In literature, poetry and philosophical essays continued to be popular, but historical writing became the primary form of literary creativity. Historians such as Sima Qian and Ban Gu (the dynasty's official historian and the older brother of the female historian Ban Zhao) wrote works that became models for later dynastic histories. These historical works combined political and social history with biographies of key figures. Like so much literary work in China, their primary purpose was moral and political—to explain the underlying reasons for the rise and fall of individual human beings and dynasties.

Painting—often in the form of wall frescoes—became increasingly popular, although little has survived the ravages of time. In the plastic arts, bronze was steadily being replaced by iron as a medium of choice. Less expensive to produce, it was better able to satisfy the growing popular demand during a time of increasing economic affluence.

The trend toward reduced expenditures was also evident in the construction of imperial mausoleums. Qin Shi Huangdi's ambitious effort to provide for his immortality became a pattern for his successors during the Han dynasty, although apparently on a somewhat more modest scale. In 1990, Chinese workers discovered a similar underground army for a Han emperor of the second century B.C.E. Like the imperial guard of the First Qin Emperor, the underground soldiers were buried in parallel pits and possessed their own weapons and individual facial features. But they were smaller—only one-third the height of the average human adult—and were armed with wooden weapons and dressed in silk clothing, now decayed. A burial pit nearby indicated that as many as ten thousand workers, probably slaves or prisoners, died in the process of building the emperor's mausoleum, which took an estimated ten years to construct.

©William J. Duiker

Han Dynasty Horse. This terra-cotta horse head is a striking example of Han artistry. Although the Chinese had domesticated the smaller Mongolian pony as early as 2000 B.C.E., it was not until toward the end of the first millennium B.C.E. that the Chinese acquired horses as a result of military expeditions into Central Asia. Admired for their power and grace, horses made of terra-cotta or bronze were often placed in Qin and Han tombs. This magnificent head suggests the divine power that the Chinese of this time attributed to horses.

power continued. Weak rulers were isolated within their imperial chambers and dominated by eunuchs and other powerful court insiders. Official corruption and the concentration of land in the hands of the wealthy led to widespread peasant unrest. The Han also continued to have problems with the Xiongnu beyond the Great Wall to the north. Nomadic raids on Chinese territory continued intermittently to the end of the dynasty, once reaching almost to the gates of the capital city. One Chinese source reported with bitterness the conditions of the times:

The houses of the powerful are compounds where several hundreds of ridgebeams are linked together. Their fertile fields fill the countryside. Their slaves throng in thousands, and their military dependents can be counted in tens of thousands. Their boats, carts, and merchants are spread throughout the four quarters. Their stocks of goods held back for speculation fill up the principal cities. Their great mansions cannot contain their precious stones and treasure. The upland valleys cannot hold their horses, cattle, sheep, and swine. Their elegant apartments are full of seductive lads and lovely concubines. Singing-girls and courtesans are lined up in their deep halls.[9]

Buffeted by insurmountable problems within and without, in the late second century C.E., the dynasty entered a period of inexorable decline. The population of the empire, which had been estimated at about sixty million in China's first census in the year 2 C.E., had shrunk to less than one-third that number two hundred years later. In the early third century C.E., the dynasty was finally brought to an end when power was seized by Cao Cao (Ts'ao Ts'ao), a general known to later generations as one of the main characters in the famous Chinese epic *The Romance of the Three Kingdoms*. But Cao Cao was unable to consolidate his power, and China entered a period of almost constant anarchy and internal division, compounded by invasions by northern tribal peoples. The next great dynasty did not arise until the beginning of the seventh century, four hundred years later.

CHRONOLOGY The Han Dynasty

Overthrow of Qin dynasty	206 B.C.E.
Formation of Han dynasty	202 B.C.E.
First silk goods arrive in Europe	Second century B.C.E.
Reign of Han Wudi	141–87 B.C.E.
Zhang Qian's first mission to Central Asia	138–126 B.C.E.
First Buddhist merchants arrive in China	First century C.E.
Wang Mang interregnum	9–23 C.E.
Collapse of Han dynasty	221 C.E.

The Decline and Fall of the Han

In 9 C.E., the reformist official Wang Mang, who was troubled by the plight of the peasants, seized power from the Han court and declared the foundation of the Xin (New) dynasty. The empire had been crumbling for decades. As frivolous or depraved rulers amused themselves with the pleasures of court life, the power and influence of the central government began to wane, and the great noble families filled the vacuum, amassing vast landed estates and transforming free farmers into tenants. Wang Mang tried to confiscate the great estates, restore the ancient well field system, and abolish slavery. In so doing, however, he alienated powerful interests, who conspired to overthrow him. In 23 C.E., beset by administrative chaos and a collapse of the frontier defenses, Wang Mang was killed in a coup d'état.

For a time, strong leadership revived some of the glory of the early Han. The court did attempt to reduce land taxes and carry out land resettlement programs. The growing popularity of nutritious crops like rice, wheat, and soybeans, along with the introduction of new crops such as alfalfa and grapes, helped boost food production. But the great landed families' firm grip on land and

CONCLUSION

At the beginning of the first millennium C.E., two great empires—the Roman Empire in the West and the Han Empire in the East—dominated large areas of the world. Although there was little contact between them, the two empires had some remarkable similarities. Both lasted for centuries, and both had remarkable success in establishing centralized control. They built elaborate systems of roads in order to rule efficiently and relied on provincial officials, and especially on towns and cities, for local administration. In both empires, settled conditions led to a high level of agricultural production that sustained large populations, estimated at between fifty and sixty million in each empire. Although both empires expanded into areas that had

different languages, ethnic groups, and ways of life, they managed to carry their legal and political institutions, their technical skills, and their languages throughout their territory.

The Roman and Han Empires had similar social and economic structures. The family stood at the heart of the social structure, with the male head of the family as all-powerful. Duty, courage, obedience, discipline—all were values inculcated by the family that helped make the empires strong. The wealth of both societies also depended on agriculture. Although a free peasantry was a backbone of strength and stability in each, the gradual conversion of free peasants into tenant farmers by wealthy landowners was common to both societies and ultimately served to undermine the power of their imperial governments.

Of course, there were also significant differences. Merchants were more highly regarded and allowed more freedom in Rome than they were in China. One key reason seems clear: whereas many subjects of the Roman Empire depended to a considerable degree on commerce to provide them with items of daily use such as wheat, olives, wine, cloth, and timber, the vast majority of Chinese were subsistence farmers whose needs—when they were supplied—could normally be met by the local environment. As a result, social mobility was undoubtedly more limited in China than in Rome, and many Chinese peasants never ventured in their entire lives far beyond their village gate.

On the other hand, political instability was more pronounced in the Roman Empire. With the mandate of Heaven and the strong dynastic principle, Chinese rulers had authority that was easily passed on to other family members. Although Roman emperors were accorded divine status by the Roman senate after their death, accession to the Roman imperial throne depended less on solid dynastic principles and more on pure military force. As a result, over a period of centuries, Chinese imperial authority was far more stable.

Both empires were eventually overcome by invasions of nomadic peoples: the Han dynasty was weakened by the incursions of the Xiongnu, and the western Roman Empire eventually collapsed in the face of incursions by the Germanic peoples. However, although the Han dynasty collapsed, the Chinese imperial tradition, along with the class structure and values that sustained it, survived, and the Chinese Empire, under new dynasties, continued into the twentieth century as a unified political entity. The Roman Empire, by contrast, collapsed and lived on only as an idea.

Nevertheless, Roman achievements were bequeathed to the future. The Romance languages of today (French, Italian, Spanish, Portuguese, and Romanian) are based on Latin. Western practices of impartial justice and trial by jury owe much to Roman law. As great builders, the Romans left monuments to their skills throughout Europe, some of which, such as aqueducts and roads, are still in use today. Aspects of Roman administrative practices survived in the Western world for centuries. The Romans also preserved the intellectual heritage of the Greco-Roman world of antiquity. But the heirs of Rome went on to create new civilizations—European, Islamic, and Byzantine—that led to a dramatically different phase in the development of human society.

TIMELINE

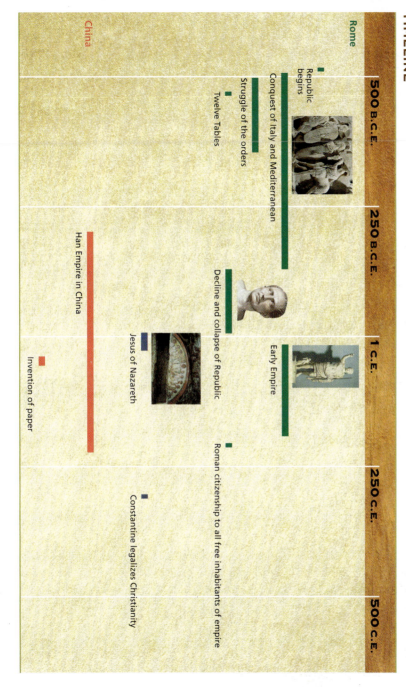

Rome

China

500 B.C.E.   250 B.C.E.   1 C.E.   250 C.E.   500 C.E.

Republic begins

Struggle of the orders

Twelve Tables

Conquest of Italy and Mediterranean

Decline and collapse of Republic

Early Empire

Jesus of Nazareth

Roman citizenship to all free inhabitants of empire

Constantine legalizes Christianity

Han Empire in China

Invention of paper

CHAPTER NOTES

1. Livy, *The Early History of Rome*, trans. A. de Selincourt, 1:16. The words were spoken by Julius Proculus, reportedly relaying to the Roman assembly a message from Romulus, one of Rome's founders, who appeared to him in a dream.

2. Tacitus, *The Annals of Imperial Rome*, trans. M. Grant (Harmondsworth, England, 1964), p. 31.

3. Virgil, *The Aeneid*, trans. C. Day Lewis (Garden City, N.Y., 1952), p. 154.

4. Juvenal, *The Sixteen Satires*, trans. P. Green (New York, 1967), p. 207.

5. Quoted in C. Starr, *Past and Future in Ancient History* (Lanham, Md., 1987), pp. 38–39.

6. Matthew 7:12.

7. Mark 12:30–31.

8. Quoted in L. E. Eastman, *Family, Fields, and Ancestors: Constancy and Change in China's Social and Economic History, 1500–1949* (New York, 1988), p. 19.

9. Quoted in M. Elvin, *The Pattern of the Chinese Past* (Stanford, Calif., 1973), p. 28.

SUGGESTED READING

General Surveys For a general account of Roman history, see M. T. Boatwright, D. J. Gargola, and R. J. A. Talbert, *The Romans: From Village to Empire* (New York, 2004). Good surveys of the Roman Republic include M. H. Crawford, *The Roman Republic*, 2d ed. (Cambridge, Mass., 1993); C. S. Mackay, *Ancient Rome: A Military and Political History* (Cambridge, 2004); H. H. Scullard, *History of the Roman World, 753–146 B.C.*, 4th ed. (London, 1978); M. Le Glay, J.-L. Voisin, and Y. Le Bohec, *A History of Rome*, trans. A. Nevill (Oxford, 1996); and A. Kamm, *The Romans* (London, 1995). The history of early Rome is well covered in T. J. Cornell, *The Beginnings of Rome: Italy and Rome from the Bronze Age to the Punic Wars (c. 1000–264 B.C.)* (London, 1995).

Roman Expansion Accounts of Rome's expansion in the Mediterranean world are provided by J.-M. David, *The Roman Conquest of Italy*, trans. A. Nevill (Oxford, 1996), and R. M. Errington, *The Dawn of Empire: Rome's Rise to World Power* (Ithaca, N.Y., 1971). On Rome's struggle with Carthage, see A. Goldsworthy, *The Punic Wars* (New York, 2001). The Roman army is examined in A. Goldsworthy, *The Complete Roman Army* (London, 2003).

The Late Republic An excellent account of basic problems in the late republic can be found in M. Beard and M. H. Crawford, *Rome in the Late Republic* (London, 1984). Also valuable are D. Shotter, *The Fall of the Roman Republic* (London, 1994), and E. Hildinger, *Swords Against the Senate: The Rise of the Roman Army and the Fall of the Republic* (Cambridge, Mass., 2002). On the role of Caesar, see A. Goldsworthy, *Caesar: Life of a Colossus* (New Haven, Conn., 2006).

Early Roman Empire Good surveys of the Early Roman Empire include P. Garnsey and R. Saller, *The Roman Empire: Economy, Society and Culture* (London, 1987); C. Wells, *The Roman Empire*, 2d ed. (London, 1992); M. Goodman, *The Roman World, 44 B.C.–A.D. 180* (London, 1997); and R. Mellor, *Augustus and the Creation of the Roman Empire* (Boston, 2005), for a brief history with documents.

Roman Society and Culture A good survey of Roman literature can be found in R. M. Ogilvie, *Roman Literature and Society* (Harmondsworth, England, 1980). On Roman art and architecture, see F. S. Kleiner, *A History of Roman Art* (Belmont, Calif., 2006). A general study of daily life in Rome is F. Dupont, *Daily Life in Ancient Rome* (Oxford, 1994). On the city of Rome, see O. F. Robinson, *Ancient Rome: City Planning and Administration* (New York, 1992). On the Roman family, see S. Dixon, *The Roman Family* (Baltimore, 1992). Roman women are examined in R. Baumann, *Women and Politics in Ancient Rome* (New York, 1995). On slavery, see K. R. Bradley, *Slavery and Society at Rome* (New York, 1994). On the gladiators, see F. Meijer, *The Gladiators: History's Most Deadly Sport* (Boston, 2005).

Late Roman Empire On the Late Roman Empire, see S. Mitchell, *History of the Later Roman Empire, A.D. 284–641* (Oxford, 2006), and A. Cameron, *The Later Roman Empire* (Cambridge, Mass., 1993). On the fourth century, see T. D. Barnes, *The New Empire of Diocletian and Constantine* (Cambridge, Mass., 1982). Studies analyzing the aristocratic circles, the barbarian invasions, and the military problem include E. A. Thompson, *Romans and Barbarians* (Madison, Wis., 1982); A. Ferrill, *The Fall of the Roman Empire: The Military Explanation* (London, 1986); and P. Heather, *The Fall of the Roman Empire: A New History of Rome and the Barbarians* (New York, 2006). On the relationship between the Romans and the Germans, see T. S. Burns, *Rome and the Barbarians, 100 B.C.–A.D. 400* (Baltimore, 2003), and M. Kulikowski, *Rome's Gothic Wars* (New York, 2007).

Early Christianity For a general introduction to early Christianity, see J. Court and K. Court, *The New Testament World* (Cambridge, 1990). Useful works on early Christianity include W. H. C. Frend, *The Rise of Christianity* (Philadelphia, 1984), and R. MacMullen, *Christianizing the Roman Empire* (New Haven, Conn., 1984). For a detailed analysis of Christianity in the 30s and 40s of the first century C.E., see J. D. Crossan, *The Birth of Christianity* (New York, 1998). On Christian women, see D. M. Scholer, ed., *Women in Early Christianity* (New York, 1993), and R. Kraemer, *Her Share of the Blessings: Women's Religion Among the Pagans, Jews and Christians in the Graeco-Roman World* (Oxford, 1995).

The Han Empire There are a number of useful books on the Han dynasty. Two very good recent histories are M. E. Lewis, *Early Chinese Empires: Qin and Han* (Cambridge, Mass., 2007), and C. Holcombe, *The Genesis of East Asia, 221 B.C.–A.D. 207*

(Honolulu, 2001). The latter study places Han China in a broader East Asian perspective. **Z. Wang,** *Han Civilization* (New Haven, Conn., 1982), presents evidence from the mainland on excavations from Han tombs and the old imperial capital of Chang'an. Also see the lavishly illustrated *Han Civilization of China* (Oxford, 1982) by **M. P. Serstevens.**

CENGAGE**NOW**

Enter *CengageNOW* using the access card that is available with this text. *CengageNOW* will help you understand the content in this chapter with lesson plans generated for your needs, as well as provide you with a connection to the *Wadsworth World History Resource Center* (see description below for details).

WORLD HISTORY RESOURCE CENTER

Enter the Resource Center using either your *CengageNOW* access card or your separate access card for the *World History Resource Center.* Organized by topic, this Website includes quizzes; images; over 350 primary source documents; interactive simulations, maps, and timelines; movie explorations; and a wealth of other resources. You can read the following documents, and many more, at the *World History Resource Center:*

Plutarch, *Life of Caesar*

Virgil, *The Aeneid,* book 1

Visit the *World History Companion Website* for chapter quizzes and more:

www.cengage.com/history/Duiker/World6e

2000 B.C.E.

3000 B.C.E.

4000 B.C.E.

5000 B.C.E.

6000 B.C.E.

Middle East

Agriculture and Neolithic towns

Sumerian civilization

India

First agricultural settlements

Harappan civilization

China

First settled agriculture

Egypt and the Mediterranean

Agriculture in the Nile Valley

Flowering of Egyptian civilization

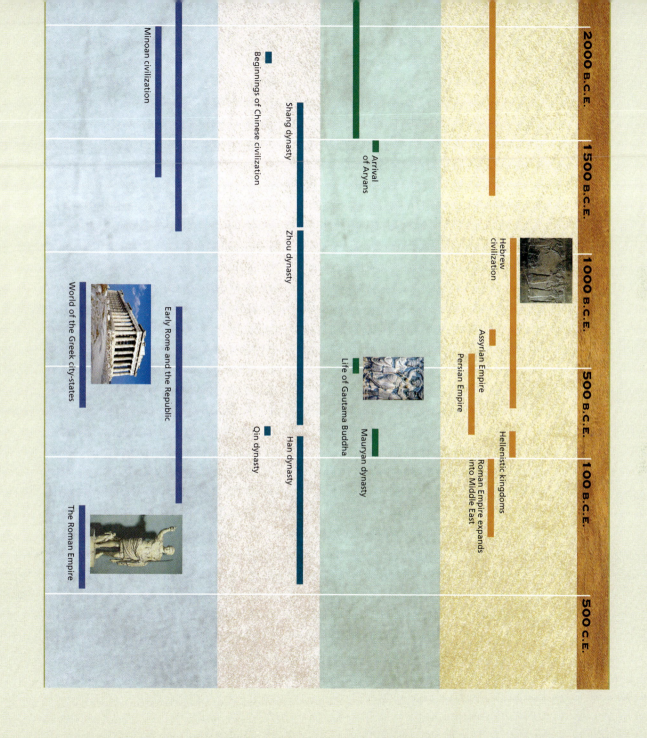

2000 B.C.E. 1500 B.C.E. 1000 B.C.E. 500 B.C.E. 100 B.C.E. 500 C.E.

Minoan civilization

Beginnings of Chinese civilization

Shang dynasty

Arrival of Aryans

Zhou dynasty

Hebrew civilization

World of the Greek city-states

Early Rome and the Republic

Assyrian Empire

Persian Empire

Life of Gautama Buddha

Qin dynasty

Han dynasty

Mauryan dynasty

Hellenistic kingdoms

Roman Empire expands into Middle East

The Roman Empire

163

NEW PATTERNS OF CIVILIZATION

BY THE BEGINNING of the first millennium C.E., the great states of the ancient world were in decline; some were even at the point of collapse. On the ruins of these ancient empires, new patterns of civilization began to take shape between 400 and 1500 C.E. In some cases, these new societies were built on the political and cultural foundations of their predecessors. The Tang dynasty in China and the Guptas in India both looked back to the ancient period to provide an ideological model for their own time. The Byzantine Empire carried on parts of the classical Greek tradition while also adopting the powerful creed of Christianity from the Roman Empire. In other cases, new states incorporated some elements of the former classical civilizations while heading in markedly different directions, as in the Arabic states in the Middle East and in the new European civilization of the Middle Ages. In Europe, the Renaissance of the fifteenth century brought an even greater revival of Greco-Roman culture.

During this period, a number of significant forces were at work in human society. The accoutrements of advanced society gradually spread from the heartland regions of the Middle East, the Mediterranean basin, the South Asian subcontinent, and China into new areas of the world—sub-Saharan Africa, central and western Europe, Southeast Asia, and even the islands of Japan, off the eastern edge of the Eurasian landmass. Across the oceans, unique but advanced civilizations began to take shape in isolation in the Americas. In the meantime, the vast migration of peoples continued, leading not only to bitter conflicts but also to increased interchanges of technology and ideas. The result was the transformation of separate and distinct cultures and civilizations into an increasingly complex and vast world system embracing not only technology and trade but also ideas and religious beliefs.

As had been the case during antiquity, the Middle East was the heart of this activity. The Arab Empire, which took shape after the death of Muhammad in the early seventh century, provided the key link in the revived trade routes through the region. Muslim traders—both Arab and Berber—opened contacts with West African societies south of the Sahara, while their ships followed the monsoon winds eastward as far as the Spice Islands in Southeast Asia. Nomads from Central Asia, many of them Muslim, carried goods back and forth along the Silk Road between the Middle East and China. For the next several hundred years, the great cities of the Middle East—Mecca, Damascus, and Baghdad—became among the wealthiest in the known world.

Islam's contributions to the human experience during this period were cultural and technological as well as economic. Muslim philosophers preserved the works of the ancient Greeks for posterity, Muslim scientists and mathematicians made new discoveries about the nature of the universe and the human body, and Arab cartographers and historians mapped the known world and speculated about the fundamental forces in human society.

But the Middle East was not the only or necessarily even the primary contributor to world trade and civilization during this period. While the Arab Empire became the linchpin of trade between the Mediterranean and eastern and southern Asia, a new center of primary importance in world trade was emerging in East Asia, focused on China. China had been a major participant in regional trade during the Han dynasty, when its silks were already being transported to Rome via Central Asia, but its role had declined after the fall of the Han. Now, with the rise of the great Tang and Song dynasties, China reemerged as a major commercial power in East Asia, trading by sea with Southeast Asia and Japan and by land with the nomadic peoples of Central Asia. Like the Middle East, China was also a prime source of new technology. From China came paper, printing, the compass, and gunpowder. The double-hulled Chinese junks that entered the Indian Ocean during the Ming dynasty were slow and cumbersome but extremely seaworthy and capable of carrying substantial quantities of goods over long distances. Many inventions arrived in Europe by way of India or the Middle East, and their Chinese origins were therefore unknown in the West.

Increasing trade on a regional or global basis also led to the exchange of ideas. Buddhism was brought to China by merchants, and Islam first arrived in sub-Saharan Africa and the Indonesian archipelago in the same manner. Merchants were not the only means by which religious and cultural ideas spread, however. Sometimes migration, conquest, or relatively peaceful processes played a part. The case of the Bantu-speaking peoples in Central Africa is apparently an example of peaceful expansion; and while Islam sometimes followed the path of Arab warriors, they rarely imposed their religion by force on the local population. In some instances, as with the Mongols, the conquerors made no effort to convert others to their own religions. By contrast, Christian monks, motivated by missionary fervor, converted many of the peoples of central and eastern Europe. Roman Catholic monks brought Latin Christianity to the Germanic and western Slavic peoples, and monks from the Byzantine Empire largely converted the southern and eastern Slavic populations to Eastern Orthodox Christianity.

Another characteristic of the period between 500 and 1500 C.E. was the almost constant migration of nomadic and seminomadic peoples. Dynamic forces in the Gobi Desert, Central Asia, the Arabian peninsula, and Central Africa provoked vast numbers of peoples to abandon their homelands and seek their livelihood elsewhere. Sometimes the migration was peaceful. More often, however, migration produced political instability and sometimes invasion and subjugation. As had been the case during antiquity, the most active source of migrants was Central Asia. The region later gave birth to the fearsome Mongols, whose armies advanced to the gates of central Europe and the conquest of China in the thirteenth century. Wherever they went, they left a train of enormous destruction and loss of life. Inadvertently, the Mongols were also the source of a new wave of epidemics that swept through much of Europe and the Middle East in the fourteenth century. The spread of the plague—known at the time as the Black Death—took much of the population of Europe to an early grave.

But there was another side to the era of nomadic expansion. Even the invasions of the Mongols—the "scourge of God," as Europeans of the thirteenth and fourteenth centuries called them—had constructive as well as destructive consequences. After their initial conquests, for a brief period of three generations, the Mongols provided an avenue for trade throughout the most extensive empire (known as the Pax Mongolica) the world had yet seen. ◆

© Pierre Colombel/CORBIS

CHAPTER 6
THE AMERICAS

© SEF/Art Resource, NY

Warriors raiding a village to capture prisoners for the ritual of sacrifice.

CHAPTER OUTLINE AND FOCUS QUESTIONS

The Peopling of the Americas

Q Who were the first Americans, and when and how did they come?

Early Civilizations in Central America

Q What were the main characteristics of religious belief in early Mesoamerica?

The First Civilizations in South America

Q What role did the environment play in the evolution of societies in the Americas?

Stateless Societies in the Americas

Q What were the main characteristics of stateless societies in the Americas, and how did they resemble and differ from the civilizations that arose there?

CRITICAL THINKING

Q In what ways were the early civilizations in the Americas similar to those in Part I, and in what ways were they unique?

IN THE SUMMER OF 2001, a powerful hurricane swept through Central America, destroying houses and flooding villages all along the Caribbean coast of Belize and Guatemala. Farther inland, at the archaeological site of Dos Pilas, it uncovered new evidence concerning a series of dramatic events that took place nearly fifteen hundred years ago. Beneath a tree uprooted by the storm, archaeologists discovered a block of stones containing hieroglyphics that described a brutal war between two powerful city-states of the area, a conflict that ultimately contributed to the decline and fall of Mayan civilization, perhaps the most advanced society then in existence throughout Central America.

Mayan civilization, the origins of which can be traced back to about 500 B.C.E., was not as old as some of its counterparts that we have discussed in Part I of this book. But it was the most recent version of a whole series of human societies that had emerged throughout the Western Hemisphere as early as the third millennium B.C.E. Although these early societies are not yet as well known as those of ancient Egypt, Mesopotamia, and India, evidence is accumulating that advanced civilizations had existed in the Americas thousands of years before the arrival of the Spanish conquistadors led by Hernán Cortés. ◆

166

The Peopling of the Americas

Q Focus Question: Who were the first Americans, and when and how did they come?

The Maya were only the latest in a series of sophisticated societies that had sprung up at various locations in North and South America since human beings first crossed the Bering Strait several millennia earlier. Most of these early peoples, today often referred to as **Amerindians,** lived by hunting and fishing or by food gathering. But eventually organized societies, based on the cultivation of agriculture, began to take root in Central and South America. One key area of development was on the plateau of central Mexico. Another was in the lowland regions along the Gulf of Mexico and extending into modern Guatemala. A third was in the central Andes Mountains, adjacent to the Pacific coast of South America. Others were just beginning to emerge in the river valleys and Great Plains of North America.

For the next two thousand years, these societies developed in isolation from their counterparts elsewhere in the world. This lack of contact with other human populations deprived them of access to technological and cultural developments taking place in Africa, Asia, and Europe. They did not know of the wheel, for example, and their written languages were rudimentary compared to equivalents in complex civilizations elsewhere around the globe. But in other respects, their cultural achievements were the equal of those realized elsewhere. When the first European explorers arrived in the region at the turn of the sixteenth century, they described much that they observed in glowing terms.

The First Americans

When the first human beings arrived in the Western Hemisphere has long been a matter of conjecture. In the centuries following the voyages of Christopher Columbus (1492–1504), speculation centered on the possibility that the first settlers to reach the American continents had crossed the Atlantic Ocean. Were they the lost tribes of Israel? Were they Phoenician seafarers from Carthage? Were they refugees from the legendary lost continent of Atlantis? In all cases, the assumption was that they were relatively recent arrivals.

By the mid-nineteenth century, under the influence of the Darwinian concept of evolution, a new theory developed. It proposed that the peopling of America had taken place much earlier as a result of the migration of small groups across the Bering Strait, at a time when the area was a land bridge uniting the continents of Asia and North America. Recent evidence, including numerous physical similarities between most early Americans and contemporary peoples living in northeastern Asia, has confirmed this hypothesis. The debate on when the migrations began continues, however. The archaeologist Louis Leakey, one

of the pioneers in the search for the origins of humankind in Africa, suggested that the first hominids may have arrived in America as long as 100,000 years ago. Others estimate that the first Americans were *Homo sapiens sapiens* who crossed from Asia by foot between ten and fifteen thousand years ago in pursuit of herds of bison and caribou that moved into the area in search of grazing land at the end of the last ice age. Some scholars suggest the possibility that early migrants from Asia followed a maritime route down the western coast of the Americas, supporting themselves by fishing and feeding on other organisms floating in the sea.

In recent years, a number of fascinating new possibilities have opened up. A site discovered at Cactus Hill, in central Virginia, shows signs of human habitation as long as fifteen thousand years ago. Other recent discoveries indicate that some early settlers may have originally come from Africa or from the South Pacific rather than from Asia. The question has not yet been answered definitively.

Nevertheless, it is now generally accepted that human beings were living in the Americas at least fifteen thousand years ago. They gradually spread throughout the North American continent and had penetrated almost to the southern tip of South America by about 11,000 B.C.E. These first Americans were hunters and food gatherers who lived in small nomadic communities close to the sources of their food supply. Although it is not known when agriculture was first practiced, beans and squash seeds have been found at sites that date back at least ten thousand years, implying that farming arose in America almost as early as in the Middle East. The cultivation of maize (corn), and perhaps other crops as well, appears to have been under way as early as 5000 B.C.E. in the Tehuacán valley in central Mexico. A similar process may have occurred in the lowland regions near the modern city of Veracruz and in the Yucatán peninsula farther to the east. There, in the region that archaeologists call Mesoamerica, one of the first civilizations in the Americas began to appear.

Early Civilizations in Central America

Q Focus Question: What were the main characteristics of religious belief in early Mesoamerica?

The first signs of civilization in Mesoamerica appeared at the end of the second millennium B.C.E., with the emergence of what is called Olmec culture in the hot and swampy lowlands along the coast of the Gulf of Mexico south of Veracruz (see Map 6.1).

1 The Olmecs: In the Land of Rubber

Olmec civilization was characterized by intensive agriculture along the muddy riverbanks in the area and by

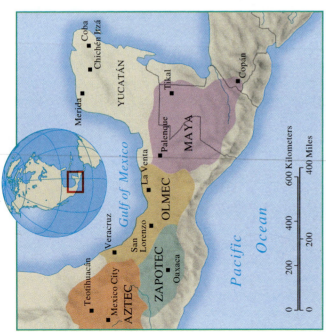

MAP 6.1 Early Mesoamerica. Mesoamerica was home to some of the first civilizations in the Western Hemisphere. This map shows the major urban settlements in the region. **Q** What types of ecological areas were most associated with Olmec, Mayan, and Aztec culture?

the carving of stone ornaments, tools, and monuments at sites such as San Lorenzo and La Venta. The site at La Venta contains a ceremonial precinct with a 30-foot-high earthen pyramid, the largest of its date in all Mesoamerica. The Olmec peoples organized a widespread trading network, carried on religious rituals, and devised an as yet undeciphered system of hieroglyphics that is similar in some respects to later Mayan writing (see "Mayan Hieroglyphs and Calendars" later in this chapter) and may be the ancestor of the first true writing systems in the New World.

Olmec society apparently consisted of several classes, including a class of skilled artisans who produced a series of massive stone heads, some of which are more than 10 feet high. The Olmec peoples supported themselves primarily by cultivating crops, such as corn and beans, but also engaged in fishing and hunting. The Olmecs apparently played a ceremonial game on a stone ball court, a ritual that would later be widely practiced throughout the region (see "The Maya" later in this chapter). The ball was made from the sap of a local rubber tree, thus providing the name Olmec: "people of the land of rubber."

Eventually, Olmec civilization began to decline and apparently collapsed around the fourth century B.C.E. During its heyday, however, it extended from Mexico City to El Salvador and perhaps to the shores of the Pacific Ocean.

The Zapotecs

Parallel developments were occurring at Monte Albán, on a hillside overlooking the modern city of Oaxaca, in central

Mexico. Around the middle of the first millennium B.C.E., the Zapotec peoples created an extensive civilization that flourished for several hundred years in the highlands. Like the Olmec sites, Monte Albán contains a number of temples and pyramids, but they are located in much more awesome surroundings on a massive stone terrace atop a 1,200-foot-high mountain overlooking the Oaxaca valley. The majority of the population, estimated at about twenty thousand, dwelled on terraces cut into the sides of the mountain known to local residents as Danibaan, or "sacred mountain."

The government at Monte Albán was apparently theocratic, with an elite class of nobles and priests ruling over a population composed primarily of farmers and artisans. Like the Olmecs, the Zapotecs devised a written language that has not been deciphered. Zapotec society survived for several centuries following the collapse of the Olmecs, but Monte Albán was abandoned for unknown reasons in the late eighth century C.E.

Teotihuacán: America's First Metropolis

The first major metropolis in Mesoamerica was the city of Teotihuacán, capital of an early state about 30 miles northeast of Mexico City that arose around the third century B.C.E. and flourished for nearly a millennium until it collapsed under mysterious circumstances about 800 C.E. Along the main thoroughfare were temples and palaces, all dominated by the massive Pyramid of the Sun (see the comparative illustration "The Pyramid" on p. 170), under which archaeologists have discovered the remains of sacrificial victims, probably put to death during the dedication of the structure. In the vicinity are the remains of a large market where goods from distant regions as well as agricultural produce grown by farmers in the vicinity were exchanged. The products traded included cacao, rubber, feathers, and various types of vegetables and meat. Pulque, a liquor extracted from the agave plant, was used in religious ceremonies. An obsidian mine nearby may explain the location of the city; obsidian is a volcanic glass that was prized in Mesoamerica for use in tools, mirrors, and the blades of sacrificial knives.

Most of the city consisted of one-story stucco apartment compounds; some were as large as 35,000 square feet, sufficient to house more than a hundred people. Each apartment was divided into several rooms, and the compounds were covered by flat roofs made of wooden beams, poles, and stucco. The compounds were separated by wide streets laid out on a rectangular grid and were entered through narrow alleys.

Living in the fertile Valley of Mexico, an upland plateau surrounded by magnificent snowcapped mountains, the inhabitants of Teotihuacán probably obtained the bulk of their wealth from agriculture. At that time, the valley floor was filled with swampy lakes containing the water runoff from the surrounding mountains. The combination of fertile soil and adequate

The Grand Plaza at Monte Albán. On the crest of a hilltop at Monte Albán, not far from the modern town of Oaxaca, the Zapotec peoples constructed this grand plaza around the seventh century C.E. In the vicinity are a palace, a ball court, three temple complexes, an observatory, and a majestic pyramid. As in other Mesoamerican cities like Teotihuacán, Tikal, Palenque, and Chichén Itzá, these religious sites functioned as immense stage sets where the entire community could observe and participate in the dramas and sacrificial rituals of their cultures. The use of poetry, music, and dance to dramatize human fears and hopes was a universal phenomenon in all ancient societies.

© Claire Duiker

water made the valley one of the richest farming areas in Mesoamerica.

Sometime during the eighth century, for unknown reasons, the wealth and power of the city began to decline, and eventually its ruling class departed, with the priests carrying stone images of local deities on their backs. The next two centuries were a time of troubles throughout the region as principalities fought over limited farmland. The problem was later compounded when peoples from surrounding areas, attracted by the rich farmlands, migrated into the Valley of Mexico and began to compete for territory with small city-states already established there. As the local population expanded, farmers began to engage in more intensive agriculture. They drained the lakes to build *chinampas,* swampy islands crisscrossed by canals that provided water for their crops and easy transportation to local markets for their excess produce.

What were the relations among these early societies in Mesoamerica? Trade contacts were quite active, as the Olmecs exported rubber to their neighbors in exchange for salt and obsidian. During its heyday, Olmec influence extended throughout the region, leading some historians to surmise that it was a "mother culture," much like the Shang dynasty was once reputed to be in ancient China (see Chapter 3). Other scholars, however, point to indigenous elements in neighboring cultures and suggest that perhaps the Olmec were merely first among equals.

The Maya

Far to the east of the Valley of Mexico, another major civilization had arisen in what is now the state of Guatemala and the Yucatán peninsula. This was the civilization of the Maya, which was older and just as sophisticated as the society at Teotihuacán.

Origins It is not known when human beings first inhabited the Yucatán peninsula, but peoples contemporaneous with the Olmecs were already cultivating such crops as corn, yams, and manioc in the area during the first millennium B.C.E. As the population increased, an early civilization began to emerge along the Pacific coast directly to the south of the peninsula and in the highlands of modern Guatemala. Contacts were already established with the Olmecs to the west.

Since the area was a source for cacao trees and obsidian, the inhabitants soon developed relations with other early civilizations in the region. Cacao trees (whose name derives from the Mayan word *kakaw*) were the source of chocolate, which was drunk as a beverage by the upper classes, while cocoa beans, the fruit of the cacao tree, were used as currency in markets throughout the region.

As the population in the area increased, the inhabitants began to migrate into the central Yucatán peninsula and farther to the north. The overcrowding forced

RELIGION & PHILOSOPHY

The Pyramid. The building of monumental structures known as pyramids was characteristic of a number of civilizations that arose in antiquity. The pyramid symbolized the link between the world of human beings and the realm of deities and was often used to house the tomb of a deceased ruler. Shown here are two prominent examples. The upper photo shows the pyramids of Giza, Egypt, built in the third millennium B.C.E. and located near the modern city of Cairo. Shown below it is the Pyramid of the Sun at Teotihuacán, erected in central Mexico in the fifth century C.E. Similar structures of various sizes were built throughout the Western Hemisphere. The concept of the pyramid was also widely applied in parts of Asia. Scholars still debate the technical aspects of constructing such pyramids.

Q How would you compare the pyramids erected in the Western Hemisphere with similar structures in other parts of the world? What were their symbolic meanings to the builders?

© Will & Dehl McIntyre/Photo Researchers, Inc.

© Superstock

farmers in the lowland areas to shift from slash-and-burn cultivation to swamp agriculture of the type practiced in the lake region of the Valley of Mexico. By the middle of the first millennium C.E., the entire area was honeycombed with a patchwork of small city-states competing for land and resources. The largest urban centers such as Tikal may have had 100,000 inhabitants at their height and displayed a level of technological and cultural achievement that was unsurpassed in the region. By the end of the third century C.E., Mayan civilization had begun to enter its classical phase.

Political Structures The power of Mayan rulers was impressive. One of the monarchs at Copán—known to scholars as "18 Rabbit" from the hieroglyphs composing his name—ordered the construction of a grand palace requiring more than 30,000 person-days of labor. Around the seventh century C.E., Pacal became king of Palenque, one of the most powerful of the Mayan city-states, through the royal line of his mother and grandmother, thereby breaking the patrilineal descent twice. His mother ruled Palenque for three years and was the

as sculptors or painters. As the society's wealth grew, so did the role of artisans and traders, who began to form a small middle class.

The majority of the population on the peninsula, however (estimated at roughly three million at the height of Mayan prosperity), were farmers. They lived on their *chinampa* plots or on terraced hills in the highlands. Houses were built of adobe and thatch and probably resembled the houses of the majority of the population in the area today. There was a fairly clear-cut division of labor along gender lines. The men were responsible for fighting and hunting, the women for homemaking and the preparation of cornmeal, the staple food of much of the population.

Some noblewomen, however, seem to have played important roles in both political and religious life. In the seventh century C.E., for example, Pacal became king of Palenque, one of the most powerful of the Mayan city-states, through the royal line of his mother and grandmother, thereby breaking the patrilineal descent twice. His mother ruled Palenque for three years and was the

© William J. Duiker

Mayan Temple at Tikal. This eighth-century temple, peering over the treetops of a jungle at Tikal, represents the zenith of the engineering and artistry of the Mayan peoples. Erected to house the body of a ruler, such pyramidal tombs contained elaborate works of jade jewelry, polychrome ceramics, and intricate bone carvings depicting the ruler's life and various deities. This temple dominates a great plaza that is surrounded by a royal palace and various religious structures.

power behind the throne for her son's first twenty-five years of rule. Pacal legitimized his kingship by transforming his mother into a divine representation of the "first mother" goddess.

Mayan Religion Like some of the early religious beliefs in Asia and the Mediterranean, Mayan religion was polytheistic. Although the names were different, Mayan gods shared many of the characteristics of deities of nearby cultures. The supreme god was named Itzamna ("Lizard House"). Deities were ranked in order of importance and had human characteristics, as in ancient Greece and India. Some, like the jaguar god of night, were evil rather than good. Many of the nature deities may have been viewed as manifestations of one supreme godhead (see the box on p. 172). As at Teotihuacán, human sacrifice (normally by decapitation) was practiced to propitiate the heavenly forces.

Physically, the Mayan cities were built around a ceremonial core dominated by a central pyramid surmounted by a shrine to the gods. Nearby were other temples, palaces, and a sacred ball court. Like many of their modern counterparts, Mayan cities suffered from urban sprawl, with separate suburbs for the poor and the middle class, and even strip malls stretched along transportation routes, where merchants hawked their wares to pedestrians passing by.

The ball court was a rectangular space surrounded by vertical walls with metal rings through which the contestants attempted to drive a hard rubber ball. Although the rules of the game are only imperfectly understood, it apparently had religious significance, and the vanquished players were sacrificed in ceremonies held after the close of the game. Most of the players were men, although there may have been some women's teams. Similar courts have been found at sites throughout Central and South America, with the earliest, located near Veracruz, dating back to around 1500 B.C.E.

Mayan Hieroglyphs and Calendars The Mayan writing system, developed during the mid-first millennium B.C.E., was based on hieroglyphs that remained undeciphered until scholars recognized that symbols appearing in many passages represented dates in the Mayan calendar (see the box on p. 173). This elaborate calendar, which measures time back to a particular date in August 3114 B.C.E., required a sophisticated understanding of astronomical events and mathematics to compile. Starting with these known symbols as a foundation, modern scholars have gradually deciphered the script. Like the scripts of the Sumerians and ancient Egyptians, the Mayan hieroglyphs were both ideographic and phonetic and were becoming more phonetic as time passed.

The responsibility for compiling official records in the Mayan city-states was given to a class of scribes, who wrote on deerskin or strips of tree bark. Unfortunately, virtually all such records have fallen victim to the ravages of a humid climate or were deliberately destroyed at the hands of Spanish missionaries after their arrival in the sixteenth century. As one Spanish bishop remarked at the time, "We found a large number of books in these characters and, as they contained nothing in which there were not to be seen superstition and lies of the devil, we burned them all, which they regretted to an amazing degree, and which caused them much affliction."[1]

As a result, almost the only surviving written records dating from the classical Mayan era are those that were carved in stone. One of the most important repositories of Mayan hieroglyphs is at Palenque, an archaeological site deep in the jungles in the neck of the Mexican peninsula, considerably to the west of the Yucatán (see Map 6.2). In a chamber located under the Temple of

THE CREATION OF THE WORLD: A MAYAN VIEW

RELIGION & PHILOSOPHY

Popul Vuh, a sacred work of the ancient Maya, is an account of Mayan history and religious beliefs. No written version in the original Mayan script is extant, but shortly after the Spanish conquest, it was written down in Quiche (the spoken language of the Maya), using the Latin script, apparently translated into Spanish. The following excerpt from the opening lines of Popul Vuh recounts the Mayan myth of the creation.

Popul Vuh: The Sacred Book of the Maya

This is the account of how all was in suspense, all calm, in silence; all motionless, still, and the expanse of the sky was empty.

This is the first account, the first narrative. There was neither man, nor animal, birds, fishes, crabs, trees, stones, caves, ravines, grasses, nor forests; there was only the sky. The surface of the earth had not appeared. There was only the calm sea and the great expanse of the sky.

There was nothing brought together, nothing which could make a noise, nor anything which might move, or tremble, or could make noise in the sky.

There was nothing standing; only the calm water, the placid sea, alone and tranquil. Nothing existed.

There was only immobility and silence in the darkness, in the night. Only the Creator, the Maker, Tepeu, Gucumatz, the Forefathers, were in the water surrounded with light. They were hidden under green and blue feathers, and were therefore called Gucumatz. By nature they were great sages and great thinkers. In this manner the sky existed and also the Heart of Heaven, which is the name of God and thus He is called.

Then came the word. Tepeu and Gucumatz came together in the darkness, in the night, and Tepeu and Gucumatz talked together. They talked then, discussing and deliberating; they agreed, they united their words and their thoughts.

Then while they meditated, it became clear to them that when dawn would break, man must appear. Then they planned the creation, and the growth of the trees and the thickets and the birth of life and the creation of man. Thus it was arranged in the darkness and in the night by the Heart of Heaven who is called Huracan.

The first is called Caculha Huracan. The second is Chipi-Caculha. The third is Raxa-Caculha. And these three are the Heart of Heaven.

So it was that they made perfect the work, when they did it after thinking and meditating upon it.

Q *What similarities and differences do you see between this account of the beginning of the world and those of other ancient civilizations?*

CENGAGENOW *To read more of Popul Vuh, enter the documents area of the World History Resource Center using the access card that is available for World History.*

A Ball Court. Throughout Mesoamerica, a dangerous game was played on ball courts such as this one. A large ball of solid rubber was propelled from the hip at such tremendous speed that players had to wear extensive padding. More than an athletic contest, the game had religious significance. The court is thought to have represented the cosmos and the ball the sun, and the losers were sacrificed to the gods in postgame ceremonies. The game is still played today in parts of Mexico (without the sacrifice, of course).

© William J. Duiker

A SAMPLE OF MAYAN WRITING

The Maya were the only Mesoamerican people to devise a complete written language. Like the Sumerian and Egyptian scripts, the Mayan system was composed of a mixture of ideographs and phonetic symbols, which were written in double columns to be read from left to right and top to bottom. The language was rudimentary in many ways. It had few adjectives or adverbs, and the numbering system used only three symbols: a shell for zero, a dot for one, and a bar for five.

During the classical era from 300 to 900 C.E., the Maya used the script to record dynastic statistics with deliberate precision, listing the date of the ruler's birth, his accession to power, and his marriage and death while highlighting victories in battle, the capture of prisoners, and ritual ceremonies. The symbols were carved on stone panels, stelae, and funerary urns or were painted with a brush on folding-screen books made of bark paper; only four of these books from the late period remain extant today. A sample of Mayan hieroglyphs is shown below.

Q *How would you compare Mayan glyphs with the early forms of writing in Egypt, China, and Mesopotamia? Consider purpose, ease of writing, and potential for development into a purely phonetic system.*

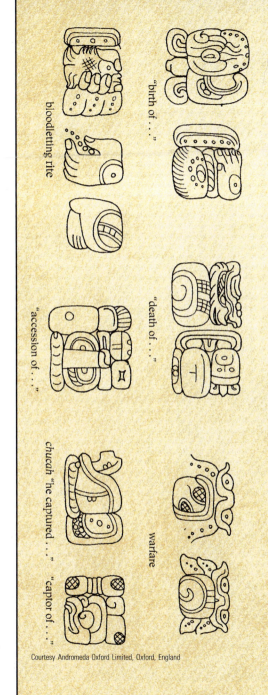

"birth of . . ."

"death of . . ."

bloodletting rite

"accession of . . ."

warfare

chuuch "he captured . . ."

"captor of . . ."

Courtesy Andromeda Oxford Limited, Oxford, England

Inscriptions, archaeologists discovered a royal tomb and a massive limestone slab covered with hieroglyphs. By deciphering the message on the slab, archaeologists for the first time identified a historical figure in Mayan history; He was the ruler named Pacal, known from his glyph as "The Shield"; Pacal ordered the construction of the Temple of Inscriptions in the mid-seventh century, and it was his body that was buried in the tomb at the foot of the staircase leading down into the crypt.

As befits their intense interest in the passage of time, the Maya also had a sophisticated knowledge of astronomy and kept voluminous records of the movements of the heavenly bodies. There were practical reasons for their concern. The arrival of the planet Venus in the evening sky, for example, was a traditional time to prepare for war. The Maya also devised the so-called Long Count, a system of calculating time based on a lunar calendar that calls for the end of the current cycle of 5,200 years in the year 2012 of the Western solar-based Gregorian calendar.

Scholars once believed that the Maya were a peaceful people who rarely engaged in violence. Now, however, it is thought that rivalry among Mayan city-states was endemic and often involved bloody clashes. Scenes from paintings and rock carvings depict a society preoccupied with war and the seizure of captives for sacrifice. The conflict mentioned at the beginning of this chapter is but a recent example. During the seventh century C.E., two powerful city-states, Tikal and Calakmul, competed for dominance throughout the region, setting up puppet regimes and waging bloody wars that wavered back and forth for years but ultimately resulted in the total destruction of Calakmul at the end of the century.

The Mystery of Mayan Decline

Sometime in the eighth or ninth century, the classical Mayan civilization in the central Yucatán peninsula began to decline. At Copán, for example, it ended abruptly in 822 C.E., when work on various stone sculptures ordered by the ruler suddenly ceased. The end of Palenque soon followed, and the city of Tikal was abandoned by 870 C.E. Whether the decline was caused by overuse of the land, incessant warfare, internal revolt, or a natural disaster such as a volcanic eruption is a question that has puzzled archaeologists for decades. Recent evidence supports the theory that overcultivation of the land due to a growing population

nearby Lake Petén, did not appear to suffer from a lack of water. Until we learn more, we must be content with the theory of multiple causes.

Whatever the case, cities like Tikal and Palenque were abandoned to the jungles. In their place, newer urban centers in the northern part of the peninsula, like Uxmal and Chichén Itzá, continued to prosper, although the level of cultural achievement in this postclassical era did not match that of previous years. According to local history, this latter area was taken over by peoples known as the Toltecs, led by a man known as Kukulcan, who migrated to the peninsula from Teotihuacán in central Mexico sometime in the tenth century. Some scholars believe this flight was associated with the legend of the departure from that city of Quetzalcoatl, a deity in the form of a feathered serpent who promised that he would someday return to reclaim his homeland.

The Toltecs apparently controlled the upper peninsula from their capital at Chichén Itzá for several centuries, but this area was less fertile and more susceptible to drought than the earlier regions of Mayan settlement, and eventually they too declined. By the early sixteenth century, the area was divided into a number of small principalities, and the cities, including Uxmal and Chichén Itzá, had been abandoned.

The Aztecs

Among the groups moving into the Valley of Mexico after the fall of Teotihuacán were the Mexica (pronounced "maysheeka"). No one knows their origins, although folk legend held that their original homeland was an island in a lake called Aztlán. From that legendary homeland

© William J. Duiker

The Art Archive/National Anthropological Museum, Mexico/Gianni Dagli Orti

MAP 6.2 **The Maya Heartland.** During the classical era, Mayan civilization was centered on modern-day Guatemala and the lower Yucatán peninsula. After the ninth century, new centers of power like Chichén Itzá and Uxmal began to emerge farther north.

Q What factors appear to have brought an end to classical Mayan civilization?

gradually reduced crop yields. A long drought, which lasted throughout most of the ninth and tenth centuries C.E., may have played a major role, although the city-state of Tikal, blessed with fertile soil and the presence of

The Role of Jade. To many early peoples, the beautiful stone we know as jade possessed magical spiritual qualities, which undoubtedly inspired the two objects shown here. The funeral mask of Lord Pacal (right), a seventh-century ruler of Palenque, was placed in his tomb in the hope that its spiritual energy would propel Pacal into the afterlife, thereby merging him with the divine in the Mayan cosmos. In China, members of the Han ruling family were buried in jade body suits, such as the one shown below. The suit was composed of jade squares sewn together with gold thread. Because of the expense, such practices were eventually banned as extravagant.

© William J. Duiker

© British Museum, London/Art Resource, NY

A Mayan Bloodletting Ceremony. The Mayan elite drew blood at various ritual ceremonies. Here we see Lady Xok, the wife of a king of Yaxchilan, passing a rope pierced with thorns along her tongue in a bloodletting ritual. Above her, the king holds a flaming torch. This vivid scene from an eighth-century C.E. palace lintel demonstrates the excellence of Mayan stone sculpture as well as the sophisticated weaving techniques shown in the queen's elegant gown.

comes the name *Aztec*, by which they are known to the modern world. Sometime during the early twelfth century, the Aztecs left their original habitat and, carrying an image of their patron deity, Huitzilopochtli, began a lengthy migration that climaxed with their arrival in the Valley of Mexico sometime late in the century.

Less sophisticated than many of their neighbors, the Aztecs were at first forced to seek alliances with stronger city-states. They were excellent warriors, however, and (like Sparta in ancient Greece and the state of Qin in Zhou dynasty China) theirs had become the dominant city-state in the lake region by the early fifteenth century. Establishing their capital at Tenochtitlán, on an island in the middle of Lake Texcoco, they set out to bring the entire region under their domination (see Map 6.3).

For the remainder of the fifteenth century, the Aztecs consolidated their control over much of what is modern Mexico, from the Atlantic to the Pacific Ocean and as far south as the Guatemalan border. The new kingdom was not a centralized state but a collection of semiautonomous territories. To provide a unifying focus for the kingdom, the Aztecs promoted their patron god, Huitzilopochtli, as the guiding deity of the entire population, which now numbered several million.

Quetzalcoatl. Quetzalcoatl was one of the favorite deities of the Central American peoples. His visage of a plumed serpent, as shown here, was prominent in the royal capital of Teotihuacán. According to legend, Quetzalcoatl, the leader of the Toltecs, was tricked into drunkenness and humiliated by a rival god. In disgrace, he left his homeland but promised to return. In 1519, the Aztec monarch Moctezuma welcomed Hernán Cortés, the leader of the Spanish expedition, believing that he was a representative of Quetzalcoatl.

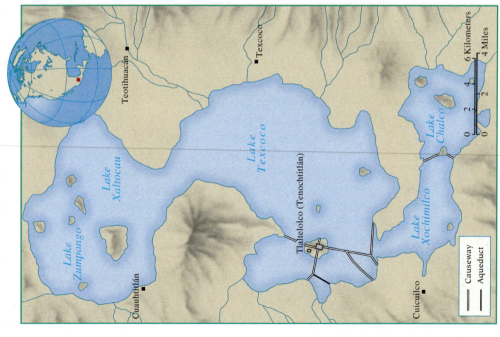

MAP 6.3 **The Valley of Mexico Under Aztec Rule.** The Aztecs were one of the most advanced peoples in pre-Columbian Central America. Their capital at Tenochtitlán (Tlaltelolco) was located at the site of modern-day Mexico City. Of the five lakes shown here, only Lake Texcoco remains today. **Q** What forms of agricultural cultivation were practiced in the Valley of Mexico, and why?

CHRONOLOGY Early Mesoamerica

Arrival of human beings in America	At least 15,000 years ago
Agriculture first practiced	c. 8000 B.C.E.
Rise of Olmec culture	1200 B.C.E.
End of Olmec era	400 B.C.E.
Origins of Mayan civilization	First millennium C.E.
Teotihuacán civilization	c. 300 B.C.E.–800 C.E.
Classical era of Mayan culture	300–900 C.E.
Tikal abandoned	870 C.E.
Migration of Mexica to Valley of Mexico	Late 1100s
Kingdom of the Aztecs	1300s–1400s

tribute, in the form of goods or captives, to the central government. The most important government officials in the provinces were the tax collectors, who collected the tribute. They used the threat of military action against those who failed to carry out their tribute obligations and therefore, understandably, were not popular with the taxpayers. According to Bernal Díaz, a Spaniard who recorded his impressions of Aztec society during a visit in the early sixteenth century:

All these towns complained about Montezuma [Moctezuma, the Aztec ruler] and his tax collectors, speaking in private so that the Mexican ambassadors should not hear them, however. They said these officials robbed them of all they possessed, and that if their wives and daughters were pretty they would violate them in front of their fathers and husbands and carry them away. They also said that the Mexicans [that is, the representatives from the capital] made the men work like slaves, compelling them to carry pine trunks and stone and firewood and maize overland and in canoes, and to perform other tasks, such as planting maize fields, and that they took away the people's lands as well for the service of their idols.[2]

Politics Like all great empires in ancient times, the Aztec state was authoritarian. Power was vested in the monarch, whose authority had both a divine and a secular character. The Aztec ruler claimed descent from the gods and served as an intermediary between the material and the metaphysical worlds. Unlike many of his counterparts in other ancient civilizations, however, the monarch did not obtain his position by a rigid law of succession. On the death of the ruler, his successor was selected from within the royal family by a small group of senior officials, who were also members of the family and were therefore eligible for the position. Once placed on the throne, the Aztec ruler was advised by a small council of lords, headed by a prime minister who served as the chief executive of the government, and a bureaucracy. Beyond the capital, the power of the central government was limited. Rulers of territories subject to the Aztecs were allowed considerable autonomy in return for paying

Social Structures Positions in the government bureaucracy were the exclusive privilege of the hereditary nobility, all of whom traced their lineage to the founding family of the Aztec clan. Male children in noble families were sent to temple schools, where they were exposed to a harsh regimen of manual labor, military training, and memorization of information about Aztec society and religion. On reaching adulthood, they would select a career in the military service, the government bureaucracy, or the priesthood. As a reward for their services, senior officials received large estates from the government, and they alone had the right to hire communal labor.

The remainder of the population consisted of commoners, indentured workers, and slaves. Most indentured workers were landless laborers who contracted to work on the nobles' estates, while slaves served in the households of the wealthy. Slavery was not an inherited status, and the children of slaves were considered free citizens. Commoners might sell themselves into slavery when in debt and then later purchase their freedom.

The vast majority of the population consisted of commoners. All commoners were members of large kinship groups called *calpulli*. Each *calpulli*, often consisting of as many as a thousand members, was headed by an elected chief, who ran its day-to-day affairs and served as an intermediary with the central government. Each *calpulli* was responsible for providing taxes (usually in the form of goods) and conscript labor to the state.

Each *calpulli* maintained its own temples and schools and administered the land held by the community. Farmland within the *calpulli* was held in common and could not be sold, although it could be passed down within the family. In the cities, each *calpulli* occupied a separate neighborhood, where its members often performed a particular function, such as metalworking, stonecutting, weaving, carpentry, or commerce. Apparently, a large proportion of the population engaged in some form of trade, at least in the densely populated Valley of Mexico, where an estimated half of the people lived in an urban environment. Many farmers, who cultivated their crops in *chinampas* as their predecessors had for centuries, brought their goods to the markets via the canals and sold them directly to retailers (see the box above).

The *calpulli* compounds themselves were divided into smaller family units. Individual families lived in small flat-roofed dwellings containing one or two rooms. Each house was separate from its neighbors and had direct access to the surrounding streets and canals. The houses of farmers living on the *chinampas* were set on raised dirt platforms built above the surrounding fields to prevent flooding.

Gender roles within the family were rigidly stratified. Male children were trained for war and were expected to serve in the army on reaching adulthood. Women were expected to work in the home, weave textiles, and raise children, although, like their brothers,

---

INTERACTION & EXCHANGE

MARKETS AND MERCHANDISE IN AZTEC MEXICO

One of our most valuable descriptions of Aztec civilization is *The Conquest of New Spain*, written by Bernal Díaz, a Spaniard who visited Mexico in 1519. In the following passage, Díaz describes the great market at Tenochtitlán.

Bernal Díaz, *The Conquest of New Spain*

Let us begin with the dealers in gold, silver, and precious stones, feathers, cloaks, and embroidered goods, and male and female slaves who are also sold there. They bring as many slaves to be sold in that market as the Portuguese bring Negroes from Guinea. Some are brought there attached to long poles by means of collars round their necks to prevent them from escaping, but others are left loose. Next there were those who sold coarser cloth, and cotton goods and fabrics made of twisted thread, and there were chocolate merchants with their chocolate. In this way you could see every kind of merchandise to be found anywhere in New Spain, laid out in the same way as goods are laid out in my own district of Medina del Campo, a center for fairs, where each line of stalls has its own particular sort. So it was in this great market. There were those who sold sisal cloth and ropes and the sandals they wear on their feet, which are made from the same plant. All these were kept in one part of the market, in the place assigned to them, and in another part were skins of tigers and lions, otters, jackals, and deer, badgers, mountain cats, and other wild animals, some tanned and some untanned, and other classes of merchandise.

There were sellers of kidney beans and sage and other vegetables and herbs in another place, and in yet another they were selling fowls, and birds with great dewlaps, also rabbits, hares, deer, young ducks, little dogs, and other such creatures. Then there were the fruiterers; and the women who sold cooked food, flour and honey cake, and tripe, had their part of the market. Then came pottery of all kinds, from big water jars to little jugs, displayed in its own place, also honey, honey paste, and other sweets like nougat. Elsewhere they sold timber too, boards, cradles, beams, blocks, and benches, all in a quarter of their own.

Then there were the sellers of pitch pine for torches, and other things of that kind, and I must also mention, with all apologies, that they sold many canoe loads of human excrement, which they kept in the creeks near the market. This was for the manufacture of salt and the curing of skins, which they say cannot be done without it. I know that many gentlemen will laugh at this, but I assure them it is true. I may add that on all the roads they have shelters made of reeds or straw or grass so that they can retire when they wish to do so, and purge their bowels unseen by passersby, and also in order that their excrement shall not be lost.

Q Which of the items offered for sale in this account might you expect to be available in a market in Asia, Africa, or Europe? What types of goods mentioned here appear to be unique to the Americas?

CENGAGENOW To read more of The Conquest of New Spain, enter the documents area of the access card World History Resource Center using the access card that is available for World History.

Aztec Midwife Ritual Chants

FAMILY & SOCIETY

Most Aztec women were burdened with time-consuming family chores, such as grinding corn into flour for tortillas and carrying heavy containers of water from local springs. Like their brothers, Aztec girls went to school, but rather than training for war, they learned spinning, weaving, and how to carry out family rituals. In the sixteenth century C.E., a Spanish priest, Bernardino de Sahagún, interviewed Aztec informants to compile a substantial account of traditional Aztec society. Here we read his narration of ritual chants used by midwives during childhood. For a boy, the highest honor was to shed blood in battle. For a girl, it was to offer herself to the work of domestic life. If a woman died in childbirth, however, she would be glorified as a "warrior woman." Compare the gender roles presented here with those of other ancient civilizations in preceding chapters.

Bernardino de Sahagún, *The Florentine Codex*

My precious son, my youngest one.… Heed, hearken: Thy home is not here, for thou art an eagle, thou art an ocelot.… Thou art the serpent, the bird of the lord of the near, of the nigh. Here is only the place of thy nest. Thou hast only been hatched here; thou hast only come, arrived.… Thou belongest out there.… Thou hast been sent into warfare. War is the desert, thy task. Thou shalt give drink, nourishment, food to the sun, the lord of the earth.… Perhaps thou wilt receive the gift, perhaps thou wilt merit death by the obsidian knife, the flowered death by the obsidian knife.

My beloved maiden.… Thou wilt be in the heart of the home, thou wilt go nowhere, thou wilt nowhere become a wanderer, thou becomest the banked fire, the hearth stones. Here our Lord planteth thee, burieth thee. And thou wilt become fatigued, thou wilt become tired; thou art to provide water, to grind maize, to drudge; thou art to sweat by the ashes, by the hearth.

Q *What does this document suggest as to the proper role to be played by a woman in Aztec society? How did the assigned roles for men and women in Mesoamerica compare with those that we have seen in other societies around the world?*

---

they were permitted to enter the priesthood. According to Bernal Díaz, a female deity presided over the rites of marriage. As in most traditional societies, chastity and obedience were desirable female characteristics. Although women in Aztec society enjoyed more legal rights than women in some traditional Old World civilizations, they were still not equal to men (see the box above). Women were permitted to own and inherit property and to enter into contracts. Marriage was usually monogamous, although noble families sometimes practiced **polygyny** (having more than one wife at a time). Wedding partners were normally selected from within the lineage group but not the immediate family. As in most societies at the time, parents usually selected their child's spouse, often for purposes of political or social advancement.

Classes in Aztec society were rigidly stratified. Commoners were not permitted to enter the nobility, although some occasionally rose to senior positions in the army or the priesthood as the result of exemplary service. As in medieval Europe, such occupations often provided a route of upward mobility for ambitious commoners. A woman of noble standing would sometimes marry a commoner because the children of such a union would inherit her higher status, and she could expect to be treated better by her husband's family, who would be proud of the marriage relationship.

Land of the Feathered Serpent: Aztec Religion and Culture The Aztecs, like their contemporaries throughout Mesoamerica, lived in an environment populated by

---

a multitude of gods. Scholars have identified more than a hundred deities in the Aztec pantheon; some of them were nature spirits, like the rain god, Tlaloc, and some were patron deities, like the symbol of the Aztecs themselves, Huitzilopochtli. A supreme deity, called Ometeotl, represented the all-powerful and omnipresent forces of the heavens, but he was rather remote, and other gods, notably the feathered serpent Quetzalcoatl, had a more direct impact on the lives of the people. Representing the forces of creation, virtue, and learning and culture, Quetzalcoatl bears a distinct similarity to Shiva in Hindu belief. According to Aztec tradition, this godlike being had left his homeland in the Valley of Mexico in the tenth century, promising to return in triumph (see "The Mystery of Mayan Decline" earlier in this chapter).

Aztec cosmology was based on a belief in the existence of two worlds, the material and the divine. The earth was the material world and took the form of a flat disk surrounded by water on all sides. The divine world, which consisted of both heaven and hell, was the abode of the gods. Human beings could aspire to a form of heavenly salvation but first had to pass through a transitional stage, somewhat like Christian purgatory, before reaching their final destination, where the soul was finally freed from the body. To prepare for the final day of judgment, as well as to help them engage in proper behavior through life, all citizens underwent religious training at temple schools during adolescence and took part in various rituals throughout their lives. The most devout were encouraged to study for the priesthood. Once accepted, they served at temples ranging from local branches at the *calpulli* level to the highest shrines in the ceremonial precinct at Tenochtitlán. In some respects, however, Aztec society may have been undergoing a process of secularization. By late Aztec times, athletic contests at the ball court had apparently lost some of their religious significance. Gambling was increasingly common, and wagering over the results of the matches was widespread. One province reportedly sent sixteen thousand rubber balls to the capital city of Tenochtitlán as its annual tribute to the royal court.

Aztec religion contained a distinct element of fatalism that was inherent in the creation myth, which described an unceasing struggle between the forces of good and evil throughout the universe. This struggle led to the creation and destruction of four worlds, or suns. The world was now living in the time of the fifth sun. But that world, too, was destined to end with the destruction of this earth and all that is within it:

Even jade is shattered,
Even gold is crushed,
Even quetzal plumes are torn....
One does not live forever on this earth:
*We endure only for an instant!*³

In an effort to postpone the day of reckoning, the Aztecs practiced human sacrifice. The Aztecs believed that by appeasing the sun god, Huitzilopochtli, with sacrifices, they could delay the final destruction of their world. Victims were prepared for the ceremony through elaborate rituals and then brought to the holy shrine, where their hearts were ripped out of their chests and presented to the gods as a holy offering. It was an honor to be chosen for sacrifice, and captives were often used as sacrificial victims, since they represented valor, the trait the Aztecs prized most.

Art and Culture

Like the art of the Olmecs, most Aztec architecture, art, and sculpture had religious significance. At the center of the capital city of Tenochtitlán was the sacred precinct, dominated by the massive pyramid dedicated to Huitzilopochtli and the rain god, Tlaloc. According to Bernal Díaz, at its base the pyramid was equal to the plots of six large European town houses and tapered from there to the top, which was surmounted by a platform containing shrines to the gods and an altar for performing human sacrifices. The entire pyramid was covered with brightly colored paintings and sculptures.

Although little Aztec painting survives, it was evidently of high quality. Díaz compared the best work with that of Michelangelo. Artisans worked with stone and with soft metals such as gold and silver, which they cast using the lost-wax technique. They did not have the knowledge for making implements in bronze or iron, however. Stoneworking consisted primarily of representations of the gods and bas-reliefs depicting religious ceremonies. Among the most famous is the massive disk called the Stone of the Fifth Sun, carved for use at the central pyramid at Tenochtitlán.

The Aztecs had devised a form of writing based on hieroglyphs that represented an object or a concept. The symbols had no phonetic significance and did not constitute a writing system as such but could give the sense of a message and were probably used by civilian or religious officials as notes or memorandums for their orations. Although many of the notes simply recorded dates in the complex calendar that had evolved since Olmec times, others provide insight into the daily lives of the Aztec peoples. A trained class of scribes carefully painted the notes on paper made from the inner bark of fig trees. Unfortunately, many of these notes were destroyed by the Spaniards as part of their effort to eradicate all aspects of Aztec religion and culture.

The First Civilizations in South America

Q **Focus Question:** What role did the environment play in the evolution of societies in the Americas?

South America is a vast continent, characterized by extremes in climate and geography. The north is dominated by the mighty Amazon River, which flows through dense tropical rain forests carrying a larger

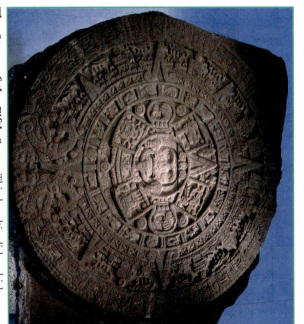

The Stone of the Fifth Sun. This basaltic disk, which weighs twenty-six tons, recorded the Aztec view of the cosmos: It portrays the perpetual struggle between forces of good and evil in the universe; in the center is an intimidating image of the sun god clutching human hearts with his talons. Having previously traversed the creation and destruction of four worlds, the Aztecs believed they were living in the world of the fifth and final sun—hence this stone carving, which was found in the central pyramid at Tenochtitlán.

© Werner Forman/Art Resource, NY

Monte Verde	10,500 B.C.E.
First organized societies in the Andes	c. 6000 B.C.E.
Agriculture first practiced	c. 3200 B.C.E.
Founding of Caral	c. 2500 B.C.E.
Chavín style	First millennium B.C.E.
Moche civilization	c. 150–800 C.E.
Civilization of Chimor	c. 1100–1450
Inka takeover in central Andes	1400s

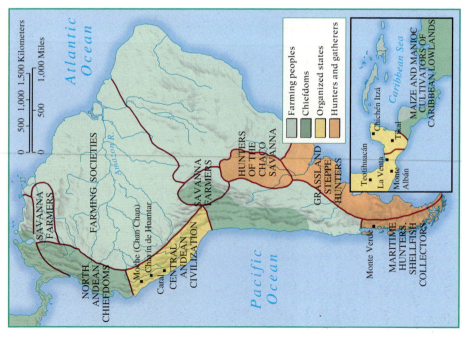

MAP 6.4 Early Peoples and Cultures of Central and South America. This map shows regions of early human settlements in Central and South America. Urban conglomerations appear in Mesoamerica (see inset) and along the western coast of South America.

Q Why do you think urban centers appeared in these areas?

Caral

By the third millennium B.C.E., complex societies had begun to emerge in the coastal regions of modern-day Peru and Ecuador. The first settlements were apparently located along the coast, but eventually farming communities watered by canals began to appear in the river valleys flowing down from the Andes Mountains. Fish and agricultural products were traded to highland peoples for wool and salt.

By 2500 B.C.E.—a thousand years earlier than the earliest known cities in Mesoamerica—the first urban settlements appeared in the region. At Caral, an archaeological site located 14 miles inland from the coast, the remnants of a 4,500-year-old city sit on the crest of a 60-foot-high pyramid. The inhabitants engaged in farming of squash, beans, and tomatoes but also provided cotton to fishing communities along the coast, where it was used to make fishnets. Land was divided in a manner similar to the well field system in ancient China (see Chapter 2).

This culture reached its height during the first millennium B.C.E. with the emergence of the Chavín style, named for a site near the modern city of Chavín de Huantar. The ceremonial precinct at the site contained an impressive stone temple complete with interior galleries, a stone-block ceiling, and a system of underground canals that probably channeled water into the temple complex for ceremonial purposes. The structure was surrounded by stone figures depicting various deities and two pyramids. Evidence of metallurgy has also been found, with objects made of copper and gold. Another impressive technological achievement was the building in 300 B.C.E. of the first solar observatory in the Americas in the form of thirteen stone towers on a hillside north of Lima, Peru. There are even signs of a rudimentary writing system (see "Inka Culture" later in this chapter).

Moche

Chavín society had broken down by 200 B.C.E., but early in the first millennium C.E., another advanced civilization appeared in northern Peru, in the valley of the Moche River, which flows from the foothills of the Andes into the Pacific Ocean. It occupied an area of more than 2,500 square miles, and its capital city, large enough to

flow of water than any other river system in the world (see Map 6.4). Farther to the south, the forests are replaced by prairies and steppes stretching westward to the Andes Mountains, which extend the entire length of the continent, from the Isthmus of Panama to the Strait of Magellan. Along the Pacific coast, on the western slopes of the mountains, are some of the driest desert regions in the world.

South America has been inhabited by human beings for more than twelve thousand years. Wall paintings discovered at the so-called Cavern of the Painted Rock in the Amazon region suggest that Stone Age peoples were living in the area at least eleven thousand years ago, and a site at Monte Verde, along the central coast of Chile, has been dated to 10,500 B.C.E. Early peoples lived by hunting, fishing, and food gathering, but there are indications that irrigated farming was being practiced on the western slopes of the Andes Mountains more than five thousand years ago.

© Ann Ronan Picture Library/HIP/Art Resource, NY

A Chimú Gold Mask. One of the most impressive achievements of the early civilizations of South America was the high quality of their metalwork. Much of their finest craftsmanship is found in the manufacture of delicate gold ornaments. Unfortunately, many of these artifacts were later melted down by Spanish conquistadors. Illustrated here is a hammered gold mask from the Chimor culture, successors to the Moche in what is present-day Peru. Such masks were often placed inside royal tombs, and this one is highly reminiscent of the famous death mask found at Mycenae, in central Greece.

contain over ten thousand people, was dominated by two massive adobe pyramids as much as 100 feet high. The largest, known as the Pyramid of the Moon, covered a total of 15 acres and was adorned with painted murals depicting battles, ritual sacrifices, and various local deities.

Artifacts found at Moche, especially the metalwork and stone and ceramic figures, exhibit a high quality of artisanship. They were imitated at river valley sites throughout the surrounding area, which suggests that the authority of the Moche rulers may have extended as far as 400 miles along the coast. The artifacts also indicate that the people at Moche, like those in Central America, were preoccupied with warfare. Paintings and pottery as well as other artifacts in stone, metal, and ceramics frequently portray warriors, prisoners, and sacrificial victims. The Moche were also fascinated by the heavens, and much of their art consisted of celestial symbols and astronomical constellations.

Environmental Problems The Moche River valley is extremely arid, receiving less than an inch of rain annually. The peoples in the area compensated by building a sophisticated irrigation system to carry water from the river to the parched fields. At its zenith, Moche culture was spectacular. By the eighth century C.E., however, the civilization was in a state of collapse, the irrigation canals had been abandoned, and the remaining population had left the area and moved farther inland or suffered from severe malnutrition.

What had happened to bring Moche culture to this untimely end? Archaeologists speculate that environmental

disruptions, perhaps brought on by changes in the temperature of the Pacific Ocean known as **El Niño**, led to alternating periods of drought and flooding of coastal regions, which caused the irrigated fields to silt up (see the comparative essay "History and the Environment" on p. 182). The warm water created by El Niño conditions also killed local marine life, severely damaging the local fishing industry.

Three hundred years later, a new power, the kingdom of Chimor, with its capital at Chan Chan, at the mouth of the Moche River, emerged in the area. Built almost entirely of adobe, Chan Chan housed an estimated thirty thousand residents in an area of more than 12 square miles that included a number of palace compounds surrounded by walls nearly 30 feet high. One compound contained an intricate labyrinth that wound its way progressively inward until it ended in a central chamber, probably occupied by the ruler. Like the Moche before them, the people of Chimor relied on irrigation to funnel the water from the river into their fields. An elaborate system of canals brought the water through hundreds of miles of hilly terrain to the fields near the coast. Nevertheless, by the fifteenth century, Chimor, too, had disappeared, a victim of floods and a series of earthquakes that destroyed the intricate irrigation system that had been the basis of its survival.

These early civilizations in the Andes were by no means isolated from other societies in the region. As early as 2000 B.C.E., local peoples had been venturing into the Pacific Ocean on wind-powered rafts constructed of balsa wood. By the late first millennium C.E., seafarers from the coast of Ecuador had established a vast trading network that extended southward to central Peru and as far north as western Mexico, over 2,000 miles away. Items transported included jewelry, beads, and metal goods. In all likelihood, technological exchanges were an important by-product of the relationship.

Transportation by land, however, was more difficult. Although roads were constructed to facilitate communication between communities, the forbidding character of the terrain in the mountains was a serious obstacle, and the only draft animal on the entire continent was the llama, considerably less hardy than the cattle, horses, and water buffalo used in much of Asia. Such problems undoubtedly hampered the development of regular contacts with distant societies in the Americas, as well as the exchange of goods and ideas that had lubricated the rise of civilizations from China to the Mediterranean Sea.

The Inka

The Chimor kingdom was eventually succeeded in the late fifteenth century by an invading force from the mountains far to the south. In the late fourteenth century, the Inka were a small community in the area of Cuzco, a city located at an altitude of 10,000 feet in the mountains of southern Peru. In the 1440s, however, under the leadership of their powerful ruler Pachakuti (sometimes called

COMPARATIVE ESSAY
HISTORY AND THE ENVIRONMENT

© F. Ardito, UNEP/Peter Arnold Inc.

In *The Decline and Fall of the Roman Empire*, published in 1788, the British historian Edward Gibbon raised a question that has fascinated historians ever since: What brought about the collapse of that once powerful civilization that dominated the Mediterranean region for over five centuries? Traditional explanations have centered on political or cultural factors, such as imperial overreach, moral decay, military weakness, or the impact of invasions. Recently, however, some historians have suggested that environmental factors, such as poisoning due to the use of lead water pipes and cups, the spread of malaria, or a lengthy drought in wheat-growing regions in North Africa, might have been at least contributory causes.

The current interest in the impact of the environment on the Roman Empire reflects a growing awareness among historians that environmental conditions may have been a key factor in the fate of several of the great societies in the ancient world. Climatic changes or natural disasters almost certainly led to the decline and collapse of civilization in the Indus River valley. In the Americas, massive flooding brought about by the El Niño effect (environmental conditions triggered by changes in water temperature in the Pacific Ocean) appears to be one possible cause for the collapse of the Moche civilization in what is today Peru, while drought and overcultivation of the land are often cited as reasons for the decline of the Maya in Mesoamerica.

Climatic changes continued to affect the fate of nations and peoples after the end of the classical era. Drought conditions and overuse of the land may have led to the gradual decline of Mesopotamia as a focal point of advanced civilization in the Middle East, while soil erosion and colder conditions doomed an early attempt by the Vikings to establish a foothold in Greenland and North America. Sometimes the problems were self-inflicted, as on Easter Island, a remote outpost in the Pacific Ocean, where Polynesian settlers

Modern-day desertification, symbolized by a boat stranded in a dried-up lake bed in Central Asia.

migrating from the west about 900 C.E. so denuded the landscape that by the fifteenth century, what had been a reasonably stable and peaceful society had descended into civil war and cannibalism.

Climatic changes, of course, have not always been detrimental to the health and prosperity of human beings. A warming trend that took place at the end of the last ice age eventually made much of the world more habitable for farming peoples about ten thousand years ago. The effects of El Niño may be beneficial to people living in some areas and disastrous in others. But human misuse of land and water resources is always dangerous to settled societies, especially those living in fragile environments.

theory) and was ruled by a governor related to the royal family. Excess inhabitants were transferred to other locations. The capital of Cuzco was divided into four quarters, or residential areas, and the social status and economic functions of the residents of each quarter were rigidly defined.

The state was built on forced labor. Often entire communities of workers were moved from one part of the country to another to open virgin lands or engage in massive construction projects. Under Pachakuti, Cuzco was transformed from a city of mud and thatch into an imposing metropolis of stone. The walls, built of close-fitting stones without the use of mortar, were a wonder to early European visitors. The most impressive

Pachacutec, or "he who transforms the world"), the Inka launched a campaign of conquest that eventually brought the entire region under their authority. Under Pachakuti and his immediate successors, Topa Inka and Huayna Inka (the word *Inka* means "ruler"), the boundaries of the kingdom were extended as far as Ecuador, central Chile, and the edge of the Amazon basin.

The Four Quarters: Inka Politics and Society   Pachakuti created a highly centralized state (see Map 6.5). With a stunning concern for mathematical precision, he divided his empire, called Tahuantinsuyu, or "the world of the four quarters," into provinces and districts. Each province contained about ten thousand residents (at least in

The Art Archive/Museo del Oro, Lima, Peru/Gianni Dagli Orti

Paracus Royal Mummy. The ancient residents of coastal Chile developed complex methods for mummifying their dead more than four thousand years ago, and this practice continued up through Inka times. In Peru, the Paracus culture (200 B.C.E.–500 C.E.) bundled up its rulers in extensive layers of sumptuously embroidered textiles. The body was placed in the fetal position, adorned with articles of value such as a crown of feathers, animal skins, and gold and bone jewelry. The mummy was then interred in a chamber with other deceased members of the community. Food offerings of maize and peanuts accompanied the mummy for sustenance in the afterlife.

structure in the city was a temple dedicated to the sun. According to a Spanish observer, "All four walls of the temple were covered from top to bottom with plates and slabs of gold."[4] Equally impressive are the ruins of the abandoned city of Machu Picchu, built on a lofty hilltop far above the Urubamba River.

Another major construction project was a system of 24,800 miles of highways and roads that extended from the border of modern Colombia to a point south of modern Santiago, Chile. Two major roadways extended in a north-south direction, one through the Andes Mountains and the other along the coast, with connecting routes between them. Rest houses and storage depots were placed along the roads. Suspension bridges made of braided fiber and fastened to stone abutments on opposite banks were built over ravines and waterways. Use of the highways was restricted to official and military purposes. Trained runners carried messages rapidly from one way station to another, enabling information to travel up to 140 miles in a single day.

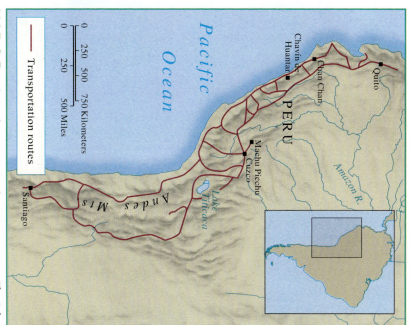

MAP 6.5 The Inka Empire About 1500 C.E. The Inka were the last civilization to flourish in South America prior to the arrival of the Spanish. The impressive system of roads constructed to facilitate communication shows the extent of Inka control throughout the Andes Mountains.

Q In what modern countries was the Inka state located?

— Transportation routes

Pacific Ocean

PERU

Quito · Chavin de Huantar · Chan Chan · Machu Picchu · Cuzco · Santiago · Lake Titicaca · Andes Mts · Amazon R.

In rural areas, the population lived mainly by farming. In the mountains, the most common form was terraced agriculture, watered by irrigation systems that carried precise amounts of water into the fields, which were planted with maize, potatoes, and other crops. The plots were tilled by collective labor regulated by the state. Like other aspects of Inka society, marriage was strictly regulated, and men and women were required to select a marriage partner from within the immediate tribal group. For women, there was one escape from a life of domestic servitude: fortunate maidens were selected to serve as "chosen virgins" in temples throughout the country (see the box on p. 185). Noblewomen were eligible to compete for service in the Temple of the Sun at Cuzco, while commoners might hope to serve in temples in the provincial capitals. Punishment for breaking the vow of chastity was harsh, and few evidently took the risk.

Inka Culture Like many other civilizations in pre-Columbian Latin America, the Inka state was built on war. Soldiers for the 200,000-man Inka army, the largest and best armed in the region, were raised by universal male conscription. Military units were moved rapidly

© Carol C. Coffin

Machu Picchu. Situated in the Andes in modern Peru, Machu Picchu reflects the glory of Inka civilization. To farm such rugged terrain, the Inka constructed terraces and stone aqueducts. To span vast ravines, they built suspension bridges made of braided fiber and fastened them to stone abutments on the opposite banks. The most revered of the many temples and stone altars at Machu Picchu was the thronelike "hitching post of the sun," so called because of its close proximity to the sun god.

along the highway system and were bivouacked in the rest houses located along the roadside. Because the Inka had no wheeled vehicles, supplies were carried on the backs of llamas. Once an area was placed under Inka authority, the local inhabitants were instructed in the Quechua language, which became the lingua franca of the state, and were introduced to the state religion. The Inka had no writing system but kept records using a system of knotted strings called **quipu** (pronounced "key-poo"), maintained by professionally trained officials, that were able to record all data of a numerical nature. What could not be recorded in such a manner was committed to memory and then recited when needed. The practice was apparently not invented by the Inka. Fragments of *quipu* have been found at Caral and dated at approximately five thousand years ago. Nor apparently was the experiment limited to the Americas. A passage in the Chinese classic *The Way of the Tao* declares, "Let the people revert to communication by knotted cords."

As in the case of the Aztecs and the Maya, the lack of a fully developed writing system did not prevent the Inka from realizing a high level of cultural achievement. Most of what survives was recorded by the Spanish and consists of entertainment for the elites. The Inka had a highly developed tradition of court theater, including both tragic and comic works. There was also some poetry, composed in blank verse and often accompanied by music played on reed instruments.

Stateless Societies in the Americas

Q Focus Question: What were the main characteristics of stateless societies in the Americas, and how did they resemble and differ from the civilizations that arose there?

Beyond Central America and the high ridges of the Andes Mountains, on the Great Plains of North America, along the Amazon River in South America, and on the islands of the Caribbean Sea, other communities of Amerindians were also beginning to master the art of agriculture and to build organized societies.

Although human beings had occupied much of the continent of North America during the early phase of human settlement, the switch to farming as a means of survival did not occur until the third millennium B.C.E. at the earliest, and much later in most areas of the continent. Until that time, most Amerindian communities lived by hunting, fishing, or foraging. As the supply of large animals began to diminish, they turned to smaller game and to fishing and foraging for wild plants, fruits, and nuts.

The Eastern Woodlands

It was probably during the third millennium B.C.E. that peoples in the Eastern Woodlands (the land in eastern North America from the Great Lakes to the Gulf of

Mexico) began to cultivate indigenous plants for food in a systematic way. As wild game and food became scarce, some communities began to place more emphasis on cultivating crops. This shift first occurred in the Mississippi River valley from Ohio, Indiana, and Illinois down to the Gulf of Mexico (see Map 6.6). Among the most commonly cultivated crops were maize, squash, beans, and various grasses.

As the population in the area increased, people began to congregate in villages, and sedentary communities began to develop in the alluvial lowlands, where the soil could be cultivated for many years at a time because of the nutrients deposited by the river water.

Village councils were established to adjudicate disputes, and in a few cases, several villages banded together under the authority of a local chieftain. Urban centers began to appear, some of them inhabited by ten thousand people or more. At the same time, regional trade increased. The people of the **Hopewell culture** in Ohio ranged from the shores of Lake Superior to the Appalachian Mountains and the Gulf of Mexico in search of metals, shells, obsidian, and manufactured items to support their economic needs and religious beliefs.

Cahokia

At the site of Cahokia, near the modern city of East Saint Louis, Illinois, archaeologists found a burial mound more than 98 feet high with a base larger than that of the Great Pyramid in Egypt. A hundred smaller mounds were also found in the vicinity. The town itself, which covered almost 300 acres and was surrounded by a wooden stockade, was apparently the administrative capital of much of the surrounding territory until its decline in the 1200s. With a population of over twenty thousand, it was reportedly the largest city in North America until Philadelphia surpassed that number in the early nineteenth century. Cahokia carried on extensive trade with other communities throughout the region, and there are some signs of regular contacts with the civilizations in Mesoamerica, such as the presence of ball courts in the Central American style. But wars were not uncommon, leading the

VIRGINS WITH RED CHEEKS

FAMILY & SOCIETY

A letter from a Peruvian chief to King Philip III of Spain written four hundred years ago gives us a firsthand account of the nature of traditional Inkan society. The purpose of author Huaman Poma was both to justify the history and culture of the Inka peoples and to record their sufferings under Spanish domination. In his letter, Poma describes Inka daily life from birth to death in minute detail. He explains the different tasks assigned to men and women, beginning with their early education. Whereas boys were taught to watch the flocks and trap animals, girls were taught to dye, spin, and weave cloth and perform other domestic chores. Most interesting, perhaps, was the emphasis that the Inka placed on virginity, as is witnessed in the document presented here. The Inka tradition of temple virgins is reminiscent of similar practices in ancient Rome, where young girls from noble families were chosen as priestesses to tend the sacred fire in the Temple of Vesta for thirty years. If an Inka temple virgin lost her virginity, she was condemned to be buried alive in an underground chamber.

Huaman Poma, Letter to a King

During the time of the Incas certain women, who were called *aclla* or "the chosen," were destined for lifelong virginity. Mostly they were confined in houses and they belonged to one of two main categories, namely sacred virgins and common virgins.

The so-called "virgins with red cheeks" entered upon their duties at the age of twenty and were dedicated to the service of the Sun, the Moon, and the Day-Star. In their whole life they were never allowed to speak to a man.

The virgins of the Inca's own shrine of Huanacauri were known for their beauty as well as their chastity. The other principal shrines had similar girls in attendance. At the less important shrines there were the older virgins who occupied themselves with spinning and weaving the silk-like clothes worn by their idols. There was a still lower class of virgins, over forty years of age and no longer very beautiful, who performed unimportant religious duties and worked in the fields or as ordinary seamstresses.

Daughters of noble families who had grown into old maids were adept at making girdles, headbands, string bags, and similar articles in the intervals of their pious observances.

Girls who had musical talent were selected to sing or play the flute and drum at Court, weddings and other ceremonies, and all the immemorable festivals of the Inca year.

There was yet another class of *acla* or "chosen," only some of whom kept their virginity and others not. These were the Inca's beautiful attendants and concubines, who were drawn from noble families and lived in his palaces. They made clothing for him out of material finer than taffeta or silk. They also prepared a maize spirit of extraordinary richness, which was matured for an entire month, and they cooked delicious dishes for the Inca. They also lay with him, but never with any other man.

Q *In this passage, one of the chief duties of a woman in Inkan society was to spin and weave. In what other traditional societies was textile making a woman's work? Why do you think this was the case?*

© British Museum, London/Art Resource, NY

A North American Village. John White, governor of the first English colony in North America, was an artist who provided us with descriptions of the activities of North Americans in eastern North Carolina, where the colony was located. His drawing of an Indian village depicts pole-and-thatch houses surrounded by a wooden stockade. The inhabitants were agriculturalists who also supported themselves with hunting and fishing. At first, relations with the English colonists were friendly, but they soon deteriorated, leading ultimately to the disappearance of the English village, today known as the "Lost Colony."

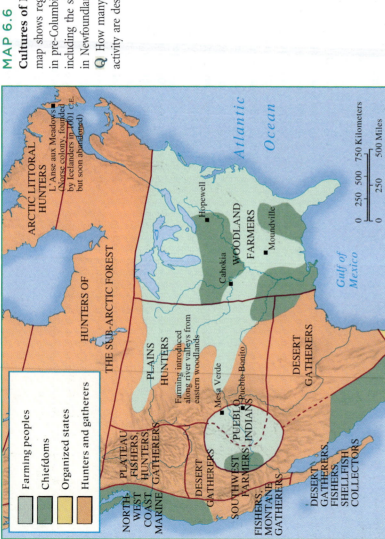

MAP 6.6 Early Peoples and Cultures of North America. This map shows regions of human settlement in pre-Columbian North America, including the short-lived Viking colony in Newfoundland.

Q How many varieties of economic activity are described on this map?

Iroquois, who inhabited much of the modern states of Pennsylvania and New York as well as parts of southern Canada, to create a tribal alliance called the League of Iroquois.

The "Ancient Ones": The Anasazi

West of the Mississippi River basin, most Amerindian peoples lived by hunting or food gathering. During the first millennium C.E., knowledge of agriculture gradually spread up the rivers to the Great Plains, and farming was practiced as far west as southwestern Colorado, where the Anasazi (Navajo for "alien ancient ones") established an extensive agricultural community in an area extending from northern New Mexico and Arizona to southwestern Colorado and parts of southern Utah. Although they apparently never discovered the wheel or used beasts of burden, the Anasazi created a system of roads that facilitated an extensive exchange of technology, products, and ideas throughout the region. By the ninth century, they had mastered the art of irrigation, which allowed them to expand their productive efforts to squash and beans, and had established an important urban center at Chaco Canyon, in southern New Mexico, where they built a

© William J. Duiker

Cliff Palace at Mesa Verde. Mesa Verde is one of the best-developed sites of the Anasazi peoples in southwestern North America. At one time they were farmers who tilled the soil atop the mesas, but eventually they were forced to build their settlements in more protected locations. At Cliff Palace, shown here, adobe houses were hidden on the perpendicular face of the mesa. Access was achieved only by a perilous descent via indented finger- and toeholds on the rock face.

walled city with dozens of three-story adobe communal houses, called *pueblos*, with timbered roofs. Community religious functions were carried out in two large circular chambers called *kivas*. Clothing was made from hides or cotton cloth. At its height, Pueblo Bonito contained several hundred compounds housing several thousand residents.

In the mid-twelfth century, the Anasazi moved north to Mesa Verde, in southwestern Colorado. At first, they settled on top of the mesa, but eventually they expanded onto the cliffs of surrounding canyons.

Sometime during the late thirteenth century, however, Mesa Verde was also abandoned, and the inhabitants migrated southward. Their descendants, the Zuni and the Hopi, now occupy pueblos in central Arizona and New Mexico (thus leading some to adopt a new name, "ancient Puebloans"). For years, archaeologists surmised that a severe drought was the cause of the migration, but new evidence has raised doubts that decreasing rainfall, by itself, was a sufficient explanation. An increase in internecine warfare, perhaps brought about by climatic changes, may also have played a role in the decision to relocate. Some archaeologists point to evidence that cannibalism was practiced at Pueblo Bonito and suggest that migrants from the south may have arrived in the area, provoking bitter rivalries within Anasazi society. In any event, with increasing aridity and the importation of the horse by the Spanish in the sixteenth century, hunting revived, and mounted nomads like the Apache and the Navajo came to dominate much of the Southwest.

South America: The Arawak

East of the Andes Mountains in South America, other Amerindian societies were beginning to make the transition to agriculture. Perhaps the most prominent were the Arawak, a people living along the Orinoco River in modern Venezuela. Having begun to cultivate manioc (a tuber also known as *cassava* or *yuca*, the source of tapioca) along the banks of the river, they gradually migrated down to the coast and then proceeded to move eastward along the northern coast of the continent. Some occupied the islands of the Caribbean Sea. In their new island habitat, they lived by a mixture of fishing, hunting, and cultivating maize, beans, manioc, and squash, as well as other crops such as peanuts, peppers, and pineapples. As the population increased, a pattern of political organization above the village level appeared, along with recognizable social classes headed by a chieftain whose authority included control over the economy. The Arawak practiced human sacrifice, and some urban centers contained ball courts, suggesting the possibility of contacts with Mesoamerica.

In most such societies, where clear-cut class stratifications had not as yet taken place, men and women were considered of equal status. Men were responsible for hunting, warfare, and dealing with outsiders, while women were accountable for the crops, the distribution of food, maintaining the household, and bearing and raising the children. Their roles were complementary and were often viewed as a divine division of labor. In such cases, women in the stateless societies of North America held positions of greater respect than their counterparts in the river valley civilizations of the Old World.

Amazonia

Substantial human activity was also apparently taking place in the Amazon River valley. Scholars have been skeptical that advanced societies could take shape in the region because the soil, contrary to popular assumptions, lacked adequate nutrients to support a large population. Recent archaeological evidence, however, suggests that in some areas where decaying organic matter produces a rich soil suitable for farming—such as the region near the modern river port of Santarem—large agricultural societies may have once existed.

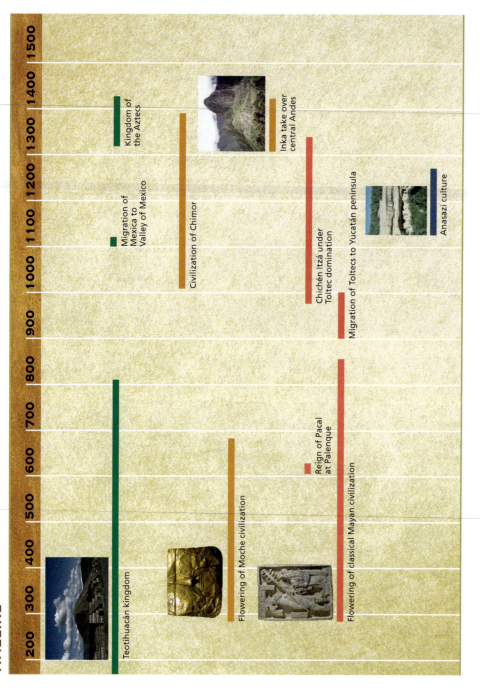

Timeline (200–1500):

- Teotihuacán kingdom
- Flowering of Moche civilization
- Reign of Pacal at Palenque
- Flowering of classical Mayan civilization
- Migration of Mexica to Valley of Mexico
- Kingdom of the Aztecs
- Civilization of Chimor
- Inka take over central Andes
- Chichén Itzá under Toltec domination
- Migration of Toltecs to Yucatán peninsula
- Anasazi culture

CONCLUSION

The first human beings did not arrive in the Americas until quite late in the prehistorical period. For the next several millennia, their descendants were forced to respond to the challenges of the environment in total isolation from other parts of the world. Nevertheless, around 5000 B.C.E., farming settlements began to appear in river valleys and upland areas in both Central and South America. Not long afterward—as measured in historical time—organized communities located along the coast of the Gulf of Mexico and the western slopes of the central Andes Mountains embarked on the long march toward creating advanced technological societies. Along the same path were the emerging societies of North America, which were beginning to expand their commercial and cultural links with civilizations farther to the south and had already laid the groundwork for future urbanization. Although the total number of people living in the Americas is a matter of debate, estimates range from ten million to as many as ninety million people.

What is perhaps most striking about the developments in the Western Hemisphere is how closely the process paralleled those of other civilizations. Irrigated agriculture, long-distance trade, urbanization, and the development of a writing system were all hallmarks of the emergence of advanced societies of the classical type. One need only point to the awed comments of early Spanish visitors, who said that the cities of the Aztecs were the equal of Seville and the other great metropolitan centers of Spain.

In some respects, the societies that emerged in the Americas were not as advanced technologically as their counterparts elsewhere. They were not familiar with the process of smelting iron, for example, and they had not yet invented wheeled vehicles. Their writing systems, by comparison with those in the Old World, were still in their infancy. Several possible reasons have been advanced to explain this technological gap. Geographical isolation—not only from people of other continents but also, in some cases, from each other—deprived them of the benefits of the diffusion of ideas that had assisted other societies in learning from their neighbors. Contacts among societies in the Americas were made much more difficult because of the topography and the diversity of the environment.

In some ways, too, they were not as blessed by nature. As the sociologist Jared Diamond has pointed out, the Americas did not possess many indigenous varieties of edible grasses that could encourage hunter-gatherers to take up farming. Nor were there abundant large mammals that could easily be domesticated for food and transport. It was not until the arrival of the Europeans that such familiar attributes of civilization became widely available for human use in the Americas.[5]

These disadvantages can help explain some of the problems that the early peoples of the Americas encountered in their efforts to master their environments. It is interesting to note that the spread of agriculture and increasing urbanization had already begun to produce a rising incidence of infectious diseases. It is also significant that in the Americas, as elsewhere, many of the first civilizations formed by the human species appear to have been brought to an end as much by environmental changes and disease as by war. In the next chapter, we shall return to Asia, where new civilizations were in the process of replacing the ancient empires.

CHAPTER NOTES

1. Quoted in S. Morley and G. W. Brainerd, *The Ancient Maya* (Stanford, Calif., 1983).
2. B. Díaz, *The Conquest of New Spain* (Harmondsworth, England, 1975), p. 513.
3. Quoted in M. D. Coe, D. Snow, and E. P. Benson, *Atlas of Ancient America* (New York, 1988), p. 210.
4. G. de la Vega (El Inca), *Royal Commentaries of the Incas and General History of Peru*, pt. 1, trans. H. V. Livermore (Austin, Tex., 1966), p. 180.
5. J. Diamond, *Guns, Germs, and Steel: The Fates of Human Societies* (New York, 1997), pp. 187–188.

SUGGESTED READING

Early Civilizations of the Americas For a profusely illustrated and informative overview of the early civilizations of the Americas, see **M. D. Coe, D. Snow, and E. P. Benson, *Atlas of Ancient America*** (New York, 1988). The first arrival of human beings in the New World is discussed in **B. Fagan, *The Great Journey: The Peopling of Ancient America*** (London, 1987). A fascinating recent account that covers the entire pre-Columbian era is **C. Mann's *1491: New Revelations of the Americas Before Columbus*** (New York, 2006).

Mayan Civilization On Mayan civilization, see **D. Webster, *The Fall of the Ancient Maya: Solving the Mystery of the Maya Collapse*** (London, 2002); **M. D. Coe, *The Maya*** (London, 1993); and **J. Sabloff, *The New Archeology and the Ancient Maya*** (New York, 1990).

Aztec Civilization For an overview of Aztec civilization in Mexico, see **B. Fagan, *The Aztecs*** (New York, 1984). **S. D. Gillespie, *The Aztec Kings: The Construction of Rulership in Mexican History*** (Tucson, Ariz., 1989), is an imaginative effort to uncover the symbolic meaning in Aztec traditions. For a provocative study of religious traditions in a comparative context, see **B. Fagan, *From Black Land to Fifth Sun*** (Reading, Mass., 1998). On the Olmecs and the Zapotecs, see **E. P. Benson, *The Olmec and Their Neighbors*** (Washington, D.C., 1981), and **R. E. Blanton, *Monte Albán: Settlement Patterns at the Ancient Zapotec Capital*** (New York, 1978).

Daily Life in Ancient Central America Much of our information about the lives of the peoples of ancient Central America comes from Spanish writers who visited or lived in the area during the sixteenth and seventeenth centuries. For a European account of Aztec society, see **B. Díaz, *The Conquest of New Spain*** (Harmondsworth, England, 1975).

Ancient South America A worthy account of developments in South America is **G. Bawden, *The Moche*** (Oxford, 1996). On the Inka and their predecessors, see **R. W. Keatinge, ed., *Peruvian Prehistory: An Overview of Pre-Inca and Inca Society*** (Cambridge, 1988).

Art and Culture of the Ancient Americas On the art and culture of the ancient Americas, see **M. E. Miller, *Maya Art and Architecture*** (London, 1999); **E. Pasztory, *Pre-Columbian Art*** (Cambridge, 1998); and **M. León-Portilla and E. Shorris, *In the Language of Kings*** (New York, 2001). Writing systems are discussed in **M. Coe, *Breaking the Maya Code*** (New York, 1992), and **G. Upton, *Signs of the Inka Quipu*** (Austin, Tex., 2003).

Social Issues of the Ancient Americas On social issues, see **L. Schele and D. Freidel, *A Forest of Kings: The Untold Story of the Ancient Maya*** (New York, 1990); **R. van Zantwijk, *The Aztec Arrangement: The Social History of Pre-Spanish Mexico*** (Norman, Okla., 1985); and **N. Shoemaker, *Negotiators of Change: Historical Perspectives on Native American Women*** (New York, 1995).

For a treatment of the role of the environment, see **B. Fagan, *Floods, Famine, and Emperors: El Niño and the Fate of Civilizations*** (New York, 1999).

CENGAGENOW Enter CengageNOW using the access card that is available with this text. CengageNOW will help you understand the content in this chapter with lesson plans generated for your needs, as well as provide you with a connection to the Wadsworth World History Resource Center (see description below for details).

WORLD HISTORY RESOURCE CENTER

Enter the Resource Center using either your *CengageNOW* access card or your separate access card for the *World History Resource Center*. Organized by topic, this Website includes quizzes; images: over 350 primary source documents; interactive simulations; maps; and timelines; movie explorations; and a wealth of other resources. You can read the following documents, and many more, at the *World History Resource Center*:

Popul Vuh

Visit the *World History Companion Website* for chapter quizzes and more:

www.cengage.com/history/Duiker/World6e

CHAPTER 7

FERMENT IN THE MIDDLE EAST: THE RISE OF ISLAM

© British Library/The Bridgeman Art Library

Muhammad rises to heaven.

CHAPTER OUTLINE AND FOCUS QUESTIONS

The Rise of Islam

Q What were the main tenets of Islam, and how does the religion compare with Judaism and Christianity?

The Arab Empire and Its Successors

Q Why did the Arabs undergo such a rapid expansion in the seventh and eighth centuries, and why were they so successful in creating an empire?

Islamic Civilization

Q What were the main features of Islamic society and culture during its era of early growth?

CRITICAL THINKING

Q In what ways did the arrival of Islam change the political, social, and cultural conditions that had existed in the area before Muhammad?

IN THE YEAR 570, in the Arabian city of Mecca, there was born a child named Muhammad whose life changed the course of world history. The son of a merchant, Muhammad grew to maturity in a time of transition. Old empires that had once ruled the entire Middle East were only a distant memory. The region was now divided into many separate states, and the people adhered to many different faiths.

According to tradition, the young Muhammad became deeply concerned at the corrupt and decadent society of his day and took to wandering in the hills outside the city to meditate on the conditions of his time. On one of these occasions, he experienced visions that he was convinced had been inspired by Allah. Muslims believe that this message had been conveyed to him by the angel Gabriel, who commanded Muhammad to preach the revelations that he would be given. Eventually, they would be transcribed into the holy book of Islam—the Qur'an—and provide inspiration to millions of people throughout the world.

Within a few decades of Muhammad's death, the Middle East was united once again. The initial triumph may have been primarily political and military, based on the transformative power of a dynamic new religion that inspired thousands of devotees to extend their faith to neighboring regions. In any event, Islamic beliefs and culture exerted a powerful influence in all areas occupied by Arab armies. Initially, Arab beliefs and customs, as reflected through the prism of Muhammad's teachings, transformed the societies and cultures of the peoples living in the new empire. But eventually, the distinctive political and cultural forces that had long characterized the region began to reassert themselves. Factional struggles led to the decline and then the destruction of the empire.

Still, the Arab conquest left a powerful legacy that survived the decline of Arab political power. The ideological and emotional appeal of Islam remained strong throughout the Middle East and eventually extended into areas not occupied by Arab armies, such as the Indian subcontinent, Southeast Asia, and sub-Saharan Africa. ◆

The Rise of Islam

Q Focus Question: What were the main tenets of Islam, and how does the religion compare with Judaism and Christianity?

The Arabs were a Semitic-speaking people of southwestern Asia with a long history. They were mentioned in Greek sources of the fifth century B.C.E. and even earlier in the Old Testament. The Greek historian Herodotus had applied the name *Arab* to the entire peninsula, calling it Arabia. In 106 B.C.E., the Romans extended their authority to the Arabian peninsula, transforming it into a province of their growing empire.

During Roman times, the region was inhabited primarily by the **Bedouin** Arabs, nomadic peoples who came originally from the northern part of the peninsula. Bedouin society was organized on a tribal basis. The ruling member of the tribe was called the **sheikh** and was selected from one of the leading families by a council of elders called the *majlis*. The *sheikh* ruled the tribe with the consent of the council. Each tribe was autonomous but felt a general sense of allegiance to the larger unity of all the clans in the region. In early times, the Bedouins had supported themselves primarily by shepherding or by raiding passing caravans, but after the domestication of the camel during the second millennium B.C.E., the Bedouins began to participate in the caravan trade themselves and became major carriers of goods between the Persian Gulf and the Mediterranean Sea.

The Arabs of pre-Islamic times were polytheistic, with a supreme god known as Allah presiding over a community of spirits. It was a communal faith, involving all members of the tribe, and had no priesthood. Spirits were believed to inhabit natural objects, such as trees, rivers, and mountains, while the supreme deity was symbolized by a sacred stone. Each tribe possessed its own stone, but by the time of Muhammad, a massive black meteorite, housed in a central shrine called the Ka'aba in the commercial city of Mecca, had come to possess especially sacred qualities.

In the fifth and sixth centuries C.E., the economic importance of the Arabian peninsula began to increase. As a result of the political disorder in Mesopotamia—a consequence of the constant wars between the Byzantine and Persian Empires—and in Egypt, the trade routes that ran directly across the peninsula or down the Red Sea became increasingly risky, and a third route, which passed from the Mediterranean through Mecca to Yemen and then by ship across the Indian Ocean, became more popular. The communities in that part of the peninsula benefited from the change and took a larger share of the caravan trade between the Mediterranean and the countries on the other side of the Indian Ocean. As a consequence, relations between the Bedouins of the desert and the increasingly wealthy merchant class of the towns began to become strained.

The Role of Muhammad

Into this world came Muhammad (also known as Mohammed), a man whose spiritual visions unified the Arab world (see Map 7.1) with a speed no one would have suspected possible. Born in Mecca to a merchant family and orphaned at the age of six, Muhammad (570–632) grew up to become a caravan manager and eventually married a rich widow, Khadija, who was also his employer. For several years, he lived in Mecca as a merchant but, according to tradition, was apparently troubled by the growing gap between the Bedouin values of honesty and generosity (he himself was a member of the local Hashemite clan of the Quraishi tribe) and the acquisitive behavior of the affluent commercial elites in the city. Deeply concerned, he began to visit the nearby hills to meditate in isolation. It was there that he encountered the angel Gabriel, who commanded him to preach the revelations that he would be given.

It is said that Muhammad was acquainted with Jewish and Christian beliefs and came to believe that while Allah had already revealed himself in part through Moses and Jesus—and thus through the Hebraic and Christian traditions—the final revelations were now being given to him. Out of his revelations, which were eventually dictated to scribes, came the Qur'an ("recitation," also spelled Koran), the holy scriptures of Islam (*Islam* means "submission," implying submission to the will of Allah). The Qur'an contained the guidelines by which followers of Allah, known as Muslims (practitioners of Islam), were to live. Like the Christians and the Jews, Muslims (also known as Moslems) were a "people of the Book," believers in a faith based on scripture.

Muslims believe that after returning home, Muhammad set out to comply with Gabriel's command by preaching to the residents of Mecca about his revelations. At first, many were convinced that he was a madman or a charlatan. Others were undoubtedly concerned that his

MAP 7.1 The Middle East in the Time of Muhammad. When Islam began to spread throughout the Middle East in the early seventh century, the dominant states in the region were the Roman Empire in the eastern Mediterranean and the Sassanian Empire in Persia.

Q What were the major territorial divisions existing at the time and the key sites connected to the rise of Islam?

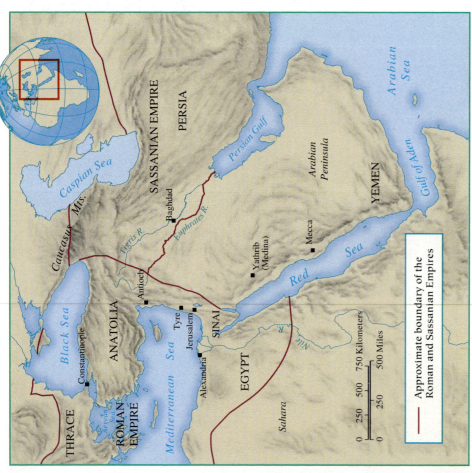

vigorous attacks on traditional beliefs and the corrupt society around him could severely shake the social and political order. After three years of proselytizing, he had only thirty followers.

Discouraged, perhaps, by the systematic persecution of his followers, which was allegedly undertaken with a brutality reminiscent of the cruelties suffered by early Christians, as well as the failure of the Meccans to accept his message, in 622 Muhammad and some of his closest supporters (mostly from his own Hashemite clan) left the city and retreated north to the rival city of Yathrib, later renamed Medina, or "city of the Prophet." That flight, known in history as the **Hegira** (*Hijrah*), marks the first date on the official calendar of Islam. At Medina, Muhammad failed in his original purpose—to convert the Jewish community in Medina to his beliefs. But he was successful in winning support from many residents of the city as well as from Bedouins in the surrounding countryside. From this mixture, he formed the first Muslim community (the **umma**). Returning to his birthplace at the head of a considerable military force, Muhammad conquered Mecca and converted the townspeople to the new faith. In 630, he made a symbolic visit to the Ka'aba, where he declared it a sacred shrine of Islam and ordered the destruction of the idols of the traditional faith. Two

years later, Muhammad died, just as Islam was beginning to spread throughout the peninsula.

The Teachings of Muhammad

Like Christianity and Judaism, Islam is monotheistic. Allah is the all-powerful being who created the universe and everything in it. Islam is also concerned with salvation and offers the hope of an afterlife. Those who hope to achieve it must subject themselves to the will of Allah. Unlike Christianity, Islam makes no claim to the divinity of its founder. Muhammad, like Abraham, Moses, and other figures of the Old Testament, was a prophet, but he was also a man like other men. Because, according to the Qur'an, earlier prophets had corrupted his revelations, Allah sent his complete revelation through Muhammad.

At the heart of Islam is the Qur'an, with its basic message that there is no God but Allah and Muhammad is his Prophet. Consisting of 114 *suras* (chapters) drawn together by a committee established after Muhammad's death, the Qur'an is not only the sacred book of Islam but also an ethical guidebook and a code of law and political theory combined.

As it evolved, Islam developed a number of fundamental tenets. Of primary importance is the need to obey

© Mehmet Biber/Photo Researchers Inc.

FILM & HISTORY

THE MESSAGE (MUHAMMAD: THE MESSENGER OF GOD) (1976)

Over the years, countless commercial films depicting the early years of Christianity have been produced in Hollywood. By contrast, cinematic portrayals of the birth of other world religions such as Buddhism, Hinduism, and Islam have been rare. In the case of Islam, the reluctance has been based in part on the traditional prohibition for Muslims to depict the face and figure of the Prophet Muhammad. Reactions to depictions of the Prophet in European media in recent years have demonstrated that this issue remains highly sensitive in Muslim communities worldwide.

In the 1970s, an American Muslim filmmaker, Moustapha Akkak, dismayed at the widespread ignorance of the tenets of Islam in Western countries, sought to produce a full-length feature film on the life of Muhammad for presentation in Europe and the United States. Failing to obtain financial help for the product from domestic sources, he sought aid abroad and finally won the support of the Libyan leader Muammar Qaddhafi, and the film was released in both English and Arabic versions in 1976.

The film seeks to present an accurate and sympathetic account of the life of the Prophet from his spiritual awakening in 610 to his peaceful return to Mecca in 630. To assuage Muslim concerns, neither the figure nor the voice of Muhammad is in the film. None of his wives, daughters, or sons-in-law appear onscreen. The narrative is carried on through comments and actions of his friends and disciples, notably the Prophet's uncle Hamzah, ably played by the American veteran actor Anthony Quinn.

The film, shot on location in Libya and Morocco, is a sometimes moving account of the emergence of Islam in

© John Bryson// Time Life Pictures/Getty Images

Hamzah, Muhammad's uncle (left, played by Anthony Quinn), is shown defending Muhammad's followers in the early years of Islam.

early-seventh-century Arabia. Although it does not dwell on the more esoteric aspects of Muslim beliefs, it stresses many of the humanistic elements of Islam, including respect for women and opposition to slavery, as well as the equality of all human beings in the eyes of God. Muhammad and his followers are shown as messengers of peace who are aroused to violence only in order to protect themselves from the acts of their enemies.

Though slow-moving in spots and somewhat lengthy in the manner of the genre, *The Message* (also known as *Muhammad: Messenger of God*) is beautifully filmed and contains a number of stirring battle scenes. Viewers come away with a fairly accurate and sympathetic portrait of the life of the Prophet and his message to the faithful.

The Ka'aba in Mecca. The Ka'aba, the shrine containing a black meteorite in the Arabian city of Mecca, is the most sacred site of the Islamic faith. Wherever Muslims pray, they are instructed to face Mecca; each thus becomes a spoke of the Ka'aba, the holy center of the wheel of Islam. If they are able to do so, all Muslims are encouraged to visit the Ka'aba at least once in their lifetime. Called the *hajj*, this pilgrimage to Mecca represents the ultimate in spiritual fulfillment.

THE QUR'AN: THE PILGRIMAGE

RELIGION & PHILOSOPHY

The Qur'an is the sacred book of the Muslims, comparable to the Bible in Christianity. This selection from Sura 22, titled "Pilgrimage," discusses the importance of making a pilgrimage to Mecca, one of the Five Pillars of Islam. The pilgrim's final destination was the Ka'aba at Mecca, containing the Black Stone.

Qur'an, Sura 22: "Pilgrimage"

Exhort all men to make the pilgrimage. They will come to you on foot and on the backs of swift camels from every distant quarter; they will come to avail themselves of many a benefit, and to pronounce on the appointed days the name of God over the cattle which He has given them for food. Eat of their flesh, and feed the poor and the unfortunate.

Then let the pilgrims tidy themselves, make their vows, and circle the Ancient House. Such is God's commandment. He that reveres the sacred rites of God shall fare better in the sight of his Lord.

The flesh of cattle is lawful for you, except for that which has been specified before. Guard yourselves against the filth of idols; and avoid the utterance of falsehoods.

Dedicate yourselves to God, and serve none besides Him. The man who serves other deities besides God is like him who falls from heaven and is snatched by the birds or carried away by the wind to some far-off region. Even such is he.

He that reveres the offerings made to God shows the piety of his heart. Your cattle are useful to you in many ways until the time of their slaughter. Then they are offered for sacrifice at the Ancient House.

For every community We have ordained a ritual, that they may pronounce the name of God over the cattle which He has given them for food. Your God is one God; to Him surrender yourselves. Give good news to the humble, whose hearts are filled with awe at the mention of God; who endure adversity with fortitude, attend to their prayers, and give in alms from what We gave them.

We have made the camels a part of God's rites. They are of much use to you. Pronounce over them the name of God as you draw them up in line and slaughter them; and when they have fallen to the ground eat of their flesh and feed the uncomplaining beggar and the demanding supplicant. Thus have We subjected them to your service, so that you may give thanks.

Their flesh and blood does not reach God; it is your piety that reaches Him. Thus has He subjected them to your service, so that you may give glory to God for guiding you.

Give good news to the righteous. God will ward off evil from true believers. God does not love the treacherous and the thankless.

Q *What is the key purpose of undertaking a pilgrimage to Mecca? What is the historical importance of the sacred stone?*

CENGAGENOW *To read more of the Qur'an, enter the documents area of the World History Resource Center using the access card that is available for World History.*

---

the will of Allah. This means following a basic ethical code that consists of what are popularly termed the **Five Pillars of Islam:** belief in Allah and Muhammad as his Prophet; standard prayer five times a day and public prayer on Friday at midday to worship Allah; observation of the holy month of **Ramadan,** including fasting from dawn to sunset; making a pilgrimage, if possible, to Mecca at least once in one's lifetime (see the box above); and giving alms (*zakat*) to the poor and unfortunate. The faithful who observe the law are guaranteed a place in an eternal paradise (*a vision of a luxurious and cool garden shared by some versions of Eastern Christianity*) with the sensuous delights so obviously lacking in the midst of the Arabian desert.

Islam is not just a set of religious beliefs but a way of life as well. After the death of Muhammad, a panel of Muslim scholars, known as the **ulama,** drew up a law code, called the **Shari'a,** to provide believers with a set of prescriptions to regulate their daily lives. Much of the *Shari'a* was drawn from existing legal regulations or from the **Hadith,** a collection of the sayings of the Prophet that

was used to supplement the revelations contained in the holy scriptures.

Believers are subject to strict behavioral requirements. In addition to the Five Pillars, Muslims are forbidden to gamble, to eat pork, to drink alcoholic beverages, and to engage in dishonest behavior. Sexual mores are also strict. Contacts between unmarried men and women are discouraged, and ideally, marriages are to be arranged by the parents (see the box on p. 195). In accordance with Bedouin custom, polygyny is permitted, but Muhammad attempted to limit the practice by restricting males to no more than four wives.

To what degree the traditional account of the exposition and inner meaning of the Qur'an can stand up to historical analysis is a matter of debate. The circumstances surrounding the life of Muhammad and his role in founding the religion of Islam, given the lack of verifiable evidence, remain highly speculative, and many Muslims are undoubtedly concerned that the consequences of rigorous examination might undercut key tenets of the Muslim faith. One of the problems connected with such

"DRAW THEIR VEILS OVER THEIR BOSOMS"

RELIGION & PHILOSOPHY

Prior to the Islamic era, many upper-class women greeted men on the street, entertained their husband's friends at home, went on pilgrimages to Mecca, and even accompanied their husbands to battle. Such women were neither veiled nor secluded. Muhammad, however, specified that his own wives, who (according to the Qur'an) were "not like any other women," should be modestly attired and should be addressed by men from behind a curtain. Over the centuries, Muslim theologians, fearful that female sexuality could threaten the established order, interpreted Muhammad's "modest attire" and his reference to curtains to mean segregated seclusion and body concealment for all Muslim women. In fact, one strict scholar in fourteenth-century Cairo went so far as to prescribe that ideally, a woman should be allowed to leave her home only three times in her life: when entering her husband's home after marriage, after the death of her parents, and after her own death.

In traditional Islamic societies, veiling and seclusion were more prevalent among urban women than among their rural counterparts. The latter, who worked in the fields and rarely saw people outside their extended family, were less restricted. In this excerpt from the Qur'an, women are instructed to "guard their modesty." Nowhere in the Qur'an, however, does it stipulate that women should be sequestered or covered from head to toe.

Qur'an, Sura 24: "The Light"

And say to the believing women
That they should lower
Their gaze and guard
Their modesty; that they
Should not display their
Beauty and ornaments except
What [must ordinarily] appear
Thereof; that they should
Draw their veils over
Their bosoms and not display
Their beauty except
To their husbands, their fathers,
Their husbands' fathers, their sons,
Their brothers or their brothers' sons,
Or their sisters' sons,
Or their women, or the slaves
Whom their right hands
Possess, or male servants
Free of physical needs,
Or small children who
Have no sense of the shame
Of sex; and that they
Should not strike their feet
In order to draw attention
To their hidden ornaments;

Q How does the role of women in Islam compare with what we have seen in other traditional societies, such as India, China, and the Americas?

CENGAGENOW To read more of the Qur'an, enter the documents area of the World History Resource Center using the access card that is available for World History.

---

an effort is that the earliest known versions of the Qur'an available today do not contain the diacritical marks that modern Arabic uses to clarify meaning, thus leaving much of the sacred text ambiguous and open to varying interpretations.

The Arab Empire and Its Successors

Q Focus Question: Why did the Arabs undergo such a rapid expansion in the seventh and eighth centuries, and why were they so successful in creating an empire?

The death of Muhammad presented his followers with a dilemma. Although Muhammad had not claimed divine qualities, Muslims saw no separation between political and religious authority. Submission to the will of Allah meant submission to his Prophet, Muhammad. According to the Qur'an, "Whoso obeyeth the messenger obeyeth Allah."[1] Muhammad's charismatic authority and political skills had been at the heart of his success. But Muslims have never agreed whether or not he named a successor, and although he had several daughters, he left no sons. In the male-oriented society of his day, who would lead the community of the faithful?

Shortly after Muhammad's death, a number of his closest followers selected Abu Bakr, a wealthy merchant from Medina who was Muhammad's father-in-law and one of his first supporters, as **caliph** (*khalifa*, literally "successor"). The caliph was the temporal leader of the Islamic community and was also considered, in general terms, to be a religious leader, or **imam**. Under Abu Bakr's prudent leadership, the movement succeeded in suppressing factional tendencies among some of the Bedouin tribes in the peninsula and began to direct its attention to wider fields. Muhammad had used the Arabic tribal custom of the *razzia*, or raid, in the struggle against his enemies. Now his successors turned to the same custom to expand the authority of the movement. The Qur'an called this activity "striving in the way of the Lord," or *jihad.* Although sometimes translated as "holy war," the term can be applied in a wide range of situations, much like the somewhat analogous English term *crusade.*

Creation of an Empire

Once the Arabs had become unified under Muhammad's successor, they began directing against neighboring peoples the energy they had formerly directed against each other. The Byzantine and Sassanian Empires were the first to feel the strength of the newly united Arabs, now aroused to a peak of zeal by their common faith. In 636, the Muslims defeated the Byzantine army on the Yarmuk River, north of the Dead Sea. Four years later, they took possession of the Byzantine province of Syria. To the east, the Arabs defeated a Persian force in 637 and then went on to conquer the entire empire of the Sassanids by 650. In the meantime, Egypt and other areas of North Africa were also brought under Arab authority (see Chapter 8).

What accounts for this rapid expansion of the Arabs after the rise of Islam in the early seventh century? Historians have proposed various explanations, ranging from a prolonged drought on the Arabian peninsula to the desire of Islam's leaders to channel the energies of their new converts. Another hypothesis is that the expansion was deliberately planned by the ruling elites in Mecca to extend their trade routes and bring surplus-producing regions under their control. Whatever the case, Islam's ability to unify the Bedouin peoples certainly played a role. Although the Arab triumph was made substantially easier by the ongoing conflict between the Byzantine and Persian Empires, which had weakened both powers, the strength and mobility of the Bedouin armies should not be overlooked. Led by a series of brilliant generals commanding a vaunted mounted cavalry, the Arabs assembled a large, highly motivated army whose valor was enhanced by the belief that Muslim warriors who died in battle were guaranteed a place in paradise.

Once the army had prevailed, Arab administration of the conquered areas was generally tolerant. Sometimes, due to a shortage of trained Arab administrators, government was left to local officials. Conversion to Islam was generally voluntary in accordance with the maxim in the Qur'an that "there shall be no compulsion in religion."[2] Those who chose not to convert were required only to submit to Muslim rule and pay a head tax in return for exemption from military service, which was required of all Muslim males. Under such conditions, the local populations often welcomed Arab rule as preferable to Byzantine rule or that of the Sassanid dynasty in Persia. Furthermore, the simple and direct character of the new religion, as well as its egalitarian qualities (all people were viewed as equal in

the eyes of Allah), were undoubtedly attractive to peoples throughout the region.

The Rise of the Umayyads

The main challenge to the growing empire came from within. Some of Muhammad's followers had not agreed with the selection of Abu Bakr as the first caliph and promoted the candidacy of Ali, Muhammad's cousin and son-in-law, as an alternative. Ali's claim was ignored by other leaders, however, and after Abu Bakr's death, the office was passed to Umar, another of Muhammad's followers. In 656, Umar's successor, Uthman, was assassinated, and Ali, who happened to be in Medina at the time, was finally selected for the position. But according to tradition, Ali's rivals were convinced that he had been implicated in the death of his predecessor, and a factional struggle broke out within the Muslim leadership. In 661, Ali himself was assassinated, and Mu'awiya, the governor of Syria and one of Ali's chief rivals, replaced him in office. Mu'awiya thereupon made the caliphate hereditary in his own family, called the Umayyads, who were a branch of the Quraishi clan. The new caliphate, with its capital at Damascus, remained in power for nearly a century.

The factional struggle within Islam did not bring an end to Arab expansion. At the beginning of the eighth century, new attacks were launched at both the western and the eastern ends of the Mediterranean world (see Map 7.2). Arab armies seized Egypt, advanced across North Africa, and conquered the Berbers, a primarily pastoral people living along the Mediterranean coast and in the mountains in the interior. Muslim fleets attacked several islands in the eastern Mediterranean. Then, around 710, Arab forces, supplemented by Berber allies under their commander, Tariq, crossed the Strait of Gibraltar and occupied southern Spain. The Visigothic kingdom, already weakened by internecine warfare, quickly collapsed, and by 725, most of the Iberian peninsula had become a Muslim state with its center in Andalusia. Seven years later, an Arab force, making a foray into southern France, was defeated by the army of Charles Martel between Tours and Poitiers. For the first time, Arab horsemen had met their match, in a disciplined Frankish infantry. Some historians think that internal exhaustion would have forced the invaders to retreat even without their defeat at the hands of the Franks. In any event, the Battle of Tours (or Poitiers) would be the high-water mark of Arab expansion in Europe.

In the meantime, in 717, another Muslim force had launched an attack on Constantinople with the hope of destroying the Byzantine Empire. But the Byzantines' use of Greek fire, a petroleum-based compound containing quicklime and sulfur, destroyed the Muslim fleet, thus saving the empire and indirectly Christian Europe, since the fall of Constantinople would have opened the door to an Arab invasion of eastern Europe. The Byzantine Empire and Islam now established an uneasy frontier in southern Asia Minor.

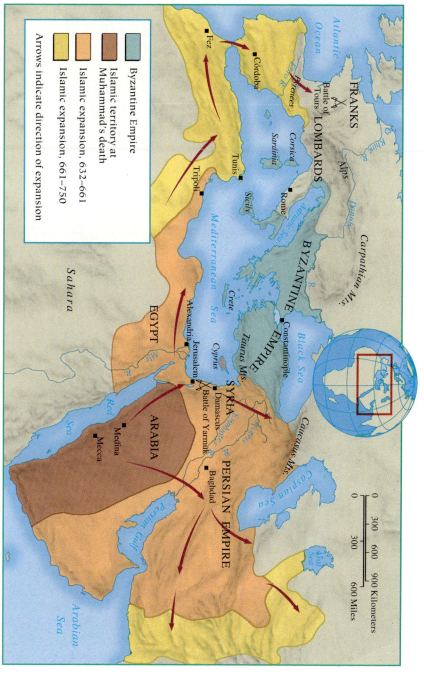

MAP 7.2 The Expansion of Islam. This map traces the expansion of the Islamic faith from its origins in the Arabian peninsula. Muhammad's followers carried the religion as far west as Spain and southern France and eastward to India and Southeast Asia.

Q In which of these areas is the Muslim faith still the dominant religion? 🖰 **View an animated version of this map or related maps at www.cengage.com/history/Duiker/Worldde**

Map legend:
- Byzantine Empire
- Islamic territory at Muhammad's death
- Islamic expansion, 632–661
- Islamic expansion, 661–750

Arrows indicate direction of expansion

the overthrow of the Umayyads and the establishment of the Abbasid dynasty (750–1258) in what is now Iraq.

The Abbasids

The Abbasid caliphs brought political, economic, and cultural change to the world of Islam. While seeking to implant their own version of religious orthodoxy, they tried to break down the distinctions between Arab and non-Arab Muslims. All Muslims were now allowed to hold both civil and military offices. This change helped open Islamic culture to the influences of the occupied civilizations. Some Arabs began to intermarry with the peoples they had conquered. In many parts of the Islamic world, notably North Africa and the eastern Mediterranean, most Muslim converts began to consider themselves Arabs. In 762, the Abbasids built a new capital city at Baghdad, on the Tigris River far to the east of the Umayyad capital at Damascus. The new capital was strategically positioned to take advantage of river traffic to the Persian Gulf and also lay astride the caravan route from the Mediterranean to Central Asia. The move eastward allowed Persian influence to come to the fore, encouraging a new cultural orientation. Under the Abbasids,

Arab power also extended to the east, consolidating Islamic rule in Mesopotamia and Persia and northward into Central Asia. But factional disputes continued to plague the empire. Many Muslims of non-Arab extraction resented the favoritism toward Arabs shown by local administrators. In some cases, resentment led to revolt, as in Iraq, where Ali's second son, Hussein, disputed the legitimacy of the Umayyads and incited his supporters—to be known in the future as **Shi'ites** (from the Arabic phrase *shi'at Ali*, "partisans of Ali")—to rise up against Umayyad rule in 680. Hussein's forces were defeated, and with the death of Hussein in the battle, a schism between Shi'ite and **Sunni** (usually translated as "orthodox") Muslims had been created that continues to this day.

Umayyad rule created resentment, not only in Mesopotamia but also in North Africa, where Berber resistance continued, especially in the mountainous areas south of the coastal plains. According to critics, the Umayyads may have contributed to their own demise by their decadent behavior. One caliph allegedly swam in a pool of wine and then imbibed enough of the contents to lower the level significantly. Finally, in 750, a revolt led by Abu al-Abbas, a descendant of Muhammad's uncle, led to

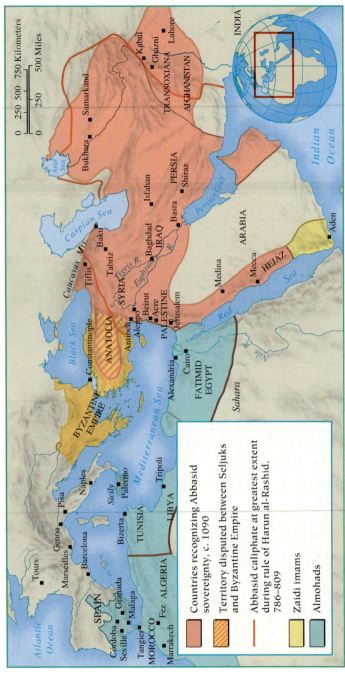

MAP 7.3 **The Abbasid Caliphate at the Height of Its Power.** The Abbasids arose in the eighth century as the defenders of the Muslim faith and established their capital at Baghdad. With its prowess as a trading state, the caliphate was the most powerful and extensive state in the region for several centuries.

Q What were the major urban centers under the influence of Islam, as shown on this map?

View an animated version of this map or related maps at www.cengage.com/history/Duiker/ World6e

Countries recognizing Abbasid sovereignty, c. 1090

Territory disputed between Seljuks and Byzantine Empire

Abbasid caliphate at greatest extent during rule of Harun al-Rashid, 786–809

Zaidi imams

Almohads

judges, merchants, and government officials, rather than warriors, were regarded as the ideal citizens.

Abbasid Rule The new Abbasid caliphate experienced a period of splendid rule well into the ninth century. Best known of the caliphs of the time was Harun al-Rashid (786–809), or Harun "the Upright," whose reign is often described as the golden age of the Abbasid caliphate. His son al-Ma'mun (813–833) was a patron of learning who founded an astronomical observatory and established a foundation for undertaking translations of classical Greek works. This was also a period of growing economic prosperity. The Arabs had conquered many of the richest provinces of the Roman Empire and now controlled the routes to the east (see Map 7.3). Baghdad became the center of an enormous commercial market that extended into Europe, Central Asia, and Africa, greatly adding to the wealth of the Islamic world and promoting an exchange of culture, ideas, and technology from one end of the known world to the other. Paper was introduced from China and eventually passed on to North Africa and Europe. Crops from India and Southeast Asia, including rice, sugar, sorghum, and cotton, moved toward the west, while glass, wine, and indigo dye were introduced into China.

Under the Abbasids, the caliphs became more regal. More kings than spiritual leaders, described by such

august phrases as the "caliph of God," they ruled by autocratic means, hardly distinguishable from the kings and emperors in neighboring civilizations. A thirteenth-century Chinese author, who compiled a world geography based on accounts by Chinese travelers, left the following description of one of the later caliphs:

The king wears a turban of silk brocade and foreign cotton stuff [buckram]. On each new moon and full moon he puts on an eight-sided flat-topped headdress of pure gold, set with the most precious jewels in the world. His robe is of silk brocade and is bound around him with a jade girdle. On his feet he wears golden shoes.... The king's throne is set with pearls and precious stones, and the steps of the throne are covered with pure gold.[3]

As the caliph took on more of the trappings of a hereditary autocrat, the bureaucracy assisting him in administering the expanding empire grew more complex as well. The caliph was advised by a council (called a *diwan*) headed by a prime minister, known as a *vizier* (*wazir*). The caliph did not attend meetings of the *diwan* in the normal manner but sat behind a screen and then communicated his divine will to the *vizier*. Some historians have ascribed the change in the caliphate to Persian influence, which permeated the empire after the capital was moved to Baghdad. Persian influence was indeed strong (the mother of the caliph

© The Bridgeman Art Library

The Great Mosque of Samarra. The ninth-century mosque of Samarra, located north of Baghdad in present-day Iraq, is the largest mosque in the Islamic world. Rising from the center of the city of Samarra, the capital of the Abbasids for over half a century and one of the largest medieval cities of its time, the imposing tower shown here is 156 feet in height. Its circular ramp may have inspired medieval artists in Europe as they imagined the ancient cultures of Mesopotamia. Although the mosque is today in ruins, its spiral tower still signals the presence of Islam to the faithful across the broad valley of the Tigris and Euphrates Rivers.

al-Ma'mun, for example, was a Persian), but more likely, the increase in pomp and circumstance was a natural consequence of the growing power and prosperity of the empire.

Instability and Division

However, an element of instability lurked beneath the surface. The lack of spiritual authority may have weakened the caliphate in competition with its potential rivals, and disputes over succession were common. At Harun's death, the rivalry between his two sons, Amin and al-Ma'mun, led to civil war and the destruction of Baghdad. As described by the tenth-century Muslim historian al-Mas'udi, "Mansions were destroyed, most remarkable monuments obliterated; prices soared.... Brother turned his sword against brother, son against father, as some fought for Amin, others for Ma'mun. Houses and palaces fueled the flames; property was put to the sack."[4]

Wealth contributed to financial corruption. By awarding important positions to court favorites, the Abbasid caliphs began to undermine the foundations of their own power and eventually became mere figureheads. Under Harun al-Rashid, members of his Hashemite clan received large pensions from the state treasury, and his wife, Zubaida, reportedly spent huge sums while shopping on a pilgrimage to Mecca. One powerful family, the Barmakids, amassed vast wealth and power until Harun al-Rashid eliminated the entire clan in a fit of jealousy.

The life of luxury enjoyed by the caliph and other political and economic elites in Baghdad seemingly undermined the stern fiber of Arab society as well as the strict moral code of Islam. Strictures against sexual promiscuity were widely ignored, and caliphs were rumored to maintain thousands of concubines in their harems. Divorce was common, homosexuality was widely practiced, and alcohol was consumed in public despite Islamic law's prohibition against imbibing spirits.

The process of disintegration was accelerated by changes that were taking place within the armed forces and the bureaucracy of the empire. Given the shortage of qualified Arabs for key positions in the army and the administration, the caliphate began to recruit officials from among the non-Arab peoples in the empire, such as Persians and Turks from Central Asia. These people gradually became a dominant force in the army and administration.

Environmental problems added to the regime's difficulties. The Tigris and Euphrates river system, lifeblood of Mesopotamia for three millennia, was beginning to silt up. Bureaucratic inertia now made things worse, as many of the country's canals became virtually unusable, leading to widespread food shortages.

The fragmentation of the Islamic empire accelerated in the tenth century. Morocco became independent, and in 973, a new Shi'ite dynasty under the Fatimids was established in Egypt with its capital at Cairo. With increasing disarray in the empire, the Islamic world was held together only by the common commitment to the Arabic language and the Qur'an.

The Seljuk Turks

In the eleventh century, the Abbasid caliphate faced yet another serious threat in the form of the Seljuk Turks. The Seljuk Turks were a nomadic people from Central Asia who had converted to Islam and flourished as military mercenaries for the Abbasid caliphate, where they were known for their ability as mounted archers. Moving gradually into Persia and Armenia as the Abbasids weakened, the Seljuk Turks grew in number until by the eleventh century, they were able to occupy the eastern provinces of the Abbasid Empire. In 1055, a Turkish leader captured Baghdad and assumed command of the empire with the title of **sultan** ("holder of power"). While the Abbasid caliph remained the chief representative of Sunni religious authority, the real military and political

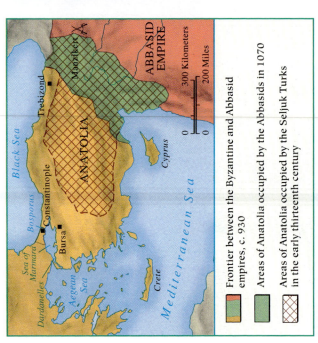

MAP 7.4 **The Turkish Occupation of Anatolia.** This map shows the expansion of Turkic-speaking peoples into the Anatolian peninsula in the tenth and eleventh centuries. The Ottoman Turks established their capital at Bursa in 1335 and eventually at Constantinople in 1453.

Q What was at the time the major obstacle to Ottoman expansion into Europe?

Legend:
- Frontier between the Byzantine and Abbasid empires, c. 930
- Areas of Anatolia occupied by the Abbasids in 1070
- Areas of Anatolia occupied by the Seljuk Turks in the early thirteenth century

power of the state was in the hands of the Seljuk Turks. The latter did not establish their headquarters in Baghdad, which now entered a period of decline. As the historian Khatib Baghdadi described:

There is no city in the world equal to Baghdad in the abundance of its riches, the importance of its business, the number of its scholars and important people, the distinctions of its leaders and its common people, the extent of its palaces, inhabitants, streets, avenues, alleys, mosques, baths, docks and caravansaries, the purity of its air, the sweetness of its water, the freshness of its dew and its shade, the temperateness of its summer and winter, the healthfulness of its spring and fall, and its great swarming crowds. The buildings and the inhabitants were most numerous during the time of Harun al-Rashid, when the city and its surrounding areas were full of cooled rooms, thriving places, fertile pastures, rich watering-places for ships. Then the riots began, an uninterrupted series of misfortunes befell the inhabitants, its flourishing conditions came to ruin to such extent that, before our time and the century preceding ours, it found itself, because of the perturbation and the decadence it was experiencing, in complete opposition to all capitals and in contradiction to all inhabited countries.[5]

Baghdad would revive, but it would no longer be the "Gift of God" of Harun al-Rashid.

Toward the end of the eleventh century, the Seljuks were exerting military pressure on Egypt and the Byzantine Empire. In 1071, when the Byzantines foolishly challenged the Turks, their army was routed at Manzikert, near Lake Van in eastern Turkey, and the victors took over most of the Anatolian peninsula (see Map 7.4). In dire straits, the Byzantine Empire turned to the west for help, setting in motion the papal pleas that led to the **Crusades** (see the next section).

In Europe, and undoubtedly within the Muslim world itself, the arrival of the Turks was regarded as a disaster. The Turks were viewed as barbarians who destroyed civilizations and oppressed populations. In fact, in many respects, Turkish rule in the Middle East was probably beneficial. Converted to Islam, the Turkish rulers temporarily brought an end to the fraternal squabbles between Sunni and Shi'ite Muslims while supporting the Sunnis. They put their energies into revitalizing Islamic law and institutions and provided much-needed political stability to the empire, which helped restore its former prosperity. Under Seljuk rule, Muslims began to organize themselves into autonomous brotherhoods, whose relatively tolerant practices characterized Islamic religious attitudes until the end of the nineteenth century, when increased competition with Europe led to confrontation with the West.

Seljuk political domination over the old Abbasid Empire, however, provoked resentment on the part of many Persian Shi'ites, who viewed the Turks as usurping foreigners who had betrayed the true faith of Islam. Among the regime's most feared enemies was Hasan al-Sabahh, a Cairo-trained Persian who formed a rebel group, popularly known as "assassins" (guardians), who for several decades terrorized government officials and

other leading political and religious figures from their base in the mountains south of the Caspian Sea. Like their modern-day equivalents, the terrorist organization known as al-Qaeda, Sabahh's followers were highly motivated and were adept at infiltrating the enemy's camp in order to carry out their clandestine activities. The organization was finally eliminated by the invading Mongols in the thirteenth century.

The Crusades

Just before the end of the eleventh century, the Byzantine emperor Alexius I desperately called for assistance from other Christian states in Europe to protect his empire against the invading Seljuk Turks. As part of his appeal, he said that the Muslims were desecrating Christian shrines in the Holy Land and molesting Christian pilgrims en route to the shrines. In actuality, the Muslims had never threatened the shrines or cut off Christian access to them. But tension between Christendom and Islam was on the rise, and the Byzantine emperor's appeal received a ready response in Europe. Beginning in 1096 and continuing into the thirteenth century, a series of Christian raids on Islamic territories known as the Crusades brought the Holy Land and adjacent areas on the Mediterranean coast from Antioch to the Sinai peninsula under Christian rule (see Chapter 12).

At first, Muslim rulers in the area were taken aback by the invading crusaders, whose armored cavalry presented

COMPARATIVE ILLUSTRATION

© Michael Nicholson/CORBIS

© Fridmar Damm/zefa/CORBIS

The Medieval Castle. Beginning in the eighth century, Muslim rulers began to erect fortified stone castles in the desert. So impressed were the crusaders by the innovative defensive features they saw that they began to incorporate similar ideas in their own European castles, which had previously been made of wood. In twelfth-century Syria, the crusaders constructed the imposing citadel known as the Krak des Chevaliers (Castle of the Knights) on the foundation of a Muslim fort (left photo). This new model of a massive fortress of solid masonry spread to western Europe, as is evident in the castle shown in the right photo, built in the late thirteenth century in Wales.

Q What types of warfare were used to defend—and attack—castles such as these?

a new challenge to local warriors, and their response was ineffectual. The Seljuk Turks by that time were preoccupied with events taking place farther to the east and took no action themselves. But in 1169, Sunni Muslims under the leadership of Saladin (Salah al-Din), vizier to the last Fatimid caliph, brought an end to the Fatimid dynasty. Proclaiming himself sultan, Saladin succeeded in establishing his control over both Egypt and Syria, thereby confronting the Christian states in the area with united Muslim power on two fronts. In 1187, Saladin's army invaded the kingdom of Jerusalem and destroyed the Christian forces concentrated there. Further operations reduced Christian occupation in the area to a handful of fortresses along the northern coast. Unlike the Christians, however, Saladin did not permit a massacre of the civilian population and even tolerated the continuation of Christian religious services in conquered territories. For a time, Christian occupation forces even carried on a lively trade relationship with Muslim communities in the region.

The Christians returned for another try a few years after the fall of Jerusalem, but the campaign succeeded only in securing some of the coastal cities. Although the Christians would retain a toehold on the coast for much of the thirteenth century (Acre, their last stronghold, fell to the Muslims in 1291), they were no longer a significant force in Middle Eastern affairs. In retrospect, the Crusades had only minimal importance in the history of the Middle East, although they may have served to unite the forces of Islam against the foreign invaders, thus creating a residue of distrust toward Christians that continues to resonate through the Islamic world today (see the box on p. 202).

Far more important in their impact were the Mongols, a pastoral people who swept out of the Gobi Desert in the early thirteenth century to seize control over much of the known world (see Chapter 10). Beginning with the advances of Genghis Khan in northern China, Mongol armies later spread across Central Asia, and in 1258, under the leadership of Hulegu, brother of the more famous Khubilai Khan, they seized Persia and Mesopotamia, bringing an end to the caliphate at Baghdad.

The Mongols

Unlike the Seljuk Turks, the Mongols were not Muslims, and they found it difficult to adapt to the settled conditions that they found in the major cities in the Middle East. Their treatment of the local population in conquered territories was brutal (according to one historian, after conquering a city, they wiped out not only entire families but also their household pets) and destructive to the economy. Cities were razed to the ground, and dams and other irrigation works were destroyed, reducing prosperous agricultural societies to the point of mass starvation. The Mongols advanced as far as the Red Sea, but their attempt to seize Egypt failed, in part because of

OPPOSING VIEWPOINTS

THE SIEGE OF JERUSALEM: CHRISTIAN AND MUSLIM PERSPECTIVES

RELIGION & PHILOSOPHY

During the First Crusade, Christian knights laid siege to Jerusalem in June 1099. The first excerpt is taken from an account by Fulcher of Chartres, who accompanied the crusaders to the Holy Land. The second selection is by a Muslim writer, Ibn al-Athir, whose account of the First Crusade can be found in his history of the Muslim world.

Fulcher of Chartres, *Chronicle of the First Crusade*

Then the Franks entered the city magnificently at the noonday hour on Friday, the day of the week when Christ redeemed the whole world on the cross. With trumpets sounding and with everything in an uproar, exclaiming: "Help, God!" they vigorously pushed into the city, and straightway raised the banner on the top of the wall. All the heathen, completely terrified, changed their boldness to swift flight through the narrow streets of the quarters. The more quickly they fled, the more quickly they put to flight.

Count Raymond and his men, who were bravely assailing the city in another section, did not perceive this until they saw the Saracens [Muslims] jumping from the top of the wall. Seeing this, they joyfully ran to the city as quickly as they could, and helped the others pursue and kill the wicked enemy.

Then some, both Arabs and Ethiopians, fled into the Tower of David; others shut themselves in the Temple of the Lord and of Solomon, where in the halls a very great attack was made on them. Nowhere was there a place where the Saracens could escape swordsmen.

On the top of Solomon's Temple, to which they had climbed in fleeing, many were shot to death with arrows and cast down headlong from the roof. Within this Temple, about ten thousand were beheaded. If you had been there, your feet would have been stained up to the ankles with the blood of the slain. What more shall I tell? Not one of

them was allowed to live. They did not spare the women and children.

Account of Ibn al-Athir

In fact Jerusalem was taken from the north on the morning of Friday 22 Sha'ban 492/15 July 1099. The population was put to the sword by the Franks, who pillaged the area for a week. A band of Muslims barricaded themselves into the Oratory of David and fought on for several days. They were granted their lives in return for surrendering. The Franks honored their word, and the group left by night for Ascalon. In the Masjid al-Aqsa the Franks slaughtered more than 70,000 people, among them a large number of Imams and Muslim scholars, devout and ascetic men who had left their homelands to live lives of pious seclusion in the Holy Place. The Franks stripped the Dome of the Rock of more than forty silver candelabra, each of them weighing 3,600 drams, and a great silver lamp weighing forty-four Syrian pounds, as well as a hundred and fifty smaller candelabra and more than twenty gold ones, and a great deal more booty. Refugees from Syria reached Baghdad in Ramadan, among them the qadi Abu sa'd al-Harawi. They told the Caliph's ministers a story that wrung their hearts and brought tears to their eyes. On Friday they went to the Cathedral Mosque and begged for help, weeping so that their hearers wept with them as they described the sufferings of the Muslims in that Holy City: the men killed, the women and children taken prisoner, the homes pillaged. Because of the terrible hardships they had suffered, they were allowed to break the fast.

Q *What happened to the inhabitants of Jerusalem when the Christian knights captured the city? How do you explain the extreme intolerance and brutality of the Christian knights? How do these two accounts differ, and how are they similar?*

---

the effective resistance posed by the Mamluks (or Mamelukes, a Turkish military class originally composed of slaves), who had recently overthrown the administration set up by Saladin and seized power for themselves.

Eventually, the Mongol rulers in the Middle East began to assimilate the culture of the peoples they had conquered. Mongol elites converted to Islam, Persian influence became predominant at court, and the cities began to be rebuilt. By the fourteenth century, the Mongol empire had begun to split into separate kingdoms and then to disintegrate. However, the old Islamic empire originally established by the Arabs in the seventh and eighth centuries had long since come to an end. The new center of Islamic civilization was in Cairo, now about

to promote a renaissance in Muslim culture under the sponsorship of the Mamluks.

To the north, another new force appeared on the horizon with the rise of the Ottoman Turks on the Anatolian peninsula. In 1453, Sultan Mehmet II[1] seized Constantinople and brought an end to the Byzantine Empire. Then the Ottomans began to turn their attention to the rest of the Middle East (see Chapter 16).

Andalusia: A Muslim Outpost in Europe

After the decline of Baghdad, perhaps the brightest star in the Muslim firmament was in Spain, where a member of the Ummayad dynasty had managed to establish himself after his family's rule in the Middle East had been overthrown in 750 C.E. Abd al-Rathman had escaped the carnage in Damascus and made his way to Spain, where Muslim power had recently replaced that of the Visigoths. By 756, he had legitimized his authority in southern Spain—known to the Arabs as *al-Andaluz* and to Europeans as Andalusia—and took the title of **emir** (commander), with his capital at Córdoba. There he and his successors sought to build a vibrant new center for Islamic culture in the region. With the primacy of Baghdad now at an end, Andalusian rulers established a new caliphate in 929.

Now that the seizure of Crete, Sardinia, Sicily, and the Balearic Islands had turned the Mediterranean Sea into a Muslim lake, Andalusia became part of a vast trade network that stretched all the way from the Strait of Gibraltar to the Red Sea and beyond. Valuable new products were introduced to the Iberian peninsula, including cotton, sugar, olives, wheat, citrus, and the date palm.

Andalusia also flourished as an artistic and intellectual center. The court gave active support to writers and artists, creating a brilliant culture focused on the emergence of three world-class cities—Córdoba, Seville, and Toledo. Intellectual leaders arrived in the area from all parts of the Islamic world, bringing their knowledge of medicine, astronomy, mathematics, and philosophy. With the establishment of a paper factory near Valencia, the means of disseminating such information dramatically improved, and the libraries of Andalusia became the wonder of their time (see "Philosophy and Science" later in this chapter).

One major reason for the rise of Andalusia as a hub of artistic and intellectual activity was the atmosphere of tolerance in social relations fostered by the state. Although Islam was firmly established as the official faith and non-Muslims were encouraged to convert as a means of furthering their careers, the policy of *convivéncia* (commingling) provided an environment for many Christians and Jews to maintain their religious beliefs and even obtain favors from the court.

A Time of Troubles

Unfortunately, the primacy of Andalusia as a cultural center was short-lived. By the end of the tenth century, factionalism was beginning to undermine the foundations of the emirate. In 1009, the royal palace at Córdoba was totally destroyed in a civil war. Twenty years later, the caliphate itself disappeared as the emirate dissolved into a patchwork of city-states.

In the meantime, the Christian kingdoms that had managed to establish themselves in the north of the Iberian peninsula were consolidating their position and beginning to expand southward. In 1085, Alfonso VI, the Christian king of Castile, seized Toledo, one of Andalusia's main intellectual centers. The new authorities continued to foster the artistic and intellectual activities of their predecessors. To recoup their recent losses, the Muslim rulers in Seville called on fellow Muslims, the Almoravids—a Berber dynasty in Morocco—to assist in halting the Christian advance. Berber mercenaries defeated Castilian forces at Badajoz in 1086 but then remained in the area to establish their own rule over remaining Muslim-held areas in southern Spain.

A warrior culture with no tolerance for heterodox ideas, the Almoravids quickly brought an end to the era of religious tolerance and intellectual achievement. But the presence of Andalusia's new warlike rulers was unable to stem the tide of Christian advance. In 1215, Pope Innocent III called for a new crusade to destroy Muslim rule in southern Spain. Over the next two hundred years, Christian armies advanced relentlessly southward, seizing the cities of Seville and Córdoba. But a single redoubt of Abd al-Rathman's glorious achievement remained: the remote mountain city of Granada, with its imposing hilltop fortress, the Alhambra.

Spain in the Eleventh Century

Atlantic Ocean

CASTILE

ARAGON

Pyrenees

Mediterranean Sea

AFRICA

Seville
Badajoz
Granada
Córdoba
Toledo
Valencia

Christian-held areas

0 100 200 300 Kilometers
0 100 200 Miles

The Alhambra in Granada. Islamic civilization reached its zenith with the fourteenth-century castle known as the Alhambra, in southern Spain (left). Like the Hindus in India, the Muslims of the Middle East and Spain lived in a hot, dry climate, making water a highly prized commodity both literally and psychologically. The quiet, refreshing coolness of water became a vital component of Muslim architecture, displayed in magnificent gardens featuring fountains and reflecting pools such as this one at the Alhambra (below).

© William J. Duiker

© William J. Duiker

Islamic Civilization

Q **Focus Question:** What were the main features of Islamic society and culture during its era of early growth?

As Thomas Lippman, author of *Understanding Islam*, has remarked, the Muslim religion is based on behavior as well as belief. Although this generalization applies in broad terms to most major religions, it seems to be particularly true of Islam. To be a Muslim is not simply to worship Allah but also to live according to his law as revealed in the Qur'an, which is viewed as fundamental and immutable doctrine, not to be revised by human beings.

Thus in Islamic society, there is no rigid demarcation between church and state, between the sacred and the secular. As Allah has decreed, so must human beings behave. Therefore, Islamic doctrine must be consulted to determine questions of politics, economic behavior, civil and criminal law, and social ethics.

To live entirely by God's law is of course difficult, if not impossible. Moreover, many issues of social organization and human behavior were not addressed in the Qur'an or in the *Hadith* or *Shari'a*. There was therefore some room for differing interpretations of holy scripture in accordance with individual preference and local practice. Still, the Islamic world is and has probably always been more homogeneous in terms of its political institutions, religious beliefs, and social practices than most of its contemporary civilizations.

Political Structures

For early converts, establishing political institutions and practices that conformed to Islamic doctrine was a daunting task. In the first place, the will of Allah, as revealed to his Prophet, was not precise about the relationship between religious and political authority, simply decreeing that human beings should "conduct their affairs by mutual consent." On a more practical plane, establishing political institutions for a large and multicultural empire presented a challenge for the Arabs, whose own political structures were relatively rudimentary and relevant only to small pastoral communities (see the box above).

During the life of Muhammad, the problem could be avoided, since he was generally accepted as both the religious and the political leader of the Islamic community—the *umma*. His death, however, raised the question of how a successor should be chosen and what authority that person should have. As we have seen, Muhammad's immediate successors were called caliphs. Their authority was purely temporal, although they were also considered in general terms to be religious leaders, with the title of *imam*. At first, each caliph was selected informally by leading members of the *umma*. Soon succession became hereditary in the Umayyad clan, but their authority was still qualified, at least in theory, by the principles of consultation with other leaders.

The Wealth of Araby: Trade and Cities in the Middle East

As we have noted, this era was probably one of the most prosperous periods in the history of the Middle East. Trade flourished, not only in the Islamic world but also with China (now in a period of efflorescence during the Tang and Song dynasties; see Chapter 10), with the Byzantine Empire, and with the trading societies in Southeast Asia (see Chapter 9). Trade goods were carried both by ship and by the "fleets of the desert," the camel caravans that traversed the arid land from Morocco in the far west to the countries beyond the Caspian Sea. From West Africa came gold and slaves; from China, silk and porcelain; from East Africa, gold, ivory, and rhinoceros horn; and from the lands of South Asia, sandalwood, cotton, wheat, sugar, and spices. Within the empire, Egypt contributed grain; Iraq, linens, dates, and precious stones; Spain, leather goods, olives, and wine; and western India, pepper and various textile goods. The exchange of goods was facilitated by the development of banking and the use of currency and letters of credit (see the comparative essay "Trade and Civilization" on p. 206).

SAGE ADVICE FROM FATHER TO SON

POLITICS & GOVERNMENT

Tahir ibn Husayn was born into an aristocratic family in Central Asia and became a key political adviser to al-Ma'mun, the Abbasid caliph of Baghdad in the early ninth century. Appointed in 821 to a senior position in Khurusan, a district near the city of Herat in what is today Afghanistan, he wrote the following letter to his son, giving advice on how to wield authority most effectively. The letter so impressed al-Ma'mun that he had it widely distributed throughout his bureaucracy.

Letter of Tahir ibn Husayn

Look carefully into the matter of the land-tax which the subjects have an obligation to pay.... Divide it among the tax payers with justice and fairness with equal treatment for all. Do not remove any part of the obligation to pay the tax from any noble person just because of his nobility or any rich person because of his richness or from any of your secretaries or personal retainers. Do not require from anyone more than he can bear, or exact more than the usual rate....

[The ruler should also devote himself to looking after the affairs of the poor and destitute, those who are unable to bring their complaints of ill-treatment to you personally and those of wretched estate who do not know how to set about claiming their rights.... Turn your attention to those who have suffered injuries and their orphans and widows and provide them with allowances from the state treasury, following the example of the Commander of the Faithful, may God exalt him, in showing compassion for them and giving them financial support, so that God may thereby bring some alleviation into their daily lives and by means of it bring you the spiritual food of His blessing and an increase of His favour. Give pensions from the state treasury to the blind, and give higher allowances to those who know of the Qur'an, or most of it by heart. Set up hospices where sick Muslims can find shelter, and appoint custodians for these places who will treat the patients with kindness and physicians who will cure their illnesses....

Keep an eye on the officials at your court and on your secretaries. Give them each a fixed time each day when they can bring you their official correspondence and any documents requiring the ruler's signature. They can let you know about the needs of the various officials and about all the affairs of the provinces you rule over. Then devote all your faculties, ears, eyes, understanding and intellect, to the business they set before you: consider it and think about it repeatedly. Finally take those actions which seem to be in accordance with good judgment and justice.

Q *How would you compare Tahir's advice with that given in the political treatise Arthasastra, discussed in Chapter 2? Would it serve as an effective model for political leadership today?*

COMPARATIVE ESSAY
TRADE AND CIVILIZATION

INTERACTION & EXCHANGE

In 2002, archaeologists unearthed the site of an ancient Egyptian port city on the shores of the Red Sea. Established sometime during the first millennium B.C.E., the city of Berenike linked the Nile River valley with ports as far away as the island of Java in Southeast Asia. The discovery of Berenike is only the latest piece of evidence confirming the importance of interregional trade in the ancient world. The exchange of goods between far-flung societies became a powerful engine behind the rise of advanced civilizations throughout the ancient world. Raw materials such as copper, tin, and obsidian; items of daily necessity like salt, fish, and other foodstuffs; and luxury goods like gold, silk, and precious stones passed from one end of the Eurasian supercontinent to the other, across the desert from the Mediterranean Sea to sub-Saharan Africa, and throughout much of the Americas. Less well known but also important was the maritime trade that stretched from the Mediterranean across the Indian Ocean to port cities on the distant coasts of Southeast and East Asia.

During the first millennium C.E., the level of interdependence among human societies intensified as three major trade routes—across the Indian Ocean, along the Silk Road, and by caravan across the Sahara—created the framework of a single system of trade. The new global network was not only commercial but informational as well, transmitting technology and ideas, such as the emerging religions of Buddhism, Christianity, and Islam, to new destinations.

There was a close relationship between missionary activities and trade. Buddhist merchants first brought the teachings of Siddhartha Gautama to China, and Muslim traders carried Muhammad's words to Southeast Asia and sub-Saharan Africa. Indian traders carried Hindu beliefs and political institutions to Southeast Asia.

What caused the rapid expansion of trade during this period? One key factor was the introduction of technology to facilitate transportation. The development of the compass, improved techniques in mapmaking and shipbuilding, and greater knowledge of wind patterns all contributed to the expansion of maritime trade. Caravan trade, once carried by wheeled chariots or on the backs of oxen, now used the camel as the preferred beast of burden through the deserts of Africa, Central Asia, and the Middle East.

Another reason for the expansion of commerce during this period was the appearance of several multinational empires that created zones of stability and affluence in key areas of the Eurasian landmass. Most important were the emergence of the Abbasid Empire in the Middle East and

the prosperity of China during the Tang and Song dynasties (see Chapter 10). The Mongol invasions in the thirteenth century temporarily disrupted the process but then established a new era of stability that fostered long-distance trade throughout the world.

The importance of interregional trade as a crucial factor in promoting the growth of human civilizations can be highlighted by comparing the social, cultural, and technological achievements of active trading states with those communities that have traditionally been cut off from contacts with the outside world. We shall encounter many of these communities in later chapters. Even in the Western Hemisphere, where regional trade linked societies from the great plains of North America to the Andes Mountains in present-day Peru, geographical barriers limited the exchange of inventions and ideas, placing these societies at a distinct disadvantage when the first contacts with peoples across the oceans occurred at the beginning of the modern era.

© Art Resource, NY

Arab traders in a caravan.

© William J. Duiker

© William J. Duiker

© William J. Duiker

© William J. Duiker

COMPARATIVE ILLUSTRATION

Early Agricultural Technology. For centuries, farmers across the globe have adopted various techniques to guarantee the flow of adequate amounts of water for their crops. One of the most effective ways to irrigate fields in hilly regions is to construct terraces to channel the flow of water from higher elevations in the most effective manner. Shown on the left is a hillside terrace in northern China, an area where dry crops like oats and millet have been cultivated since the sixth millennium B.C.E. The illustration on the right shows a terraced hillside in the southwestern corner of the Arabian peninsula. Excavations show that despite dry conditions through much of the peninsula, terraced agriculture has been practiced in mountainous parts of the region for as long as five thousand years.

Q In what other areas of the Middle East is irrigated agriculture practiced?

Under these conditions, urban areas flourished. While the Abbasids were in power, Baghdad was probably the greatest city in the empire, but after the rise of the Fatimids in Egypt, the focus of trade shifted to Cairo, described by the traveler Leo Africanus as "one of the greatest and most famous cities in all the whole world, filled with stately and admirable palaces and colleges, and most sumptuous temples."[6] Other great commercial cities included Basra at the head of the Persian Gulf, Aden at the southern tip of the Arabian peninsula, Damascus in modern Syria, and Marrakech in Morocco. In the cities, the inhabitants were generally segregated by religion, with Muslims, Jews, and Christians living in separate neighborhoods. But all were equally subject to the most common threats to urban life—fire, flood, and disease.

The most impressive urban buildings were usually the palace for the caliph or the local governor and the great mosque. Houses were often constructed of stone or brick on a timber frame. The larger houses were often built around an interior courtyard where the residents could retreat from the dust, noise, and heat of the city streets. Sometimes domestic animals such as goats or sheep would be stabled there. The houses of the wealthy were multistoried, with balconies and windows covered with latticework to provide privacy. The poor in both urban and rural areas lived in simpler houses composed of clay or unfired bricks. The Bedouins lived in tents that could be dismantled and moved according to their needs.

The Arab empire was clearly more urbanized than most other areas of the known world at the time. Yet the bulk of the population continued to live in the countryside, supported by farming or herding animals. During the early stages, most of the farmland was owned by independent peasants, but eventually some concentration of land in the hands of wealthy owners began to take place. Some lands were owned by the state or the court and were cultivated by slave labor, but plantation agriculture was not as common as would be the case later in many areas of the world. In the valleys of rivers such as the Tigris, the Euphrates, and the Nile, the majority of the farmers were probably independent peasants. A Chinese account described life along the Nile:

The peasants work their fields without fear of inundation or droughts; a sufficiency of water for irrigation is supplied by a river whose source is not known. During the seasons when no cultivation is in progress, the level of the river remains even with the banks; with the beginning of cultivation it rises day by day. Then it is that an official is appointed to watch the river and to await the highest water level, when he summons the people, who then plough and sow their fields. When they have had enough water, the river returns to its former level.[7]

Eating habits varied in accordance with economic standing and religious preference. Muslims did not eat pork, but those who could afford it often served other meats, including mutton, goat, poultry, or fish. Fruit, spices, and various sweets were delicacies. The poor were generally forced to survive on boiled millet or peas with an occasional lump of meat or fat. Bread—white or whole meal—could be found on tables throughout the region except in the deserts, where boiled grain was the staple food. Pasta was probably first introduced to the Italians by Arab traders operating in Sicily.

Islamic Society

In some ways, Arab society was probably one of the most egalitarian of its time. Both the principles of Islam, which held that all were equal in the eyes of Allah, and the importance of trade to the prosperity of the state certainly contributed to this egalitarianism. Although there was a fairly well defined upper class, consisting of the ruling families, senior officials, tribal elites, and the wealthiest merchants, there was no hereditary nobility as in many contemporary societies, and the merchants enjoyed a degree of respect that they did not receive in Europe, China, or India.

Not all benefited from the high degree of social mobility in the Islamic world, however. Slavery was widespread. Since a Muslim could not be enslaved, the supply came from sub-Saharan Africa or from non-Islamic populations elsewhere in Asia. Most slaves were employed in the army (which was sometimes a road to power, as in the case of the Mamluks) or as domestic servants, who were occasionally permitted to purchase their freedom. The slaves who worked the large estates experienced the worst living conditions and rose in revolt on several occasions.

The Islamic principle of human equality also fell short, as in most other societies of its day, in the treatment of women. Although the Qur'an instructed men to treat women with respect, and women did have the right to own and inherit property, the male was dominant in Muslim society. Polygyny was permitted, and the right of divorce was in practice restricted to the husband, although some schools of legal thought permitted women to stipulate that their husband could have only one wife or to seek a separation in certain specific circumstances. Adultery and homosexuality were stringently forbidden (although such prohibitions were frequently ignored in practice), and Islamic custom required that women be cloistered in their homes and prohibited from social contacts with males outside their own family.

A prominent example of this custom is the harem, introduced at the Abbasid court during the reign of Harun al-Rashid. Members of the royal harem were drawn from non-Muslim female populations throughout the empire. The custom of requiring women to cover virtually all parts of their body when appearing in public was common in urban areas and continues to be practiced in many Islamic societies today. It should be noted, however, that these customs owed more to traditional Arab practice than to Qur'anic law (see the box on p. 209).

The Culture of Islam

The Arabs were heirs to many elements of the remaining Greco-Roman culture of the Roman Empire, and they assimilated Byzantine and Persian culture just as readily. In the eighth and ninth centuries, numerous Greek, Syrian, and Persian scientific and philosophical works were translated into Arabic and eventually found their way to Europe. As the chief language in the southern Mediterranean and the Middle East, Arabic became an international language. Later, Persian and Turkish also came to be important in administration and culture.

The spread of Islam led to the emergence of a new culture throughout the Arab empire. This was true in all fields of endeavor, from literature to art and architecture. But pre-Islamic traditions were not extinguished and frequently combined with Muslim motifs, resulting in creative works of great imagination and originality.

Philosophy and Science   During the centuries following the rise of the Arab empire, it was the Islamic world that was most responsible for preserving and spreading the scientific and philosophical achievements of ancient civilizations. At a time when ancient Greek philosophy was largely unknown in Europe, key works by Aristotle, Plato, and other Greek philosophers were translated into Arabic and stored in a "house of wisdom" in Baghdad, where they were read and studied by Muslim scholars. Eventually, many of these works were translated into Latin and were brought to Europe, where they exercised a profound influence on the later course of Christianity and Western philosophy.

The process began in the sixth century C.E., when the Byzantine ruler Justinian (see Chapter 13) shut down the Platonic Academy in Athens, declaring that it promoted heretical ideas. Many of the scholars at the Academy fled to Baghdad, where their ideas and the classical texts they brought with them soon aroused local interest and were translated into Persian or Arabic. Later such works were supplemented by acquisitions in Constantinople and possibly also from the famous library at Alexandria.

The academies where such translations were carried out—often by families specializing in the task—were not true universities like those that would later appear in Europe but were private operations under the sponsorship of a great patron, many of them highly cultivated Persians living in Baghdad or other major cities. Dissemination of the translated works was stimulated by the arrival of paper in the Middle East, brought by Buddhist pilgrims from China passing along the Silk Road. Paper was much cheaper to manufacture than papyrus, and by the end of the eighth century, the first paper factories were up and running in Baghdad. Libraries and booksellers soon appeared.

What motives inspired this ambitious literary preservation project? At the outset, it may have simply been an effort to provide philosophical confirmation for existing

© Topkapi Palace Museum/The Bridgeman Art Library

THE GIFT OF THE ROBE

Ibn Battuta (1304–1377), a travel writer born in the Moroccan city of Tangier, is often described as the Muslim equivalent of his famous Italian counterpart Marco Polo. Over the course of a quarter of a century, he voyaged widely throughout Africa and Asia, logging over 75,000 miles in the process. The fascinating personal account of his travels is a prime source of information about his times. In the excerpt presented here, he describes a visit to the city of Balkh, one of the fabled caravan stops on the Silk Road as it passed through Central Asia.

The Travels of Ibn Battuta

After a journey of a day and a half over a sandy desert in which there was no house, we arrived at the city of Balkh, which now lies in ruins. It has not been rebuilt since its destruction by the cursed Jengiz Khan. The situation of its buildings is not very discernible, although its extent may be traced. It is now in ruins, and without society.

Its mosque was one of the largest and handsomest in the world. Its pillars were incomparable: three of which were destroyed by Jengiz Khan, because it had been told him, that the wealth of the mosque lay concealed under them, provided as a fund for its repairs. When, however, he had destroyed them, nothing of the kind was to be found: the rest, therefore he left as they were.

The story about this treasure arose from the following circumstance. It is said, that one of the Califs of the house of Abbas was very much enraged at the inhabitants of Balkh, on account of some accident which had happened, and, on this account, sent a person to collect a heavy fine from them. Upon this occasion, the women and children of the city betook themselves to the wife of their then governor, who, out of her own money, built this mosque; and to her they made a grievous complaint. She accordingly sent to the officer, who had been commissioned to collect the fine, a robe very richly embroidered and adorned with jewels, much greater in value than the amount of the fine imposed. This, she requested might be sent to the Calif as a present from herself, to be accepted instead of the fine. The officer accordingly took the robe, and sent it to the Calif, who, when he saw it, was surprised at her liberality, and said: This woman must not be allowed to exceed myself in generosity. He then sent back the robe, and remitted the fine. When the robe was returned to her, she asked, whether a look of the Calif had fallen upon it; and being told that it had, she replied: No robe shall ever come upon me, upon which the look of any man, except my own husband, has fallen. She then ordered it to be cut up and sold; and with the price of it she built the mosque, with the cell and structure in the front of it. Still, from the price of the robe there remained a third, which she commanded to be buried under one of its pillars, in order to meet any future expenses which might be necessary for its repairs. Upon Jengiz Khan's hearing this story, he ordered these pillars to be destroyed; but, as already remarked, he found nothing.

Q *From the point of view of a Muslim observer, would the actions of the governor's wife, as described in this story, be considered meritorious? If so, why?*

Preserving the Wisdom of the Greeks.

After the fall of the Roman Empire, the philosophical works of ancient Greece were virtually forgotten in Europe or were banned as heretical by the Byzantine Empire. It was thanks to Muslim scholars, who stored copies and translations in libraries in Baghdad, Alexandria, and elsewhere in the Arab world, that many classical Greek writings survived. Here young Muslim scholars are being trained in the Greek language so that they can translate classical Greek literature into Arabic. Later the works will be translated back into Western languages and serve as the catalyst for an intellectual revival in medieval and Renaissance Europe.

religious beliefs as derived from the Qur'an. Eventually, however, more adventurous minds began to use the classical texts not only to seek greater knowledge of the divine will but also to seek a better understanding of the laws of nature.

Such was the case with the physician and intellectual Ibn Sina (980–1037), known in the West as Avicenna, who in his own philosophical writings cited Aristotle to the effect that the world operated not only at the will of Allah but also by its own natural laws, laws that could be ascertained by human reason.

Such ideas eventually aroused the ire of traditional Muslim scholars, and although classical works by such ancient writers as Euclid, Ptolemy, and Archimedes continued to be translated, the influence of Greek philosophy began to wane in Baghdad by the end of the eleventh century and did not recover.

By then, however, interest in classical Greek ideas had spread to Spain, where philosophers such as Averroës (Arabic name Ibn Rushd) and Maimonides (Musa Ibn Maymun, a Jew who often wrote in Arabic) undertook their own translations and wrote in support of Avicenna's defense of the role of human reason. Both were born in Córdoba in the early twelfth century but were persecuted for their ideas by the Almohads, a Berber dynasty that had supplanted Almoravid authority in Andalusia, and both men ended their days in exile in North Africa.

By then, however, Christian rulers such as Alfonso VI in Castile and Frederick II in Sicily were beginning to sponsor their own translations of Greek classical works from Arabic into Latin, whence they made their way to the many new universities sprouting up all over Western Europe.

Although Islamic scholars are justly praised for preserving much of classical knowledge for the West, they also made considerable advances of their own. Nowhere is this more evident than in mathematics and the natural sciences. Islamic scholars adopted and passed on the numerical system of India, including the use of zero, and a ninth-century Persian mathematician founded the mathematical discipline of algebra (al-jabr, "the reduction"). Simplified "Arabic" numerals had begun to replace cumbersome Roman numerals in Italy by the thirteenth century.

In astronomy, Muslims set up an observatory at Baghdad to study the position of the stars. They were aware that the earth was round and in the ninth century produced a world map based on the tradition of the Greco-Roman astronomer Ptolemy. Aided by the astrolabe, an instrument designed to enable sailors to track their position by means of the stars, Muslim fleets and caravans opened up new trading routes connecting the Islamic world with other civilizations, and Muslim travelers such as al-Mas'udi and Ibn Battuta provide modern readers with their most accurate descriptions of political and social conditions throughout the Middle East.

Muslim scholars also made many new discoveries in optics and chemistry and, with the assistance of texts on anatomy by the ancient Greek physician Galen

© Bildarchiv Preussischer Kulturbesitz/Art Resource, NY

A Twelfth-Century Map of the World. The twelfth-century Muslim geographer Al-Idrisi received his education in the Spanish city of Córdoba while it was under Islamic rule. Later he served at the court of the Norman king of Sicily, Roger II, where he created an atlas of the world based on Arab and European sources. In Muslim practice at the time, north and south were inverted from modern practice. This map depicts the world as it was known at that time, stretching from the Spanish peninsula on the right to the civilization of China on the far left. It is also a testimonial to the vast extension of the power and influence of Islam in the six centuries since the death of Muhammad in 632.

Early Arabic poetry focused on simple pleasures, such as wine, women, song, and the faithful camel. This excerpt is from a longer work by the sixth-century Arab poet Tarafah. Tarafah was one of a group of seven poets called the "suspended ones." Their poems, having won a prize in an annual competition, were suspended on a wall for all to read.

The Ode of Tarafah

Ah, but when grief assails me, straightway I ride it
off mounted on my swift, lean-flanked camel,
night and day racing...
Her long neck is very erect when she lifts it up,
calling to mind the rudder of a Tigris-bound
vessel. Her skull is most like an anvil, the
junction of its two halves meeting together as
it might be on the edge of a file.
Her cheek is smooth as Syrian parchment, her split
lip a tanned hide of Yemen, its slit not bent
crooked; her eyes are a pair of mirrors, sheltering
in the caves of her brow-bones, the rock of a
pool's hollow....
I am at her with the whip, and my she-camel quickens
pace what time the mirage of the burning
stone-tract shimmers; elegantly she steps, as a
slave-girl at a party will sway, showing her master
skirts of a trailing white gown.

I am not one that skulks fearfully among the
hilltops, but when the folk seek my succor I
gladly give it; if you look for me in the circle
of the folk you'll find me there, and if you
hunt me in the taverns there you'll catch me.
Come to me when you will, I'll pour you a flowing
cup, and if you don't need it, well, do without
and good luck to you!
Whenever the tribe is assembled you'll come upon
me at the summit of the noble House, the oft-
frequented; my boon-companions are white as
stars, and a singing-wench comes to us in her
striped gown or her saffron robe, wide the opening
of her collar, delicate her skin to my companions'
fingers, tender her nakedness.
When we say, "Let's hear from you," she advances
to us chanting fluently; her glance languid, in
effortless song.

Q How does this poem celebrate the secular aspects of life?

CENGAGENOW To read more Arabic poetry, enter the documents area of the World History Resource Center using the access card that is available for World History.

(c. 180–200 C.E.), developed medicine as a distinctive field of scientific inquiry. Avicenna compiled a medical encyclopedia that, among other things, emphasized the contagious nature of certain diseases and showed how they could be spread by contaminated water supplies. After its translation into Latin, Avicenna's work became a basic medical textbook for medieval European university students.

Islamic Literature The literature of the Middle East is diverse, reflecting the many distinct cultures of the region. The Arabic and Persian works in particular represent a significant contribution to world literature.

An established tradition of Arabic poetry already existed prior to Muhammad. It extolled the Bedouin experience of tribal life, courage in battle, hunting, sports, and respect for the animals of the desert, especially the camel. Because the Arabic language did not possess a written script until the fourth century C.E., poetry was originally passed on by memory. Later, in the eighth and ninth centuries, it was compiled in anthologies. These personal reflections on wine, sensuous women, good companionship, and the joys of a ride on a fast camel still speak directly to modern readers (see the box above).

Pre-Muslim Persia also boasted a long literary tradition, most of it oral and later written down using the Arabic alphabet. Lacking the desert tradition of the Arabs, Persian writers focused on legends of past kings, Zoroastrian religious themes, romances, fables, and folktales. The transcendent literary monument of early Persian literature is *The Book of Lords*, an early-sixth-century compilation of poetry about Persian myths and legendary heroes. Transmitted orally by generations of poet-musicians, these vivid stories of battles, hunting, and drinking bouts constitute the national epic of ancient Persia, its answer to the *Mahabharata* of India.

Islam brought major changes to the culture of the Middle East, not least to literature. Muslims regarded the Qur'an as their greatest literary work, but pre-Islamic traditions continued to influence writers throughout the region. Poetry is the Persian art par excellence. *The Book of Kings*, a ten-volume epic poem by the Persian poet Ferdowzi (940–1020), is one of the greatest achievements of Persian literature. It traces the history of the country from legendary times to the arrival of Islam. Iranian schoolchildren still learn its verses, which serve to reaffirm pride in their ancient heritage. But love poetry remained popular. Here Rabe'a of Qozdar, Persia's first known woman poet, who wrote in the second half of the tenth century, expresses her anguish at the suffering love brings:

The love of him threw me in chains again,
Struggle against them proved of no avail.

Love is a sea of invisible shores.

How can one swim in it, O clever one?
If you want to pursue love to the end,
Be content to endure much unpleasantness.

Ugliness you must see and imagine it is beauty,
Poison you must take and think it is sugar.

Beset with impatience I did not know
That the more one seeks to pull away, the tighter
becomes the rope.[8]

In the West, the most famous works of Middle Eastern literature are undoubtedly the *Rubaiyat* of Omar Khayyam and *Tales from 1001 Nights* (also called *The Arabian Nights*). Paradoxically, these two works are not as popular with Middle Eastern readers. In fact, both were freely translated into Western languages for nineteenth-century European readers, who developed a taste for stories set in exotic foreign places—a classic example of the tendency of Western observers to regard the customs and cultures of non-Western societies as strange or exotic.

Unfortunately, very little is known of the life or the poetry of the twelfth-century poet Omar Khayyam. Skeptical, reserved, and slightly contemptuous of his peers, he combined poetry with scientific works on mathematics and astronomy and a revision of the calendar that was more accurate than the Gregorian version devised in Europe hundreds of years later. Omar Khayyam did not write down his poems but composed them orally over wine with friends at a neighborhood tavern. They were recorded later by friends or scribes. Many poems attributed to him were actually written long after his death. Among them is the well-known couplet translated into English in the nineteenth century: "Here with a loaf of bread beneath the bough, / A flask of wine, a book of verse, and thou."

Omar Khayyam's poetry is simple and down to earth. Key themes are the impermanence of life, the impossibility of knowing God, and disbelief in an afterlife. Ironically, recent translations of his work appeal to modern attitudes of skepticism and minimalist simplicity that may make him even more popular in the West:

In youth I studied for a little while;
Later I boasted of my mastery.
Yet this was all the lesson that I learned:
We come from dust, and with the wind are gone.

Of all the travelers on this endless road
No one returns to tell us where it leads.

There's little in this world but greed and need:
Leave nothing here, for you will not return....

Since no one can be certain of tomorrow,
It's better not to fill the heart with care.
Drink wine by moonlight, darling, for the moon
Will shine long after this, and find us not.[9]

Like Omar Khayyam's verse, *The Arabian Nights* was loosely translated into European languages and adapted to Western tastes. A composite of folktales, fables, and romances of Indian and indigenous origin, the stories interweave the natural with the supernatural. The earliest stories were told orally and were later transcribed, with many later additions, in Arabic and Persian versions. The famous story of Aladdin and the Magic Lamp, for example, was an eighteenth-century addition. Nevertheless, *The Arabian Nights* has entertained readers for centuries, allowing them to enter a land of wish fulfillment through extraordinary plots, sensuality, comic and tragic situations, and a cast of unforgettable characters.

Sadi (1210–1292), considered the Persian Shakespeare, remains to this day the favorite author in Iran. His *Rose Garden* is a collection of entertaining stories written in prose sprinkled with verse. He is also renowned for his sonnetlike love poems, which set a model for generations to come. Sadi was a master of the pithy maxim:

A cat is a lion in catching mice
But a mouse in combat with a tiger.

He has found eternal happiness who lived a good life,
Because, after his end, good repute will keep his
name alive.

When thou fightest with anyone, consider
Whether thou wilt have to flee from him or he
from thee.[10]

Such maxims are typical of the Middle East, where the proverb, a one-line witty observation on the vagaries of life, has long been popular. Proverbs are not only a distinctive feature of Middle Eastern verse, especially Persian, but are also a part of daily life—a scholar recently recovered over four thousand in one Lebanese village! The following are some typical examples:

Trust in God, but tie up your camel. (Persian)
The world has not promised anything to anybody. (Moroccan)
An old cat will not learn how to dance. (Moroccan)
Lower your voice and strengthen your argument. (Lebanese)
He who has money can eat sherbet in Hell. (Lebanese)
What is brought by the wind will be carried away by the wind. (Persian)
You can't pick up two melons with one hand. (Persian)

Some Arabic and Persian literature reflected the deep spiritual and ethical concerns of the Qur'an. Many writers, however, carried Islamic thought in novel

© William J. Duiker

© Nik Wheeler/CORBIS

the Middle East, this skill reached an apogee in the art of the knotted woolen rug. Originating in the pre-Muslim era, rugs were initially used to insulate stone palaces against the cold as well as to warm shepherds' tents. Eventually, they were applied to religious purposes, since every practicing Muslim is required to pray five times a day on clean ground. Small rugs served as prayer mats for individual use, while larger and more elaborate ones were given by rulers as rewards for political favors. Bedouins in the Arabian desert covered their sandy floors with rugs to create a cozy environment in their tents.

In villages throughout the Middle East, the art of rug weaving has been passed down from mother to daughter over the centuries. Girls as young as four years old took part in the process by helping to spin and prepare the wool shorn from the family sheep. By the age of six, girls would begin their first rug, and before adolescence, their slender fingers would be producing fine carpets. Skilled artisanship represented an extra enticement to prospective bridegrooms, and rugs often became an important part of a woman's dowry to her future husband. After the wedding, the wife would continue to make rugs for home use, as well as for sale to augment the family income.

Eventually, rugs began to be manufactured in workshops by professional artisans, who reproduced the designs from detailed painted diagrams.

Most decorations on the rugs, as well as on all forms of Islamic art, consisted of Arabic script and natural plant and figurative motifs. Repeated continuously in naturalistic or semiabstract geometrical patterns called arabesques, these decorations completely covered the surface and left no area undecorated. This dense decor was also evident in brick, mosaic, and stucco ornamentation and culminated in the magnificent tile work of later centuries.

Representation of the Prophet Muhammad, in painting or in any other art form, has traditionally been strongly discouraged. Although no passage of the Qur'an forbids representational painting, the *Hadith* warned against any attempt to imitate God through artistic creation or idolatry, and this has been interpreted as an outright ban on any such depictions.

Human beings and animals could still be represented in secular art, but relatively little survives from the early centuries aside from a very few wall paintings from the royal palaces. Although the Persians used calligraphy and art to decorate their books, the Arabs had no pictorial

The Recycled Mosque. The Great Mosque at Córdoba was built on a site previously dedicated to the Roman God Janus, which later boasted a Christian church built by the Visigoths. In the eighth century, the Muslims incorporated parts of the old church into their new mosque, aggrandizing it over the centuries. After the Muslims were driven from Spain, the mosque reverted to Christianity, and in 1523, a soaring cathedral sprouted from its spine (shown below). Inside, the mosque and the cathedral seem to blend well aesthetically, a prototype for harmonious religious coexistence. Throughout history, societies have destroyed past architectural wonders, robbing older marble glories to erect new marvels. It is rare and wonderful that the Great Mosque survived to vaunt its glittering dome in the *mihrab* chamber (shown in the upper photo).

The Qur'an as Sculptured Design. Muslim sculptors and artists, reflecting the traditional view that any visual representation of the prophet Muhammad was blasphemous, turned to geometric patterns, as well as to flowers and animals, as a means of fulfilling their creative urges. The predominant motif, however, was the reproduction of Qur'anic verses in the Arabic script. Calligraphy, which was almost as important in the Middle East as it was in traditional China, used the Arabic script to decorate all of the Islamic arts, from painting to pottery, tile and ironwork, and wall decorations such as this carved plaster panel in a courtyard of the Alhambra palace in Spain. Since a recitation from the Qur'an was an important component of the daily devotional activities for all practicing Muslims, elaborate scriptural panels such as this one perfectly blended the spiritual and the artistic realms.

© William J. Duiker

tradition of their own and only began to develop the art of book illustration in the late twelfth century to adorn translations of Greek scientific works.

In the thirteenth century, a Mongol dynasty established at Tabriz, west of the Caspian Sea, offered the Middle East its first direct contact with the art of East Asia. Mongol painting, done in the Chinese manner with a full brush and expressing animated movement and intensity (see Chapter 10), freed Islamic painters from traditional confines and enabled them to experiment with new techniques. The most famous paintings of the Tabriz school are found in the illustrations accompanying

Ferdowzi's *Book of Kings.* They express a new realistic detail and a concern for individual human qualities.

Chinese art also influenced Islamic art with its sense of space. A new sense of perspective pervaded Islamic painting, leading to some of the great paintings of the Herat School under the fifteenth-century autocrat Tamerlane. Artists working in the Herat style often depicted mounted warriors battling on a richly detailed background of trees and birds. These paintings served as the classical models for later Islamic painting, which culminated in the glorious artistic tradition of sixteenth-century Iran, Turkey, and India (see Chapter 16).

CONCLUSION

After the collapse of Roman power in the west, the Eastern Roman Empire, centered on Constantinople, continued in the eastern Mediterranean and eventually emerged as the unique Christian civilization known as the Byzantine Empire, which flourished for hundreds of years. One of the greatest challenges to the Byzantine Empire, however, came from a new force—Islam—that blossomed in the Arabian peninsula and spread rapidly throughout the Middle East. In the eyes of some Europeans during the Middle Ages, the Arab empire was a malevolent force that posed a serious threat to the security of Christianity. Their fears were not entirely misplaced, for within half a century after the death of Islam's founder, Muhammad, Arab armies overran Christian states in North Africa and the Iberian peninsula, and Turkish Muslims moved eastward onto the fringes of the Indian subcontinent. But although the teachings of Muhammad brought war and conquest to much of the known world, they also brought hope and a sense of political and economic

stability to peoples throughout the region. Thus for many people in the medieval Mediterranean world, the arrival of Islam was a welcome event. Islam brought a code of law and a written language to societies that had previously lacked them. Finally, by creating a revitalized trade network stretching from West Africa to East Asia, it established a vehicle for the exchange of technology and ideas that brought untold wealth to thousands and a better life to millions.

Like other empires in the region, the Arab empire did not last. It fell victim to a combination of internal and external pressures, and by the end of the thirteenth century, it was no more than a memory. But it left a powerful legacy in Islam, which remains one of the great religions of the world. In succeeding centuries, Islam began to penetrate into new areas beyond the edge of the Sahara and across the Indian Ocean into the islands of the Indonesian archipelago.

TIMELINE

500 | 750 | 1000 | 1250 | 1500

Life of Muhammad

Muhammad's flight to Medina

Election of Ali to caliphate

Founding of Abbasid caliphate

Reign of Harun al-Rashid

Conquest of Mecca

Spread of Islam to Spain and northwestern India

Construction of city of Baghdad

Arab defeat of Byzantines at Yarmuk

Battle of Manzikert

Seljuk Turks seize Baghdad

Conquest of Anatolia by Seljuk Turks

The Crusades

Mongols destroy city of Baghdad

Ottoman Turks seize Constantinople

CHAPTER NOTES

1. M. M. Pickthall, trans., *The Meaning of the Glorious Koran* (New York, 1953), p. 89.
2. Quoted in T. W. Lippman, *Understanding Islam: An Introduction to the Moslem World* (New York, 1982), p. 118.
3. F. Hirth and W. W. Rockhill, trans., *Chau Ju-kua: His Work on the Chinese and Arab Trade in the Twelfth and Thirteenth Centuries, Entitled Chu-fan-chi* (New York, 1966), p. 115.
4. al-Mas'udi, *The Meadows of Gold: The Abbasids*, ed. P. Lunde and C. Stone (London, 1989), p. 151.
5. Quoted in G. Wiet, *Baghdad: Metropolis of the Abbasid Caliphate*, trans. S. Feiler (Norman, Okla., 1971), pp. 118–119.
6. L. Africanus, *The History and Description of Africa and of the Notable Things Therein Contained* (New York, n.d.), pp. 820–821.
7. Hirth and Rockhill, *Chau Ju-kua*, p. 116.
8. E. Yarshater, ed., *Persian Literature* (Albany, N.Y., 1988), pp. 125–126.
9. Ibid., pp. 154–159.
10. E. Rehatsek, trans., *The Gulistan or Rose Garden of Sa'di* (New York, 1964), pp. 65, 67, 71.

SUGGESTED READING

The Rise of Islam

Standard works on the rise of Islam include T. W. Lippman, *Understanding Islam: An Introduction to the Moslem World* (New York, 1982), and J. Bloom and S. Blair, *Islam: A Thousand Years of Faith and Power* (New Haven, Conn., 2002). Also see K. Armstrong, *Islam: A Short History* (New York, 2000).

Other worthwhile studies include B. Lewis, *The Middle East: A Brief History of the Last 2,000 Years* (New York, 1986), and J. L. Esposito, ed., *The Oxford History of Islam* (New York, 1999). For anthropological background, see D. Bates and A. Rassam, *Peoples and Cultures of the Middle East* (Englewood Cliffs, N.J., 1983).

Specialized works on various historical periods are numerous. For a view of the Crusades from an Arab perspective, see A. Maalouf, *The Crusades Through Arab Eyes* (London, 1984), and C. Hillenbrand, *The Crusades: Islamic Perspectives* (New York, 2001). On the Mamluks, see R. Irwin, *The Middle East in the Middle Ages: The Early Mamluk Sultanate, 1250–1382* (Carbondale, Ill., 1986). In *God of Battles: Christianity and Islam* (Princeton, N.J., 1998), P. Partner compares the expansionist tendencies of the two great religions. Also see R. Fletcher, *The Cross and the Crescent: Christianity and Islam from Muhammad to the Reform* (New York, 2005).

Abbasid Empire

On the Abbasid Empire, see H. Kennedy's highly readable *When Baghdad Ruled the Muslim World: The Rise and Fall of Islam's Greatest Dynasty* (Cambridge, Mass., 2004). Christian–Muslim contacts are discussed in S. O'Shea, *Sea of Faith: Islam and Christianity in the Medieval Mediterranean World* (New York, 2006). On the situation in Spain during the Abbasid era, see M. Menocal's elegant study, *Ornament of the World: How Muslims, Jews, and Christians Created a Culture of Tolerance in Medieval Spain* (New York, 2002).

For an excellent overview of world textiles, see K. Wilson *A History of Textiles* (Boulder, Colo. 1982).

CENGAGENOW Enter *CengageNOW* using the access card that is available with this text. *CengageNOW* will help you understand the content in this chapter with lesson plans generated for your needs, as well as provide you with a connection to the *Wadsworth World History Resource Center* (see description below for details).

WORLD HISTORY RESOURCE CENTER

Enter the Resource Center using either your *CengageNOW* access card or your separate access card for the *World History Resource Center*. Organized by topic, this Website includes quizzes; images; over 350 primary source documents; interactive simulations, maps, and timelines; movie explorations; and a wealth of other resources. You can read the following documents, and many more, at the *World History Resource Center*:

Muhammad's Last Sermon

Visit the *World History* Companion Website for chapter quizzes and more:

www.cengage.com/history/Duiker/World6e

Economy On the economy, see E. Ashtor, *A Social and Economic History of the Near East in the Middle Ages* (Berkeley, Calif., 1976); K. N. Chaudhuri, *Asia Before Europe: Economy and Civilization of the Indian Ocean from the Rise of Islam to 1750* (Cambridge, 1990); C. Issawi, *The Middle East Economy: Decline and Recovery* (Princeton, N.J., 1995); and P. Crone, *Meccan Trade and the Rise of Islam* (Princeton, N.J., 1987).

Women On women, see F. Hussain, ed., *Muslim Women* (New York, 1984); G. Nashat and J. E. Tucker, *Women in the Middle East and North Africa* (Bloomington, Ind., 1998); S. S. Hughes and B. Hughes, *Women in World History,* vol. 1 (London, 1995); and L. Ahmed, *Women and Gender in Islam* (New Haven, Conn., 1992).

Islamic Literature and Art For the best introduction to Islamic literature, consult J. Kritzeck, ed., *Anthology of Islamic Literature* (New York, 1964), with its concise commentaries and introduction. An excellent introduction to Persian literature can be found in E. Yarshater, ed., *Persian Literature* (Albany, N.Y., 1988). H. Haddawy, trans., *The Arabian Nights* (New York, 1990) is the most accessible version for students. It presents 271 "nights" in a clear and colorful style.

For the best introduction to Islamic art, consult the concise yet comprehensive work by D. T. Rice, *Islamic Art*, rev. ed. (London, 1975). Also see J. Bloom and S. Blair, *Islamic Arts* (London, 1997).

CHAPTER 8

EARLY CIVILIZATIONS IN AFRICA

© Nick Greaves/Alamy

The Temple at Great Zimbabwe

CHAPTER OUTLINE AND FOCUS QUESTIONS

The Emergence of Civilization

Q How did the advent of farming and pastoralism affect the various peoples of Africa in the classical era? How did the consequences of the agricultural revolution in Africa differ from those in other societies in Eurasia and America?

The Coming of Islam

Q What effects did the coming of Islam have on African religion, society, political structures, trade, and culture?

States and Stateless Societies in Central and Southern Africa

Q What role did migration play in the evolution of early African societies? How did the impact of these migrations compare with similar population movements elsewhere?

African Society

Q What role did lineage groups, women, and slavery play in African societies? In what ways did African societies in various parts of the continent differ? What accounted for these differences?

African Culture

Q What are some of the chief characteristics of African sculpture and carvings, music, and architecture, and what purpose did these forms of creative expression serve in African society?

CRITICAL THINKING

Q With the exception of the Nile River valley, organized states did not emerge in the continent of Africa until much later than in many regions of the Eurasian supercontinent. Why do you think this was the case?

IN 1871, THE GERMAN EXPLORER Karl Mauch began to search southern Africa's central plateau for the colossal stone ruins of a legendary lost civilization. In late August, he found what he had been looking for. According to his diary, "Presently I stood before it and beheld a wall of a height of about 20 feet of granite bricks. Very close by there was a place where a kind of footpath led over rubble into the interior. Following this path I stumbled over masses of rubble and parts of walls and dense thickets. I stopped in front of a towerlike structure. Altogether it rose to a height of about 30 feet." Mauch was convinced that "a civilized nation must once have lived here." Like many other nineteenth-century Europeans, however, Mauch was equally convinced that the Africans who had lived there could never have built such splendid structures as the ones he had found at Great Zimbabwe. To Mauch and other archaeologists, Great Zimbabwe must have been the work of "a northern race closely akin to the Phoenician and Egyptian." It was not until the twentieth century that Europeans could overcome their prejudices and finally admit that Africans south of Egypt had also developed advanced civilizations with spectacular achievements.

The continent of Africa has played a central role in the long evolution of humankind. It was in Africa that the

219

The Land

Africa is as physically diverse as it is vast. The northern coast, washed by the Mediterranean Sea, is mountainous for much of its length. South of the mountains lies the greatest desert on earth, the Sahara, which stretches from the Atlantic to the Indian Ocean. To the east is the Nile River, heart of the ancient Egyptian civilization. Beyond that lies the Red Sea, separating Africa from Asia.

The Sahara acts as a great divide separating the northern coast from the rest of the continent. Africa south of the Sahara contains a number of major regions. In the west is the so-called hump of Africa, which juts like a massive shoulder into the Atlantic Ocean. Here the Sahara gradually gives way to grasslands in the interior and then to tropical rain forests along the coast. This region, dominated by the Niger River, is rich in natural resources and was the home of many ancient civilizations.

Far to the east, bordering the Indian Ocean, is a very different terrain of snowcapped mountains, upland plateaus, and lakes. Much of this region is grassland populated by wild beasts, which have given it the modern designation of Safari Country. Here, in the East African Rift valley in the lake district of modern Kenya, early hominids began their long trek toward civilization several million years ago.

Farther to the south lies the Congo basin, with its jungles watered by the mighty Congo River. The jungles of equatorial Africa then fade gradually into the hills, plateaus, and deserts of the south. This rich land contains some of the most valuable mineral resources known today.

Kush

It is not certain when agriculture was first practiced on the continent of Africa. Until recently, historians assumed that crops were first cultivated in the lower Nile valley (the northern part near the Mediterranean) about seven or eight thousand years ago, when wheat and barley were introduced, possibly from the Middle East. Eventually, as explained in Chapter 1, this area gave rise to the civilization of ancient Egypt.

Recent evidence suggests that this hypothesis may need some revision. South of Egypt, near the junction of the White Nile and the Blue Nile, is an area known historically as Nubia. Some archaeologists suggest that agriculture may have appeared first in Nubia rather than farther north. Stone Age farmers from Nubia may have begun to cultivate local crops such as sorghum and millet along the banks of the upper Nile (the southern part near the river's source) as early as the eleventh millennium B.C.E. It was this area that eventually gave birth to the kingdom of Kush (see Chapter 1).

In the absence of extensive written records, confirmed evidence about the nature of Kushite society is limited, but it seems likely that it was predominantly urban. Initially, foreign trade was probably a monopoly of the state, but the presence of luxury goods in the numerous private

---

first hominids appeared more than three million years ago. It was probably in Africa that the immediate ancestors of modern human beings—*Homo sapiens*—emerged. The domestication of animals may have occurred first in Africa. Certainly, one of the first states appeared in Africa, in the Nile valley in the northeastern corner of the continent, in the form of the kingdom of the pharaohs. Recent evidence suggests that Egyptian civilization was significantly influenced by cultural developments taking place to the south, in Nubia, in modern Sudan. Egypt in turn exercised a profound influence on scientific and cultural developments throughout the eastern Mediterranean region, including the civilization of the Greeks.

After the decline of the Egyptian empire during the first millennium B.C.E., the focus of social change began to shift from the lower Nile valley to other areas of the continent: to West Africa, where a series of major trading states began to take part in the caravan trade with the Mediterranean through the vast wastes of the Sahara; to the region of the upper Nile River, where the states of Kush and Axum dominated trade for several centuries; and to the eastern coast from the Horn of Africa (formally known as Cape Guardafui) to the straits between the continent and the island of Madagascar, where African peoples began to play an active role in the commercial traffic in the Indian Ocean. In the meantime, a gradual movement of agricultural peoples brought Iron Age farming to the central portion of the continent, leading eventually to the creation of several states in the Congo River basin and the plateau region south of the Zambezi River.

The peoples of Africa, then, have played a significant role in the changing human experience since ancient times. Yet the landmass of Africa is so vast and its topography so diverse that communication within the continent and between Africans and peoples living elsewhere in the world has often been more difficult than in many other regions. As a consequence, while some parts of the continent were directly exposed to the currents of change sweeping across Eurasia and were influenced by them to varying degrees, other regions were virtually isolated from the "great tradition" cultures discussed in Part I of this book and developed in their own directions, rendering generalizations about Africa difficult, if not impossible, to make. ◆

The Emergence of Civilization

Q Focus Questions: How did the advent of farming and pastoralism affect the various peoples of Africa in the classical era? How did the consequences of the agricultural revolution in Africa differ from those in other societies in Eurasia and America?

After Asia, Africa is the largest of the continents (see Map 8.1). It stretches nearly 5,000 miles from the Cape of Good Hope in the south to the Mediterranean in the north and extends a similar distance from Cape Verde on the west coast to the Horn of Africa on the Indian Ocean.

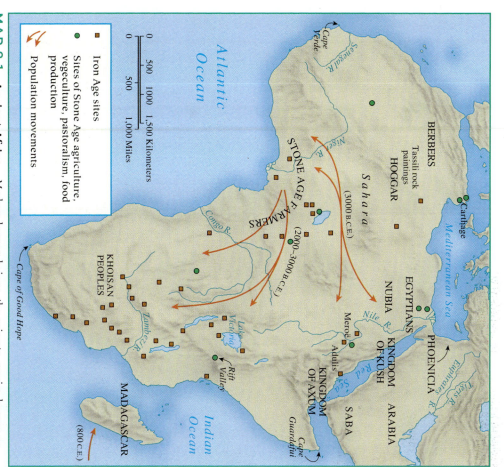

MAP 8.1 Ancient Africa. Modern human beings, the primate species known as *Homo sapiens*, first evolved on the continent of Africa. Some key sites of early human settlement are shown on this map.

Q Which are the main river systems on the continent of Africa? **View an animated version of this map or related maps at www.cengage.com/history/Duiker/Worlde**

Map legend:
- ■ Iron Age sites
- ● Sites of Stone Age agriculture, vegeculture, pastoralism, food production
- ↗ Population movements

tombs in the vicinity indicate that at one time material prosperity was relatively widespread. This suggests that commercial activities were being conducted by a substantial merchant class. Beyond the immediate confines of the Nile River valley lived pastoral peoples little affected by the currents of ancient Egyptian civilization.

Axum and Saba

In the first millennium C.E., Kush declined and was eventually conquered by Axum, a new power located in the highlands of modern Ethiopia (see Map 8.2). Axum had been founded during the first millennium B.C.E., possibly by migrants from the kingdom of Saba (popularly known as Sheba) across the Red Sea on the southern tip of the Arabian peninsula. During antiquity, Saba was a major trading state, serving as a transit point for goods carried from South Asia into the lands surrounding the Mediterranean. Biblical sources credited the "queen of Sheba" with vast wealth and resources. In fact, much of that wealth had

originated much farther to the east and passed through Saba en route to the countries adjacent to the Mediterranean.

When Saba declined, perhaps because of the desiccation (drying up) of the Arabian Desert, Axum survived for centuries as an independent state. Like Saba, Axum owed much of its prosperity to its location on the commercial trade route between India and the Mediterranean, and Greek ships from the Ptolemaic kingdom in Egypt stopped regularly at the port of Adulis on the Red Sea. Axum exported ivory, frankincense, myrrh, and slaves, while its primary imports were textiles, metal goods, wine, and olive oil (see the box on p. 223). For a time, Axum competed for control of the ivory trade with the neighboring state of Kush, and hunters from Axum armed with imported iron weapons scoured the entire region for elephants. Probably as a result of this competition, in the fourth century C.E., the Axumite ruler, claiming he had been provoked, launched an invasion of Kush and conquered it.

Perhaps the most distinctive feature of Axumite civilization was its religion. Originally, the rulers of Axum (who claimed descent from King Solomon through the visit of the queen of Sheba to Israel in biblical times) followed the

religion of their predecessors in Saba. But in the fourth century C.E., Axumite rulers adopted Christianity, possibly from Egypt. This commitment to the Egyptian form of Christianity (often called **Coptic**, from the local language of the day) was retained even after the collapse of Axum and the expansion of Islam through the area in later centuries. Later, Axum (renamed Ethiopia) would be identified by some Europeans as the "hermit kingdom" and the home of Prester John, a legendary Christian king of East Africa (see Chapter 14).

The Sahara and Its Environs

Kush and Axum were part of the ancient trading network that extended from the Mediterranean Sea to the Indian Ocean and were affected in various ways by the cross-cultural contacts that took place throughout that region. Elsewhere in Africa, somewhat different patterns prevailed; they varied from area to area, depending on the geography and climate.

At one time, when the world's climate was much cooler and wetter than it is today, Central Africa may have been one of the few areas that was habitable for the first hominids. Later, from 8000 to 4000 B.C.E., a warm, humid climate prevailed in the Sahara, creating lakes and ponds, as well as vast grasslands (known as savannas) replete with game. Rock paintings found in what are today some of the most uninhabitable parts of the region are a clear indication that the environment was much different several thousand years ago.

By 7000 B.C.E., the peoples of the Sahara were herding animals—first sheep and goats and later cattle. Unlike many other areas of the ancient world, there was as yet no pressure to introduce farming. During the sixth and fifth millennia B.C.E., however, the climate became more arid, and the desertification of the Sahara began. From the rock paintings, which for the most part date from the fourth and third millennia B.C.E., we know that by that time the herds were being supplemented by fishing and the limited cultivation of crops such as millet, sorghum, and a drought-resistant form of dry rice. After 3000 B.C.E., as the desiccation of the Sahara proceeded and the lakes dried up, the local inhabitants began to migrate eastward toward the Nile River and southward into the grasslands. As a result, farming began to spread into the savannas on the southern fringes of the desert and eventually into the tropical forest areas to the south, where crops were no longer limited to drought-resistant cereals but could include tropical fruits and tubers.

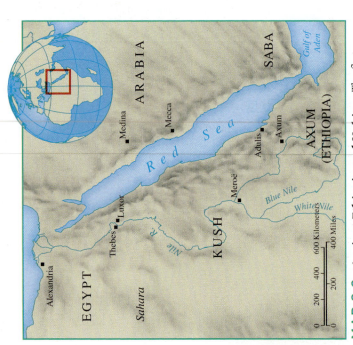

MAP 8.2 **Ancient Ethiopia and Nubia.** The first civilizations to appear on the African continent emerged in the Nile River valley. Early in the first century C.E., the state of Axum emerged in what is today the states of Ethiopia and Eritrea.
Q Where are the major urban settlements in the region, as shown on this map? 🔊 **View an animated version of this map or related maps at** www.cengage.com/history/Duiker/World6e

Fleets of the Desert. Since the dawn of history, caravans have transported food and various manufactured articles southward across the Sahara in exchange for salt, gold, copper, skins, and slaves. Once carried on by donkey carts, the trade expanded dramatically with the introduction of the one-humped camel into the region from the Arabian peninsula. Unlike most other draft animals, the camel can go great distances without water, a scarce item in the desert.

© Frans Lemmens/zefa/CORBIS

Historians do not know when goods first began to be exchanged across the Sahara in a north-south direction, but during the first millennium B.C.E., the commercial center of Carthage on the Mediterranean had become a focal point of the trans-Saharan trade. The **Berbers**, a pastoral people of North Africa (see Chapter 7), served as intermediaries, carrying food products and manufactured goods from Carthage across the desert and exchanging them for salt, gold and copper, skins, various agricultural products, and perhaps slaves (see the box on p. 225).

This trade initiated a process of cultural exchange that would exert a significant impact on the peoples of tropical Africa. Among other things, it may have spread the knowledge of ironworking south of the desert. Although historians once believed that ironworking knowledge reached sub-Saharan Africa from Meroë in the upper Nile valley in the first centuries C.E., recent finds suggest that the peoples along the Niger River were smelting iron five or six hundred years earlier. Some scholars believe that the technique developed independently there, but others surmise that it was introduced by the Berbers, who had learned it from the Carthaginians.

Whatever the case, the **Nok culture** in northern Nigeria eventually became one of the most active ironworking societies in Africa. Excavations have unearthed numerous terra-cotta and metal figures, as well as stone and iron farm implements, dating back as far as 500 B.C.E. The remains of smelting furnaces confirm that the iron was produced locally.

Early in the first millennium C.E., the introduction of the camel provided a major stimulus to the trans-Saharan trade. With its ability to store considerable amounts of food and water, the camel was far better equipped to handle the arduous conditions of the desert than the donkey, which had been used previously. The "camel caravans" of the Berbers became known as the "fleets of the desert."

The Garamantes

Not all the peoples involved in trade across the Sahara were nomadic. Recent exploratory work in the Libyan Desert has revealed the existence of an ancient kingdom that for over a thousand years transported goods between societies along the Mediterranean Sea and sub-Saharan Africa. The Garamantes, as they were known to the Romans, carried salt, glass, metal, olive oil, and wine to Central Africa in return for gold, slaves, and various tropical products. To provide food for their communities in the heart of the desert,

---

THE GOLD RUSH, AFRICAN STYLE

INTERACTION & EXCHANGE

Attractive to the eye, malleable in shape, and resistant to corrosion, gold has been a valuable commodity in human societies since ancient times. Because of its relative rarity in the natural world, efforts to locate sources of the precious metal have often resulted in the establishment of contacts between previously unacquainted peoples. The commercial transaction portrayed in this excerpt took place in the region of Axum and was described by the Egyptian monk Cosmas Indicopleustes.

The Christian Topography of Cosmas Indicopleustes

The country known as that of Sasu is itself near the ocean, just as the ocean is near the frankincense country, in which there are many gold mines. The King of the Axomites accordingly, every other year, through the governor of Agau, sends thither special agents to bargain for the gold, and these are accompanied by many other traders—upwards, say, of five hundred—bound on the same errand as themselves. They take along with them to the mining district oxen, lumps of salt, and iron, and when they reach its neighbourhood they make a halt at a certain spot and form an encampment, which they fence round with a great hedge of thorns. Within this they live, and having slaughtered the oxen, cut them in pieces, and lay the pieces on the top of the thorns, along with the lumps of salt and the iron. Then come the natives bringing gold in nuggets like peas, called *tancharas*, and lay one or two or more of these upon what pleases them—the pieces of flesh or the salt or the iron, and then they retire to some distance off. Then the owner of the meat approaches, and if he is satisfied he takes the gold away, and upon seeing this its owner comes and takes the flesh or the salt or the iron. If, however, he is not satisfied, he leaves the gold, when the native seeing that he has not taken it, comes and either puts down more gold, or takes up what he had laid down, and goes away. Such is the mode in which business is transacted with the people of that country, because their language is different and interpreters are hardly to be found. The time they stay in that country is five days more or less, according as the natives more or less readily coming forward buy up all their wares. On the journey homeward they all agree to travel well-armed, since some of the tribes through whose country they must pass might threaten to attack them from a desire to rob them of their gold. The space of six months is taken up with this trading expedition, including both the going and the returning. In going they march very slowly, chiefly because of the cattle, but in returning they quicken their pace lest on the way they should be overtaken by winter and its rains.

Q *Does this form of exchange appear to you to be essentially fair to both sides of the commercial transaction, or is there an element of exploitation involved? Explain your answer.*

Beginning in the second millennium B.C.E., new peoples began to migrate into East Africa from the west. Farming peoples speaking dialects of the Bantu family of languages began to move from the region of the Niger River into East Africa and the Congo River basin (see the comparative essay "The Migration of Peoples" on p. 226). They were probably responsible for introducing the widespread cultivation of crops and knowledge of iron-working to much of East Africa, although there are signs of some limited iron smelting in the area before their arrival.

The Bantu settled in rural communities based on subsistence farming. The primary crops were millet and sorghum, along with yams, melons, and beans. The land was often tilled with both iron and stone tools, and the former were usually manufactured in a local smelter. Some people kept domestic animals such as cattle, sheep, goats, or chickens or supplemented their diets by hunting and food gathering. Because the population was minimal and an ample supply of cultivable land was available, most settlements were relatively small; each village formed a self-sufficient political and economic entity.

As early as the era of the New Kingdom in the second millennium B.C.E., Egyptian ships had plied the waters off the East African coast in search of gold, ivory, palm oil, and perhaps slaves. By the first century C.E., the region was an established part of a trading network that included the Mediterranean and the Red Sea. In that century, a Greek seafarer from Alexandria wrote an account of his travels down the coast from Cape Guardafui at the tip of the Horn of Africa to the Strait of Madagascar, thousands of miles to the south. Called the *Periplus*, this work provides generally accurate descriptions of the peoples and settlements along the African coast and the trade goods they supplied.

According to the *Periplus*, the port of Rhapta (probably modern Dar es Salaam) was a commercial metropolis, exporting ivory, rhinoceros horn, and tortoise shell and importing glass, wine, grain, and metal goods such as weapons and tools. The identity of the peoples taking part in this trade is not clear, but it seems likely that the area was already inhabited by a mixture of local peoples and immigrants from the Arabian peninsula. Out of this mixture would eventually emerge an African-Arabian **Swahili** culture (see "East Africa: The Land of Zanj" later in this chapter) that continues to exist in coastal areas today. Beyond Rhapta was "unexplored ocean." Some contemporary observers believed that the Indian and Atlantic Oceans were connected. Others were convinced that the Indian Ocean was an enclosed sea and that the continent of Africa could not be circumnavigated.

Trade across the Indian Ocean and down the coast of East Africa, facilitated by the monsoon winds, would gradually become one of the most lucrative sources of commercial profit in the ancient and medieval worlds. Although the origins of the trade remain shrouded in mystery, traders eventually came by sea from as far away

© Scala/Art Resource, NY

Nok Pottery Head. The Nok peoples of the Niger River are the oldest known culture in West Africa to have created sculpture. This is a typical terra-cotta head of the Nok culture produced between 500 B.C.E. and 200 C.E. Discovered by accident in the twentieth century by tin miners, these heads feature perforated eyes set in triangles or circles, stylized eyebrows, open thick lips, broad noses with wide nostrils, and large ears. Perhaps the large facial openings permitted the hot air to escape as the heads were fired. Although the function of these statues is not known for certain, they were likely connected with religious rituals or devotion to ancestors.

they constructed a complex irrigation system consisting of several thousand miles of underground channels. The technique is reminiscent of similar systems in Persia and Central Asia. Scholars believe that the kingdom declined as a result of the fall of the Roman Empire and the desiccation of the desert. As the historian Felipe Fernández-Armesto has noted in his provocative book, *Civilizations*, advanced societies do not easily thrive in desert conditions.[1]

East Africa

South of Axum, along the shores of the Indian Ocean and in the inland plateau that stretches from the mountains of Ethiopia through the lake district of Central Africa, lived a mixture of peoples, some depending on hunting and food gathering and others following pastoral pursuits.

INTERACTION & EXCHANGE

Little is known regarding Antonius Malfante, the Italian adventurer who in 1447 wrote this letter relating his travels along the trade route used by the Hausa city-states of northern Nigeria. In this passage, he astutely described the various peoples who inhabited the Sahara: Arabs, Jews, Berbers, Tuaregs (a subgroup of the Berber peoples), and African blacks, who lived in uneasy proximity as they struggled to coexist in the stark conditions of the desert. The mutual hostility between settled and pastoral peoples in the area continues today.

Antonius Malfante, Letter to Genoa

Though I am a Christian, no one ever addressed an insulting word to me. They said they had never seen a Christian before. It is true that on my first arrival they were scornful of me, because they all wished to see me, saying with wonder, "This Christian has a countenance like ours"—for they believed that Christians had disguised faces. Their curiosity was soon satisfied, and now I can go alone anywhere, with no one to say an evil word to me.

There are many Jews, who lead a good life here, for they are under the protection of the several rulers, each of whom defends his own clients. Thus they enjoy very secure social standing. Trade is in their hands, and many of them are to be trusted with the greatest confidence.

This locality is a mart of the country of the Moors [Berbers] to which merchants come to sell their goods: gold is carried hither, and bought by those who come up from the coast....

It never rains here: if it did, the houses, being built of salt in the place of reeds, would be destroyed. It is scarcely ever cold here: in summer the heat is extreme, wherefore they are almost all blacks. The children of both sexes go naked up to the age of fifteen. These people observe the religion and law of Muhammad.

In the lands of the blacks, as well as here, dwell the Philistines [the Tuareg], who live, like the Arabs, in tents.

They are without number, and hold sway over the land of Gazola from the borders of Egypt to the shores of the Ocean, as far as Massa and Safi, and over all the neighboring towns of the blacks. They are fair, strong in body and very handsome in appearance. They ride without stirrups, with simple spurs. They are governed by kings, whose heirs are the sons of their sisters—for such is their law. They keep their mouths and noses covered. I have seen many of them here, and have asked them through an interpreter why they cover their mouths and noses thus. They replied: "We have inherited this custom from our ancestors." They are sworn enemies of the Jews, who do not dare to pass hither. Their faith is that of the Blacks. Their sustenance is milk and flesh, no corn or barley, but much rice. Their sheep, cattle, and camels are without number. One breed of camel, white as snow, can cover in one day a distance which would take a horseman four days to travel. Great warriors, these people are continually at war amongst themselves.

The states which are under their rule border upon the land of the blacks...which have inhabitants of the faith of Muhammad. In all, the great majority are blacks, but there are a small number of whites....

To the south of these are innumerable great cities and territories, the inhabitants of which are all blacks and idolators, continually at war with each other in defense of their law and faith of their idols. Some worship the sun, others the moon, the seven planets, fire, or water; others a mirror which reflects their faces, which they take to be the images of gods; others groves of trees, the seats of a spirit to whom they make sacrifice; others again, statues of wood and stone, with which, they say, they commune by incantations.

Q *What occupations does Malfante mention? To what degree do they refer to specific peoples living in the area?*

---

as the mainland of Southeast Asia. Early in the first millennium C.E., Malay peoples bringing cinnamon to the Middle East began to cross the Indian Ocean directly and landed on the southeastern coast of Africa. Eventually, a Malay settlement was established on the island of Madagascar, where the population is still of mixed Malay-African origin. Historians suspect that Malay immigrants were responsible for introducing such Southeast Asian foods as the banana and the yam to Africa, although recent archaeological evidence suggests that they may have arrived in Africa as early as the third millennium B.C.E. The banana, with its high yield and ability to grow in uncultivated rain forest, became the preferred crop of many Bantu peoples.

The Coming of Islam

Q **Focus Question:** What effects did the coming of Islam have on African religion, society, political structures, trade, and culture?

As noted in Chapter 7, the rise of Islam during the first half of the seventh century C.E. had ramifications far beyond the Arabian peninsula. Arab armies swept across North Africa, incorporating it into the Arab empire and isolating the Christian state of Axum to the south. Although East Africa and West Africa south of the Sahara were not conquered by the Arab forces, Islam eventually penetrated these areas as well.

COMPARATIVE ESSAY
The Migration of Peoples

© Erich Lessing/Art Resource, NY

INTERACTION & EXCHANGE

About fifty thousand years ago, a small band of humans crossed the Sinai peninsula from Africa and began to spread out across the Eurasian supercontinent. Thus began a migration of peoples that continued with accelerating speed throughout the ancient era and beyond. By 40,000 B.C.E., their descendants had spread across Eurasia as far as China and eastern Siberia and had even settled the distant continent of Australia.

Who were these peoples, and what provoked their decision to change their habitat? Undoubtedly, the first migrants were foragers or hunters in search of wild game, but with the advent of agriculture and the domestication of animals about twelve thousand years ago, other peoples began to migrate vast distances in search of fertile farming and pasturelands.

The ever-changing climate was undoubtedly a major factor driving the process. In the fourth millennium B.C.E., the drying up of rich pasturelands in the Sahara forced the local inhabitants to migrate eastward toward the Nile River valley and the grasslands of East Africa. At about the same time, Indo-European-speaking farming peoples left the region of the Black Sea and moved gradually into central Europe in search of new farmlands. They were eventually followed by nomadic groups from Central Asia who began to occupy lands along the frontiers of the Roman Empire, while other bands of nomads threatened the plains of northern China from the Gobi Desert. In the meantime, Bantu-speaking farmers migrated from the Niger River southward into the rain forests of Central Africa and beyond. Similar movements took place in Southeast Asia and the Americas.

This steady flow of migrating peoples often had a destabilizing effect on sedentary societies in their path. Nomadic incursions represented a constant menace to the security of China, Egypt, and the Roman Empire and ultimately brought them to an end. But this vast movement of peoples often had beneficial effects as well, spreading new technologies and means of livelihood. Although some migrants, like the Huns, came for plunder and left havoc in their wake, other groups, like the Celtic peoples and the Bantus, prospered in their new environment.

The most famous of all nomadic invasions is a case in point. In the thirteenth century C.E., the Mongols left their

Rock Paintings of the Sahara. Even before the Egyptians built their pyramids at Giza, other peoples far to the west in the vast wastes of the Sahara were creating their own art forms. These rock paintings, some of which date back to the fourth millennium B.C.E. and are reminiscent of similar examples from Europe, Asia, and Australia, provide a valuable record of a society that supported itself by a combination of farming, hunting, and herding animals. After the introduction of the horse from Arabia around 1200 B.C.E., subsequent rock paintings depicted chariots and horseback riding. Eventually, camels began to appear in the paintings, a consequence of the increasing desiccation of the Sahara.

homeland in the Gobi Desert, advancing westward into the Russian steppes and southward in China and Central Asia, leaving death and devastation in their wake. At the height of their empire, the Mongols controlled virtually all of Eurasia except its western and southern fringes, thus creating a zone of stability in which a global trade and informational network could thrive that stretched from China to the shores of the Mediterranean.

African Religious Beliefs Before Islam

When Islam arrived, most African societies already had well-developed systems of religious beliefs. Like other aspects of African life, early African religious beliefs varied from place to place, but certain characteristics appear to have been shared by most African societies. One of these common features was **pantheism,** belief in a single creator god from whom all things came. Sometimes the creator

god was accompanied by a whole pantheon of lesser deities. The Ashanti people of Ghana in West Africa believed in a supreme being called Nyame, whose sons were lesser gods. Each son served a different purpose: one was the rainmaker, another was the source of compassion, and a third was responsible for the sunshine. This heavenly hierarchy paralleled earthly arrangements: worship of Nyame was the exclusive preserve of the king through his priests; lesser officials and the common people worshiped

Nyame's sons, who might intercede with their father on behalf of ordinary Africans.

Many African religions also shared a belief in a form of afterlife during which the soul floated in the atmosphere through eternity. Belief in an afterlife was closely connected to the importance of ancestors and the **lineage group**, or clan, in African society. Each lineage group could trace itself back to a founding ancestor or group of ancestors. These ancestral souls would not be extinguished as long as the lineage group continued to perform rituals in their name. The rituals could also benefit the lineage group on earth, for the ancestral souls, being closer to the gods, had the power to influence the lives of their descendants, for good or evil.

Such beliefs were challenged but not always replaced by the arrival of Islam. In some ways, the tenets of Islam were in conflict with traditional African beliefs and customs. Although the concept of a single transcendent deity presented no problems in many African societies, Islam's rejection of spirit worship and a priestly class ran counter to the beliefs of many Africans and was often ignored in practice. Similarly, as various Muslim travelers observed, Islam's insistence on the separation of the sexes contrasted with the relatively informal relationships that prevailed in many African societies and was probably slow to take root. In the long run, imported ideas were synthesized with native beliefs to create a unique brand of Africanized Islam.

The Arabs in North Africa

In 641, Arab forces advanced into Egypt, seized the delta of the Nile River, and brought two centuries of Byzantine rule to an end. To guard against attacks from the Byzantine fleet, the Arabs eventually built a new capital at Cairo, inland from the previous Byzantine capital of Alexandria, and began to consolidate their control over the entire region.

The Arab conquerors were probably welcomed by many of the local inhabitants, if not the majority. Although Egypt had been a thriving commercial center under the Byzantines, the average Egyptian had not shared in this prosperity. Tax rates were generally high, and Christians were subjected to periodic persecution by the Byzantines, who viewed the local Coptic faith and other sects in the area as heresies. Although the new rulers continued to obtain much of their revenue from taxing the local farming population, tax rates were generally lower than they had been under the corrupt Byzantine government, and conversion to Islam brought exemption from taxation. During the next generations, many Egyptians converted to the Muslim faith, but Islam did not move into the upper Nile valley until several hundred years later. As Islam spread southward, it was adopted by many lowland peoples, but it had less success in the mountains of Ethiopia, where Coptic Christianity continued to win adherents.

In the meantime, Arab rule was gradually being extended westward along the Mediterranean coast. When the Romans conquered Carthage in 146 B.C.E., they had called their new province Africa, thus introducing a name that would eventually be applied to the entire continent. After the fall of the Roman Empire, much of the area had reverted to the control of local Berber chieftains, but the Byzantines captured Carthage in the mid-sixth century C.E. In 690, the city was seized by the Arabs, who then began to extend their control over the entire area, which they called *al-Maghrib* ("the west").

At first, the local Berber peoples resisted their new conquerors. The Berbers were tough fighters, and for several generations, Arab rule was limited to the towns and lowland coastal areas. But Arab persistence eventually paid off, and by the early eighth century, the entire North African coast as far west as the Strait of Gibraltar was under Arab rule. The Arabs were now poised to cross the strait and expand into southern Europe and to push south beyond the fringes of the Sahara.

The Spread of Islam in Africa

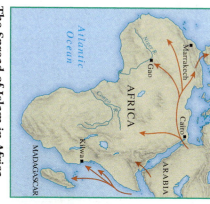

The Kingdom of Ethiopia: A Christian Island in a Muslim Sea

By the end of the sixth century C.E., the kingdom of Axum, long a dominant force in the trade network through the Red Sea, was in a state of decline. Both overexploitation of farmland and a shift in trade routes away from the Red Sea to the Arabian peninsula and Persian Gulf contributed to this decline. By the beginning of the ninth century, the capital had been moved farther into the mountainous interior, and Axum was gradually transformed from a maritime power into an isolated agricultural society.

The rise of Islam on the Arabian peninsula hastened this process, as the Arab world increasingly began to serve as the focus of the regional trade passing through the area. By the eighth century, a number of Muslim trading states had been established on the African coast of the Red Sea, a development that contributed to the transformation of Axum into a landlocked society with primarily agricultural interests. At first, relations between Christian Axum and its Muslim neighbors were relatively peaceful, as the larger and more powerful Axumite kingdom attempted with some success to compel the coastal Islamic states to accept a tributary relationship. Axum's role in the local commercial network temporarily revived, and the area became a prime source for ivory, gold, resins like frankincense and myrrh, and slaves. Slaves came primarily from the south, where Axum had been attempting to subjugate restive tribal peoples living in the Amharic plateau beyond its southern border (see the box on p. 229).

Beginning in the twelfth century, however, relations between Axum and its neighbors deteriorated as the Muslim states along the coast began to move inland to gain control over the growing trade in slaves and ivory. Axum responded with force and at first had some success in reasserting its hegemony over the area. But in the early fourteenth century, the Muslim state of Adal, located at the juncture of the Indian Ocean and the Red Sea, launched a new attack on the Christian kingdom.

Axum also underwent significant internal change during this period. The Zagwe dynasty, which seized control of the country in the mid-twelfth century, centralized the government and extended the Christian faith throughout the kingdom, now known as Ethiopia. Military commanders or civilian officials who had personal or kinship ties with the royal court established vast landed estates to maintain security and facilitate the collection of taxes from the local population. In the meantime, Christian missionaries established monasteries and churches to propagate the faith in outlying areas. Close relations were reestablished with leaders of the Coptic church in Egypt and with Christian officials in the Holy Land. This process was continued by the Solomonids, who succeeded the Zagwe dynasty in 1270. But by the early fifteenth century, the state had become more deeply involved in an expanding conflict with Muslim Adal to the east, a conflict that lasted for over a century and gradually took on the characteristics of a holy war.

East Africa: The Land of Zanj

The rise of Islam also had a lasting impact on the coast of East Africa, which the Greeks had called Azania and the Arabs called Zanj. During the seventh and eighth centuries, peoples from the Arabian peninsula and the Persian Gulf began to settle at ports along the coast and on the small islands offshore. Then, according to legend, in the middle of the tenth century, a Persian from the city of Shiraz sailed to the area with his six sons. As his small fleet stopped along the coast, each son disembarked on one of the coastal islands and founded a small community; these settlements eventually grew into important commercial centers such as Mombasa, Pemba, Zanzibar (literally, "the coast of Zanj"), and Kilwa.

The Swahili Coast

Although the legend underestimates the degree to which the area had already become a major participant in local commerce as well as the role of the local inhabitants in the process, it does reflect the importance of Arab and Persian immigrants in the formation of a string of trading ports stretching from Mogadishu (today the capital of Somalia) in the north to Kilwa (south of present-day Dar es Salaam) in the south. Kilwa became especially important because it was near the southern limit for a ship hoping to complete the round-trip journey in a single season. Goods such as ivory, gold, and rhinoceros horn were exported across the Indian Ocean to countries as far away as China, while imports included iron goods, glassware, Indian textiles, and Chinese porcelain. Merchants in these cities often amassed considerable profit, as evidenced by their lavish stone palaces, some of which still stand in the modern cities of Mombasa and Zanzibar. Though now in ruins, Kilwa was one of the most magnificent cities of its day. The fourteenth-century Arab traveler Ibn Battuta described it as "amongst the most beautiful of cities and most elegantly built. All of it is of wood, and the ceilings of its houses are of *al-dis* [reeds]."[2] One particularly impressive structure was the Husini Kubwa, a massive palace with vaulted roofs capped with domes and elaborate stone carvings, surrounding an inner courtyard. Ordinary townspeople and the residents in smaller towns did not live in such luxurious conditions, of course, but even so, affluent urban residents lived in spacious stone buildings, with indoor plumbing and consumer goods imported from as far away as China and southern Europe.

BEWARE THE TROGODYTES!

FAMILY & SOCIETY

In Africa, as elsewhere, relations between pastoral peoples and settled populations living in cities or in crowded river valleys were frequently marked by distrust and conflict. Such was certainly the case in the state of Kush, where residents living in the Nubian city of Meroë viewed the nomadic peoples in the surrounding hills and deserts with a mixture of curiosity and foreboding. The following excerpt was written by the second century B.C.E. Greek historian Agatharchides, as he described the so-called Trogodyte people living in the mountains east of the Nile River.

On the Erythraean Sea

Now, the Trogodytes are called "Nomads" by the Greeks and live a wandering life supported by their herds in groups ruled by tyrants. Together with their children they have their women in common except for the one belonging to the tyrant. Against a person who has sexual relations with her the chief levies as a fine a specified number of sheep.

This is their way of life. When it is winter in their country—this is at the time of the Etesian winds—and the god inundates their land with heavy rains, they draw their sustenance from blood and milk, which they mix together and stir in jars which have been slightly heated. When summer comes, however, they live in the marshlands, fighting among themselves over the pasture. They eat those of their animals that are old and sick after they have been slaughtered by butchers whom they call "Unclean."

For armament the tribe of Trogodytes called Megabari have circular shields made of raw ox-hide and clubs tipped with iron knobs; but the others have bows and spears.

They do not fight with each other, as the Greeks do, over land or some other pretext but over the pasturage as it sprouts up at various times. In their feuds, they first pelt each other with stones until some are wounded. Then for the remainder of the battle they resort to a contest of bows and arrows. In a short time many die as they shoot accurately because of their practice in this pursuit and their aiming at a target bare of defensive weapons. The older women, however, put an end to the battle by rushing in between them and meeting with respect. For it is their custom not to strike these women on any account so that immediately upon their appearance the men cease shooting.

They do not, he says, sleep as do other men. They possess a large number of animals which accompany them, and they ring cowbells from the horns of all the males in order that their sound might drive off wild beasts. At nightfall, they collect their herds into byres and cover these with hurdles made from palm branches. Their women and children mount up on one of these. The men, however, light fires in a circle and sing additional tales and thus ward off sleep, since in many situations discipline imposed by nature is able to conquer nature.

Q *Does the author of this passage appear to describe the customs of the Trogodytes in an impartial manner, or do you detect a subtle attitude of disapproval or condescension?*

Most of the coastal states were self-governing, although sometimes several towns were grouped together under a single dominant authority. Government revenue came primarily from taxes imposed on commerce. Some trade went on between these coastal city-states and the peoples of the interior, who provided gold and iron, ivory, and various agricultural goods and animal products in return for textiles, manufactured articles, and weapons (see the box on p. 231). Relations apparently varied, and the coastal merchants sometimes resorted to force to obtain goods from the inland peoples. A Portuguese visitor recounted that "the men [of Mombasa] are oft-times at war and but seldom at peace with those of the mainland, and they carry on trade with them, bringing thence great store of honey, wax, and ivory."[3]

By the twelfth and thirteenth centuries, a mixed African-Arabian culture, eventually known as Swahili (from the Arabic *sahel*, meaning "coast"), began to emerge throughout the seaboard area. Intermarriage between the immigrants and the local population was common, although a distinct Arab community, made up primarily of merchants, persisted in many areas. The members of the ruling class were often of mixed heritage but usually traced their genealogy to Arab or Persian ancestors. By this time, too, many members of the ruling class had converted to Islam. Middle Eastern urban architectural styles and other aspects of Arab culture were implanted within a society still predominantly African. Arabic words and phrases were combined with Bantu grammatical structures to form a mixed language, also known as Swahili; it is the national language of Kenya and Tanzania today.

The States of West Africa

During the eighth century, merchants from the Maghrib began to carry Muslim beliefs to the savanna areas south of the Sahara. At first, conversion took place on an individual basis and primarily among local merchants, rather than through official encouragement. The first rulers to convert to Islam were the royal family of Gao at the end of the tenth century. Five hundred years later, most of the population in the grasslands south of the Sahara had accepted Islam.

The expansion of Islam into West Africa had a major impact on the political system. By introducing Arabic as the first written language in the region and Muslim law codes and administrative practices from the Middle East, Islam provided local rulers with the tools to increase their authority and the efficiency of their governments. Moreover, as Islam gradually spread throughout the region, a common religion united previously diverse peoples into a more coherent community.

When Islam arrived in the grasslands south of the Sahara, the region was beginning to undergo significant political and social change. A number of major trading states were in the making, and they eventually transformed the Sahara into one of the leading avenues of world trade, crisscrossed by caravan routes leading to destinations as far away as the Atlantic Ocean, the Mediterranean, and the Red Sea (see Map 8.3).

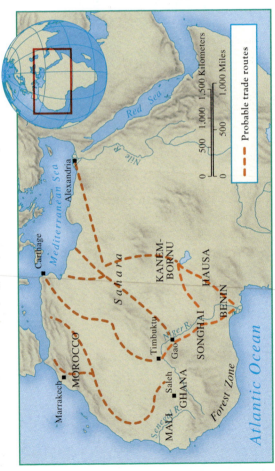

MAP 8.3 Trans-Saharan Trade Routes. Trade across the Sahara began during the first millennium B.C.E. With the arrival of the camel from the Middle East, trade expanded dramatically.

Q What were the major cities involved in the trade, as shown on this map?

View an animated version of this map or related maps at www.cengage.com/history/Duiker/World6e

Ghana The first of these great commercial states was Ghana, which emerged in the fifth century C.E. in the upper Niger valley, a grassland region between the Sahara and the tropical forests along the West African coast. (The modern state of Ghana, which takes its name from the trading society under discussion here, is located in the forest region to the south.) The majority of the people in the area were Iron Age farmers living in villages under the authority of a local chieftain. Gradually, these local communities were united to form the kingdom of Ghana.

Although the people of the region had traditionally lived from agriculture, a primary reason for Ghana's growing importance was gold. The heartland of the state was located near one of the richest gold-producing areas in all of Africa. Ghanaian merchants transported the gold to Morocco, whence it was distributed throughout the known world. As was the case with the gold trade in East Africa (see the box on p. 223), the exchange of goods became quite ritualized. As the ancient Greek historian Herodotus relates:

The Carthaginians also tell us that they trade with a race of men who live in a part of Libya beyond the Pillars of Heracles [the Strait of Gibraltar]. On reaching this country, they unload their goods, arrange them tidily along the beach, and then, returning to their boats, raise a smoke. Seeing the

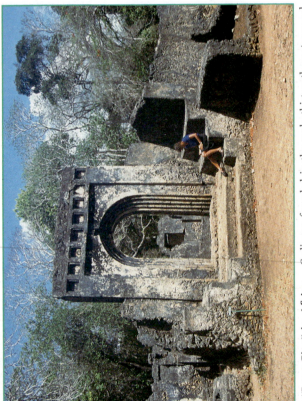

A "Lost City" in Africa. Gedi was founded in the early thirteenth century and abandoned three hundred years later. Its romantic ruins suggest the grandeur of the Swahili civilization that once flourished along the eastern coast of Africa. Located 60 miles north of Mombasa, in present-day Kenya, Gedi once contained several thousand residents but was eventually abandoned after it was attacked by nomadic peoples from the north. Today the ruins of the town, surrounded by a 9-foot wall, seem dwarfed by towering baobab trees populated only by chattering monkeys. Shown here is the entrance to the palace, which probably served as the residence of the chief official in the town. Neighboring houses, constructed of coral stone, contain sumptuous rooms, with separate women's quarters and enclosed lavatories with urinal channels and double-sink washing benches. Artifacts found at the site came from as far away as Venice and China.

© William J. Duiker

THE COAST OF ZANJ

From early times, the people living on the coast of East Africa took an active part in trade along the coast and across the Indian Ocean. The process began with the arrival of Arab traders early in the first millennium C.E. According to local legends, Arab merchants often married the daughters of the local chieftains and then received title to coastal territories as part of their wife's dowry. This description of the area was written by the Arab traveler al-Mas'udi, who visited the "land of Zanj" in 916.

Al-Mas'udi in East Africa

The land of Zanj produces wild leopard skins. The people wear them as clothes, or export them to Muslim countries. They are the largest leopard skins and the most beautiful for making saddles.... They also export tortoise shell for making combs, for which ivory is likewise used.... The Zanj are settled in that area, which stretches as far as Sofala, which is the furthest limit of the land and the end of the voyages made from Oman and Siraf on the sea of Zanj.... The Zanj use the ox as a beast of burden, for they have no horses, mules or camels in their land.... There are many wild elephants in this land but no tame ones. The Zanj do not use them for war or anything else, but only hunt and kill them for their ivory. It is from this country that come tusks weighing fifty pounds and more. They usually go to Oman, and from there are sent to China and India. This is the chief trade route....

The Zanj have an elegant language and men who preach in it. One of their holy men will often gather a crowd and exhort his hearers to please God in their lives and to be obedient to him. He explains the punishments that follow upon disobedience, and reminds them of their ancestors and kings of old. These people have no religious law; their kings rule by custom and by political expediency.

The Zanj eat bananas, which are as common among them as they are in India; but their staple food is millet and a plant called *kalari* which is pulled out of the earth like truffles. They also eat honey and meat. They have many islands where the coconut grows: its nuts are used as fruit by all the Zanj peoples. One of these islands, which is one or two days' sail from the coast, has a Muslim population and a royal family. This is the island of Kanbulu [thought to be modern Pemba].

Q *Why did Arab traders begin to settle along the coast of East Africa? What impact did the Arab presence have on the lives of the local population?*

---

smoke, the natives come down to the beach, place on the ground a certain quantity of gold in exchange for the goods, and go off again to a distance. The Carthaginians then come ashore and take a look at the gold; and if they think it represents a fair price for their wares, they collect it and go away; if, on the other hand, it seems too little, they go back aboard and wait, and the natives come and add to the gold until they are satisfied. There is perfect honesty on both sides; the Carthaginians never touch the gold until it equals in value what they have offered for sale, and the natives never touch the goods until the gold has been taken away.[4]

Later, Ghana became known to Arab-speaking peoples in North Africa as "the land of gold." Actually, the name was misleading, for the gold did not come from Ghana but from a neighboring people, who sold it to merchants from Ghana in much the same way as we saw with the gold trade in Axum earlier in this chapter.

Eventually, other exports from Ghana found their way to the bazaars of the Mediterranean coast and beyond—ivory, ostrich feathers, hides, leather goods, and ultimately slaves. The origins of the slave trade in the area probably go back to the first millennium B.C.E., when Berber tribesmen seized African villagers in the regions south of the Sahara and sold them for profit to buyers in Europe and the Middle East. In return, Ghana imported metal goods (especially weapons), textiles, horses, and salt. Much of the trade across the desert was still conducted by the nomadic Berbers, but Ghanaian merchants played an active role as intermediaries, trading tropical products such as bananas, kola nuts, and palm oil from the forest states of Guinea along the Atlantic coast to the south. By the eighth and ninth centuries, much of this trade was conducted by Muslim merchants, who purchased the goods from local traders (using iron and copper cash or cowrie shells from Southeast Asia as the primary means of exchange) and then sold them to Berbers, who carried them across the desert. The merchants who carried on this trade often became quite wealthy and lived in splendor in cities like Saleh, the capital of Ghana. So did the king, of course, who taxed the merchants as well as the farmers and the producers.

Like other West African monarchs, the king of Ghana ruled by divine right and was assisted by a hereditary aristocracy composed of the leading members of the prominent clans, who also served as district chiefs responsible for maintaining law and order and collecting taxes. The king was responsible for maintaining the security of his kingdom, serving as an intermediary with local deities, and functioning as the chief law officer to adjudicate disputes. The kings of Ghana did not convert to Islam themselves, although they welcomed Muslim merchants and apparently did not discourage their subjects from adopting the new faith (see the box on p. 234).

Mali The state of Ghana flourished for several hundred years, but by the twelfth century, weakened by ruinous wars with Berber tribesmen, it had begun to decline, and it

A Great Gate at Marrakech. The Moroccan city of Marrakech, founded in the ninth century C.E., was a major northern terminus of the trans-Saharan trade and one of the chief commercial centers in pre-modern Africa. Widely praised by such famous travelers as Ibn Battuta, the city was an architectural marvel in that all its major public buildings were constructed of red sandstone. Shown here is the Great Gate to the city, through which camel caravans passed en route to and from the vast desert. In the Berber language, Marrakech means "pass without making a noise," a reference to the need for caravan traders to be aware of the danger of thieves in the vicinity.

© William J. Duiker.

collapsed at the end of the century. In its place rose a number of new trading societies, including large territorial states like Mali and Songhai in the west, Kanem-Bornu in the east, and small commercial city-states like the Hausa states, located in what is today northern Nigeria (see Map 8.4).

The greatest of the states that emerged after the destruction of Ghana was Mali. Extending from the Atlantic coast inland as far as the trading cities of Timbuktu and Gao on the Niger River, Mali built its wealth and power on the gold trade. But the heartland of Mali was situated south of the Sahara in the savanna region, where sufficient moisture enabled farmers to grow such crops as sorghum, millet, and rice. The farmers lived in villages ruled by a local chieftain (called a *mansa*), who served as

both religious and administrative leader and was responsible for forwarding tax revenues from the village to higher levels of government.

The primary wealth of the country was accumulated in the cities. Here lived the merchants, who were primarily of local origin, although many were now practicing Muslims. Commercial activities were taxed but were apparently so lucrative that both the merchants and the kings prospered. One of the most powerful kings of Mali was Mansa Musa (r. 1312–1337), whose primary contribution to his people was probably not economic prosperity but the Muslim faith. Mansa Musa strongly encouraged the building of mosques and the study of the Qur'an in his kingdom and imported scholars and books to introduce his subjects to the message of Allah. One visitor from

Mansa Musa. Mansa Musa, king of the West African state of Mali, was one of the richest and most powerful rulers of his day. During a famous pilgrimage to Mecca, he arrived in Cairo with a hundred camels laden with gold and gave away so much gold that its value depreciated there for several years. To promote the Islamic faith in his country, he bought homes in Cairo and Mecca to house pilgrims en route to the holy shrine, and he brought back to Mali a renowned Arab architect to build mosques in the trading centers of Gao and Timbuktu. His fame spread to Europe as well, evidenced by this Spanish map of 1375, which depicts Mansa Musa seated on his throne in Mali, holding an impressive gold nugget.

© British Library/HIP/Art Resource, NY

The Art Archive/Gianni Dagli Orti

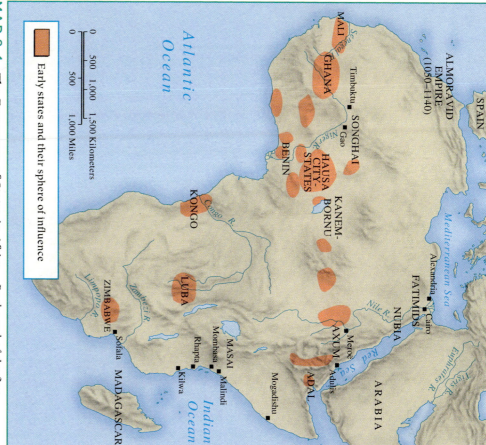

MAP 8.4   The Emergence of States in Africa. By the end of the first millennium C.E., organized states had begun to appear in various parts of Africa.
Q Why did organized states appear at these particular spots and not in other areas of Africa? View an animated version of this map or related maps at **www.cengage.com/history/Duiker/World6e**

□ Early states and their sphere of influence

Europe, writing in the late fifteenth century, reported:

> The rich king of Timbuktu has many plates and scepters of gold, some whereof weigh 1,300 pounds; and he keeps a magnificent and well-furnished court. When he travels anywhere, he rides upon a camel which is led by some of his noblemen; and so he does likewise when he goes to warfare, and all his soldiers ride upon horses.... They often have skirmishes with those that refuse to pay tribute and, so many as they may take, they sell unto the merchants of Timbuktu.... Here are a great store of doctors, judges, priests and other learned men, that are bountifully maintained at the king's cost and charges. And hither are brought divers manuscripts of written books out of Barbary [North Africa] which are sold for more money than any other merchandise. The coin of Timbuktu is of gold without any stamp or superscription: but in matters of small value they use certain shells [cowrie shells] brought hither out of the kingdom of Persia.[5]

The city of Timbuktu ("well of Bouctu," a Tuareg woman who lived in the area) was founded in 1100 C.E. as a seasonal camp for caravan traders on the Niger River. Under Mansa Musa and his successors, the city gradually emerged

The City of Timbuktu. The city of Timbuktu sat astride one of the major trade routes that passed through the Sahara between the kingdoms of West Africa and the Mediterranean Sea. Caravans transported food and various manufactured articles southward in exchange for salt, gold, copper, skins, agricultural goods, and slaves. Salt was at such a premium in Timbuktu that a young Moroccan wrote in 1513 that one camel's load brought 500 miles by caravan sold for 80 gold ducats, while a horse sold for only 40 ducats. Timbuktu became a prosperous city as well as a great center of Islamic scholarship. By 1550, it had three universities connected to its principal mosques and 180 Qur'anic schools.

ROYALTY AND RELIGION IN GHANA

RELIGION & PHILOSOPHY

After its first appearance in West Africa in the decades following the death of Muhammad, Islam competed with native African religions for followers. Eventually, several local rulers converted to the Muslim faith. This passage by the Arab geographer al-Bakri reflects religious tolerance in the state of Ghana during the eleventh century under a non-Muslim ruler with many Muslim subjects.

Al-Bakri's Description of Royalty in Ghana

The king's residence comprises a palace and conical huts, the whole surrounded by a fence like a wall. Around the royal town are huts and groves of thorn trees where live the magicians who control their religious rites. These groves, where they keep their idols and bury their kings, are protected by guards who permit no one to enter or find out what goes on in them.

None of those who belong to the imperial religion may wear tailored garments except the king himself and the heir-presumptive, his sister's son. The rest of the people wear wrappers of cotton, silk or brocade according to their means. Most of the men shave their beards and the women their heads. The king adorns himself with female

ornaments around the neck and arms. On his head he wears gold-embroidered caps covered with turbans of finest cotton. He gives audience to the people for the redressing of grievances in a hut around which are placed 10 horses covered in golden cloth. Behind him stand 10 slaves carrying shields and swords mounted with gold. On his right are the sons of vassal kings, their heads plaited with gold and wearing costly garments. On the ground around him are seated his ministers, whilst the governor of the city sits before him. On guard at the door are dogs of fine pedigree, wearing collars adorned with gold and silver. The royal audience is announced by the beating of a drum, called *daba*, made out of a long piece of hollowed-out wood. When the people have gathered, his coreligionists draw near upon their knees sprinkling dust upon their heads as a sign of respect, whilst the Muslims clap hands as their form of greeting.

Q *Why might an African ruler find it advantageous to adopt the Muslim faith? What kinds of changes would the adoption of Islam entail for the peoples living in West Africa?*

as a major intellectual and cultural center in West Africa and the site of schools of law, literature, and the sciences.

States and Stateless Societies in Central and Southern Africa

Q Focus Questions: What role did migration play in the evolution of early African societies? How did the impact of these migrations compare with similar population movements elsewhere?

In the southern half of the African continent, from the great basin of the Congo River to the Cape of Good Hope, states formed somewhat more slowly than in the north. Until the eleventh century C.E., most of the peoples in this region lived in what are sometimes called **stateless societies,** characterized by autonomous villages organized by clans and ruled by a local chieftain or clan head. Beginning in the eleventh century, in some parts of southern Africa, these independent villages gradually began to consolidate. Out of these groupings came the first states.

The Congo River Valley

One area where this process occurred was the Congo River valley, where the combination of fertile land and nearby deposits of copper and iron enabled the inhabitants to enjoy an agricultural surplus and engage in regional commerce. Two new states in particular underwent this transition.

Sometime during the fourteenth century, the kingdom of Luba was founded in the center of the continent, in a rich agricultural and fishing area near the shores of Lake Kisale. Luba had a relatively centralized government, in which the king appointed provincial governors, who were responsible for collecting tribute from the village chiefs. At about the same time, the kingdom of Kongo was formed just south of the mouth of the Congo River on the Atlantic coast.

These new states were primarily agricultural, although both had a thriving manufacturing sector and took an active part in the growing exchange of goods throughout the region. As time passed, both began to expand southward to absorb the mixed farming and pastoral peoples in the area of modern Angola. In the drier grassland area to the south, other small communities continued to support themselves by herding, hunting, or food gathering. A Portuguese sailor who encountered them in the late sixteenth century reported:

These people are herdsmen and cultivators.... Their main crop is millet, which they grind between two stones or in wooden mortars to make flour.... Their wealth consists mainly in their huge number of dehorned cows.... They live together in small villages, in houses made of reed mats, which do not keep out the rain.[6]

Zimbabwe

Farther to the east, the situation was somewhat different. In the grassland regions immediately to the south of the Zambezi River, a mixed economy involving farming, cattle herding, and commercial pursuits had begun to develop during the early centuries of the first millennium C.E. Characteristically, villages in this area were constructed inside walled enclosures to protect the animals at night. The most famous of these communities was Zimbabwe, located on the plateau of the same name between the Zambezi and Limpopo Rivers. From the twelfth century to the middle of the fifteenth, Zimbabwe was the most powerful and most prosperous state in the region and played a major role in the gold trade with the Swahili trading communities on the eastern coast.

The ruins of Zimbabwe's capital, known as Great Zimbabwe (the term *Zimbabwe* means "sacred house" in the Bantu language), provide a vivid illustration of the kingdom's power and influence. Strategically situated between substantial gold reserves to the west and a small river leading to the coast, Great Zimbabwe was well placed to benefit from the expansion of trade between the coast and the interior. The town sits on a hill overlooking the river and is surrounded by stone walls, which enclosed an area large enough to hold over ten thousand residents. Like the Inka in South America (see Chapter 6), the local people stacked stone blocks without mortar to build their walls. The houses of the wealthy were built of cement on stone foundations, while those of the common people were of dried mud with thatched roofs. In the valley below is the royal palace, surrounded by a stone wall 30 feet high (see the illustration on the opening page of this chapter). Artifacts found at the site include household implements and ornaments made of gold and copper, as well as jewelry and porcelain imported from China.

Most of the royal wealth probably came from two sources: the ownership of cattle and the king's ability to levy heavy taxes on the gold that passed through the kingdom en route to the coast. By the middle of the fifteenth century, however, the city was apparently abandoned, possibly because of environmental damage caused by overgrazing. With the decline of Zimbabwe, the focus of economic power began to shift northward to the valley of the Zambezi River.

Southern Africa

South of the East African plateau and the Congo basin is a vast land of hills, grasslands, and arid desert stretching almost to the Cape of Good Hope at the tip of the continent. As Bantu-speaking farmers spread southward during the final centuries of the first millennium B.C.E., they began to encounter Stone Age peoples in the area who still lived primarily by hunting and foraging.

Available evidence suggests that early relations between these two peoples were relatively harmonious. Intermarriage between members of the two groups was apparently not unusual, and many of the hunter-gatherers were gradually absorbed into what became a dominantly Bantu-speaking pastoral and agricultural society that spread throughout much of southern Africa during the first millennium C.E.

The Khoi and the San Two such peoples were the Khoi and the San. The two were related because of their language, known as Khoisan, distinguished by the use of "clicking" sounds. The Khoi were herders, while the San were hunter-gatherers who lived in small family communities of twenty to twenty-five members throughout southern Africa from Namibia in the west to the Drakensberg Mountains near the southeastern coast. Scholars have learned about the early life of the San by interviewing their modern descendants and by studying rock paintings found in caves throughout the area. These multicolored paintings, which predate the coming of the Europeans, were drawn with a brush made of small feathers fastened to a reed. They depict various aspects of the San's lifestyle, including their hunting techniques and religious rituals.

African Society

Q Focus Questions: What role did lineage groups, women, and slavery play in African societies? In what ways did African societies in various parts of the continent differ? What accounted for these differences?

As noted earlier, generalizing about social organization, cultural development, and daily life in traditional Africa is difficult because of the extreme diversity of the continent and its inhabitants. One-quarter of all the languages in the world are spoken in Africa, and five of the major language families are located there. Ethnic divisions are equally pronounced. Because many of these languages did not have a system of writing until fairly recently, historians must rely on accounts of the occasional visitor, such as al-Mas'udi and Ibn Battuta. Such travelers, however, tended to come into contact mostly with the wealthy and the powerful, leaving us to speculate about what life was like for ordinary Africans during this early period.

Urban Life

African towns often began as fortified walled villages and gradually evolved into larger communities serving several purposes. Here, of course, were the center of government and the teeming markets filled with goods from distant regions. Here also were artisans skilled in metalworking or woodworking, pottery making, and other crafts. Unlike the rural areas, where a village was usually composed of a single lineage group or clan, the towns drew their residents from several clans, although individual clans usually lived in their own compounds and were governed by their own clan heads.

In the states of West Africa, the focal point of the major towns was the royal precinct. The relationship between the ruler and the merchant class differed from the situation in most Asian societies, where the royal family and the aristocracy were largely isolated from the remainder of the population. In Africa, the chasm between the king and the common people was not so great. Often the ruler would hold an audience to allow people to voice their complaints or to welcome visitors from foreign countries. In the city-states of the East African coast as well, the ruler was frequently forced to share political power with a class of wealthy merchants and often, as in the case of the town of Kilwa, "did not possess more power than the city itself."[7]

This is not to say that the king was not elevated above all others in status. In wealthier states, the walls of the audience chamber would be covered with sheets of beaten silver and gold, and the king would be surrounded by hundreds of armed soldiers and some of his trusted advisers. Nevertheless, the symbiotic relationship between the ruler and merchant class served to reduce the gap between the king and his subjects. The relationship was mutually beneficial, since the merchants received honors and favors from the palace while the king's coffers were filled with taxes paid by the merchants. Certainly, it was to the benefit of the king to maintain law and order in his domain so that the merchants could ply their trade. As Ibn Battuta observed, among the good qualities of the peoples of West Africa was the prevalence of peace in the region. "The traveler is not afraid in it," he remarked, "nor is he who lives there in fear of the thief or of the robber by violence."[8]

Village Life

The vast majority of Africans lived in small rural villages. Their identities were established by their membership in

a nuclear family and a lineage group. At the basic level was the nuclear family of parents and preadult children; sometimes it included an elderly grandparent and other family dependents as well. They lived in small, round huts constructed of packed mud and topped with a conical thatch roof. In most African societies, these nuclear family units would be combined into larger kinship communities known as households or lineage groups.

The lineage group was similar in many respects to the clan in China or the caste system in India in that it was normally based on kinship ties, although sometimes outsiders such as friends or other dependents may have been admitted to membership. Throughout the precolonial era, lineages served, in the words of one historian, as the "basic building blocks" of African society. The authority of the leading members of the lineage group was substantial. As in China, the elders had considerable power over the economic functions of the other people in the group, which provided mutual support for all members.

A village would usually be composed of a single lineage group, although some communities may have consisted of several unrelated families. At the head of the village was the familiar "big man," who was often assisted by a council of representatives of the various households in the community. Often the "big man" was believed to possess supernatural powers, and as the village grew in size and power, he might eventually be transformed into a local chieftain or monarch.

The Role of Women

Although generalizations are risky, we can say that women were usually subordinate to men in Africa, as in most early societies. In some cases, they were valued for the work they could do or for their role in increasing the size of the lineage group. Polygyny was not uncommon, particularly in Muslim societies. Women often worked in the fields while the men of the village tended the cattle or went on hunting expeditions. In some communities, the women specialized in commercial activities. In one area in southern Africa, young girls were sent into the mines to extract gold because of their smaller physiques.

But there were some key differences between the role of women in Africa and elsewhere. In many African societies, lineage was **matrilinear** rather than **patrilinear.** In the words of Ibn Battuta during his travels in West Africa, "A man does not pass on inheritance except to the sons of his sister to the exclusion of his own sons."[9] He said he had never encountered this custom before except among the unbelievers of the Malabar coast in India. Women were often permitted

The Tellem Tombs. Sometime in the eleventh century C.E., the Bantu-speaking Tellem peoples moved into an area just south of the Niger River called the Bandiagara Escarpment, where they built mud dwellings and burial tombs into the side of a vast cliff overlooking a verdant valley. To support themselves, the Tellem planted dry crops like millet and sorghum in the savanna plateau above the cliff face. They were eventually supplanted in the area by the Dogon peoples, who continue to use their predecessors' structures for housing and granaries today. The site is highly reminiscent of Mesa Verde, the Anasazi settlement mentioned in Chapter 6.

© Ruth Petzold

to inherit property, and the husband was often expected to move into his wife's house.

Relations between the sexes were also sometimes more relaxed than in China or India, with none of the taboos characteristic of those societies. Again, in the words of Ibn Battuta, himself a Muslim:

> With regard to their women, they are not modest in the presence of men, they do not veil themselves in spite of their perseverance in the prayers.... The women there have friends and companions amongst men outside the prohibited degrees of marriage [that is, other than brothers, fathers, or other closely related males]. Likewise for the men, there are companions from amongst women outside the prohibited degrees. One of them would enter his house to find his wife with her companion and would not disapprove of that conduct.[10]

When Ibn Battuta asked an African acquaintance about these customs, the latter responded, "Women's companionship with men in our country is honorable and takes place in a good way: there is no suspicion about it. They are not like the women in your country," Ibn Battuta noted his astonishment at such a "thoughtless" answer and did not accept further invitations to visit his friend's house.[11]

Such informal attitudes toward the relationship between the sexes were not found everywhere in Africa and were probably curtailed as many Africans converted to Islam (see the box above). But it is a testimony to the tenacity of traditional customs that the relatively puritanical views about the role of women in society brought by Muslims from the Middle East made little impression even among Muslim families in West Africa.

Slavery

African slavery is often associated with the period after 1500. Indeed, the slave trade did reach enormous proportions in the seventeenth and eighteenth centuries, when European slave ships transported millions of unfortunate victims abroad to Europe or the Americas (see Chapter 14).

However, slavery did not originate with the coming of the Europeans. It had been practiced in Africa since ancient times and probably originated with prisoners of war who were forced into perpetual servitude. Slavery was common in ancient Egypt and became especially prevalent during the New Kingdom, when slaving expeditions brought back thousands of captives from the upper Nile to be used in labor gangs, for tribute, and even as human sacrifices.

Slavery persisted during the early period of state building, well more than a thousand years into the Common Era. Berber tribes may have regularly raided agricultural communities south of the Sahara for captives who were transported northward and eventually sold throughout the Mediterranean. Some were enrolled as soldiers, while others, often women, were put to work as domestic servants in the homes of the well-to-do. The use of captives for forced labor or for sale was apparently also common in African societies farther to the south and along the eastern coast.

FAMILY & SOCIETY

WOMEN AND ISLAM IN NORTH AFRICA

In Muslim societies in North Africa, as elsewhere, women were required to cover their bodies to avoid tempting men, but Islam's puritanical insistence on the separation of the sexes contrasted with the relatively informal relationships that prevailed in many African societies. In this excerpt from *The History and Description of Africa*, Leo Africanus describes the customs along the Mediterranean coast of Africa. A resident of Spain of Muslim parentage who was captured by Christian corsairs in 1518 and later served under Pope Leo X, Leo Africanus undertook many visits to Africa.

Leo Africanus, *The History and Description of Africa*

Their women (according to the guise of that country) go very gorgeously attired: they wear linen gowns dyed black, with exceeding wide sleeves, over which sometimes they cast a mantle of the same color or of blue, the corners of which mantle are very [attractively] fastened about their shoulders with a fine silver clasp. Likewise they have rings hanging at their ears, which for the most part are made of silver; they wear many rings also upon their fingers. Moreover they usually wear about their thighs and ankles certain scarfs and rings, after the fashion of the Africans. They cover their faces with certain masks having only two holes for the eyes to peep out at. If any man have a chance to meet with them, they presently hide their faces, passing by him with silence, except it be some of their allies or kinsfolks; for unto them they always [uncover] their faces, neither is there any use of the said mask so long as they be in presence. These Arabians when they travel any journey (as they oftentimes do) they set their women upon certain saddles made handsomely of wicker for the same purpose, and fastened to their camel backs, neither be they anything too wide, but fit only for a woman to sit in. When they go to the wars each man carries his wife with him, to the end that she may cheer up her good man, and give him encouragement. Their damsels which are unmarried do usually paint their faces, breasts, arms, hands, and fingers with a kind of counterfeit color: which is accounted a most decent custom among them.

Q *Which of the practices described here are dictated by the social regulations of Islam? Does the author approve of the behavior of African women as described in this passage?*

Life was difficult for the average slave. The least fortunate were probably those who worked on plantations owned by the royal family or other wealthy landowners. Those pressed into service as soldiers were sometimes more fortunate, since in Muslim societies in the Middle East, they might at some point win their freedom. Many slaves were employed in the royal household or as domestic servants in private homes. In general, these slaves probably had the most tolerable existence. Although they were not ordinarily permitted to purchase their freedom, their living conditions were often decent and sometimes practically indistinguishable from those of the free individuals in the household. In some societies in North Africa, slaves reportedly made up as much as 75 percent of the entire population. Elsewhere, the percentage was much lower, in some cases less than 10 percent.

African Culture

Q **Focus Question:** What are some of the chief characteristics of African sculpture and carvings, music, and architecture, and what purpose did these forms of creative expression serve in African society?

In early Africa, as in much of the rest of the world at the time, creative expression, whether in the form of painting, literature, or music, was above all a means of serving religion and the social order. Though to the uninitiated a wooden mask or the bronze and iron statuary of southern Nigeria is simply a work of art, to the artist it was often a means of

expressing religious convictions and communal concerns. Indeed, some African historians reject the use of the term *art* to describe such artifacts because they were produced for spiritual or moral rather than aesthetic purposes.

Painting and Sculpture

The oldest extant art forms in Africa are rock paintings. The most famous examples are in the Tassili Mountains in the central Sahara, where the earliest paintings may date back as far as 5000 B.C.E., though the majority are a millennium or so younger. Some of the later paintings depict the two-horse chariots used to transport goods prior to the introduction of the camel. Rock paintings are also found elsewhere in the continent, including the Nile valley and eastern and southern Africa. Those of the San peoples of southern Africa are especially interesting for their illustrations of ritual ceremonies in which village shamans induce rain, propitiate the spirits, or cure illnesses.

More familiar, perhaps, are African wood carvings and sculpture. The remarkable statues, masks, and headdresses were carved from living trees, to the spirit of which the artists had made a sacrifice. These masks and headdresses were worn by costumed singers and dancers in performances to the various spirits, revealing the identification and intimacy of the African with the natural world. In Mali, for example, the 3-foot-tall Ci Wara headdresses, one female, the other male, expressed meaning in performances that celebrated the mythical hero who had introduced agriculture.

In the thirteenth and fourteenth centuries C.E., metal workers at Ife in what is now southern Nigeria produced handsome bronze and iron statues using the lost-wax method, in which melted wax in a mold is replaced by molten metal. The Ife sculptures may in turn have influenced artists in Benin, in West Africa, who produced equally impressive works in bronze during the same period. The Benin sculptures include bronze heads, relief plaques depicting life at court, ornaments, and figures of various animals.

Westerners once regarded African wood carvings and metal sculpture as a form of "primitive art," but the label is not appropriate. The metal sculpture of Benin, for example, is highly sophisticated, and some of the best works are considered masterpieces. Such artistic works were often created by artisans in the employ of the royal court.

African Metalwork. The rulers of emerging West African states frequently commissioned royal artifacts to adorn their palaces and promote their temporal grandeur. Elaborate stools, weaponry, shields, and sculpted heads of members of the royal family served to commemorate their reign and preserve their memory for later generations. This regal thirteenth-century brass head attests to the technical excellence and sophistication of Ife metal artisans. The small holes along the scalp and the mouth permitted either hair, a veil, or a crown to be attached to the head, which itself was often attached to a wooden mannequin dressed in elaborate robes for display during memorial services.

Music

Like sculpture and wood carving, African music and dance often served a religious function. With their characteristic heavy rhythmic beat, dances were a means of communicating with the spirits, and the frenzied movements that are often identified with African dance were intended to represent the spirits acting through humans.

African music during the traditional period varied from one society to another. A wide variety of instruments were used, including drums and other percussion instruments, xylophones, bells, horns and flutes, and stringed instruments like the fiddle, harp, and zither. Still, the music throughout the continent had sufficient common characteristics to justify a few generalizations. In the first place, a strong rhythmic pattern was an important feature of most African music, although the desired effect was achieved through a wide variety of means, including gourds, pots, bells, sticks beaten together, and hand clapping as well as drums.

Another important feature of African music was the integration of voice and instrument into a total musical experience. Musical instruments and the human voice were often woven together to tell a story, and instruments, such as the famous "talking drum," were often used to represent the voice. Choral music and individual voices were frequently used in a pattern of repetition and variation, sometimes known as "call and response." Through this technique, the audience participated in the music by uttering a single phrase over and over as a choral response to the changing call sung by the soloist. This tradition was carried by slaves to the Americas and survives to this day in the gospel music sung in many African American congregations. Sometimes instrumental music achieved a similar result.

Much music was produced in the context of social rituals, such as weddings and funerals, religious ceremonies, and official inaugurations. It could also serve an educational purpose by passing on to the young people information about the history and social traditions of the community. In the absence of written languages in sub-Saharan Africa (except for the Arabic script, used in Muslim societies in East and West Africa), music served as the primary means of transmitting folk legends and religious traditions from generation to generation. Storytelling, which was usually undertaken by a priestly class or a specialized class of storytellers, served a similar function.

Architecture

No aspect of African artistic creativity is more varied than architecture. From the pyramids along the Nile to the ruins of Great Zimbabwe south of the Zambezi River, from the Moorish palaces at Zanzibar to the turreted mud mosques of West Africa, African architecture shows a striking diversity of approach and technique that is unmatched in other areas of creative endeavor.

The earliest surviving architectural form found in Africa is the pyramid. The Kushite kingdom at Meroë apparently adopted the pyramidal form from Egypt during the last centuries of the first millennium B.C.E. Although used for the same purpose as their earlier counterparts at Giza, the pyramids at Meroë were distinctive in style; they were much smaller and were topped with a flat platform rather than rising to a point. Remains of temples with massive carved pillars at Meroë also reflect Egyptian influence.

Farther to the south, the kingdom of Axum was developing its own architectural traditions. Most distinctive were the carved stone pillars, known as stelae (see the comparative illustration on p. 240), that were used to mark the tombs of dead kings. Some stood as high as 100 feet. The advent of Christianity eventually had an impact on Axumite architecture. During the Zagwe dynasty, churches carved out of solid rock were constructed throughout the country. The earliest may have been built in the eighth century C.E. Stylistically, they combined indigenous techniques inherited from the pre-Christian period with elements borrowed from Christian churches in the Holy Land (an illustration of such a church appears on p. 261).

In West Africa, buildings constructed in stone were apparently a rarity until the emergence of states during the first millennium C.E. At that time, the royal palace, as well as other buildings of civic importance, were often built of stone or cement, while the houses of the majority of the population continued to be constructed of dried mud. On his visit to the state of Guinea on the West African coast, the sixteenth-century traveler Leo Africanus noted that the houses of the ruler and other elites were built of chalk with roofs of straw. Even then, however, well into the state-building period, mosques were often built of mud.

Along the east coast, the architecture of the elite tended to reflect Middle Eastern styles. In the coastal towns and islands from Mogadishu to Kilwa, the houses of the wealthy were built of stone and reflected Moorish (Spanish Muslim) influence. As elsewhere, the common people lived in huts of mud, thatch, or palm leaves (see the box on p. 241). Mosques were built of stone.

The most famous stone buildings in sub-Saharan Africa are those at Great Zimbabwe. Constructed without mortar, the outer wall and public buildings at Great Zimbabwe are an impressive monument to the architectural creativity of the peoples of the region.

Literature

Literature in the sense of written works did not exist in sub-Saharan Africa during the early traditional period, except in regions where Islam had brought the Arabic script from the Middle East. But African societies compensated for the absence of a written language with a rich tradition of oral lore. The **bard**, a professional storyteller, was an ancient African institution by which

© Werner Forman/Art Resource, NY

© William J. Duiker

© Bortomeo/Art Resource, NY

COMPARATIVE ILLUSTRATION

The Stele. A stele is a stone slab or pillar, usually decorated or inscribed and placed upright. Stelae were often used to commemorate the accomplishments of a ruler or significant figure. Shown at the left is the tallest of the Axum stelae still standing, in present-day Ethiopia. The stone stelae in Axum in the fourth century B.C.E. marked the location of royal tombs with inscriptions commemorating the glories of the kings. An earlier famous stele, seen in the center, is the obelisk at Luxor in southern Egypt. A similar kind of stone pillar, shown at the right, was erected in India during the reign of Ashoka in the third century B.C.E. (see Chapter 2) to commemorate events in the life of the Buddha. Archaeologists have also found stelae in ancient China, Greece, and Mexico.

history was transmitted orally from generation to generation. In many West African societies, bards were highly esteemed and served as counselors to kings as well as protectors of local tradition. Bards were revered for their oratory and singing skills, phenomenal memory, and astute interpretation of history. As one African scholar wrote, the death of a bard was equivalent to the burning of a library.

Bards served several necessary functions in society. They were chroniclers of history, preservers of social customs and proper conduct, and entertainers who possessed a monopoly over the playing of several musical instruments, which accompanied their narratives. Because of their unique position above normal society, bards often played the role of mediator between hostile families or

clans in a community. They were also credited with possessing occult powers and could read divinations and give blessings and curses. Traditionally, bards also served as advisers to the king, sometimes inciting him to action (such as going to battle) through the passion of their poetry. When captured by the enemy, bards were often treated with respect and released or compelled to serve the victor with their art.

One of the most famous West African poems is *The Epic of Son-Jara.* Passed down orally by bards for more than seven hundred years, it relates the heroic exploits of Son-Jara (also known as Sunjata or Sundiata), the founder of Mali's empire and its ruler from 1230 to 1255. Although Mansa Musa is famous throughout the world because of his flamboyant pilgrimage to Mecca in the fourteenth

A CHINESE VIEW OF AFRICA

FAMILY & SOCIETY

This passage from Chau Ju-kua's thirteenth-century treatise on geography describes various aspects of life along the eastern coast of Africa in what is now Somalia, including the urban architecture. The author was an inspector of foreign trade in the city of Quanzhou (sometimes called Zayton) on the southern coast of China. His account was compiled from reports of seafarers. Note the varied uses that the local people make of a whale carcass.

Chau Ju-kua on East Africa

The inhabitants of the Chung-li country [the Somali coast] go bareheaded and barefooted; they wrap themselves in cotton stuffs, but they dare not wear jackets, for the wearing of jackets and turbans is a privilege reserved to the ministers and the king's courtiers. The king lives in a brick house covered with glazed tiles, but the people live in huts made of palm leaves and covered with grass-thatched roofs. Their daily food consists of baked flour cakes, sheep's and camel's milk. There are great numbers of cattle, sheep, and camels. . . .

There are many sorcerers among them who are able to change themselves into birds, beasts, or aquatic animals, and by these means keep the ignorant people in a state of terror. If some of them in trading with some foreign ship have a quarrel, the sorcerers pronounce a charm over the ship so that it can neither go forward nor backward, and they only release the ship when it has settled the dispute. The government has formally forbidden this practice.

When one of the inhabitants dies, and they are about to bury him in his coffin, his kinsfolk from near and far come to condole. Each person, flourishing a sword in his hand, goes in and asks the mourners the cause of the person's death. If he was killed by the hand of man, each one says, we will revenge him on the murderer with these swords. Should the mourners reply that he was not killed by any one, but that he came to his end by the will of Heaven, they throw away their swords and break into violent wailing.

Every year there are driven on the coast a great many dead fish measuring two hundred feet in length and twenty feet through the body. The people do not eat the flesh of these fish, but they cut out their brains, marrow, and eyes, from which they get oil. They mix this oil with lime to caulk their boats, and use it also in lamps. The poor people use the ribs of these fish to make rafters, the backbones for door leaves, and they cut off vertebrae to make mortars with.

Q *How does this passage compare with the earlier document by the Arab traveler al-Mas'udi? What does it offer in terms of information about housing and consumption habits?*

© Jenny Pate/Getty Images

The Mosque at Jenne, Mali. With the opening of the gold fields south of Mali, in present-day Ghana, Jenne became an important trading center for gold. Shown here is its distinctive fourteenth-century mosque made of unbaked clay without reinforcements. The projecting timbers offer easy access for repairing the mud exterior, as was regularly required.

A WEST AFRICAN ORAL TRADITION

ARTS & IDEAS

Like other great epics of world literature, the West African *Epic of Son-Jara* describes the ordeals of a male protagonist as he hurdles superhuman obstacles while fulfilling his heroic destiny. It is interesting, however, to observe the role played by women in the epic hero's calamitous journey. Although he is often opposed by evil witches and temptresses, he can also be assisted in the foiling of his foes by the courageous acts of a woman. Penelope in the *Odyssey* outwits her enemies, as does Sita in the Ramayana and Draupadi in the Mahabharata.

In this pivotal passage, Son-Jara's sister, Sugulun Kulunkan, offers to seduce his enemy Sumamuru in order to obtain the Manden secret, or magic spell, needed to control the kingdom of Mali. Sumamuru divulges his all-powerful secret and is rebuked by his mother; both son and mother then disown each other with the trenchant symbols of the slashed breast and cut cloth. After each line of verse recited by the bard, an assistant would respond with the endorsement "true." This practice is perhaps the distant ancestor of today's African American custom, called "call and response," of following each line of religious oratory with "Amen."

The Epic of Son-Jara

Son-Jara's flesh-and-blood sister, Sugulun Kulunkan,
She said, "O Magan Son-Jara,
"One person cannot fight this war.
"Let me go seek Sumamuru.
"Were I then to reach him,
"To you I will deliver him,
"So that the folk of the Manden be yours,
"And all the Mandenland you shield."
Sugulun Kulunkan arose,
And went up to the gates of Sumamuru's fortress:
…
"Come open the gates, Susu Mountain Sumamuru!
"Come make me your bed companion!"
Sumamuru came to the gates:

"What manner of person are you?"
"It is I, Sugulun Kulunkan!"
"Well, now, Sugulun Kulunkan,
"If you have come to trap me,
"To turn me over to some person,
"Know that none can ever vanquish me.
"I have found the Manden secret,
"And made the Manden sacrifice.
"And in five score millet stalks placed it.
"And buried them here in the earth.
"'Tis I who found the Manden secret,
"And made the Manden sacrifice.
"And in a red piebald bull did place it.
"And buried it here in the earth.
"Know that none can vanquish me.
"'Tis I who found the Manden secret
"And made a sacrifice to it.
"And in a pure white cock did place it.
"Were you to kill it,
"And uproot some barren groundnut plants,
"And strip them of their leaves,
"And spread them round the fortress,
"And uproot more barren peanut plants,
"And fling them into the fortress.
"Only then can I be vanquished."
His mother sprang forward at that:
"Heh! Susu Mountain Sumamuru!
"Never tell all to a woman,
"To a one-night woman!
"The woman is not safe, Sumamuru."
Sumamuru sprang towards his mother,
And came and seized his mother,
And slashed off her breast with a knife, magasi!
She went and got the old menstrual cloth.
"Ah! Sumamuru!" she swore.
"If your birth was ever a fact,
"I have cut your old menstrual cloth!"

Q What do you think the purpose of the call and response is in such epics? What effect does the technique have on the audience?

century, Son-Jara is more celebrated in West Africa because of the dynamic and unbroken oral traditions of the West African peoples (see the box above).

Like the bards, women were appreciated for their storytelling talents, as well as for their role as purveyors of the moral values and religious beliefs of African societies. In societies that lacked a written tradition, women represented the glue that held the community together. Through the recitation of fables, proverbs, poems, and songs, mothers conditioned the communal bonding and moral fiber of succeeding generations in a way that was rarely encountered in the patriarchal societies of Europe, Asia, and the Middle East. Such activities were not only vital aspects of education in traditional Africa but also offered a welcome respite from the drudgery of everyday life and a spark to develop the imagination and artistic awareness of the young. Renowned for its many proverbs, Africa also offers the following: "A good story is like a garden carried in the pocket."

TIMELINE

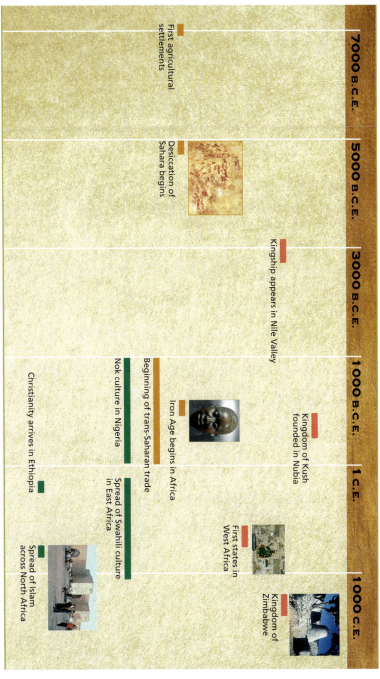

7000 B.C.E.	5000 B.C.E.	3000 B.C.E.	1000 B.C.E.	1 C.E.	1000 C.E.

First agricultural settlements

Desiccation of Sahara begins

Kingship appears in Nile Valley

Kingdom of Kush founded in Nubia

Nok culture in Nigeria

Beginning of trans-Saharan trade

Iron Age begins in Africa

Christianity arrives in Ethiopia

Spread of Swahili culture in East Africa

First states in West Africa

Spread of Islam across North Africa

Kingdom of Zimbabwe

CONCLUSION

Thanks to the dedicated work of a generation of archaeologists, anthropologists, and historians, we have a much better understanding of the evolution of human societies in Africa than we did a few decades ago. Intensive efforts by archaeologists have demonstrated beyond reasonable doubt that the first hominids lived there. Recent evidence suggests that farming may have been practiced in Africa more than twelve thousand years ago, and the concept of kingship may have originated not in Sumer or in Egypt but in the upper Nile valley as long ago as the fourth millennium B.C.E.

Less is known about more recent African history, partly because of the paucity of written records. Still, historians have established that the first civilizations had begun to take shape in sub-Saharan Africa by the first millennium C.E., while the continent as a whole was an active participant in emerging regional and global trade with the Mediterranean world and across the Indian Ocean.

Thus the peoples of Africa were not as isolated from the main currents of human history as was once assumed. Although the state-building process in sub-Saharan Africa was still in its early stages compared with the ancient civilizations of India, China, and Mesopotamia, in many respects these new states were as impressive and as sophisticated as their counterparts elsewhere in the world.

In the fifteenth century, a new factor was added to the equation. Urged on by the tireless efforts of Prince Henry the Navigator, Portuguese fleets began to probe southward along the coast of West Africa. At first, their sponsors were in search of gold and slaves, but at the end of the century, Vasco da Gama's voyage around the Cape of Good Hope signaled Portugal's determination to dominate the commerce of the Indian Ocean in the future. The new situation posed a challenge to the peoples of Africa, whose nascent states and technology would be severely tested by the rapacious demands of the Europeans (see Chapter 14).

CHAPTER NOTES

1. F. Fernández-Armesto, *Civilizations* (London, 2000), pp. 66–68.
2. S. Hamdun and N. King, eds., *Ibn Battuta in Africa* (London, 1975), p. 19.
3. *The Book of Duarte Barbosa* (Nedeln, Liechtenstein, 1967), p. 28.
4. Herodotus, *The Histories*, trans. A. de Sélincourt (Baltimore, 1964), p. 307.
5. Quoted in M. Shinnie, *Ancient African Kingdoms* (London, 1965), p. 60.
6. C. R. Boxer, ed., *The Tragic History of the Sea, 1589–1622* (Cambridge, 1959), pp. 121–122.

7. Quoted in D. Nurse and T. Spear, *The Swahili: Reconstructing the History and Language of an African Society, 800–1500* (Philadelphia, 1985), p. 84.

8. Hamdun and King, *Ibn Battuta in Africa*, p. 47.

9. Ibid., p. 28.

10. Ibid.

11. Ibid., p. 30.

SUGGESTED READING

In few areas of world history is scholarship advancing as rapidly as in African history. New information is constantly forcing archaeologists and historians to revise their assumptions about the early history of the continent. Standard texts therefore quickly become out-of-date as their conclusions are supplanted by new evidence.

General Surveys Several general surveys provide a useful overview of the early period of African history. The dean of African historians, and certainly one of the most readable, is **B. Davidson.** For a sympathetic portrayal of the African people, see his **African History** (New York, 1968) and **Lost Cities in Africa**, rev. ed. (Boston, 1970). Other respected accounts are **R. Oliver and J. D. Fage, A Short History of Africa** (Middlesex, England, 1986), and **V. B. Khapoya,** *The African Experience: An Introduction* (Englewood Cliffs, N.J., 1994). **R. O. Collins, ed.,** *Problems in African History: The Precolonial Centuries* (New York, 1993), provides a useful collection of scholarly articles on key issues in precolonial Africa.

Specialized Studies Specialized studies are beginning to appear with frequency on many areas of the continent. For a popular account of archaeological finds, see **B. Fagan,** *New Treasures of the Past: Fresh Finds That Deepen Our Understanding of the Archaeology of Man* (Leicester, England, 1987), and **D. W. Phillipson,** *African Archaeology* (Cambridge, 2005). For a more detailed treatment of the early period, see the multivolume *General History of Africa,* sponsored by UNESCO (Berkeley, Calif., 1998). **R. O. Collins** has provided a useful service with his **African History in Documents,** (Princeton, N.J., 1990). C. **Ehret,** *An African Classical Age: Eastern and Southern Africa in World History, 1000 B.C. to A.D. 400* (Charlottesville, Va., 1998), applies historical linguistics to make up for the lack of documentary evidence in the precolonial era. **J. D. Clarke and S. A. Brandt, eds.,** *From Hunters to Farmers* (Berkeley, Calif., 1984), takes an economic approach. Also see **D. A. Welsby,** *The Kingdom of Kush: The Napatacan Meroitic Empire* (London, 1996), and **J. Middleton, Swahili: An African Mercantile Civilization** (New Haven, Conn., 1992). For a fascinating account of trans-Saharan trade, see **E. W. Bovill,** *The Golden Trade of the Moors: West African Kingdoms in the Fourteenth Century,* 2d ed. (Princeton, N.J., 1995). On the cultural background, see **R. Olaniyan, ed.,**

African History and Culture (Lagos, Nigeria, 1982), and **J. Vansina, Paths in the Rainforest: Toward a History of Political Tradition in Equatorial Africa** (Madison, Wis., 1990). Although there exist many editions of **The Epic of Son-Jara,** based on recitations of different bards, the most conclusive edition is by **F. D. Sisòkò,** translated and annotated by **J. W. Johnson** (Bloomington, Ind., 1992).

East Africa On East Africa, see **D. Nurse and T. Spear,** *The Swahili: Reconstituting the History and Language of an African Society, 800–1500* (Philadelphia, 1985). The maritime story is recounted with documents in **G. S. P. Freeman-Grenville,** *The East African Coast: Select Documents from the First to the Earlier Nineteenth Century* (Oxford, 1962). For the larger picture, see **K. N. Chaudhuri,** *Trade and Civilization in the Indian Ocean: An Economic History from the Rise of Islam to 1750* (Cambridge, 1985). On the early history of Ethiopia, see **S. Burstein, ed.,** *Ancient African Civilizations: Kush and Axum* (Princeton, N.J., 1998).

Southern Africa For useful general surveys of southern Africa, see **N. Parsons,** *A New History of Southern Africa* (New York, 1983), and **K. Shillington,** *A History of Southern Africa* (Essex, England, 1987), a profusely illustrated account. For an excellent introduction to African art, see **M. B. Visond et al,** *A History of Art in Africa* (New York, 2001); **R. Hackett,** *Art and Religion in Africa* (London, 1996); and **F. Willet,** *African Art,* rev. ed. (New York, 1993).

Enter **CengageNOW** using the access card that is available with this text. *CengageNOW* will help you understand the content in this chapter with lesson plans generated for your needs, as well as provide you with a connection to the *Wadsworth World History Resource Center* (see description below for details).

WORLD HISTORY RESOURCE CENTER

Enter the Resource Center using either your *CengageNOW* access card or your separate access card for the *World History Resource Center*. Organized by topic, this Website includes quizzes; images; over 350 primary source documents; interactive simulations, maps, and timelines; movie explorations; and a wealth of other resources. You can read the following documents, and many more, at the *World History Resource Center:*

   An African story of the creation of humanity

   A hymn to Mawari

Visit the *World History Companion Website* for chapter quizzes and more:

   www.cengage.com/history/Duiker/World6e

One of the two massive carved statues of the Buddha formerly at Bamiyan

© Thomas J. Abercrombie/National Geographic Image Collection

CHAPTER OUTLINE AND FOCUS QUESTIONS

The Silk Road

Q What were some of the chief destinations along the Silk Road, and what kinds of products and ideas traveled along the route?

India After the Mauryas

Q How did Buddhism change in the centuries after Siddhartha Gautama's death, and why did the religion ultimately decline in popularity in India?

The Arrival of Islam

Q How did Islam arrive in the Indian subcontinent, and why were Muslim peoples able to establish states here?

Society and Culture

Q What impact did Muslim rule have on Indian society? To what degree did the indigenous population convert to the new religion, and why?

The Golden Region: Early Southeast Asia

Q What were the main characteristics of Southeast Asian social and economic life, culture, and religion before 1500 C.E.?

CRITICAL THINKING

Q New religions had a significant impact on the social and cultural life of peoples living in southern Asia during the period covered in this chapter. What factors caused the spread of these religions in the first place? What changes occurred as a result of the introduction of these new faiths? Were the religions themselves affected by their spread into new regions of Asia?

WHILE TRAVELING from his native China to India along the Silk Road in the early fifth century C.E., the Buddhist monk Fa Xian stopped en route at a town called Bamiyan, a rest stop located deep in the mountains of what is today known as Afghanistan. At that time, Bamiyan was a major center of Buddhist studies, with dozens of temples and monasteries filled with students, all overlooked by two giant standing statues of the Buddha hewn directly out of the side of a massive cliff. Fa Xian was thrilled at the sight. "The law of Buddha," he remarked with satisfaction in his account of the experience, "is progressing and flourishing." He then continued southward to India, where he spent several years visiting Buddhists throughout the country. Because little of the literature from that period survives, Fa Xian's observations are a valuable resource for our knowledge of the daily lives of the Indian people.

The India that Fa Xian visited was no longer the unified land it had been under the Mauryan dynasty. The overthrow of the Mauryas in the early second century B.C.E. had been followed by several hundred years of disunity, when the subcontinent was divided into a number of separate kingdoms and principalities. The dominant force in the north was the Kushan state, established by Indo-European-speaking pastoral peoples who had been driven

245

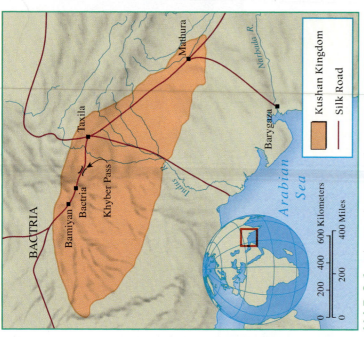

MAP 9.1 The Kushan Kingdom and the Silk Road.
After the collapse of the Mauryan Empire, a new state formed by recent migrants from the north arose north of the Indus River valley. For the next four centuries, the Kushan kingdom played a major role in regional trade via the Silk Road until it declined in the third century C.E.

Q What were the major products shipped along the Silk Road? Which countries beyond the borders of this map took an active part in trade along the Silk Road?

out of what is now China's Xinjiang province either by the Xiongnu or perhaps by the increasing aridity of the region (see Chapter 3). The Kushans penetrated into the mountains north of the Indus River, where they eventually formed a kingdom with its capital at Bactria, not far from modern Kabul. Over the next two centuries, the Kushans established their supremacy along the Indus River and in the central Ganges valley.

Meanwhile, to the south, a number of kingdoms arose among the Dravidian-speaking peoples of the Deccan Plateau, which had been only partly under Mauryan rule. The most famous of these kingdoms was Chola (sometimes spelled Cola) on the southeastern coast. Chola developed into a major trading power and sent merchant fleets eastward across the Bay of Bengal, where they introduced Indian culture as well as Indian goods to the peoples of Southeast Asia. In the fourth century C.E., Chola was overthrown by the Pallavas, who ruled from their capital at Kanchipuram (known today as Kanchi), just southwest of modern Chennai (Madras), for the next four hundred years. ◆

The Silk Road

Q Focus Question: What were some of the chief destinations along the Silk Road, and what kinds of products and ideas traveled along the route?

The Kushan kingdom, with its power base beyond the Khyber Pass in modern Afghanistan, became the dominant political force in northern India in the centuries immediately after the fall of the Mauryas. Sitting astride the main trade routes across the northern half of the subcontinent, the Kushans thrived on the commerce that passed through the area (see Map 9.1). The bulk of that trade was between the Roman Empire and China and was transported along the route now known as the Silk Road, one segment of which passed through the mountains northwest of India (see Chapter 10). From there, goods were shipped to Rome through the Persian Gulf or the Red Sea.

Trade between India and Europe had begun even before the rise of the Roman Empire, but it expanded rapidly in the first century C.E., when sailors mastered the pattern of the monsoon winds in the Indian Ocean (from the southwest in the summer and the northeast in the winter). Commerce between the Mediterranean and the Indian Ocean, as described in the *Periplus*, a first-century C.E. account by a Greek merchant, was extensive and often profitable, and it resulted in the establishment of several small trading settlements along the Indian coast. Rome imported ivory, indigo, precious stones, and pepper from India and silk from China. The Romans sometimes paid cash for these goods but also exported silver, wine, perfume, slaves, and glass and cloth from Egypt. Overall, Rome appears to have imported much more than it sold to the Far East, leading Emperor Tiberius to

grumble that "the ladies and their baubles are transferring our money to foreigners."

The Silk Road was a conduit not only of material goods but also of technology and of ideas. The first Indian monks to visit China may have traveled over the road during the second century C.E. By the time of Fa Xian, Buddhist monks from China were beginning to arrive in increasing numbers to visit holy sites in India. The visits not only enriched the study of Buddhism in the two countries but also led to a fruitful exchange of ideas and technological advances in the realms of astronomy, mathematics, and linguistics. According to one scholar, the importation of Buddhist writings from India encouraged the development of printing in China, while the Chinese obtained lessons in health care from monks returned from the Asian subcontinent.

Indeed, the emergence of the Kushan kingdom as a major commercial power was due not only to its role as an intermediary in the Rome-China trade but also to the rising popularity of Buddhism. During the second century C.E., Kanishka, the greatest of the Kushan monarchs, began to patronize Buddhism. Under Kanishka and his successors, an intimate and mutually beneficial relationship was established between Buddhist monasteries and the local

A PORTRAIT OF MEDIEVAL INDIA

INTERACTION & EXCHANGE

Much of what we know about life in medieval India comes from the accounts of Chinese missionaries who visited the subcontinent in search of documents recording the teachings of the Buddha. Here the Buddhist monk Fa Xian, who spent several years there in the fifth century C.E., reports on conditions in the kingdom of Mathura (Mo-tu-lo), a vassal state in western India that was part of the Gupta Empire. Although he could not have been pleased that the Gupta monarchs in India had adopted the Hindu faith, he found that the people were contented and prosperous except for the outcastes, whom he called Chandalas.

Fa Xian, *The Travels of Fa Xian*

Going southeast…somewhat less than 80 *joyanas* [about 640 miles], we passed very many temples one after another, with some myriad of priests in them. Having passed these places, we arrived at a certain country. This country is called Mo-tu-lo. Once more we followed the Pu-na river. On the sides of the river, both right and left, are twenty *sangharamas* [monasteries] with perhaps 3,000 priests. The law of Buddha is progressing and flourishing. Beyond the deserts are the countries of western India. The kings of these countries are all firm believers in the law of Buddha. They remove their caps of state when they make offerings to the priests. The members of the royal household and the chief ministers personally direct the food giving; when the distribution of food is over, they spread a carpet on the ground opposite the chief seat (the president's seat) and sit down before it. They dare not sit on couches in the presence of the priests. The rules relating to the almsgiving of kings have been handed down from the time of Buddha till now. Southward from this is the so-called middle country (Madhyadesa). The climate of this country is warm and equable, without frost or snow. The people are very well off, without poll tax or official restrictions. Only those who till the royal lands return a portion of profit of the land. If they desire to go, they go; if they like to stop, they stop. The kings govern without corporal punishment; criminals are fined, according to circumstances, lightly or heavily. Even in cases of repeated rebellion they only cut off the right hand. The king's personal attendants, who guard him on the right and left, have fixed salaries. Throughout the country the people kill no living thing nor drink wine, nor do they eat garlic or onions, with the exception of Chandalas only. The Chandalas are named "evil men" and dwell apart from others; if they enter a town or market, they sound a piece of wood in order to separate themselves; then men, knowing who they are, avoid coming in contact with them. In this country they do not keep swine nor fowls, and do not deal in cattle; they have no shambles [slaughterhouses] or wine shops in their marketplaces. In selling they use cowrie shells. The Chandalas only hunt and sell flesh.

Q *To what degree do the practices described here appear to conform to the principles established by Siddhartha Gautama in his own teachings? Would political advisers such as Kautilya and the Chinese philosopher Mencius have approved of governmental policies?*

---

merchant community in thriving urban centers like Taxila and Varanasi. Merchants were eager to build stupas and donate money to monasteries in return for social prestige and the implied promise of a better life in this world or the hereafter.

For their part, the wealthy monasteries ceased to be simple communities where monks could find a refuge from the material cares of the world; instead they became major consumers of luxury goods provided by their affluent patrons. Monasteries and their inhabitants became increasingly involved in the economic life of society, and Buddhist architecture began to be richly decorated with precious stones and glass purchased from local merchants or imported from abroad. The process was very similar to the changes that would later occur in the Christian church in medieval Europe.

It was from the Kushan kingdom that Buddhism began its long journey across the wastes of Central Asia to China and other societies in eastern Asia. As trade between the two regions increased, merchants and missionaries flowed from Bactria over the trade routes snaking through the mountains toward the northeast. At various stopping points on the trail, pilgrims erected statues and decorated mountain caves with magnificent frescoes depicting the life of the Buddha and his message to his followers. One of the most prominent of these centers was at Bamiyan, not far from modern-day Kabul, where believers carved two mammoth statues of the Buddha out of a sheer sandstone cliff. According to the Chinese pilgrim Fa Xian (see the box above), when he visited the area in 400 C.E., over a thousand monks were attending a religious ceremony at the site.

India After the Mauryas

Q Focus Question: How did Buddhism change in the centuries after Siddhartha Gautama's death, and why did the religion ultimately decline in popularity in India?

The Kushan kingdom came to an end under uncertain conditions sometime in the third century C.E. In 320, a new state was established in the central Ganges valley by a local raja named Chandragupta (no relation to

CHRONOLOGY Medieval India

Kushan kingdom	c. 150 B.C.E.–c. 200 C.E.
Gupta dynasty	320–600s
Chandragupta I	320–c. 335
Samudragupta	335–375
Chandragupta II	375–415
Arrival of Fa Xian in India	c. 406
First Buddhist temples at Ellora	Seventh century
Travels of Xuan Zang in India	630–643
Conquest of Sind by Arab armies	c. 711
Mahmud of Ghazni	997–1030
Delhi sultanate at peak	1220
Mongol invasion of northern India	1221
Invasion of Tamerlane	1398

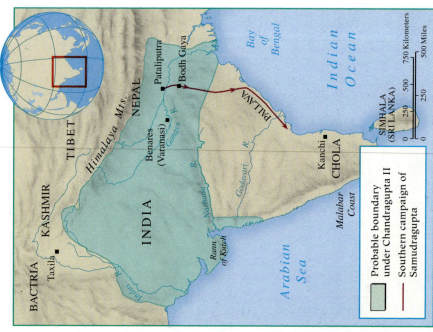

MAP 9.2 The Gupta Empire. This map shows the extent of the Gupta Empire, the only major state to arise in the Indian subcontinent during the first millennium C.E. The arrow indicates the military campaign into southern India led by King Samudragupta.

Q How did the Gupta Empire differ in territorial extent from its great predecessor, the Mauryan Empire? View an animated version of this map or related maps at www.cengage.com/history/Duiker/World6e

China, Southeast Asia, and the Mediterranean. Great cities, notable for their temples and Buddhist monasteries as well as for their economic prosperity, rose along the main trade routes throughout the subcontinent. The religious trade also prospered as pilgrims from across India and as far away as China came to visit the major religious centers.

As in the Mauryan Empire, much of the trade in the Gupta Empire was managed or regulated by the government. The Guptas owned mines and vast crown lands and earned massive profits from their commercial dealings. But there was also a large private sector, dominated by *jati* (caste) guilds that monopolized key sectors of the economy. A money economy had probably been in operation since the second century B.C.E., when copper and gold coins had been introduced from the Middle East. This in turn led to the development of banking. Nevertheless, there are indications that the circulation of coins was limited. The Chinese missionary Xuan Zang, who visited India early in the seventh century, remarked that most commercial transactions were conducted by barter.[1]

But the good fortunes of the Guptas proved to be relatively short-lived. Beginning in the late fifth century C.E., incursions by nomadic warriors from the northwest gradually reduced the power of the empire. Soon northern India was once more divided into myriad small kingdoms engaged in seemingly constant conflict. In the south, however, emerging states like Chola and Pallava prospered from their advantageous position athwart the regional trade network stretching from the Red Sea eastward into Southeast Asia.

The Transformation of Buddhism

The Chinese pilgrims who traveled to India during the Gupta era encountered a Buddhism that had changed in a number of ways in the centuries since the time of Siddhartha Gautama. They also found a doctrine that was

Chandragupta Maurya, the founder of the Mauryan dynasty). Chandragupta located his capital at Pataliputra, the site of the now-decaying palace of the Mauryas. Under his successor, Samudragupta, the territory under Gupta rule was extended into surrounding areas, and eventually the new kingdom became the dominant political force throughout northern India. It also established a loose suzerainty over the Dravidian state of Pallava to the south, thus becoming the greatest state in the subcontinent since the decline of the Mauryan Empire. Under a succession of powerful, efficient, and highly cultured monarchs, notably Samudragupta (r. 335–375 C.E.) and Chandragupta II (r. 375–415 C.E.), India enjoyed a new "classical age" of civilization (see Map 9.2).

The Gupta Dynasty: A New Golden Age?

Historians of India have traditionally viewed the Gupta era as a time of prosperity and thriving commerce with

beginning to decline in popularity in the face of the rise of Hinduism, as the Brahmanic religious beliefs of the Aryan people would eventually be called.

The transformation in Buddhism had come about in part because the earliest written sources were transcribed two centuries after Siddhartha's death and in part because his message was reinterpreted as it became part of the everyday life of the people. Abstract concepts of a Nirvana that cannot be described began to be replaced, at least in the popular mind, with more concrete visions of heavenly salvation, and Siddhartha was increasingly regarded as a divinity rather than as a sage. The Buddha's teachings that all four classes were equal gave way to the familiar Brahmanic conviction that some people, by reason of previous reincarnations, were closer to Nirvana than others.

Theravada These developments led to a split in the movement. Purists emphasized what they insisted were the original teachings of the Buddha, describing themselves as the school of **Theravada**, or "the teachings of the elders." Followers of Theravada considered Buddhism a way of life, not a salvationist creed. Theravada stressed the importance of strict adherence to personal behavior and the quest for understanding as a means of release from the wheel of life.

Mahayana In the meantime, another interpretation of Buddhist doctrine was emerging in the northwest. Here Buddhist believers, perhaps hoping to compete with other salvationist faiths circulating in the region, began to promote the view that Nirvana could be achieved through devotion and not just through painstaking attention to one's behavior. According to advocates of this school, eventually to be known as **Mahayana** ("greater vehicle"), Theravada teachings were too demanding or too strict for ordinary people to follow and therefore favored the wealthy, who were more apt to have the time and resources to spend weeks or months away from their everyday occupations. Mahayana Buddhists referred to their rivals as **Hinayana**, or "lesser vehicle," because in Theravada fewer would reach enlightenment. Mahayana thus attempted to provide hope for the masses in their efforts to reach Nirvana, but to the followers of Theravada, it did so at the expense of an insistence on proper behavior.

To advocates of the Mahayana school, salvation could also come from the intercession of a **bodhisattva** ("he who possesses the essence of Buddhahood"). According to Mahayana beliefs, some individuals who had achieved *bodhi* and were thus eligible to enter the state of Nirvana after death chose instead, because of their great compassion, to remain on earth in spirit form to help all human beings achieve release from the life cycle. Followers of Theravada, who believed the concept of bodhisattva applied only to Siddhartha Gautama himself, denounced such ideas as "the teaching of demons." But to their proponents, such ideas extended the hope of

salvation to the masses. Mahayana Buddhists revered the saintly individuals who, according to tradition, had become bodhisattvas at death and erected temples in their honor where the local population could pray and render offerings. The most famous bodhisattva was Avalokitesvara, a mythic figure whose name in Sanskrit means "Lord of Compassion." Perhaps because of the identification of Avalokitesvara with the concept of mercy, in China he was gradually transformed into a female figure known as Guan Yin (Kuan Yin).

A final distinguishing characteristic of Mahayana Buddhism was its reinterpretation of Buddhism as a religion rather than as a philosophy. Although Mahayana had philosophical aspects, its adherents increasingly regarded the Buddha as a divine figure, and an elaborate Buddhist cosmology developed. Nirvana was not a form of extinction but a true heaven with many rest stations along the way for the faithful.

Under Kushan rule, Mahayana achieved considerable popularity in northern India and for a while even made inroads in such Theravada strongholds as the island of Sri Lanka. But in the end, neither Mahayana nor Theravada was able to retain its popularity in Indian society. By the seventh century C.E., Theravada had declined rapidly on the subcontinent, although it retained its foothold in Sri Lanka and across the Bay of Bengal in Southeast Asia, where it remained an influential force to modern times (see Map. 9.3). Mahayana prospered in the northwest for centuries, but eventually it was supplanted by a revived Hinduism and later by a new arrival, Islam. But Mahayana too would find better fortunes abroad, as it was carried over the Silk Road or by sea to China and then to Korea and Japan (see Chapters 10 and 11). In all three countries, Buddhism has coexisted with Confucian doctrine and indigenous beliefs to the present.

The Decline of Buddhism in India

Why was Buddhism unable to retain its popularity in its native India, although it became a major force elsewhere in Asia? Some have speculated that in denying the existence of the soul, Buddhism ran counter to traditional Indian belief. Perhaps, too, one of Buddhism's strengths was also a weakness. In rejecting the class divisions that defined the Indian way of life, Buddhism appealed to those very groups who lacked an accepted place in Indian society, such as the untouchables. But at the same time, it represented a threat to those with a higher status. Moreover, by emphasizing the responsibility of each person to seek an individual path to Nirvana, Buddhism undermined the strong social bonds of the Indian class system.

Perhaps a final factor in the decline of Buddhism was the transformation of Brahmanism into a revised faith known as Hinduism. In its early development, Brahmanism had been highly elitist. Not only was observance of court ritual a monopoly of the *brahmin*

MAP 9.3 The Spread of Religions in Southern and Eastern Asia, 600–1900 C.E.
Between 600 and 1900 C.E., three of the world's great religions—Buddhism, Hinduism, and Islam—continued to spread from their original sources to different parts of southern and eastern Asia.

Q Which religion had the greatest impact? How might the existence of major trade routes help explain the spread of these religions?

class (see the box on p. 252), but the major route to individual salvation, asceticism, was hardly realistic for the average Indian. However, in the centuries after the fall of the Mauryas, a growing emphasis on devotion (*bhakti*) as a religious observance brought the possibility of improving one's *karma* by means of ritual acts within the reach of Indians of all classes. It seems likely that Hindu devotionalism rose precisely to combat the inroads of Buddhism and reduce the latter's appeal among the Indian population. The Chinese Buddhist missionary Fa Xian reported that mutual hostility between the Buddhists and the *brahmins* in the Gupta era was quite strong:

Leaving the southern gate of the capital city, on the east side of the road is a place where Buddha once dwelt. Whilst here he bit [a piece from] the willow stick and fixed it in the earth; immediately it grew up seven feet high, neither more nor less. The unbelievers and Brahmans, filled with jealousy, cut it down and scattered the leaves far and wide, but yet it always sprang up again in the same place as before.[2]

For a while, Buddhism was probably able to stave off the Hindu challenge by its own salvationist creed of Mahayana, which also emphasized the role of devotion, but the days of Buddhism as a dominant faith in the subcontinent were numbered. By the eighth century C.E.,

Hindu missionaries spread throughout southern India, where their presence was spearheaded by new Shaivite temples in Kanchi, the site of a famous Buddhist monastery, and at Mamallapuram.

The Arrival of Islam

Q Focus Question: How did Islam arrive in the Indian subcontinent, and why were Muslim peoples able to establish states here?

While India was still undergoing a transition after the collapse of the Gupta Empire, a new and dynamic force in the form of Islam was arising in the Arabian peninsula to the west. As we have seen, during the seventh and eighth centuries, Arab armies carried the new faith westward to the Iberian peninsula and eastward across the arid wastelands of Persia and into the rugged mountains of the Hindu Kush. Islam first reached India through the Arabs in the eighth century, but a second onslaught in the tenth and eleventh centuries by Turkic-speaking converts had a more lasting effect (see Map 9.3 above).

Although Arab merchants had been active along the Indian coasts for centuries, Arab armies did not reach

© William J. Duiker

India until the early eighth century. When Indian pirates attacked Arab shipping near the delta of the Indus River, the Muslim ruler in Iraq demanded an apology from the ruler of Sind, a Hindu state in the Indus valley. When the latter refused, Muslim forces conquered lower Sind in 711 and then moved northward into the Punjab, bringing Arab rule into the frontier regions of the subcontinent for the first time.

The Empire of Mahmud of Ghazni

For the next three centuries, Islam made no further advances into India. But a second phase began at the end of the tenth century with the rise of the state of Ghazni, located in the area of the old Kushan kingdom in present-day Afghanistan. The new kingdom was founded in 962 when Turkic-speaking slaves seized power from the Samanids, a Persian dynasty. When the founder of the new state died in 997, his son, Mahmud of Ghazni (997–1030),

succeeded him. Brilliant and ambitious, Mahmud used his patrimony as a base of operations for sporadic forays against neighboring Hindu kingdoms to the southeast. Before his death in 1030, he was able to extend his rule throughout the upper Indus valley and as far south as the Indian Ocean (see Map 9.4). In wealth and cultural brilliance, his court at Ghazni rivaled that of the Abbasid dynasty in Baghdad. But his achievements had a dark side. Describing Mahmud's conquests in northwestern India, the contemporary historian al-Biruni wrote:

Mahmud utterly ruined the prosperity of the country, and performed wonderful exploits by which the Hindus became like atoms scattered in all directions, and like a tale of old in the mouth of the people. Their scattered remains cherish, of course, the most inveterate aversion towards all Muslims. This is the reason, too, why Hindu sciences have retired far away from those parts of the country conquered by us, and have fled to places which our hand cannot yet reach, to Kashmir, Benares, and other places.[3]

Resistance against the advances of Mahmud and his successors into northern India was led by the Rajputs, aristocratic Hindu clans who were probably descended from tribal groups that had penetrated into northwestern India from Central Asia in earlier centuries. The Rajputs possessed a strong military tradition and fought bravely, but their military tactics, based on infantry supported by elephants, were no match for the fearsome cavalry of the invaders, whose ability to strike with lightning speed contrasted sharply with the slow-footed forces of their adversaries. Moreover, the incessant squabbling among the Rajput leaders put them at a disadvantage against the single-minded intensity and religious fervor of Mahmud's armies. Although the power of

© William J. Duiker

Mamallapuram Shore Temple. Mamallapuram ("The City of the Great Warrior") was so named by one of the powerful kings of the Pallavan kingdom on the eastern coast of South India. From this port, ships embarked on naval expeditions to Sri Lanka and far-off destinations in Southeast Asia. Although the site was originally identified with the Hindu deity Vishnu, in the eighth century C.E. a Pallavan monarch built this shore temple in honor of Vishnu's rival deity, Shiva. It stands as a visual confirmation of the revival of the Hindu faith in southern India at the time. Centuries of wind and rain have eroded the ornate carvings that originally covered the large granite blocks. Nearby stands a group of five rock-cut monoliths named after heroes in the Mahabharata. The seventh-century rock cutters carved these impressive shrines out of giant boulders.

RELIGION & PHILOSOPHY

THE EDUCATION OF A *BRAHMIN*

Although the seventh-century Chinese traveler Xuan Zang was a Buddhist, he faithfully recorded his impressions of the Hindu religion in his memoirs. Here he describes the education of a *brahmin*, the highest class in Indian society. *Brahmin* youths were educated at what were called *ashramas*, where they received instruction in medicine, science, astronomy, and the Vedas. Their Buddhist counterparts were taught at monasteries, including a famous one at Sarnath, where Siddhartha gave his first sermon.

Xuan Zang, *Records of Western Countries*

The Brahmans study the four *Veda Sastras.* The first is called *Shau* [longevity]; it relates to the preservation of life and the regulation of the natural condition. The second is called *Se* [sacrifice]; it relates to the [rules of] sacrifice and prayer. The third is called *Ping* [peace or regulation]; it relates to decorum, casting of lots, military affairs, and army regulations. The fourth is called *Shue* [secret mysteries]; it relates to various branches of science, incantations, medicine.

The teachers [of these works] must themselves have closely studied the deep and secret principles they contain, and penetrated to their remotest meaning. They then explain their general sense, and guide their pupils in understanding the words that are difficult. They urge them on and skillfully conduct them. They add luster to their poor knowledge, and stimulate the desponding. If they find that their pupils are satisfied with their acquirements, and so

wish to escape to attend to their worldly duties, then they use means to keep them in their power. When they have finished their education, and have attained thirty years of age, then their character is formed and their knowledge ripe. When they have secured an occupation they first of all thank their master for his attention. There are some, deeply versed in antiquity, who devote themselves to elegant studies, and live apart from the world, and retain the simplicity of their character. These rise above mundane presents, and are as insensible to the contempt of the world. Their name having spread afar, the rulers appreciate them highly, but are unable to draw them to the court. The chief of the country honors them on account of their [mental] gifts, and the people exalt their fame and render them universal homage.... They search for wisdom, relying on their own resources. Although they are possessed of large wealth, yet they will wander here and there to seek their subsistence. There are others who, whilst attaching value to letters, will yet without shame consume their fortunes in wandering about for pleasure, neglecting their duties. They squander their substance in costly food and clothing. Having no virtuous principle, and no desire to study, they are brought to disgrace, and their infamy is widely circulated.

Q *How would you compare the educational practices described here with the training provided to young men in other traditional societies in Europe, Asia, and the Americas? What was distinctive, if anything, about the educational system in India?*

Ghazni declined after his death, a successor state in the area resumed the advance in the late twelfth century, and by 1200, Muslim power, in the form of a new Delhi sultanate, had been extended over the entire plain of northern India.

The Delhi Sultanate

South of the Ganges River valley, Muslim influence spread more slowly and in fact had little immediate impact. Muslim armies launched occasional forays into the Deccan Plateau, but at first they had little success, even though the area was divided among a number of warring kingdoms, including the Cholas along the eastern coast and the Pandyas far to the south.

One reason the Delhi sultanate failed to take advantage of the disarray of its rivals was the threat posed by the Mongols on the northwestern frontier (see Chapter 10). Mongol armies unleashed by the great tribal warrior Genghis Khan occupied Baghdad and destroyed the Abbasid caliphate in the 1250s, while other forces occupied

the Punjab around Lahore, from which they threatened Delhi on several occasions. For the next half-century, the attention of the sultanate was focused on the Mongols. That threat finally declined in the early fourteenth century with the gradual breakup of the Mongol Empire, and a new Islamic state emerged in the form of the Tughluq dynasty (1320–1413), which extended its power into the Deccan Plateau. In praise of his sovereign, the Tughluq monarch Ala-ud-din, the poet Amir Khusrau exclaimed:

Happy be Hindustan, with its splendor of religion,
Where Islamic law enjoys perfect honor and dignity:
In learning Delhi now rivals Bukhara;
Islam has been made manifest by the rulers.
From Ghazni to the very shore of the ocean
You see Islam in its glory.[4]

Such happiness was not destined to endure, however. During the latter half of the fourteenth century, the Tughluq dynasty gradually fell into decline. In 1398, a new military force crossed the Indus River from the

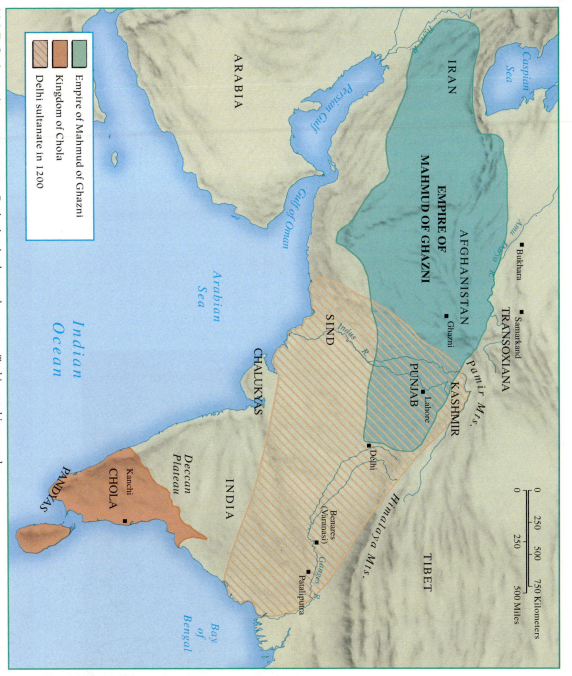

MAP 9.4 India, 1000–1200. Beginning in the tenth century, Turkic-speaking peoples invaded northwestern India and introduced Islam to the peoples in the area. Most famous was the empire of Mahmud of Ghazni.

Q Locate the major trade routes passing through the area. What geographical features explain the location of those routes?

northwest, raided the capital of Delhi, and then with-drew. According to some contemporary historians, as many as 100,000 Hindu prisoners were massacred be-fore the gates of the city. Such was India's first en-counter with Tamerlane.

Tamerlane

Tamerlane (b. 1330s), also known as Timur-i-lang (Timur the Lame), was the ruler of a Mongol khanate based in Samarkand to the north of the Pamir Moun-tains. His kingdom had been founded on the ruins of the Mongol Empire, which had begun to disintegrate as a result of succession struggles in the thirteenth century. Tamerlane, the son of a local aristocrat, seized power in

Samarkand in 1369 and immediately launched a program of conquest. During the 1380s, he brought the entire region east of the Caspian Sea under his authority and then conquered Baghdad and occupied Mesopotamia (see Map 9.5). After his brief foray into northern India, he turned to the west and raided the Anatolian peninsula. Defeating the army of the Ottoman Turks, he advanced almost as far as the Bosporus before withdrawing. "The last of the great nomadic conquerors," as one modern historian described him, died in 1405 in a final military campaign.

The passing of Tamerlane removed a major menace from the diverse states of the Indian subcontinent. But the respite from external challenge was not long. By the end of the fifteenth century, two new challenges had

© William J. Duiker

© William J. Duiker

Kutub Minar. To commemorate their religious victory in 1192, the Muslim conquerors of northern India constructed a magnificent mosque on the site of Delhi's largest Hindu temple. Much of the material for the mosque came from twenty-seven local Hindu and Jain shrines (right). Adjacent to the mosque soars the Kutub Minar, symbol of the new conquering faith. Originally 238 feet high, the tower's inscription proclaimed its mission to cast the long shadow of God over the realm of the Hindus.

appeared from beyond the horizon: the Mughals, a newly emerging nomadic power beyond the Khyber Pass in the north, and the Portuguese traders, who arrived by sea from the eastern coast of Africa in search of gold and spices. Both, in different ways, would exert a major impact on the later course of Indian civilization.

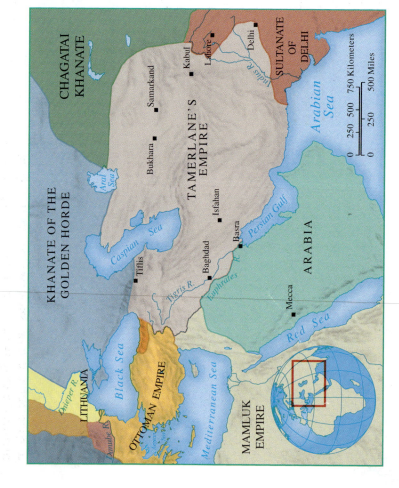

MAP 9.5   The Empire of Tamerlane. In the fourteenth century, Tamerlane, a feared conqueror of Mongolian extraction, established a brief empire in Central Asia with his capital at Samarkand. **Q** Which of the states in this map were part of Muslim civilization?

Society and Culture

© William J. Duiker

Samarkand, Gem of the Empire. The city of Samarkand has a long history. Originating during the first millennium B.C.E. as a caravan stop on the Silk Road, it was later occupied by Alexander the Great, the Abbasids, and the Mongols before becoming the capital of Tamerlane's expanding empire. Tamerlane expended great sums in creating a city worthy of his imperial ambitions. Shown here is the great square, known as the Registan. Site of a mosque, a library, and a Muslim university, all built in the exuberant Persian style, Samarkand was the jumping-off point for trade with China far to the east. The inset highlights the fanciful tile mosaics, showing lions chasing deer while a rising sun smiles on the scene.

© William J. Duiker

Q Focus Questions: What impact did Muslim rule have on Indian society? To what degree did the indigenous population convert to the new religion, and why?

The establishment of Muslim rule over the northern parts of the subcontinent had a significant impact on the society and culture of the Indian people.

Religion

Like their counterparts in other areas that came under Islamic rule, many Muslim rulers in India were relatively tolerant of other faiths and used peaceful means, if any, to encourage nonbelievers to convert to Islam. Even the more enlightened, however, could be fierce when their religious zeal was aroused. One ruler, on being informed that a Hindu fair had been held near Delhi, ordered the promoters of the event put to death. Hindu temples were razed, and mosques were erected in their place. Eventually, however, most Muslim rulers realized that not all Hindus could be converted and recognized the necessity of accepting what to them was an alien and repugnant religion. While Hindu religious practices were generally tolerated, non-Muslims were compelled to pay a tax to the state. Some Hindus likely converted to Islam to avoid paying the tax, but they were then expected to make the

traditional charitable contribution required of Muslims in all Islamic societies.

Over time, millions of Hindus did turn to the Muslim faith. Some were individuals or groups in the employ of the Muslim ruling class, such as government officials, artisans, or merchants catering to the needs of the court. But many others were probably peasants from the *sudra* class or even untouchables who found in the egalitarian message of Islam a way of removing the stigma of low-class status in the Hindu social hierarchy.

Seldom have two major religions been so strikingly different. Where Hinduism tolerated a belief in the existence of several deities (although admittedly they were all considered by some to be manifestations of one supreme god), Islam was uncompromisingly monotheistic. Where Hinduism was hierarchical, Islam was egalitarian. Where Hinduism featured a priestly class to serve as an intermediary with the ultimate force of the universe, Islam permitted no one to come between believers and their god. Such differences contributed to the mutual hostility that developed between the adherents of the two faiths in the Indian subcontinent, but more mundane issues, such as the Muslim habit of eating beef and the idolatry and sexual frankness of Hindu art, were probably a greater source of antagonism at the popular level (see the box on p. 256).

In other cases, the two peoples borrowed from each other. Some Muslim rulers found the Indian idea of divine kingship appealing. In their turn, Hindu rajas

The Islamic Conquest of India

INTERACTION & EXCHANGE

One consequence of the Muslim conquest of northern India was the imposition of many Islamic customs on Hindu society. In this excerpt, the fourteenth-century Muslim historian Zia-ud-din Barani describes the attempt of one Muslim ruler, Ala-ud-din, to prevent the use of alcohol and gambling, two practices expressly forbidden in Muslim society. Ala-ud-din had seized power in Delhi from a rival in 1294.

A Muslim Ruler Suppresses Hindu Practices

He forbade wine, beer, and intoxicating drugs to be used or sold; dicing, too, was prohibited. Vintners and beer sellers were turned out of the city, and the heavy taxes which had been levied from them were abolished. All the china and glass vessels of the Sultan's banqueting room were broken and thrown outside the gate of Badaun, where they formed a mound. Jars and casks of wine were emptied out there till they made mire as if it were the season of the rains. The Sultan himself entirely gave up wine parties. Self-respecting people at once followed his example; but the ne'er-do-wells went on making wine and spirits and hid the leather bottles in loads of hay or firewood and by various such tricks smuggled it into the city. Inspectors and gatekeepers and spies diligently sought to seize the contraband and the smugglers; and when seized the wine was given to the elephants, and the importers and sellers and drinkers [were] flogged and given short terms of imprisonment. So many were they, however, that holes had to be dug for their incarceration outside the great thoroughfare of the Badaun gate, and many of the wine bibbers died from the rigor of their confinement and others were taken out half-dead and were long in recovering their health. The terror of these holes deterred many from drinking. Those who could not give it up had to journey ten or twelve leagues [30 to 36 miles] to get a drink, for at half that distance, four or five leagues from Delhi, wine could not be publicly sold or drunk. The prevention of drinking proving very difficult, the Sultan enacted that people might distill and drink privately in their own homes, if drinking parties were not held and the liquor not sold. After the prohibition of drinking, conspiracies diminished.

Q *The ruler described here is a Muslim, establishing regulations for moral behavior in a predominantly Hindu society. Based on information available to you in Chapter 8, was a similar approach often adopted by Muslim rulers in African societies?*

---

learned by bitter experience the superiority of cavalry mounted on horses instead of elephants, the primary assault weapon in early India. Some upper-class Hindu males were attracted to the Muslim tradition of *purdah* and began to keep their women in seclusion (termed locally "behind the curtain") from everyday society. Hindu sources claimed that one reason for adopting the custom was to protect Hindu women from the roving eyes of foreigners. But it is likely that many Indian families adopted the practice for reasons of prestige or because they were convinced that *purdah* was a practical means of protecting female virtue. Adult Indian women had already begun to cover their heads with a scarf during the Gupta era.

All in all, Muslim rule probably did not have a significant impact on the lives of most Indian women (see the comparative essay "Caste, Class, and Family" on p. 257). *Purdah* was practiced more commonly among high castes than among the lower castes. Though it was probably of little consolation, sexual relations in poor and low-class families were relatively egalitarian, as men and women worked together on press gangs or in the fields. Muslim customs apparently had little effect on the Hindu tradition of *sati* (widow burning) (see the box on p. 258). In fact, in many respects, Muslim women had more rights than their Hindu counterparts. They had more property rights than Hindu women and were legally permitted to divorce under certain conditions and

to remarry after the death of their husband. The primary role for Indian women in general, however, was to produce children. Sons were preferred over daughters, not only because they alone could conduct ancestral rites but also because a daughter was a financial liability. A daughter required that her father provide a costly dowry when she married, yet after the wedding, she would transfer her labor and assets to her husband's family. Still, women shared with men a position in the Indian religious pantheon. The cult of the mother-goddess, which had originated in the Harappan era, revived during the Gupta era stronger than ever. The Hindu female deity known as Devi was celebrated by both men and women as the source of cosmic power, bestower of wishes, and symbol of fertility.

Overall, the Muslims continued to view themselves as foreign conquerors and generally maintained a strict separation between the Muslim ruling class and the mass of the Hindu population. Although a few Hindus rose to important positions in the local bureaucracy, most high posts in the central government and the provinces were reserved for Muslims. Only with the founding of the Mughal dynasty was a serious effort undertaken to reconcile the differences.

One result of this effort was the religion of the Sikhs ("disciples"). Founded by the guru Nanak in the early sixteenth century in the Punjab, Sikhism attempted to integrate the best of the two faiths in a single religion.

COMPARATIVE ESSAY
CASTE, CLASS, AND FAMILY

Why have men and women played such different roles throughout human history? Why have some societies historically adopted the joint family or the nuclear family, while others preferred the joint family or the clan? Such questions are controversial and often subject to vigorous debate, yet they are crucial to our understanding of the human experience.

As we know, the first human beings practiced hunting and foraging, living in small bands composed of one or more lineage groups and moving from place to place in search of sustenance. Individual members of the community were assigned different economic and social roles—usually with men as the hunters and women as the food gatherers—but such roles were not rigidly defined. The concept of private property did not exist, and all members shared the goods possessed by the community according to need.

The agricultural revolution brought about dramatic changes in human social organizations. Although women, as food gatherers, may have been the first farmers, men—now increasingly deprived of their traditional role as hunters—began to replace them in the fields. As communities gradually adopted a sedentary lifestyle, women were increasingly assigned to domestic tasks in the home while raising the children. As farming communities grew in size and prosperity, vocational specialization and the concept of private property appeared, leading to the family as a legal entity and the emergence of a class system composed of elites, commoners, and slaves. Women were deemed inferior to men and placed in a subordinate status.

This trend toward job specialization and a rigid class system was less developed in pastoral societies, some of which still practiced a nomadic style of life and shared communal goods on a roughly equal basis within the community. Even within sedentary societies, there was considerable variety in the nature of social organizations. In some areas, the nuclear family consisted of parents and their dependent children. Other societies, however, adopted (either in theory or in practice) the idea of the joint family (ideally consisting of three generations of a family living under one roof) and sometimes even going a step further, linking several families under the larger grouping of the caste or the clan. Prominent examples of the latter tendency include India and China, although the degree to which such concepts conformed to reality is a matter of debate.

Such large social organizations, where they occurred, often established a rigid hierarchy of status within the community, including the subordination of women. On the other hand, they sometimes played a useful role in society, providing a safety net or a ladder of upward mobility for disadvantaged members of the group, as well as a form of stability in societies where legitimate and effective authority at the central level was lacking.

The Good Life. On the walls of the Buddhist temple of Borobudur are a series of bas reliefs in stone depicting the path to enlightenment. The lower levels depict the pleasures of the material world. Shown here is a woman of leisure, assisted by her maidservants, at her toilette.

© William J. Duiker

Sikhism originated in the devotionalist movement in Hinduism, which taught that God was the single true reality. All else is illusion. But Nanak rejected the Hindu tradition of asceticism and mortification of the flesh and, like Muhammad, taught his disciples to participate in the world. Sikhism achieved considerable popularity in northwestern India, where Islam and Hinduism confronted each other directly, and eventually evolved into a militant faith that fiercely protected its adherents against its two larger rivals. In the end, Sikhism did not reconcile Hinduism and Islam but provided an alternative to them.

One complication for both Muslims and Hindus as they tried to come to terms with the existence of a mixed society was the problem of class and caste. Could non-Hindus form castes, and if so, how were these castes related to the Hindu castes? Where did the Turkic-speaking elites who made up the ruling class in many of the Islamic states fit into the equation?

The problem was resolved in a pragmatic manner that probably followed an earlier tradition of assimilating non-Hindu tribal groups into the system. Members of the Turkic ruling groups formed social groups that were roughly equivalent to the Hindu *brahmin* or *kshatriya*

THE PRACTICE OF SATI

FAMILY & SOCIETY

In the course of his extensive travels throughout Africa and Asia, the Muslim diarist Ibn Battuta—whom we have encountered in Chapters 7 and 8—spent several months in Muslim-held territories in India. In the following excerpt, he describes the Hindu practice of *sati*, according to which a widow immolates herself on her deceased husband's funeral pyre as a means of expressing her fealty to her lord and master.

The Travels of Ibn Battuta

In this part, I also saw those women who burn themselves when their husbands die. The woman adorns herself, and is accompanied by a cavalcade of the infidel Hindoos and Brahmans, with drums, trumpets, and men, following her, both Moslems and Infidels for mere pastime. The fire had been already kindled, and into it they threw the dead husband. The wife then threw herself upon him, and both were entirely burnt. A woman's burning herself, however, with her husband is not considered as absolutely necessary among them, but it is encouraged; and when a woman burns herself with her husband, her family is considered as being ennobled, and supposed to be worthy of trust. But when she does not burn herself, she is ever after clothed coarsely, and remains in constraint among her relations, on account of her want of fidelity to her husband.

The woman who burns herself with her husband is generally surrounded by women, who bid her farewell, and commission her with salutations for their former friends, while she laughs, plays, or dances to the very time in which she is to be burnt.

Some of the Hindoos, moreover, drown themselves in the river Ganges to which they perform pilgrimages; and into which they pour the ashes of those who have been burnt. When any one intends to drown himself, he opens his mind on the subject to one of his companions, and says: You are not to suppose that I do this for the sake of any thing worldly; my only motive is to draw near to Kisāī, which is a name of God with them. And when he is drowned, they draw him out of the water, burn the body, and pour the ashes into the Ganges.

Historians today evaluate documents such as this one with caution, since every observer approaches a society not his own from the perspective of his own experience and applies the values of his own experience. That being the case, are there reasons to doubt the reliability of a report by a Muslim on conditions in Hindu civilization?

class. During the Delhi sultanate in the north, members of the local Rajput nobility who converted to Islam were occasionally permitted to join such class groupings. Ordinary Indians who converted to Islam also formed Muslim castes, although at a lower level on the social scale. Many who did so were probably artisans who converted en masse to obtain the privileges that conversion could bring.

In most of India, then, Muslim rule did not substantially disrupt the class and caste system, although it may have become more fluid than was formerly the case. One perceptive European visitor in the early sixteenth century reported that in Malabar, along the southwestern coast, there were separate castes for fishing, pottery making, weaving, carpentry and metalworking, salt mining, sorcery, and labor on the plantations. There were separate castes for doing the laundry, one for the elite and the other for the common people.

Economy and Daily Life

India's landed and commercial elites lived in the cities, often in conditions of considerable opulence. The rulers possessed the most wealth. One maharaja of a relatively small state in southern India, for example, had over 100,000 soldiers in his pay along with nine hundred elephants and twenty thousand horses. Another maintained a thousand high-caste women to serve as sweepers of his palace. Each carried a broom and a brass basin containing a mixture of cow dung and water and followed him from one house to another, plastering the path where he was to tread. Most urban dwellers, of course, did not live in such style. Xuan Zang, the Chinese Buddhist missionary, left us a description of ordinary homes in seventh-century urban areas:

Their houses are surrounded by low walls.... The earth being soft and muddy, the walls of the towns are mostly built of brick or tiles. The towers on the walls are constructed of wood or bamboo; the houses have balconies and belvederes, which are made of wood, with a coating of lime or mortar, and covered with tiles. The different buildings have the same form as those in China; rushes, or dry branches, or tiles, or boards are used for covering them. The walls are covered with lime and mud, mixed with cow's dung for purity. At different seasons they scatter flowers about. Such are some of their different customs.[5]

Agriculture

The majority of India's population (estimated at slightly more than 100 million by the year 1000), however, lived on the land. Most were peasants who tilled small plots with a wooden plow pulled by oxen and paid a percentage of the harvest to their landlord. The landlord in turn forwarded part of the payment to the local ruler. In effect, the landlord functioned as a tax collector for the king, who retained ultimate ownership of all farmland in his domain. At worst, they were forced into debt and fell victim to moneylenders who charged exorbitant rates of interest.

In the north and in the upland regions of the Deccan Plateau, the primary grain crops were wheat and barley. In the Ganges valley and the southern coastal plains, the main crop was rice. Vegetables were grown everywhere, and southern India produced many spices and fruits, sugarcane, and cotton. The cotton plant apparently originated in the Indus River valley and spread from there. Although some cotton was cultivated in Spain and North Africa by the eighth and ninth centuries, India remained the primary producer of cotton goods. Spices such as cinnamon, pepper, ginger, sandalwood, cardamom, and cumin were also major export products.

Foreign Trade

Agriculture, of course, was not the only source of wealth in India. Since ancient times, the subcontinent had served as a major entrepôt for trade between the Middle East and the Pacific basin, as well as the source of other goods shipped throughout the known world. Although civil strife and piracy, heavy taxation of the business community by local rulers to finance their fratricidal wars, and increased customs duties between principalities may have contributed to a decline in internal trade, the level of foreign trade remained high, particularly in the Dravidian kingdoms in the south and along the northwestern coast, which were located along the traditional trade routes to the Middle East and the Mediterranean Sea. Much of this foreign trade was carried on by wealthy Hindu castes with close ties to the royal courts. But there were other participants as well, including such non-Hindu minorities as the Muslims, the Parsis, and the Jains. The Parsis, expatriates from Persia who practiced the Zoroastrian religion, dominated banking and the textile industry in the cities bordering the Rann of Kutch. Later they would become a dominant economic force in the modern city of Mumbai (Bombay). The Jains became prominent in trade and manufacturing even though their faith emphasized simplicity and the rejection of materialism.

According to early European travelers, merchants often lived quite well. One Portuguese observer described the "Moorish" population in Bengal as follows:

They have girdles of cloth, and over them silk scarves; they carry in their girdles daggers garnished with silver and gold, according to the rank of the person who carries them; on their fingers many rings set with rich jewels, and cotton turbans on their heads. They are luxurious, eat well and spend freely, and have many other extravagances as well. They bathe often in great tanks which they have in their houses. Everyone has three or four wives or as many as he can maintain. They keep them carefully shut up, and treat them very well, giving them great store of gold, silver and apparel of fine silk.[6]

Outside these relatively small, specialized trading communities, most manufacturing and commerce were in the hands of petty traders and artisans, who were generally limited to local markets. This failure to build on the promise of antiquity has led some historians to ask why India failed to produce an expansion of commerce and growth of cities similar to the developments that began in Europe during the High Middle Ages or even in China during the Song dynasty (see Chapter 10). Some have pointed to the traditionally low status of artisans and merchants in Indian society, symbolized by the comment in the *Arthasastra* that merchants were "thieves that are not called by the name of thief."[7] Yet commercial activities were frowned on in many areas in Europe throughout the Middle Ages, a fact that did not prevent the emergence of capitalist societies in much of the West.

Another factor may have been the monopoly on foreign trade held by the government in many areas of India. More important, perhaps, was the impact of the class and caste system, which reduced the ability of entrepreneurs to expand their activities and have dealings with other members of the commercial and manufacturing community. Successful artisans, for example, normally could not set up as merchants to market their products, nor could merchants compete for buyers outside their normal area of operations. The complex interlocking relationships among the various classes in a given region were a powerful factor inhibiting the development of a thriving commercial sector in medieval India.

Science and Technology

Indian thinkers played an important role during this period in promoting knowledge of the sciences throughout the Eurasian world. One example is the fifth-century astronomer Aryabhata, who accurately calculated the value of pi and measured the length of the solar year at slightly more than 365 days. Indian writings on astronomy, mathematics, and medicine were influential elsewhere in the region, while—as noted in Chapter 7—the Indian system of numbers, including the concept of zero, was introduced into the Middle East and ultimately replaced the Roman numerals then in use in medieval Europe.

The Wonder of Indian Culture

The era between the Mauryas and the Mughals in India was a period of cultural evolution as Indian writers and artists built on the literary and artistic achievements of their predecessors. This is not to say, however, that Indian culture rested on its ancient laurels. To the contrary, it was an era of tremendous innovation in all fields of creative endeavor.

Art and Architecture

At the end of antiquity, the primary forms of religious architecture were the Buddhist cave temples and monasteries. The next millennium witnessed the evolution of religious architecture from underground cavity to monumental structure.

© William J. Duiker

Ajanta Caves. The twenty-eight caves of Ajanta are among the wonders of India. Begun in the second century B.C.E., most of the excavations occurred in the fifth century C.E. only to disappear under jungle growth as Buddhism in India waned. Rediscovered accidentally in the nineteenth century by soldiers on a tiger hunt, the caves have subsequently attracted world acclaim. Some caves contain temple halls; others serve as monasteries. They are most famous for their paintings and sculptures (right).

The twenty-eight caves of Ajanta in the Deccan Plateau are among India's greatest artistic achievements. They are as impressive for their sculpture and painting as for their architecture. Except for a few examples from the second century B.C.E., most of the caves were carved out of solid rock over an incredibly short period of eighteen years, from 460 to 478 C.E. In contrast to the early unadorned temple halls, these caves were exuberantly decorated with ornate pillars, friezes, beamed ceilings, and statues of the Buddha and bodhisattvas. Several caves served as monasteries, which by then had been transformed from simple holes in the wall to large complexes with living apartments, halls, and shrines to the Buddha. Other temples, such as the one at Ellora, were carved directly out of the mountains (see the comparative illustration on p. 261).

All of the inner surfaces of the caves, including the ceilings, sculptures, walls, door frames, and pillars, were painted in vivid colors. Perhaps best known are the wall paintings, which illustrate the various lives and incarnations of the Buddha. These paintings are in an admirable state of preservation, making it possible to reconstruct the customs, dress, house interiors, and physical characteristics of the peoples of fifth-century India. Similar rock paintings focusing on secular subjects can be found at Sigiriya, a fifth-century royal palace on the island of Sri Lanka. As a defensive measure, the palace was located on top of a gigantic volcanic rock.

Among the most impressive rock carvings in southern India are the cave temples at Mamallapuram (also known as Mahabalipuram), south of the modern city of Chennai (Madras). The sculpture, called *Descent of the Ganges River*, depicts the role played by Shiva in intercepting the heavenly waters of the Ganges and allowing them to fall gently on the earth. Mamallapuram also boasts an eighth-century shore temple (see the illustration on p. 251), which is one of the earliest surviving freestanding structures in the subcontinent.

From the eighth century until the time of the Mughals, Indian architects built a multitude of magnificent Hindu temples, now constructed exclusively aboveground. Each temple consisted of a central shrine surmounted by a sizable tower, a hall for worshipers, a vestibule, and a porch, all set in a rectangular courtyard that might also contain other minor shrines. Temples became progressively more ornate until the eleventh century, when sculpture began to dominate the structure. The towers became higher and the temple complexes more intricate, some becoming virtual walled compounds set one within the other and resembling small towns.

Among the best examples of temple art are those in the eastern state of Orissa. The Sun Temple at Konarak, standing at the edge of the sea and covered with intricate carvings, is generally considered the masterpiece of its genre. Although now in ruins, the Sun Temple still boasts some of India's most memorable sculptures. Especially renowned are the twelve pairs of carved wheels, each 10 feet high, representing the twelve signs of the zodiac.

The greatest example of medieval Hindu temple art, however, is probably Khajuraho. Of the original eighty-five temples, dating from the tenth century, twenty-five remain standing today. All of the towers are

© William J. Duiker

© Werner Forman/Art Resource, NY

COMPARATIVE ILLUSTRATION

Rock Architecture. Along with the caves at Ajanta, one of the greatest examples of Indian rock architecture remains the eighth-century temple at Ellora, in central India, shown on the left. Named after Shiva's holy mountain in the Himalayas, the temple is approximately the size of the Parthenon in Athens but was literally carved out of a hillside. The builders dug nearly 100 feet straight down into the top of the mountain to isolate a single block of rock, removing in the process over 3 million cubic feet of stone. Unlike earlier rock-cut shrines, which had been constructed in the form of caves, the Ellora temple is open to the sky and filled with some of India's finest sculpture. The overall impression is one of massive grandeur.

This form of architecture also found expression in parts of Africa. In 1200 C.E., Christian monks in Ethiopia began to construct a remarkable series of eleven churches carved out of solid volcanic rock (right). After a 40-foot trench was formed by removing the bedrock, the central block of stone was hewed into the shape of a Greek cross; then it was hollowed out and decorated. These churches, which are still in use today, testify to the fervor of Ethiopian Christianity, which plays a major role in preserving the country's cultural and national identity.

Q Why do you think some early cultures made frequent use of the concept of rock architecture, while others did not? Why do you think the process was discontinued?

buttressed at various levels on the sides, giving the whole a sense of unity and creating a vertical movement similar to Mount Kailasa in the Himalayas, sacred to Hindus. Everywhere the viewer is entertained by voluptuous temple dancers bringing life to the massive structures. One is removing a thorn from her foot, another is applying eye makeup, and yet another is wringing out her hair.

In the Deccan Plateau, a different style prevailed. The southern temple style was marked by massive oblong stone towers, some 200 feet high. The towers were often covered with a profusion of sculpted figures and were visible for miles. The walls surrounding the temple complex were also surmounted with impressive gate towers, known as *gopuras*.

Literature

During this period, Indian authors produced a prodigious number of written works, both religious and secular. Indian religious poetry was written in Sanskrit and also in the languages of southern India. As Hinduism was transformed from a contemplative to a more devotional religion, its poetry became more ardent and erotic and prompted a sense of divine ecstasy. Much of the religious verse extolled the lives and heroic acts of Shiva, Vishnu, Rama, and Krishna by repeating the same themes over and over, which is also a characteristic of Indian art. In the eighth century, a tradition of poet-saints inspired by intense mystical devotion to a deity emerged in southern India. Many were women who sought to escape the drudgery of domestic toil through an imagined sexual union with the god-lover. Such was the case for the twelfth-century mystic whose poem here expresses her sensuous joy in the physical-mystical union with her god:

> *It was like a stream*
> *running into the dry bed*
> *of a lake,*

emotional scene in just a few lines. Witness this poem by the poet Amaru:

We'll see what comes of it, I thought,
and I hardened my heart against her.
What, won't the villain speak to me? she
thought, flying into a rage.
And there we stood, sedulously refusing to look one
another in the face,
Until at last I managed an unconvincing laugh,
and her tears robbed me of my resolution.[9]

One of India's most famous authors was Kalidasa, who lived during the Gupta dynasty. Although little is known of him, including his dates, he probably wrote for the court of Chandragupta II (375–415 C.E.). Even today, Kalidasa's hundred-verse creation *The Cloud Messenger* remains one of the most popular Sanskrit poems.

In addition to being a poet, Kalidasa was also a great dramatist. He wrote three plays, all dramatic romances that blend the erotic with the heroic and the comic. *Shakuntala*, perhaps the best-known play in all Indian literature, tells the story of a king who, while out hunting, falls in love with the maiden Shakuntala. He asks her to marry him and offers her a ring of betrothal but is suddenly recalled to his kingdom on urgent business. Shakuntala, who is pregnant, goes to him, but the king has been cursed by a hermit and no longer recognizes her. With the help of the gods, the king eventually does recall their love and is reunited with Shakuntala and their son.

Each of Kalidasa's plays is propelled by the magic powers of a goddess, and each ends in affirmation and unity. Another interesting aspect of Kalidasa's plays is that they combine several languages as well as poetry and prose. The language and form of the characters' speeches correspond to their position in the social hierarchy. Thus the king speaks in Sanskrit poetry, while the other characters in the play use prose in three different vernaculars of everyday life.

Kalidasa was one of the greatest Indian dramatists, but he was by no means the only one. Sanskrit plays typically contained one to ten acts. They were performed in theaters in the palaces or in court temples by troupes of actors of both sexes who were trained and supported by the royal family. The plots were usually taken from Indian legends of gods and kings. No scenery or props were used, but costumes and makeup were elaborate. The theaters had to be small because much of the drama was conveyed through intricate gestures and dance conventions. There were many different positions for various parts of the body, including one hundred for the hands alone.

Like poetry, prose developed in India from the Vedic period. The use of prose was well established by the sixth and seventh centuries C.E. This is truly astonishing considering that the novel did not appear until the tenth century in Japan and until the seventeenth century in Europe.

The great secular literature of traditional India was also written in Sanskrit in the form of poetry, drama, and prose. Some of the best medieval Indian poetry is found in single-stanza poems, which create an entire

Sculptural Decorations at Khajuraho. This Hindu temple, one of the greatest in India, is literally covered with statues, both mortal and divine, depicted in erotic poses and thought to promote Hindu cosmology. Many represent the ideal couple or divine lovers, who symbolize the union of the worshipers with the deity, thus blending physical and spiritual beauty. Evolving from the traditional female earth spirit (see Chapter 2), women have been represented in Indian art as the sensuous bearers of fertility and prosperity. As a contemporary Indian text stated, "As a house without a wife, as frolic without a woman, so without the figure of woman the monument will be of inferior quality and will bear no fruit."

like rain pouring on plants
parched to sticks.
It was like this world's pleasure
and the way to the other,
both walking towards me.
Seeing the feet of the master,
O lord white as jasmine
I was made worthwhile.[8]

© Lynn McLaren/Photo Researchers, Inc.

ARTS & IDEAS

The writings of the seventh-century author Dandin provide a lively portrait of Indian society. In this excerpt from his novel *The Ten Princes* are revealed the frustrations of a mother determined to mold her daughter into a wealthy courtesan, one who could assure herself and her family of a life of ease. Rather than focusing on attracting wealthy patrons, however, the daughter has preferred to share her charms with a handsome youth of no fortune.

Dandin, *The Ten Princes*

At this point the mother lifted her hands, touched the earth with hair dappled with grey, lifted her head, and spoke: "Holy sir, this your maid-servant acquaints you with my own wrongdoing. And this wrongdoing of mine lay in the performance of my obvious duty. For obvious duty is as follows for the mother of a *fille de joie:* care of her daughter's person from the hour of birth; nourishment by a diet so regulated as to develop stateliness, vigor, complexion, intelligence, while harmonizing the humors, gastric calefaction, and secretions; not permitting her to see too much even of her father after the fifth year; festive ritual on birthdays and holy days; instruction in the arts of flirtation, both major and minor; thorough training in dance, song, instrumental music, acting, painting, also judgment of foods, perfumes, flowers, not forgetting writing and graceful speech; a conversational acquaintance with grammar, with logical inference and conclusion; profound skill in money-making, sport, and betting on cockfights or chess; assiduous use of go-betweens in the passages of coquetry; display of numerous well-dressed attendants at religious or secular celebrations; careful selection of teachers to insure success at unpremeditated vocal and other exhibitions; advertising on a national scale by a staff of trained specialists; publicity for beautymarks through astrologers and such; eulogistic mention in gatherings of men about town of her beauty, character, accomplishments, charm, and sweetness by hangers-on, gay dogs, buffoons, female

religionists, and others; raising her price considerably when she has become an object of desire to young gentlemen; surrender to a lover of independent fortune, a philogynist or one intoxicated by seeing her charms, a gentleman eminent for rank, figure, youth, money, vigor, purity, generosity, cleverness, gallantry, art, character, and sweetness of disposition; delivery, with gracious exaggeration of value received, to one less affluent, but highly virtuous and cultivated (the alternative is levying on his natural guardians, after informal union with such a gentleman); collection of bad debts by vamping judge and jury; mothering a lover's daughter; abstraction by ingenious tricks of money left in an admirer's possession after payment for periodical pleasures; steady quarreling with a defaulter or miser; simulation of the spirit of generosity in an overthrifty adorer by the incentive of jealousy; repulse of the impecunious by biting speeches, by public taunts, by cutting his daughters, and by other embarrassing habits, as well as by simple contempt; continued clinging to the open-handed, the chivalrous, the blameless, the wealthy, with full consideration of the interrelated chances of money and misery.

"Besides, a courtesan should show readiness indeed, but no devotion to a lover; and, even if fond of him, she should not disobey mother or grandmother. In spite of all, the girl disregards her God-given vocation and has spent a whole month of amusement—at her own expense!—with a Brahman youth, a fellow from nowhere whose face is his fortune. Her snippiness has offended several perfectly solvent admirers and has pauperized her own family. And when I scolded her and told her, 'This is no kind of a scheme. This isn't pretty,' she was angry and took to the woods. And if she is obstinate, this whole family will stay right here and starve to death. There is nothing else to do." And the mother wept.

Q *How would you define in a few words the advice given here on the training of a courtesan in medieval India? How has the daughter responded to this advice from her mother? Was she justified in her actions?*

One of the greatest masters of Sanskrit prose was Dandin, who lived during the seventh century. In *The Ten Princes,* he created a fantastic and exciting world that fuses history and fiction. His keen powers of observation, details of low life, and humor give his writing considerable vitality. Witness the passage in which the mother of a courtesan describes the demanding education required for her most accomplished daughter (see the box above).

Music   Another area of Indian creativity that developed during this era was music. Ancient Indian music had come from the chanting of the Vedic hymns and thus had a strong metaphysical and spiritual flavor. The actual physical vibrations of music (*nada*) were believed to be related to the spiritual world. An off-key or sloppy rendition of a sacred text could upset the harmony and balance of the entire universe.

In form, Indian classical music is based on a scale, called a *raga.* There are dozens, if not hundreds, of separate scales, which are grouped into separate categories depending on the time of day during which they are to be performed. The performers use a stringed instrument called a *sitar* and various types of wind instruments and drums. The performers select a basic *raga* and then are free to improvise the melodic structure and rhythm. A good performer never performs a particular *raga* the same way twice. As with jazz music in the West, the audience is concerned not so much with faithful reproduction as with the performer's creativity.

The Golden Region: Early Southeast Asia

Q Focus Question: What were the main characteristics of Southeast Asian social and economic life, culture, and religion before 1500 C.E.?

Between China and India lies the region that today is called Southeast Asia. It has two major components: a mainland region extending southward from the Chinese border down to the tip of the Malay peninsula and an extensive archipelago, most of which is part of present-day Indonesia and the Philippines. Travel between the islands and regions to the west, north, and east was not difficult, so Southeast Asia has historically served as a vast land bridge for the movement of peoples between China, the Indian subcontinent, and the more than 25,000 islands of the South Pacific.

Mainland Southeast Asia consists of several north-south mountain ranges, separated by river valleys that run in a southerly or southeasterly direction. Between the sixth and thirteenth centuries C.E., two groups of migrants—the Thai from southwestern China and the Burmese from the Tibetan highlands—came down these valleys in search of new homelands, as earlier peoples had done before them. Once in Southeast Asia, most of these migrants settled in the fertile deltas of the rivers—the Irrawaddy and the Salween in Burma, the Chao Phraya in Thailand, and the Red River and the Mekong in Vietnam—or in lowland areas in the islands to the south.

Although the river valleys facilitated north-south travel on the Southeast Asian mainland, movement between east and west was relatively difficult. The mountains are densely forested and infested with malaria-carrying mosquitoes. Consequently, the lowland peoples in the river valleys were often isolated from each other and had only limited contacts with the upland peoples in the mountains. These geographical barriers may help explain why Southeast Asia is one of the few regions in Asia that was never unified under a single government.

Given Southeast Asia's location between China and India, it is not surprising that both civilizations influenced developments in the region. In 111 B.C.E., Vietnam was conquered by the Han dynasty and remained under Chinese control for more than a millennium, as will be discussed in Chapter 11. The Indian states never exerted much political control over Southeast Asia, but their influence was pervasive nevertheless. The first

contacts had taken place by the fourth century B.C.E., when Indian merchants began sailing to Southeast Asia; they were soon followed by Buddhist and Hindu missionaries. Indian influence can be seen in many aspects of Southeast Asian culture, from political institutions to religion, architecture, language, and literature.

Paddy Fields and Spices: The States of Southeast Asia

The traditional states of Southeast Asia can generally be divided between agricultural societies and trading societies. The distinction between farming and trade was a product of the environment. The agricultural societies—notably, Vietnam, and what is now Cambodia, and the Burmese state of Pagan—were situated in fertile river deltas that were conducive to the development of a wet rice economy (see Map 9.6). Although all produced some goods for regional markets, none was tempted to turn to commerce as the prime source of national income. In

MAP 9.6 Southeast Asia in the Thirteenth Century. This map shows the major states that arose in Southeast Asia after the year 1000 C.E. Some, like Angkor and Dai Viet, were predominantly agricultural. Others, like Srivijaya and Champa, were commercial.

Q Which of these empires would soon disappear? Why?

THE KINGDOM OF ANGKOR

INTERACTION & EXCHANGE

Angkor was the greatest kingdom of its time in Southeast Asia. This passage was written in the thirteenth century by the Chinese customs inspector Chau Ju-kua, in the city of Quanzhou (sometimes called Zaiton) on the southern coast of China. His account, compiled from reports of seafarers, includes a brief description of the great archaeological sites of the region. Angkor was already in decline when Chau Ju-kua described the kingdom, and the capital was abandoned in 1432.

Chau Ju-kua, *Records of Foreign Nations*

The officials and the common people dwell in houses with sides of bamboo matting and thatched with reeds. Only the king resides in a palace of hewn stone. It has a granite lotus pond of extraordinary beauty with golden bridges, some three hundred odd feet long. The palace buildings are solidly built and richly ornamented. The throne on which the king sits is made of gharu wood and the seven precious substances; the dais is jewelled, with supports of veined wood [possibly ebony]; the screen [behind the throne] is of ivory.

When all the ministers of state have audience, they first make three full prostrations at the foot of the throne; they then kneel and remain thus, with hands crossed on their breasts, in a circle round the king, and discuss the affairs of state. When they have finished, they make another prostration and retire....

[The people] are devout Buddhists. There are serving [in the temples] some three hundred foreign women; they dance and offer food to the Buddha. They are called *a-nan* or slave dancing girls.

As to their customs, lewdness is not considered criminal; theft is punished by cutting off a hand and a foot and by branding on the chest.

The incantations of the Buddhist and Taoist priests [of this country] have magical powers. Among the former those who wear yellow robes may marry, while those who dress in red lead ascetic lives in temples. The Taoists clothe themselves with leaves; they have a deity called P'o-to-li which they worship with great devotion.

[The people of this country] hold the right hand to be clean, the left unclean, so when they wish to mix their rice with any kind of meat broth, they use the right hand to do so and also to eat with.

The soil is rich and loamy; the fields have no bounds. Each one takes as much as he can cultivate. Rice and cereals are cheap; for every tael [1.3 ounces] of lead one can buy two bushels of rice.

The native products comprise elephants' tusks, the *chan* and *su* [varieties of gharu wood], good yellow wax, kingfisher's feathers,...resin, foreign oils, ginger peel, gold-colored incense.... raw silk and cotton fabrics.

The foreign traders offer in exchange for these gold, silver, porcelainware, sugar, preserves, and vinegar.

Q *Because of the paucity of written records about Angkor society, documents such as this one from a Chinese source are important in providing knowledge about local conditions. What does this excerpt tell us about the political system, religious beliefs, and land use in thirteenth-century Angkor?*

---

fact, none was situated astride the main trade routes that crisscrossed the region.

The Mainland States

One exception to this general rule was the kingdom of Funan, which arose in the fertile valley of the lower Mekong River in the second century C.E. At that time, much of the regional trade between India and the South China Sea moved across the narrow neck of the Malay peninsula. With access to copper, tin, and iron, as well as a variety of tropical agricultural products, Funan played an active role in this process, and Oc Eo, on the Gulf of Thailand, became one of the primary commercial ports in the region. Funan declined in the fifth century when trade began to pass through the Strait of Malacca and was eventually replaced by the agricultural state of Chenla and then, three hundred years later, by the great kingdom of Angkor.

Angkor was the most powerful state to emerge in mainland Southeast Asia before the sixteenth century (see the box above). The remains of its capital city, Angkor Thom, give a sense of the magnificence of Angkor civilization. The city formed a square 2 miles on each side. Its massive stone walls were several feet thick and were surrounded by a moat. Four main gates led into the city, which at its height had a substantial population. Like its predecessor, the wealth of Angkor was based primarily on the cultivation of wet rice, which had been introduced to the Mekong River valley from China in the third millennium B.C.E. Other products were honey, textiles, fish, and salt. By the fourteenth century, however, Angkor had begun to decline, a product of incessant wars with its neighbors and the silting up of its irrigation system, and in 1432, Angkor Thom was destroyed by the Thai, who had migrated into the region from southwestern China in the thirteenth century and established their capital at Ayuthaya, in lower Thailand, in 1351.

As the Thai expanded southward, however, their main competition came from the west, where the Burmese peoples had formed their own agricultural society in the valleys of the Salween and Irrawaddy

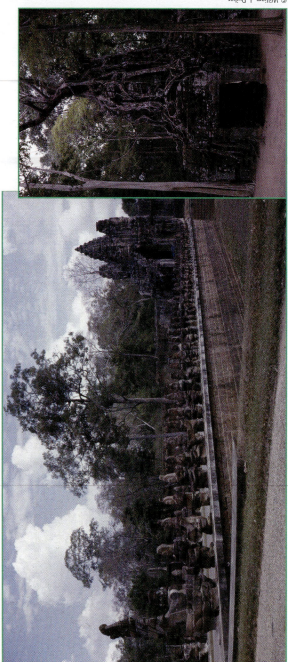

© William J. Duiker

© William J. Duiker

A Lost City in Asia. The city of Angkor Thom was the capital of the Angkor empire. Founded in the late twelfth century by the powerful ruler Jayavarman VII (r. 1181–1219), the city contained a palace, several Buddhist temples, crematoria for deceased rulers, and a vast parade ground for royal processions. Shown here is one of the massive gates leading into the city. After destruction by invading Thai armies in the fifteenth century, the city sank into the surrounding rain forest, only to be rediscovered four hundred years later by a wandering French naturalist. The inset shows the Buddhist temple Ta Prohm, constructed by Jayavarman VII as a memorial to his mother, still struggling to emerge from its surroundings.

Rivers. Like the Thai, they were relatively recent arrivals in the area, having migrated southward from the highlands of Tibet beginning in the seventh century C.E. After subjugating weaker societies already living in the area, in the eleventh century they founded the first great Burmese state, the kingdom of Pagan. Like the Thai, they quickly converted to Buddhism and adopted Indian political institutions and culture. For a while, they were a major force in the western part of Southeast Asia, but attacks from the Mongols in the late thirteenth century (see Chapter 10) weakened Pagan, and the resulting vacuum may have benefited the Thai as they moved into areas occupied by Burmese migrants in the Chao Phraya valley.

The Malay World   In the Malay peninsula and the Indonesian archipelago, a different pattern emerged. For centuries, this area had been linked to regional trade networks, and much of its wealth had come from the export of tropical products to China, India, and the Middle East. The vast majority of the inhabitants of the region were Malays, a people who spread from their original homeland in southeastern China into island Southeast Asia and even to more distant locations in the South Pacific, such as Tahiti, Hawaii, and Easter Island.

Eventually, the islands of the Indonesian archipelago gave rise to two of the region's most notable trading societies—Srivijaya and Majapahit. Both were based in large part on spices. As the wealth of the Arab empire in

the Middle East and then of western Europe increased, so did the demand for the products of East Asia. Merchant fleets from India and the Arabian peninsula sailed to the Indonesian islands to buy cloves, pepper, nutmeg, cinnamon, precious woods, and other exotic products coveted by the wealthy. In the eighth century, Srivijaya, located along the eastern coast of Sumatra, became a powerful commercial state that dominated the trade passing through the Strait of Malacca, at that time the most convenient route from East Asia into the Indian Ocean. The rulers of Srivijaya had helped bring the route to prominence by controlling the pirates who had previously plagued shipping in the strait. Another inducement was Srivijaya's capital at Palembang, a deepwater port where sailors could wait out the monsoon season before making their return voyage. In 1025, however, Chola, one of the kingdoms of southern India and a commercial rival of Srivijaya, inflicted a devastating defeat on the island kingdom. Although Srivijaya survived, it was unable to regain its former dominance, in part because the main trade route had shifted to the east, through the Strait of Sunda and directly out into the Indian Ocean. In the late thirteenth century, this shift in trade patterns led to the founding of the new kingdom of Majapahit on the island of Java. In the mid-fourteenth century, Majapahit succeeded in uniting most of the archipelago and perhaps even part of the Southeast Asian mainland under its rule (see the box on p. 267).

The Role of India

Indian influence was evident in all of these societies to various degrees. Based on models from the Dravidian kingdoms of southern India, Southeast Asian kings were believed to possess special godlike qualities that set them apart from ordinary people. In some societies such as Angkor, the most prominent royal advisers constituted a *brahmin* class on the Indian model. In Pagan and Angkor, some division of the population into separate classes based on occupation and ethnic background seems to have occurred, although these divisions do not seem to have developed the rigidity of the Indian class system.

India also supplied Southeast Asians with a writing system. The societies of the region had no written scripts for their spoken languages before the arrival of the Indian merchants and missionaries. Indian phonetic symbols were borrowed and used to record the spoken language. Initially, Southeast Asian literature was written in the Indian Sanskrit but eventually came to be written in the local languages. Southeast Asian authors borrowed popular Indian themes, such as stories from the Buddhist scriptures and tales from the Ramayana.

A popular form of entertainment among the common people, the *wayang kulit*, or shadow play, may have come originally from India or possibly China, but it became a distinctive art form in Java and other islands of the Indonesian archipelago. In a shadow play, flat leather puppets were manipulated behind an illuminated screen while the narrator recited tales from the Indian classics. The plays were often accompanied by a gamelan, an orchestra composed primarily of percussion instruments such as gongs and drums that apparently originated in Java.

Daily Life

Because of the diversity of ethnic backgrounds, religions, and cultures, making generalizations about daily life in Southeast Asia during the early historical period is difficult. Nevertheless, it appears that societies in the region did not always apply the social distinctions that prevailed in India. For example, although the local population, as elsewhere, was divided according to a variety of economic functions, the dividing lines between classes were not as rigid and imbued with religious significance as they were in the Indian subcontinent.

Social Structures Still, traditional societies in Southeast Asia had some clearly hierarchical characteristics. At the top of the social ladder were the hereditary aristocrats, who monopolized both political power and economic

---

POLITICS & GOVERNMENT

THE LEGENDARY GRANDEUR OF MAJAPAHIT

The *Nagarkertagama*, written by the court poet Prapanca in 1365, was the national epic of the kingdom of Majapahit. This passage describes the relationship between the kingdom and neighboring countries in the region.

Prapanca, Nagarkertagama

Such is the excellence of His Majesty the Prince who reigns at Majapahit as absolute monarch. His is praised like the moon in autumn, since he fills all the world with joy. The evil-doers are like the red lotus, the good—who love him wholeheartedly—are like the white lotus. His retinue, treasures, chariots, elephants, horses, etc., are [immeasurable] like the sea.

The land of Java is becoming more and more famous for its blessed state throughout the world. "Only Jambudwipa [India] and Java," so people say, "are mentioned for their superiority, good countries as they are; because of the multitude of men experienced in the doctrine...; whatever 'work' turns up, they are very able to handle it."

First comes the Illustrious Brahmaraja, the excellent *brahmin*, an irreproachable, great poet and expert of the religious traditions; he has complete knowledge of the speculative as well as all the other philosophies,...the system of dialectical [logic], etc. And [then] the holy Shamana, very pious, virtuous, experienced in the Vedas and the six pure activities. And also the Illustrious Vishnu, powerful in Samaveda incantations, with which he aims to increase the country's prosperity.

For this reason all kinds of people have continually come from other countries, in multitudes. There are Jambudwipa, Kamboja [Cambodia], China, Yawana [Annam], Champa, Kannataka [in South China], etc., Goda [Gaur] and Siam—these are the places whence they come from. They come by ship with numerous merchants; monks and *brahmins* are the principal ones who as they come are regaled and are well pleased during their stay.

And in each month of Phalguna [February-March] His Majesty the Prince is honored and celebrated in his residence. Then the high state officials come from all over Java, the heads of districts, and the judicial officials...; also the [people from] other islands, Bali, etc., all come with tributes so numerous that they are uninterrupted, to honor him. Traders and merchants fill the market in dense crowds with all their wares in great variety.

Q *What does this passage tell us about the nature of Majapahit and the qualities of its ruler? Is it as useful a description of Javanese society as, for example, those by the Chinese monks Fa Xian and Xuan Zang appearing earlier in this chapter?*

CHRONOLOGY Early Southeast Asia

Chinese conquest of Vietnam	111 B.C.E.
Arrival of Burmese peoples	c. seventh century C.E.
Formation of Srivijaya	c. 670
Construction of Borobudur	c. eighth century
Creation of Angkor kingdom	c. ninth century
Thai migrations into Southeast Asia	c. thirteenth century
Rise of Majapahit empire	1292
Fall of Angkor kingdom	1432

farmers, fishers, or artisans, lived in small *kampongs* (Malay for "villages") in wooden houses built on stilts to avoid flooding during the monsoon season. Some of the farmers were probably sharecroppers who paid a part of their harvest to a landlord, who was often a member of the aristocracy. But in other areas, the tradition of free farming was strong. In some cases, some of the poorer land belonged to the village as a collective unit and was assigned for use by the neediest families.

wealth and enjoyed a borrowed aura of charisma by virtue of their proximity to the ruler. Most aristocrats lived in the major cities, which were the main source of power, wealth, and foreign influence. Beyond the major cities lived the mass of the population, composed of farmers, fishers, artisans, and merchants. In most Southeast Asian societies, the vast majority were probably rice farmers, living at a bare level of subsistence and paying heavy rents or taxes to a landlord or a local ruler.

The average Southeast Asian peasant was not actively engaged in commerce except as a consumer of various necessities. But accounts by foreign visitors indicate that in the Malay world, some were involved in growing or mining products for export, such as tropical food products, precious woods, tin, and precious gems. Most of the regional trade was carried on by local merchants, who purchased products from local growers and then transported them to the major port cities. During the early state-building era, roads were few and relatively primitive, so most of the trade was transported by small boats down rivers to the major ports along the coast. There the goods were loaded onto larger ships for delivery outside the region. Growers of export goods in areas near the coast were thus indirectly involved in the regional trade network but received few economic benefits from the relationship.

As we might expect from an area of such ethnic and cultural diversity, social structures differed significantly from country to country. In the Indianized states on the mainland, the tradition of a hereditary tribal aristocracy was probably accentuated by the Hindu practice of dividing the population into separate classes, called *varna* in imitation of the Indian model. In Angkor and Pagan, for example, the divisions were based on occupation or ethnic background. Some people were considered free subjects of the king, although there may have been legal restrictions against changing occupations. Others, however, may have been indentured to an employer. Each community was under a chieftain, who was in turn subordinated to a higher official responsible for passing on the tax revenues of each group to the central government.

In the kingdoms in the Malay peninsula and the Indonesian archipelago, social relations were generally less formal. Most of the people in the region, whether

Women and the Family The women of Southeast Asia during this era have been described as the most fortunate in the world. Although most women worked side by side with men in the fields, as in Africa they often played an active role in trading activities. Not only did this lead to a higher literacy rate among women than among their male counterparts, but it also allowed them more financial independence than their counterparts in China and India, a fact that was noticed by the Chinese traveler Zhou Daguan at the end of the thirteenth century: "In Cambodia it is the women who take charge of trade. For this reason a Chinese arriving in the country loses no time in getting himself a mate, for he will find her commercial instincts a great asset."[10]

Although, as elsewhere, warfare was normally part of the male domain, women sometimes played a role as bodyguards as well. According to Zhou Daguan, women were used to protect the royal family in Angkor, as well as in kingdoms located on the islands of Java and Sumatra. While there is no evidence that such female units ever engaged in battle, they did give rise to wondrous tales of "amazon" warriors in the writings of foreign travelers such as the fourteenth-century Muslim adventurer Ibn Battuta.

One reason for the enhanced status of women in traditional Southeast Asia is that the nuclear family was more common than the joint family system prevalent in China and the Indian subcontinent. Throughout the region, wealth in marriage was passed from the male to the female, in contrast to the dowry system applied in China and India. In most societies, virginity was usually not a valued commodity in brokering a marriage, and divorce proceedings could be initiated by either party. Still, most marriages were monogamous, and marital fidelity was taken seriously.

The relative availability of cultivable land in the region may help explain the absence of joint families. Joint families under patriarchal leadership tend to be found in areas where land is scarce and individual families must work together to conserve resources and maximize income. With the exception of a few crowded river valleys, few areas in Southeast Asia had a high population density per acre of cultivable land. Throughout most of the area, water was plentiful, and the land was relatively fertile. In parts of Indonesia, it was possible to survive by living off the produce of wild fruit trees—bananas, coconuts, mangoes, and a variety of other tropical fruits.

World of the Spirits: Religious Belief

Indian religions also had a profound effect on Southeast Asia. Traditional religious beliefs in the region took the familiar form of spirit worship and animism that we have seen in other cultures. Southeast Asians believed that spirits dwelled in the mountains, rivers, streams, and other sacred places in their environment. Mountains were probably particularly sacred, since they were considered to be the abode of ancestral spirits, the place to which the souls of all the departed would retire after death.

When Hindu and Buddhist ideas began to penetrate the area early in the first millennium C.E., they exerted a strong appeal among local elites. Not only did the new doctrines offer a more convincing explanation of the nature of the cosmos, but they also provided local rulers with a means of enhancing their prestige and power and conferred an aura of legitimacy on their relations with their subjects. In the Javanese kingdoms and in Angkor, Hindu gods like Vishnu and Shiva provided a new and more sophisticated veneer for existing beliefs in nature deities and ancestral spirits. In Angkor, the king's duties included performing sacred rituals on the mountain in the capital city; in time, the ritual became a state cult

uniting Hindu gods with local nature deities and ancestral spirits in a complex pantheon.

This state cult, financed by the royal court, eventually led to the construction of temples throughout the country. Many of these temples housed thousands of priests and retainers and amassed great wealth, including vast estates farmed by local peasants. It has been estimated that there were as many as 300,000 priests in Angkor at the height of its power. This vast wealth, which was often exempt from taxes, may be one explanation for the gradual decline of Angkor in the thirteenth and fourteenth centuries.

Initially, the spread of Hindu and Buddhist doctrines was essentially an elite phenomenon. Although the common people participated in the state cult and helped construct the temples, they did not give up their traditional beliefs in local deities and ancestral spirits. A major transformation began in the eleventh century, however, when Theravada Buddhism began to penetrate the mainland kingdom of Pagan from the island of Sri Lanka. From Pagan, it spread rapidly to other areas in Southeast Asia and eventually became the religion of the masses throughout the mainland west of the Annamite Mountains.

Theravada's appeal to the peoples of Southeast Asia is reminiscent of the original attraction of Buddhist thought

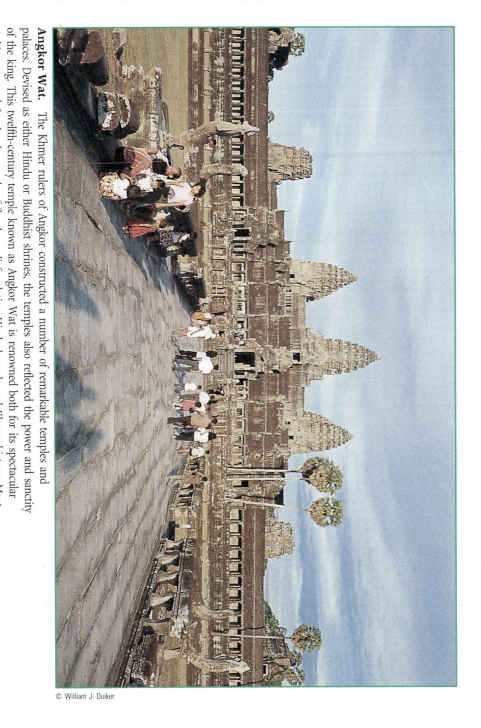

© William J. Duiker

Angkor Wat. The Khmer rulers of Angkor constructed a number of remarkable temples and palaces. Devised as either Hindu or Buddhist shrines, the temples also reflected the power and sanctity of the king. This twelfth-century temple known as Angkor Wat is renowned both for its spectacular architecture and for the thousands of fine bas-reliefs relating Hindu legends and Khmer history. Most memorable are the heavenly dancing maidens and the royal processions with elephants and soldiers.

centuries earlier on the Indian subcontinent. By teaching that individuals could seek Nirvana through their own actions rather than through the intercession of the ruler or a priest, Theravada was more accessible to the masses than the state cults promoted by the rulers. During the next centuries, Theravada gradually undermined the influence of state-supported religions and became the dominant faith in several mainland societies, including Burma, Thailand, Laos, and Cambodia. In the process, however, it was gradually appropriated by local rulers, who portrayed themselves as "immanent Buddhas," higher than ordinary mortals on the scale of human existence.

Theravada did not penetrate far into the Malay peninsula or the Indonesian island chain, perhaps because it entered Southeast Asia through Burma farther to the north. But the Malay world found its own popular alternative to state religions when Islam began to enter the area in the thirteenth and fourteenth centuries.

Because Islam's expansion into Southeast Asia took place for the most part after 1500, its emergence as a major force in the region will be discussed later in the book.

Not surprisingly, Indian influence extended to the Buddhist and Hindu temples of Southeast Asia. Temple architecture reflecting Gupta or southern Indian styles began to appear in Southeast Asia during the first centuries C.E. Most famous is the Buddhist temple at Borobudur, in central Java. Begun in the late eighth century at the behest of a king of Sailendra (an agricultural kingdom based in eastern Java), Borobudur is a massive stupa with nine terraces. Sculpted on the sides of each terrace are bas-reliefs depicting the nine stages in the life of Siddhartha Gautama, from childhood to his final release from the chain of human existence. Surmounted by hollow bell-like towers containing representations of the Buddha and capped by a single stupa, the structure dominates the landscape for miles around.

© William J. Duiker

© William J. Duiker

The Temple of Borobudur. The colossal pyramid temple at Borobudur, on the island of Java, is one of the greatest Buddhist monuments. Constructed in the eighth century C.E., it depicts the path to spiritual enlightenment in stone. Sculptures and relief portrayals of the life of the Buddha at the lower level depict the world of desire. At higher elevations, they give way to empty bell towers (see inset) and culminate at the summit with an empty and closed stupa, signifying the state of Nirvana. Shortly after it was built, Borobudur was abandoned when a new ruler switched his allegiance to Hinduism and ordered the erection of the Hindu temple of Prambanan nearby. Buried for a thousand years under volcanic ash and jungle, Borobudur was rediscovered in the nineteenth century and has recently been restored to its former splendor.

© William J. Duiker

Second only to Borobudur in technical excellence and even more massive in size are the ruins of the old capital city of Angkor Thom. The temple of Angkor Wat is the most famous and arguably the most beautiful of all the existing structures at Angkor Thom. Built on the model of the legendary Mount Meru (the home of the gods in Hindu tradition), it combines Indian architectural techniques with native inspiration in a structure of impressive delicacy and grace.

In existence for more than six hundred years, Angkor Thom serves as a bridge between the Hindu and Buddhist architectural styles. The last of its great temples, known as the Bayon, followed the earlier Hindu model but was topped with sculpted towers containing four-sided representations of a bodhisattva, searching, it is said, for souls to save. Shortly after the Bayon was built, Theravada Buddhist societies in Burma and Thailand began to create a new Buddhist architecture based on the concept of a massive stupa surmounted by a spire. Most famous, perhaps, is the Shwedagon Pagoda in Yangon (Rangoon), capital of modern Myanmar (Burma), which is covered with gold leaf contributed by devout Buddhists from around the country.

Giant Heads of Easter Island. When the Malayo-Polynesian-speaking peoples spread out from their homeland into the islands of the Pacific, they eventually settled in areas as far distant as Hawaii and Easter Island. Some of these peoples first arrived on Easter Island in the fifth century C.E. and soon began to erect giant stone statues. It is thought that they were devised by rival chiefdoms for reasons of prestige. Moving them from the quarry (shown here) by rolling them on a bed of rounded logs resulted in the eventual devastation of the forests and the total erosion of the landscape, nearly wiping out the entire population.

Expansion into the Pacific

One of the great maritime feats of human history was the penetration of the islands of the Pacific Ocean by Malayo-Polynesian-speaking peoples originating on the island of Taiwan and along the southeastern coast of China. By 2000 B.C.E., these seafarers had migrated as far as the Bismarck Archipelago, northeast of the island of New Guinea, where they encountered Melanesian peoples whose ancestors had taken part in the first wave of human settlement into the region thirty thousand years previously.

From there, the Polynesian peoples—as they are now familiarly known—continued their explorations eastward in large sailing canoes up to 100 feet long that carried more than forty people and many of their food staples, such as chickens, chili peppers, and a tuber called taro, the source of poi. Stopping in Fiji, Samoa, and the Cook Islands during the first millennium C.E., their descendants pressed onward, eventually reaching Tahiti, Hawaii, and even Easter Island, one of the most remote sites of human habitation in the world. Other peoples, now known as the Maori, sailed southwestward from the island of Rarotonga and settled in New Zealand, off the coast of Australia. The final frontier of human settlement had been breached.

CONCLUSION

During the more than fifteen hundred years from the fall of the Mauryas to the rise of the Mughals, Indian civilization faced a number of severe challenges. One challenge was primarily external and took the form of a continuous threat from beyond the mountains in the northwest. A second had internal causes, stemming from the tradition of factionalism and internal rivalry that had marked relations within the aristocracy since the Aryan influx in the second millennium B.C.E. (see Chapter 2). Despite the abortive efforts of the Guptas, that tradition continued almost without interruption down to the founding of the Mughal Empire in the sixteenth century.

The third challenge was primarily cultural and religious. One appeared in the religious divisions between Hindus and Buddhists, and later between Hindus and Muslims, that took place throughout much of this period. It is a measure of the strength and resilience of Hindu tradition that it was able to surmount the challenge of Buddhism and by the late first millennium C.E. had managed to reassert its dominant position in Indian society. But that triumph was short-lived. Like so many other areas in the region of southern Asia, it was now beset by a new challenge presented by nomadic forces from Central Asia. One result of the foreign conquest of northern India was the introduction of Islam into the region. As we shall see later, the new religion was about to become a serious rival to traditional beliefs among the people of India.

During the same period that Indian civilization faced these challenges at home, it was having a profound impact on the emerging states of Southeast Asia. Situated at the crossroads between two oceans and two great civilizations, Southeast Asia has long served as a bridge linking peoples and cultures, and as complex societies began to develop in the area, it is not surprising that they were strongly influenced by the older civilizations of neighboring China and India. At the same time, the Southeast Asian peoples put their own unique stamp on the ideas that they adopted and eventually rejected those that were inappropriate to local conditions.

The result was a region characterized by an almost unparalleled cultural richness and diversity, reflecting influences from as far away as the Middle East yet preserving indigenous elements that were deeply rooted in the local culture. Unfortunately, that very diversity posed potential problems for the peoples of Southeast Asia as they faced a new challenge from beyond the horizon. We shall deal with that challenge when we return to the region later in the book. In the meantime, we must turn our attention to the other major civilization that spread its shadow over the societies of southern Asia—China.

TIMELINE

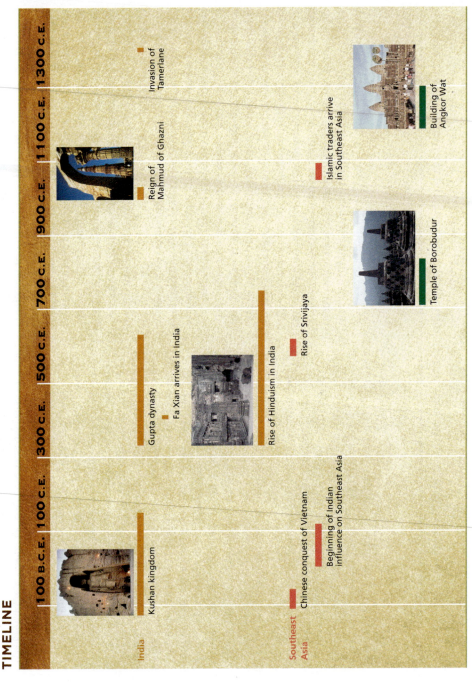

	100 B.C.E.	100 C.E.	300 C.E.	500 C.E.	700 C.E.	900 C.E.	1100 C.E.	1300 C.E.

India
- Kushan kingdom
- Gupta dynasty
- Fa Xian arrives in India
- Rise of Hinduism in India
- Reign of Mahmud of Ghazni
- Invasion of Tamerlane

Southeast Asia
- Chinese conquest of Vietnam
- Beginning of Indian influence on Southeast Asia
- Rise of Srivijaya
- Temple of Borobudur
- Islamic traders arrive in Southeast Asia
- Building of Angkor Wat

CHAPTER NOTES

1. Hiuen Tsiang, *Si-Yu-Ki: Buddhist Records of the Western World*, trans. S. Beal (London, 1982), pp. 89–90.
2. "Fo-Kwo-Ki" (Travels of Fa Xian), ch. 20, p. 43, in ibid.
3. E. C. Sachau, *Alberoni's India* (London, 1914), vol. 1, p. 22.
4. Quoted in S. M. Ikram, *Muslim Civilization in India*, (New York, 1964), p. 68.
5. Hiuen Tsiang, *Si-Yu-Ki*, pp. 73–74.
6. D. Barbosa, *The Book of Duarte Barbosa* (Nedeln, Liechtenstein, 1967), pp. 147–148.
7. Quoted in R. Lannoy, *The Speaking Tree: A Study of Indian Culture and Society* (London, 1971), p. 232.
8. Quoted in S. Tharu and K. Lalita, *Women Writing in India*, vol. 1 (New York, 1991), p. 77.

9. Quoted in A. L. Basham, *The Wonder That Was India* (London, 1954), p. 426.

10. Quoted in S. Hughes and B. Hughes, *Women in World History*, vol. 1 (Armonk, N.Y., 1995), p. 217.

SUGGESTED READING

General   The period from the decline of the Mauryas to the rise of the Mughals in India is not especially rich in terms of materials in English. Still, a number of the standard texts on Indian history contain useful sections on the period. Particularly good are **A. L. Basham**, *The Wonder That Was India* (London, 1954), and **S. Wolpert**, *India*, 3d ed. (New York, 2005).

Indian Society and Culture   A number of studies of Indian society and culture deal with this period. See, for example, **R. Thapar**, *Early India, from the Origins to A.D. 1300* (London, 2002), for an authoritative interpretation of Indian culture during the medieval period. On Buddhism, see **H. Nakamura**, *Indian Buddhism: A Survey with Bibliographical Notes* (Delhi, 1987), and **H. Akira**, *A History of Indian Buddhism from Sakyamuni to Early Mahayana* (Honolulu, 1990). For an interesting treatment of the Buddhist influence on commercial activities that is reminiscent of the role of Christianity in Europe, see **L. Xinru**, *Ancient India and Ancient China: Trade and Religious Changes, A.D. 1–600* (Delhi, 1988).

Women's Issues   For a discussion of women's issues, see **S. Hughes and B. Hughes**, *Women in World History*, vol. 1 (Armonk, N.Y., 1995); **S. Tharu and K. Lalita**, *Women Writing in India*, vol. 1 (New York, 1991); and **V. Dehejia**, *Devi: The Great Goddess* (Washington, D.C., 1999).

Indian Economy   The most comprehensive treatment of the Indian economy and regional trade throughout the Indian Ocean is **K. N. Chaudhuri**, *Trade and Civilization in the Indian Ocean: An Economic History from the Rise of Islam to 1750* (Cambridge, 1985), a groundbreaking comparative study. See also his more recent and massive *Asia Before Europe: Economy and Civilization of the Indian Ocean from the Rise of Islam to 1750* (Cambridge, 1990), which owes a considerable debt to F. Braudel's classical work on the Mediterranean region.

Central Asia   For an overview of events in Central Asia during this period, see **D. Christian**, *Inner Eurasia from Prehistory to the Mongol Empire* (Oxford, 1998) and **C. E. Bosworth**, *The Later Ghaznavids: Splendor and Decay* (New York, 1977). On the career of Tamerlane, see **B. F. Manz**, *The Rise and Rule of Tamerlane* (Cambridge, 1989).

Medieval Indian Art   On Indian art during the medieval period, see **S. Huntington**, *The Art of Ancient India: Buddhist, Hindu, and Jain* (New York, 1985), and **V. Dehejia**, *Indian Art* (London, 1997).

Early Southeast Asia   The early history of Southeast Asia is not as well documented as that of China or India. Except for

Vietnam, where histories written in Chinese appeared shortly after the Chinese conquest, written materials on societies in the region are relatively sparse. Historians were therefore compelled to rely on stone inscriptions and the accounts of travelers and historians from other countries. As a result, the history of precolonial Southeast Asia was presented, as it were, from the outside looking in. For an overview of modern scholarship on the region, see **N. Tarling**, ed., *The Cambridge History of Southeast Asia*, vol. 1 (Cambridge, 1999).

Impressive advances are now being made in the field of prehistory. See **P. Bellwood**, *Prehistory of the Indo-Malaysian Archipelago* (Honolulu, 1997), and **C. Higham**, *The Bronze Age of Southeast Asia* (Cambridge, 1996). Also see the latter's *Civilization of Angkor* (Berkeley, Calif., 2001), which discusses the latest evidence on that major empire.

Southeast Asian Commerce   The role of commerce has been highlighted as a key aspect in the development of the region. For two fascinating accounts, see **K. R. Hall**, *Maritime Trade and State Development in Early Southeast Asia* (Honolulu, 1985), and **A. Reid**, *Southeast Asia in the Era of Commerce, 1450–1680: The Lands Below the Winds* (New Haven, Conn., 1989). The latter is also quite useful on the role of women. On the region's impact on world history, see the impressive *Strange Parallels: Southeast Asia in Global Context, c. 800–1300*, vol. 1, by **V. Lieberman** (Cambridge, 2003).

WORLD HISTORY RESOURCE CENTER

Enter the Resource Center using either your CengageNOW access card or your separate access card for the World History Resource Center. Organized by topic, this Website includes quizzes; images; over 350 primary source documents; interactive simulations, maps, and timelines; movie explorations; and a wealth of other resources. You can read the following documents, and many more, at the *World History Resource Center*:

Acts and Rewards of Devotion to the Buddha

The Buddhist Conception of the Intermediate State

Visit the *World History Companion Website* for chapter quizzes and more:

www.cengage.com/history/Duiker/World6e

CENGAGE**NOW**   Enter CengageNOW using the access card that is available with this text. *CengageNOW* will help you understand the content in this chapter with lesson plans generated for your needs, as well as provide you with a connection to the *Wadsworth World History Resource Center* (see description below for details).

CHAPTER 10

THE FLOWERING OF TRADITIONAL CHINA

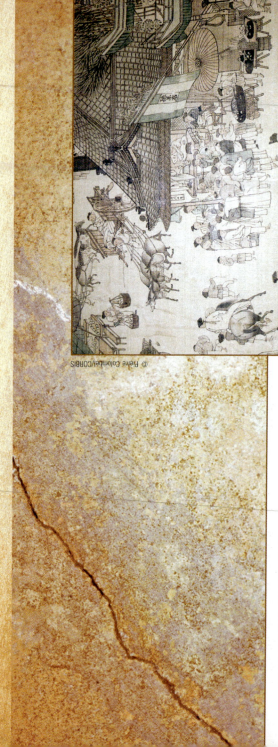

Detail of a Chinese scroll, Spring Festival on the River

© Pierre Colombel/CORBIS

CHAPTER OUTLINE AND FOCUS QUESTIONS

China After the Han

Q After the decline of the Han dynasty, China went through several centuries of internal division. Why do you think this occurred, and what impact did it have on Chinese society?

China Reunified: The Sui, the Tang, and the Song

Q What major changes in political structures and social and economic life occurred during the Sui, Tang, and Song dynasties?

Explosion in Central Asia: The Mongol Empire

Q Why were the Mongols able to amass an empire, and what were the main characteristics of their rule in China?

The Ming Dynasty

Q What were the chief initiatives taken by the early rulers of the Ming dynasty to enhance the role of China in the world? Why did the imperial court order the famous voyages of Zhenghe, and then why were they discontinued?

In Search of the Way

Q What roles did Buddhism, Daoism, and Neo-Confucianism play in Chinese intellectual life in the period between the Sui dynasty and the Ming?

The Apogee of Chinese Culture

Q What were the main achievements in Chinese literature and art in the period between the Tang dynasty and the Ming, and what technological innovations and intellectual developments contributed to these achievements?

CRITICAL THINKING

Q The civilization of ancient China fell under the onslaught of nomadic invasions, as had some of its counterparts elsewhere in the world. But China, unlike other classical empires, was later able to reconstitute itself on the same political and cultural foundations. How do you account for the difference?

ON HIS FIRST VISIT to the city, the traveler was mightily impressed. Its streets were so straight and wide that he could see through the city from one end to the other. Along the wide boulevards were beautiful palaces and inns in great profusion. The city was laid out in squares like a chessboard, and within each square were spacious courts and gardens. Truly, said the visitor, this must be one of the largest and wealthiest cities on earth—a city "planned out to a degree of precision and beauty impossible to describe."

The visitor was Marco Polo, and the city was Khanbaliq (later known as Beijing), capital of the Yuan dynasty (1279–1368) and one of the great urban centers of the Chinese Empire. Marco Polo was an Italian merchant who had traveled to China in the late thirteenth century and then served as an official at the court of Khubilai Khan. In later travels in China, Polo visited a number of other great cities, including the commercial hub of Ken-Zan-fu (Kaifeng) on the Yellow River. It is a city, he remarked,

of great commerce, and eminent for its manufactures. Raw silk is produced in large quantities, and tissues of gold and every other kind of silk are woven there. At this place likewise they prepare every article necessary for the equipment of an army. All species of provisions are in abundance, and to be procured at a moderate price.[1]

China After the Han

Focus Question: After the decline of the Han dynasty, China went through several centuries of internal division. Why do you think this occurred, and what impact did it have on Chinese society?

Polo's diary, published after his return to Italy almost twenty years later, astonished readers with tales of this magnificent but unknown civilization far to the east.

When Marco Polo arrived, China was ruled by the Mongols, a nomadic people from Central Asia who had overthrown the Song (Sung) dynasty and assumed control of the Chinese Empire. The Yuan dynasty, as the Mongol rulers were called, was only one of a succession of dynasties to rule China after the collapse of the Han dynasty in the third century C.E. The end of the Han had led to a period of internal division and civil war that lasted nearly four hundred years and was aggravated by the threat posed by nomadic peoples from the north. This time of troubles ended in the early seventh century, however, when the dynamic Tang dynasty led China to some of its finest achievements.

To this point, Chinese history appeared to be following a pattern similar to that of India. There, as we have seen, the passing of the Mauryan dynasty in the second century B.C.E. unleashed a period of internal division that, except for the interval of the Guptas, lasted several hundred years. It was not until the rise of the Mughal Empire in the early sixteenth century that unity returned to the subcontinent.

But China did not repeat the Indian experience. The Tang dynasty collapsed in 907, but after a brief interregnum, China was reunified under the Song, who ruled most of China for nearly three hundred years. The Song were in turn overthrown by the Mongols in the late thirteenth century, and they then gave way to a powerful new native dynasty, the Ming, in 1368. Dynasty followed dynasty, with periods of extraordinary cultural achievement alternating with periods of internal disorder, but in general Chinese society continued to build on the political and cultural foundations of the Zhou and the Han.

Chinese historians, viewing this vast process as it evolved over time, began to hypothesize that Chinese history was cyclical, driven by the dynamic interplay of the forces of good and evil, *yang* and *yin*, growth and decay. Beyond the forces of conflict and change lay the essential continuity of Chinese history, based on the timeless principles established by Confucius and other thinkers during the Zhou dynasty in antiquity. In actuality, this picture of a succession of dynasties, each seeking to replicate the glories of China's golden age under the early Zhou dynasty, disguises the reality that under the surface Chinese society was undergoing significant changes and bore scant resemblance to the kingdom that had been founded by the house of Zhou more than twenty centuries earlier.

After the collapse of the Han dynasty at the beginning of the third century C.E., China fell into an extended period of division and civil war. Taking advantage of the absence of organized government in China, nomadic forces from the Gobi Desert penetrated south of the Great Wall and established their own rule over northern China. In the Yangtze valley and farther to the south, native Chinese rule was maintained, but constant civil war and instability led later historians to refer to the period as the "era of the six dynasties."

The collapse of the Han Empire had a marked effect on the Chinese psyche. The Confucian principles that emphasized hard work, the subordination of the individual to community interests, and belief in the essentially rational order of the universe came under severe challenge, and many Chinese began to turn to more messianic creeds that emphasized the supernatural or the promise of earthly or heavenly salvation. Intellectuals began to reject the stuffy moralism and complacency of State Confucianism and sought emotional satisfaction in hedonistic pursuits or philosophical Daoism (see the box on p. 276).

Eccentric behavior and a preference for philosophical Daoism became a common response to a corrupt age. A group of writers known as the "seven sages of the bamboo forest" exemplified the period. Among the best known was the poet Liu Ling, whose odd behavior is described in this oft-quoted passage:

Liu Ling was an inveterate drinker and indulged himself to the full. Sometimes he stripped off his clothes and sat in his room stark naked. Some men saw him and rebuked him. Liu Ling said, "Heaven and earth are my dwelling, and my house is my trousers. Why are you all coming into my trousers?"[2]

But neither popular beliefs in the supernatural nor philosophical Daoism could satisfy deeper emotional needs or provide solace in time of sorrow or the hope of a better life in the hereafter. Buddhism filled that gap.

Buddhism was brought to China in the first or second century C.E., probably by missionaries and merchants traveling over the Silk Road. The concept of rebirth was probably unfamiliar to most Chinese, and the intellectual hairsplitting that often accompanied discussion of the Buddha's message in India was too esoteric for Chinese tastes. Still, in the difficult years surrounding the decline of the Han dynasty, Buddhist ideas, especially those of the Mahayana school, began to find adherents among intellectuals and ordinary people alike. As Buddhism increased in popularity, it was frequently attacked by supporters of Confucianism and Daoism for its foreign origins. Some even claimed that Siddhartha Gautama had been a disciple of Lao Tzu. But such sniping did not halt the progress of Buddhism, and eventually the new faith was assimilated into Chinese culture, assisted by the efforts of such tireless advocates as the missionaries Fa Xian and Xuan Zang and the support of ruling elites in both northern and southern China (see "The Rise and Decline of Buddhism and Daoism" later in this chapter).

OPPOSING VIEWPOINTS

ACTION OR INACTION: AN IDEOLOGICAL DISPUTE IN MEDIEVAL CHINA

RELIGION & PHILOSOPHY

During the interregnum between the fall of the Han dynasty in 220 C.E. and the rise of the Tang four hundred years later, Daoist critics lampooned the hypocrisy of the "Confucian gentleman" and the Master's emphasis on ritual and the maintenance of proper relations among individuals in society. In the first selection, a third-century Daoist launches an attack on the type of pompous and hypocritical Confucian figure who feigns high moral principles while secretly engaging in corrupt and licentious behavior.

By the eighth century, the tables had turned. Han Yu (768–824), a key figure in the emergence of Neo-Confucian thought as the official ideology of the state, responded to such remarks with his own withering analysis of the dangers of "doing nothing"—a clear reference to the famous Daoist doctrine of "inaction." An excerpt is provided in the second selection.

Biography of a Great Man

What the world calls a gentleman [*chün-tzu*] is someone who is solely concerned with moral law [*fa*], and cultivates exclusively the rules of propriety [*li*]. His hand holds the emblem of jade [authority]; his foot follows the straight line of the rule. He likes to think that his actions set a permanent example; he likes to think that his words are everlasting models. In his youth, he has a reputation in the villages of his locality; in his later years, he is well known in the neighboring districts. Upward, he aspires to the dignity of the Three Dukes; downward, he does not disdain the post of governor of the nine provinces.

Have you ever seen the lice that inhabit a pair of trousers? They jump into the depths of the seams, hiding themselves in the cotton wadding, and believe they have a pleasant place to live. Walking, they do not risk going beyond the edge of the seam; moving, they are careful not to emerge from the trouser leg; and they think they have kept to the rules of etiquette. But when the trousers are ironed, the flames invade the hills, the fire spreads, the villages are set on fire and the towns burned down; then the lice that inhabit the trousers cannot escape.

What difference is there between the gentleman who lives within a narrow world and the lice that inhabit trouser legs?

Han Yu, *Essentials of the Moral Way*

In ancient times men confronted many dangers. But sages arose who taught them the way to live and to grow

together. They served as rulers and as teachers. They drove out reptiles and wild beasts and had the people settle the central lands. The people were cold, and they clothed them; hungry, and they fed them. Because the people dwelt in trees and fell to the ground, dwelt in caves and became ill, the sages built houses for them.

They fashioned crafts so the people could provide themselves with implements. They made trade to link together those who had and those who had not and medicine to save them from premature death. They taught the people to bury and make sacrifices [to the dead] to enlarge their sense of gratitude and love. They gave rites to set order and precedence, music to vent melancholy, government to direct idleness, and punishments to weed out intransigence. When the people cheated each other, the sages invented tallies and seals, weights and measures to make them honest. When they attacked each other, they fashioned walls and towns, armor and weapons for them to defend themselves. So when dangers came, they prepared the people; and when calamity arose, they defended the people.

But now the Daoists maintain:

Till the sages are dead,
theft will not end....
so break the measures, smash the scales,
and the people will not contend.

These are thoughtless remarks indeed, for humankind would have died out long ago if there had been no sages in antiquity. Men have neither feathers nor fur, neither scales nor shells to ward off heat and cold, neither talons nor fangs to fight for food....

But now the Daoists advocate "doing nothing" as in high antiquity. Such is akin to criticizing a man who wears furs in winter by asserting that it is easier to make linen, or akin to criticizing a man who eats when he is hungry by asserting that it is easier to take a drink....

This being so, what can be done? Block them or nothing will flow; stop them or nothing will move. Make humans of these people, burn their books, make homes of their dwellings, make clear the way of the former kings to guide them, and "the widowers, the widows, the orphans, the childless, and the diseased all shall have care." This can be done.

Q *How might the author of the first excerpt respond to Han Yu's remarks? Based on information available to you, which author appears to make the better case for his chosen ideological preference?*

China Reunified: The Sui, the Tang, and the Song

Q **Focus Question:** What major changes in political structures and social and economic life occurred during the Sui, Tang, and Song dynasties?

After nearly four centuries of internal division, China was unified once again in 581 when Yang Jian (Yang Chien), a member of a respected aristocratic family in northern China, founded a new dynasty, known as the Sui (581–618). Yang Jian (who is also known by his reign title of Sui Wendi, or Sui Wen Ti) established his capital at the historic metropolis of Chang'an and began to extend his authority throughout the heartland of China.

The Sui Dynasty

Like his predecessors, the new emperor sought to create a unifying ideology for the state to enhance its efficiency. But where Liu Bang, the founder of the Han dynasty, had adopted Confucianism as the official doctrine to hold the empire together, Yang Jian turned to Daoism and Buddhism. He founded monasteries for both doctrines in the capital and appointed Buddhist monks to key positions as political advisers.

SCIENCE & TECHNOLOGY

COMPARATIVE ILLUSTRATION

The Grand Canal. Built over centuries, the Grand Canal is one of the engineering wonders of the world and a crucial conduit for carrying goods between northern and southern China. After the Song dynasty, when the region south of the Yangtze River became the heartland of the empire, the canal was used to carry rice and other agricultural products to the food-starved northern provinces. Many of the towns and cities located along the canal became famous for their wealth and cultural achievements. Among the most renowned was Suzhou, a center for silk manufacture, which is sometimes described as the "Venice of China" because of its many canals. Shown here at the top right is a classic example of a humpback bridge crossing an arm of the canal in downtown Suzhou. The resemblance to the Bridge of Marvels in Venice (lower left) seems more than coincidental.

Q In what ways do you think the roles that the Grand Canal in China and the city of Venice played in the regional and global marketplace might differ?

© William J. Duiker

© William J. Duiker

Yang Jian was a builder as well as a conqueror, ordering the construction of a new canal from the capital to the confluence of the Wei and Yellow Rivers nearly 100 miles to the east. His son, Emperor Sui Yangdi (Sui Yang Ti), continued the process, and the 1,400-mile-long Grand Canal, linking the two great rivers of China, the Yellow and the Yangtze, was completed during his reign (see the comparative illustration below). The new canal facilitated the shipment of grain and other commodities from the rice-rich southern provinces to the densely populated north. The canal also served other purposes, such as speeding communications between the two regions and permitting the rapid dispatch of troops to troubled provinces. Sui Yangdi also used the canal as an imperial highway for inspecting his empire. One imperial procession from the capital to the central Yangtze region was described as follows:

The emperor caused to be built dragon boats . . . red battle cruisers, multi-decked transports, lesser vessels of bamboo slats. Boatmen hired from all the waterways . . . pulled the vessels by ropes of green silk on the imperial progress to Chiang-tu [Yangzhou]. The emperor rode in the dragon boat, and civil and military officials of the fifth grade and above rode in the multi-decked transports; those of the ninth grade and above were given the vessels of yellow bamboo. The boats followed one another from prow to prow for more than 200 leagues [about 65 miles]. The prefectures and counties through which they passed were ordered to prepare to offer provisions. Those who made bountiful arrangements were given an additional office or title; those who fell short were given punishments up to the death penalty.[3]

Despite such efforts to project the majesty of the imperial personage, the Sui dynasty came to an end immediately after Sui Yangdi's death. The Sui emperor was a tyrannical ruler, and his expensive military campaigns aroused widespread unrest. After his return from a failed campaign against Korea in 618, the emperor was murdered in his palace. One of his generals, Li Yuan, took advantage of the instability that ensued and declared the foundation of a new dynasty, known as the Tang (T'ang). Building on the successes of its predecessor, the Tang lasted for three hundred years, until 907.

The Tang Dynasty

Li Yuan ruled for a brief period and then was elbowed aside by his son, who assumed the reign title Tang Taizong (T'ang T'ai-tsung). Under his vigorous leadership, the Tang launched a program of internal renewal and external expansion that would make it one of the greatest dynasties in the long history of China (see Map 10.1). Under the Tang, the northwest was pacified and given the

name of Xinjiang, or "new region." A long conflict with Tibet led for the first time to the extension of Chinese control over the vast and desolate plateau north of the Himalaya Mountains. The southern provinces below the Yangtze were fully assimilated into the Chinese Empire, and the imperial court established commercial and diplomatic relations with the states of Southeast Asia. With reason, China now claimed to be the foremost power in East Asia, and the emperor demanded fealty and tribute from all his fellow rulers beyond the frontier. Korea accepted tribute status and attempted to adopt the Chinese model, and the Japanese dispatched official missions to China to learn more about its customs and institutions (see Chapter 11).

Finally, the Tang dynasty witnessed a flowering of Chinese culture. Many modern observers feel that the era represents the apogee of Chinese creativity in poetry and sculpture. One reason for this explosion of culture was the influence of Buddhism, which affected art, literature, and philosophy, as well as religion and politics. Monasteries sprang up throughout China, and as under the Sui, Buddhist monks served as advisers at the Tang imperial court. The city of Chang'an, now restored to the glory it had known as the capital of the Han dynasty, once again became the seat of the empire. It was possibly the greatest

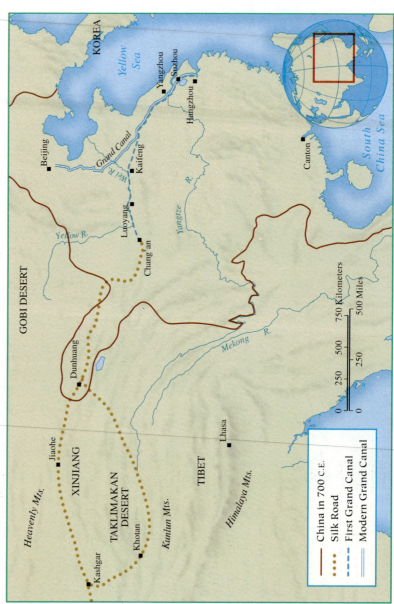

MAP 10.1 China Under the Tang. The era of the Tang dynasty was one of the greatest periods in the long history of China. Tang influence spread from heartland China into neighboring regions, including Central and Southeast Asia.

Q What was the main function of the Grand Canal during this period, and why was it built?

Legend:
China in 700 C.E.
Silk Road
First Grand Canal
Modern Grand Canal

View an animated version of this map or related maps at www.cengage.com/history/Duiker/World6e

© William J. Duiker

Buddhist Sculpture at Longmen. The Silk Road was an avenue for ideas as well as trade. Over the centuries, Christian, Buddhist, and Muslim teachings came to China across the sandy wastes of the Taklimakan Desert. In the seventh century, the Tang emperor Gaozong commissioned this massive temple carving as part of the large complex of cave art devoted to Buddha at Longmen in central China. Bold and grandiose in their construction, these statues reflect the glory of the Tang dynasty.

Map: Forbidden Park · Outer City · Imperial City · Palace City · 0 2 4 6 Kilometers · 0 2 4 Miles

---

Chang'an Under the Sui and the Tang

city in the world of its time, with an estimated population of nearly two million. The city was filled with temples and palaces, and its markets teemed with goods from all over the known world (see the box on p. 280).

But the Tang, like the Han, sowed the seeds of their own destruction.

Tang rulers could not prevent the rise of internal forces that would ultimately weaken the dynasty and bring it to an end. Two ubiquitous problems were court intrigues and official corruption. Xuanzong (Hsuan Tsung, r. 712–756), one of the great Tang emperors and a renowned patron of the arts, was dominated in later life by one of his favorite concubines, the beautiful Yang Guifei (Yang Kuei-fei). One of her protégés launched a rebellion in 755 and briefly seized power in the capital of Chang'an. The revolt was eventually suppressed, and Yang Guifei, who is viewed as one of the great villains of Chinese history, was put to death. But the Tang never fully recovered from the catastrophe. The loss of power by the central government led to increased influence by great landed families inside China and chronic instability along the northern and western frontiers, where local military commanders ruled virtually without central government interference. Some historians also speculate that a prolonged drought may have played a role in the decline of the dynasty. It was an eerie repetition of the final decades of the Han.

The end finally came in the early tenth century, when border troubles with northern nomadic peoples called the Khitan increased, leading to the final collapse of the dynasty in 907. The Tang had followed the classic strategy of "using a barbarian to oppose a barbarian" by allying with a trading people called the Uighurs (a Turkic-speaking people who had taken over many of the caravan routes along the Silk Road) against their old rivals. But yet another nomadic people called the Kirghiz defeated the Uighurs and then turned on the Tang government in its moment of weakness and overthrew it.

The Song Dynasty

China slipped once again into chaos. This time, the period of foreign invasion and division was much shorter. In 960, a new dynasty, known as the Song (960–1279), rose to power. From the start, however, the Song (Sung) rulers encountered more problems than their predecessors. Although the founding emperor, Song Taizu (Sung T'ai-tsu), was able to co-opt many of the powerful military commanders whose rivalry had brought the Tang dynasty to an end, he was unable to reconquer the northwestern part of the country from the nomadic Khitan peoples. The emperor therefore established his capital farther to the east, at Kaifeng, where the Grand Canal intersected the Yellow River. Later, when pressures from the nomads in the north increased, the court was forced to move the capital even farther south, to Hangzhou (Hangchow), on the coast just south of the Yangtze River delta; the emperors who ruled from Hangzhou are known as the southern Song. The Song also lost control over Tibet. Despite its political and military weaknesses, the dynasty nevertheless ruled during a period of economic expansion, prosperity, and cultural achievement and is therefore considered among the more successful Chinese dynasties. The population of the empire had risen to an estimated forty million people, slightly more than that of the continent of Europe.

Yet the Song dynasty was never able to surmount the external challenge from the north, and that failure

The Good Life in the High Tang

ARTS & IDEAS

At the height of the Tang dynasty, China was at the apex of its power and magnificence. Here the Tang poet Du Fu (Tu Fu) describes a gala festival in the capital of Chang'an (Ch'ang-an) attended by the favored elite. The author's distaste for the spectacle of arrogance and waste is expressed in muted sarcasm.

Du Fu, "A Poem"

Third day of the third month
The very air seems new
In Chang-an along the water
Many beautiful girls...
Firm, plump contours,
Flesh and bone proportioned.
Dresses of gauze brocade
Mirror the end of spring
Peacocks crimped in thread of gold
Unicorns in silver....
Some are kin to the imperial favorite
Among them the Lady of Kuo and the Lady
of Ch'in [Qin].
Camel-humps of purple meat
Brought in shining pans
The white meat of raw fish
Served on crystal platters
Don't tempt the sated palate.
All that is cut with fancy and
Prepared with care—left untouched.
Eunuchs, reins a-flying
Disturb no dust
Bring the "eight chef d'oeuvres"
From the palace kitchens.
Music of strings and pipes...
Accompanying the feasting
Moving the many guests
All of rank and importance.
Last comes a horseman
See him haughtily
Dismount near the screen
And step on the flowery carpet....
The chancellor is so powerful
His mere touch will scorch.
Watch you don't come near
Lest you displease him.

Q *Why does the author of this poem appear to be so angry at the site of the festival he described here? Compare his feelings here with those he expresses in the short poem included in the box on p. 301.*

---

eventually brought about the end of the dynasty. During its final decades, the Song rulers were forced to pay tribute to the Jurchen peoples from Manchuria. In the early thirteenth century, the Song, ignoring precedent and the fate of the Tang, formed an alliance with the Mongols, a new and obscure nomadic people from the Gobi Desert. As under the Tang, the decision proved to be a disaster. Within a few years, the Mongols had become a much more serious threat to China than the Jurchen. After defeating the Jurchen, the Mongols turned their attention to the Song, advancing on Song territory from both the north and the west. By this time, the Song empire had been weakened by internal factionalism and a loss of tax revenues. After a series of river battles and sieges marked by the use of catapults and gunpowder, the Song were defeated, and the conquerors announced the creation of a new Yuan (Mongol) dynasty. Ironically, the Mongols had first learned about gunpowder from the Chinese.

Political Structures: The Triumph of Confucianism

During the nearly seven hundred years from the Sui to the end of the Song, a mature political system based on principles originally established during the Qin and Han dynasties gradually emerged in China. After the Tang dynasty's brief flirtation with Buddhism, State Confucianism became the ideological cement that held the system together. The development of this system took several centuries, and it did not reach its height until the period of the Song dynasty.

Equal Opportunity in China: The Civil Service Examination

At the apex of the government hierarchy was the **Grand Council**, assisted by a secretariat and a chancellery; it included representatives from all three authorities—civil, military, and censorate. Under the Grand Council was the Department of State Affairs, composed of ministries responsible for justice, military affairs, personnel, public works, revenue, and rites (ritual). This department was in effect the equivalent of a modern cabinet.

The Tang dynasty adopted the practice of selecting bureaucrats through civil service examinations but was unable to curb the influence of the great aristocratic clans. The Song were more successful at limiting aristocratic control over the bureaucracy, in part because the power of the nobility had been irreparably weakened during the final years of the Tang dynasty and did not recover during the interregnum that followed its collapse.

Arrival of Buddhism in China	c. first century C.E.
Fall of the Han dynasty	220 C.E.
Sui dynasty	581–618
Tang dynasty	618–907
Li Bo (Li Po) and Du Fu (Tu Fu)	700s
Emperor Xuanzong	712–756
Song dynasty	960–1279
Wang Anshi	1021–1086
Southern Song dynasty	1127–1279
Life of Genghis Khan	c. 1162–1227
Mongol conquest of China	1279
Reign of Khubilai Khan	1260–1294
Fall of the Yuan dynasty	1368
Ming dynasty	1369–1644

One way of strengthening the power of the central administration was to make the civil service examination system the primary route to an official career. To reduce the power of the noble families, relatives of individuals serving in the imperial court, as well as eunuchs, were prohibited from taking the examinations. But if the Song rulers' objective was to make the bureaucracy more subservient to the court, they may have been disappointed. The rising professionalism of the bureaucracy, which numbered about ten thousand in the imperial capital, with an equal number at the local level, provided it with an esprit de corps and an influence that sometimes enabled it to resist the whims of individual emperors.

Under the Song, the examination system attained the form that it would retain in later centuries. In general, three levels of examinations were administered. The first was a qualifying examination given annually at the provincial capital. Candidates who succeeded in this first stage were considered qualified but normally were not given positions in the bureaucracy except at the local level. Many stopped at this level and accepted positions as village teachers to train other candidates. Candidates who wished to go on could take a second examination given at the capital every three years. Successful candidates could apply for an official position. Some went on to take the final examination, which was given in the imperial palace once every three years. Those who passed were eligible for high positions in the central bureaucracy or for appointments as district magistrates.

During the early Tang, the examinations included questions on Buddhist and Daoist as well as Confucian texts, but by Song times, examinations were based entirely on the Confucian classics. Candidates were expected to memorize passages and to be able to define the moral lessons they contained. The system guaranteed that successful candidates—and therefore officials—would have received a full dose of Confucian political and social

ethics. Whether they followed those ethics, of course, was another matter. Many students complained about the rigors of memorization and the irrelevance of the process. Others brought crib notes into the examination hall (one enterprising candidate concealed an entire Confucian text in the lining of his cloak). One famous Tang scholar complained that if Mencius and other Confucian worthies had lived in his own day, they would have refused to sit for the examinations.

The Song authorities ignored such criticisms, but they did open the system to more people by allowing all males except criminals or members of certain restricted occupations to take the examinations. To provide potential candidates with schooling, training academies were set up at the provincial and district levels. Without such academies, only individuals fortunate enough to receive training in the classics in family-run schools would have had the expertise to pass the examinations. Such policies represented a considerable improvement over earlier times, when most candidates came from the ranks of the elite. According to one historian, more than half of the successful candidates during the mid-Song period came from families that had not previously had a successful candidate for at least three generations. In time, the majority of candidates came from the landed gentry, nonaristocratic landowners who controlled much of the wealth in the countryside. Because the gentry prized education and became the primary upholders of the Confucian tradition, they were often called the

scholar-gentry.

But certain aspects of the system still prevented it from truly providing equal opportunity to all. In the first place, only males were eligible. Then again, the Song did not attempt to establish a system of universal elementary education. In practice, only those who had been given a basic education in the classics at home were able to enter the state-run academies and compete for a position in the bureaucracy. Unless they were fortunate to have a wealthy relative willing to serve as a sponsor, the poor had little chance.

Nor could the system guarantee an honest, efficient bureaucracy. Official arrogance, bureaucratic infighting, corruption, and legalistic interpretations of government regulations were as prevalent in medieval China as in bureaucracies the world over. Another problem was that officials were expected to use their positions to help their relatives. As we observed earlier, even Confucius held that filial duty transcends loyalty to the community. What is nepotism in Western eyes was simply proper behavior in China. Chinese rulers attempted to circumvent this problem by assigning officials outside their home region, but this policy met with only limited success.

Despite such weaknesses, the civil service examination system was an impressive achievement for its day and probably provided a more efficient government and more opportunity for upward mobility than were found in any other civilization of its time. Most Western governments, for example, began to recruit officials on the basis of merit only in the nineteenth century. Furthermore, by regulating the content of the examinations, the system helped provide China with a cultural uniformity lacking in empires elsewhere in Asia.

The court also attempted to curb official misbehavior through the censorate. Specially trained officials known as censors were assigned to investigate possible cases of official wrongdoing and report directly to the court. The censorate was supposed to be independent of outside pressures to ensure that its members would feel free to report wrongdoing wherever it occurred. In practice, censors who displeased high court officials were often removed or even subjected to more serious forms of punishment, which reduced the effectiveness of the system.

Local Government

The Song dynasty maintained the local government institutions that it had inherited from its predecessors. At the base of the government pyramid was the district (or county), governed by a magistrate. The magistrate, assisted by his staff of three or four officials and several other menial employees, was responsible for maintaining law and order and collecting taxes within his jurisdiction. A district could exceed 100,000 people. Below the district was the basic unit of Chinese government, the village. Because villages were so numerous in China, the central government did not appoint an official at that level and allowed the villages to administer themselves. Village government was normally in the hands of a council of elders, most often assisted by a chief. The council, usually made up of the heads of influential families in the village, maintained the local irrigation and transportation network, adjudicated local disputes, organized and maintained a militia, and assisted in collecting taxes (usually paid in grain) and delivering them to the district magistrate.

As a rule, most Chinese had little involvement with government matters. When they had to deal with the government, they almost always turned to their village officials. Although the district magistrate was empowered to settle local civil disputes, most villagers preferred to resolve problems among themselves. It was expected that the magistrate and his staff would supplement their income by charging for such services, a practice that reduced the costs of the central government but also provided an opportunity for bribes, a problem that plagued the Chinese bureaucracy down to modern times.

The Economy

During the long period between the Sui and the Song, the Chinese economy, like the government, grew considerably in size and complexity. China was still an agricultural society, but major changes were taking place within the economy and the social structure. The urban sector of the economy was becoming increasingly important, new social classes were beginning to appear, and the economic

focus of the empire was beginning to shift from the Yellow River valley in the north to the Yangtze River valley in the center—a process that was encouraged both by the expansion of cultivation in the Yangtze delta and by the control exerted over the north by nomadic peoples during the Song.

The Land Reform

The economic revival began shortly after the rise of the Tang. During the long period of internal division, land had become concentrated in the hands of aristocratic families, with most peasants reduced to serfdom or slavery. The early Tang tried to reduce the power of the landed nobility and maximize tax revenues by adopting the ancient "equal field" system, in which land was allocated to farmers for life in return for an annual tax payment and three weeks of conscript labor.

At first, the new system was vigorously enforced and led to increased rural prosperity and government revenue. But eventually, the rich and the politically influential learned to manipulate the system for their own benefit and accumulated huge tracts of land. The growing population, bolstered by a rise in food production and the extended period of social stability, also put steady pressure on the system. Finally, the government abandoned the effort to equalize landholdings and returned the land to private hands while attempting to prevent inequalities through the tax system. The failure to resolve the land problem contributed to the fall of the Tang dynasty in the early tenth century.

The Song tried to resolve the land problem by returning to the successful programs of the early Tang and reducing the power of the wealthy landed aristocrats. During the late eleventh century, the reformist official Wang Anshi (Wang An-shih) attempted to limit the size of landholdings through progressive land taxes and provided cheap credit to poor farmers to help them avoid bankruptcy. His reforms met with some success, but other developments probably contributed more to the general agricultural prosperity under the Song. These included the opening of new lands in the Yangtze River valley, improvements in irrigation techniques such as the chain pump (a circular chain of square pallets on a treadmill that enabled farmers to lift considerable amounts of water or mud to a higher level), and the introduction of a new strain of quick-growing rice from Southeast Asia, which permitted farmers in warmer regions to plant and harvest two crops each year.

The Urban Economy

Major changes also took place in the Chinese urban economy, which witnessed a significant increase in trade and manufacturing. This process began under the Tang dynasty, but it was not entirely a product of deliberate state policy. In fact, early Tang rulers shared some of the traditional prejudice against commercial activities that had been prevalent under the Han and enacted a number of regulations that restricted trade. As under the Han, the state maintained monopolies over key commodities such as salt.

SCIENCE & TECHNOLOGY

From the invention of stone tools and the discovery of fire to the introduction of agriculture and the writing system, mastery of technology has been a driving force in the history of human evolution. But why do some human societies appear to be much more advanced in their use of technology than others? People living on the island of New Guinea, for example, began cultivating local crops like taro and bananas as early as ten thousand years ago but never took the next steps toward creating a complex society until the arrival of Europeans many millennia later. Advanced societies had begun to emerge in the Western Hemisphere during the Classical era, but none had discovered the use of the wheel or the smelting of metals for toolmaking. Writing was in its infancy there.

Technological advances appear to take place for two reasons: need and opportunity. Farming peoples throughout the world needed to control the flow of water, so in areas where water was scarce or unevenly distributed, they learned to practice irrigation to make resources available throughout the region. Some-times, however, opportunity strikes by ac-cident (as in the legendary story of the Chinese princess who dropped a silkworm cocoon in her cup of hot tea, thus opening a series of discoveries that resulted in the manufacture of silk) or when new technology is introduced from a neighboring region (as when the discovery of tin in Anatolia launched the Bronze Age throughout the Middle East).

Copper astrolabe from the Middle East, circa ninth century.

© Bibliothèque Nationale de Cartes et Plans/The Bridgeman Art Library

The most important factor enabling societies to keep abreast of the latest advances in technology, it would appear, is participation in the global trade and communications network. In this respect, the relative ease of communications between the Mediterranean Sea and the Indus River valley represented a major advantage for the Abbasid Empire, since the peoples living there had rapid access to all the resources and technological advances in that part of the world. China was more isolated from such developments because of distance and the obstacle represented by the Himalaya Mountains. But because of its size and high level of cultural achievement, China was almost a continent in itself and was soon communicating with countries to the west via the Silk Road.

Societies that were not linked to this vast network were at an enormous disadvantage in keeping up with new developments in the field of technology. The peoples of New Guinea, at the far end of the Indonesian archipelago, had little or no contact with the outside world. In the Western Hemisphere, a trade network did begin to take shape between societies in the Andes and their counterparts in Mesoamerica. But because of difficulties in communication (see Chapter 6), contacts were more inter-mittent. As a result, technological developments taking place in distant Eurasia did not reach the Americas until the arrival of the conquistadors.

Despite the restrictive policies of the state, the urban sector grew steadily larger and more complex, helped by several new technological developments (see the comparative essay "The Spread of Technology" above). During the Tang, the Chinese mastered the art of manufacturing steel by mixing cast iron and wrought iron. The blast furnace was heated to a high temperature by burning coal, which had been used as a fuel in China from about the fourth century C.E. The resulting product was used in the manufacture of swords, sickles, and even suits of armor. By the eleventh century, more than 35,000 tons of steel were being produced annually. The intro-duction of cotton offered new opportunities in textile manufacturing. Gunpowder was invented by the Chinese during the Tang dynasty and used primarily for explosives and a primitive flamethrower; it reached the West via the Arabs in the twelfth century.

The Silk Road   The nature of trade was also changing. In the past, most long-distance trade had been undertaken by state monopoly. By the time of the Song, private commerce was being actively encouraged, and many merchants engaged in shipping as well as in wholesale and retail trade. Guilds began to appear, along with a new money economy. Paper currency began to be used in the eighth and ninth centuries. Credit (at first called "flying money") also made its first appearance during the Tang. With the increased circulation of paper money, banking began to develop as merchants found that strings of copper coins were too cumbersome for their increasingly complex operations.

© Museum of Fine Arts, Boston, Massachusetts, USA, Special Chinese and Japanese Fund/ The Bridgeman Art Library

Court Ladies Preparing Silk. Since antiquity, human beings have fashioned textiles out of hemp, flax, wool, cotton, and silk. The Shang dynasty produced both hemp and silk cloth, while wool was prominent in the Middle East and Greece. Linen, woven in Egypt, was used by the Roman Empire to clothe its army. Fine Indian cotton was introduced to China along the Silk Road, just as Chinese satin was carried by Mongol warriors to Europe, where it was used for making banners. Sometimes the Chinese government demanded not only grain but also bolts of cloth as a tax from peasants. Silk, produced mostly by peasants as an agricultural by-product, was also woven, as seen here, by the elegant court ladies of the Song dynasty, and its use as a fabric was restricted to the elite classes until the nineteenth century.

Unfortunately, early issues of paper currency were not backed by metal coinage and led to price inflation. Equally useful, if more prosaic, was the invention of the abacus, an early form of calculator that simplified the computations needed for commercial transactions.

Long-distance trade, both overland and by sea, expanded under the Tang and the Song. Trade with countries and peoples to the west had been carried on for centuries (see Chapter 3), but it had declined dramatically between the fourth and sixth centuries C.E. as a result of the collapse of the Han and Roman Empires. It began to revive with the rise of the Tang and the simultaneous unification of much of the Middle East under the Arabs. During the Tang era, the Silk Road reached its zenith. Much of the trade was carried by the Turkic-speaking Uighurs. During the Tang, Uighur caravans of two-humped Bactrian camels (a hardy variety native to Iran and regions to the northeast) carried goods back and forth between China and the countries of South Asia and the Middle East.

In actuality, the Silk Road was composed of a number of separate routes. The first to be used, probably because of the jade found in the mountains south of Khotan, ran along the southern rim of the Taklimakan Desert via Kashgar and thence through the Pamir Mountains into Bactria. The first Buddhist missionaries traveled this route from India to China. Eventually, however, this area began to dry up, and traders were forced to seek other routes. From a climatic standpoint, the best route for the Silk Road was to the north of the Tian Shan (Heavenly Mountains), where moisture-laden northwesterly winds created pastures where animals could graze. But the area was frequently infested by bandits who preyed on unwary travelers. Most caravans therefore followed the southern route, which passed along the northern fringes of the Taklimakan Desert to Kashgar and down into northwestern India. Travelers avoided the direct route through the desert (in the Uighur language, the name means "go in and you won't come out") and trudged from oasis to oasis along the southern slopes of the Tian Shan. The oases were created by the water runoff from winter snows in the mountains, which then dried up in the searing heat of the desert.

The Maritime Route   The Silk Road was so hazardous that shipping goods by sea became increasingly popular. China had long been engaged in sea trade with other countries in the region, but most of the commerce was originally in the hands of Korean, Japanese, or Southeast Asian merchants. Chinese maritime trade, however, was stimulated by the invention of the compass and technical improvements in shipbuilding such as the widespread use of the sternpost rudder and the lug sail (which enabled ships to sail close to the wind). If Marco Polo's observations can be believed, by the thirteenth century, Chinese junks had multiple sails and weighed up to 2,000 tons, much more than contemporary ships in the West. The Chinese governor of Canton in the early twelfth century remarked:

According to the government regulations concerning seagoing ships, the larger ones can carry several hundred men, and the smaller ones may have more than a hundred men on board. . . . The ships' pilots are acquainted with the configuration of the coasts; at night they steer by the stars, and in the daytime by the Sun. In dark weather they look at the south-pointing needle. They also use a line a hundred feet long with a hook at the end, which they let down to take samples of mud from the seabottom; by its appearance and smell they can determine their whereabouts.[4]

A wide variety of goods passed through Chinese ports. The Chinese exported tea, silk, and porcelain to the countries beyond the South China Sea, receiving exotic woods, precious stones, and various tropical goods in exchange. Seaports on the southern China coast exported sweet oranges, lemons, and peaches in return for grapes, walnuts, and pomegranates. Along the Silk Road to China came raw hides, furs, and horses. Chinese aristocrats, their appetite for material consumption stimulated by the affluence of Chinese society during much of the Tang and Song periods, were fascinated by the exotic goods and the flora and the fauna of the desert and the tropical lands of the South Seas. The city of Chang'an became the eastern terminus of the Silk Road and perhaps the wealthiest city in the world during the Tang era. The major port of exit in southern China was Canton, where an estimated 100,000 merchants lived. Their activities were controlled by an imperial commissioner sent from the capital.

Some of this trade was a product of the tribute system, which the Chinese rulers used as an element of their foreign policy. The Chinese viewed the outside world as they viewed their own society—in a hierarchical manner. Rulers of smaller countries along the periphery were viewed as "younger brothers" of the Chinese emperor and owed fealty to him. Foreign rulers who accepted the relationship were required to pay tribute and to promise not to harbor enemies of the Chinese Empire. But the foreign rulers also benefited from the relationship. Not only did it confer legitimacy on them, but they often received magnificent gifts from their "elder brother" as a reward for good behavior. Merchants from their countries also gained access to the vast Chinese market.

Society in Traditional China

These political and economic changes affected Chinese society during the Tang and Song era. For one thing, it became much more complex. Whereas previously China had been almost exclusively rural, with a small urban class of merchants, artisans, and workers almost entirely dependent on the state, the cities had now grown into an important, if statistically still insignificant, part of the population. Urban life, too, had changed. Cities were no longer primarily administrative centers dominated by officials and their families but now included a much broader mix of officials, merchants, artisans, peddlers, and entertainers. Unlike the situation in Europe, however, Chinese cities did not possess special privileges that protected their residents from the rapacity of the central government.

In the countryside, equally significant changes were taking place as the relatively rigid demarcation between the landed aristocracy and the mass of the rural population gave way to a more complex mixture of landed gentry, free farmers, sharecroppers, and landless laborers. There was also a class of "base people," consisting of actors, butchers, and prostitutes, who possessed only limited legal rights and were not permitted to take the civil service examination.

The Rise of the Gentry   Perhaps the most significant development was the rise of the landed gentry as the most influential force in Chinese society. The gentry class controlled much of the wealth in the rural areas and produced the majority of the candidates for the bureaucracy. By virtue of their possession of land and specialized knowledge of the Confucian classics, the gentry

© Claire L. Duiker

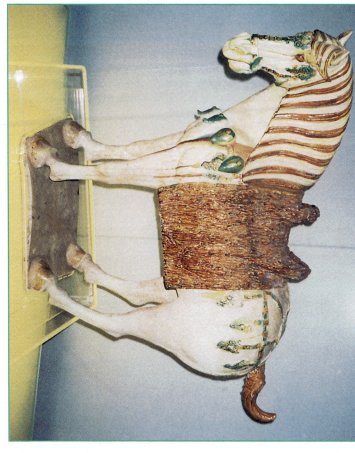

A Tang Horse. During the Tang dynasty, trade among China, India, and the Middle East along the Silk Road increased rapidly and introduced new Central Asian motifs to Chinese culture. Ceramic representations of the sturdy Central Asian horse and the two-humped Bactrian camel were often produced as tomb figures or as decorative objects in the homes of the wealthy. Preserved for us today, these ceramic studies of horses and camels, as well as of officials, court ladies, and servants, painted in brilliant gold, green, and blue lead glazes, are impressive examples of Tang cultural achievement.

had replaced the aristocracy as the political and economic elite of Chinese society. Unlike the aristocracy, however, the gentry did not form an exclusive class separated by the accident of birth from the remainder of the population. Upward and downward mobility between the scholar-gentry class and the remainder of the population was not uncommon and may have been a key factor in the stability and longevity of the system. A position in the bureaucracy opened the doors to wealth and prestige for the individual and his family, but it was no guarantee of success, and the fortunes of individual families might experience a rapid rise and fall. The soaring ambitions and arrogance of China's landed gentry are vividly described in the following wish list set in poetry by a young bridegroom of the Tang dynasty:

Chinese slaves to take charge of treasury and barn,
Foreign slaves to take care of my cattle and sheep.
Strong-legged slaves to run by saddle and stirrup
*   when I ride,*
Powerful slaves to till the fields with might
*   and main,*
Handsome slaves to play the harp and hand
*   the wine;*
Slim-waisted slaves to sing me songs, and dance;
Dwarfs to hold the candle by my dining-couch.[5]

For affluent Chinese in this era, life offered many more pleasures than had been available to their forebears. There were new forms of entertainment, such as playing cards and chess (brought from India, although an early form had been invented in China during the Zhou dynasty); new forms of transportation, such as the paddlewheel boat and horseback riding (made possible by the introduction of the stirrup); better means of communication (block printing was first invented in the eighth century C.E.); and new tastes for the palate introduced from lands beyond the frontier. Tea had been introduced from the Burmese frontier by monks as early as the Han dynasty, and brandy and other concentrated spirits produced by the distillation of alcohol made their appearance in the seventh century.

Village China The vast majority of the Chinese people still lived off the land in villages ranging in size from a few dozen residents to several thousand. The life of the farmers was bounded by their village. Although many communities were connected to the outside world by roads or rivers, the average Chinese rarely left the confines of their native village except for an occasional visit to a nearby market town. This isolation was psychological as well as physical, for most Chinese identified with their immediate environment and had difficulty envisioning themselves living beyond the bamboo hedges or mud walls that marked the limit of their horizon.

An even more basic unit than the village in the lives of most Chinese, of course, was the family. The ideal was the joint family with at least three generations under one roof. Because of the heavy labor requirements of rice farming, the tradition of the joint family was especially prevalent in the south. When a son married, he was expected to bring his new wife back to live in his parents' home (see the box on p. 287). Often the parents added a new wing to the house for the new family. Women who did not marry remained in the home where they grew up.

Chinese village architecture reflected these traditions. Most family dwellings were simple, consisting of one or at most two rooms. They were usually constructed of dried mud, stone, or brick, depending on available materials and the prosperity of the family. Roofs were of thatch or tile, and the floors were usually of packed dirt. Large houses were often built in a square around an inner courtyard, thus guaranteeing privacy from the outside world.

Within the family unit, the eldest male theoretically ruled as an autocrat. He was responsible for presiding over ancestral rites at an altar, usually in the main room of the house. He had traditional legal rights over his wife, and if she did not provide him with a male heir, he was permitted to take a second wife. She, however, had no recourse to divorce. As the old saying went, "Marry a chicken, follow the chicken; marry a dog, follow the dog." Wealthy Chinese might keep concubines, who lived in a separate room in the house and sometimes competed with the legal wife for precedence.

In accordance with Confucian tradition, children were expected, above all, to obey their parents, who not only determined their children's careers but also selected their marriage partners. Filial piety was viewed as an absolute moral good, above virtually all other moral obligations. Even today, duty to one's parents is considered important in traditional Chinese families, and the tombstones of deceased Chinese are often decorated with tile paintings depicting the filial acts that they performed during their lifetime.

The Role of Women The tradition of male superiority continued from ancient times into the medieval era, especially under the southern Song when it was reinforced by Neo-Confucianism. Female children were considered less desirable than males because they could not undertake heavy work in the fields or carry on the family traditions. Poor families often sold their daughters to wealthy villagers to serve as concubines, and female infanticide was not uncommon in times of famine to ensure that there would be food for the remainder of the family. Concubines had few legal rights; female domestic servants, even fewer.

During the Song era, two new practices emerged that changed the equation for women seeking to obtain a successful marriage contract. First, a new form of dowry appeared. Whereas previously the prospective husband offered the bride's family a bride price, now the reverse became the norm, with the bride's parents paying the groom's family a dowry. With the prosperity that characterized Chinese society during much of the Song era, affluent parents sought to buy a satisfactory husband for their daughter, preferably one with a higher social standing and good prospects for an official career.

A second source of marital bait during the Song period was the promise of a bride with tiny bound feet. The process of **foot binding**, carried out on girls aged five to thirteen, was excruciatingly painful, since it bent and compressed the foot to half its normal size by imprisoning it in restrictive bandages. But the procedure was often performed by ambitious mothers intent on assuring their daughters of the best possible prospects for marriage. The zealous mother also wanted her daughter to possess a competitive edge in dealing with the other wives and concubines of her future husband. Bound feet represented submissiveness and self-discipline, two required attributes for the ideal Confucian wife.

Throughout northern China, foot binding became a common practice for women of all social classes. It was less common in southern China, where the cultivation of wet rice could not be carried out with bandaged feet; there it tended to be limited to the scholar-gentry class. Still, most Chinese women with bound feet contributed to the labor force to supplement the family income. Although foot binding was eventually prohibited, the practice lasted into the twentieth century, particularly in rural villages, and the author of this chapter frequently observed older women with bound feet in Chinese cities as late as the 1980s.

As in most traditional cultures, there were exceptions to the low status of women in Chinese society. Women had substantial property rights and retained control over their dowries even after divorce or the death of their husband. Wives were frequently an influential force in the home, often handling the accounts and taking primary responsibility for raising the children. Some were active in politics. The outstanding example was Wu Zhao (c. 625–c. 706), popularly known as Empress Wu. Selected by Emperor Tang Taizong as a concubine, after his death she rose to a position of supreme power at court.

THE SAINTLY MISS WU

FAMILY & SOCIETY

The idea that a wife should sacrifice her wants to the needs of her husband and family was deeply embedded in traditional Chinese society. Widows in particular had few rights, and their remarriage was strongly condemned. In this account from a story by Hung Mai, a twelfth-century writer, the widowed Miss Wu wins the respect of the entire community by faithfully serving her mother-in-law.

Hung Mai, *A Song Family Saga*

Miss Wu served her mother-in-law very filially. Her mother-in-law had an eye ailment and felt sorry for her daughter-in-law's solitary and poverty-stricken situation, so she suggested that they call in a son-in-law for her and thereby get an adoptive heir. Miss Wu announced in tears, "A woman does not serve two husbands. I will support you. Don't talk this way." Her mother-in-law, seeing that she was determined, did not press her. Miss Wu did spinning, washing, sewing, cooking, and cleaning for her neighbors, earning perhaps a hundred cash a day, all of which she gave to her mother-in-law to cover the cost of firewood and food. If she was given any meat, she would wrap it up to take home....

Once when her mother-in-law was cooking rice, a neighbor called to her, and to avoid overcooking the rice she dumped it into a pan. Owing to her bad eyes, however, she mistakenly put it in the dirty chamber pot. When Miss Wu returned and saw it, she did not say a word. She went to a neighbor to borrow some cooked rice for her mother-in-law and took the dirty rice and washed it to eat herself.

One day in the daytime neighbors saw [Miss Wu] ascending into the sky amid colored clouds. Startled, they told her mother-in-law, who said, "Don't be foolish. She just came back from pounding rice for someone, and is lying down on the bed. Go and look." They went to the room and peeked in and saw her sound asleep. Amazed, they left.

When Miss Wu woke up, her mother-in-law told her what happened, and she said, "I just dreamed of two young boys in blue clothes holding documents and riding on the clouds. They grabbed my clothes and said the Emperor of Heaven had summoned me. They took me to the gate of heaven and I was brought in to see the emperor, who was seated beside a balustrade. He said 'Although you are just a lowly ignorant village woman, you are able to serve your old mother-in-law sincerely and work hard. You really deserve respect.' He gave me a cup of aromatic wine and a string of cash, saying, 'I will supply you. From now on you will not need to work for others.' I bowed to thank him and came back, accompanied by the two boys. Then I woke up."

There was in fact a thousand cash on the bed, and the room was filled with a fragrance. They then realized that the neighbors' vision had been a spirit journey. From this point on even more people asked her to work for them, and she never refused. But the money that had been given to her she kept for her mother-in-law's use. Whatever they used promptly reappeared, so the thousand cash was never exhausted. The mother-in-law also regained her sight in both eyes.

Q *What is the moral of this story? How do the supernatural elements in the account strengthen the lesson intended by the author?*

© The Art Archive/Topkapi Museum/Gianni Dagli Orti

A Young Chinese Bride and Her Dowry. A Chinese bride had to leave her parental home for that of her husband, transferring her filial allegiance to her in-laws. For this reason, the mother-son relationship would be the most important one in a Chinese woman's life. With the expansion of the gentry class during the Song dynasty, young men who passed the civil service examination became the most sought-after marriage prospects, requiring that the families of young women offer a substantial dowry as an enticement to the groom's family. But some women were destined for more distant locations. In this Persian miniature, a Chinese bride leads a procession along the Silk Road to marry a Turkish bridegroom, transporting her dowry of prized Chinese porcelain to her new home.

At first, she was content to rule through her sons, but in 690, she declared herself empress of China. To bolster her claim of legitimacy, she cited a Buddhist *sutra* to the effect that a woman would rule the world seven hundred years after the death of Siddhartha Gautama. For her presumption, she has been vilified by later Chinese historians, but she was actually a quite capable ruler. She was responsible for giving meaning to the civil service examination system and was the first to select graduates of the examinations for the highest positions in government. During her last years, she reportedly fell under the influence of courtiers and was deposed in 705, when she was probably around eighty.

Explosion in Central Asia: The Mongol Empire

Q Focus Question: Why were the Mongols able to amass an empire, and what were the main characteristics of their rule in China?

The Mongols, who succeeded the Song as the rulers of China in the late thirteenth century, rose to power in Asia with stunning rapidity. When Genghis Khan (also known

as Chinggis Khan), the founder of Mongol greatness, was born, the Mongols were a relatively obscure pastoral people in the area of modern-day Outer Mongolia. Like most of the nomadic peoples in the region, they were organized loosely into clans and tribes and even lacked a common name for themselves. Rivalry among the various tribes over pastureland, livestock, and booty was intense and increased at the end of the twelfth century as a result of a growing population and the consequent overgrazing of pastures. Since they had no source of subsistence besides their herds, the Mongols were, in the words of one historian, in a "state of stress."

This challenge was met by the great Mongol chieftain Genghis Khan. Born during the 1160s, Genghis Khan, whose original name was Temuchin (or Temujin), was the son of an impoverished noble of his tribe. When Temuchin was still a child, his father was murdered by a rival, and the boy was forced to seek refuge in the wilderness. Described by one historian as tall, adroit, and vigorous, young Temuchin gradually unified the Mongol tribes through his prowess and the power of his personality. In 1206, he was elected Genghis Khan ("universal ruler") at a massive tribal meeting in the Gobi Desert. From that time on, he devoted himself to military pursuits. Mongol nomads were now forced to pay taxes and

© National Palace Museum, Taipei/The Bridgeman Art Library

Genghis Khan. Founder of the Mongol Empire, Temuchin (later to be known as Genghis Khan) died in 1227, long before Mongol warriors defeated the armies of the Song in China and established the Yuan Dynasty (1279–1368). In this portrait by a Chinese court artist, the ruler appears in a stylized version, looking much like other Chinese emperors from the period. Such techniques were used by painters in many societies to render their subjects in a manner more familiar to the prospective observer.

were subject to military conscription. "Man's highest joy," Genghis Khan reportedly remarked, "is in victory: to conquer one's enemies, to pursue them, to deprive them of their possessions, to make their beloved weep, to ride on their horses, and to embrace their wives and daughters."[6]

The army that Genghis Khan unleashed on the world was not exceptionally large—totaling less than 130,000 in 1227, at a time when the total Mongol population numbered between one and two million. But their mastery of military tactics set the Mongols apart from their rivals. Their tireless flying columns of mounted warriors surrounded their enemies and harassed them like cattle, luring them into pursuit and then ambushing them with flank attacks. John Plano Carpini, a contemporary Franciscan friar, remarked:

As soon as they discover the enemy they charge and each one unleashes three or four arrows. If they see that they can't break him, they retire in order to entice the enemy to pursue, thus luring him into an ambush prepared in advance. If they conclude that the enemy army is stronger, they retire for a day or two and ravage neighboring areas.... Or they strike camp in a well chosen position, and when the army begins to pass by, they appear unexpectedly.... Their military stratagems are numerous. At the moment of an enemy cavalry attack, they place prisoners and foreign auxiliaries in the forefront of their own position, while positioning the bulk of their own troops on the right and left wings to envelop the adversary, thus giving the enemy the impression that they are more numerous than in reality. If the adversary defends himself well, they open their ranks to let him pass through in flight, after which they launch in pursuit and kill as many as possible.[7]

In the years after the election of Temuchin as universal ruler, the Mongols defeated tribal groups to their west and then turned their attention to the seminomadic non-Chinese kingdoms of northern China. There they discovered that their adversaries were armed with a weapon called a fire-lance, an early form of flamethrower. Gunpowder had been invented in China during the late Tang period, and by the early thirteenth century, a fire-lance had been developed that could spew out flames and projectiles a distance of 30 or 40 yards, inflicting considerable damage on the enemy. The following account of a battle in the 1230s between Mongol forces and the army of the state of Qin (Chin) in northern China describes the effects of this weapon:

On the fifth day of the fifth month they sacrificed to Heaven, secretly prepared fire-lances, and embarked 450 Chin soldiers outside the south gate, whence they sailed first east and then north. During the night they killed the enemy guards outside the dikes, and reached the Wang family temple.... Kuan-Nu divided his small craft into squadrons of five, seven and ten boats, which came out from behind the defenses and caught the Mongols both from front and rear, using the fire-spouting lances. The Mongols could not stand up to this and fled, losing more than 3500 men drowned. Finally their stockades were burnt, and our force returned.[8]

Before the end of the thirteenth century, the fire-lance had evolved into the much more effective handgun and cannon. These inventions came too late to save China from the Mongols, however, and were transmitted to Europe by the early fourteenth century by foreigners employed by the Mongol rulers of China.

While some Mongol armies were engaged in the conquest of northern China, others traveled farther afield and advanced as far as central Europe. Only the death of Genghis Khan in 1227 may have prevented an all-out Mongol attack on western Europe (see the box on p. 290). In 1231, the Mongols

The Mongol Conquest of China

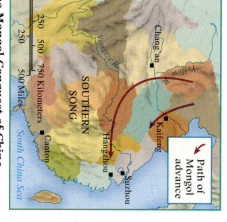

Chang'an · Yellow · Yangtze R. · SOUTHERN SONG · Kaifeng · Hangzhou · Suzhou · Canton · South China Sea

0 250 500 750 Kilometers
0 250 500 Miles

Path of Mongol advance

A LETTER TO THE POPE

In 1243, Pope Innocent IV dispatched the Franciscan friar John Plano Carpini to the Mongol headquarters at Karakorum to appeal to the great khan Kuyuk to cease his attacks on Christians. After a considerable wait, Carpini was given the following reply, which could not have pleased the pope. The letter was discovered recently in the Vatican archives.

A Letter from Kuyuk Khan to Pope Innocent IV

By the power of the Eternal Heaven, We are the all-embracing Khan of all the Great Nations. It is our command:

This is a decree, sent to the great Pope that he may know and pay heed.

After holding counsel with the monarchs under your suzerainty, you have sent us an offer of subordination, which we have accepted from the hands of your envoy.

If you should act up to your word, then you, the great Pope, should come in person with the monarchs to pay us homage and we should thereupon instruct you concerning the commands of the Yasak.

Furthermore, you have said it would be well for us to become Christians. You write to me in person about this matter, and have addressed to me a request. This, your request, we cannot understand.

Furthermore, you have written me these words: "You have attacked all the territories of the Magyars and other Christians, at which I am astonished. Tell me, what was their crime?" These, your words, we likewise cannot understand. Jenghiz Khan and Ogatai Khakan revealed the commands of Heaven. But those whom you name would not believe the commands of Heaven. Those of whom you speak showed themselves highly presumptuous and slew our envoys. Therefore, in accordance with the commands of the Eternal Heaven the inhabitants of the aforesaid countries have been slain and annihilated. If not by the command of Heaven, how can anyone slay or conquer out of his own strength?

And when you say: "I am a Christian. I pray to God. I arraign and despise others," how do you know who is pleasing to God and to whom He allots His grace? How can you know it, that you speak such words?

Thanks to the power of the Eternal Heaven, all lands have been given to us from sunrise to sunset. How could anyone act other than in accordance with the commands of Heaven? Now your own upright heart must tell you: "We will become subject to you, and will place our powers at your disposal." You in person, at the head of the monarchs, all of you, without exception, must come to tender us service and pay us homage, then only will we recognize your submission. But if you do not obey the commands of Heaven, and run counter to our orders, we shall know that you are our foe.

That is what we have to tell you. If you fail to act in accordance therewith, how can we foresee what will happen to you? Heaven alone knows.

Q *Based on the account shown here, what message was the pope seeking to convey to the great khan in Karakorum? What is the nature of the latter's reply?*

---

attacked Persia and then defeated the Abbasids at Baghdad in 1258 (see Chapter 7). Mongol forces attacked the Song from the west in the 1260s and finally defeated the remnants of the Song navy in 1279.

By then, the Mongol Empire was quite different from what it had been under its founder. Prior to the conquests of Genghis Khan, the Mongols had been purely nomadic. They spent their winters in the southern plains, where they found suitable pastures for their cattle, and traveled north in the summer to wooded areas where the water was sufficient. They lived in round, felt-covered tents (called yurts), which were lightly constructed so that they could be easily transported. For food, the Mongols depended on milk and meat from their herds and game from hunting.

To administer the new empire, Genghis Khan had set up a capital city at Karakorum, in present-day Outer Mongolia, but prohibited his fellow Mongols from practicing sedentary occupations or living in cities. But under his successors, the Mongols began to adapt to their conquered areas. As one khan remarked, quoting his Chinese adviser, "Although you inherited the Chinese Empire on horseback, you cannot rule it from that position." Mongol aristocrats began to enter administrative positions, while commoners took up sedentary occupations as farmers or merchants.[9]

The territorial nature of the empire also changed. Following tribal custom, at the death of the ruling khan, the territory was distributed among his heirs. The once-united empire of Genghis Khan was thus divided into several separate **khanates**, each under the autonomous rule of one of his sons by his principal wife. One of his sons was awarded the khanate of Chaghadai in Central Asia with its capital at Samarkand; another ruled Persia from the conquered city of Baghdad; a third took charge of the khanate of Kipchak (commonly known as the Golden Horde). But it was one of his grandsons, named Khubilai Khan (1215–1294), who completed the conquest of the Song and established a new Chinese dynasty, called the Yuan (from a phrase in the *Book of Changes* referring to the "original creative force" of the universe). Khubilai moved the capital of China northward from Hangzhou to Khanbaliq ("city of the khan"), which was located on a major trunk route from the Great Wall to the plains of northern China (see Map 10.2). Later the city would be known by the Chinese name Beijing, or Peking ("northern capital").

Mongol Rule in China

At first, China's new rulers exhibited impressive vitality. Under the leadership of the talented Khubilai Khan, the Yuan continued to flex their muscles by attempting to expand their empire. Mongol armies advanced into the Red River valley and reconquered Vietnam, which had declared its independence after the fall of the Tang three hundred years earlier. Mongol fleets were launched against Malay kingdoms in Java and Sumatra and also against the islands of Japan. Only the expedition against Vietnam succeeded, however, and even that success was temporary. The Vietnamese counterattacked and eventually drove the Mongols back across the border. The attempted conquest of Japan was even more disastrous. On one occasion, a massive storm destroyed the Mongol fleet, killing thousands (see Chapter 11).

Logistics may explain why the Mongol army failed elsewhere after succeeding in China. The Mongol attacks on Japan, Vietnam, and the Indonesian kingdoms were too far afield for the army to be easily supported and resupplied. The terrain may also have contributed to their defeat. Mongol tactics, such as cavalry charges and siege warfare, were less effective in tropical and hilly regions than they were closer to the arid Mongol heartland.

The Mongols had more success in governing China. After a failed attempt to administer their conquest as they had ruled their own tribal society (some advisers reportedly even suggested that the plowed fields be transformed into pastures), Mongol rulers adapted to the Chinese political system and made use of local talents in the bureaucracy. The tripartite division of the administration into civilian, military, and censorate was retained, as were the six ministries. The civil service system, which had been abolished in the north in 1237 and in the south forty years later, was revived in the early fourteenth century. The state cult of Confucius was also restored, although Khubilai Khan himself remained a Buddhist.

But there were some key differences. Culturally, the Mongols were nothing like the Chinese and remained a

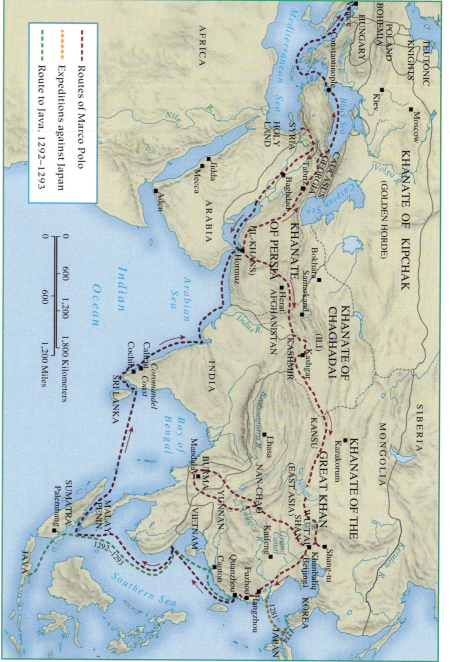

MAP 10.2 Asia Under the Mongols. This map traces the expansion of Mongol power throughout Eurasia in the thirteenth century. After the death of Genghis Khan in 1227, the empire was divided into four separate khanates.

Q Why was the Mongol Empire divided into four separate khanates? ● View an animated version of this map or related maps at www.cengage.com/history/Duiker/World6e

FILM & HISTORY

THE ADVENTURES OF MARCO POLO (1938) AND MARCO POLO (2007)

© Everett Collection

Scene from *The Adventures of Marco Polo* (1938). Marco Polo (Gary Cooper, gesturing on the right) confers with Kaidu (Alan Hale), leader of the Mongols.

The famous story of Marco Polo's trip to East Asia in the late thirteenth century has sparked the imagination of Western readers ever since. The son of an Italian merchant from Venice, Polo went to China in 1270 and did not return for twenty-four years, traveling eastward via the Silk Road and returning by sea across the Indian Ocean. Captured by the Genoese in 1298 and tossed into prison, he recounted his experiences to a professional writer known as Rusticello of Pisa. Copies of the resultant book, originally titled *Description of the World*, were soon circulating throughout Europe, and one even found its way into the luggage of Christopher Columbus, who used it as a source for information on the eastern lands he sought during his own travels. Marco Polo's adventures have appeared in numerous languages, thrilling readers around the world, and filmmakers have done their part, producing feature films that have promoted his exploits to modern audiences.

But did Marco Polo actually visit China, or was the book an elaborate hoax? In recent years, some historians have expressed doubts about the veracity of his account. Frances Wood, author of *Did Marco Polo Go to China?* (1996), suggested that he might have simply recounted tales that he had heard from contemporaries, thus provoking a lively debate about the topic in the halls of academe.

Such reservations have not brought the fascination with Polo's exploits to an end, as is indicated by the fact that a number of commercial films on the subject have appeared in recent years. The first to be produced in Hollywood, titled *The Adventures of Marco Polo* (1938), starred the prewar screen idol Gary Cooper, with Basil Rathbone as his evil nemesis in China. Like many film epics of the era, it was highly entertaining but lacked historical accuracy. The most recent version, a Hallmark Channel production

titled *Marco Polo*, appeared in 2007 and starred the young American actor Ian Somerholder in the title role. The film is a reasonably faithful rendition of the book, with stirring battle scenes, the predictable "cast of thousands," and a somewhat unlikely love interest between Polo and a Mongolian princess thrown in. Although the lead character is not particularly convincing in the title role—after two grueling decades in Asia, he still bears a striking resemblance to a teenage surfing idol—the producers should be credited for their efforts to portray China as the most advanced civilization of its day. A number of Chinese inventions then unknown in Europe, such as paper money, explosives, and the compass, make their appearance in the film. Emperor Khubilai Khan (played by the veteran actor Brian Dennehy) does not project an imperial presence, however, and is unconvincing when he expresses his preference for someone who can speak truth to power.

unity, and economic prosperity that the Mongols initially brought to China.

Indeed, the Mongols' greatest achievement may have been the prosperity they fostered. At home, they continued the relatively tolerant economic policies of the southern Song, and by bringing the entire Eurasian landmass under a single rule, they encouraged long-distance trade, particularly along the Silk Road, now dominated by Muslim merchants from Central Asia. To promote trade, the Grand Canal was extended from the Yellow River to the capital. Adjacent to the canal, a paved highway was constructed that extended all the way from the Song capital of Hangzhou to its Mongol counterpart at Khanbaliq.

separate class with its own laws. The highest positions in the bureaucracy were usually staffed by Mongols. Although some leading Mongols followed their ruler in converting to Buddhism, most commoners retained their traditional religion. Even those who adopted Buddhism chose the Lamaist variety from Tibet, which emphasized divination and magic.

Despite these differences, some historians believe that the Mongol dynasty won considerable support from the majority of the Chinese. The people of the north, after all, were used to foreign rule, and although those living farther to the south may have resented their alien conquerors, they probably came to respect the stability,

Khanbaliq (Beijing) Under the Mongols

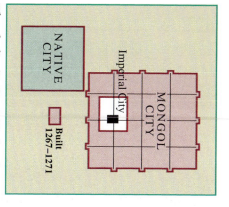

NATIVE CITY

Imperial City

MONGOL CITY

Imperial City

■ Built 1267–1271

The capital was a magnificent city, unusual in a society where commitments were ordinarily of a tribal nature. According to the Italian merchant Marco Polo, who resided there during the reign of Khubilai Khan, it was 24 miles in diameter and surrounded by thick walls of earth penetrated by a dozen massive gates. He described the old Song capital of Hangzhou as a noble city where "so many pleasures may be found that one fancies himself to be in Paradise."

Ironically, while many of their subjects prospered, the Mongols themselves often did not. Burdened by low salaries and heavy military obligations that left them little time for their herds, many Mongol warriors became so impoverished that they were forced to sell their sons and daughters into slavery. Eventually, the Yuan government had to provide funds from the imperial treasury to buy them back and return them to their families.

The magnificence of the empire impressed foreign visitors, including Marco Polo, whose tales of the glories of Cathay (a name adapted from Kitai, the Russian name for China) were not believed when he returned to Europe (see the box on p. 294). But the Yuan eventually fell victim to the same fate that had afflicted other powerful dynasties in China. In fact, it was one of the shortest-lived of the great dynasties, lasting less than a century. Excessive spending on foreign conquest, inadequate tax revenues, factionalism and corruption at court and in the bureaucracy, and growing internal instability, brought about in part by a famine in central China in the 1340s, all contributed to the dynasty's demise. Khubilai Khan's successors lacked his administrative genius, and by the middle of the next century, the Yuan dynasty in China, like the Mongol khanates elsewhere in Central Asia, had begun to decline rapidly (see Chapter 13).

The Mongols' Place in History

The Mongols were the last, and arguably the greatest, of the nomadic peoples who came thundering out of the steppes of Central Asia, pillaging and conquering the territories of their adversaries. What caused this extraordinary burst of energy, and why were the Mongols so much more successful than their predecessors? Historians are divided. Some have suggested that drought and overpopulation may have depleted the available pasture on the steppes, yet another example of the unseen impact of environmental changes on human history. Others have cited the ambition and genius of Genghis Khan, who was able to arouse a sense of personal loyalty unusual in a society where commitments were ordinarily of a tribal nature. Still others point to his reliance on the organizational unit known as the *ordos*, described by the historian Samuel Adshead as "a system of restructuring tribes into decimal units whose top level of leadership was organized on bureaucratic lines."[10] Although the *ordos* system had been used by the Xiongnu and other nomadic peoples before them, the Mongols applied it to create disciplined military units that were especially effective against the relatively freewheeling tactics of their rivals on the steppes and devastating against the relatively immobile armies of the sedentary states in their path. Once organized, the Mongols used their superior horsemanship and blitzkrieg tactics effectively, while taking advantage of divisions within the enemy ranks and borrowing more advanced military technology.

Once in power, however, the Mongols' underlying weaknesses eventually proved fatal. Unlike some of their predecessors, the Mongols had difficulty making the transition from the nomadic life of the steppes to the sedentary life of the villages, and their unwieldy system of royal succession led to instability in their leadership ranks. Still, although the Mongol era was just a brief interlude in the long sweep of human history, it was rich in consequences.

The era of Mongol expansion has usually been portrayed as a tragic period in human history. The Mongols' conquest resulted in widespread death and suffering throughout the civilized world. Nations and empires were humbled, cities destroyed, and irrigation systems laid waste. Then, just when the ravages of the era appeared to come to an end, the Black Death, probably carried by lice hidden in the saddlebags of Mongol horsemen, decimated the population of Europe and the Middle East. Some regions lost as much as one-third of their population, with severe economic consequences.

Few modern historians would dispute the brutality that characterized Mongol expansion. But some are now beginning to point out that beyond its legacy of death and destruction, the Mongol era also brought widespread peace (known as the Pax Mongolica) and inaugurated what one scholar has described as "the idea of the unified conceptualization of the globe" creating a "basic information circuit" that spread commodities, ideas, and inventions from one end of the Eurasian supercontinent to the other. Unfortunately, such conditions were not destined to last.

The immediate instrument of Mongol defeat was Zhu Yuanzhang (Chu Yuan-chang), the son of a poor peasant in the lower Yangtze valley. After losing most of his family in the famine of the 1340s, Zhu became an itinerant monk and then the leader of a gang of bandits. In the 1360s, unrest spread throughout the country, and after defeating a number of rivals, Zhu put an end to the disintegrating Yuan regime and declared the foundation of the new Ming ("bright") dynasty (1369–1644).

KHANBALIQ, KHUBILAI KHAN'S CAPITAL

POLITICS & GOVERNMENT

When the Italian merchant and adventurer Marco Polo returned from China to Europe in the late thirteenth century, he wrote a lengthy description of his experiences, later to be popularized in book form as *The Travels of Marco Polo*. Here he describes the Chinese capital city of Khanbaliq, which he called Cambaluc and would later be known as Peking or Beijing, as it existed during the height of the Mongol dynasty. Although the magnificent gates and palaces that he saw no longer exist today, the layout of modern Beijing is much as it is presented here, with wide streets built at right angles and ending at massive gates that once offered an entryway through the wall that surrounded the imperial city.

The Travels of Marco Polo

Now there was on that spot in old times a great and noble city called Cambaluc, which is as much as to say in our tongue "The city of the emperor." But the great Khan was informed by his astrologers that this city would prove rebellious, and raise great disorders against his imperial authority. So he caused the present city to be built close beside the old one, with only a river between them. And he caused the people of the old city to be removed to the new town that he had founded; and this is called Taidu. However, he allowed a portion of the people which he did not suspect to remain in the old city, because the new one could not hold the whole of them, big as it is.

As regards the size of this new city you must know that it has a compass of twenty-four miles, for each side of it hath a length of six miles, and it is four square. And it is all walled round with walls of earth which have a thickness of full ten paces at bottom, and a height of more than ten paces; but they are not so thick at top, for they diminish in thickness as they rise, so that at top they are only about

three paces thick. And they are provided throughout with loop-holed battlements, which are all whitewashed.

There are twelve gates, and over each gate there is a great and handsome palace, so that there are on each side of the square three gates and five palaces; for I ought to mention there is at each angle also a great and handsome palace. In those palaces are vast halls in which are kept the arms of the city garrison.

The streets are so straight and wide that you can see right along them from end to end and from one gate to the other. And up and down the city there are beautiful palaces, and many great and fine hostelries, and fine houses in great numbers. All the plots of ground on which the houses of the city are built are four square, and laid out with straight lines; all the plots being occupied by great and spacious palaces, with courts and gardens of proportionate size. All these plots were assigned to different heads of families. Each square plot is encompassed by handsome streets for traffic; and thus the whole city is arranged in squares just like a chessboard, and disposed in a manner so perfect and masterly that it is impossible to give a description that should do it justice.

Moreover, in the middle of the city there is a great clock—that is to say, a bell—which is struck at night. And after it has struck three times no one must go out in the city, unless it be for the needs of a woman in labor, or of the sick. And those who go about on such errands are bound to carry lanterns with them. Moreover, the established guard at each gate of the city is one thousand armed men; not that you are to imagine this guard is kept up for fear of any attack, but only as a guard of honor for the sovereign, who resides there, and to prevent thieves from doing mischief in the town.

Q *How would you compare this city with the layout of Rome under the Roman Empire? What do you think accounts for the differences and similarities?*

The Ming Dynasty

Q Focus Questions: What were the chief initiatives taken by the early rulers of the Ming dynasty to enhance the role of China in the world? Why did the imperial court order the famous voyages of Zhenghe, and then why were they discontinued?

The Ming inaugurated a new era of greatness in Chinese history. Under a series of strong rulers, China extended its rule into Mongolia and Central Asia. The Ming even briefly reconquered Vietnam, which, after a thousand years of Chinese rule, had reclaimed its independence following the collapse of the Tang dynasty in the tenth century. Along the northern frontier, the Emperor Yongle (Yung Lo; 1402–1424) strengthened the Great Wall and pacified the nomadic tribes that had troubled China in previous centuries. A tributary relationship was established with the Yi dynasty in Korea.

The internal achievements of the Ming were equally impressive. When they replaced the Mongols in the fourteenth century, the Ming turned to traditional Confucian institutions as a means of ruling their vast empire. These included the six ministries at the apex of the bureaucracy, the use of the civil service examinations to select members of the bureaucracy, and the division of the empire into provinces, districts, and counties. As before, Chinese villages were relatively autonomous, and local councils of elders continued to be responsible for adjudicating disputes, initiating local construction and irrigation projects, mustering a militia, and assessing and collecting taxes.

The society that was governed by this vast hierarchy of officials was a far cry from the predominantly agrarian society that had been ruled by the Han. In the burgeoning cities near the coast and along the Yangtze River valley, factories and workshops were vastly increasing the variety and output of their manufactured goods. The population had doubled, and new crops had been introduced, greatly expanding the food output of the empire.

The Voyages of Zhenghe

In 1405, in a splendid display of Chinese maritime might, Emperor Yongle sent a fleet of Chinese trading ships under the eunuch admiral Zhenghe (Cheng Ho) through the Strait of Malacca and out into the Indian Ocean; there they traveled as far west as the east coast of Africa, stopping on the way at ports in South Asia. The size of the fleet was impressive: nearly 28,000 sailors on sixty-two ships, some of them junks larger by far than any other oceangoing vessels the world had yet seen. China seemed about to become a direct participant in the vast trade network that extended as far west as the Atlantic Ocean, thus culminating the process of opening China to the wider world that had begun with the Tang dynasty.

Why the expeditions were undertaken has been a matter of some debate. Some historians assume that economic profit was the main reason. Others point to Yongle's native curiosity and note that the voyage—and the six others that followed it—returned not only with goods but also with a plethora of information about the outside world as well as with some items unknown in China (the emperor was especially intrigued by the giraffes brought back from East Africa and placed them in the imperial zoo, where they were identified by sooth-sayers with the coming of good government). Others speculate that the emperor was seeking to ascertain the truth of rumors that his immediate predecessor, Emperor Jianwen (Chien Wen; 1398–1402), had escaped to Southeast Asia to live in exile.

Whatever the case, the voyages resulted in a dramatic increase in Chinese knowledge about the world and the nature of ocean travel. They also brought massive profits for their sponsors, including individuals connected with Admiral Zhenghe at court. This aroused resentment

© William J. Duiker

© William J. Duiker

The Great Wall of China. Although the Great Wall is popularly believed to be over two thousand years old, the part of the wall that is most frequently visited by tourists was a reconstruction undertaken during the early Ming dynasty as a means of protection against invasion from the north. Part of that wall, which was built to protect the imperial capital of Beijing, is shown here. The original walls, which stretched from the shores of the Pacific Ocean to the deserts of Central Asia, were often composed of loose stone, dirt, or piled rubble. The section shown on the right is located north of the Turfan Depression in Xinjiang Province.

© William J. Duiker

The Temple of Heaven. This temple, located in the capital city of Beijing, is one of the most important historical structures in China. Built in 1420 at the order of the Ming emperor Yongle, it served as the location for the emperor's annual ceremony appealing to Heaven for a good harvest. Yongle's temple burned to the ground in 1889 but was immediately rebuilt following the original design.

among conservatives within the bureaucracy, some of whom viewed commercial activities with a characteristic measure of Confucian disdain. One commented that an end to the voyages would provide the Chinese people with a respite "so that they can devote themselves to husbandry [agriculture] and schooling."

An Inward Turn

Shortly after Yongle's death, the voyages were discontinued, never to be revived. The decision had long-term consequences and in the eyes of many modern historians marks a turning inward of the Chinese state, away from commerce and toward a more traditional emphasis on agriculture, away from the exotic lands to the south and toward the heartland of the country in the Yellow River valley.

Ironically, the move toward the Yellow River had been initiated by Yongle himself when he had decided to move the Ming capital from Nanjing, in central China, where the ships were built and the voyages launched, back to Beijing, where official eyes were firmly focused on the threat from beyond the Great Wall to the north. As a means of reducing that threat, Yongle ordered the resettlement of thousands of families from the fertile Yangtze valley. The emperor had presumably not intended to set forces in motion that would divert the country from its contacts with the external world. After all, he had been the driving force behind Zhenghe's voyages. But the end result was a shift in the balance of power from central China, where it had been since the southern Song dynasty, back to northern China, where it had originated and would remain for the rest of the Ming era. China would not look outward again for more than four centuries.

Why the Ming government discontinued Zhenghe's voyages and turned its attention back to domestic concerns has long been a quandary. Was it simply a consequence of court intrigues or the replacement of one emperor by another, or were there deeper issues involved? A recent theory that has gained wide attention and spurred scholarly debate speculates that the Chinese fleets did not limit their explorations to the Indian Ocean but actually circled the earth and discovered the existence of the Western Hemisphere. Although that theory has won few scholarly adherents, the voyages, and their abrupt discontinuance, remain one of the most fascinating enigmas in the history of China.

In Search of the Way

Q **Focus Question:** What roles did Buddhism, Daoism, and Neo-Confucianism play in Chinese intellectual life in the period between the Sui dynasty and the Ming?

By the time of the Sui dynasty, Buddhism and Daoism had emerged as major rivals of Confucianism as the ruling ideology of the state. But during the last half of the Tang dynasty, Confucianism revived and once again became dominant at court, a position it would retain to the end of the dynastic period in the early twentieth century. Buddhist and Daoist beliefs, however, remained popular at the local level.

The Rise and Decline of Buddhism and Daoism

As noted earlier, Buddhism arrived in China with merchants from India and found its first adherents among the merchant community and intellectuals intrigued by the new ideas. During the chaotic centuries following the collapse of the Han dynasty, Buddhism and Daoism appealed to those who were searching for more emotional and spiritual satisfaction than Confucianism could provide.

THE WAY OF THE GREAT BUDDHA

According to Buddhists, it is impossible to describe the state of Nirvana, which is sometimes depicted as an extinction of self. Yet Buddhist scholars found it difficult to avoid trying to interpret the term for their followers. The following passage by the Chinese monk Shen-Hui, one of the leading exponents of *Chan* Buddhism, dates from the eighth century and attempts to describe the means by which an individual may hope to seek enlightenment. There are clear similarities with philosophical Daoism.

Shen-Hui, *Elucidating the Doctrine*

"Absence of thought" is the doctrine.

"Absence of action" is the foundation.

True Emptiness is the substance.

And all wonderful things and beings are the function.

True Thusness is without thought; it cannot be known through conception and thought.

The True State is noncreated—can it be seen in matter and mind?

There is no thought except that of True Thusness.

There is no creation except that of the True State.

Abiding without abiding, forever abiding in Nirvana.

Acting without acting, immediately crossing to the Other Shore.

Thusness does not move, but its motion and functions are inexhaustible.

In every instant of thought, there is no seeking; the seeking itself is no thought.

Perfect wisdom is not achieved, and yet the Five Eyes all become pure and the Three Bodies are understood.

Great Enlightenment has no knowledge, and yet the Six Supernatural Powers of the Buddha are utilized and the Four Wisdoms of the Buddha are made great.

Thus we know that calmness is at the same time no calmness, wisdom at the same time no wisdom, and action at the same time no action.

The nature is equivalent to the void and the substance is identical with the Realm of Law.

In this way, the Six Perfections are completed.

None of the ways to arrive at Nirvana is wanting.

Thus we know that the ego and the dharmas are both empty in reality and being and nonbeing are both obliterated.

The mind is originally without activity; the Way is always without thought.

No thought, no reflection, no seeking, no attainment;

No this, no that, no coming, no going.

With such reality one understands the True Insight into previous and future mortal conditions and present mortal suffering].

With such a mind one penetrates the Eight Emancipations [through the eight stages of mental concentration].

By merits one accomplishes the Ten Powers of the Buddha.

Q *What similarities with philosophical Daoism are expressed in this passage? Compare and contrast the views expressed here with the Neo-Confucian worldview.*

CENGAGENOW *To read "Buddha Enters Nirvana," enter the documents area of the World History Resource Center using the access card that is available for World History.*

Both faiths reached beyond the common people and found support among the ruling classes as well. There was even a small Christian church in the capital of Chang'an, introduced to China by Syrian merchants in the sixth century C.E.

The Sinification of Buddhism

As Buddhism attracted more followers, it began to take on Chinese characteristics and divided into a number of separate sects. Some, like the **Chan** (Zen in Japanese) sect, called for mind training and a strict regimen as a means of seeking enlightenment, a technique that reflected Daoist ideas and appealed to many intellectuals (see the box above). Others, like the **Pure Land** sect, stressed the role of devotion, an approach that was more appealing to ordinary Chinese, who lacked the time and inclination for strict monastic discipline. Still others were mystical sects, like **Tantrism**, which emphasized the importance of magical symbols and ritual in seeking a preferred way to enlightenment. Some Buddhist groups, like their Daoist counterparts, had political objectives. The **White Lotus** sect, founded in 1133, often adopted the form of a rebel movement, seeking political reform or the overthrow of a dynasty and forecasting a new era when a "savior Buddha" would come to earth to herald the advent of a new age. Most believers, however, assimilated Buddhism into their daily lives, where it joined Confucian ideology and spirit worship as an element in the highly eclectic and tolerant Chinese worldview.

The burgeoning popularity of Buddhism continued into the early years of the Tang dynasty. Early Tang rulers lent their support to the Buddhist monasteries that had been established throughout the country. Buddhist scriptures were regularly included in the civil service examinations, and Buddhist and Daoist advisers replaced shamans and Confucian scholar-officials

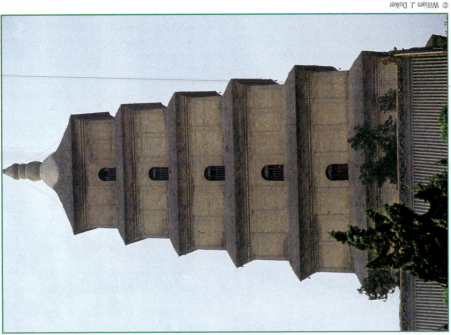

© William J. Duiker

The Spread of Buddhism in Asia

as advisers at court. But ultimately, Buddhism and Daoism lost favor at court and were increasingly subjected to official persecution. Part of the reason was xenophobia. Envious Daoists and Confucianists made a point of criticizing the foreign origins of Buddhist doctrines, which one prominent Confucian scholar characterized as nothing but "silly relics." To deflect such criticism, Buddhists attempted to make the doctrine more Chinese, equating the Indian concept of *dharma* (law) with the Chinese concept of *Dao* (the Way). Emperor Tang Taizong ordered the Buddhist monk Xuan Zang to translate Lao Tzu's classic, *The Way of the Dao*, into Sanskrit, reportedly to show visitors from India that China had its own equivalent to the Buddhist scriptures. But another reason for this change of heart may have been financial. The great Buddhist monasteries had accumulated thousands of acres of land and serfs that were exempt from paying taxes to the state. Such wealth contributed to the corruption of the monks and other Buddhist officials and in turn aroused popular resentment and official disapproval. As the state attempted to eliminate the great landholdings of the aristocracy, the large monasteries also attracted its attention. During the later Tang, countless temples and monasteries were destroyed, and over 100,000 monks were compelled to leave the monasteries and return to secular life.

Buddhism Under Threat There were probably deeper political and ideological reasons for the growing antagonism between Buddhism and the state. By preaching the illusory nature of the material world, Buddhism was denying the very essence of Confucian teachings—the necessity for filial piety and hard work. By encouraging young Chinese to abandon their rice fields and seek refuge and wisdom in the monasteries, Buddhism was undermining the foundation stones of Chinese society—the family unit and the work ethic. In the final analysis, Buddhism was incompatible with the activist element in Chinese society, an orientation that was most effectively expressed by State Confucianism. In the competition with Confucianism for support by the state, Buddhism, like Daoism, was almost certain to lose, at least in the more this-worldly, secure, and prosperous milieu of late Tang and Song China. The two doctrines continued to win converts at the local level, but official support ceased. In the meantime, Buddhism was under attack in Central Asia as well. In the eighth century, the Uighur kingdom adopted **Manichaeanism**, an offshoot of the ancient Zoroastrian

The Big Goose Pagoda. When the Buddhist pilgrim Xuan Zang returned to China from India in the mid-seventh century C.E., he settled in the capital of Chang'an, where, under orders from the Tang emperor, he began to translate Buddhist texts in his possession from Sanskrit into Chinese. The Big Goose Pagoda, shown here, was erected shortly afterward to house them. Originally known as the Pagoda of the Classics, the structure consists of seven stories and is over 240 feet tall.

religion with some influence from Christianity. Manichaeanism spread rapidly throughout the area and may have been a reason for the European belief that a Christian king (the legendary Prester John) ruled somewhere in Asia. By the tenth century, Islam was beginning to move east along the Silk Road, posing a severe threat to both Manichaean and Buddhist centers in the area.

Neo-Confucianism: The Investigation of Things

Into the vacuum left by the decline of Buddhism and Daoism stepped a revived Confucianism. But it was a Confucianism that had been significantly altered by its competition with Buddhist and Daoist teachings. Challenged by Buddhist and Daoist ideas about the nature of the universe, Confucian thinkers began to flesh out the

FAMILY & SOCIETY

During the twelfth century, the philosopher Zhu Xi attempted to reinvigorate Confucian teachings in a contemporary setting that would be more accessible in its appeal to a broad audience. His goal was militantly Confucian, to combat both popular Buddhist doctrines and the superstitious practices of the common people. With his new moral code, Zhu Xi hoped to put Chinese society back on the Confucian track, with its emphasis on proper behavior. He therefore set forth the proper rituals required to carry out the special days that marked the lives of all Chinese: entry into adolescence, marriage, and funeral and ancestral rites. In the following excerpt, he prescribes the proper protocol for the Confucian wedding ceremony.

Zhu Xi's *Family Rituals*

4. Welcoming in Person

On the day before the wedding, the bride's family sends people to lay out the dowry furnishings in the groom's chamber. At dawn the groom's family sets places in the chamber. Meanwhile, the bride's family sets up places outside. As the sun goes down, the groom puts on full attire. After the presiding man makes a report at the offering hall, he pledges the groom and orders him to go to fetch the bride. The groom goes out and mounts his horse. When he gets to the bride's home he waits at his place. The presiding man of the bride's family makes a report at the offering hall, after which he pledges the bride and instructs her. Then he goes out to greet the groom. When the groom enters, he presents a goose. The duenna takes the girl out to climb into the conveyance. The groom mounts his horse and leads the way for the bridal vehicle. When they arrive at his house he leads the bride in and they take their seats. After the eating and drinking are done, the groom leaves the chamber. On reentering, he takes off his clothes and the candles are removed.

5. The Bride Is Presented to Her Parents-in-Law

The next day, having risen at dawn, the bride meets her parents-in-law, who entertain her. Then the bride is presented to the elders. If she is the wife of the eldest son, she serves food to her parents-in-law. Then the parents-in-law feast the bride.

6. Presentation at the Family Shrine

On the third day the presiding man takes the bride to be presented at the offering hall.

7. The Groom Is Presented to the Wife's Parents

The day after that the groom goes to see his wife's parents. Afterward he is presented to his wife's relatives. The bride's family entertains the groom, as in ordinary etiquette.

Q *What is the apparent purpose for describing proper etiquette as expressed in this passage? How does adherence to such rigid rituals contribute to becoming a good Confucian?*

---

spare metaphysical structure of classical Confucian doctrine with a set of sophisticated theories about the nature of the cosmos and humans' place in it. Although the origins of this effort can be traced to the early Tang period, it reached fruition during the intellectually prolific Song dynasty, when it became the dominant ideology of the state.

The fundamental purpose of **Neo-Confucianism,** as the new doctrine was called, was to unite the metaphysical speculations of Buddhism and Daoism with the pragmatic Confucian approach to society. In response to Buddhism and Daoism, Neo-Confucianism maintained that the world is real, not illusory, and that fulfillment comes from participation, not withdrawal.

The primary contributor to this intellectual effort was the philosopher Zhu Xi (Chu Hsi) (see the box above). Raised during the southern Song era, Zhu Xi accepted the division of the world into a material world and a transcendent world (called by Neo-Confucianists the **Supreme Ultimate,** or *Tai Ji*). The latter was roughly equivalent to the *Dao,* or Way, in classical Confucian philosophy. To Zhu Xi, this Supreme Ultimate was a set of abstract principles governed by the law of *yin* and *yang* and the five elements.

Human beings served as a link between the two halves of this bifurcated universe. Although human beings live in the material world, each individual has an identity that is linked with the Supreme Ultimate, and the goal of individual action is to transcend the material world in a Buddhist sense to achieve an essential identity with the Supreme Ultimate. According to Zhu Xi and his followers, the means of transcending the material world is self-cultivation, which is achieved by the "investigation of things."

The School of Mind   During the remainder of the Song dynasty and into the early years of the Ming, Zhu Xi's ideas became the central core of Confucian ideology and a favorite source of questions for the civil service examinations. But during the mid-Ming era, his ideas came under attack from a Confucian scholar named Wang Yangming. Wang and his supporters disagreed with Zhu Xi's focus on learning through an investigation of the outside world and asserted that the correct way to transcend the material world was through an understanding of self. According to this so-called **School of Mind,** the mind and the universe were a single unit. Knowledge was thus intuitive rather than empirical and was obtained through internal self-searching rather than through an investigation of the outside world. The debate is reminiscent of a similar disagreement between followers of the ancient Greek philosophers Plato and Aristotle. Plato had argued that all knowledge comes from within, while Aristotle argued that knowledge resulted from an examination of the external world. Wang Yangming's ideas attracted many followers during the Ming dynasty, and the school briefly rivaled that of Zhu Xi in popularity among Confucian scholars. Nevertheless, it never won official acceptance, probably because it was too much like Buddhism in denying the importance of a life of participation and social action.

Neo-Confucianism remained the state doctrine until the end of the dynastic system in the twentieth century. Some historians have asked whether the doctrine can help explain why China failed to experience scientific and industrial revolutions of the sort that occurred in the West (see the comparative essay "The Scientific Revolution" in Chapter 18). In particular, it has been suggested that Neo-Confucianism tended to encourage an emphasis on the elucidation of moral principles rather than the expansion of scientific knowledge. Though the Chinese excelled in practical technology, inventing gunpowder, the compass (first used by seafarers during the Song dynasty), printing and paper, and cast iron, among other things, they had less interest in scientific theory. Their relative backwardness in mathematics is a good example. Chinese scholars had no knowledge of the principles of geometry and lagged behind other advanced civilizations in astronomy, physics, and optics. Until the Mongol era, they had no knowledge of Arabic numerals and lacked the concept of zero. Even after that time, they continued to use a cumbersome numbering system based on Chinese characters.

Furthermore, intellectual affairs in China continued to be dominated by the scholar-gentry, the chief upholders of Neo-Confucianism, who not only had little interest in the natural sciences or economic change but also viewed them as a threat to their own dominant status in Chinese society. The commercial middle class, who lacked social status and an independent position in society, had little say in intellectual matters. In contrast, in the West, an urban middle class emerged that was a source not only of wealth but also of social prestige, political power, and intellectual ideas. The impetus for the intellectual revolution in the West came from the members of the commercial bourgeoisie, who were interested in the conquest of nature and the development of technology. In China, however, the scholar-gentry continued to focus on the sources of human behavior and a correct understanding of the relationship between humankind and the universe. The result was an intellectual environment that valued continuity over change and tradition over innovation.

The Apogee of Chinese Culture

Q **Focus Question:** What were the main achievements in Chinese literature and art in the period between the Tang dynasty and the Ming, and what technological innovations and intellectual developments contributed to these achievements?

The period between the Tang and the Ming dynasties was in many ways the great age of achievement in Chinese literature and art. Enriched by Buddhist and Daoist images and themes, Chinese poetry and painting reached the pinnacle of their creativity. Porcelain emerged as the highest form of Chinese ceramics, and sculpture flourished under the influence of styles imported from India and Central Asia.

Literature

The development of Chinese literature was stimulated by two technological innovations: the invention of paper during the Han dynasty and the invention of woodblock printing during the Tang. At first, paper was used for clothing, wrapping material, toilet tissue, and even armor, but by the first century B.C.E., it was being used for writing as well.

In the seventh century C.E., the Chinese developed the technique of carving an entire page of text into a wooden block, inking it, and then pressing it onto a sheet of paper. Ordinarily, a text was printed on a long sheet of paper like a scroll. Then the paper was folded and stitched together to form a book. The earliest printed book known today is a Buddhist text published in 868 C.E.; it is more than 16 feet long. Although the Chinese eventually developed movable type as well, block printing continued to be used until relatively modern times because of the large number of Chinese characters needed to produce a lengthy text. Even with printing, books remained too expensive for most Chinese, but they did help popularize all forms of literary writing among the educated elite. Although literature was primarily a male occupation, a few women achieved prominence as a result of their creative prowess.

During the post-Han era, historical writing and essays continued to be favorite forms of literary activity. Each dynasty produced an official dynastic history of its predecessor to elucidate sober maxims about the qualities of good and evil in human nature, and local gazetteers added to the general knowledge about the various regions. Encyclopedias brought together in a single location information and documents about all aspects of Chinese life.

Li Bo was one of the great poets of the Tang dynasty. The first selection, "Quiet Night Thoughts," is probably the best-known poem in China and has been memorized by schoolchildren for centuries. The second poem, "Drinking Alone in Moonlight," reflects the poet's carefree attitude toward life.

Du Fu, Li Bo's prime competitor as the greatest poet of the Tang dynasty, was often the more reflective of the two. In "Spring Prospect," the poet has returned to his home in the capital after a rebellion against the dynasty has left the city in ruins.

Li Bo, "Quiet Night Thoughts"

Beside my bed the bright moonbeams bound
Almost as if there were frost on the ground.
Raising up, I gaze at the Mountain moon;
Lying back, I think of my old hometown.

Li Bo, "Drinking Alone in Moonlight"

Among the flowers, with a jug of wine,
I drink all alone—no one to share.
Raising my cup, I welcome the moon,
And my shadow joins us, making a threesome.
Alas! the moon won't take part in the drinking
And my shadow just does whatever I do.
But I'm friends for a while with the moon and my shadow,
And we caper in revels well suited to spring
As I sing the moon seems to sway back and forth;
As I dance my shadow goes flopping about.
As long as I'm sober we'll enjoy one another,
And when I get drunk, we'll go our own ways;
Forever committed to carefree play,
We'll all meet again in the Milky Way!

Du Fu, "Spring Prospect"

The capital is taken. The hills and streams are left,
And with spring in the city the grass and trees grown dense.
Mourning the times, the flowers trickle their tears;
Saddened with parting, the birds make my heart flutter.
The army beacons have flamed for three months;
A letter from home would be worth ten thousand in gold.
My white hairs I have anxiously scratched ever shorter,
But such disarray! Even hairpins will do no good!

Q Historians often contrast these two famous poets in terms of their personalities and their approach to life. Can you see any differences in their points of view as conveyed in these short poems?

The Importance of Poetry

But it was in poetry, above all, that Chinese from the Tang to the Ming dynasties most effectively expressed their literary talents. Chinese poems celebrated the beauty of nature, the changes of the seasons, the joys of friendship and drink, sadness at the brevity of life, and old age and parting. Given the frequency of imperial banishment and the requirement that officials serve away from their home district, it is little wonder that separation was an important theme. Love poems existed but were neither as intense as Western verse nor as sensual as Indian poetry.

The nature of the Chinese language imposed certain characteristics on Chinese poetry, the first being compactness. The most popular forms were four-line and eight-line poems, with five or seven words in each line. Because Chinese grammar does not rely on case or gender and makes no distinction between verb tenses, five-character Chinese poems were not only brief but often cryptic and ambiguous.

Two Tang poets, Li Bo (Li Po, sometimes known as Li Bai or Li Taibo) and Du Fu (Tu Fu), symbolized the genius of the era as well as the two most popular styles.

Li Bo was a free spirit. His writing often centered on nature and melancholy. Two of his best-known poems are "Resolution on Waking with a Hangover on a Spring Morning" and "Drinking Alone in Moonlight" (see the box above).

Where Li Bo was a carefree Daoist, Du Fu was a sober Confucian. His poems often dealt with historical issues or ethical themes, befitting a scholar-official living during the chaotic times of the late Tang era. Many of his works reflect a concern with social injustice and the plight of the unfortunate rarely to be found in the writings of his contemporaries (see the box on p. 280). Neither the poetry nor the prose of the great writers of the Tang and Song dynasties was written for or ever reached the majority of the Chinese population. The millions of Chinese peasants and artisans living in rural villages and market towns acquired their knowledge of Chinese history, Confucian moralisms, and even Buddhist scripture from stories, plays, and songs passed down by storytellers, wandering minstrels, and itinerant monks in a rich oral tradition.

© The Art Archive/British Museum

surviving the rigors of the Silk Road. The entrances to the caves were filled with stones after the tenth century, when Muslim zealots began to destroy Buddhist images throughout Central Asia, and have only recently been uncovered. Like the few surviving Tang scroll paintings, these wall paintings display a love of color and refinement that are reminiscent of styles in India and Persia (see the illustration below).

Daoism ultimately had a greater influence than Buddhism on Chinese painting. From early times, Chinese artists removed themselves to the mountains to write and paint and find the *Dao*, or *Way*, in nature. In the fifth century, one Chinese painter, too old to travel, began to paint mountain scenes from memory and announced that depicting nature could function as a

Cave Art at Dunhuang. Dunhuang was a major rest stop on the eastern section of the Silk Road. Many merchants from Central Asia paused there while awaiting permission to travel on to the Tang capital at Chang'an. Before embarking on the last stage of their journey, some travelers endowed the creation of Buddhist frescoes and statuary in caves on a cliffside not far from their lodgings. Shown here is an eighth-century wall banner of the Buddha that shows distinct Indian influence. After the Muslim faith penetrated into the area, the caves were abandoned, not to be rediscovered until late in the nineteenth century.

Popular Culture By the Song dynasty, China had sixty million people, one million in Hangzhou alone. With the growth of cities came an increased demand for popular entertainment. Although the Tang dynasty had imposed a curfew on urban residents, the Song did not. The city gates and bridges were closed at dark, but food stalls and entertainment continued through the night. At fairgrounds throughout the year, one could find comedians, musicians, boxers, fencers, wrestlers, acrobats, puppets and marionettes, shadow plays, and especially storytellers. Many of these arts had come from India centuries before and were now the favorite forms of amusement of the Chinese people.

The Chinese Novel During the Yuan dynasty, new forms of literary creativity, including popular theater and the novel, began to appear. The two most famous novels were *Romance of the Three Kingdoms* and *Tale of the Marshes*. The former had been told orally for centuries, appearing in written form during the Song as a scriptbook for storytellers. It was first printed in 1321 but was not published for mass consumption until 1522. Each new edition was altered in some way, making the final edition a composite effort of generations of the Chinese imagination. The plot recounts the power struggle that took place among competing groups after the fall of the Han dynasty. Packed with court intrigues, descriptions of peasant life, and gripping battles, *Romance of the Three Kingdoms* stands as a magnificent epic, China's counterpart to the Mahabharata.

Tale of the Marshes is an often violent tale of outlaw heroes who at the end of the northern Song banded together to oppose government taxes and official oppression. They rob from those in power to share with the poor. *Tale of the Marshes* is the first prose fiction that describes the daily ordeal of ordinary Chinese people in their own language. Unlike the picaresque novel in the West, *Tale of the Marshes* does not limit itself to the exploits of one hero, offering instead 108 different story lines. This multitude of plots is a natural outgrowth of the tradition of the professional storyteller, who attempts to keep the audience's attention by recounting as many adventures as the market will bear.

Art

Although painting flourished in China under the Han and reached a level of artistic excellence under the Tang, little remains from those periods. The painting of the Song and the Yuan, however, is considered the apogee of painting in traditional China.

Like literature, Chinese painting found part of its inspiration in Buddhist and Daoist sources. Some of the best surviving examples of the Tang period are the Buddhist wall paintings in the caves at Dunhuang, in Central Asia. These paintings were commissioned by Buddhist merchants who stopped at Dunhuang and, while awaiting permission to enter China, wished to give thanks for

© The Art Archive/National Palace Museum, Taipei

substitute for contemplating nature itself. Painting, he said, could be the means of realizing the *Dao*. This explains in part the emphasis on nature in traditional Chinese painting. The word for *landscape* in Chinese means "mountain-water," and the Daoist search for balance between earth and water, hard and soft, *yang* and *yin*, is at play in the tradition of Chinese painting. To enhance the effect, poems were added to the paintings, underscoring the fusion of the visual and the verbal in Chinese art. Many artists were proficient in both media, the poem inspiring the painting and vice versa.

To represent the totality of nature, Chinese artists attempted to reveal the quintessential forms of the landscape. Rather than depicting the actual realistic shape of a specific mountain, they tried to portray the "idea" of a mountain. Empty spaces were left in the paintings because in the Daoist vision, one cannot know the whole truth. Daoist influence was also evident in the tendency to portray human beings as insignificant in the midst of nature. In contrast to the focus on the human body and personality in Western art, Chinese art presented people as tiny figures fishing in a small boat, meditating on a cliff, or wandering up a hillside trail, co-existing with but not dominating nature.

The Chinese displayed their paintings on long scrolls of silk or paper that were attached to a wooden cylindrical bar at the bottom. Varying in length from 3 to 20 feet, the paintings were unfolded slowly so that the eye could enjoy each segment, one after the other, beginning at the bottom with water or a village and moving upward into the hills to the mountain peaks and the sky.

By the tenth century, Chinese painters began to eliminate color from their paintings, preferring the challenge of capturing the distilled essence of the landscape in washes of black ink on white silk. Borrowing from calligraphy, now a sophisticated and revered art, they emphasized the brush stroke and created black-and-white landscapes characterized by a gravity of mood and dominated by overpowering mountains.

Other artists turned toward more expressionist and experimental painting. These so-called literati artists were scholars and administrators, highly educated and adept in music, poetry, and painting. Being scholars first and artists second, however, they believed that the purpose of painting was not representation but expression. No longer did painters wish to evoke the feeling of wandering in nature. Instead they tried to reveal to the viewer their own mind and feelings. Like many Western painters in the nineteenth and twentieth centuries, many of these artists were misunderstood by the public and painted only for themselves and one another.

Second only to painting in creativity was the field of ceramics, notably the manufacture of porcelain. Made of fine clay baked at unusually high temperatures in a kiln, porcelain was first produced during the period after the fall of the Han and became popular during the Tang era. During the Song, porcelain came into its own. Most renowned perhaps are the celadons, in a delicate gray-green, but Song artists also excelled in other colors and techniques. As in painting, Song delicacy and grace contrasted with the bold and often crude styles popular under the Tang. The translucency of Chinese porcelain resulted from a technique that did not reach Europe until the eighteenth century. During the Yuan and the Ming, new styles appeared. Most notable is the cobalt blue-and-white porcelain usually identified with the Ming dynasty, which actually originated during the Yuan. The Ming also produced a multicolored porcelain—often in green, yellow, and red—covered with exotic designs.

Emperor Ming-huang Traveling to Shu. Although the Tang dynasty was a prolific period in the development of Chinese painting, few examples have survived. Fortunately, the practice of copying the works of previous masters was a common tradition in China. Here we see an eleventh-century copy of an eighth-century painting depicting the precipitous journey of Emperor Ming-huang as he was driven by a revolt from the capital into the mountains of southwestern China. Rather than portraying the bitterness of the emperor's precarious escape, however, the artist reflected the confidence and brilliance of the Tang dynasty through cheerful color and an idyllic landscape.

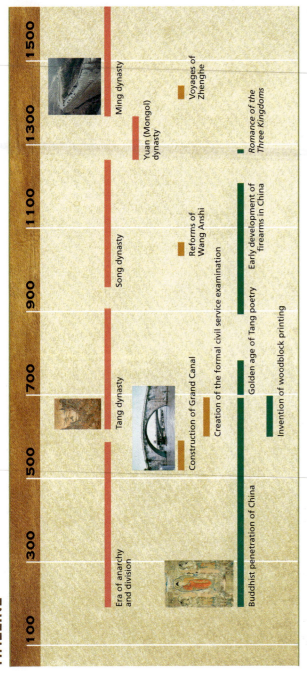

| 100 | 300 | 500 | 700 | 900 | 1100 | 1300 | 1500 |

Era of anarchy and division

Tang dynasty

Song dynasty

Yuan (Mongol) dynasty

Ming dynasty

Construction of Grand Canal

Creation of the formal civil service examination

Reforms of Wang Anshi

Voyages of Zhenghe

Buddhist penetration of China

Golden age of Tang poetry

Early development of firearms in China

Romance of the Three Kingdoms

Invention of woodblock printing

CONCLUSION

Traditionally, Chinese historians believed that Chinese history tended to be cyclical. The pattern of history was marked by the rise and fall of great dynasties, interspersed with periods of internal division and foreign invasion. Underlying the waxing and waning of dynasties was the essential continuity of Chinese civilization.

This view of the dynamic forces of Chinese history was long accepted as valid by historians in China and in the West and led many to assert that Chinese history was unique and could not be placed in a European or universal framework. Whereas Western history was linear, leading steadily away from the past, China's always returned to its moorings and was rooted in the values and institutions of antiquity.

In recent years, however, this traditional view of a changeless China has come under increasing challenge from historians who see patterns of change that made the China of the late fifteenth century a very different place from the country that had existed at the rise of the Tang dynasty in 600. To these scholars, China had passed through its own version of the "middle ages" and was on the verge of beginning a linear evolution into a posttraditional society.

As we have seen, China at the beginning of the Ming had advanced in many ways since the end of the great Han dynasty over a thousand years earlier. The industrial and commercial sector had grown considerably in size, complexity, and technological capacity, while in the countryside the concentration of political and economic power in the hands of the aristocracy had been replaced by a more stable and more equitable mixture of landed gentry, freehold farmers, and sharecroppers. In addition, Chinese society had achieved a level of stability and social tranquillity that not only surpassed conditions during the final years of the Han but was the envy of observers from other lands, near and far. The civil service provided an avenue of upward mobility that was unavailable elsewhere in the world, and the state tolerated a diversity of beliefs that responded to the emotional needs and preferences of the Chinese people. In many respects, China's achievements were unsurpassed throughout the world and marked a major advance beyond antiquity.

Yet there were also some key similarities between the China of the Ming and the China of late antiquity. Ming China was still a predominantly agrarian society, with wealth based primarily on the ownership of land. Commercial activities flourished but remained under a high level of government regulation and by no means represented a major proportion of the national income. China also remained a relatively centralized empire based on an official ideology that stressed the virtue of hard work, social conformity, and hierarchy. In foreign affairs, the long frontier struggle with the nomadic peoples along the northern and western frontiers continued unabated.

Thus the significant change that China experienced during its medieval era can probably be best described as change within continuity, an evolutionary working out of trends that had first become visible during the Han dynasty or even earlier. The result was a civilization that was the envy of its neighbors and of the known world. It also influenced other states in the region, including Japan, Korea, and Vietnam. It is to these societies along the Chinese rimlands that we now turn.

CHAPTER NOTES

1. *The Travels of Marco Polo* (New York, n.d.), pp. 128, 179.
2. Quoted in A. F. Wright, *Buddhism in Chinese History* (Stanford, Calif., 1959), p. 30.
3. Quoted in A. F. Wright, *The Sui Dynasty* (New York, 1978), p. 180.
4. Chu-yu, *P'ing-chow Table Talks*, quoted in R. Temple, *The Genius of China: 3,000 Years of Science, Discovery, and Invention* (New York, 1986), p. 150.
5. Quoted in E. H. Schafer, *The Golden Peaches of Samarkand: A Study of T'ang Exotics* (Berkeley, Calif., 1963), p. 43.
6. Quoted in J. K. Fairbank, E. O. Reischauer, and A. M. Craig, *East Asia: Tradition and Transformation* (Boston, 1973), p. 164.
7. Quoted in R. Grousset, *L'Empire des Steppes* (Paris, 1939), p. 285.
8. Temple, *Genius of China*, pp. 242–243.
9. A. M. Khazanov, *Nomads and the Outside World* (Cambridge, 1983), p. 241.
10. S. A. M. Adshead, *China in World History* (New York, 2000), p. 132.

SUGGESTED READING

General   For an authoritative overview of the early imperial era in China, see **M. Elvin, *The Pattern of the Chinese Past*** (Stanford, Calif., 1973). A global perspective is presented in **S. A. M. Adshead, *China in World History*** (New York, 2000). For an informative treatment of China's relations with its neighbors, see **C. Holcombe, *The Genesis of East Asia, 220 B.C.E.–A.D. 907*** (Honolulu, 2001).

A vast body of material is available on almost all periods of early Chinese history. For the post-Han period, see **A. E. Dien, ed., *State and Society in Early Medieval China*** (Stanford, Calif., 1990); **F. Mote, *Imperial China*** (Cambridge, 1999); and **D. Twitchett and M. Loewe, *Cambridge History of China*, vol. 3, *Medieval China*** (Cambridge, 1986).

The Sui, Tang, and Song Dynasties   For a readable treatment of the brief but tempestuous Sui dynasty, see **A. F. Wright, *The Sui Dynasty*** (New York, 1978). On the Tang, see **C. Benn, *China's Golden Age: Everyday Life in the Tang Dynasty*** (Oxford, 2004). The Song dynasty has been studied in considerable detail. For an excellent interpretation, see **J. T. C. Liu, *China Turning Inward: Intellectual Changes in the Early Twelfth Century*** (Cambridge, Mass., 1988). Song problems with the northern frontier are chronicled in **Tao Jing-shen, *Two Sons of Heaven: Studies in Sung–Liao Relations*** (Tucson, Ariz., 1988).

The Mongol Period   Among a number of good studies on the Mongol period in Chinese history is **W. A. Langlois, *China Under Mongol Rule*** (Princeton, N.J., 1981). **M. Rossabi, *Khubilai Khan: His Life and Times*** (Berkeley, Calif., 1988), is a good biography of the dynasty's greatest emperor, while **M. Rossabi, ed., *China Among Equals: The Middle Kingdom and Its Neighbors*** (Berkeley, Calif., 1983), deals with foreign affairs. For a provocative interpretation of Chinese relations with nomadic peoples, see **T. J. Barfield, *The Perilous Frontier: Nomadic Empires and China*** (Cambridge, 1989). An analytical account of the dynamics of nomadic society is **A. M. Khazanov, *Nomads and the Outside World*** (Cambridge, 1983).

Miscellaneous Topics   The emergence of urban culture during the Mongol era is analyzed in **C. K. Heng, *Cities of Aristocrats and Bureaucrats: The Development of Medieval Chinese Cityscapes*** (Honolulu, 1999). For perspectives on China as viewed from the outside, see **J. Spence, *The Chan's Great Continent: China in a Western Mirror*** (New York, 1998). China's contacts with foreign cultures are discussed in **J. Waley-Cohen, *The Sextants of Beijing*** (New York, 1999). On the controversial belief that Chinese fleets circled the globe in the fifteenth century, see **G. Menzies, *1421: The Year China Discovered America*** (New York, 2002).

Chinese Women's Issues   For an introduction to women's issues during this period, consult **P. B. Ebrey, *The Inner Quarters: Marriage and the Lives of Chinese Women in the Sung Period*** (Berkeley, Calif., 1993); **Chu Hsi's *Family Rituals*** (Princeton, N.J., 1991); and **"Women, Marriage, and the Family in Chinese History,"** in P. S. Ropp, *Heritage of China: Contemporary Perspectives on Chinese Civilization* (Berkeley, Calif., 1990). For an overview of Chinese foot binding, see C. F. Blake, "Foot-Binding in Neo-Confucian China and the Appropriation of Female Labor," *Signs* 19 (Spring 1994).

Central Asia   On Central Asia, two popular accounts are **J. Myrdal, *The Silk Road*** (New York, 1979), and **N. Marty, *The Silk Road*** (Methuen, Mass., 1987). A more interpretive approach is found in **S. A. M. Adshead, *Central Asia in World History*** (New York, 1993). See also **E. T. Grotenhuis, ed., *Along the Silk Road*** (Washington, D.C., 2002). Xuan Zang's journey to India is re-created in R. Bernstein, *Ultimate Journey: Retracing the Path of an Ancient Buddhist Monk Who Crossed Asia in Search of Enlightenment* (New York, 2000).

Chinese Literature   On Chinese literature, consult **S. Owen, *An Anthology of Chinese Literature: Beginnings to 1911*** (New York, 1996), and V. Mair, *The Columbia Anthology of Traditional Chinese Literature* (New York, 1994). For poetry, see **Liu Wu-Chi and I. Yucheng Lo, *Sunflower Splendor: Three Thousand Years of Chinese Poetry*** (Bloomington, Ind., 1975), and **S. Owen, *The Great Age of Chinese Poetry: The High Tang*** (New Haven, Conn., 1981), the latter presenting poems in both Chinese and English.

Chinese Art   For a comprehensive introduction to Chinese art, see the classic **M. Sullivan, *The Arts of China*, 4th ed.** (Berkeley, Calif., 1999); **M. Tregear, *Chinese Art*, rev ed.** (London, 1997); and **C. Clunas, *Art in China*** (Oxford, 1997). The standard introduction to Chinese painting can be found in **J. Cahill, *Chinese Painting*** (New York, 1985), and **Yang Xin et al., *Three Thousand Years of Chinese Painting*** (New Haven, Conn., 1997).

CENGAGENOW   Enter CengageNOW using the access card that is available with this text. *CengageNOW* will help you understand the content in this chapter with lesson plans generated for your needs, as well as provide you with a connection to the Wadsworth *World History Resource Center* (see description below for details).

WORLD HISTORY RESOURCE CENTER

Enter the Resource Center using either your CengageNOW access card or your separate access card for the *World History Resource Center*. Organized by topic, this Website includes quizzes; images; over 350 primary source documents; interactive simulations, maps, and timelines; movie explorations; and a wealth of other resources. You can read the following documents, and many more, at the *World History Resource Center*:

> Buddha Enters Nirvana
> Confucius, *The Doctrine of the Mean*
> Dao De Jing, Daoism

Visit the *World History Companion Website* for chapter quizzes and more at

www.cengage.com/history/Duiker/World6e

© William J. Duiker

Turtle Island, Hanoi

CHAPTER 11

THE EAST ASIAN RIMLANDS: EARLY JAPAN, KOREA, AND VIETNAM

CHAPTER OUTLINE AND FOCUS QUESTIONS

Japan: Land of the Rising Sun

Q How did Japan's geographical location affect the course of early Japanese history, and how did it influence the political structures and social institutions that arose there?

Korea: Bridge to the East

Q What were the main characteristics of economic and social life in early Korea?

Vietnam: The Smaller Dragon

Q What were the main developments in Vietnamese history before 1500? Why were the Vietnamese able to restore their national independence after a millennium of Chinese rule?

CRITICAL THINKING

Q How did Chinese civilization influence the societies that arose in Japan, Korea, and Vietnam during their early history?

THERE IS A SMALL body of water in the heart of the Vietnamese national capital of Hanoi that is known affectionately to local city-dwellers as Returned Sword Lake. The lake owes its name to a legend that Le Loi, founder of the later Le dynasty in the fifteenth century, had drawn a magic sword from the lake that enabled him to achieve a great victory over Chinese occupation forces. It thus symbolizes to many Vietnamese their nation's historical resistance to domination by its powerful northern neighbor.

Ironically, however, a temple that was later erected on tiny Turtle Island in the middle of the lake reflects the strong influence that China continued to exert on traditional Vietnamese culture. After Le Loi's victory, the sword was allegedly returned to the water, and the Vietnamese ruler accepted a tributary relationship to his "elder brother," the Chinese emperor in Beijing. China's philosophy, political institutions, and social mores served as hallmarks for the Vietnamese people down to the early years of the twentieth century. That is why Vietnam was for centuries known as "the smaller dragon."

Le Loi's deferential attitude toward his larger neighbor should not surprise us. During ancient times, China was the most technologically advanced society in East Asia. To its north and west were pastoral peoples whose military exploits were often impressive but whose political and cultural attainments were still limited, at least by comparison with the great river valley civilizations of the day. In inland areas south of the Yangtze River were scattered clumps of rice farmers and hill peoples, most of whom had not yet entered the era of state building and had little knowledge of the niceties of Confucian ethics. Along the fringes of Chinese civilization were a number of other agricultural societies that were beginning to follow a pattern of development similar to that of China, although somewhat later in time. One of these was the land of Yueh (Vietnam), where a relatively advanced agricultural civilization had been in existence for several hundred years before the area was finally conquered by the Han dynasty in the second century C.E. Another was in the islands of Japan, where an organized society was beginning to take shape just as Chinese administrators were attempting to consolidate imperial rule over the Vietnamese people. On the Korean peninsula, an advanced Neolithic society had already begun to develop a few centuries earlier.

All of these early agricultural societies were eventually influenced to some degree by their great neighbor, China. Vietnam remained under Chinese rule for a thousand years. Korea retained its separate existence but was long a tributary state of China and in many ways followed the cultural example of its larger patron. Only Japan retained both its political independence and its cultural uniqueness. Yet even the Japanese were strongly influenced by the glittering culture of their powerful neighbor, and today many Japanese institutions and customs still bear the imprint of several centuries of borrowing from China. In this chapter, we will take a closer look at these emerging societies along the Chinese rimlands and consider how their cultural achievements reflected or contrasted with those of the Chinese Empire. ◆

Japan: Land of the Rising Sun

Q **Focus Question:** How did Japan's geographical location affect the course of early Japanese history, and how did it influence the political structures and social institutions that arose there?

Geography accounts for many of the historical differences between Chinese and Japanese society. Whereas China is a continental civilization, Japan is an island country. It consists of four main islands (see Map 11.1): Hokkaido in the north, the main island of Honshu in the center, and the two smaller islands of Kyushu and Shikoku in the southwest. Its total land area is about 146,000 square miles, about the size of the state of Montana. Japan's main islands are at approximately the same latitude as the eastern seaboard of the United States.

Like the eastern United States, Japan is blessed with a temperate climate. It is slightly warmer on the east coast, which is washed by the Pacific Current sweeping up from the south, and has a number of natural harbors that provide protection from the winds and high waves of the Pacific Ocean. As a consequence, in recent times, the majority of the Japanese people have tended to live along the east coast, especially in the flat plains surrounding the cities of Tokyo, Osaka, and Kyoto. In these favorable environmental conditions, Japanese farmers have been able to harvest two crops of rice annually since early times.

By no means, however, is Japan an agricultural paradise. Like China, much of the country is mountainous, with only about 20 percent of the total land area suitable for cultivation. These mountains are of volcanic origin, since the Japanese islands are located at the juncture of the Asian and Pacific tectonic plates. This location is both an advantage and a disadvantage. Volcanic soils are extremely fertile, which helps explain the exceptionally high productivity of Japanese farmers. At the same time, the area is prone to earthquakes, such as the famous quake of 1923, which destroyed almost the entire city of Tokyo.

The fact that Japan is an island country has had a significant impact on Japanese history. As we have seen, the continental character of Chinese civilization, with its constant threat of invasion from the north, had a number of consequences for Chinese history. One effect was to make the Chinese more sensitive to the preservation of their culture from destruction at the hands of non-Chinese invaders. As one fourth-century C.E. Chinese ruler remarked when he was forced to move his capital southward under pressure from nomadic incursions, "The King takes All Under Heaven as his home."[1] Proud of their own considerable cultural achievements and their dominant position throughout the region, the Chinese have traditionally been reluctant to dilute the purity of their culture with foreign innovations. Culture more than race is a determinant of the Chinese sense of identity.

MAP 11.1 Early Japan. This map shows key cities in Japan during the early development of the Japanese state. Q What was the original heartland of Japanese civilization on the main island of Honshu? View an animated version of this map or related maps at www.cengage.com/history/Duiker/World6e

By contrast, the island character of Japan probably had the effect of strengthening the Japanese sense of ethnic and cultural distinctiveness. Although the Japanese view of themselves as the most ethnically homogeneous people in East Asia may not be entirely accurate (the modern Japanese probably represent a mix of peoples, much like their neighbors on the continent), their sense of racial and cultural homogeneity has enabled them to import ideas from abroad without worrying that the borrowings will destroy the uniqueness of their own culture.

A Gift from the Gods: Prehistoric Japan

According to an ancient legend recorded in historical chronicles written in the eighth century C.E., the islands of Japan were formed as a result of the marriage of the god Izanagi and the goddess Izanami. After giving birth to Japan, Izanami gave birth to a sun goddess whose name was Amaterasu. A descendant of Amaterasu later descended to earth and became the founder of the Japanese nation. This Japanese creation myth is reminiscent of similar beliefs in other ancient societies, which often saw themselves as the product of a union of deities. What is interesting about the Japanese version is that it has survived into modern times as an explanation for the uniqueness of the Japanese people and the divinity of the

Japanese emperor, who is still believed by some Japanese to be a direct descendant of the sun goddess Amaterasu.

Modern scholars have a more prosaic explanation for the origins of Japanese civilization. According to archaeological evidence, the Japanese islands have been occupied by human beings for at least 100,000 years. The earliest known Neolithic inhabitants, known as the Jomon people (named for the cord pattern of their pottery), lived in the islands as much as ten thousand years ago. They lived by hunting, fishing, and food gathering.

Agriculture may have appeared in Japan sometime during the first millennium B.C.E., although some archaeologists believe that the Jomon people had learned to cultivate some food crops considerably earlier than that. About 400 B.C.E., rice cultivation was introduced, probably by immigrants from the mainland by way of the Korean peninsula. Until recently, historians believed that these immigrants drove out the existing inhabitants of the area and gave rise to the emerging Yayoi culture (named for the site near Tokyo where pottery from the period was found). It is now thought, however, that Yayoi culture was a product of a mixture between the Jomon people and the new arrivals, enriched by imports such as wet-rice agriculture, which had been brought by the immigrants from the mainland. In any event, it seems clear that the Yayoi peoples were the ancestors of the vast majority of present-day Japanese.

© William J. Duiker

© William J. Duiker

© William J. Duiker

COMPARATIVE ILLUSTRATION

The Longhouse. Many early peoples built longhouses of wood and thatch to store their goods and carry on community activities. Many such structures were erected on heavy pilings to protect the interior from flooding, insects, or wild animals. On the left is a model of a sixth-century C.E. warehouse in Osaka, Japan. The original was apparently used by local residents to store grain and other foodstuffs. In the center is a reconstruction of a similar structure built originally by Vikings in Denmark. The longhouses on the right are still occupied by families living on Nias, a small island off the coast of Sumatra. The outer walls were built to resemble the hulls of Dutch galleons that plied the seas near Nias during the seventeenth and eighteenth centuries.

Q The longhouse served as a communal structure in many human communities in early times. What types of structures serve communities in modern societies today?

RELIGION & PHILOSOPHY

THE EASTERN EXPEDITION OF EMPEROR JIMMU

Japanese myths maintained that the Japanese nation could be traced to the sun goddess Amaterasu, who was the ancestor of the founder of the Japanese imperial family, Emperor Jimmu. This passage from the *Nihon Shoki* (Chronicles of Japan) describes the campaign in which the "divine warrior" Jimmu occupied the central plains of Japan, symbolizing the founding of the Japanese nation. Legend dates this migration to about 660 B.C.E., but modern historians believe that it took place much later (perhaps as late as the fourth century C.E.) and that the account of the "divine warrior" may represent an effort by Japanese chroniclers to find a local equivalent to the Sage Kings of prehistoric China.

The Chronicles of Japan

Emperor Jimmu was forty-five years of age when he addressed the assemblage of his brothers and children:

"Long ago, this central land of the Reed Plains was bequeathed to our imperial ancestors by the heavenly deities, Takamimusubi-no-Kami and Amaterasu Omikami.... However, the remote regions still do not enjoy the benefit of our imperial rule, with each town having its own master and each village its own chief. Each of them sets up his own boundaries and contends for supremacy against other masters and chiefs.

"I have heard from an old deity knowledgeable in the affairs of the land and sea that in the east there is a beautiful land encircled by blue mountains. This must be the land from which our great task of spreading our benevolent rule can begin, for it is indeed the center of the universe.... Let us go there, and make it our capital...."

In the winter of that year...the Emperor personally led imperial princes and a naval force to embark on his eastern expedition....

When Nagasunehiko heard of the expedition, he said: "The children of the heavenly deities are coming to rob me of my country." He immediately mobilized his troops and intercepted Jimmu's troops at the hill of Kusaka and engaged in a battle.... The imperial forces were unable to advance. Concerned with the reversal, the Emperor formulated a new divine plan and said to himself: "I am the descendant of the Sun Goddess, and it is against the way of heaven to face the sun in attacking my enemy. Therefore our forces must retreat to make a show of weakness. After making sacrifice to the deities of heaven and earth, we shall march with the sun on our backs. We shall trample down our enemies with the might of the sun. In this way, without staining our swords with blood, our enemies can be conquered."... So he ordered the troops to retreat to the port of Kusaka and regroup there....

[After withdrawing to Kusaka, the imperial forces sailed southward, landed at a port in the present-day Kita peninsula, and again advanced north toward Yamato.]

The precipitous mountains provided such effective barriers that the imperial forces were not able to advance into the interior, and there was no path they could tread. Then one night Amaterasu Omikami appeared to the Emperor in a dream: "I will send you the Yatagarasu, let it guide you through the land." The following day, indeed, the Yatagarasu appeared flying down from the great expanse of the sky. The Emperor said: "The coming of this bird signifies the fulfillment of my auspicious dream. How wonderful it is! Our imperial ancestor, Amaterasu Omikami, desires to help us in the founding of our empire."

Q   How does the author of this document justify the actions taken by Emperor Jimmu to defeat his enemies? What evidence does he present to demonstrate that Jimmu has the support of divine forces?

CENGAGENOW   To read about Emperor Jimmu, enter the documents area of the *World History Resource Center* using the access card that is available for World History.

At first, the Yayoi lived primarily on the southern island of Kyushu, but eventually they moved northward onto the main island of Honshu, conquering, assimilating, or driving out the previous inhabitants of the area, some of whose descendants, known as the Ainu, still live in the northern islands. Finally, in the first centuries C.E., the Yayoi settled in the Yamato plain in the vicinity of the modern cities of Osaka and Kyoto. Japanese legend recounts the story of a "divine warrior," Jimmu, who led his people eastward from the island of Kyushu to establish a kingdom in the Yamato plain (see the box above).

In central Honshu, the Yayoi set up a tribal society based on a number of clans, called **uji**. Each **uji** was ruled by a hereditary chieftain, who provided protection to the local population in return for a portion of the annual harvest. The population itself was divided between a small aristocratic class and the majority, composed of rice farmers, artisans, and other household servants of the aristocrats. Yayoi society was highly decentralized, although eventually the chieftain of the dominant clan in the Yamato region, who claimed to be descended from the sun goddess Amaterasu, achieved a kind of titular primacy. There is no evidence, however, of a central ruler equivalent in power to the Chinese rulers of the Shang and the Zhou eras.

The Rise of the Japanese State

Although the Japanese had been aware of China for centuries, they paid relatively little attention to their more advanced neighbor until the early seventh century, when the rise of the centralized and expansionistic Tang dynasty presented a challenge. The Tang began to meddle in the affairs of the Korean peninsula, conquering the southwestern coast and arousing anxiety in Japan. Yamato rulers attempted to deal with the potential threat posed by the Chinese in two ways. First, they sought alliances with the remaining Korean states. Second, they attempted to centralize their authority so that they could mount a more effective resistance in the event of a Chinese invasion. The key figure in this effort was Shotoku Taishi (572–622), a leading aristocrat in one of the dominant clans in the Yamato region. Prince Shotoku sent missions to the Tang capital of Chang'an to learn about the political institutions already in use in the relatively centralized Tang kingdom (see Map 11.2).

Emulating the Chinese Model   Shotoku Taishi then launched a series of reforms to create a new system based roughly on the Chinese model. In the so-called seventeen-article constitution, he called for the creation of a centralized government under a supreme ruler and a merit system for selecting and ranking public officials (see the box on p. 311). His objective was to limit the powers of the hereditary nobility and enhance the prestige and authority of the Yamato ruler, who claimed divine status and was now emerging as the symbol of the unique character of the Japanese nation. In reality, there is evidence that places the origins of the Yamato clan on the Korean peninsula.

After Shotoku Taishi's death in 622, his successors continued to introduce reforms to make the government more efficient. In a series of so-called **Taika reforms** (*taika* means "great change") that began in the mid-seventh century, the Grand Council of State was established, presiding over a cabinet of eight ministries. To the traditional six ministries of Tang China were added ministers representing the central secretariat and the imperial household. Official communications were to be based on the Chinese written language. The territory of Japan was divided into administrative districts on the Chinese pattern. The rural village, composed ideally of fifty households, was the basic unit of government. The village chief was responsible for "the maintenance of the household registers, the assigning of the sowing of crops and the cultivation of mulberry trees, the prevention of offenses, and the requisitioning of taxes and forced labor." A law code was introduced, and a new tax system was established; now all farmland technically belonged to the state, so taxes were paid directly to the central government rather than through the local nobility, as had previously been the case.

As a result of their new acquaintance with China, the Japanese also developed a strong interest in Buddhism. Some of the first Japanese to travel to China during this period were Buddhist pilgrims hoping to learn more about the exciting new doctrine and bring back scriptures. Buddhism became quite popular among the aristocrats, who endowed wealthy monasteries that became active in Japanese politics. At first, the new faith did not penetrate to the masses, but eventually, popular sects such as the Pure Land sect, an import from China, won many adherents among the common people.

The Nara Period   Initial efforts to build a new state modeled roughly after the Tang state were successful. After Shotoku Taishi's death in 622, political influence fell into the hands of the powerful Fujiwara clan, which managed to marry into the ruling family and continue the reforms Shotoku had begun. In 710, a new capital, laid out on a grid similar to the great Tang city of Chang'an, was established at Nara, on the eastern edge of the Yamato plain. The Yamato ruler began to use the title "son of Heaven" in the Chinese

The Yamato Plain

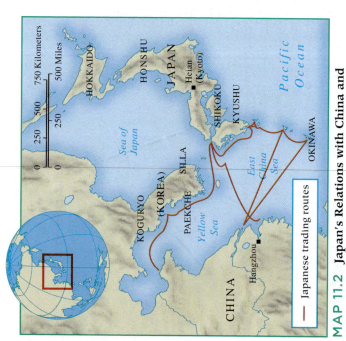

MAP 11.2   Japan's Relations with China and Korea. This map shows the Japanese islands at the time of the Yamato state. Maritime routes taken by Japanese traders and missionaries to China are indicated.

Q Where did Japanese traders travel after reaching the mainland?   View an animated version of this map or related maps at www.cengage.com/history/Duiker/World6e

THE SEVENTEEN-ARTICLE CONSTITUTION

POLITICS & GOVERNMENT

The following excerpt from the *Nihon Shoki* (Chronicles of Japan) is a passage from the seventeen-article constitution promulgated in 604 C.E. Although the opening section reflects Chinese influence in its emphasis on social harmony, there is also a strong focus on obedience and hierarchy. The constitution was put into practice during the reign of the famous Prince Shotoku.

The Chronicles of Japan

Summer, 4th month, 3rd day [12th year of Empress Suiko, 604 C.E.]. The Crown Prince personally drafted and promulgated a constitution consisting of seventeen articles, which are as follows:

I. Harmony is to be cherished, and opposition for opposition's sake must be avoided as a matter of principle. Men are often influenced by partisan feelings, except a few sagacious ones. Hence there are some who disobey their lords and fathers, or who dispute with their neighboring villages. If those above are harmonious and those below are cordial, their discussion will be guided by a spirit of conciliation, and reason shall naturally prevail. There will be nothing that cannot be accomplished.

II. With all our heart, revere the three treasures. The three treasures, consisting of Buddha, the Doctrine, and the Monastic Order, are the final refuge of the four generated beings, and are the supreme objects of worship in all countries. Can any man in any age ever fail to respect these teachings? Few men are utterly devoid of goodness, and men can be taught to follow the teachings. Unless they take refuge in the three treasures, there is no way of rectifying their misdeeds.

III. When an imperial command is given, obey it with reverence. The sovereign is likened to heaven, and his subjects are likened to earth. With heaven providing the cover and earth supporting it, the four seasons proceed in orderly fashion, giving sustenance to all that which is in nature. If earth attempts to overtake the functions of heaven, it destroys everything.... If there is no reverence shown to the imperial command, ruin will automatically result....

VII. Every man must be given his clearly delineated responsibility. If a wise man is entrusted with office, the sound of praise arises. If a wicked man holds office, disturbances become frequent.... In all things, great or small, find the right man, and the country will be well governed.... In this manner, the state will be lasting and its sacerdotal functions will be free from danger.

Q *What are the key components in this first constitution in the history of Japan? To what degree do its provisions conform to Confucian principles in China?*

© William J. Duiker

A Worship Hall in Nara. Buddhist temple compounds in Japan traditionally offered visitors an escape from the tensions of the outside world. The temple site was normally comprised of an entrance gate, a central courtyard, a worship hall, a pagoda, and a cloister, as well as support buildings for the monks. The pagoda, a multitiered tower, harbored a sacred relic of the Buddha and served as the East Asian version of the Indian stupa. The worship hall corresponded to the Vedic carved chapel. Here we see the Todaiji worship hall in Nara. Originally constructed in the mid-eighth century C.E., it is reputed to be the largest wooden structure in the world and is the centerpiece of a vast temple complex on the outskirts of the old capital city.

edly divine character of the ruling family, the mandate remained in perpetuity in the imperial house rather than being bestowed on an individual who was selected by Heaven because of his talent and virtue, as was the case in China.

Had these reforms succeeded, Japan might have followed the Chinese pattern and developed a centralized bureaucratic government. But as time passed, the central government proved unable to curb the power of the aristocracy. Unlike in Tang China, the civil service examinations in Japan were not open to all but were restricted to individuals of noble birth. Leading officials were awarded large tracts of land, and they and other powerful families were able to keep the taxes from the lands for themselves. Increasingly starved for revenue, the central government steadily lost power and influence.

In deference to the alleg-

fashion.

The Heian Period The influence of powerful Buddhist monasteries in the city of Nara soon became oppressive, and in 794, the emperor moved the capital to his family's original power base at nearby Heian, on the site of present-day Kyoto. Like its predecessor, the new capital was laid out in the now familiar Chang'an checkerboard pattern, but on a larger scale than at Nara. Now increasingly self-confident, the rulers ceased to emulate the Tang and sent no more missions to Chang'an. At Heian, the emperor—as the royal line descended from the sun goddess was now styled—continued to rule in name, but actual power was in the hands of the Fujiwara clan, which had managed through intermarriage to link its fortunes closely with the imperial family. A senior member of the clan began to serve as regent (in practice, the chief executive of the government) for the emperor.

What was occurring was a return to the decentralization that had existed prior to Shotoku Taishi. The central government's attempts to impose taxes directly on the rice lands failed, and rural areas came under the control of powerful families whose wealth was based on the ownership of tax-exempt farmland (called *shoen*). To avoid paying taxes, peasants would often surrender their lands to a local aristocrat, who would then allow the peasants to cultivate the lands in return for the payment of rent. To obtain protection from government officials, these local aristocrats might in turn grant title of their lands to a more powerful aristocrat with influence at court. In return, these individuals would receive inheritable rights to a portion of the income from the estate.

With the decline of central power at Heian, local aristocrats tended to take justice into their own hands and, increasingly used military force to protect their interests. A new class of military retainers called the **samurai** emerged whose purpose was to protect the security and property of their patron. They frequently drew their leaders from disappointed aristocratic office seekers, who thus began to occupy a prestigious position in local society, where they often served an administrative as well as a military function. The samurai lived a life of simplicity and self-sacrifice and were expected to maintain an intense and unquestioning loyalty to their lord (see the comparative essay "Feudal Orders Around the World" on p. 313). Bonds of loyalty were also quite strong among members of the samurai class, and homosexuality was common. Like the knights of medieval Europe, the samurai fought on horseback (although a samurai carried a sword and a bow and arrows rather than lance and shield) and were supposed to live by a strict warrior code, known in Japan as **Bushido**, or "way of the warrior" (see the box on p. 314). As time went on, they became a major force and almost a surrogate government in much of the Japanese countryside.

The Kamakura Shogunate and After By the end of the twelfth century, as rivalries among noble families led to almost constant civil war, centralizing forces again asserted themselves. This time the instrument was a powerful noble from a warrior clan named Minamoto Yoritomo (1142–1199), who defeated several rivals and set up his power base on the Kamakura peninsula, south of the modern city of Tokyo. To strengthen the state, he created a more centralized government (the **bakufu**, or "tent government") under a powerful military leader,

The Burning of the Palace. The Kamakura era is represented in this action-packed thirteenth-century scene from the *Scroll of the Heiji Period*, which depicts the burning of a retired emperor's palace in the middle of the night. Servants and ladies of the court flee the massive flames; confusion and violence reign. The determined faces of the samurai warriors only add to the ferocity of the attack.

© Museum of Fine Arts, Boston/The Bridgeman Art Library

COMPARATIVE ESSAY
FEUDAL ORDERS AROUND THE WORLD

When we use the word *feudalism*, we usually think of European knights on horseback clad in iron and armed with sword and lance. However, zation that modern historians called feudalism developed in different parts of the world. Historians use the term to refer to a decentralized political order in which local lords owed loyalty and provided military service to a king or more powerful lord. In Europe, a feudal order based on lords and vassals arose between 800 and 900 and flourished for the next four hundred years.

In Japan, a feudal order much like that found in Europe developed between 800 and 1500. By the end of the ninth century, powerful nobles in the countryside, while owing a loose loyalty to the Japanese emperor, began to exercise political and legal power in their own extensive lands. To protect their property and security, these nobles retained samurai, warriors who owed loyalty to the nobles and provided military service for them. Like knights in Europe, the samurai followed a warrior code and fought on horseback, clad in iron. However, they carried a sword and a bow and arrow rather than a sword and a lance.

In some respects, the political relationships among the Indian states beginning in the fifth century took on the character of the feudal system that emerged in Europe in the Middle Ages. Like medieval European lords, local Indian rajas were technically vassals of the king, but unlike in European feudalism, the relationship was not a contractual one. Still, the Indian model became highly complex, with "inner" and "outer" vassals, depending on their physical or political proximity to the king, and "greater" or "lesser" vassals, depending on their power and influence. As in Europe, the vassals themselves often had vassals.

In the Valley of Mexico, the Aztecs developed a political system between 1300 and 1500 that bore some similarities to the Japanese, Indian, and European feudal orders. Although the Aztec king was a powerful, authoritarian ruler, the local rulers of lands outside the capital city were allowed considerable freedom. However, they did pay tribute to the king and also provided him with military forces. Unlike the knights and samurai of Europe and Japan, however, Aztec warriors were armed with sharp knives made of stone and spears of wood fitted with razor-sharp blades cut from stone.

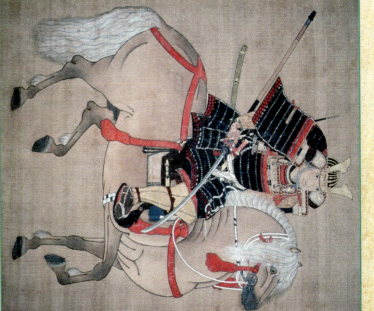

Samurai. During the Kamakura period, painters began to depict the adventures of the new warrior class. Here is an imposing mounted samurai warrior, the Japanese equivalent of the medieval knight in fief-holding Europe. Like his European counterpart, the samurai was supposed to live by a strict moral code and was expected to maintain an unquestioning loyalty to his liege lord. Above all, a samurai's life was one of simplicity and self-sacrifice.

© Sakamoto Photo Research Laboratory/CORBIS

---

known as the **shogun** (general). The shogun attempted to increase the powers of the central government while reducing rival aristocratic clans to vassal status. This **shogunate system**, in which the emperor was the titular authority while the shogun exercised actual power, served as the political system in Japan until the second half of the nineteenth century.

The system worked effectively, and it was fortunate that it did, because during the next century, Japan faced the most serious challenge it had confronted yet. The Mongols, who had destroyed the Song dynasty in China, were now attempting to assert their hegemony throughout all of Asia (see Chapter 10). In 1266, Emperor Khubilai Khan demanded tribute from Japan. When the Japanese refused, he invaded with an army of more than thirty thousand troops. Bad weather and difficult conditions forced a retreat, but the Mongols tried again in 1281. An army nearly 150,000 strong landed on the northern coast of Kyushu. The Japanese were able to contain them for two months until virtually the entire Mongol fleet was destroyed by a massive typhoon—a "divine wind" (*kamikaze*). Japan would not face a foreign invader again until American forces landed on the Japanese islands in the summer of 1945.

POLITICS & GOVERNMENT

JAPAN'S WARRIOR CLASS

The samurai was the Japanese equivalent of the medieval European knight. Like the latter, the samurai fought on horseback and was expected to adhere to a strict moral code. Although this passage comes from a document dating only to the 1500s, a distinct mounted warrior class had already begun to emerge in Japan as early as the tenth century. It shows the importance of hierarchy and duty in a society influenced by the doctrine of Confucius. Note the similarity with Krishna's discourse on the duties of an Indian warrior in Chapter 2.

The Way of the Samurai

The master once said:... Generation after generation men have taken their livelihood from tilling the soil, or devised and manufactured tools, or produced profit from mutual trade, so that people's needs were satisfied. Thus the occupations of farmer, artisan, and merchant necessarily grew up as complementary to one another. However, the samurai eats food without growing it, uses utensils without manufacturing them, and profits without buying or selling.... The samurai is one who does not cultivate, does not manufacture, and does not engage in trade, but it cannot be that he has no function at all as a samurai....

If one deeply fixes [one's] attention on what I have said and examines closely one's own function, it will become clear what the business of the samurai is. The business of the samurai consists in reflecting on his own station in life, in discharging loyal service to his master if he has one, in deepening his fidelity in associations with friends, and, with due consideration of his own position, in

devoting himself to duty above all.... The samurai dispenses with the business of the farmer, artisan, and merchant and confines himself to practicing this Way; should there be someone in the three classes of the common people who transgresses against these moral principles, the samurai summarily punishes him and thus upholds proper moral principles in the land.... Outwardly he stands in physical readiness for any call to service, and inwardly he strives to fulfill the Way of the lord and subject, friend and friend, father and son, older and younger brother, and husband and wife. Within his heart he keeps to the ways of peace, but without he keeps his weapons ready for use. The three classes of the common people make him their teacher and respect him. By following his teachings, they are enabled to understand what is fundamental and what is secondary.

Herein lies the Way of the samurai, the means by which he earns his clothing, food, and shelter; and by which his heart is put at ease, and he is enabled to pay back at length his obligation to his lord and the kindness of his parents. Were there no such duty, it would be as though one were to steal the kindness of one's parents, greedily devour the income of one's master, and make one's whole life a career of robbery and brigandage. This would be very grievous.

Q *How would you compare the duties of the samurai with those of a knight in medieval Europe? Are his responsibilities closer to those of a Confucian "gentleman" in China?*

Resistance to the Mongols had put a heavy strain on the system, however, and in 1333, the Kamakura shogunate was overthrown by a coalition of powerful clans. A new shogun, supplied by the Ashikaga family, arose in Kyoto and attempted to continue the shogunate system. But the Ashikaga were unable to restore the centralized power of their predecessors. With the central government reduced to a shell, the power of the local landed aristocracy increased to an unprecedented degree. Heads of great noble families, now called **daimyo** ("great names"), controlled vast landed estates that owed no taxes to the government or to the court in Kyoto. As clan rivalries continued, the daimyo relied increasingly on the samurai for protection, and political power came into the hands of a loose coalition of noble families.

By the end of the fifteenth century, Japan was again close to anarchy. A disastrous civil conflict known as the Onin War (1467–1477) led to the virtual destruction of the capital city of Kyoto and the disintegration of the shogunate. With the disappearance of central authority, powerful aristocrats in rural areas now seized total

control over large territories and ruled as independent lords. Territorial rivalries and claims of precedence led to almost constant warfare in this period of "warring states," as it is called (in obvious parallel with a similar era during the Zhou dynasty in China). The trend back toward central authority did not begin until the last quarter of the sixteenth century.

Economic and Social Structures

From the time the Yayoi culture was first established on the Japanese islands, Japan was a predominantly agrarian society. Although Japan lacked the spacious valleys and deltas of the river valley societies, its inhabitants were able to take advantage of their limited amount of tillable land and plentiful rainfall to create a society based on the cultivation of wet rice.

Trade and Manufacturing   As in China, commerce was slow to develop in Japan. During ancient times, each *uji* had a local artisan class, composed of weavers, carpenters, and ironworkers, but trade was essentially local and was regulated by the local clan leaders. With the rise of the Yamato state, a money economy gradually began to develop, although most trade was still conducted through barter until the twelfth century, when metal coins introduced from China became more popular.

Trade and manufacturing began to develop more rapidly during the Kamakura period, with the appearance of quarterly markets in the larger towns and the emergence of such industries as paper, iron casting, and porcelain. Foreign trade, mainly with Korea and China, began during the eleventh century. Japan exported raw materials, paintings, swords, and other manufactured items in return for silk, porcelain, books, and copper cash. Some Japanese traders were so aggressive in pressing their interests that authorities in China and Korea attempted to limit the number of Japanese commercial missions that could visit each year. Such restrictions were often ignored, however, and encouraged some Japanese traders to turn to piracy.

Significantly, manufacturing and commerce developed rapidly during the more decentralized period of the Ashikaga shogunate and the era of the warring states, perhaps because of the rapid growth in the wealth and autonomy of local daimyo families. Market towns, now operating on a full money economy, began to appear, and local manufacturers formed guilds to protect their mutual interests. Sometimes local peasants would sell at the markets products made in their homes, such as silk or hemp clothing, household items, or food. In general, however, trade and manufacturing remained under the control of the local daimyo, who would often provide tax breaks to local guilds in return for other benefits. Although Japan remained a primarily agricultural society, it was on the verge of a major advance in manufacturing.

Daily Life One of the first descriptions of the life of the Japanese people comes from a Chinese dynastic history from the third century C.E. It describes lords and peasants living in an agricultural society that was based on the cultivation of wet rice. Laws had been enacted to punish offenders, local trade was conducted in markets, and government granaries stored the grain that was paid as taxes (see the box on p. 316).

Life for the common people probably changed very little over the next several hundred years. Most were peasants, who worked on land owned by their lord or, in some cases, by the state or by Buddhist monasteries. By no means, however, were all peasants equal economically or socially. Although in ancient times, all land was owned by the state and peasants working the land were taxed at an equal rate depending on the nature of the crop, after the Yamato era, variations began to develop. At the top were local officials, who were often well-to-do peasants. They were responsible for organizing collective labor services and collecting tax grain from the peasants and were in turn exempt from such obligations themselves.

The majority of the peasants were under the authority of these local officials. In general, peasants were free to dispose of their harvest as they saw fit after paying their tax quota, but in practical terms, their freedom was limited. Those who were unable to pay the tax sank to the level of **genin**, or landless laborers, who could be bought and sold by their proprietors like slaves along with the land on which they worked. Some fled to escape such a fate and attempted to survive by clearing plots of land in the mountains or by becoming bandits.

In addition to the **genin**, the bottom of the social scale was occupied by the **eta**, a class of hereditary slaves who, like the outcastes in India, were responsible for what were considered degrading occupations, such as curing leather and burying the dead. The origins of the eta are not entirely clear, but they probably were descendants of prisoners of war, criminals, or mountain dwellers who were not related to the dominant Yamato peoples. As we shall see, the eta are still a distinctive part of Japanese society, and although their full legal rights are guaranteed under the current constitution, discrimination against them is not uncommon.

Daily life for ordinary people in early Japan resembled that of their counterparts throughout much of Asia. The vast majority lived in small villages, several of which normally made up a single *shoen*. Housing was simple. Most lived in small two-room houses of timber, mud, or thatch, with dirt floors covered by straw or woven mats (the origin, perhaps, of the well-known *tatami*, or woven-mat floor, of more modern times). Their diet consisted of rice (if some was left after the payment of the grain tax), wild grasses, millet, roots, and some fish and birds. Life must have been difficult at best; as one eighth-century poet lamented:

> Here I lie on straw
> Spread on bare earth,
> With my parents at my pillow,
> My wife and children at my feet,
> All huddled in grief and tears.
> No fire sends up smoke
> At the cooking place,
> And in the cauldron
> A spider spins its web.[2]

LIFE IN THE LAND OF WA

FAMILY & SOCIETY

Some of the earliest descriptions of Japan come from Chinese sources. The following passage from the *History of the Wei Dynasty* was written in the late third century C.E. *Wa* is a derogatory word meaning "dwarf" frequently used in China to refer to the Japanese people. The author of this passage, while remarking on the strange habits of the Japanese, writes without condescension.

History of the Wei Dynasty

The people of Wa make their abode in the mountainous islands located in the middle of the ocean to the southeast of the Taifang prefecture....

All men, old or young, are covered by tattoos. Japanese fishers revel in diving to catch fish and shell-fish. Tattoos are said to drive away large fish and water predators. They are considered an ornament.... Men allow their hair to cover both of their ears and wear head-bands. They wear loincloths wrapped around their bodies and seldom use stitches. Women gather their hair at the ends and tie it in a knot and then pin it to the tops of their heads. They make their clothes in one piece, and cut an opening in the center for their heads. They plant wet-field rice, China-grass [a type of nettle], and mulberry trees. They raise cocoons and reel the silk off the cocoons. They produce clothing made of China-grass, of coarse silk, and of cotton. In their land, there are no cows, horses, tigers, leopards, sheep, or swan. They fight with halberds, shields, and wooden bows.... Their arrows are made of bamboo, and iron and bone points make up the arrowhead.

People...live long, some reaching one hundred years of age, and others to eighty or ninety years. Normally men of high echelon have four or five wives, and the plebeians may have two or three. When the law is violated, the light offender loses his wife and children by confiscation, and the grave offender has his household and kin exterminated. There are class distinctions within the nobility and the base, and some are vassals of others. There are mansions and granaries erected for the purpose of collecting taxes....

When plebeians meet the high-echelon men on the road, they withdraw to the grassy area [side of the road] hesitantly. When they speak or are spoken to, they either crouch or kneel with both hands on the ground to show their respect. When responding they say "aye," which corresponds to our affirmative "yes."

Q *What does this document tell us about the nature of Japanese society in the third century C.E.? What does it tell us about the point of view of the author?*

The Role of Women Evidence about the relations between men and women in early Japan presents a mixed picture. The Chinese dynastic history reports that "in their meetings and daily living, there is no distinction between...men and women." It notes that a woman "adept in the ways of shamanism" had briefly ruled Japan in the third century C.E. But it also remarks that polygyny was common, with nobles normally having four or five wives and commoners two or three.[3] An eighth-century law code guaranteed the inheritance rights of women, and wives abandoned by their husbands were permitted to obtain a divorce and remarry. A husband could divorce his wife if she did not produce a male child, committed adultery, disobeyed her in-laws, talked too much, engaged in theft, was jealous, or had a serious illness.[4]

When Buddhism was introduced, women were initially relegated to a subordinate position in the new faith. Although they were permitted to take up monastic life—many widows entered a monastery at the death of their husbands—they were not permitted to visit Buddhist holy places, nor were they even (in the accepted wisdom) equal with men in the afterlife. One Buddhist commentary from the late thirteenth century said that a woman could not attain enlightenment because "her sin is grievous, and so she is not allowed to enter the lofty palace of the great Brahma, nor to look upon the clouds which hover over his ministers and people."[5] Other Buddhist scholars were more egalitarian: "Learning the Law of Buddha and achieving release from illusion have nothing to do with whether one happens to be a man or a woman."[6] Such views ultimately prevailed, and women were eventually allowed to participate fully in Buddhist activities in medieval Japan.

Although women did not possess the full legal and social rights of their male counterparts, they played an active role at various levels of Japanese society. Aristocratic women were prominent at court, and some, such as the author known as Lady Murasaki, became renowned for their artistic or literary talents (see the box on p. 318). Though few commoners could aspire to such prominence, women often appear in the scroll paintings of the period along with men, doing the spring planting, threshing and hulling the rice, and acting as carriers, peddlers, salespersons, and entertainers.

In Search of the Pure Land: Religion in Early Japan

In Japan, as elsewhere, religious belief began with the worship of nature spirits. Early Japanese worshiped spirits called **kami** who resided in trees, rivers and streams, and mountains. They also believed in ancestral spirits present in the atmosphere. In Japan, these beliefs

The Japanese director Akira Kurosawa is one of the most respected filmmakers of the second half of the twentieth century. In a series of films produced during the post–World War II period, he sought to evoke the mood of a long-lost era—the Japan of the Middle Ages. The first to attract broad world attention was *Rashomon*, produced in 1950, in which the filmmaker adopted an unusual technique to explore the ambiguity of truth. The film became so famous that the expression "Rashomon effect" has come to stand for the difficulty of establishing the veracity of an incident.

In the movie, a woman is accosted and raped in a forest glen by the local brigand Tajomaru, and her husband is killed in the encounter. The true facts remain obscure, however, as the testimony of each of the key figures in the story—including the ghost of the deceased—seems to present a different version of the facts. Was the husband murdered by the brigand, or did he commit suicide in shame for failing to protect his wife's virtue? Did she herself kill her husband in anger after he rejected her as soiled goods, or is it even possible that she actually hoped to run away with the bandit?

Although the plot line in *Rashomon* is clearly fictional, the film sheds light on several key features of life in medieval Japan. The hierarchical nature of the class system provides a fascinating backdrop, as the traveling couple are members of the aristocratic elite while the bandit—played by the director's favorite actor, Toshiro Mifune—is a rough-hewn commoner. The class distinctions between the two men are clearly displayed during their physical confrontation, which involves a lengthy bout of spirited swordplay. A second theme centers on the question of honor. While the husband's outrage at the violation of his wife is quite understandable, his anger is directed primarily at her because her reputation has been irreparably tarnished. She in turn harbors a deep sense of shame that she has been physically possessed by two men, one in the presence of the other.

Over the years, Kurosawa followed his success in *Rashomon* with a series of films that made use of themes

from premodern Japanese history. In *The Seven Samurai* (1954), a village hires a band of warriors to provide itself with protection against nearby bandits. The warrior-for-hire theme reappears in the satirical film *Yojimbo* (1961), while in *Ran*, produced in 1985, the director borrows a theme from Shakespeare's play *King Lear* by depicting a power struggle among the sons of an aging local warlord. Hollywood has in turn provided its own testimonial to Kurosawa by producing a number of films that pay homage to his work, including *Ocean's Eleven*, *The Magnificent Seven*, and *Hostage*.

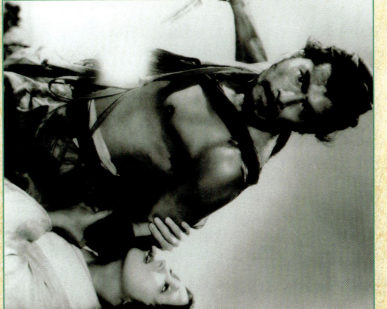

In this still from Kurosawa's *Rashomon*, the samurai's wife, Masako (Machiko Kyo) pleads with the brigand Tajomaru (Toshiro Mifune).

Daiei/The Kobal Collection

eventually evolved into a kind of state religion called **Shinto** (the Sacred Way or Way of the Gods) that is still practiced today. Shinto still serves as an ideological and emotional force that knits the Japanese into a single people and nation.

Shinto does not have a complex metaphysical superstructure or an elaborate moral code. It does require certain ritual acts, usually undertaken at a shrine, and a process of purification, which may have originated in primitive concerns about death, childbirth, illness, and menstruation. This traditional concern about physical purity may help

explain the strong Japanese concern for personal cleanliness and the practice of denying women entrance to the holy places.

Another feature of Shinto is its stress on the beauty of nature and the importance of nature itself in Japanese life. Shinto shrines are usually located in places of exceptional beauty and are often dedicated to a nearby physical feature. As time passed, such primitive beliefs contributed to the characteristic Japanese love of nature. In this sense, early Shinto beliefs have been incorporated into the lives of all Japanese.

FAMILY & SOCIETY

Out of the Japanese tradition of female introspective prose appeared one of the world's truly great novels, *The Tale of Genji*, written around the year 1000 by the diarist and court author Murasaki Shikibu, known as Lady Murasaki. It is even today revered for its artistic refinement and sensitivity and has influenced Japanese writing for more than a thousand years. A panoramic portrayal of court life in tenth-century Japan, it traces the life and loves of the courtier Genji as he strives to remain in favor with those in power while at the same time pursuing his cult of love and beauty. Truly remarkable is the character of Genji himself, revealed to the reader through myriad psychological observations. In this excerpt, Genji has just seduced a lady at court and now feels misgivings at having betrayed his child bride. A *koto* is a Japanese stringed instrument similar to a zither.

Lady Murasaki, *The Tale of Genji*

A curtain string brushed against a koto, to tell him that she had been passing a quiet evening at her music.

"And will you not play for me on the koto of which I have heard so much?" ...

This lady had not been prepared for an incursion and could not cope with it. She fled to an inner room. How she could have contrived to bar it he could not tell, but it was very firmly barred indeed. Though he did not exactly force his way through, it is not to be imagined that he left matters as they were. Delicate, slender—she was almost too beautiful. Pleasure was mingled with pity at the thought that he was imposing himself upon her. She was even more pleasing than reports from afar had had her. The autumn night, usually so long, was over in a trice. Not wishing to be seen, he hurried out, leaving affectionate assurances behind.

Genji called in secret from time to time. The two houses being some distance apart, he feared being seen by fishers, who were known to relish a good rumor, and sometimes several days would elapse between his visits....

[Genji dreaded having Murasaki [his bride] learn of the affair. He still loved her more than anyone, and he did not want her to make even joking reference to it. She was a quiet, docile lady, but she had more than once been unhappy with him. Why, for the sake of brief pleasure, had he caused her pain? He wished it were all his to do over again. The sight of the Akashi lady only brought new longing for the other lady.

He got off a more earnest and affectionate letter than usual, at the end of which he said: "I am in anguish at the thought that, because of foolish occurrences for which I have been responsible but have had little heart, I might appear in a guise distasteful to you. There has been a strange, fleeting encounter. That I should volunteer this story will make you see, I hope, how little I wish to have secrets from you. Let the gods be my judges.

"It was but the fisherman's brush with the salty sea
                pine,
Followed by a tide of tears of longing."

Her reply was gentle and unreproachful, and at the end of it she said: "That you should have deigned to tell me a dreamlike story which you could not keep to yourself calls to mind numbers of earlier instances.

"Naive of me, perhaps; yet we did make our vows.
And now see the waves that wash the Mountain of
                Waiting!"

It was the one note of reproach in a quiet, undemanding letter. He found it hard to put down, and for some nights he stayed away from the house in the hills.

Q *Why does this thousand-year-old passage speak to readers today with such a contemporary meaning?*

whom were considered later manifestations of the Buddha. Most of the Buddhist sects that had achieved popularity in China were established in Japan, and many of them attracted powerful patrons at court. Great monasteries were built that competed in wealth and influence with the noble families that had traditionally ruled the country.

Perhaps the two most influential Buddhist sects were the **Pure Land** (Jodo) sect and **Zen** (in Chinese, Chan or Ch'an). The Pure Land sect, which taught that devotion alone could lead to enlightenment and release, was very popular among the common people, for whom monastic life was one of the few routes to upward mobility. Among the aristocracy, the most influential school was Zen, which exerted a significant impact on Japanese life and culture during the era of the warring states. In its

In time, Shinto evolved into a state doctrine that was linked with belief in the divinity of the emperor and the sacredness of the Japanese nation. A national shrine was established at Ise, north of the early capital of Nara, where the emperor annually paid tribute to the sun goddess. But although Shinto had evolved well beyond its primitive origins, like its counterparts elsewhere, it could not satisfy all the religious and emotional needs of the Japanese people. For those needs, the Japanese turned to Buddhism.

As we have seen, Buddhism was introduced into Japan from China during the sixth century C.E. and had begun to spread beyond the court to the general population by the eighth century. As in China, most Japanese saw no contradiction between worshiping both the Buddha and their local nature gods (*kami*), many of

emphasis on austerity, self-discipline, and communion with nature, Zen complemented many traditional beliefs in Japanese society and became an important component of the samurai warrior's code.

In Zen teachings, there were various ways to achieve enlightenment (*satori* in Japanese). Some stressed that it could be achieved suddenly. One monk, for example, reportedly achieved *satori* by listening to the sound of a bamboo stick striking against roof tiles; another did so by carefully watching the opening of peach blossoms in the spring. But other practitioners, sometimes called adepts, said that enlightenment could come only through studying the scriptures and arduous self-discipline (known as *zazen*, or "seated Zen"). Seated Zen involved a lengthy process of meditation that cleansed the mind of all thoughts so that it could concentrate on the essential.

Sources of Traditional Japanese Culture

Nowhere is the Japanese genius for blending indigenous and imported elements into an effective whole better demonstrated than in the national culture. In such widely diverse fields as art, architecture, sculpture, and literature, the Japanese from early times showed an impressive ability to borrow selectively from abroad without destroying essential native elements.

Growing contact with China during the rise of the Yamato state stimulated Japanese artists. Missions sent to China and Korea during the seventh and eighth centuries returned with examples of Tang literature, sculpture, and painting, all of which influenced the Japanese.

Literature

Borrowing from Chinese models was somewhat complicated, however, since the early Japanese had no system for recording their own spoken language and initially adopted the Chinese pictographic language for writing. The challenge was complicated by the fact that spoken Japanese is not part of the Sino-Tibetan family of languages. But resourceful Japanese soon adapted the Chinese written characters so that they could be used for recording the Japanese language. In some cases, Chinese characters were given Japanese pronunciations. But Chinese characters ordinarily could not be used to record Japanese words, which normally contain more than one syllable. Sometimes the Japanese simply used Chinese characters as phonetic symbols that were combined to form Japanese words. Later they simplified the characters into phonetic symbols that were used alongside Chinese characters. This hybrid system continues to be used today.

At first, most educated Japanese preferred to write in Chinese, and a court literature—consisting of essays, poetry, and official histories—appeared in the classical Chinese language. But spoken Japanese never totally disappeared among the educated classes and eventually became the instrument of a unique literature. With the lessening of Chinese cultural influence in the

tenth century, Japanese verse resurfaced. Between the tenth and fifteenth centuries, twenty imperial anthologies of poetry were compiled. Initially, they were written primarily by courtiers, but with the fall of the Heian court and the rise of the warrior and merchant classes, all literate segments of society began to produce poetry.

Japanese poetry is unique. It expresses its themes in a simple form, a characteristic stemming from traditional Japanese aesthetics, Zen religion, and the language itself. The aim of the Japanese poet was to create a mood, perhaps the melancholic effect of gently falling cherry blossoms or leaves. With a few specific references, the poet suggested a whole world, just as Zen Buddhism sought enlightenment from a sudden perception. Poets often alluded to earlier poems by repeating their images with small changes, a technique that was viewed not as plagiarism but as an elaboration on the meaning of the earlier poem.

By the fourteenth century, the technique of the "linked verse" had become the most popular form of Japanese poetry. Known as *haiku*, it is composed of seventeen syllables divided into lines of five, seven, and five syllables, respectively. The poems usually focused on images from nature and the mutability of life. Often the poetry was written by several individuals alternately composing verses and linking them into long sequences of hundreds and even thousands of lines (see the box on p. 320).

Poetry served a unique function at the Heian court, where it was the initial means of communication between lovers. By custom, aristocratic women were isolated from all contact with men outside their immediate family and spent their days hidden behind screens. Some amused themselves by writing poetry. When courtship began, poetic exchanges were the only means a woman had to attract her prospective lover, who would be enticed solely by her poetic art.

During the Heian period, male courtiers wrote in Chinese, believing that Chinese civilization was superior and worthy of emulation. Like the Chinese, they viewed prose fiction as "vulgar gossip." Nevertheless, from the ninth century to the twelfth, Japanese women were prolific writers of prose fiction in Japanese (see the box on p. 318). Excluded from school, they learned to read and write at home and wrote diaries and stories to pass the time. Some of the most talented women were invited to court as authors in residence.

In the increasingly pessimistic world of the warring states of Kamakura (1185–1333), Japanese novels typically focused on a solitary figure who is aloof from the refinements of the court and faces battle and possibly death. Another genre, that of the heroic war tale, came out of the new warrior class. These works described the military exploits of warriors, coupled with an overwhelming sense of sadness and loneliness.

The famous classical Japanese drama known as *No* also originated during this period. *No* developed out of

A SAMPLE OF LINKED VERSE

ARTS & IDEAS

One of the distinctive features of medieval Japanese literature was the technique of "linked verse." In a manner similar to *haiku* poetry today, such poems, known as *renga*, were written by groups of individuals who would join together to compose the poem, verse by verse. The following example, by three famous poets named Sogi, Shohaku, and Socho, is one of the most famous of the period.

The Three Poets at Minase

Snow clinging to slope,
On mist-enshrouded mountains
At eveningtime.   Sogi

In the distance flows
Through plum-scented villages.   Shohaku

Willows cluster
In the river breeze
As spring appears.   Socho

The sound of a boat being poled
In the clearness at dawn   Sogi

Still the moon lingers
As fog o'er-spreads
The night.   Shohaku

A frost-covered meadow;
Autumn has drawn to a close.   Socho

Against the wishes
Of droning insects
The grasses wither.   Sogi

Q *How do these Japanese poems differ from the poems produced in China during the Tang dynasty and quoted in Chapter 10?*

CENGAGENOW *To read more early Japanese poetry, enter the documents area of the World History Resource Center using the access card that is available for World History.*

---

a variety of entertainment forms, such as dancing and juggling, that were part of the native tradition or had been imported from China and other regions of Asia. The plots were normally based on stories from Japanese history or legend. Eventually, *No* evolved into a highly stylized drama in which the performers wore masks and danced to the accompaniment of instrumental music. Like much of Japanese culture, *No* was restrained, graceful, and refined.

Art and Architecture In art and architecture, as in literature, the Japanese pursued their interest in beauty, simplicity, and nature. To some degree, Japanese artists and architects were influenced by Chinese forms. As they became familiar with Chinese architecture, Japanese rulers and aristocrats tried to emulate the splendor of Tang civilization and began constructing their palaces and temples in Chinese style.

During the Heian period (794–1185), the search for beauty was reflected in various art forms, such as narrative hand scrolls, screens, sliding door panels, fans, and lacquer decoration. As in the case of literature, nature themes dominated—seashore scenes, a spring rain, moon and mist, flowering wisteria and cherry blossoms. All were intended to evoke an emotional response on the part of the viewer. Japanese painting suggested the frail beauty of nature by presenting it on a smaller scale. The majestic mountain in a Chinese painting became a more intimate Japanese landscape with rolling hills and a rice field. Faces were rarely shown, and human drama was indicated by a woman lying prostrate or hiding her

face in her sleeve. Tension was shown by two people talking at a great distance or with their backs to one another.

During the Kamakura period (1185–1333), the hand scroll with its physical realism and action-packed paintings of the new warrior class achieved great popularity. Reflecting these chaotic times, the art of portraiture flourished, and a scroll would include a full gallery of warriors and holy men in starkly realistic detail, including such unflattering features as stubble, worry lines on a forehead, and crooked teeth. Japanese sculptors also produced naturalistic wooden statues of generals, nobles, and saints. By far the most distinctive, however, were the fierce heavenly "guardian kings," who still intimidate the viewer today.

Zen Buddhism, an import from China in the thirteenth century, also influenced Japanese aesthetics. With its emphasis on immediate enlightenment without recourse to intellectual analysis and elaborate ritual, Zen reinforced the Japanese predilection for simplicity and self-discipline. During this era, Zen philosophy found expression in the Japanese garden, the tea ceremony, the art of flower arranging, pottery and ceramics, and miniature plant display (the famous *bonsai*, literally "pot scenery").

Landscapes served as an important means of expression in both Japanese art and architecture. Japanese gardens were initially modeled on Chinese examples. Early court texts during the Heian period emphasized the importance of including a stream or pond when creating a garden. The landscape surrounding the fourteenth-century

© William J. Duiker

© William J. Duiker

Guardian Kings. Larger than life and intimidating in its presence, this thirteenth-century wooden statue departs from the refined atmosphere of the Heian court and pulsates with the masculine energy of the Kamakura period. Placed strategically at the entrance to Buddhist shrines, guardian kings such as this one protected the temple and the faithful. In contrast to the refined atmosphere of the Fujiwara court, the Kamakura era was a warrior's world.

Golden Pavilion in Kyoto displays a harmony of garden, water, and architecture that makes it one of the treasures of the world. Because of the shortage of water in the city, later gardens concentrated on rock composition, using white pebbles to represent water.

Like the Japanese garden, the tea ceremony represents the fusion of Zen and aesthetics. Developed in the fifteenth century, it was practiced in a simple room devoid of external ornament except for a *tatami* floor, sliding doors, and an alcove with a writing desk and asymmetrical shelves. The participants could therefore focus completely on the activity of pouring and drinking tea. "Tea and Zen

The Golden Pavilion in Kyoto. The landscape surrounding the Golden Pavilion displays a harmony of garden, water, and architecture that makes it one of the treasures of the world. Constructed in the fourteenth century as a retreat for the shoguns named for the gold foil that covered its exterior. Completely destroyed by an arsonist in 1950 as a protest against the commercialism of modern Buddhism, it was rebuilt and reopened in 1987. The use of water as a backdrop is especially noteworthy in Chinese and Japanese landscapes, as well as in the Middle East.

have the same flavor" goes the Japanese saying. Considered the ultimate symbol of spiritual deliverance, the tea ceremony had great aesthetic value and moral significance in traditional times as well as today.

Japan and the Chinese Model

Few societies in Asia have been as isolated as Japan. Cut off from the mainland by 120 miles of frequently turbulent ocean, the Japanese had only minimal contact with the outside world during most of their early development.

Whether this isolation was ultimately beneficial to Japanese society cannot be determined. On the one hand, lack of knowledge of developments taking place elsewhere probably delayed the process of change in Japan. On the other hand, the Japanese were spared the destructive

© William J. Duiker

COMPARATIVE ILLUSTRATION

RELIGION & PHILOSOPHY

In the Garden. In traditional China and Japan, gardens were meant to free the observer's mind of mundane concerns, offering spiritual refreshment in the quiet of nature. Chinese gardens were designed to reconstruct an orderly microcosm of nature, where the harassed Confucian official could find spiritual renewal. Wandering within constantly changing perspectives of ponds, trees, rocks, and pavilions, he could imagine himself immersed in a monumental landscape. In the garden in Suzhou on the left, the rocks represent towering mountains to suggest a Daoist sense of withdrawal and eternity, reducing the viewer to a tiny speck in the grand flow of life.

In Japan, the traditional garden reflected the Zen Buddhist philosophy of simplicity, restraint, allusion, and tranquility. In the garden at the right, at the Ryoanji temple in Kyoto, the rocks are meant to suggest mountains rising from a sea of pebbles. Such gardens served as an aid to meditation, inspiring the viewer to join with comrades in composing "linked verse" (see the box on p. 320).

Q How do gardens in traditional China and Japan differ in their form and purpose from those in Western societies? Why do you think this is the case?

invasions that afflicted other ancient civilizations. Certainly, once the Japanese became acquainted with Chinese culture at the height of the Tang era, they were quick to take advantage of the opportunity. In the space of a few decades, the young state adopted many aspects of Chinese society and culture and thereby introduced major changes into Japanese life.

Nevertheless, Japanese political institutions failed to follow all aspects of the Chinese pattern. Despite Prince Shotoku's effort to make effective use of the imperial traditions of Tang China, the decentralizing forces in Japanese society remained dominant throughout the period under discussion in this chapter. Adoption of the Confucian civil service examination did not lead to a breakdown of Japanese social divisions; instead, the examination was administered in a manner that preserved and strengthened them. Although Buddhist and Daoist doctrines made a significant contribution to Japanese religious practices, Shinto beliefs continued to play a major role in shaping the Japanese worldview.

Why Japan did not follow the Chinese road to centralized authority has been a subject of debate among historians. Some argue that the answer lies in differing cultural traditions, while others suggest that Chinese institutions and values were introduced too rapidly to be assimilated effectively by Japanese society. One factor may have been the absence of a foreign threat (except for the brief incursion by the Mongols). A recent view holds that diseases (such as smallpox and measles) imported inadvertently from China led to a marked decline in the population of the islands, reducing food output and preventing the population from coalescing in more compact urban centers.

In any event, Japan was not the only society in Asia to assimilate ideas from abroad while at the same time preserving customs and institutions inherited from the past. Across the Sea of Japan to the west and several thousand miles to the southwest, other Asian peoples were embarked on a similar journey. We now turn to their experience.

Korea: Bridge to the East

Q **Focus Question:** What were the main characteristics of economic and social life in early Korea?

Few of the societies on the periphery of China have been as directly influenced by the Chinese model as Korea. However, the relationship between China and Korea has often been characterized by tension and conflict, and

Koreans have often resented what they perceive to be Chinese chauvinism and arrogance.

A graphic example of this attitude has occurred in recent years as officials and historians in both countries have vociferously disputed differing interpretations of the early history of the Korean people. Slightly larger than the state of Minnesota, the Korean peninsula was probably first settled by Altaic-speaking fishing and hunting peoples from neighboring Manchuria during the Neolithic Age. Because the area is relatively mountainous (only about one-fifth of the peninsula is adaptable to cultivation), farming was apparently not practiced until about 2000 B.C.E. From that point, the peoples living in the area began to form organized communities.

It is at this point also that disagreement arises. In 2004, Chinese official sources claimed that the first organized kingdom in the area, known as Koguryo (37 B.C.E.–668 C.E.), occupied a wide swath of Manchuria as well as the northern section of the Korean peninsula and was thus an integral part of Chinese history. Korean scholars, basing their contentions on both legend and scattered historical evidence, countered that the first kingdom established on the peninsula, known as Gojoseon, was created by the Korean ruler Dangun in 2333 B.C.E. and was ethnically Korean. It was at that time, these scholars maintain, that the Bronze Age got under way in northeastern Asia.

Although the facts relating to this issue continue to be in dispute, most scholars today do agree that in 109 B.C.E., the northern part of the peninsula came under direct Chinese influence. During the next several generations, the area was ruled by the Han dynasty, which divided the territory into provinces and introduced Chinese institutions. With the decline of the Han in the third century C.E., power gradually shifted to local leaders, who drove out the Chinese administrators but continued to absorb Chinese cultural influences. Eventually, three separate kingdoms emerged on the peninsula: Koguryo in the north, Paekche in the southwest, and Silla in the southeast. The Japanese, who had recently established their own state on the Yamato plain, may have maintained a small colony on the southern coast.

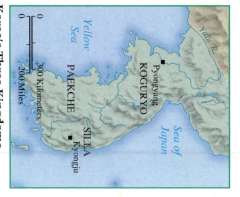

Korea's Three Kingdoms

The Three Kingdoms

From the fourth to the seventh centuries, the three kingdoms were bitter rivals for influence and territory on the peninsula. At the same time, all began to absorb Chinese political and cultural institutions. Chinese influence was most notable in Koguryo, where Buddhism was introduced in the late fourth century C.E. and the first Confucian academy on the peninsula was established in the capital at Pyongyang. All three kingdoms also appear to have accepted a tributary relationship with one or another of the squabbling states that emerged in China after the fall of the Han. The kingdom of Silla, less exposed than its two rivals to Chinese influence, was at first the weakest of the three, but eventually its greater internal cohesion—perhaps a consequence of the tenacity of its tribal traditions—enabled it to become the dominant power on the peninsula. Then the rulers of Silla forced the Chinese to withdraw from all but the area adjacent to the Yalu River. To pacify the haughty Chinese, Silla accepted tributary status under the Tang dynasty. In the meantime, any remaining Japanese colonies in the south were eliminated.

With the country unified for the first time, the rulers of Silla attempted to use Chinese political institutions and ideology to forge a centralized state. Buddhism, rising in popularity, became the state religion, and Korean monks followed the paths of their Japanese counterparts on journeys to Buddhist sites in China. Chinese architecture and art became dominant in the capital at Kyongju and other urban centers, and the written Chinese language became the official means of legal communication. But powerful aristocratic families, long dominant in the southeastern part of the peninsula, were still influential at court. They were able to prevent the adoption of the Tang civil service examination system and resisted the distribution of manorial lands to the poor. The failure to adopt the Chinese model was fatal. Squabbling among noble families steadily increased, and after the assassination of the king of Silla in 780, civil war erupted.

The Rise of the Koryo Dynasty

In the early tenth century, a new dynasty called Koryo (the root of the modern name of the country in English) arose in the north. The new kingdom adopted Chinese political institutions in an effort to strengthen its power and unify its territory. The civil service examination system was introduced in 958, but as in Japan, the bureaucracy continued to be dominated by influential aristocratic families.

The Koryo dynasty remained in power for four hundred years, protected from invasion by the absence of a strong dynasty in neighboring China. Under the Koryo, industry and commerce slowly began to develop, but as in China, agriculture was the prime source of wealth. In theory, all land was the property of the king, but in actuality, noble families controlled their holdings. The lands were worked by peasants who were subject to burdens similar to those of European serfs. At the bottom of society was a class of "base people" (chonmin), composed of slaves, artisans, and other specialized workers.

Pulguksa Bell Tower. Among the greatest architectural achievements on the Korean peninsula is the Pulguksa (Monastery of the Land of Buddha), built near Kyongju, the ancient capital of Silla, in the eighth century C.E. Shown here is the bell tower, located in the midst of beautiful parklands on the monastery grounds. Young Korean couples often come to this monastery after their weddings to be photographed in the stunning surroundings.

© William J. Duiker

From a cultural point of view, the Koryo era was one of high achievement. Buddhist monasteries, run by sects introduced from China, including Pure Land and Zen (Chan), controlled vast territories, while their monks served as royal advisers at court. At first, Buddhist themes dominated in Korean art and sculpture, and the entire Tripitaka (the "three baskets," or sections, of the Buddhist canon) was printed using wooden blocks. Eventually, however, with the appearance of landscape painting and porcelain, Confucian themes began to predominate.

Under the Mongols

Like its predecessor in Silla, the kingdom of Koryo was unable to overcome the power of the nobility and the absence of a reliable tax base. In the thirteenth century, the Mongols seized the northern part of the country and assimilated it into the Yuan empire. The weakened kingdom of Koryo became a tributary of the great khan in Khanbaliq (see Chapter 10).

The era of Mongol rule was one of profound suffering for the Korean people, especially the thousands of peasants and artisans who were compelled to perform conscript labor to help build the ships in preparation for Khubilai Khan's invasion of Japan. On the positive side,

the Mongols introduced many new ideas and technology from China and farther afield. The Koryo dynasty had managed to survive, but only by accepting Mongol authority, and when the power of the Mongols declined, the kingdom declined with it. With the rise to power of the Ming in China, Koryo collapsed, and power was seized by the military commander Yi Song-gye, who declared the founding of the new Yi dynasty in 1392. Once again, the Korean people were in charge of their own destiny.

Vietnam: The Smaller Dragon

Q Focus Questions: What were the main developments in Vietnamese history before 1500? Why were the Vietnamese able to restore their national independence after a millennium of Chinese rule?

While the Korean people were attempting to establish their own identity in the shadow of the powerful Chinese empire, the peoples of Vietnam, on China's southern frontier, were seeking to do the same. The Vietnamese (known as the Yueh in Chinese, from the peoples of that name inhabiting the southeastern coast of mainland China) began to practice irrigated agriculture in the flooded regions of

© Bulguksa Temple, South Korea/The Bridgeman Art Library

the Red River delta at an early date and entered the Bronze Age sometime during the second millennium B.C.E. By about 200 B.C.E., a young state had begun to form in the area but immediately encountered the expanding power of the Qin empire (see Chapter 3). The Vietnamese were not easy to subdue, however, and the collapse of the Qin dynasty temporarily enabled them to preserve their independence (see the box on p. 326). Nevertheless, a century later, they were absorbed into the Han empire.

At first, the Han were satisfied to rule the delta as an autonomous region under the administration of the local landed aristocracy. But Chinese taxes were oppressive, and in 39 C.E., a revolt led by the Trung sisters (widows of local nobles who had been executed by the Chinese) briefly brought Han rule to an end. The Chinese soon suppressed the rebellion, however, and began to rule the area directly through officials dispatched from China. The first Chinese officials to serve in the region became exasperated at the uncultured ways of the locals, who wandered around "naked without shame."[7] In time, however, these foreign officials began to intermarry with the local nobility and form a Sino-Vietnamese ruling class who, though trained in Chinese culture, began to identify with the cause of Vietnamese autonomy.

For nearly a thousand years, the Vietnamese were exposed to the art, architecture, literature, philosophy, and written language of China as the Chinese attempted to integrate the area culturally as well as politically and administratively into their empire. It was a classic case of the Chinese effort to introduce advanced Confucian civilization to the "backward peoples" along the perimeter. To all intents and purposes, the Red River delta, then known to the Chinese as the "pacified South" (Annam), became a part of China.

The Rise of Great Viet

Despite Chinese efforts to assimilate Vietnam, the Vietnamese sense of ethnic and cultural identity proved inextinguishable, and in the tenth century, the Vietnamese took advantage of the collapse of the Tang dynasty in China to overthrow Chinese rule.

The new Vietnamese state, which called itself Dai Viet (Great Viet), became a dynamic new force on the Southeast Asian mainland. As the population of the Red River delta expanded, Dai Viet soon came into conflict with Champa, its neighbor to the south. Located along the central coast of modern Vietnam, Champa was a trading society based on Indian cultural traditions. Over the next several centuries, the two states fought on numerous occasions. By the end of the fifteenth century, Dai Viet had conquered Champa. The Vietnamese then

The Sokkuram Buddha. As Buddhism spread from India to other parts of Asia, so did the representation of the Buddha in human form. From the first century C.E., statues of the Buddha began to absorb various cultural influences. Some early sculptures, marked by flowing draperies, reflected the Greco-Roman culture introduced to India during the era of Alexander the Great. Others were reminiscent of traditional male earth spirits, with broad shoulders and staring eyes. Under the Guptas, artists emphasized the Indian ideal of spiritual and bodily perfection.

As the faith spread along the Silk Road, representations of the Buddha began to reflect cultural influences from Persia and China and eventually from Korea and Japan. Shown here is the eighth-century Sokkuram Buddha, created during the Silla dynasty. Unable to build structures similar to the cave temples in China and India due to the hardness of the rock in the nearby hills, Korean builders fashioned a small domed cave out of granite blocks, adorned with a wooden veranda (upper right). Today, pilgrims still climb the steep hill to pay homage to this powerful and serene Buddha, one of the finest in Asia.

© William J. Duiker

POLITICS & GOVERNMENT

THE FIRST VIETNAM WAR

In the third century B.C.E., the armies of the Chinese state of Qin (Ch'in) invaded the Red River delta to launch an attack on the small Vietnamese state located there. As this passage from a Han dynasty philosophical text shows, the Vietnamese were not easy to conquer, and the new state soon declared its independence from the Qin. It was a lesson that was too often forgotten by would-be conquerors in later centuries.

Masters of Huai Nan

Ch'in Shih Huang Ti [the first emperor of Qin] was interested in the rhinoceros horn, the elephant tusks, the kingfisher plumes, and the pearls of the land of Yüeh [Viet]; he therefore sent Commissioner T'u Sui at the head of five hundred thousand men divided into five armies.... For three years the sword and the crossbow were in constant readiness. Superintendent Lu was sent; there was no means of assuring the transport of supplies so he employed soldiers to dig a canal for sending grain, thereby making it possible to wage war on the people of Yüeh. The lord of Western Ou, I Hsu Sung, was killed; consequently, the Yüeh people entered the wilderness and lived there with the animals; none consented to be a slave of Ch'in; choosing from among themselves men of valor, they made them their leaders and attacked the Ch'in by night, inflicting on them a great defeat and killing Commissioner T'u Sui; the dead and wounded were many. After this, the emperor deported convicts to hold the garrisons against the Yüeh people.

The Yüeh people fled into the depths of the mountains and forests, and it was not possible to fight them. The soldiers were kept in garrisons to watch over the abandoned territories. This went on for a long time, and the soldiers grew weary. Then the Yüeh came out and attacked; the Ch'in soldiers suffered a great defeat. Subsequently, convicts were sent to hold the garrisons against the Yüeh.

Q How would the ancient Chinese military strategist Sun Tzu mentioned in Chapter 3, have advised the Qin military commanders to carry out their operations? Would he have approved of the tactics adopted by the Vietnamese?

---

resumed their march southward, establishing agricultural settlements in the newly conquered territory. By the seventeenth century, the Vietnamese had reached the Gulf of Siam.

The Vietnamese faced an even more serious challenge from the north. The Song dynasty in China, beset with its own problems on the northern frontier, eventually accepted the Dai Viet ruler's offer of tribute status (see the box on p. 328), but later dynasties attempted to reintegrate the Red River delta into the Chinese empire. The first effort was made in the late thirteenth century by the Mongols, who attempted on two occasions to conquer the Vietnamese. After a series of bloody battles, during which the Vietnamese displayed an impressive capacity for guerrilla warfare, the invaders were driven out. A little over a century later, the Ming dynasty tried again, and for twenty years Vietnam was once more under Chinese rule. In 1428, the Vietnamese evicted the Chinese again, but the experience had contributed to the strong sense of Vietnamese identity.

The Chinese Legacy   Despite their stubborn resistance to Chinese rule, after the restoration of independence in the tenth century, Vietnamese rulers quickly discovered the convenience of the Confucian model in administering a river valley society and therefore attempted to follow Chinese practice in forming their own state. The ruler styled himself an emperor like his counterpart to the north (although he prudently termed himself a king in his direct dealings with the Chinese court), adopted Chinese court rituals, claimed the Mandate of Heaven, and arrogated to himself the same authority and privileges in his dealings with his subjects. But unlike a Chinese emperor, who had no particular symbolic role as defender of the Chinese people or Chinese culture, a Vietnamese monarch was viewed, above all, as the symbol and defender of Vietnamese independence.

Like their Chinese counterparts, Vietnamese rulers fought to preserve their authority from the challenges of powerful aristocratic families and turned to the Chinese bureaucratic model, including civil service examinations, as a means of doing so. Under the pressure of strong monarchs, the concept of merit eventually took hold, and the power of the landed aristocracy was weakened if not entirely broken. The Vietnamese adopted much of the Chinese

---

Map labels: CHINA · DAI VIET · Red R. · Thanglong (Hanoi) · Gulf of Tonkin · HAINAN ISLAND · CHAMPA · ANGKOR · South China Sea · Gulf of Siam · 0 150 300 Kilometers · 0 100 200 Miles

The Kingdom of Dai Viet, 1100

© William J. Duiker

© William J. Duiker

A Lost Civilization. Before the spread of Vietnamese settlers into the area early in the second millennium C.E., much of the coast along the South China Sea was occupied by the kingdom of Champa. A trading people who were directly engaged in the regional trade network between China and the Bay of Bengal, the Cham received their initial political and cultural influence from India. This shrine-tower, located on a hill in the modern city of Nha Trang, was constructed in the eleventh century and clearly displays the influence of Indian architecture. Champa finally succumbed to a Vietnamese invasion in the fifteenth century.

Another aspect of the Chinese legacy was the spread of Buddhist, Daoist, and Confucian ideas, which

administrative structure, including the six ministries, the censorate, and the various levels of provincial and local administration.

supplemented the Viets' traditional belief in nature spirits. Buddhist precepts became popular among the local population, who integrated the new faith into their existing belief system by founding Buddhist temples dedicated to the local village deity in the hope of

The Temple of Literature, Hanoi. When the Vietnamese regained their independence from China in the tenth century C.E., they retained Chinese institutions that they deemed beneficial. A prime example was the establishment of the Temple of Literature, Vietnam's first university, in 1076. Here sons of mandarins (officials) were educated in the Confucian classics in preparation for an official career. Beginning in the fifteenth century, those receiving doctorates had stelae erected to identify their achievements. Over eighty of these stelae were erected on the school grounds over a space of three hundred years.

A PLEA TO THE EMPEROR

INTERACTION & EXCHANGE

Like many other societies in premodern East and Southeast Asia, the kingdom of Vietnam regularly paid tribute to the imperial court in China. The arrangement was often beneficial to both sides, as the tributary states received a form of international recognition from the massive Chinese market. China, for its part, assured itself that neighboring areas would not harbor dissident elements hostile to its own security.

In this document, contained in a historical chronicle written by Le Tac in the fourteenth century, a claimant to the Vietnamese throne seeks recognition from the Song emperor while offering tribute to the Son of Heaven in China. Note the way in which the claimant, Le Hoan, founder of the early Le dynasty (980–1009), demeans the character of the Vietnamese people in comparison with the sophisticated ways of imperial China.

Le Tac, *Essay on Annam*

My ancestors have received favors from the Imperial Court. Living in a faraway country at a corner of the sea [Annam], they have been granted the seals of investiture for that barbarian area and have always paid to the Imperial ministers the tribute and respect they owed. But recently our House has been little favored by Heaven; however, the death of our ancestors has not prevented us from promptly delivering the tribute....

But now the leadership of the country is in dispute and investiture has not yet been conferred by China. My father, Pou-ling, and my eldest brother, Lienn, formerly enjoyed the favors of the [Chinese] Empire, which endowed them with the titles and functions of office. They zealously and humbly protected their country, neither daring to appear lazy or negligent.... [But then] the good fortune of our House began to crumble. The mandarins [officials], the army, the people, the court elders, and members of my family, all... entreated me to lead the army.... My people, who are wild mountain-dwellers, have unpleasant and violent customs; they are a people who live in caves and have disorderly and impetuous habits. I feared that trouble would arise if I did not yield to their wishes. From prudence I therefore assumed power temporarily.... I hope that His Majesty will place my country among His other tributary states by granting me the investiture. He will instill peace in the heart of His little servant by allowing me to govern the patrimony my parents left me. Then shall I administer my barbarian and remote people.... I shall send tributes of precious stones and ivory, and before the Golden Gate I shall express my loyalty.

Q *What is the tribute system as described in this document? Does it provide benefits to both parties in the arrangement, and if so, how and why?*

guaranteeing an abundant harvest. Upper-class Vietnamese were educated in the Confucian classics tended to follow the more agnostic Confucian doctrine, but some joined Buddhist monasteries. Daoism also flourished at all levels of society and, as in China, provided a structure for animistic beliefs and practices that still predominated at the village level.

During the early period of independence, Vietnamese culture also borrowed liberally from its larger neighbor. Educated Vietnamese tried their hand at Chinese poetry, and followed Chinese models in sculpture, architecture, and porcelain. Many of the notable buildings of the medieval period, such as the Temple of Literature and the famous One-Pillar Pagoda in Hanoi, are classic examples of Chinese architecture.

But there were signs that Vietnamese creativity would eventually transcend the bounds of Chinese cultural norms. Although most classical writing was undertaken in literary Chinese, the only form of literary expression deemed suitable by Confucian conservatives, an adaptation of Chinese written characters,

called *chu nom* ("southern characters"), was devised to provide a written system for spoken Vietnamese. In use by the early ninth century, it eventually began to be used for the composition of essays and poetry in the Vietnamese language. Such pioneering efforts would lead in later centuries to the emergence of a vigorous national literature totally independent of Chinese forms.

Society and Family Life

Vietnamese social institutions and customs were also strongly influenced by those of China. As in China, the introduction of a Confucian system and the adoption of civil service examinations undermined the role of the old landed aristocrats and led eventually to their replacement by the scholar-gentry class. Also as in China, the examinations were open to most males, regardless of family background, which opened the door to a degree of social mobility unknown in most of the states elsewhere in the region. Candidates for the bureaucracy read many of the same Confucian classics and absorbed the same ethical principles as their counterparts in China. At the same time, they were also exposed to the classic works of Vietnamese history, which strengthened their sense that Vietnam was a distinct culture similar to, but separate from, that of China.

The vast majority of the Vietnamese people, however, were peasants. Most were small landholders or share-croppers who rented their plots from wealthier farmers, but large estates were rare due to the systematic efforts of the central government to prevent the rise of a powerful local landed elite.

Family life in Vietnam was similar in many respects to that in China. The Confucian concept of family took hold during the period of Chinese rule, along with the related concepts of filial piety and gender inequality. Perhaps the most striking difference between family traditions in China and Vietnam was that Vietnamese women possessed more rights both in practice and by law. Since ancient times, wives had been permitted to own property and initiate divorce proceedings. One consequence of Chinese rule was a growing emphasis on male dominance, but the tradition of women's rights was never totally extinguished and was legally recognized in a law code promulgated in 1460.

Moreover, Vietnam had a strong historical tradition associating heroic women with the defense of the homeland. The Trung sisters were the first but by no means the only example. In the following passage, a Vietnamese historian of the eighteenth century recounts their story:

The imperial court was far away; local officials were greedy and oppressive. At that time the country of one hundred sons was the country of the women of Lord To. The ladies [the Trung sisters] used the female arts against their irreconcilable foe; skirts and hairpins sang of patriotic righteousness, uttered a solemn oath at the inner door of the ladies' quarters, expelled the governor, and seized the capital.... Were they not grand heroines?... Our two ladies brought forward an army of all the people, and, establishing a royal court that settled affairs in the territories of the sixty-five strongholds, shook their skirts over the Hundred Yueh [the Vietnamese people].[8]

CHRONOLOGY   Early Korea and Vietnam

Foundation of Gojoseon state in Korea	c. 2333 B.C.E.
Chinese conquest of Korea and Vietnam	First century B.C.E.
Trung Sisters' Revolt	39 C.E.
Founding of Champa	192
Era of Three Kingdoms in Korea	300s–600s
Restoration of Vietnamese independence	939
Mongol invasions of Korea and Vietnam	1257–1285
Founding of Yi dynasty in Korea	1392
Vietnamese conquest of Champa	1471

CONCLUSION

Like many other great civilizations, the Chinese were traditionally convinced of the superiority of their culture and, when the opportunity arose, sought to introduce it to neighboring peoples. Although the latter were viewed with a measure of condescension, Confucian teachings suggested the possibility of redemption. As the Master had remarked in the *Analects*, "By nature, people are basically alike; in practice they are far apart."[9] As a result, Chinese policies in the region were often shaped by the desire to introduce Chinese values and institutions to non-Chinese peoples living on the periphery.

As this chapter has shown, when conditions were right, China's "civilizing mission" sometimes had some marked success. All three countries that we have dealt with here borrowed liberally from the Chinese model. At the same time, all adapted Chinese institutions and values to the conditions prevailing in their own societies. Though all expressed admiration and respect for China's achievement, all sought to keep Chinese power at a distance.

As an island nation, Japan was the most successful of the three in protecting its political sovereignty and its cultural identity. Both Korea and Vietnam were compelled on various occasions to defend their independence by force of arms. That experience may have shaped their strong sense of national distinctiveness, which we shall discuss further in a later chapter.

The appeal of Chinese institutions can undoubtedly be explained by the fact that Japan, Korea, and Vietnam were all agrarian societies, much like their larger neighbor. But it is undoubtedly significant that the aspect of Chinese political culture that was least amenable to adoption abroad was the civil service examination system. The Confucian concept of meritocracy ran directly counter to the strong aristocratic tradition that flourished in all three societies during their early stage of development. Even when the system was adopted, it was put to quite different uses. Only in Vietnam did the concept of merit eventually triumph over that of birth, as strong rulers of Dai Viet attempted to initiate the Chinese model as a means of creating a centralized system of government.

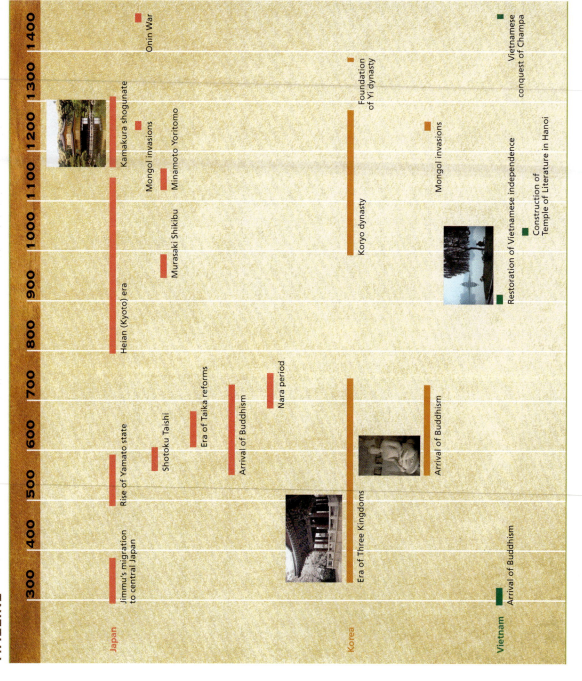

Japan

Jimmu's migration to central Japan
Rise of Yamato state
Shotoku Taishi
Era of Taika reforms
Arrival of Buddhism
Nara period
Heian (Kyoto) era
Murasaki Shikibu
Minamoto Yoritomo
Mongol invasions
Kamakura shogunate
Onin War

Korea

Era of Three Kingdoms
Arrival of Buddhism
Koryo dynasty
Mongol invasions
Foundation of Yi dynasty

Vietnam

Arrival of Buddhism
Restoration of Vietnamese independence
Construction of Temple of Literature in Hanoi
Vietnamese conquest of Champa

300 400 500 600 700 800 900 1000 1100 1200 1300 1400

CHAPTER NOTES

1. Cited in C. Holcombe, *The Genesis of East Asia, 221 B.C.–A.D. 907* (Honolulu, 2001), p. 41.
2. Quoted in D. J. Lu, *Sources of Japanese History*, vol. 1 (New York, 1974), p. 7.
3. From "The History of Wei," quoted in ibid., p. 10.
4. From "The Law of Households," quoted in ibid., p. 32.
5. From "On the Salvation of Women," quoted in ibid., p. 127.
6. Quoted in B. Ruch, "The Other Side of Culture in Medieval Japan," in K. Yamamura, ed., *The Cambridge History of Japan*, vol. 3, *Medieval Japan* (Cambridge, 1990). p. 506.
7. K. W. Taylor, *The Birth of Vietnam* (Berkeley, Calif., 1983), p. 76.
8. Quoted in ibid., pp. 336–337.
9. Confucius, *Analects*, 17:2.

SUGGESTED READING

Rise of Japanese Civilization   Some of the standard treatments of the rise of Japanese civilization appear in textbooks

dealing with the early history of East Asia. Two of the best are J. K. Fairbank, E. O. Reischauer, and A. M. Craig, *East Asia: Tradition and Transformation* (Boston, 1989), and C. Schirokauer et al., *A Brief History of Chinese and Japanese Civilizations* (San Diego, Calif., 2005). For the latest scholarship on the early period, see the first three volumes of *The Cambridge History of Japan*, ed. J. W. Hall, M. B. Jansen, M. Kanai, and D. Twitchett (Cambridge, 1988).

Early History of Japan   The best available collections of documents on the early history of Japan are D. J. Lu, ed., *Sources of Japanese History*, vol. 1 (New York, 1974), and W. T. de Bary et al., eds, *Sources of Japanese Tradition*, vol. 1 (New York, 2001).

For specialized books on the early historical period, see R. J. Pearson, ed., *Windows on the Japanese Past: Studies in Archaeology and Prehistory* (Ann Arbor, Mich., 1986). Also see M. Ashkenazi, *Handbook of Japanese Mythology* (Santa Barbara, Calif., 2003). The relationship between disease and state building is analyzed in W. W. Farris, *Population, Disease, and Land in Early Japan, 645–900* (Cambridge, 1985). The Kamakura period is covered in J. P. Mass, ed., *Court and Bakufu in Japan: Essays in Kamakura History* (New Haven, Conn., 1982). See also **H. P. Varley**, *The Onin War* (New York, 1977). On Japanese Buddhism, see **W. T. de Bary**, ed., *The Buddhist Tradition in India, China, and Japan* (New York, 1972).

Women's Issues in Early Japan A concise and provocative introduction to women's issues during this period in Japan, as well as in other parts of the world, can be found in **S. S. Hughes and B. Hughes**, *Women in World History* (Armonk, N.Y., 1995). For a tenth-century account of daily life for women at the Japanese court, see **I. Morris**, trans. and ed., *The Pillow Book of Sei Shonagon* (New York, 1991).

Japanese Literature The best introduction to Japanese literature for college students is still the concise and insightful **D. Keene**, *Japanese Literature: An Introduction for Western Readers* (London, 1953). The most comprehensive anthology is **Keene's** *Anthology of Japanese Literature* (New York, 1955), and the best history of Japanese literature, also by **Keene**, is *Seeds in the Heart: Japanese Literature from Earlier Times to the Late Sixteenth Century* (New York, 1993).

For the text of *Lady Murasaki's Tale of Genji*, see the translation by **E. Seidensticker** (New York, 1976). The most accessible edition for college students is the same author's abridged Vintage Classics edition of 1990, which captures the spirit of the original in 360 pages.

Japanese Art For the most comprehensive introduction to Japanese art, consult **P. Mason**, *History of Japanese Art* (New York, 1993). Also see the concise **J. Stanley-Baker**, *Japanese Art* (London, 1984). For a stimulating text with magnificent illustrations, see **D. Elisseeff and V. Elisseeff**, *Art of Japan* (New York, 1985). See also **J. E. Kidder Jr.**, *The Art of Japan* (London, 1985), for an insightful text accompanied by beautiful photographs.

Korea For an informative and readable history of Korea, see **Lee Ki-baik**, *A New History of Korea* (Cambridge, 1984).

P. H. Lee, ed., *Sourcebook of Korean Civilization*, vol. 1 (New York, 1993), is a rich collection of documents dating from the period prior to the sixteenth century.

Vietnam Vietnam often receives little attention in general studies of Southeast Asia because it was part of the Chinese empire for much of the traditional period. For a detailed investigation of the origins of Vietnamese civilization, see **K. W. Taylor**, *The Birth of Vietnam* (Berkeley, Calif., 1983). For an overview of Vietnamese history, with chapters on various themes, see **W. J. Duiker**, *Vietnam: Revolution in Transition* (Boulder, Colo., 1995).

CENGAGENOW Enter *CengageNOW* using the access card that is available with this text. *CengageNOW* will help you understand the content in this chapter with lesson plans generated for your needs, as well as provide you with a connection to the *Wadsworth World History Resource Center* (see description below for details).

WORLD HISTORY RESOURCE CENTER

Enter the Resource Center using either your *CengageNOW* access card or your separate access card for the *World History Resource Center*. Organized by topic, this Website includes quizzes; images; over 350 primary source documents; interactive simulations, maps, and timelines; movie explorations; and a wealth of other resources. You can read the following documents, and many more, at the *World History Resource Center:*

Japanese Creation Myth

The Legend of King Onjo of Paekche

The Story of the Trung Sisters

Visit the *World History Companion Website* for chapter quizzes and more:

www.cengage.com/history/Duiker/World6e

The coronation of Charlemagne by Pope Leo III, as depicted in a medieval French manuscript

© Scala/Art Resource, NY

CHAPTER OUTLINE AND FOCUS QUESTIONS

The Emergence of Europe in the Early Middle Ages

Q What contributions did the Romans, the Christian church, and the Germanic peoples make to the new civilization that emerged in Europe after the collapse of the Western Roman Empire? What was the significance of Charlemagne's coronation as emperor?

Europe in the High Middle Ages

Q What roles did aristocrats, peasants, and townspeople play in medieval European civilization, and how did their lifestyles differ? How did cities in Europe compare to those in China and the Middle East? What were the main aspects of the political, economic, spiritual, and cultural revivals that took place in Europe during the High Middle Ages?

Medieval Europe and the World

Q In what ways did Europeans begin to relate to peoples in other parts of the world after 1000 C.E.? What were the reasons for the Crusades, and who or what benefited the most from them?

CRITICAL THINKING

Q In what ways was the civilization that developed in Europe in the Middle Ages similar to those in China and the Middle East? How were they different?

IN 800, CHARLEMAGNE, the king of the Franks, journeyed to Rome to help Pope Leo III, head of the Catholic church, who was barely clinging to power in the face of rebellious Romans. On Christmas Day, Charlemagne and his family, attended by Romans and Franks, crowded into Saint Peter's Basilica to hear Mass. Quite unexpectedly, according to a Frankish writer, "as the king rose from praying before the tomb of the blessed apostle Peter, Pope Leo placed a golden crown on his head." The people in the church shouted, "Long life and victory to Charles Augustus, crowned by God the great and peace-loving Emperor of the Romans." Seemingly, the Roman Empire in the west had been reborn, and Charles had become the first Roman emperor since 476. But this "Roman emperor" was actually a German king, and he had been crowned by the head of the western Christian church. In truth, the coronation of Charlemagne was a sign not of the rebirth of the Roman Empire but of the emergence of a new European civilization that came into being in western Europe after the collapse of the Western Roman Empire.

This new civilization—European civilization—was formed by the coming together of three major elements: the legacy of the Romans, the Christian church, and the Germanic peoples who moved in and settled the western

The Emergence of Europe in the Early Middle Ages

Q Focus Questions: What contributions did the Romans, the Christian church, and the Germanic peoples make to the new civilization that emerged in Europe after the collapse of the Western Roman Empire? What was the significance of Charlemagne's coronation as emperor? ◆

As we saw in Chapter 10, China descended into political chaos and civil wars after the end of the Han Empire, and it was almost four hundred years before a new imperial dynasty established political order. Similarly, after the collapse of the Western Roman Empire in the fifth century, it would also take hundreds of years to establish a new society.

The New Germanic Kingdoms

Germanic peoples in large numbers had begun to move into the lands of the Roman Empire in the third century C.E., and by 500, the Western Roman empire had been supplanted politically by a series of successor states ruled by German kings. The fusion of Romans and Germans took different forms in the various Germanic kingdoms, with occasional parallels. Both the kingdom of the Ostrogoths in Italy and the kingdom of the Visigoths in Spain (see Map 12.1) favored coexistence between the Roman and German populations, both featured a warrior caste dominating a larger native population, and both continued to maintain much of the Roman structure of government while largely excluding Romans from power. Over time, Germans and natives began to fuse. In Britain, however, when the Roman armies left at the beginning of the fifth century, the Angles and Saxons, Germanic tribes from Denmark and northern Germany, moved in and settled there.

The Kingdom of the Franks

One of the most prominent German states on the European continent was the kingdom of the Franks. The establishment of a Frankish kingdom was the work of Clovis (c. 482–511), a member of the Merovingian dynasty who became a Catholic Christian around 500. He was not the first German king to convert to Christianity, but the others had joined the Arian sect of Christianity, a group who believed that Jesus

had been human and thus not truly God. The Christian church in Rome, which had become known as the Roman Catholic Church, regarded the Arians as heretics, people who believed in teachings different from the official church doctrine. To Catholics, Jesus was human, but of the "same substance" as God and therefore also truly God. Clovis found that his conversion to Catholic Christianity gained him the support of the Roman Catholic Church, which was only too eager to obtain the friendship of a major Germanic ruler who was a Catholic Christian.

By 510, Clovis had established a powerful new Frankish kingdom stretching from the Pyrenees in the west to German lands in the east (modern France and western Germany). After Clovis's death, however, as his sons divided his newly created kingdom, as was the Frankish custom. During the sixth and seventh centuries, the once-united Frankish kingdom came to be divided into three major areas: Neustria, in northern Gaul; Austrasia, consisting of the ancient Frankish lands on both sides of the Rhine; and the former kingdom of Burgundy.

The Society of the Germanic Peoples

As Germans and Romans intermarried and began to form a new society, some of the social customs of the Germanic peoples came to play an important role. The crucial social bond among the Germanic peoples was the family, especially the extended family of husbands, wives, children, brothers, sisters, cousins, and grandparents. The German family structure was quite simple. Males were dominant and made all the important decisions. A woman obeyed her father until she married and then fell under the legal domination of her husband. For most women in the new Germanic kingdoms, their legal status reflected the material conditions of their lives. Most women had life expectancies of only thirty or forty years, and perhaps 15 percent of women died in their childbearing years, no doubt due to complications associated with childbirth. For most women, life consisted of domestic labor: providing food and clothing for the household, caring for the children, and assisting with farming chores.

The German conception of family affected the way Germanic law treated the problem of crime and punishment. In the Roman system, as in our own, a crime such as murder was considered an offense against society or the state and was handled by a court that heard evidence and arrived at a decision. Germanic law was personal. An injury by one person against another could lead to a blood feud in which the family of the injured party took revenge on the family of the wrongdoer. Feuds could lead to savage acts of revenge, such as hacking off hands or feet or gouging out eyes. Because this system could easily get out of control, an alternative system arose that made use of a fine called *wergeld*, which was the amount paid by a wrongdoer to the family of the person injured or killed. *Wergeld*, which literally means "man money," was the value of a person in monetary terms. That value varied considerably according to social status. An offense

the official Roman state disintegrated, the Christian church played an increasingly important role in the growth of the new European civilization.

The Organization of the Church

By the fourth century, the Christian church had developed a system of government. The Christian community in each city was headed by a bishop, whose area of jurisdiction was known as a bishopric, or **diocese**; the bishoprics of each Roman province were joined together under the direction of an archbishop. The bishops of four great cities—Rome, Jerusalem, Alexandria, and Antioch—held positions of special power in church affairs because the churches in these cities all asserted that they had been founded by the original apostles sent out by Jesus. Soon, however, one of them—the bishop of Rome—claimed that he was the sole leader of the western Christian church. According to church tradition, Jesus had given the keys to the kingdom of heaven to Peter, who was considered the chief apostle and the first bishop of Rome. Subsequent bishops of Rome were considered Peter's successors and came to be known as popes (from the Latin word *papa*, meaning "father"). By the sixth century, popes had been successful in extending papal authority over the Christian church in the west and converting the pagan peoples of Germanic Europe. Their primary instrument of conversion was the monastic movement.

The Monks and Their Missions

A **monk** (in Latin, *monachus*, meaning "one who lives alone") was a man who sought to live a life divorced from the world, cut off from ordinary human society, in order to pursue an ideal of total dedication to God. As the monastic ideal spread, a new form of **monasticism** based on living together in a community soon became the dominant form. Saint Benedict (c. 480–c. 543), who founded a

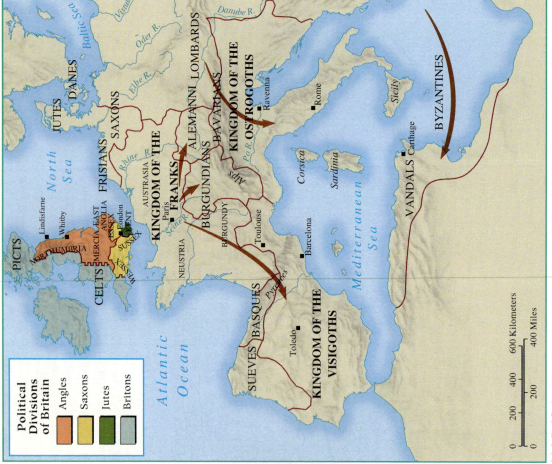

MAP 12.1 **The Germanic Kingdoms of the Old Western Empire.** Germanic tribes filled the power vacuum caused by the demise of the Roman Empire, founding states that blended elements of Germanic customs and laws with those of Roman culture, including large-scale conversions to Christianity. The Franks established the most durable of these Germanic states.

Q How did the movements of Franks during this period correspond to the borders of present-day France? **View an animated version of this map or related maps at www.cengage.com/history/Duiker/World6e**

against a nobleman, for example, cost considerably more than one against a freeman or a slave.

Germanic law also provided a means of determining guilt: the ordeal. The ordeal was based on the idea of divine intervention: divine forces (whether pagan or Christian) would not allow an innocent person to be harmed (see the box on p. 335).

The Role of the Christian Church

By the end of the fourth century, Christianity had become the predominant religion of the Roman Empire. As

FAMILY & SOCIETY

In Germanic customary law, the ordeal was used as a means by which accused persons might clear themselves. Although the ordeal took different forms, all involved a physical trial of some sort, such as holding a red-hot iron. It was believed that God would protect the innocent and allow them to come through the ordeal unharmed. This sixth-century account by Gregory of Tours describes an ordeal by hot water.

Gregory of Tours, *An Ordeal of Hot Water* (c. 580)

An Arian presbyter disputing with a deacon of our religion made venomous assertions against the Son of God and the Holy Ghost, as is the habit of that sect [the Arians]. But when the deacon had discoursed a long time concerning the reasonableness of our faith and the heretic, blinded by the fog of unbelief, continued to reject the truth,... the former said: "Why weary ourselves with long discussions? Let acts approve the truth; let a kettle be heated over the fire and someone's ring be thrown into the boiling water. Let him who shall take it from the heated liquid be approved as a follower of the truth, and afterward let the other party be converted to the knowledge of the truth. And do you also understand, O heretic, that this our party will fulfill the conditions with the aid of the Holy Ghost; you shalt confess that there is no discordance, no dissimilarity in the Holy Trinity." The heretic consented to the proposition and they separated after appointing the next morning for the trial. But the fervor of faith in which the deacon had first made this suggestion began to cool through the instigation of the enemy. Rising with the dawn he bathed his arm in oil and smeared it with ointment. But nevertheless he made the round of the sacred places and called in prayer on the Lord... About the third hour they met in the marketplace. The people came together to see the show. A fire was lighted, the kettle was placed upon it, and when it grew very hot the ring was thrown into the boiling water. The deacon invited the heretic to take it out of the water first. But he promptly refused, saying, "You who did propose this trial are the one to take it out." The deacon all of a tremble bared his arm. And when the heretic presbyter saw it besmeared with ointment he cried out: "With magic arts you have thought to protect yourself, that you have made use of these salves, but what you have done will not avail." While they were thus quarreling there came up a deacon from Ravenna named Iacinthus and inquired what the trouble was about. When he learned the truth he drew his arm out from under his robe at once and plunged his right hand into the kettle. Now the ring that had been thrown in was a little thing and very light so that it was thrown about by the water as chaff would be blown about by the wind, and searching for it a long time he found it after about an hour. Meanwhile the flame beneath the kettle blazed up mightily so that the greater heat might make it difficult for the ring to be followed by the hand; but the deacon extracted it at length and suffered no harm, protesting rather that at the bottom the kettle was cold while at the top it was just pleasantly warm. When the heretic beheld this he was greatly confused and audaciously thrust his hand into the kettle saying, "My faith will aid me." As soon as his hand had been thrust in all the flesh was boiled off the bones clear up to the elbow. And so the dispute ended.

Q *What was the purpose of the ordeal of hot water? What does it reveal about the nature of the society that used it?*

---

monastic house for which he wrote a set of rules, established the basic form of monastic life in the western Christian church.

Benedict's rules divided each day into a series of activities, with primary emphasis on prayer and manual labor. Physical work of some kind was required of all monks for several hours a day because idleness was "the enemy of the soul." At the very heart of community practice was prayer, the proper "work of God." Although this included private meditation and reading, all monks gathered together seven times during the day for communal prayer and chanting of psalms. The Benedictine life was a communal one. Monks ate, worked, slept, and worshiped together.

Each Benedictine monastery was strictly ruled by an **abbot,** or "father" of the monastery, who had complete authority over his fellow monks. Unquestioning obedience to the will of the abbot was expected of every monk. Each Benedictine monastery held lands that enabled it to be a self-sustaining community, isolated from and independent of the world surrounding it. Within the monastery, however, monks were to fulfill their vow of poverty: "Let all things be common to all, as it is written, lest anyone should say that anything is his own."[1] Only men could be monks, but women, called **nuns,** also began to withdraw from the world to dedicate themselves to God.

Monasticism played an indispensable role in early medieval civilization. Monks became the new heroes of Christian civilization, and their dedication to God became the highest ideal of Christian life. They were the social workers of their communities; monks provided schools for the young, hospitality for travelers, and hospitals for the sick. Monks also copied Latin works and passed on the legacy of the ancient world to the new European civilization. Monasteries became centers of

© Snark/Art Resource, NY

Saint Benedict. Benedict was the author of a set of rules that was instrumental in the development of monastic groups in the Roman Catholic Church. In this medieval Latin manuscript, Benedict is shown handing the rules of the Benedictine order to a monk.

officers of the king's household—assumed more control of the kingdom. One of these mayors, Pepin, finally took the logical step of assuming the kingship of the Frankish state for himself and his family. Upon his death in 768, his son came to the throne of the Frankish kingdom.

This new king was the dynamic and powerful ruler known to history as Charles the Great (768–814), or Charlemagne (from the Latin for Charles the Great, *Carolus Magnus*). He was determined and decisive, intelligent and inquisitive, a strong statesman, and a pious Christian. Himself unable to read or write, he was a wise patron of learning. In a series of military campaigns, he greatly expanded the territory he had inherited and created what came to be known as the Carolingian Empire. At its height, Charlemagne's empire covered much of western and central Europe; not until the time of Napoleon in the nineteenth century would an empire of its size be seen again in Europe (see the box on p. 337).

Charlemagne continued the efforts of his father in organizing the Carolingian kingdom. Besides his household staff, Charlemagne's administration of the empire depended on the use of counts as the king's chief representatives in local areas. As an important check on the power of the counts, Charlemagne established the *missi dominici* ("messengers of the lord king"), two men who were sent out to local districts to ensure that the counts were executing the king's wishes.

The Significance of Charlemagne As Charlemagne's power grew, so did his prestige as the most powerful Christian ruler of what one monk called the "kingdom of Europe." In 800, Charlemagne acquired a new title: emperor of the Romans. The significance of this imperial coronation has been much debated by historians. We are not even sure if the pope or Charlemagne initiated the idea when they met in the summer of 799 in Paderborn in German lands or whether Charles was pleased or displeased.

In any case, Charlemagne's coronation as Roman emperor demonstrated the strength, even after three hundred years, of the concept of an enduring Roman Empire. More important, it symbolized the fusion of Roman, Christian, and Germanic elements: a Germanic king had been crowned emperor of the Romans by the spiritual leader of western Christendom. Charlemagne had assembled an empire that stretched from the North Sea to Italy and from the Atlantic Ocean to the Danube River. This differed significantly from the Roman Empire, which encompassed much of the Mediterranean world. Had a new civilization emerged? And should Charlemagne be regarded, as one of his biographers has argued, as the "father of Europe"?²

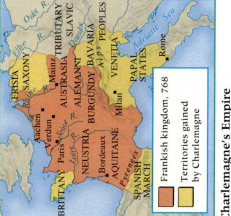

Charlemagne's Empire

Frankish kingdom, 768

Territories gained by Charlemagne

learning wherever they were located, and monks worked to spread Christianity to all of Europe.

Women played an important role in the monastic missionary movement and the conversion of the Germanic kingdoms. Some served as **abbesses** (an abbess was the head of a monastery for nuns, known as a *convent*); many abbesses came from aristocratic families, especially in Anglo-Saxon England. In the kingdom of Northumbria, for example, Saint Hilda founded the monastery of Whitby in 657. As abbess, she was responsible for making learning an important part of the life of the monastery.

Charlemagne and the Carolingians

During the seventh and eighth centuries, as the kings of the Frankish kingdom gradually lost their power, the mayors of the palace—the chief

THE ACHIEVEMENTS OF CHARLEMAGNE

POLITICS & GOVERNMENT

Einhard, the biographer of Charlemagne, was born in the valley of the Main River in Germany about 775. Raised and educated in the monastery of Fulda, an important center of learning, he arrived at the court of Charlemagne in 791 or 792. Although he did not achieve high office under Charlemagne, he served as private secretary to Louis the Pious, Charlemagne's son and successor. In this selection, Einhard discusses some of Charlemagne's accomplishments.

Einhard, *Life of Charlemagne*

Such are the wars, most skillfully planned and successfully fought, which this most powerful king waged during the forty-seven years of his reign. He so largely increased the Frank kingdom, which was already great and strong when he received it at his father's hands, that more than double its former territory was added to it.... He subdued all the wild and barbarous tribes dwelling in Germany between the Rhine and the Vistula, the Ocean and the Danube, all of which speak very much the same language, but differ widely from one another in customs and dress....

He added to the glory of his reign by gaining the good will of several kings and nations; so close, indeed, was the alliance that he contracted with Alfonso, King of Galicia and Asturias, that the latter, when sending letters or ambassadors to Charles, invariably styled himself his man.... The Emperors of Constantinople [the Byzantine emperors] sought friendship and alliance with Charles by several embassies; and even when the Greeks [the Byzantines] suspected him of designing to take the empire from them, because of his assumption of the title Emperor, they made a close alliance with him, that he might have no cause of offense. In fact, the power of the Franks was always viewed with a jealous eye, whence the Greek proverb, "Have the Frank for your friend, but not for your neighbor."

This King, who showed himself so great in extending his empire and subduing foreign nations, and was constantly occupied with plans to that end, undertook also very many works calculated to adorn and benefit his kingdom, and brought several of them to completion. Among these, the most deserving of mention are the basilica of the Holy Mother of God at Aix-la-Chapelle [Aachen], built in the most admirable manner, and a bridge over the Rhine River at Mainz, half a mile long, the breadth of the river at this point.... Above all, sacred buildings were the object of his care throughout his whole kingdom; and whenever he found them falling to ruin from age, he commanded the priests and fathers who had charge of them to repair them, and made sure by commissioners that his instructions were obeyed.... Thus did Charles defend and increase as well as beautify his kingdom....

He cherished with the greatest fervor and devotion the principles of the Christian religion, which had been instilled into him from infancy. Hence it was that he built the beautiful church at Aix-la-Chapelle, which he adorned with gold and silver and lamps, and with rails and doors of solid brass. He had the columns and marbles for this structure brought from Rome and Ravenna, for he could not find such as were suitable elsewhere. He was a constant worshiper at this church as long as his health permitted, going morning and evening, even after nightfall, besides attending mass....

He was very forward in caring for the poor, so much so that he not only made a point of giving in his own country and his own kingdom, but when he discovered that there were Christians living in poverty in Syria, Egypt, and Africa, at Jerusalem, Alexandria, and Carthage, he had compassion on their wants, and used to send money over the seas to them.... He sent great and countless gifts to the popes, and throughout his whole reign the wish that he had nearest at heart was to reestablish the ancient authority of the city of Rome under his care and by his influence, and to defend and protect the Church of St. Peter, and to beautify and enrich it out of his own store above all other churches.

Q *How long did Einhard know Charlemagne? Does this excerpt reflect close, personal knowledge of the man, his court, and his works or hearsay and legend?*

CENGAGENOW *To read more of Einhard's Life of Charlemagne, enter the documents area of the World History Resource Center using the access card that is available for World History.*

The World of Lords and Vassals

The Carolingian Empire began to disintegrate soon after Charlemagne's death in 814, and less than thirty years later, in 843, it was divided among his grandsons into three major sections: the western Frankish lands, which formed the core of the eventual kingdom of France; the eastern lands, which eventually became Germany; and a "middle kingdom" extending from the North Sea to the Mediterranean. The territories of the middle kingdom became a source of incessant struggle between the other two Frankish rulers and their heirs. At the same time, powerful nobles gained even more dominance in their local territories while the Carolingian rulers fought each other, and incursions by outsiders into various parts of the Carolingian world furthered the process of disintegration.

Invasions of the Ninth and Tenth Centuries In the ninth and tenth centuries, western Europe was beset by a wave of invasions. Muslims attacked the southern coasts of Europe and sent raiding parties into southern France. The Magyars, a people from western Asia, moved into

© Robert Harding Picture Library Ltd (G. Richardson)/Alamy

© The Pierpont Morgan Library, New York/Art Resource, NY

The Vikings Attack England. The illustration on the left, from an eleventh-century English manuscript, depicts a group of armed Vikings invading England. Two ships have already reached the shore, and a few Vikings are shown walking down a long gangplank onto English soil. On the right is a replica of a well-preserved Viking ship found at Oseberg, Norway. The Oseberg ship was one of the largest Viking ships in its day.

central Europe at the end of the ninth century and settled on the plains of Hungary, launching forays from there into western Europe. Finally crushed at the Battle of Lechfeld in Germany in 955, the Magyars converted to Christianity, settled down, and established the kingdom of Hungary.

The most far-reaching attacks of the time came from the Northmen or Norsemen of Scandinavia, also known to us as the Vikings. The Vikings were warriors whose love of adventure and search for booty and new avenues of trade may have led them to invade other areas of Europe. Viking ships were the best of the period. Long and narrow with beautifully carved arched prows, the Viking "dragon ships" carried about fifty men. Their shallow draft enabled them to sail up European rivers and attack places at some distance inland. In the ninth century, Vikings sacked villages and towns, destroyed churches, and easily defeated small local armies. Viking attacks frightened people and led many a clergyman to plead with them to change their

behavior and appease God's anger, as is revealed in this sermon in 1014 by an English archbishop:

Things have not gone well now for a long time at home or abroad, but there has been devastation and persecution in every district again and again, and the English have been for a long time now completely defeated and too greatly disheartened through God's anger; and the pirates [Vikings] so strong with God's consent that often in battle one puts to flight ten, and sometimes less, sometimes more, all because of our sins.... We pay them continually and they humiliate us daily; they ravage and they burn, plunder, and rob and carry on board; and lo, what else is there in all these events except God's anger clear and visible over this people?[3]

By the middle of the ninth century, the Norsemen had begun to build winter settlements in different areas of Europe. By 850, groups from Norway had settled in Ireland, and Danes occupied northeastern England by 878. Beginning in 911, the ruler of the western Frankish lands gave one band of Vikings land at the mouth of the

Seine River, forming a section of France that came to be known as Normandy. This policy of settling the Vikings and converting them to Christianity was a deliberate one; by their conversion to Christianity, the Vikings were soon made a part of European civilization.

The Development of Fief-Holding

The disintegration of central authority in the Carolingian world and the invasions by Muslims, Magyars, and Vikings led to the emergence of a new type of relationship between free individuals. When governments ceased to be able to defend their subjects, it became important to find some powerful lord who could offer protection in return for service. The contract sworn between a lord and his subordinate (known as a **vassal**) is the basis of a form of social organization that modern historians called *feudalism*. But feudalism was never a cohesive system, and many historians today prefer to avoid using the term (see the comparative essay "Feudal Orders Around the World" on p. 313).

With the breakdown of royal governments, powerful nobles took control of large areas of land. They needed men to fight for them, so the practice arose of giving grants of land to vassals who in return would fight for their lord. The Frankish army had originally consisted of foot soldiers, dressed in coats of mail and armed with swords. But in the eighth century, a military change began to occur with the use of larger horses and the stirrup, which was introduced by nomadic horsemen from Asia. Earlier, horsemen had been throwers of spears. Now they came to be armored in coats of mail (the larger horse could carry the weight) and wielded long lances that enabled them to act as battering rams (the stirrups kept them on their horses). For almost five hundred years, warfare in Europe would be dominated by heavily armored cavalry, or *knights*, as they were called. The knights came to have the greatest social prestige and formed the backbone of the European aristocracy.

Of course, it was expensive to have a horse, armor, and weapons. It also took time and much practice to learn to wield these instruments skillfully from horseback. Consequently, lords who wanted men to fight for them had to grant each vassal a piece of land that provided for the support of the vassal and his family. In return for the land, the vassal provided his lord with his fighting skills. Each needed the other. In the society of the Early Middle Ages, where there was little trade and wealth was based primarily on land, land became the most important gift a lord could give to a vassal in return for his loyalty and military service.

By the ninth century, the grant of land made to a vassal had become known as a **fief**. A fief was a piece of land held from the lord by a vassal in return for military service, but vassals who held such grants of land came to exercise rights of jurisdiction or political and legal authority within these fiefs. As the Carolingian world disintegrated politically under the impact of internal dissension and invasions, an increasing number of powerful lords arose who were now responsible for keeping order.

The Practice of Fief-Holding

Fief-holding also became increasingly complicated with the development of **subinfeudation.** The vassals of a king, who were themselves great lords, might also have vassals who would owe them military service in return for a grant of land taken from their estates. Those vassals, in turn, might likewise have vassals, who at such a level would be simple knights with barely enough land to provide their equipment. The lord-vassal relationship, then, bound together both greater and lesser landowners. At all levels, the lord-vassal relationship was always an honorable relationship between free men and did not imply any sense of servitude.

Fief-holding came to be characterized by a set of practices that determined the relationship between a lord and his vassal. The major obligation of a vassal to his lord was to perform military service, usually about forty days a year. A vassal was also required to appear at his lord's court when summoned to give advice to the lord. He might also be asked to sit in judgment in a legal case, since the important vassals of a lord were his peers and only they could judge each other. Finally, vassals were also responsible for aids, or financial payments to the lord on a number of occasions, among them the knighting of the lord's eldest son, the marriage of his eldest daughter, and the ransom of the lord's person if he were captured.

In turn, a lord had responsibilities toward his vassals. His major obligation was to protect his vassal, either by defending him militarily or by taking his side in a court of law. The lord was also responsible for the maintenance of the vassal, usually by granting him a fief.

The Manorial System

The landholding class of nobles and knights contained a military elite whose ability to function as warriors depended on having the leisure time to pursue the arts of war. Landed estates, located on the fiefs given to a vassal by his lord and worked by a dependent peasant class, provided the economic sustenance that made this way of life possible. A **manor** was an agricultural estate operated by a lord and worked by peasants (see Map 12.2). Although a large class of free peasants continued to exist, increasing numbers of free peasants became **serfs**—persons bound to the land and required to provide labor services, pay rents, and be subject to the lord's jurisdiction. By the ninth century, probably 60 percent of the population of western Europe had become serfs.

Labor services consisted of working the lord's **demesne,** the land retained by the lord, which might consist of one-third to one-half of the cultivated lands scattered throughout the manor. The rest would be used by the peasants for themselves. Building barns and digging ditches were also part of the labor services. Serfs usually worked about three days a week for their lord and paid rents by giving the lord a share of every product they raised.

Serfs were legally bound to the lord's lands and could not leave without his permission. Although free to marry, serfs could not marry anyone outside their manor without the lord's approval. Moreover, lords sometimes

Ages, the number of people nearly doubled to 74 million. What accounted for this dramatic increase? For one thing, conditions in Europe were more settled and more peaceful after the invasions of the Early Middle Ages had ended. For another, agricultural production surged after 1000.

The New Agriculture

During the High Middle Ages, Europeans began to farm in new ways. An improvement in climate resulted in better growing conditions, but an important factor in increasing food production was the expansion of cultivated or arable land, accomplished by clearing forested areas. Peasants of the eleventh and twelfth centuries cut down trees and drained swamps until by the thirteenth century, Europeans had more acreage available for farming than at any time before or since.

Technological changes also furthered the development of farming. The Middle Ages saw an explosion of laborsaving devices, many of which were made from iron, which was mined in different areas of Europe. Iron was used to make scythes, axes, and hoes for use on farms as well as saws, hammers, and nails for building purposes. Iron was crucial in making the *carruca*, a heavy, wheeled plow with an iron plowshare pulled by teams of horses, which could turn over the heavy clay soil north of the Alps.

Besides using horsepower, the High Middle Ages harnessed the power of water and wind to do jobs formerly done by human or animal power. Although the watermill had been invented as early as the second century B.C.E., it did not come into widespread use until the High Middle Ages. Located along streams, watermills were used to grind grain into flour. Often dams were constructed to increase the waterpower. The development of the cam enabled millwrights to mechanize entire industries; waterpower was used in certain phases of cloth production and to run trip-hammers for the working of metals. The Chinese had made use of the cam in operating trip-hammers for hulling rice by the third century C.E. but had apparently not extended its use to other industries.

Where rivers were unavailable or not easily dammed, Europeans developed windmills to yoke the power of the wind. Historians are uncertain whether windmills were imported into Europe (they were invented in Persia) or designed independently by Europeans. In either case, by the end of the twelfth century, they were beginning to dot the European landscape. The watermill and windmill were the most important devices for the harnessing of power before the invention of the steam engine in the eighteenth century.

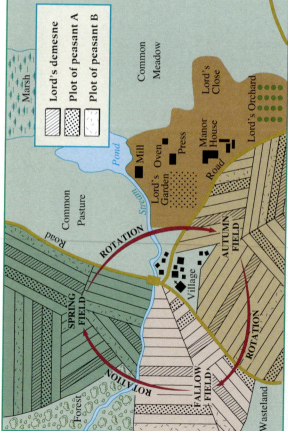

MAP 12.2 A Typical Manor. The manorial system created small, tightly knit communities in which peasants were economically and physically bound to their lord. Crops were rotated, with roughly one-third of the fields lying fallow at any one time, which helped replenish soil nutrients.

Q How does the area of the lord's manor, other buildings, garden, and orchard compare to that of the peasant holdings in the village? 🖱 **View an animated version of this map or related maps at** www.cengage.com/history/Duiker/World6e

exercised public rights or political authority on their lands, which gave them the right to try peasants in their own courts.

Europe in the High Middle Ages

Q Focus Questions: What roles did aristocrats, peasants, and townspeople play in medieval European civilization, and how did their lifestyles differ? How did cities in Europe compare to those in China and the Middle East? What were the main aspects of the political, economic, spiritual, and cultural revivals that took place in Europe during the High Middle Ages?

The new European civilization that had emerged in the Early Middle Ages began to flourish in the High Middle Ages (1000–1300). New agricultural practices that increased the food supply spurred commercial and urban expansion. Both lords and vassals recovered from the invasions and internal dissension of the Early Middle Ages, and medieval kings began to exert a centralizing authority. The recovery of the Catholic church made it a forceful presence in every area of life. The High Middle Ages also gave birth to a cultural revival.

Land and People

In the Early Middle Ages, Europe had a relatively small population of about 38 million, but in the High Middle

EARTH & ENVIRONMENT

The New Agriculture in the Medieval World.

New agricultural methods and techniques in the Middle Ages enabled peasants in both Europe and China to increase food production. This general improvement in diet was a factor in supporting noticeably larger populations in both areas. Below, a thirteenth-century illustration shows a group of English peasants harvesting grain. Overseeing their work is a bailiff, or manager, who supervised the work of the peasants. To the right, a thirteenth-century painting shows Chinese peasants harvesting rice, which became the staple food in China.

Q How important were staple foods (such as wheat and rice) to the diet and health of people in Europe and China during the Middle Ages?

© The Art Archive/British Library

© The Art Archive/Freer Gallery of Art

The shift from a two-field to a three-field system also contributed to the increase in food production (see the comparative illustration above). In the Early Middle Ages, peasants had planted one field while another of equal size was allowed to lie fallow to regain its fertility. Now estates were divided into three parts. One field was planted in the fall with winter grains, such as rye and wheat, while spring grains, such as oats or barley, and vegetables, such as peas or beans, were planted in the second field. The third was allowed to lie fallow. By rotating their use, only one-third rather than one-half of the land lay fallow at any time. The rotation of crops also kept the soil from being exhausted so quickly, and more crops could now be grown.

Daily Life of the Peasantry The lifestyle of the peasants was quite simple. Their cottages consisted of wood frames surrounded by sticks with the space between them filled with straw and rubble and then plastered over with clay. Roofs were simply thatched. The houses of poorer peasants consisted of a single room, but others had at least two rooms—a main room for cooking, eating, and other activities and another room for sleeping.

Peasant women occupied an important but difficult position in manorial society. They were expected to carry and bear their children and at the same time fulfill their obligation to labor in the fields. Their ability to manage the household might determine whether a peasant family would starve or survive in difficult times.

Though simple, a peasant's daily diet was adequate when food was available. The staple of the peasant diet, and the medieval diet in general, was bread. Women made the dough for the bread at home and then brought their loaves to be baked in community ovens, which were owned by the lord of the manor. Peasant bread was highly nutritious, containing not only wheat and rye but also barley, millet, and oats, giving it a dark appearance and a very heavy, hard texture. Bread was supplemented by numerous vegetables from the household gardens, cheese from cow's or goat's milk, nuts and berries from wood-lands, and fruits, such as apples, pears, and cherries. Chickens provided eggs and sometimes meat.

The Nobility of the Middle Ages
In the High Middle Ages, European society, like that of Japan during the same period, was dominated by men whose chief concern was warfare. Like the Japanese samurai, many Western nobles loved war. As one nobleman wrote:

And well I like to hear the call of "Help" and see the
wounded fall,
Loudly for mercy praying,
And see the dead, both great and small,
Pierced by sharp spearheads one and all.[4]

The men of war were the lords and vassals of medieval society.

The lords were the kings, dukes, counts, barons, and viscounts (and even bishops and archbishops) who had extensive landholdings and wielded considerable political influence. They formed an **aristocracy** or nobility of people who held real political, economic, and social power. Both the great lords and ordinary knights were warriors, and the institution of knighthood united them. But there were also social divisions among them based on extremes of wealth and landholdings.

In the eleventh and twelfth centuries, under the influence of the church, an ideal of civilized behavior called **chivalry** gradually evolved among the nobility. Chivalry represented a code of ethics that knights were supposed to uphold. In addition to defending the church and the defenseless, knights were expected to treat captives as honored guests instead of putting them in dungeons. Chivalry also implied that knights should fight only for glory, but this account of English knights by a medieval writer reveals another motive for battle: "The whole city was plundered to the last farthing, and then they proceeded to rob all the churches throughout the city, . . . and seizing gold and silver, cloth of all colors, women's ornaments, gold rings, goblets, and precious stones . . . they all returned to their own lords rich men."[5] Apparently, not all the ideals of chivalry were taken seriously.

Although aristocratic women could legally hold property, most women remained under the control of men—their fathers until they married and their husbands after that. Nevertheless, these women had many opportunities for playing important roles. Because the lord was often away at war or at court, the lady of the castle had to manage the estate. Households could include large numbers of officials and servants, so

this was no small responsibility. Maintaining the financial accounts alone took considerable financial knowledge. The lady of the castle was also responsible on a regular basis for overseeing the food supply and maintaining all the other supplies needed for the smooth operation of the household.

Although women were expected to be subservient to their husbands, there were many strong women who advised and sometimes even dominated their husbands. Perhaps most famous was Eleanor of Aquitaine (c. 1122–1204). Married to King Louis VII of France, Eleanor accompanied her husband on a Crusade, but her alleged affair with her uncle during the Crusade led Louis to have their marriage annulled. Eleanor then married Henry, duke of Normandy, who became King Henry II of England (1154–1189). She took an active role in politics, even assisting her sons in rebelling against Henry in 1173 and 1174 (see "Film & History: *The Lion in Winter*" on p. 343).

The New World of Trade and Cities
Medieval Europe was overwhelmingly agrarian, with most people living in small villages. In the eleventh and twelfth centuries, however, new elements were introduced that began to transform the economic foundation of European civilization: a revival of trade, the emergence of specialized craftspeople and artisans, and the growth and development of towns.

The Revival of Trade The revival of trade was a gradual process. During the chaotic conditions of the Early Middle Ages, large-scale trade had declined in western Europe except for Byzantine contacts with Italy and the Jewish traders who moved back and forth between the Muslim and Christian worlds. By the end of the tenth century, however, people were emerging in Europe with both the skills and the products for commercial activity. Cities in Italy took the lead in this revival of trade. Venice, for example, emerged as a town by the end of the eighth century, developed a mercantile fleet, and by the end of the tenth century had become the chief western trading center for Byzantine and Islamic commerce.

While the northern Italian cities were busy trading in the Mediterranean, the towns of Flanders were doing likewise in northern Europe. Flanders, the area along the coast of present-day Belgium and northern France, was known for its high-quality woolen cloth. The location of Flanders made it an ideal center for the traders of northern Europe. Merchants from England, Scandinavia, France, and Germany converged there to trade their goods

Flanders as a Trade Center

Directed by Anthony Harvey, *The Lion in Winter* is based on a play by James Goldman, who also wrote the script for the movie and won an Oscar for best adapted screenplay for it. The action takes place in a castle in Chinon, France, over the Christmas holidays in 1183. The setting is realistic: medieval castles had dirt floors covered with rushes, under which lay, according to one observer, "an ancient collection of grease, fragments, bones, excrement of dogs and cats, and everything that is nasty." The powerful but world-weary King Henry II (played by Peter O'Toole), ruler of England and a number of French lands (the "Angevin Empire"), wants to establish his legacy and plans a Christmas gathering to decide which of his sons should succeed him. He favors his overindulged youngest son John (Nigel Terry), but he is opposed by his strong-willed and estranged wife, Eleanor of Aquitaine (Katharine Hepburn). She has been imprisoned by the king for leading a rebellion against him but has been temporarily freed for the holidays. Eleanor favors their son Richard (Anthony Hopkins), the most military minded of the brothers. The middle brother, Geoffrey (John Castle), is not a candidate but manipulates the other brothers to gain his own advantage. All three sons are portrayed as treacherous and traitorous, and Henry is distrustful of them. At one point, he threatens to imprison and even kill his sons; marry his mistress Alais (Jane Merrow), who is also the sister of the king of France; and have a new family to replace them.

In contemporary terms, Henry and Eleanor are an unhappily married couple, and their family is acutely dysfunctional. Sparks fly as family members plot against each other, using intentionally cruel comments and sarcastic responses to wound each other as much as possible. When Eleanor says to Henry, "What would you have me do? Give up? Give in?" he responds, "Give me a little peace." To which Eleanor replies, "A little? Why so modest? How about eternal peace? Now there's a thought." At one point, John responds to bad news about his chances for the throne with "Poor John. Who says poor John? Don't everybody sob at once. My God, if I went up in flames, there's not a living soul who'd pee on me to put the fire out!" His brother Richard replies, "Let's strike a flint and see." Henry is not

Eleanor of Aquitaine (Katharine Hepburn) and Henry II (Peter O'Toole) at dinner at Henry's palace in Chinon, France.

Avco Embassy/The Kobal Collection

can also be cruel to his sons: "You're not mine! We're not connected! I deny you! None of you will get my crown. I leave you nothing, and I wish you plague!"

In developing this well-written, imaginative re-creation of a royal family's hapless Christmas gathering, James Goldman had a great deal of material to work with to fashion his story. Henry II was one of the most powerful monarchs of his day, and Eleanor of Aquitaine was one of the most powerful women. She had first been queen of France, but that marriage was annulled. Next she married Henry, who was then count of Anjou, and became queen of England when he became king in 1154. During their stormy marriage, Eleanor and Henry had five sons and three daughters. She is supposed to have murdered Rosamond, one of her husband's mistresses, and aided her sons in a rebellion against their father in 1173, causing Henry to distrust his sons ever after. But Henry struck back, imprisoning Eleanor for sixteen years. After his death, however, Eleanor returned to Aquitaine and lived on to play an influential role in the reigns of her two sons, Richard and John, who succeeded their father.

---

for woolen cloth. Flanders prospered in the eleventh and twelfth centuries, and such Flemish towns as Bruges and Ghent became centers of the medieval cloth trade.

By the twelfth century, a regular exchange of goods had developed between Flanders and Italy, the two major centers of northern and southern European trade. To encourage this trade, the counts of Champagne in northern France devised a series of six fairs held annually in the chief towns of their territory. At these fairs, northern merchants brought the furs, woolen cloth, tin, and honey of northern Europe and exchanged them for the cloth and swords of northern Italy and the silks, sugar, and spices of the East.

As trade increased, both gold and silver came to be in demand at fairs and trading markets of all kinds. Slowly, a money economy began to emerge. New trading companies and banking firms were set up to manage the exchange and sale of goods. All of these new practices were part of

AN ITALIAN BANKER DISCUSSES TRADE BETWEEN EUROPE AND CHINA

INTERACTION & EXCHANGE

Working on behalf of a banking guild in Florence, Francesco Balducci Pegolotti journeyed to England and Cyprus. As a result of his contacts with many Italian merchants, he acquired considerable information about long-distance trade between Europe and China. In this account, written in 1340, he provides advice for Italian merchants.

Francesco Balducci Pegolotti, An Account of Traders Between Europe and China

In the first place, you must let your beard grow long and not shave. And at Tana [modern Rostov] you should furnish yourself with a guide. And you must not try to save money in the matter of guides by taking a bad one instead of a good one. For the additional wages of the good one will not cost you so much as you will save by having him. And besides the guide it will be well to take at least two good menservants who are acquainted with the Turkish tongue.…

The road you travel from Tana to China is perfectly safe, whether by day or night, according to what the merchants say who have used it. Only if the merchant, in going or coming, should die upon the road, everything belonging to him will become the possession of the lord in the country in which he dies.… And in like manner if he dies in China.…

China is a province which contains a multitude of cities and towns. Among others there is one in particular, that is to say the capital city, to which many merchants are attracted, and in which there is a vast amount of trade; and this city is called Khanbaliq [modern Beijing]. And the said city has a circuit of one hundred miles, and is all full of people and houses.…

Whatever silver the merchants may carry with them as far as China, the emperor of China will take from them and put into his treasury. And to merchants who thus bring silver they give that paper money of theirs in exchange … and with this money you can readily buy silk and all other merchandise that you have a desire to buy. And all the people of the country are bound to receive it. And yet you shall not pay a higher price for your goods because your money is of paper.

Q *What were Francesco Pegolotti's impressions of China? Were they positive or negative? Explain your answer.*

---

the rise of **commercial capitalism,** an economic system in which people invested in trade and goods in order to make profits.

Trade Outside Europe In the High Middle Ages, Italian merchants became even more daring in their trade activities. They established trading posts in Cairo, Damascus, and a number of Black Sea ports, where they acquired spices, silks, jewelry, dyestuffs, and other goods brought by Muslim merchants from India, China, and Southeast Asia.

The spread of the Mongol Empire in the thirteenth century (see Chapter 10) also opened the door to Italian merchants in the markets of Central Asia, India, and China (see the box above). As nomads who relied on trade with settled communities, the Mongols maintained safe trade routes for merchants moving through their lands. Two Venetian merchants, the brothers Niccolò and Maffeo Polo, began to travel in the Mongol Empire around 1260.

The creation of the crusader states in Syria and Palestine in the twelfth and thirteenth centuries (discussed later in this chapter) was especially favorable to Italian merchants. In return for taking the crusaders to the east, Italian merchant fleets received trading concessions in Syria and Palestine. Venice, for example, who profited the most from this trade, was given a quarter, soon known as "a little Venice in the east," in Tyre on the coast of what is now Lebanon. Such quarters here and in other cities soon became bases for carrying on lucrative trade practices.

The Growth of Cities The revival of trade led to a revival of cities. Towns had greatly declined in the Early Middle Ages, especially in Europe north of the Alps. Old Roman cities continued to exist but had dwindled in size and population. With the revival of trade, merchants began to settle in these old cities, followed by craftspeople or artisans, people who on manors or elsewhere had developed skills and now saw an opportunity to ply their trade and make goods that could be sold by the merchants. In the course of the eleventh and twelfth centuries, the old Roman cities came alive with new populations and growth.

Beginning in the late tenth century, many new cities or towns were also founded, particularly in northern Europe. Usually, a group of merchants established a settlement near some fortified stronghold, such as a castle or monastery. (This explains why so many place names in Europe end in *borough, burgh, burg,* or *bourg,* all of which mean "fortress" or "walled enclosure.") Castles were particularly favored because they were generally located along trade routes; the lords of the castle also offered protection. If the settlement prospered and expanded, new walls were built to protect it.

Although lords wanted to treat towns and townspeople as they would their vassals and serfs, cities had totally different needs and a different perspective. Townspeople needed mobility to trade. Consequently, these merchants and artisans (who came to be called *burghers* or *bourgeois,* from the same root as *borough* and *burg*) needed their own unique laws to meet their requirements and were willing to pay for them. In many instances, lords and kings saw that they could also make money and were willing to sell to the townspeople the liberties they were beginning to demand, including the right to bequeath goods and sell property, freedom from any military obligation to the lord, and written urban laws that guaranteed their freedom. Some towns also obtained the right to govern themselves by choosing their own officials and administering their own courts of law.

Where townspeople experienced difficulties in obtaining privileges, they often swore an oath, forming an association called a **commune**, and resorted to force against their lay or ecclesiastical lords. Communes made their first appearance in northern Italy, in towns that were governed by their bishops, whom the emperors used as their chief administrators. In the eleventh century, city residents swore communal associations with the bishops' noble vassals and overthrew the authority of the bishops by force. Communes took over the rights of government and created new offices for self-rule. Although communes were also sworn in northern Europe, townspeople did not have the support of rural nobles, and revolts against lay lords were usually suppressed. When they succeeded, communes received the right to choose their own officials and run their own cities. Unlike the towns in Italy, however, where the decline of the emperor's authority ensured that the northern Italian cities could function as self-governing republics, towns in France and England, like their counterparts in the Islamic and Chinese empires, did not become independent city-states but remained ultimately subject to royal authority.

Medieval cities in Europe, then, possessed varying degrees of self-government, depending on the amount of control retained over them by the lord or king in whose territory they were located. Nevertheless, all towns, regardless of the degree of outside control, evolved institutions of government for running the affairs of the community. Only males who were born in the city or had lived there for a particular length of time were defined as citizens. In many cities, these citizens elected members of a city council who served as judges and city officials and passed laws.

Medieval cities remained relatively small in comparison to either ancient or modern cities (see the comparative essay "Cities in the Medieval World" on page 346.) A large trading city would number about 5,000 inhabitants. By 1200, London was the largest city in England with 30,000 people. On the Continent north of the Alps, only a few urban centers of commerce, such as Bruges and Ghent, had populations close to 40,000. Italian cities tended to be larger, with Venice, Florence, Genoa, Milan, and Naples numbering almost 100,000. Even the largest European city, however, seemed small alongside the Byzantine capital of Constantinople or the Arab cities of Damascus, Baghdad, and Cairo.

Daily Life in the Medieval City

Medieval towns were surrounded by stone walls that were expensive to build,

Shops in a Medieval Town. Most urban residents were merchants involved in trade and artisans who manufactured a wide variety of products. Master craftsmen had their workshops in the ground-level rooms of their homes. In this illustration, two well-dressed burghers are touring the shopping district of a French town. Tailors, furriers, a barber, and a grocer (from left to right) are visible at work in their shops.

© Snark/Art Resource, NY

so the space within was precious. Consequently, most medieval cities featured narrow, winding streets with houses crowded against each other and second and third stories extending out over the streets. Because dwellings were built mostly of wood before the fourteenth century and candles and wood fires were used for light and heat, fire was a constant threat. Medieval cities burned rapidly once a fire started.

Most of the people who lived in cities were merchants involved in trade and artisans engaged in manufacturing a wide range of goods, such as cloth, metalwork, shoes, and leather goods. Generally, merchants and artisans had their own sections within a city. The merchant area included warehouses, inns, and taverns. Artisan sections were usually divided along craft lines. From the twelfth century on, craftspeople began to organize themselves into **guilds,** and by the thirteenth century, there were individual guilds for virtually every craft. Each craft had its own street where its activity was pursued.

The physical environment of medieval cities was not pleasant. They were dirty and smelled of animal and human wastes deposited in backyard privies or on the streets. The rivers in most cities were polluted with wastes, especially from the tanning and animal-slaughtering industries. Because of the pollution, cities did not use the rivers for drinking water but relied instead on wells.

Private and public baths also existed in medieval towns. Paris, for example, had thirty-two public baths for men and women. City laws did not allow lepers and people with "bad reputations" to use them. This did not, however,

COMPARATIVE ESSAY

CITIES IN THE MEDIEVAL WORLD

© British Library, London//HIP/Art Resource, NY

INTERACTION & EXCHANGE

The exchange of goods between societies was a feature of both the ancient and medieval worlds. Trade routes crisscrossed the lands of the medieval world, and with increased trade came the growth of cities. In Europe, towns had greatly declined after the collapse of the Western Roman Empire, but with the revival of trade in the eleventh and twelfth centuries, the cities came back to life. This revival occurred first in the old Roman cities, but soon new cities arose as merchants and artisans sought additional centers for their activities. As cities grew, so did the number of fortified houses, town halls, and churches whose towers punctuated the urban European skyline. Nevertheless, in the Middle Ages, cities in western Europe, especially north of the Alps, remained relatively small. Even the larger cities found in Italy, with populations of 100,000, seemed insignificant compared to Constantinople and the great cities of the Middle East and China.

With a population of possibly 300,000 people, Constantinople, the capital city of the Byzantine Empire (see Chapter 13), was the largest city in Europe in the Early and High Middle Ages, and until the twelfth century, it was Europe's greatest commercial center, important for the exchange of goods between west and east. Although it had its share of palaces, cathedrals, and monastic buildings, Constantinople also had numerous gardens and orchards that occupied large areas inside its fortified walls. Despite the extensive open and cultivated spaces, the city was not self-sufficient and relied on imports of food under close government direction.

As trade flourished in the Islamic world, cities prospered. When the Abbasids were in power, Baghdad, with a population close to 700,000, was probably the largest city in the empire and one of the greatest cities in the world. After the rise of the Fatimids in Egypt, however, the focus of trade shifted to Cairo. Islamic cities had a distinctive physical appearance. Usually, the most impressive urban buildings were the palaces for the caliphs or the local governors and the great mosques for worship. There were also public buildings with fountains and secluded courtyards, public baths, and bazaars. The bazaar, a covered market, was a crucial part of every Muslim settlement and an important trading center where goods from all the known world were available. Food prepared for sale at the market was carefully supervised. A rule in one Muslim city stated, "Grilled meats should only be made with fresh meat and not with meat coming from a sick animal and bought for its cheapness." Merchants gained the most benefit from the growth of cities in the Islamic world.

During the medieval period, cities in China were the largest in the world. The southern port of Hangzhou had

Crime and Punishment in the Medieval City. Violence was a common feature of medieval life. Criminals, if apprehended, were punished quickly and severely, and public executions, like the one seen here, were considered a deterrent to crime.

at least a million residents by 1000, and a number of other cities, including Chang'an and Kaifeng, may also have reached that size. Chinese cities were known for their broad canals and wide, tree-lined streets. They were no longer administrative centers dominated by officials and their families but now included a broader mix of officials, merchants, artisans, and entertainers. The prosperity of Chinese cities was well known. Marco Polo, in describing Hangzhou to unbelieving Europeans in the late thirteenth century, said, "So many pleasures can be found that one fancies himself to be in Paradise."

Q *Based on a comparison of these medieval cities, which of these civilizations do you think was the most advanced? Why?*

© Musée de la Tapisserie, Bayeux, France/The Bridgeman Art Library

The Norman Conquest of England. The Bayeux tapestry, a magnificent wall hanging of woolen embroidery on a linen backing, was made by English needlewomen before 1082 for Bayeux Cathedral. It depicts scenes from the Norman invasion of England a decade and a half earlier. This segment shows the Norman cavalry charging the shield wall of the Saxon infantry during the Battle of Hastings.

prevent public baths from being known for permissiveness due to public nudity. One contemporary commented on what occurred in public bathhouses: "Shameful things. Men make a point of staying all night in the public baths and women at the break of day come in and through 'ignorance' find themselves in the men's rooms."[6]

In medieval cities, women, in addition to supervising the household, purchasing food and preparing meals, raising the children, and managing the family finances, were also often expected to help their husbands in their trades. Some women also developed their own trades to earn extra money. When some master craftspeople died, their widows even carried on their trades. Some women in medieval towns were thus able to lead lives of considerable independence.

Evolution of the European Kingdoms

The recovery and growth of European civilization in the High Middle Ages also affected the state. Although lords and vassals seemed forever mired in endless petty conflicts, some medieval kings inaugurated the process of developing new kinds of monarchical states that were based on the centralization of power rather than the decentralized political order that was characteristic of fiefholding. By the thirteenth century, European monarchs were solidifying their governmental institutions in pursuit of greater power.

England in the High Middle Ages

In late September 1066, an army of heavily armed knights under William of Normandy landed on the coast of England, and soon, on October 14, they soundly defeated King Harold and his Anglo-Saxon foot soldiers in the Battle of Hastings. William (1066–1087) was crowned king of England at Christmastime in London and promptly began a process of combining Anglo-Saxon and Norman institutions that would change England forever. Many of the Norman knights were given parcels of land that they held as fiefs from the new English king. William made all nobles swear an oath of loyalty to him as sole ruler of England and insisted that all people owed loyalty to the king. The Normans also took over existing Anglo-Saxon institutions, such as the office of sheriff. William took a census and more fully developed the system of taxation and royal courts begun by the Anglo-Saxon kings of the tenth and eleventh centuries. All in all, William of Normandy established a strong, centralized monarchy.

The Norman Conquest had numerous repercussions. Because the new king of England was still the duke of Normandy, he was both a king (of England) and at the same time a vassal to a king (of France), but a vassal who was now far more powerful than his lord. This connection with France kept England heavily involved in European affairs throughout the High Middle Ages.

In the twelfth century, the power of the English monarchy was greatly enlarged during the reign of Henry II (1154–1189; see "Film & History: *The Lion in Winter*" on p. 343). The new king was particularly successful in strengthening the power of the royal courts. Henry expanded the number of criminal cases to be tried in the king's court and also devised means for taking property cases from local courts to the royal courts. Henry's goals were clear: expanding the power of the royal courts expanded the king's power and, of course, brought revenues into his coffers. Moreover, since the royal courts were now found throughout England, a body of **common law** (law that was common to the whole kingdom) began to replace the different law codes that often varied from place to place.

Henry was less successful at imposing royal control over the church and became involved in a famous struggle between church and state. Henry claimed the right to punish clergymen in the royal courts, but Thomas à Becket, as archbishop of Canterbury, the highest-ranking English cleric, claimed that only church courts could try clerics. Attempts at compromise failed, and the angry king publicly expressed the desire to be rid of Becket: "Who will free me of this priest?" he screamed. Four knights took the challenge, went to Canterbury, and murdered the archbishop in the cathedral (see the box on p. 348). Met with public outrage, Henry was forced to allow the right of appeal from English church courts to the papal court.

Many English nobles came to resent the growth of the king's power and rose in

POLITICS & GOVERNMENT

MURDER IN THE CATHEDRAL

The most famous church-state controversy in medieval England arose between King Henry II and Thomas à Becket, the archbishop of Canterbury. This excerpt is from a letter by John of Salisbury, who served as Becket's secretary and was present at the archbishop's murder in 1170.

Letter from John of Salisbury to John of Canterbury, Bishop of Poitiers

The martyr [Becket] stood in the cathedral, before Christ's altar, as we have said, ready to suffer; the hour of slaughter was at hand. When he heard that he was sought—heard the knights who had come for him shouting in the throng of clerks and monks "Where is the archbishop?"—he turned to meet them on the steps which he had almost climbed, and said with steady countenance: "Here am I! What do you want?" One of the knight-assassins flung at him in fury. "That you die now! That you should live longer is impossible." "No martyr seems ever to have been more steadfast in his agony than he . . . and thus, steadfast in speech as in spirit, he replied: "And I am prepared to die for my God, to preserve justice and my church's liberty. If you seek my head, I forbid you on behalf of God almighty and on pain of anathema to do any hurt to any other man, monk, clerk, or layman, of high or low degree. Do not involve them in the punishment, for they have not been involved in the cause: on my head not on theirs be it if any of them have supported the Church in its troubles. I embrace death readily, so long as peace and liberty for the

Church follow from the shedding of my blood. . . . " He spoke, and saw that the assassins had drawn their swords; and bowed his head like one in prayer. His last words were "To God and St. Mary and the saints who protect and defend this church, and to the blessed Denis, I commend myself and the Church's cause." No one could dwell on what followed without deep sorrow and choking tears. A son's affection forbids me to describe each blow the savage assassins struck, spurning all fear of God, forgetful of all fealty and any human feeling. They defiled the cathedral and the holy season [Christmas] with a bishop's blood and with slaughter; but that was not enough. They sliced off the crown of his head, which had been specially dedicated to God by anointing with holy chrism—a fearful thing even to describe; then they used their evil swords, when he was dead, to spill his brain and cruelly scattered it, mixed with blood and bones, over the pavement. . . . Through all the agony the martyr's spirit was unconquered, his steadfastness marvelous to observe; he spoke not a word, uttered no cry, let slip no groan, raised no arm nor garment to protect himself from an assailant, but bent his head, which he had laid bare to their swords with wonderful courage, till all might be fulfilled. Motionless he held it, and when at last he fell his body lay straight; and he moved neither hand nor foot.

Q *What was the cause of the conflict between Henry II and the archbishop of Canterbury? What argument does the archbishop make to defend his position? How was the conflict resolved?*

---

lords. Eventually, barons and church lords formed the House of Lords; knights and burgesses, the House of Commons. The Parliaments of Edward I approved taxes, discussed politics, passed laws, and handled judicial business. The law of the realm was beginning to be determined not by the king alone but by the king in consultation with representatives of various groups that constituted the community.

Growth of the French Kingdom The Carolingian Empire had been divided into three major sections in 843. The western Frankish lands formed the core of the eventual kingdom of France. In 987, after the death of the last Carolingian king, the western Frankish nobles chose Hugh Capet as the new king, thus establishing the Capetian dynasty of French kings. Although they carried the title of kings, the Capetians had little real power. They controlled as the royal domain only the lands around Paris known as the Île-de-France. As kings of France, the Capetians were formally the overlords of the great lords of France, such as the dukes of Normandy, Brittany, Burgundy, and Aquitaine. In reality, however, many of

rebellion during the reign of King John (1199–1216). At Runnymede in 1215, John was forced to seal Magna Carta (Great Charter) guaranteeing feudal liberties. Feudal custom had always recognized that the relationship between king and vassals was based on mutual rights and obligations. Magna Carta gave written recognition to that fact and was used in later years to support the idea that a monarch's power was limited.

During the reign of Edward I (1272–1307), an institution of great importance in the development of representative government—the English Parliament—also emerged. Originally, the word *parliament* was applied to the meetings of the king's Great Council, in which the greater barons and chief prelates of the church met with the king's judges and principal advisers to deal with judicial affairs. But in his need for money, Edward in 1295 invited two knights from every county and two residents from each town to meet with the Great Council to consent to new taxes. This was the first Parliament.

The English Parliament, then, came to be composed of two knights from every county and two burgesses from every borough as well as the barons and ecclesiastical

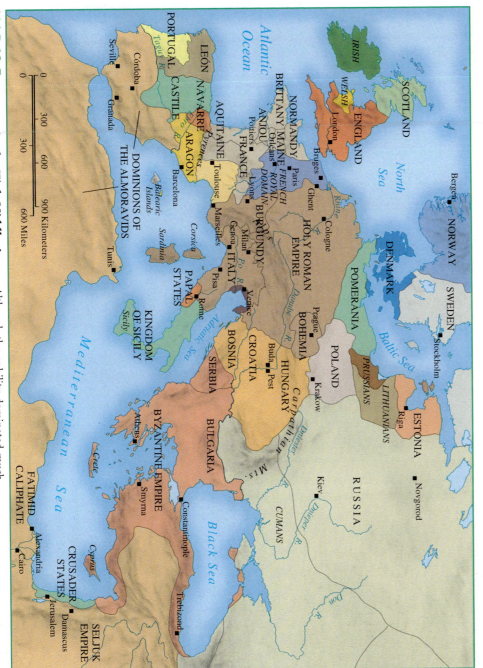

MAP 12.3 Europe in the High Middle Ages. Although the nobility dominated much of European society in the High Middle Ages, kings began the process of extending their power in more effective ways, creating the monarchies that would form the European states.

Q Which were the strongest monarchical states by 1300? Why? ● **View an animated version of this map or related maps at** www.cengage.com/history/Duiker/World6e

the dukes were considerably more powerful than the French Capetian kings. All in all, it would take the Capetian dynasty hundreds of years to create a truly centralized monarchical authority in France.

The reign of King Philip II Augustus (1180–1223) was an important turning point in the growth of the French monarchy. Philip II waged war against the Plantagenet rulers of England, who also ruled the French territories of Normandy, Maine, Anjou, and Aquitaine, and was successful in gaining control of most of these territories, thus enlarging the power of the French monarchy (see Map 12.3). To administer justice and collect royal revenues in his new territories, Philip appointed new royal officials, thus inaugurating a French royal bureaucracy in the thirteenth century.

Capetian rulers after Philip II continued to add lands to the royal domain. Philip IV the Fair (1285–1314) was especially effective in strengthening the French monarchy. He reinforced the royal bureaucracy and also brought a French parliament into being by asking representatives of the three estates, or classes—the clergy (First Estate), the nobles (Second Estate), and the townspeople (Third Estate)—to meet with him. They did so in 1302, inaugurating the Estates-General, the first French parliament, although it had little real power. By the end of the thirteenth century, France was the largest, wealthiest, and best-governed monarchical state in Europe.

The Lands of the Holy Roman Empire In the tenth century, the powerful dukes of the Saxons became kings of the eastern Frankish kingdom (or Germany, as it came to be called). The best known of the Saxon kings of Germany was Otto I (936–973), who intervened in Italian politics and for his efforts was crowned by the pope in 962 as emperor of the Romans, reviving a title that had not been used since the time of Charlemagne.

In the eleventh century, German kings created a strong monarchy and a powerful empire by leading armies into Italy. To strengthen their grip, they relied on their ability to control the church and select bishops, whom they could then use as royal administrators. But the struggle between church and state during the reign of

Henry IV (1056–1106) weakened the king's ability to use church officials in this way (see "Reform of the Papacy" later in this chapter). The German kings also tried to bolster their power by using their position as emperors to exploit the resources of Italy. But this strategy tended to backfire; many a German king lost armies in Italy in pursuit of a dream of empire, and no German dynasty demonstrates this better than the Hohenstaufens.

The two most famous members of the Hohenstaufen dynasty, Frederick I Barbarossa (1152–1190) and Frederick II (1212–1250), tried to create a new kind of empire. Previous German kings had focused on building a strong German kingdom, but Frederick I planned to get his chief revenues from Italy as the center of a "holy empire," as he called it (hence the name Holy Roman Empire). But his attempt to conquer northern Italy ran into severe problems. The pope opposed him, fearful that the emperor wanted to absorb Rome and the Papal States into his empire. The cities of northern Italy, which had become used to their freedom, were also not willing to be Frederick's subjects. An alliance of these northern Italian cities, with the support of the pope, defeated the emperor's forces in 1176.

The main goal of Frederick II was the establishment of a strong centralized state in Italy dominated by the kingdom in Sicily he had inherited from his mother. Frederick's major task was to gain control of northern Italy. In the attempt, however, he became involved in a deadly struggle with the popes, who feared that a single ruler of northern and southern Italy would mean the end of papal power in the center of the peninsula. Furthermore, the northern Italian cities were unwilling to give up their freedom. Frederick nevertheless waged a bitter battle, winning many battles but ultimately losing the war.

The struggle between popes and emperors had dire consequences for the Holy Roman Empire. By spending their time fighting in Italy, the German emperors left Germany in the hands of powerful German lords who ignored the emperor and created their own independent kingdoms. This ensured that the German monarchy would remain weak and incapable of maintaining a centralized monarchical state; thus the German Holy Roman Emperor had no real power over either Germany or Italy. Unlike France and England, neither

Germany nor Italy had a centralized national monarchy in the Middle Ages. Both of these regions consisted of many small, independent states, a situation that changed little until the nineteenth century.

The Slavic Peoples of Central and Eastern Europe The Slavs were originally a single people in central Europe, but they gradually divided into three major groups: western, southern, and eastern (see Map 12.4). The western Slavs eventually formed the Polish and Bohemian kingdoms. German Christian missionaries converted both the Czechs in Bohemia and the Slavs in Poland by the tenth century. German Christians also converted the non-Slavic kingdom of Hungary, which emerged after the Magyars settled down after their defeat in 955. The Poles, Czechs, and Hungarians all accepted Catholic or western Christianity and became closely tied to the Roman Catholic Church and its Latin culture.

The southern and eastern Slavic populations took a different path: the Slavic peoples of Moravia were converted to the Orthodox Christianity of the Byzantine Empire (see Chapter 13) by two Byzantine missionary brothers, Cyril and Methodius, who began their activities in 863. The southern Slavic peoples included the Croats, Serbs, and Bulgarians. For the most part, they too

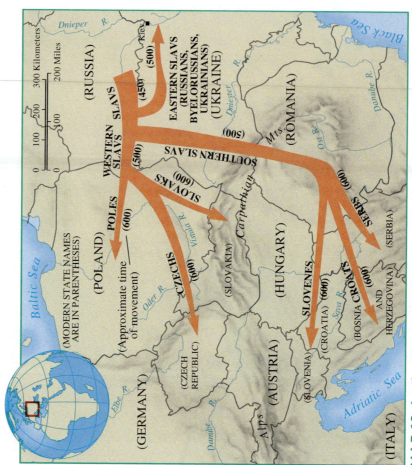

MAP 12.4 **The Migrations of the Slavs.** Originally from east-central Europe, the Slavic people broke into three groups. The western Slavs converted to Catholic Christianity, while most of the eastern and southern Slavs, under the influence of the Byzantine Empire, embraced the Eastern Orthodox faith.

Q What connections do these Slavic migrations have with what we today characterize as eastern Europe?

embraced Eastern Orthodoxy, although the Croats came to accept the Roman Catholic faith. The adoption of Eastern Orthodoxy by the Serbs and Bulgarians tied their cultural life to the Byzantine state.

The eastern Slavic peoples, from whom the modern Russians and Ukrainians are descended, had settled in the territory of present-day Ukraine and European Russia. There, beginning in the late eighth century, they began to encounter Swedish Vikings who moved down the extensive network of rivers into the lands of the eastern Slavs in search of booty and new trade routes (see the box above). These Vikings built trading settlements and eventually came to dominate the native peoples, who called them "the Rus," from which the name Russia is derived.

The Development of Russia: Impact of the Mongols A Viking leader named Oleg (c. 873–913) settled in Kiev at the beginning of the tenth century and founded the Rus state known as the principality of Kiev. His successors extended their control over the eastern Slavs and expanded the territory of Kiev until it included the area between the Baltic and Black Seas and the Danube and Volga Rivers. By marrying Slavic wives, the Viking ruling class was gradually assimilated into the Slavic population.

The growth of the principality of Kiev attracted religious missionaries, especially from the Byzantine Empire. One Rus ruler, Vladimir (c. 980–1015), married the Byzantine emperor's sister and in 987 officially accepted Christianity for himself and his people. By the end of the tenth century, Byzantine Christianity had become the model for Russian religious life.

The Kievan Rus state prospered and reached its high point in the first half of the eleventh century. But civil wars and new invasions by Asian nomads caused the principality of Kiev to collapse, and its sack by north Russian princes in 1169 brought an end to the first Russian state, which had remained closely tied to the Byzantine Empire, not to Europe. In the thirteenth century, the Mongols conquered Russia and cut it off even more from Europe.

The Mongols had exploded onto the scene in the thirteenth century, moving east into China and west into the Middle East and central Europe. Although they conquered Russia, they were not numerous enough to settle the vast Russian lands. They occupied only part of Russia

FAMILY & SOCIETY

Despite the difficulties that travel presented, early medieval civilization did witness some contact among the various cultures. This might occur through trade, diplomacy, or the conquest and migration of peoples. This document is a description of the Swedish Rus, who eventually merged with the native Slavic peoples to form the principality of Kiev, commonly regarded as the first Russian state. It was written by Ibn Fadlan, a Muslim diplomat sent from Baghdad in 921 to a settlement on the Volga River. His comments on the filthiness of the Rus reflect the Muslim preoccupation with cleanliness.

Ibn Fadlan, *The Rus*

I saw the Rus folk when they arrived on their trading mission and settled at the river Atul (Volga). Never had I seen people of more perfect physique. They are tall as date palms, and reddish in color. They wear neither coat nor kaftan, but each man carried a cape which covers one half of his body, leaving one hand free. No one is ever parted from his axe, sword, and knife. Their swords are Frankish in design, broad, flat, and fluted. Each man has a number of trees, figures, and the like from the fingernails to the neck. Each woman carried on her bosom a container made of iron, silver, copper, or gold–its size and substance depending on her man's wealth.

[The Rus] are the filthiest of God's creatures. They do not wash after discharging their natural functions, neither do they wash their hands after meals. They are as lousy as donkeys. They arrive from their distant lands and lay their ships alongside the banks of the Atul, which is a great river, and there they build big houses on its shores. Ten or twenty of them may live together in one house, and each of them has a couch of his own where he sits and diverts himself with the pretty slave girls whom he had brought along for sale. He will make love with one of them while a comrade looks on; sometimes they indulge in a communal orgy, and, if a customer should turn up to buy a girl, the Rus man will not let her go till he has finished with her.

They wash their hands and faces every day in incredibly filthy water. Every morning the girl brings her master a large bowl of water in which he washes his hands and face and hair, then blows his nose into it and spits into it. When he has finished the girl takes the bowl to his neighbor–who repeats the performance. Thus the bowl goes the rounds of the entire household....

If one of the Rus folk falls sick they put him in a tent by himself and leave bread and water for him. They do not visit him, however, or speak to him, especially if he is a serf. Should he recover he rejoins the others; if he dies they burn him. But if he happens to be a serf they leave him for the dogs and vultures to devour. If they catch a robber they hang him to a tree until he is torn to shreds by wind and weather.

Q *What was Ibn Fadlan's impression of the Rus? Why do you think he was so critical of their behavior?*

service. Of course, lords assumed the right to choose their vassals and thus came to appoint bishops and abbots. Because lords often chose their vassals from other noble families for political reasons, these bishops and abbots were often worldly figures who cared little about their spiritual responsibilities.

By the eleventh century, church leaders realized the need to free the church from the interference of lords in the appointment of church officials. **Lay investiture** was the practice by which secular rulers both chose nominees to church offices and invested them with (bestowed on them) the symbols of their office. Pope Gregory VII (1073–1085) decided to fight this practice. Gregory claimed that he, as pope, was God's "vicar on earth" and that the pope's authority extended over all of Christendom, including its rulers. In 1075, he issued a decree forbidding high-ranking clerics from receiving their investiture from lay leaders.

Gregory soon found himself in conflict with the German king over his actions. King Henry IV was also a determined man who had appointed high-ranking clerics, especially bishops, as his vassals in order to use them as administrators. Henry had no intention of obeying a decree that challenged the very heart of his administration.

The struggle between Henry IV and Gregory VII, which is known as the Investiture Controversy, was one of the great conflicts between church and state in the High Middle Ages. It dragged on until a new German king and a new pope reached a compromise in 1122 called the Concordat of Worms. Under this agreement, a bishop in Germany was first elected by church officials. After election, the nominee paid homage to the king as his lord, who then invested him with the symbols of temporal office. A representative of the pope, however, then invested the new bishop with the symbols of his spiritual office.

The Church Supreme: The Papal Monarchy The popes of the twelfth century did not abandon the reform ideals of Pope Gregory VII, but they were more inclined to consolidate their power and build a strong administrative system. During the papacy of Pope Innocent III (1198–1216), the Catholic church reached the height of its power. At the beginning of his pontificate, in a letter to a priest, the pope made a clear statement of his views on papal supremacy:

As God, the creator of the universe, set two great lights in the firmament of heaven, the greater light to rule the day, and the lesser light to rule the night, so He set two great dignities in the firmament of the universal church, ... the greater to rule the day, that is, souls, and the lesser to rule the night, that is, bodies. These dignities are the papal authority and the royal power. And just as the moon gets her light from the sun, and is inferior to the sun ... so the royal power gets the splendor of its dignity from the papal authority.[7]

Innocent III's actions were those of a man who believed that he, as pope, was the supreme judge of European affairs. To achieve his political ends, he did not

CHRONOLOGY The European Kingdoms

England	
Norman Conquest	1066
William the Conqueror	1066–1087
Henry II	1154–1189
John	1199–1216
Magna Carta	1215
Edward I	1272–1307
First Parliament	1295
France	
Philip II Augustus	1180–1223
Philip IV	1285–1314
First Estates-General	1302
Germany and the Holy Roman Empire	
Otto I	936–973
Henry IV	1056–1106
Frederick I	1152–1190
Northern Italian cities defeat Frederick	1176
Frederick II	1212–1250
The Eastern World	
Alexander Nevsky, prince of Novgorod	c. 1220–1263
Mongol conquest of Russia	1230s

but required Russian princes to pay tribute to them. One Russian prince soon emerged as more powerful than the others. Alexander Nevsky, prince of Novgorod, defeated a German invading army in northwestern Russia in 1242. His cooperation with the Mongols won him their favor. The khan, leader of the western part of the Mongol Empire, rewarded Alexander Nevsky with the title of grand-prince, enabling his descendants to become the princes of Moscow and eventually leaders of all Russia.

Christianity and Medieval Civilization

Christianity was an integral part of the fabric of European society and the consciousness of Europe. Papal directives affected the actions of kings and princes alike, and Christian teachings and practices touched the lives of all Europeans.

Reform of the Papacy Since the fifth century, the popes of the Catholic church had reigned supreme over church affairs. They had also come to exercise control over the territories in central Italy that came to be known as the Papal States, which kept the popes involved in political matters, often at the expense of their spiritual obligations. At the same time, the church became increasingly entangled in the evolving feudal relationships. High officials of the church, such as bishops and abbots, came to hold their offices as fiefs from nobles. As vassals, they were obliged to carry out the usual duties, including military

RELIGION & PHILOSOPHY

A MIRACLE OF SAINT BERNARD

Saint Bernard of Clairvaux has been called the most widely respected holy man of the twelfth century. He was an outstanding preacher, wholly dedicated to the service of God. His reputation reportedly influenced many young men to join the Cistercian order. He also inspired a myriad of stories dealing with his miracles.

A Miracle of Saint Bernard

A certain monk, departing from his monastery..., threw off his habit, and returned to the world at the persuasion of the Devil. And he took a certain parish living; for he was a priest. Because sin is punished with sin, the deserter from his Order lapsed into the vice of lechery. He took a concubine to live with him, as in fact is done by many, and by her he had children.

But as God is merciful and does not wish anyone to perish, it happened that many years after, the blessed abbot [Saint Bernard] was passing through the village in which this same monk was living, and went to stay at his house. The renegade monk recognized him, and received him very reverently, and waited on him devoutly... but as yet the abbot did not recognize him.

On the morrow, the holy man said Matins and prepared to be off. But as he could not speak to the priest, since he had got up and gone to the church for Matins, he said to the priest's son, "Go, give this message to your master." Now the boy had been born [mute]. He obeyed the command and feeling in himself the power of him who had given it, he ran to his father and uttered the words of the Holy Father clearly and exactly. His father, on hearing his son's voice for the first time, wept for joy, and made him repeat the same words... and he asked what the abbot had done to him. "He did nothing to me," said the boy, "except to say, 'Go and say this to your father.'"

At so evident a miracle the priest repented, and hastened after the holy man and fell at his feet saying, "My Lord and Father, I was your monk so-and-so, and at such-and-such a time I ran away from your monastery. I ask your Paternity to allow me to return with you to the monastery, for in your coming God has visited my heart." The saint replied unto him, "Wait for me here, and I will come back quickly when I have done my business, and I will take you with me." But the priest, fearing death (which he had not done before), answered, "Lord, I am afraid of dying before then." But the saint replied, "Know this for certain, that if you die in this condition, and in this resolve, you will find yourself a monk before God."

The saint [eventually] returned and heard that the priest had recently died and been buried. He ordered the tomb to be opened. And when they asked him what he wanted to do, he said, "I want to see if he is lying as a monk or a clerk in his tomb." "As a clerk," they said, "we buried him in his secular habit." But when they had dug up the earth, they found that he was not in the clothes in which they had buried him; but he appeared in all points, tonsure and habit, as a monk. And they all praised God.

Q *What two miracles occur in this tale of Saint Bernard? What does this document reveal about popular religious practices during the Middle Ages?*

CENGAGENOW *To read two accounts of the early career of Saint Bernard, enter the documents area of the World History Resource Center using the access card that is available for World History.*

hesitate to use the spiritual weapons at his command, especially the **interdict**, which forbade priests to dispense the **sacraments** of the church in the hope that the people, deprived of the comforts of religion, would exert pressure against their ruler. Apparently, Pope Innocent's interdicts worked: for example, one of them forced the king of France, Philip Augustus, to take back his wife and queen after Philip had tried to have his marriage annulled.

New Religious Orders and New Spiritual Ideals

Between 1050 and 1150, a wave of religious enthusiasm seized Europe, leading to a spectacular growth in the number of monasteries and the emergence of new monastic orders. Most important was the Cistercian order, founded in 1098 by a group of monks dissatisfied with the moral degeneration and lack of strict discipline at their own Benedictine monastery. The Cistercians were strict. They ate a simple diet and possessed only a single robe apiece. More time for prayer and manual labor was provided by shortening the number of hours spent at religious services. The Cistercians played a major role in developing a new, activist spiritual model for twelfth-century Europe. A Benedictine monk often spent hours in prayer to honor God. The Cistercian ideal had a different emphasis: "Arise, soldier of Christ, arise! Get up off the ground and return to the battle from which you have fled! Fight more boldly after your flight, and triumph in glory!"[8] These were the words of Saint Bernard of Clairvaux (1090–1153), who more than any other person embodied the new spiritual ideal of Cistercian monasticism (see the box above).

Women were also actively involved in the spiritual movements of the age. The number of women joining religious houses grew dramatically in the High Middle Ages. Most nuns were from the ranks of the landed aristocracy. Convents were convenient for families unable or unwilling to find husbands for their daughters and for aristocratic women who did not wish to marry. Female

© Archives Charmet/The Bridgeman Art Library

A Group of Nuns. Although still viewed by the medieval church as inferior to men, women were as susceptible to the spiritual fervor of the twelfth century as men, and female monasticism grew accordingly. This manuscript illustration shows at the left a group of nuns welcoming a novice (dressed in white) to their order. At the right, a nun receives a sick person on a stretcher for the order's hospital care.

intellectuals found them a haven for their activities. Most of the learned women of the Middle Ages were nuns.

In the thirteenth century, two new religious orders emerged that had a profound impact on the lives of ordinary people. Like their founder, Saint Francis of Assisi (1182–1226), the Franciscans lived among the people, preaching repentance and aiding the poor. Their calls for a return to the simplicity and poverty of the early church, reinforced by their own example, were especially effective and made them very popular.

The Dominican order arose out of the desire of a Spanish priest, Dominic de Guzmán (1170–1221), to defend church teachings from **heresy**—beliefs contrary to official church doctrine. Unlike Francis, Dominic was an intellectual who was appalled by the growth of heresy. He came to believe that a new religious order of men who lived lives of poverty but were learned and capable of preaching effectively would best be able to attack heresy. The Dominicans became especially well known for their roles as the inquisitors of the papal Inquisition.

The Holy Office, as the papal Inquisition was formally called, was a court that had been established by the church to find and try heretics. Anyone accused of heresy who refused to confess was considered guilty and was turned over to the state for execution. So were relapsed heretics—those who confessed, did penance, and then reverted to heresy again. Most heretics, however, were put in prison or made to do various forms of penance. To the Christians of the thirteenth century, who believed that there was only one path to salvation, heresy was a crime against God and against humanity. In their minds, force should be used to save souls from damnation.

Popular Religion in the High Middle Ages We have witnessed the actions of popes, bishops, and monks. But what of ordinary clergy and laypeople? What were their religious hopes and fears? What were their spiritual aspirations?

The sacraments of the Catholic church ensured that the church was an integral part of people's lives, from birth to death. There were (and still are) seven sacraments, administered only by the clergy. Sacraments, such as baptism and the Eucharist, were viewed as outward symbols of an inward grace and were considered imperative for a Christian's salvation. Therefore, the clergy were seen to have a key role in the attainment of salvation.

Other church practices were also important to ordinary people. Saints were seen as men and women who, through their holiness, had achieved a special position in heaven, enabling them to act as intercessors with God. The saints' ability to protect poor souls enabled them to take on great importance at the popular level. Jesus' apostles were, of course, recognized throughout Europe as saints, but there were also numerous local saints who were of special significance to a single area. New cults developed rapidly, especially in the intense religious atmosphere of the eleventh and twelfth centuries. The English, for example, introduced Saint Nicholas, the patron saint of children, who is known today as Santa Claus.

In the High Middle Ages, the foremost position among the saints was occupied by the Virgin Mary, the mother of Jesus. Mary was viewed as the most important mediator with her son, Jesus, the judge of all sinners. Moreover, from the eleventh century on, a fascination with Mary as Jesus' human mother became more evident. A sign of Mary's importance was the growing number of churches all over Europe that were dedicated to her in the twelfth and thirteenth centuries.

Emphasis on the role of the saints was closely tied to the use of relics, which also increased noticeably in the High Middle Ages. Relics were usually the bones of saints or objects intimately connected to saints that were considered worthy of veneration by the faithful. A twelfth-century English monk began his description of the abbey's relics by saying that "there is kept there a thing more precious than gold.... the right arm of St. Oswald.... This we have seen with our own eyes and have kissed, and have handled with our own hands.... There are kept here also part of his ribs and of the soil on which he fell."9 The monk went on to list additional relics possessed by the abbey, including two pieces of Jesus' swaddling clothes, pieces of Jesus' manger, and part of the five loaves of bread with which Jesus fed five thousand people. Because the holiness of the saint was considered to be inherent in his relics, these objects were believed to be capable of healing people or producing other miracles.

The Culture of the High Middle Ages

The High Middle Ages was a time of extraordinary intellectual and artistic vitality. It witnessed the birth of universities and a building spree that left Europe bedecked with churches and cathedrals.

The Rise of Universities

The university as we know it—with faculty, students, and degrees—was a product of the High Middle Ages. The word *university* is derived from the Latin word *universitas*, meaning a corporation or guild, and referred to either a corporation of teachers or a corporation of students. Medieval universities were educational guilds or corporations that produced educated and trained individuals.

The first European university appeared in Bologna, Italy, where a great teacher named Irnerius (1088–1125), who taught Roman law, attracted students from all over Europe. Most of them were laymen, usually older individuals who were administrators for kings and princes and were eager to learn more about law to apply it in their own jobs. To protect themselves, students at Bologna formed a guild or *universitas*, which was recognized by Emperor Frederick Barbarossa and given a charter in 1158. Kings, popes, and princes soon competed to found new universities, and by the end of the Middle Ages, there were eighty universities in Europe, most of them in England, France, Italy, and Germany (see the box above).

University students (all men—women did not attend universities in the Middle Ages) began their studies with the traditional **liberal arts** curriculum, which consisted of grammar, rhetoric, logic, arithmetic, geometry, music, and astronomy. Teaching was done by the lecture method. The word *lecture* is derived from the Latin verb for "read." Before the development of the printing press in the fifteenth century, books were expensive and few students could afford them, so teachers read from a basic text (such as a collection of laws if the subject was law) and then added their explanations. No exams were given after a series of lectures, but when a student applied for a degree, he was given a comprehensive oral examination

UNIVERSITY STUDENTS AND VIOLENCE AT OXFORD

ARTS & IDEAS

Medieval universities shared in the violent atmosphere of their age. Town and gown quarrels often resulted in bloody conflicts, especially during the universities' formative period. This selection is taken from an anonymous description of a student riot at Oxford at the end of the thirteenth century.

A Student Riot at Oxford

They [the townsmen] seized and imprisoned all scholars on whom they could lay hands, invaded their inns [halls of residence], made havoc of their goods and trampled their books under foot. In the face of such provocation the proctors [university officials] sent their assistants about the town, forbidding the students to leave their inns. But all commands and exhortations were in vain. By nine o'clock next morning, bands of scholars were parading the streets in martial array. If the proctors failed to restrain them, the mayor was equally powerless to restrain his townsmen. The great bell of St. Martin's rang out an alarm; oxhorns were sounded in the streets; messengers were sent into the country to collect rustic allies. The clerks [students and teachers], who numbered 3,000 in all, began their attack simultaneously in various quarters. They broke open warehouses in the Spicery, the Cutlery and elsewhere. Armed with bow and arrows, swords and bucklers, slings and stones, they fell upon their opponents. Three they slew, and wounded fifty or more. One band... took up a position in High Street between the Churches of St. Mary and All Saints', and attacked the house of a certain Edward Hales. This Hales was a longstanding enemy of the clerks. There were no half measures with him. He seized his crossbow, and from an upper chamber sent an unerring shaft into the eye of the pugnacious rector. The death of their valiant leader caused the clerks to lose heart. They fled, closely pursued by the townsmen and country-folk. Some were struck down in the streets, and others who had taken refuge in the churches were dragged out and driven mercilessly to prison, lashed with thongs and goaded with iron spikes.

Complaints of murder, violence and robbery were lodged straightway with the king by both parties. The townsmen claimed 3,000 pounds' damage. The commissioners, however, appointed to decide the matter, condemned them to pay 200 marks, removed the bailiffs, and banished twelve of the most turbulent citizens from Oxford.

Q *Who do you think was responsible for this conflict between town and gown? Why? Why do you think the king supported the university?*

by a committee of teachers. The exam was taken after a four- or six-year period of study. The first degree a student could earn was a bachelor of arts; later he might receive a master of arts degree.

After completing the liberal arts curriculum, a student could go on to study law, medicine, or theology. This last was the most highly regarded subject at the medieval university. The study of any of these three disciplines could take a decade or more. A student who passed his final oral examinations was granted a doctor's degree, which officially enabled him to teach his subject. Students who received degrees from medieval universities could pursue other careers besides teaching that proved to be much more lucrative. A law degree was necessary for those who wished to serve as advisers to kings and princes. The growing administrative bureaucracies of popes and kings also demanded a supply of clerks with a university education who could keep records and draw up official documents. Universities provided the teachers, administrators, lawyers, and doctors for medieval society.

The Development of Scholasticism The importance of Christianity in medieval society made it certain that theology would play a central role in the European intellectual world. Theology, the formal study of religion, was "queen of the sciences" in the new universities.

Beginning in the eleventh century, the effort to apply reason or logical analysis to the church's basic theological doctrines had a significant impact on the study of theology. The word *scholasticism* is used to refer to the medieval philosophical and theological system of the medieval schools. Scholasticism tried to reconcile faith and reason, to demonstrate that what was accepted on faith was in harmony with what could be learned by reason.

The overriding task of scholasticism was to harmonize Christian teachings with the work of the Greek philosopher Aristotle. In the twelfth century, due largely to the work of Muslim and Jewish scholars in Spain, western Europe was introduced to a large number of Greek scientific and philosophical works, including the works of Aristotle. However, Aristotle's works threw many theologians into consternation. Aristotle was so highly regarded that he was called "the philosopher," yet he had arrived at his conclusions by rational thought, not by faith, and some of his doctrines contradicted the teachings of the church. The most famous attempt to reconcile Aristotle and the doctrines of Christianity was that of Saint Thomas Aquinas.

Aquinas (1225–1274) is best known for his *Summa Theologica* (Summa of Theology—a summa was a compendium of knowledge that attempted to bring together all the received learning of the preceding centuries on a given subject). Aquinas' masterpiece was organized according to the dialectical method of the scholastics. Aquinas first posed a question, cited sources that offered opposing opinions on the question, and then resolved the matter by arriving at his own conclusions. In this fashion, Aquinas raised and discussed some six hundred articles.

Aquinas' reputation derives from his masterful attempt to reconcile faith and reason. He took it for granted that there were truths derived by reason and truths derived by faith. He was certain, however, that the two truths could not be in conflict. The natural mind, unaided by faith, could arrive at truths concerning the physical universe. Without the help of God's grace, however, reason alone could not grasp spiritual truths, such as the Trinity (the manifestation of God in three separate yet identical persons—Father, Son, and Holy Spirit) or the Incarnation (Jesus' simultaneous identity as God and human).

Romanesque Architecture The eleventh and twelfth centuries witnessed an explosion of building, both private and public. The construction of castles and churches absorbed most of the surplus resources of medieval society and at the same time reflected its basic preoccupations, God and warfare. The churches were by far the most conspicuous of the public buildings.

The cathedrals of the eleventh and twelfth centuries were built in the **Romanesque** style, prominent examples of which can be found in Germany, France, and Spain. Romanesque churches were normally built in the basilica shape used in the construction of churches in the Late Roman Empire. Basilicas were rectangular churches with flat wooden roofs. Romanesque builders made a significant innovation by replacing the flat wooden roof with a long, round stone vault called a barrel vault (or a cross vault where two barrel vaults intersected). Although barrel and cross vaults were technically difficult to create, they were considered aesthetically more pleasing than flat wooden roofs and were also less apt to catch fire.

Because stone roofs were extremely heavy, Romanesque churches required massive pillars and walls to hold them up. This left little space for windows, and Romanesque churches were correspondingly dark on the inside. Their massive walls and pillars gave Romanesque churches a sense of solidity and almost the impression of a fortress.

The Gothic Cathedral Begun in the twelfth century and brought to perfection in the thirteenth, the **Gothic** cathedral remains one of the greatest artistic triumphs of the High Middle Ages. Soaring skyward, as if to reach heaven, it was a fitting symbol for medieval people's preoccupation with God.

Two fundamental innovations of the twelfth century made Gothic cathedrals possible. The combination of ribbed vaults and pointed arches replaced the barrel vault of Romanesque churches and enabled builders to make Gothic churches higher than Romanesque ones. The use of pointed arches and ribbed vaults created an impression of upward movement, a sense of weightless upward thrust that implied the energy of God. Another technical innovation, the flying buttress, a heavy arched pier of stone built onto the outside of the walls, made it possible to distribute the weight of the church's vaulted ceilings outward and down and thus eliminate the heavy walls used in Romanesque churches to hold the

Barrel Vaulting. The eleventh and twelfth centuries witnessed an enormous amount of church construction. Using the basilica shape, master builders replaced flat wooden roofs with long, round stone vaults, known as barrel vaults. As this illustration of a Romanesque church in Vienne, France, indicates, the barrel vault limited the size of a church and left little room in the walls for windows.

© The Art Archive/Gianni Dagli Orti

weight of the massive barrel vaults. Thus Gothic cathedrals could be built with thin walls containing magnificent stained-glass windows, which created a play of light inside that varied with the sun at different times of the day. The extensive use of colored light in Gothic cathedrals was not accidental but was executed by people who believed that natural light was a symbol of the divine light of God.

The first fully Gothic church was the abbey of Saint-Denis near Paris, inspired by its famous Abbot Suger (1122–1151) and built between 1140 and 1150. By the mid-thirteenth century, French Gothic architecture, most brilliantly executed in cathedrals in Paris (Notre-Dame), Reims, Amiens, and Chartres, had spread to virtually all of Europe.

A Gothic cathedral was the work of the entire community. All classes contributed to its construction. Master masons, who were both architects and engineers, designed them, and stonemasons and other craftspeople were paid a daily wage and provided the skilled labor to build them. A Gothic cathedral symbolized the chief preoccupation of a medieval Christian community, its dedication to a spiritual ideal. As we have observed before, the largest buildings of an era reflect the values of its

society. The Gothic cathedral, with its towers soaring toward heaven, gave witness to an age when a spiritual impulse underlay most aspects of its existence.

Medieval Europe and the World

Q **Focus Questions:** In what ways did Europeans begin to relate to peoples in other parts of the world after 1000 C.E.? What were the reasons for the Crusades, and who or what benefited the most from them?

As it developed, European civilization remained largely confined to its home continent. Some Europeans, especially merchants, had contacts with parts of Asia and Africa. The goods of Asia and Africa made their way into medieval castles; the works of Muslim philosophers were read in medieval universities. The Vikings were also daring explorers. After 860, they sailed westward in their long ships across the North Atlantic Ocean, reaching Iceland in 874. Erik the Red, a Viking exiled from Iceland, traveled even farther west and discovered Greenland in 985. The only known Viking site in North America was found in Newfoundland, but it proved to be short-lived as Viking expansion drew to a close by the tenth century. At the end of the eleventh century, however, Europeans

The Gothic Cathedral. The Gothic cathedral was one of the great artistic triumphs of the High Middle Ages. Shown here is the cathedral of Notre-Dame in Paris. Begun in 1163, it was not completed until the beginning of the fourteenth century.

© S. Grandadam/Photo Researchers, Inc.

France toward the end of 1095, Urban challenged Christians to take up their weapons and join in a holy war to recover the Holy Land. The pope promised remission of sins: "All who die by the way, whether by land or by sea, or in battle against the pagans, shall have immediate remission of sins. This I grant them through the power of God with which I am invested."[10] The enthusiastic crowd cried out in response: "It is the will of God, it is the will of God."

The initial response to Urban's speech reveals how appealing many people found this combined call to military arms and religious fervor. A self-appointed leader, Peter the Hermit, who preached of his visions of the Holy City of Jerusalem, convinced a large mob, most of them poor and many of them peasants, to undertake a Crusade to liberate the city. One person who encountered Peter described him in these words: "Outdoors he wore a woolen tunic, which revealed his ankles, and above it a hood; he wore a cloak to cover his upper body, a bit of his arms, but his feet were bare. He drank wine and ate fish, but scarcely ever ate bread. This man, partly because of his reputation, partly because of his preaching, [assembled] a very large army."[1]

This "Peasant's Crusade" or "Crusade of the Poor" consisted of a ragtag rabble that moved through the

© Scala/Art Resource, NY

The First Crusade. Recruited from the noble class of western Europe, the first crusading army reached Constantinople by 1097. By 1098, the crusaders had taken Antioch. Working down the coast of Palestine, they captured Jerusalem in 1099. Shown here in a fifteenth-century Flemish painting is a fanciful re-creation of the punishments that were meted out to the defeated Muslim forces. Seen in the background is a panoramic view of mutilations, crucifixions, and hangings.

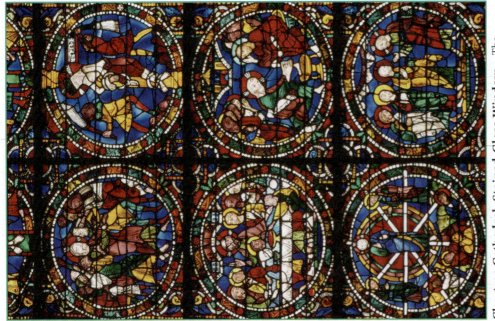

© Adam Woolfitt/CORBIS

Chartres Cathedral: Stained-Glass Window. The stained glass of Gothic cathedrals is remarkable for the beauty and variety of its colors. Stained-glass windows depicted a remarkable variety of scenes. The windows of Chartres Cathedral, for example, present the saints, views of the everyday activities of ordinary men and women, and, as in this panel, scenes from the life of Jesus.

began their first concerted attempt to expand beyond the frontiers of Europe by conquering the land of Palestine.

The First Crusades

The Crusades were based on the idea of a holy war against infidels (unbelievers). Christian wrath against Muslims had already found some expression in the attempt to wrest Spain from the Moors and the success of the Normans in reclaiming Sicily. At the end of the eleventh century, Christian Europe found itself with a glorious opportunity to go after the Muslims when the Byzantine emperor, Alexius I, asked Pope Urban II for help against the Seljuk Turks (see Chapter 13). The pope saw this as a chance to rally the warriors of Europe for the liberation of Jerusalem and the Holy Land of Palestine from the infidels. The Holy City of Jerusalem had long been the focus of Christian pilgrimages. At the Council of Clermont in southern

Balkans, terrorizing natives and looting for their food and supplies. Their misplaced religious enthusiasm led to another tragic by-product as well, the persecution of the Jews, long pictured by the church as the murderers of Christ. As a contemporary chronicler described it, "They persecuted the hated race of the Jews wherever they were found." Two bands of peasant crusaders, led by Peter the Hermit, managed to reach Constantinople. The Byzantine emperor wisely shipped them over to Asia Minor, where the Turks massacred the undisciplined and poorly armed mob.

Pope Urban II did not share the wishful thinking of the peasant crusaders but was more inclined to trust knights who had been well trained in the art of war. Three organized crusading bands of noble warriors, most of them French, made their way eastward. The crusading army probably numbered several thousand cavalry and as many as ten thousand infantry. After the capture of Antioch in 1098, much of the crusading host proceeded down the Palestinian coast, evading the well-defended coastal cities, and reached Jerusalem in June 1099. After a five-week siege, the Holy City was taken amid a horrible massacre of the inhabitants—men, women, and children (see the box on p. 202).

After further conquest of Palestinian lands, the crusaders ignored the wishes of the Byzantine emperor and organized four Latin crusader states.

Because the crusader kingdoms were surrounded by Muslims hostile to them, they grew increasingly dependent on the Italian commercial cities for supplies from Europe. Some Italian cities, such as Genoa, Pisa, and especially Venice, grew rich and powerful in the process.

But it was not easy for the crusader kingdoms to maintain themselves. Already by the 1120s, the Muslims had begun to strike back. The fall of one of the Latin kingdoms in 1144 led to renewed calls for another Crusade, especially from the monastic firebrand Saint Bernard of Clairvaux. He exclaimed, "Now, on account of our sins, the enemies of the cross have begun to show their faces.... What are you doing, you servants of the cross? Will you throw to the dogs that which is most holy? Will you cast pearls before swine?"12 Bernard even managed to enlist two powerful rulers, but their Second Crusade proved to be a total failure.

The Third Crusade was a reaction to the fall of the Holy City of Jerusalem in 1187 to the Muslim forces under Saladin. Now all of Christendom was ablaze with calls for a new Crusade. Three major monarchs agreed to lead their forces in person: Emperor Frederick Barbarossa of Germany (1152–1190), Richard I the Lionhearted of England (1189–1199), and Philip II Augustus, king of France (1180–1223). Some of the crusaders finally arrived in the Holy Land by 1189 only to encounter problems. Frederick Barbarossa drowned while swimming in a local river, and his army quickly disintegrated. The English and French arrived by sea and met with success against the coastal cities, where they had the support of their fleets, but when they moved inland, they failed miserably. Eventually, after Philip went home, Richard the Lionhearted negotiated a settlement whereby Saladin agreed to allow Christian pilgrims free access to Jerusalem.

The Later Crusades

After the death of Saladin in 1193, Pope Innocent III initiated the Fourth Crusade. On its way east, the crusading army became involved in a dispute over the succession to the Byzantine throne. The Venetian leaders of the Fourth Crusade saw an opportunity to neutralize their greatest commercial competitor, the Byzantine Empire. Diverted to Constantinople, the crusaders sacked the great capital city of Byzantium in 1204 and set up the new Latin Empire of Constantinople (see Chapter 13). Not until 1261 did a Byzantine army recapture Constantinople. In the meantime, additional Crusades were undertaken to reconquer the Holy Land. All of them were largely disasters, and by the end of the thirteenth century, the European military effort to capture Palestine was recognized as a complete failure.

Crusader Kingdoms in Palestine

Effects of the Crusades

Whether the Crusades had much effect on European civilization is debatable. The crusaders made little long-term impact on the Middle East, where the only visible remnants of their conquests were their castles. There may

CHRONOLOGY The Crusades	
Pope Urban II's call for a Crusade at Clermont	1095
First Crusade	1096–1099
Second Crusade	1147–1149
Saladin's conquest of Jerusalem	1187
Third Crusade	1189–1192
Fourth Crusade—sack of Constantinople	1204
Latin Empire of Constantinople	1204–1261

have been some broadening of perspective that comes from the exchange between two cultures, but the interaction of Christian Europe with the Muslim world was actually both more intense and more meaningful in Spain and Sicily than in the Holy Land.

Did the Crusades help stabilize European society by removing large numbers of young warriors who would have fought each other in Europe? Some historians think so and believe that Western monarchs established their control more easily as a result. There is no doubt that the Crusades did contribute to the economic growth of the Italian port cities, especially Genoa, Pisa, and Venice. But it is important to remember that the growing wealth and

population of twelfth-century Europe had made the Crusades possible in the first place. The Crusades may have enhanced the revival of trade, but they certainly did not cause it. Even without the Crusades, Italian merchants would have pursued new trade contacts with the Eastern world.

The Crusades prompted evil side effects that would haunt European society for generations. The first widespread attacks on the Jews began with the Crusades. As some Christians argued, to undertake holy wars against infidel Muslims while the "murderers of Christ" ran free at home was unthinkable. The massacre of Jews became a regular feature of medieval European life.

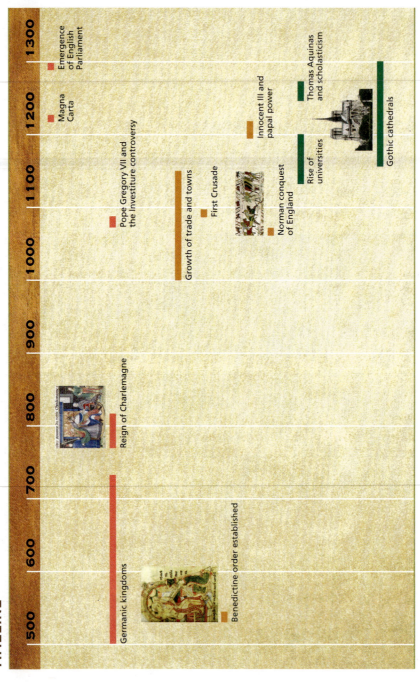

500	600	700	800	900	1000	1100	1200	1300

Germanic kingdoms

Benedictine order established

Reign of Charlemagne

Pope Gregory VII and the Investiture controversy

Growth of trade and towns

First Crusade

Norman conquest of England

Innocent III and papal power

Rise of universities

Thomas Aquinas and scholasticism

Magna Carta

Emergence of English Parliament

Gothic cathedrals

CONCLUSION

After the collapse of the Han dynasty in the third century C.E., China experienced nearly four centuries of internal chaos, until the Tang dynasty in the seventh century attempted to follow the pattern of the Han dynasty and restore the power of the Chinese empire. The fall of the Western Roman Empire in the fifth century brought a quite different result as three new civilizations emerged out of the collapse of Roman power in the Mediterranean.

A new world of Islam emerged in the east; it occupied large parts of the old Roman Empire, preserved much of Greek culture, and created its own flourishing civilization. As we shall see in Chapter 13, the eastern part of the old Roman Empire, increasingly Greek in culture, continued to survive as the Christian Byzantine Empire. At the same time, a new Christian European civilization was establishing its roots in the west. By the eleventh and twelfth centuries, these three heirs of Rome began their own conflict for control of the lands of the eastern Mediterranean.

The coronation of Charlemagne, the descendant of a Germanic tribe converted to Christianity, as Roman emperor in 800 symbolized the fusion of the three chief components of the new European civilization: the German tribes, the Roman legacy, and the Christian church. Charlemagne's Carolingian Empire fostered the idea of a distinct European identity. With the disintegration of that empire, however, power fell into the hands of many different lords, who came to constitute a nobility that dominated Europe's political, economic, and social life. But quietly and surely, within this world of castles and private power, kings gradually began during the High Middle Ages to develop the machinery of government and accumulate political authority. Although they could not know it then, the actions of these medieval monarchs laid the foundation for the European kingdoms that in one form or another have dominated the European political scene ever since.

The revival of trade, the expansion of towns and cities, and the development of a money economy did not mean the end of a predominantly rural European society, but they did open the door to new ways to make a living and new opportunities for people to expand and enrich their lives. At the same time, the High Middle Ages also gave birth to a cultural revival that led to new centers of learning in the universities, to the use of reason to systematize the study of theology, and to a dramatic increase in the number and size of churches.

The Roman Catholic Church shared in the challenge of new growth by reforming itself and striking out on a path toward greater papal power, both within the church hierarchy and over European society. The High Middle Ages witnessed a spiritual renewal that enhanced papal leadership and the religious lives of the clergy and the laity. At the same time, this spiritual renewal also gave rise to the crusading "holy warrior" who killed for God, thereby creating an animosity between Christians and Muslims that still has repercussions to this day.

CHAPTER NOTES

1. Quoted in N. F. Cantor, ed., *The Medieval World, 300–1300* (New York, 1963), p. 104.
2. A. Barbero, *Charlemagne: Father of a Continent*, trans. A. Cameron (Berkeley, Calif., 2004), p. 4.
3. Quoted in S. Keynes, "The Vikings in England, c. 790–1016," in P. Sawyer, ed., *The Oxford Illustrated History of the Vikings* (Oxford, 1997), p. 81.
4. Quoted in M. Perry, J. Peden, and T. von Laue, *Sources of the Western Tradition*, vol. 1 (Boston, 1987), p. 218.
5. Quoted in J. Gies and F. Gies, *Life in a Medieval Castle* (New York, 1974), p. 175.
6. Quoted in J. Gimpel, *The Medieval Machine* (Harmondsworth, England, 1977), p. 92.
7. O. J. Thatcher and E. H. McNeal, eds., *A Source Book for Medieval History* (New York, 1905), p. 208.
8. Quoted in R. H. C. Davis, *A History of Medieval Europe from Constantine to Saint Louis*, 2d ed. (New York, 1988), p. 252.
9. Quoted in R. Brooke and C. Brooke, *Popular Religion in the Middle Ages* (London, 1984), p. 19.
10. Quoted in Thatcher and McNeal, *Source Book for Medieval History*, p. 517.
11. Quoted in T. Asbridge, *The First Crusade: A New History* (Oxford, 2004), pp. 79–80.
12. Quoted in H. E. Mayer, *The Crusades*, trans. J. Gillingham (New York, 1972), pp. 99–100.

SUGGESTED READING

General Histories of the Middle Ages

For general histories of the Middle Ages, see **E. Peters, *Europe and the Middle Ages***, 2d ed. (Englewood Cliffs, N.J., 1989); **D. Nicholas, *The Evolution of the Medieval World: Society, Government, and Thought in Europe, 312–1500*** (London, 1993); and **B. Rosenwein, *A Short History of the Middle Ages*** (Orchard Park, N.Y., 2002). A brief history of the Middle Ages can be found in **R. Collins, *Early Medieval Europe, 300–1000*** (New York, 1991).

Carolingian Europe

Carolingian Europe is examined in **P. Riche, *The Carolingians: A Family Who Forged Europe*** (Philadelphia, 1993). On Charlemagne, see **A. Barbero, *Charlemagne: Father of a Continent***, trans. A. Cameron (Berkeley, Calif., 2004).

The Vikings and Fief-Holding

The Vikings are examined in **M. Arnold, *The Vikings: Culture and Conquest*** (London, 2006), and **R. Hall, *The World of the Vikings*** (New York, 2007). Two introductory works on fief-holding are **J. R. Strayer, *Feudalism*** (Princeton, N.J., 1985), and the classic work by **M. Bloch, *Feudal Society*** (London, 1961). For an important revisionist view, see **S. Reynolds, *Fiefs and Vassals*** (Oxford, 1994).

General Works on the High Middle Ages

For a good introduction to the High Middle Ages, see **W. C. Jordan, *Europe in the High Middle Ages*** (New York, 2003); **J. H. Mundy, *Europe in the High Middle Ages, 1150–1309*, 3d ed.** (New York, 1999); and **M. Barber, *The Two Cities: Medieval Europe, 1050–1320*** (London, 1992).

Economic and Social Conditions

On economic conditions in the Middle Ages, see **N. J. G. Pounds, *An Economic History of Medieval Europe*** (New York, 1974). Urban history is covered in **D. Nicholas, *The Growth of the Medieval City: From Late Antiquity to the Early Fourteenth Century*** (New York, 1997). On women in general, see **L. Bitel, *Women in Early Medieval Europe, 400–1100*** (Cambridge, 2002), and **M. P. P. Cosman, *Women at Work in Medieval Europe*** (New York, 2001). On peasant life, see **R. Fossier, *Peasant Life in the Medieval West*** (New York, 1988). On daily life in the medieval city, see **C. Frugoi, *A Day in a Medieval City***, trans. W. McCuaig (Chicago, 2006).

The Medieval States

There are numerous works on the various medieval states. On England, see **R. Frame, *The Political Development of the British Isles, 1100–1400*, 2d ed.** (Oxford, 1995).

On Germany, see H. Fuhrmann, *Germany in the High Middle Ages, c. 1050–1250* (Cambridge, 1986), an excellent account, and B. Arnold, *Princes and Territories in Medieval Germany* (Cambridge, 1991). On France, see J. Dunbabib, *France in the Making, 843–1180*, 2d ed. (Oxford, 2000). On Italy, see P. Jones, *The Italian City-State: From Commune to Signoria* (Oxford, 1997). On eastern Europe, see N. Davies, *God's Playground: A History of Poland*, vol. 1: *The Origins to 1795*, rev. ed. (New York, 2004), and S. Franklin and J. Shephard, *The Emergence of Rus, 750–1200* (New York, 1996).

The Christian Church in the Middle Ages For a general survey of Christianity in the Middle Ages, see J. H. Lynch, *The Medieval Church: A Brief History* (London, 1995). For a superb introduction to early Christianity, see P. Brown, *The Rise of Western Christendom: Triumph and Adversity, A.D. 200–1000*, 2d ed. (Oxford, 2002). On the papacy in the High Middle Ages, see I. S. Robinson, *The Papacy* (Cambridge, 1990). The papacy of Innocent III is covered in J. E. Sayers, *Innocent III, Leader of Europe, 1198–1216* (New York, 1994), and J. C. Moore, *Pope Innocent III* (New York, 2003). Works on monasticism include C. H. Lawrence, *Medieval Monasticism*, 3d ed. (London, 2000), a good general account, and H. Leyser, *Hermits and the New Monasticism* (London, 1984).

Culture of the High Middle Ages On medieval intellectual life, see M. L. Colish, *Medieval Foundations of the Western Intellectual Tradition, 400–1400* (New Haven, Conn., 1997). A good introduction to Romanesque style is A. Petzold, *Romanesque Art*, rev. ed. (New York, 2003). On the Gothic movement, see M. Camille, *Gothic Art: Glorious Visions*, rev. ed. (New York, 2003), and C. Wilson, *The Gothic Cathedral* (London, 1990).

The Crusades For a detailed survey of the Crusades, see C. Tyerman, *God's War: A New History of the Crusades* (Cambridge, Mass., 2006). Also see J. Riley-Smith, ed., *The Oxford Illustrated History of the Crusades* (New York, 1995); A. Konstan, *Historical Atlas of the Crusades* (New York, 2002); and N. Housley, *Contesting the Crusades* (Oxford, 2006), which discusses the historical debate about the Crusades. On the later Crusades, see N. Housley, *The Later Crusades, 1274–1580* (New York, 1992).

CENGAGENOW Enter *CengageNOW* using the access card that is available with this text. *CengageNOW* will help you understand the content in this chapter with lesson plans generated for your needs, as well as provide you with a connection to the *Wadsworth World History Resource Center* (see description below for details).

WORLD HISTORY RESOURCE CENTER

Enter the Resource Center using either your *CengageNOW* access card or your separate access card for the *World History Resource Center*. Organized by topic, this Website includes quizzes; images; over 350 primary source documents; interactive simulations, maps, and timelines; movie explorations; and a wealth of other resources. You can read the following documents, and many more, at the *World History Resource Center*:

Grant of an Estate to the Monks of Saint-Denis

Thomas Aquinas, *Summa Theologica*

Visit the *World History Companion* Website for chapter quizzes and more:

www.cengage.com/history/Duiker/Worldbe

CHAPTER 13

THE BYZANTINE EMPIRE AND CRISIS AND RECOVERY IN THE WEST

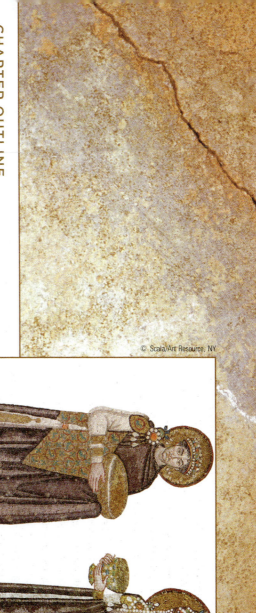

© Scala/Art Resource, NY

CHAPTER OUTLINE AND FOCUS QUESTIONS

From Eastern Roman to Byzantine Empire

Q How did the Byzantine Empire that had emerged by the eighth century differ from the empire of Justinian and from the Germanic kingdoms in the west? How were they alike?

The Zenith of Byzantine Civilization (750–1025)

Q What were the chief developments in the Byzantine Empire between 750 and 1025?

The Decline and Fall of the Byzantine Empire (1025–1453)

Q What impact did the Crusades have on the Byzantine Empire? How and why did Constantinople and the Byzantine Empire fall?

The Crises of the Fourteenth Century

Q What impact did the Black Death have on Europe and Asia in the fourteenth century? What problems did Europeans face during the fourteenth century, and what impact did they have on European economic, social, and religious life?

Recovery: The Renaissance

Q What were the main features of the Renaissance in Europe, and how did it differ from the Middle Ages?

CRITICAL THINKING

Q In what ways did the Byzantine, European, and Islamic civilizations resemble and differ from each other? Were their relationships overall based on cooperation or conflict?

Justinian and Theodora

AT THE SAME TIME that medieval European civilization was emerging in the West, the eastern part of the old Roman Empire, increasingly Greek in culture, continued to survive as the Byzantine Empire. While serving as a buffer between Europe and the peoples to the east, especially the growing empire of Islam, the Byzantine or Eastern Roman Empire also preserved the intellectual and legal accomplishments of the Greeks and Romans.

The early Byzantine Empire was beset by crises. Soon after the beginning of his reign, the emperor Justinian was faced with a serious revolt in the capital city of Constantinople. In 532, followers of both the Blues and the Greens, two factions of supporters of chariot teams that competed in the Hippodrome, a huge amphitheater, joined together and rioted to protest the emperor's taxation policies. The riots soon became a revolt as insurgents burned and looted the center of the city, shouting *"Nika!"* (victory), a word normally used to cheer on their favorite teams. Aristocratic factions joined the revolt and put forward a nobleman named Hypatius as a new emperor. Justinian seemed ready to flee, but his wife, the empress Theodora, strengthened his resolve by declaring,

363

The Reign of Justinian (527–565)

In the sixth century, the empire in the east came under the control of one of its most remarkable rulers, the emperor Justinian. As the nephew and heir of the previous emperor, Justinian had been well trained in imperial administration. He was determined to reestablish the Roman Empire in the entire Mediterranean world and began his attempt to reconquer the west in 533.

Justinian's army under Belisarius, probably the best general of the late Roman world, presented a formidable force. Belisarius sailed to North Africa and quickly defeated the Vandals in two major battles. From North Africa, he led his forces onto the Italian peninsula after occupying Sicily in 535. But it was not until 552 that the Ostrogoths were finally defeated. The struggle devastated Italy, which suffered more from Justinian's reconquest than from all of the previous barbarian invasions.

Justinian has long been criticized for overextending his resources and bankrupting the empire. Historians now think, however, that a devastating plague in 542 and long-term economic factors were far more damaging to the Eastern Roman Empire than Justinian's conquests. Before he died, Justinian appeared to have achieved his goals. He had restored the imperial Mediterranean world; his empire included Italy, part of Spain, North Africa, Asia Minor, Palestine, and Syria (see Map 13.1). But the conquest of the western empire proved fleeting. Only three years after Justinian's death, the Lombards entered Italy. Although the eastern empire maintained the fiction of Italy as a province, its forces were limited to small pockets here and there.

The Codification of Roman Law

Though his conquests proved short-lived, Justinian made a lasting contribution to Western civilization through his codification of Roman law. The eastern empire was heir to a vast quantity of materials connected to the development of Roman law. These included laws passed by the senate and assemblies, legal commentaries of jurists, decisions of praetors, and the edicts of emperors. Justinian had been well trained in imperial government and was thoroughly acquainted with Roman law. He wished to codify and simplify this mass of materials.

To accomplish his goal, Justinian authorized the jurist Trebonian to make a systematic compilation of imperial edicts. The result was the Code of Law, the first part of the *Corpus Iuris Civilis* (Body of Civil Law), completed in 529. Four years later, two other parts of the *Corpus* appeared: the *Digest*, a compendium of writings of Roman jurists, and the *Institutes*, a brief summary of the chief principles of Roman law that could be used as a textbook. The fourth part of the *Corpus* was the *Novels*, a compilation of the most important new edicts issued during Justinian's reign.

Justinian's codification of Roman law became the basis of imperial law in the Byzantine Empire until its end in 1453. More important, however, since it was

according to the historian Procopius, "If now, it is your wish to save yourself, O Emperor, there is no difficulty. For we have much money, and there is the sea, here the boats. However, consider whether it will not come about after you have been saved that you would gladly exchange that safety for death. For as for myself, I approve a certain ancient saying that royalty is a good burial-shroud."[1] Shamed by his wife's words, Justinian resolved to fight. A Byzantine army, newly returned from fighting the Persians, was ordered to attack a large crowd that had gathered in the Hippodrome to acclaim Hypatius as emperor. In the ensuing massacre, the imperial troops slaughtered thirty thousand of the insurgents, about 5 percent of the city's population. After crushing the Nika Revolt, Justinian began a massive rebuilding program and continued the autocratic reign that established the foundations of the Byzantine Empire.

Despite the early empire's reversals, the Macedonian emperors in the ninth, tenth, and eleventh centuries enlarged the empire, achieved economic prosperity, and expanded its cultural influence to eastern Europe and Russia. But after the Macedonian dynasty ended in 1056 C.E., the empire began a slow but steady decline. Involvement in the Crusades proved especially disastrous, leading to the occupation of Constantinople by Western crusading forces in 1204. Although the empire was restored under Byzantine rule in 1261, it limped along for another 190 years until its weakened condition finally enabled the Ottoman Turks to conquer it in 1453.

In the fourteenth century, Europe, too, sustained a series of crises and reversals after flourishing during the three centuries of the High Middle Ages. Unlike the Byzantine Empire, however, European civilization rebounded in the fifteenth century, experiencing an artistic and intellectual revival in the Renaissance as well as a renewal of monarchical authority among the western European states. Europe was poised to begin its dramatic entry into world affairs. ◆

From Eastern Roman to Byzantine Empire

Q **Focus Questions:** How did the Byzantine Empire that had emerged by the eighth century differ from the empire of Justinian and from the Germanic kingdoms in the west? How were they alike?

As noted earlier, the western and eastern parts of the Roman Empire began to drift apart in the fourth century. As the Germanic peoples moved into the western part of the empire and established various kingdoms over the course of the fifth century, the Roman Empire in the east, centered on Constantinople, solidified and prospered.

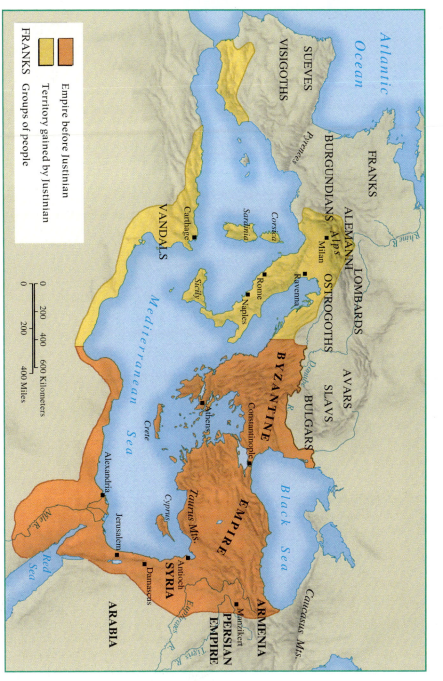

Look back at Map 5.3. What former Roman territories lay outside Justinian's control?

MAP 13.1 The Byzantine Empire in the Time of Justinian. The Byzantine emperor Justinian briefly restored much of the Mediterranean portion of the old Roman Empire. His general, Belisarius, conquered the Vandals in North Africa quite easily but wrested Italy from the Ostrogoths only after a long and devastating struggle.

FRANKS Groups of people

Empire before Justinian

Territory gained by Justinian

written in Latin (it was, in fact, the last product of eastern Roman culture to be written in Latin, which was soon replaced by Greek), it was also eventually used in the West and in fact became the basis of the legal system of all of continental Europe.

The Empress Theodora Theodora was the daughter of the "keeper of bears" for the games at Constantinople, who died when she was a child. Theodora followed in her mother's footsteps by becoming an actress, which at that time was considered a lower-class activity. Often actresses also worked as prostitutes, and Theodora was no exception. At the age of twenty-five, she met Justinian, who was forty. His father, the emperor Justin, had to change the law to allow his aristocratic senator son to marry a woman who had been an actress. After his father died in 527, Justinian became emperor and Theodora empress, a remarkable achievement for a woman from the lower classes.

Justinian and Theodora were close and loving companions. She also influenced her husband in both church and state affairs. A strong-willed and intelligent woman, she proved especially valuable in 532, when her steely resolve during the Nika Revolt caused Justinian not to flee but to fight and crush the protesters.

Theodora also helped establish a number of churches and monasteries, including a convent for former prostitutes.

The Emperor's Building Program After the riots destroyed much of Constantinople, Justinian rebuilt the city and gave it the appearance it would keep for almost a thousand years (see Map 13.2). Earlier, Emperor Theodosius II (408–450) had constructed an enormous defensive wall to protect the capital on its land side. The city was dominated by an immense palace complex, a huge arena known as the Hippodrome, and hundreds of churches. No residential district was particularly fashionable; palaces, tenements, and slums ranged alongside one another. Justinian added many new buildings. His public works projects included roads, bridges, walls, public baths, law courts, and colossal underground reservoirs to hold the city's water supply. He also built hospitals, schools, monasteries, and churches. Churches were his special passion, and in Constantinople he built or rebuilt thirty-four of them. His greatest achievement was the famous Hagia Sophia, the Church of the Holy Wisdom.

Completed in 537, Hagia Sophia was designed by two Greek scientists who departed radically from the

© Scala/Art Resource, NY

The Emperor Justinian and His Court. As the seat of Byzantine power in Italy, the town of Ravenna became adorned with examples of Byzantine art. The Church of San Vitale at Ravenna contains some of the finest examples of sixth-century Byzantine mosaics, in which small pieces of colored glass were set in mortar on the wall to form these figures and their surroundings. The emperor is seen as both head of state (he wears a jeweled crown and a purple robe) and head of the church (he carries a gold bowl symbolizing the body of Jesus).

simple, flat-roofed basilica of Western architecture. The center of Hagia Sophia consisted of four huge piers crowned by an enormous dome, which seemed to be floating in space. This effect was emphasized by Procopius, the court historian, who at Justinian's request wrote a treatise on the emperor's building projects: "From the lightness of the building, it does not appear to rest upon a solid foundation, but to cover the place beneath as though it were suspended from heaven by the fabled golden chain." In part, this impression was created by putting forty-two windows around the base of the dome, which allowed an incredible play of light within the cathedral. Light served to remind the worshipers of God; as Procopius commented:

Whoever enters there to worship perceives at once that it is not by any human strength or skill, but by the favor of God that this work has been perfected; his mind rises sublime to commune with God, feeling that He cannot be far off, but must especially

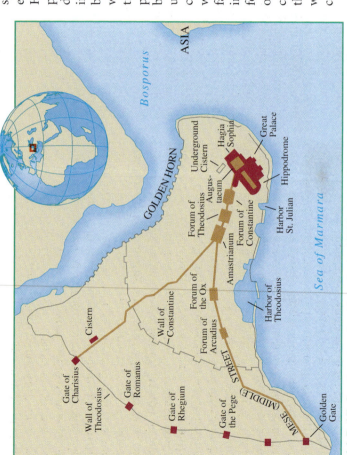

MAP 13.2 Constantinople. In the Middle Ages, Constantinople was the largest European city and a nexus of trade between east and west. Emperor Justinian oversaw a massive building program that produced important architectural monuments such as Hagia Sophia.

Q What natural and human-built aspects of the city helped protect it from invasion?

© Scala/Art Resource, NY

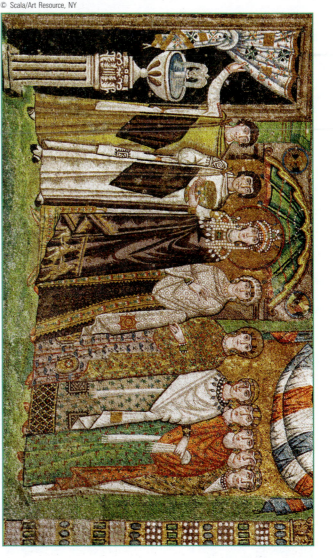

Theodora and Attendants.   This mosaic, located on the south wall of the apse of the Church of San Vitale (Justinian is on the north wall), depicts Theodora and her attendants. Her presence on the wall of this church indicates the important role she played in the Byzantine state. At the bottom of her robe is a scene of the Three Wise Men, an indication that Theodora was special enough to have belonged in the company of the three kings who visited the newborn Jesus.

love to dwell in the place which He has chosen; and this takes place not only when a man sees it for the first time, but it always makes the same impression upon him, as though he had never beheld it before.[2]

As darkness is illuminated by invisible light, so too, it was believed, the world is illuminated by invisible spirit.

The royal palace complex, Hagia Sophia, and the Hippodrome were the three greatest buildings in Constantinople. This last was a huge amphitheater, constructed of brick covered by marble, holding as many as sixty thousand spectators. Although gladiator fights were held there, the main events were the chariot races; twenty-four races usually be presented in one day. The citizens of Constantinople were passionate fans of chariot racing. Successful charioteers were acclaimed as heroes and honored with public statues. Crowds in the Hippodrome also took on political significance. Being a member of the two chief factions of charioteers—the Blues or the Greens—was the only real outlet for political expression. Even emperors had to be aware of their demands and attitudes: the loss of a race in the Hippodrome frequently resulted in bloody riots, and rioting could threaten the emperor's power.

A New Kind of Empire

Justinian's accomplishments had been spectacular, but when he died, he left the Eastern Roman Empire with serious problems: too much distant territory to protect, an empty treasury, a smaller population after a devastating plague, and renewed threats to the frontiers. The seventh

century proved to be an important turning point in the history of Byzantine Empire.

Problems of the Seventh Century   In the first half of the century, during the reign of Heraclius (610–641), the empire faced attacks from the Persians to the east and the Slavs to the north. A new system of defense was put in place, using a new and larger administrative unit, the *theme*, which combined civilian and military offices in the hands of the same person. Thus the civil governor was also the military leader of the area. Although this innovation helped the empire survive, it also fostered an increased militarization of the empire. By the mid-seventh century, it had become apparent that a restored Mediterranean empire was simply beyond the resources of the empire, which now increasingly turned its back on the Latin west. A renewed series of external threats in the second half of the seventh century strengthened this development.

The most serious challenge to the empire was the rise of Islam, which unified the Arab tribes and created a powerful new force that swept through the region (see Chapter 7). The defeat of an eastern Roman army at Yarmuk in 636 meant the loss of the provinces of Syria and Palestine. The Arabs also moved into the old Persian Empire and conquered it. An Arab attempt to besiege Constantinople that began in 674 failed, in large part due to the use of Greek fire against the Arab fleets. Greek fire was a petroleum-based compound containing quicklime and sulfur. Because it would burn under water, the Byzantines created the equivalent of modern

CHRONOLOGY The Byzantine Empire to 750

Justinian codifies Roman law	529–533
Reconquest of Italy by the Byzantines	535–552
Completion of Hagia Sophia	537
Attacks on the empire in the reign of Heraclius	610–641
Arab defeat of the Byzantines at Yarmuk	636
Defeat by the Bulgars; losses in the Balkans	679
Leo III and iconoclasm	717–741

eastern Mediterranean state. These external challenges had important internal repercussions as well. By the eighth century, the Eastern Roman Empire had been transformed into what historians call the Byzantine Empire, a civilization with its own unique character that would last until 1453 (Constantinople was built on the site of an older city named Byzantium, hence the name *Byzantine*).

The Byzantine Empire in the Eighth Century The Byzantine Empire was a Greek state. Justinian's *Corpus Iuris Civilis* had been the last official work published in Latin. Increasingly, Latin fell into disuse as Greek became not only the common language of the Byzantine Empire but its official language as well.

The Byzantine Empire was also a Christian state, built on a faith in Jesus that was shared in a profound way by almost all its citizens. An enormous amount of artistic talent was poured into the construction of churches, church ceremonies, and church decoration. Spiritual principles deeply permeated Byzantine art. The importance of religion to the Byzantines explains why theological disputes took on an exaggerated form. The most famous of these disputes, the so-called iconoclastic controversy, threatened the stability of the empire in the first half of the eighth century.

Beginning in the sixth century, the use of religious images, especially in the form of icons or pictures of sacred figures, became so widespread that charges of idolatry, the worship of images, began to be heard. The use of images or icons had been justified by the argument that icons were not worshiped but were simply used to help illiterate people understand their religion. This argument failed to stop the **iconoclasts,** as the opponents of icons were called.

Iconoclasm was not unique to the Byzantine Empire. In the neighboring Islamic empire, religious art did not include any physical representations of Muhammad (see the comparative illustration on p. 369). Iconoclasm would also play a role among some of the new religious groups that emerged in the Protestant Reformation in sixteenth-century Europe (see Chapter 15).

Beginning in 730, the Byzantine emperor Leo III (717–741)

© Erich Lessing/Art Resource, NY

Interior View of Hagia Sophia. Pictured here is the interior of the Church of the Holy Wisdom in Constantinople (modern Istanbul), constructed under Justinian by Anthemius of Tralles and Isidore of Milan. Some of the stones used in the construction of the church had been plundered from the famous classical Temple of Diana, near Ephesus, in Turkey. This view gives an idea of how the windows around the base of the dome produced a special play of light within the cathedral. The pulpits and plaques bearing inscriptions from the Qur'an were introduced when the Turks converted this church to a mosque in the fifteenth century.

flamethrowers by using tubes to blow Greek fire onto wooden ships, with frightening effect. Arabs and eastern Roman forces now faced each other along a frontier in southern Asia Minor.

Problems also arose along the northern frontier, especially in the Balkans, where an Asiatic people known as the Bulgars had arrived earlier in the sixth century. In 679, the Bulgars defeated the eastern Roman forces and took possession of the lower Danube valley, setting up a strong Bulgarian kingdom.

By the beginning of the eighth century, the Eastern Roman Empire was greatly diminished in size, consisting only of a portion of the Balkans and Asia Minor. It was now an

The Byzantine Empire, c. 750

© Art Resource, NY

COMPARATIVE ILLUSTRATION

ARTS & IDEAS

Religious Imagery in the Medieval World.

The Middle Ages was a golden age of religious art, which reflects the important role of religion itself in medieval society. These three illustrations show different aspects of medieval religious imagery.

Illuminated manuscripts were an especially valuable source for Christian art in Europe. The illustration at top left shows a page centered on the figure of Jesus from *The Book of Kells*, a richly decorated illustrated manuscript of the Christian gospels produced by the monks of Iona in the British Isles. Byzantine art was also deeply religious, which was especially evident in the icon. At top right is an icon of the Virgin and Child (Mary and Jesus) from the monastery of Saint Catherine at Mount Sinai in Egypt dating to around the year 600. Painted on wood, this icon shows the enthroned Virgin and Child between Saints Theodore and George with two angels behind them looking upward to a beam of light containing the hand of God. The figures are not realistic; the goal of the icon was to bridge the gap between the divine and the outer material world. Artists in the Muslim world faced a different challenge—Muslims warned against imitating God by creating pictures of living beings, thus effectively prohibiting the representation of humans, especially Muhammad. Islamic religious artists therefore used decorative motifs based on geometric patterns and the Arabic script. The scriptural panel in the lower illustration is an artistic presentation of a verse from the Qur'an, thus blending the spiritual and artistic spheres.

Q How is the importance of religious imagery in the Middle Ages evident in these three illustrations?

© Vanni/Art Resource, NY

© Erich Lessing/Art Resource, NY

outlawed the use of icons. Strong resistance ensued, especially from monks. Leo also used the iconoclastic controversy to add to the prestige of the patriarch of Constantinople, the highest church official in the east and second in dignity only to the bishop of Rome. The Roman popes were opposed to the iconoclastic edicts, and their opposition created considerable dissension between the popes and the Byzantine emperors. Late in the eighth century, the Byzantine rulers reversed their stand on the use of images, but not before considerable damage had been done to the unity of the Christian church. Although the final separation between Roman Catholicism and Greek Orthodoxy (as the Christian church in the Byzantine Empire was called) did not occur until 1054, the iconoclastic controversy was important in moving both sides in that direction.

The Byzantine Empire was characterized by what might be called a permanent war economy. Byzantine emperors maintained the late Roman policy of state regulation of economic affairs. Of course, it was easy to justify; the survival of the empire was dependent on careful shepherding of economic resources and the maintenance of the army. Thus the state encouraged agricultural production, regulated the guilds or corporations responsible for industrial production and the various stages of manufacturing, and controlled commerce by making trade in grain and silk, the two most valuable products, government monopolies.

The emperor occupied a crucial position in the Byzantine state. Portrayed as chosen by God, the Byzantine emperor was crowned in elaborate sacred ceremonies, and his subjects were expected to prostrate themselves in his presence. The wives of the emperors also played significant roles in the court rituals that upheld imperial authority. The emperors' power was considered absolute and was limited in practice only by deposition or assassination. Emperors were assisted by a rather unusual ruling class. Civil servants and high churchmen essentially stemmed from the same ranks of the urban society of Constantinople. They received the same education and often followed the same careers in civil service until they went their separate ways into church and government offices. A strong bureaucracy was one of the most basic features of the Byzantine Empire.

Because of their many foreign enemies, Byzantine emperors spent considerable energy on war and preparation for war. Common to Byzantine literature were manuals on war, instructing people in the ways of fighting (see the box on p. 371). Byzantine armies, often led by the emperors, were well trained and equipped with the latest weapons. The Byzantines, however, often preferred the use of diplomacy to offset the need to fight. Our word *byzantine*—often defined as "extremely complicated" or "carried on by underhanded methods"—stems from the complex and crafty instructions that Byzantine rulers sent to their envoys.

Because the emperor appointed the patriarch, he also exercised control over both church and state. The Byzantines believed that God had commanded their state to preserve the true faith, Orthodox Christianity. Emperor, clergy, and civic officials were all bound together in service to this ideal. It can be said that spiritual values truly held the Byzantine state together.

By 750, it was apparent that two of Rome's heirs, the Germanic kingdoms and the Byzantine Empire, were moving in different directions. Nevertheless, Byzantine influence on the Western world was significant. The images of a Roman imperial state that continued to haunt the west lived on in Byzantium. As noted, the legal system of the west came to owe much to Justinian's codification of Roman law. In addition, the Byzantine Empire served in part as a buffer state, protecting the west for a long time from incursions from the east.

Intellectual Life   The intellectual life of the Byzantine Empire was greatly influenced by the traditions of classical civilization. Scholars actively strived to preserve the works of the ancient Greeks and based a great deal of their own literature on classical models. Although the Byzantines produced a substantial body of literature, much of it was of a very practical nature, focusing on legal, military, and administrative matters. The most outstanding literary achievements of the early Byzantine Empire, however, were historical and religious works. Many of the latter were theological treatises, often of an extremely combative nature because of the intense theological controversies. More popular were biographies of saints, which traced the adventures of religious figures who after many struggles achieved a life of virtue.

The best known of the early Byzantine historians was Procopius (c. 500–c. 562), court historian during the reign of Justinian. Procopius served as secretary to the great general Belisarius and accompanied him on his wars on behalf of Justinian. Procopius' best historical work, the *Wars*, is a firsthand account of Justinian's wars of reconquest in the western Mediterranean and his wars against the Persians in the east. Deliberately modeled after the work of his hero, the Greek historian Thucydides (see Chapter 4), Procopius' narrative features vivid descriptions of battle scenes, clear judgment, and noteworthy objectivity.

Procopius also wrote a work that many historians consider mostly scandalous gossip, his infamous *Secret History*. At the start, Procopius informs his readers that "what I shall write now follows a different plan, supplementing the previous formal chronicle with a disclosure of what really happened throughout the Roman Empire."[3] What he reveals constitutes a scathing attack on Justinian and his wife, Theodora, for their alleged misdeeds.

Life in Constantinople: The Importance of Trade   With a population estimated in the hundreds of thousands, Constantinople was the largest city in Europe during the Middle Ages. It viewed itself as the center of an empire and a special Christian city. The Byzantines believed that the city was under the protection of God and the Virgin Mary.

A BYZANTINE EMPEROR GIVES MILITARY ADVICE

POLITICS & GOVERNMENT

To an empire surrounded by enemies on all sides, military prowess was an absolute necessity. Both Byzantine emperors and the military forces alone would not suffice and consequently fostered the art of diplomacy and military intelligence. This document is from an early-seventh-century work known as the *Strategikon*, a manual of strategy written by the emperor Maurice (582–602), himself a strong military leader who led his troops into battle. The work is based on the assumption that a detailed knowledge of the habits and fighting skills of their enemies would give the Byzantines an advantage if they had to fight them.

Maurice, *Strategikon*

The light-haired races [Germanic peoples] place great value on freedom. They are bold and undaunted in battle. Daring and impetuous as they are, they consider any timidity and even a short retreat as a disgrace. They calmly despise death as they fight violently in hand-to-hand combat either on horseback or on foot. If they are hard pressed in cavalry actions, they dismount at a single prearranged sign and line up on foot. Although only a few against many horsemen, they do not shrink from the fight. They are armed with shields, lances, and short swords slung from their shoulders. They prefer fighting on foot and rapid charges.

Whether on foot or on horseback, they draw up for battle, not in any fixed measure and formation, or in regiments or divisions, but according to tribes, their kinship with one another, and common interest. Often, as a result, when things are not going well and their friends have been killed, they will risk their lives fighting to avenge them. In combat they make the front of their battle line even and dense. Either on horseback or on foot they are impetuous and undisciplined in charging, as if they were the only people in the world who are not cowards. They are disobedient to their leaders. They are not interested in anything that is at all complicated and pay little attention to external security and their own advantage. They despise good order, especially on horseback. They are easily corrupted by money, greedy as they are.

They are hurt by suffering and fatigue. Although they possess bold and daring spirits, their bodies are pampered and soft, and they are not able to bear pain calmly. In addition, they are hurt by heat, cold, rain, lack of provisions, especially of wine, and postponement of battle. When it comes to a cavalry battle, they are hindered by uneven and wooded terrain. They are easily ambushed along the flanks and to the rear of their battle line, for they do not concern themselves at all with scouts and the other security measures. Their ranks are easily broken by a simulated flight and a sudden turning back against them. Attacks at night by archers often inflict damage, since they are very disorganized in setting up camp.

Above all, therefore, in warring against them one must avoid engaging in pitched battles, especially in the early stages. Instead, make use of well-planned ambushes, sneak attacks, and stratagems. Delay things and ruin their opportunities. Pretend to come to agreements with them. Aim at reducing their boldness and zeal by shortage of provisions or the discomfort of heat or cold. This can be done when our army has pitched camp on rugged and difficult ground. On such terrain this enemy cannot attack successfully because they are using lances. But if a favorable opportunity for a regular battle occurs, line up the army as set forth in the book on formations....

Q *According to Maurice, what are the strengths and weaknesses of the Germanic peoples? Based on his analysis of their traits, what advice does he give his military forces in the event of facing the Germans in battle?*

One thirteenth-century Byzantine said, "About our city you shall know: until the end she will fear no nation whatsoever, for no one will entrap or capture her, not by any means, for she has been given to the Mother of God and no one will snatch her out of Her hands. Many nations will break their horns against her walls and withdraw with shame."[4]

Until the twelfth century, Constantinople was Europe's greatest commercial center. The city was the chief entrepôt for the exchange of products between west and east, and trade formed the basis for its fabulous prosperity. This trade, however, was largely carried on by foreign merchants. As one contemporary said:

All sorts of merchants come here from the land of Babylon, from ...Persia, Media, and all the sovereignty of the land of Egypt, from the lands of Canaan, and from the empire of Russia, from Hungaria, Khazaria [the Caspian region], and the land of Lombardy and Sepharad [Spain]. It is a busy city, and merchants come to it from every country by sea or land, and there is none like it in the world except Baghdad, the great city of Islam.[5]

Highly desired in Europe were the products of the east: silk from China, spices from Southeast Asia and India, jewelry and ivory from India (used by artisans for church items), wheat and furs from southern Russia, and flax and honey from the Balkans. Many of these eastern goods were then shipped to the Mediterranean area and northern Europe. Despite the Germanic incursions, trade with Europe did not entirely end.

Moreover, imported raw materials were used in Constantinople for local industries. During Justinian's reign, two Christian monks smuggled silkworms from China to begin a silk industry. The state had a monopoly on the production of silk cloth, and the workshops themselves were housed in Constantinople's royal palace complex. European demand for silk cloth made it the city's most lucrative product. It is interesting to note that the upper classes, including emperors and empresses, were not discouraged from making money through trade and manufacturing. Indeed, one empress even manufactured perfumes in her bedroom.

The Zenith of Byzantine Civilization (750–1025)

Q Focus Question: What were the chief developments in the Byzantine Empire between 750 and 1025?

In the seventh and eighth centuries, the Byzantine Empire lost much of its territory to Slavs, Bulgars, and Muslims. By 750, the empire consisted only of Asia Minor, some lands in the Balkans, and the southern coast of Italy. Although Byzantium was beset with internal dissension and invasions in the ninth century, it was able to deal with them and not only endured but even expanded, reaching its high point in the tenth century, which some historians have called the golden age of Byzantine civilization.

The Beginning of a Revival

During the reign of Michael III (842–867), the Byzantine Empire began to experience a revival. Iconoclasm was finally abolished in 843, and reforms were made in education, church life, the military, and the peasant economy. There was a noticeable intellectual renewal. But the empire was still plagued by persistent problems. The Bulgars mounted new attacks, and the Arabs continued to harass the periphery. Moreover, a new religious dispute with political repercussions erupted over differences between the pope as leader of the western Christian church and the patriarch of Constantinople as leader of the eastern Christian church. Patriarch Photius condemned the pope as a heretic for accepting a revised form of the Nicene Creed stating that the Holy Spirit proceeded from the Father and the Son instead of from the Father alone. A council of eastern bishops followed Photius' wishes and excommunicated the pope, creating the so-called Photian schism. Although the differences were later papered over, this controversy inserted a greater wedge between the eastern and western Christian churches.

The Macedonian Dynasty

The problems that arose during Michael's reign were effectively dealt with by a new dynasty of Byzantine emperors known as the Macedonians (867–1056). The dynasty was founded by Basil I (867–886), a Macedonian

of uncertain background who came to Constantinople to improve his lot in life. After impressing Emperor Michael III with his wrestling skills, he married the emperor's mistress and was made co-emperor. One year later, he arranged the murder of Michael and then became sole ruler, establishing a dynasty that would last almost two hundred years.

The Macedonian dynasty managed to hold off Byzantium's external enemies and reestablish domestic order. Supported by the church, the emperors thought of the Byzantine Empire as a continuation of the Christian Roman Empire of late antiquity. Although for diplomatic reasons they occasionally recognized the imperial titles of earlier western emperors, such as Charlemagne and Otto I, they still regarded them as little more than barbarian parvenus.

Economic and Religious Policies The Macedonian emperors could boast of a remarkable number of achievements in the late ninth and tenth centuries. They worked to strengthen the position of the free farmers, who felt threatened by the attempts of landed aristocrats to expand their estates at the farmers' expense. The emperors were well aware that the free farmers made up the rank and file of the Byzantine cavalry and provided the military strength of the empire. Nevertheless, despite their efforts, the Macedonian emperors found that it was not easy to control the power of the landed nobles, and many free farmers continued to lose their lands to the nobles.

The Macedonian emperors also fostered a burst of economic prosperity by expanding trade relations with western Europe, especially by selling silks and metalwork, and the city of Constantinople flourished. Foreign visitors continued to be astounded by its size, wealth, and physical surroundings. To western Europeans, it was the stuff of legends and fables (see the box on p. 373).

In this period of prosperity, Byzantine cultural influence expanded due to the active missionary efforts of eastern Byzantine Christians. Eastern Orthodox Christianity was spread to eastern European peoples, such as the Bulgars and Serbs. Perhaps the greatest missionary success occurred when the prince of Kiev in Russia converted to Christianity in 987. From the end of the tenth century on, Byzantine Christianity became the model for Russian religious life, just as Byzantine imperial ideals came to influence the outward forms of Russian political life.

Political and Military Achievements Under the Macedonian rulers, Byzantium enjoyed a strong civil service, talented emperors, and military advances. The Byzantine civil service was staffed by well-educated, competent aristocrats from Constantinople who oversaw the collection of taxes, domestic administration, and foreign policy. At the same time, the Macedonian dynasty produced some truly outstanding emperors skilled in administration and law, including Leo VI and Constantine VII. Leo VI (886–912),

A WESTERN VIEW OF THE BYZANTINE EMPIRE

POLITICS & GOVERNMENT

Bishop Liudprand of Cremona undertook diplomatic missions to Constantinople on behalf of two western kings, Berengar of Italy and Otto I of Germany. This selection is taken from his description of his mission to the Byzantine emperor Constantine VII in 949 as an envoy for Berengar, king of Italy from 950 until his overthrow by Otto I of Germany in 964. Liudprand had mixed feelings about Byzantium: admiration, yet also envy and hostility because of its superior wealth.

Liudprand of Cremona, *Antapodosis*

Next to the imperial residence at Constantinople there is a palace of remarkable size and beauty which the Greeks call Magnavra . . . the name being equivalent to "fresh breeze." In order to receive some Spanish envoys, who had recently arrived, as well as myself . . . , Constantine gave orders that this palace should be got ready. . . .

Before the emperor's seat stood a tree, made of bronze gilded over, whose branches were filled with birds, also made of gilded bronze, which uttered different cries, each according to its varying species. The throne itself was so marvelously fashioned that at one moment it seemed a low structure, and at another it rose high into the air. It was of immense size and was guarded by lions, made either of bronze or of wood covered over with gold, who beat the ground with their tails and gave a dreadful roar with open mouth and quivering tongue. Leaning upon the shoulders of two eunuchs I was brought into the emperor's presence. At my approach the lions began to roar and the birds to cry out, each according to its kind; but I was neither terrified nor surprised, for I had previously made enquiry about all these things from people who were well acquainted with them. So after I had three times made obeisance to the emperor with my face upon the ground, I lifted my head, and behold! The man whom just before I had seen sitting on a moderately elevated seat had now changed his raiment and was sitting on the level of the ceiling. How it was done I could not imagine, unless perhaps he was lifted up by some such sort of device as we use for raising the timbers of a wine press. On that occasion he did not address me personally, . . . but by the intermediary of a secretary he enquired about Berengar's doings and asked after his health. I made a fitting reply and then, at a nod from the interpreter, left his presence and retired to my lodging.

It would give me some pleasure also to record here what I did then for Berengar. . . . The Spanish envoys . . . had brought handsome gifts from their masters to the emperor Constantine. I for my part had brought nothing from Berengar except a letter and that was full of lies. I was very greatly disturbed and shamed at this and began to consider anxiously what I had better do. In my doubt and perplexity it finally occurred to me that I might offer the gifts, which on my account I had brought for the emperor, as coming from Berengar, and trick out my humble present with fine words. I therefore presented him with nine excellent cuirasses, seven excellent shields with gilded bosses, two silver gilt cauldrons, some swords, spears, and spits, and what was more precious to the emperor than anything, four carzimasia, that being the Greek name for young eunuchs who have had both their testicles and their penis removed. This operation is performed by traders at Verdun, who take the boys into Spain and make a huge profit.

Q *What impressions of the Byzantine court do you get from Liudprand's account? What is the modern meaning of the word* byzantine? *How does this account help explain the modern meaning of the word?*

CENGAGENOW

To read more accounts by Liudprand, enter the documents area of the World History Resource Center using the access card that is available for World History.

---

known as Leo the Wise, was an accomplished scholar who composed works on politics and theology; systematized rules for regulating both trade and court officials, and arranged for a new codification of all Byzantine law. Constantine VII (945–959) wrote a detailed treatise on foreign policy to instruct his officials, as well as his son, on running the empire wisely.

In the tenth century, competent emperors combined with a number of talented generals to mobilize the empire's military resources and take the offensive. Especially important was Basil II (976–1025), who defeated the Bulgars and annexed Bulgaria to the empire (see the box on p. 375). After his final victory over the Bulgars in 1014, Basil blinded fourteen thousand Bulgar captives before allowing them to return to their homes. The Byzantines went on to add the islands of Crete and Cyprus to the empire and to defeat the Muslim forces in Syria, expanding the empire to the upper Euphrates. By the end of Basil's reign in 1025, the Byzantine Empire was the largest it had been since the beginning of the seventh century.

The Byzantine Empire, 1025

Venice · CROATIA · PAPAL STATES · SERBIA · Rome · Sicily · BULGARIA · MACEDONIA · BYZANTINE · Athens · *Mediterranean Sea* · Crete · Ephesus · EMPIRE · Constantinople · *Black Sea* · Cyprus · PERSIA · SYRIA · Danube R. · Balkan Mts. · Caucasus Mts. · Euphrates R. · Tigris R.

0 300 600 Miles
0 300 600 Kilometers

© Erich Lessing/Art Resource, NY

Emperor Leo VI. Under the Macedonian dynasty, the Byzantine Empire achieved economic prosperity through expanded trade and gained new territories through military victories. This mosaic over the western door of Hagia Sophia in Constantinople depicts the Macedonian emperor Leo VI prostrating himself before Jesus. This act of humility symbolized the emperor's function as an intermediary between God and the people. Leo's son characterized him as the "Christ-loving and glorious emperor."

The Decline and Fall of the Byzantine Empire (1025–1453)

Q Focus Questions: What impact did the Crusades have on the Byzantine Empire? How and why did Constantinople and the Byzantine Empire fall?

The Macedonian dynasty of the tenth and eleventh centuries had restored much of the power of the Byzantine Empire; its incompetent successors, however, reversed most of the gains.

New Challenges and New Responses

After the Macedonian dynasty was extinguished in 1056, the empire was beset by internal struggles for power between ambitious military leaders and aristocratic families who bought the support of the great landowners of Anatolia by allowing them greater control over their peasants. This policy was self-destructive, however, because the peasant-warrior was an important source of military strength in the Byzantine state. By the middle of the eleventh century, the Byzantine army began to decline; with fewer peasant recruits, military leaders also began to rely more on mercenaries.

A Christian Schism The growing division between the Roman Catholic Church of the west and the Eastern Orthodox Church of the Byzantine Empire also weakened the Byzantine state. The Eastern Orthodox Church was unwilling to accept the pope's claim that he was the sole head of the Christian church. This dispute reached a climax in 1054 when Pope Leo IX and Patriarch Michael Cerularius, head of the Byzantine church, formally excommunicated each other, initiating a schism between the two branches of Christianity that has not been healed to this day.

Islam and the Seljuk Turks The Byzantine Empire faced external threats to its security as well. In the west, the Normans were menacing the remaining Byzantine possessions in Italy. A much greater threat, however, came from the world of Islam. By the mid-tenth century, the Islamic empire led by the Abbasid caliphate in Baghdad (see Chapter 7) was disintegrating. An attempt was made around that time to unify the Islamic world under the direction of a Shi'ite dynasty known as the Fatimids. Originating in North Africa, they conquered Egypt and founded the new city of Cairo as their capital. In establishing a Shi'ite caliphate, they became rivals to the Sunni caliphate of Baghdad and divided the Islamic world.

The Fatimid dynasty prospered and soon surpassed the Abbasid caliphate as the dynamic center of Islam. Benefiting from their position in the heart of the Nile delta, the Fatimids played a major role in the regional trade passing from the Mediterranean to the Red Sea and beyond. They were tolerant in matters of religion and created a strong army by using nonnative peoples as mercenaries. One of these peoples, the Seljuk Turks, soon posed a threat to the Fatimids themselves.

A nomadic people from Central Asia, the Seljuk Turks had been converted to Islam. As their numbers increased, they moved into the eastern provinces of the Abbasid empire and in 1055 captured Baghdad and occupied the rest of the empire. When they moved into Asia Minor—the heartland of the Byzantine Empire and its main source of food and manpower—the Byzantines were forced to react. Emperor Romanus IV led an army of recruits and mercenaries into Asia Minor in 1071 and met Turkish forces at Manzikert, where the Byzantines were soundly defeated. Seljuk Turks then went on to occupy much of Anatolia, where many peasants, already disgusted by their exploitation at the hands of Byzantine landowners, readily accepted Turkish control (see Map 7.4 on p. 200).

A New Dynasty After the loss at Manzikert, factional fighting erupted over the emperorship until the throne was seized by Alexius Comnenus (1081–1118), who established a dynasty that breathed new life into the Byzantine Empire. Under Alexius, the Byzantines were victorious on the

Greek Adriatic coast against the Normans, defeated their enemies in the Balkans, and stopped the Turks in Anatolia. In the twelfth century, the Byzantine Empire experienced a cultural revival and a period of prosperity, fueled by an expansion of trade. The era was also marked by the increased importance of aristocratic families, especially those from a military background. In fact, Alexus' power was built on an alliance of the Comnenus family with other aristocratic families. But both the Comneni dynasty and the revival of the twelfth century were ultimately threatened by Byzantium's encounters with crusaders from the west.

Impact of the Crusades

Lacking the resources to undertake additional campaigns against the Turks, Emperor Alexus turned to the west for

THE ACHIEVEMENTS OF BASIL II

Basil II came to power at the age of eighteen and during his long reign greatly enlarged the Byzantine Empire. During his reign, an alliance with the Russian prince Vladimir was instrumental in bringing Orthodox Christianity to the Russians. We know a great deal about Basil II from an account by Michael Psellus (1018–c. 1081), one of the foremost Byzantine historians. He wrote the *Chronographia*, a series of biographies of the Byzantine emperors from 976 to 1078, much of it based on his own observations. In this selection, Psellus discusses the qualities of Basil as a leader.

Michael Psellus, *Chronographia*

In his dealings with his subjects, Basil behaved with extraordinary circumspection. It is perfectly true that the great reputation he built up as a ruler was founded rather on terror than on loyalty. As he grew older and became more experienced he relied less on the judgment of men wiser than himself. He alone introduced new measures, he alone disposed his military forces. As for the civil administration, he governed, not in accordance with the written laws, but following the unwritten dictates of his own intuition, which was most excellently equipped by nature for the purpose....

Having purged the empire of the barbarians [Bulgars] he dealt with his own subjects and completely subjugated them too—I think "subjugate" is the right word to describe it. He decided to abandon his former policy, and after the great families had been humiliated and put on an equal footing with the rest, Basil found himself playing the game of power-politics with considerable success. He surrounded himself with favorites who were neither remarkable for brilliance of intellect, nor of noble lineage, nor too learned. To them were entrusted the imperial rescripts [official announcements], and with them he was accustomed to share the secrets of state....

By humbling the pride or jealousy of his people, Basil made his own road to power an easy one. He was careful, moreover, to close the exit-doors on the monies contributed to the treasury. So a huge sum of money was built up, partly by the exercise of strict economy, partly by fresh additions from abroad.... He himself took no pleasure in any of it: quite the reverse indeed, for the majority of the white ones (which we call pearls) and the colored brilliants, far from being inlaid in diadems or collars, were hidden away in his underground vaults....

On his expedition against the barbarians, Basil did not follow the customary procedure of other emperors, setting out at the middle of spring and returning home at the end of summer. For him the time to return was when the task in hand was accomplished. He endured the rigors of winter and the heat of summer with equal indifference. He disciplined himself against thirst. In fact, all his natural desires were kept under stern control, and the man was as hard as steel.... He professed to conduct his wars and draw up the troops in line of battle, himself planning each campaign, but he preferred not to engage in combat personally. A sudden retreat might otherwise prove embarrassing....

Basil's character was two-fold, for he readily adapted himself no less to the crises of war than to the calm of peace. Really, if the truth be told, he was more of a villain in wartime, more of an emperor in time of peace. Outbursts of wrath he controlled and like the proverbial "fire under the ashes," kept anger hid in his heart, but if his orders were disobeyed in war, on his return to the palace he would kindle his wrath and reveal it. Terrible then was the vengeance he took on the miscreant. Generally, he persisted in his opinions, but there were occasions when he did change his mind. In many cases, too, he traced crimes back to their original causes, and the final links in the chain were exonerated. So most defaulters obtained forgiveness, either through his sympathetic understanding or because he showed some other interest in their affairs. He was slow to adopt any course of action, but never would he willingly alter the decision, once it was [made]; Consequently, his attitude to friends was unvaried, unless perchance he was compelled by necessity to revise his opinion of them. Similarly, where he had burst out in anger against someone, he did not quickly moderate his wrath. Whatever estimate he formed, indeed, was to him an irrevocable and divinely-inspired judgment.

Q *Based on this account, what were the personal qualities that made Basil II successful, and how would you characterize the nature of the Byzantine government? Compare the achievements of Basil II with those of Charlemagne on p. 337. How were the two rulers alike? How were they different? How would you explain the differences?*

military assistance and asked Pope Urban II for help against the Seljuk Turks. Instead of the military aid he had expected, the pope set in motion the First Crusade (see Chapter 12), a decision that created enormous difficulties for the First Crusade. To pursue the goal of liberating Palestine from the Muslims, western crusading armies would have to go through Byzantine lands to reach their objective. Alexius, and especially his daughter, Anna Comnena (who was also the Byzantine Empire's only female historian), were fearful that "to all appearances they were on pilgrimage; in reality they planned to dethrone Alexius and seize the capital."[6]

The Byzantines became cautious; Alexius requested that the military leaders of the First Crusade take an oath of loyalty to him and promise that any territory they conquered would be under Byzantine control. The crusaders ignored the emperor's wishes, and after their conquest of Antioch, Jerusalem, and additional Palestinian lands, they organized the four crusading states of Edessa, Antioch, Tripoli, and Jerusalem. The Byzantines now had to worry not only about the Turks in Anatolia but also about westerners in the crusading states. The Second and Third Crusades posed similar difficulties for the Byzantine emperors.

The Crusades also increased the impact of western ideas on the Byzantine Empire. In the mid-twelfth century, the Byzantine emperor Manuel I (1140–1183) introduced the western practice of knightly jousting to the Byzantine aristocracy. The Byzantine emperors also conferred trading concessions on the Italian city-states of Venice, Pisa, and Genoa, and in the course of the century, probably sixty thousand western Europeans came to live in Constantinople. But the presence of westerners and western practices also led to a growing hostility. Byzantine writers began to denounce western attitudes, and westerners often expressed jealousy of Constantinople's wealth. In 1171, Emperor Manuel I expelled the Venetians and seized their goods and ships, arousing in Venice a desire for revenge, no doubt a factor behind the disastrous Fourth Crusade in 1204.

The Latin Empire of Constantinople After the death of Saladin in 1193 (see Chapter 7), Pope Innocent III launched the Fourth Crusade. Judging the moment auspicious, Innocent encouraged the nobility of Europe to don the crusader's mantle. The Venetians agreed to ship the crusading army to the east but subverted it from its goal by using it first to capture Zara, a Christian port on the Dalmatian coast. The crusading army thus became enmeshed in Byzantine politics.

At the start of the thirteenth century, the Byzantine Empire was experiencing yet another struggle for the imperial throne. One contender, Alexius, son of the overthrown Emperor Isaac II, appealed to the crusaders in Zara for assistance, offering them 200,000 marks in silver (the Venetians were getting 85,000 as a transport fee) and reconciliation of the Eastern Orthodox Church with the Roman Catholic Church. The Crusade leaders now

diverted their forces to Constantinople. When the crusading army arrived, the deposed Isaac II was reestablished with his son, Alexius IV, as co-emperor. Unfortunately, the emperors were unable to pay the promised sum. Relations between the crusaders and the Byzantines deteriorated, leading to an attack on Constantinople by the crusaders in the spring of 1204. On April 12, they stormed and sacked the city (see the box on p. 377). Christian crusaders took gold, silver, jewelry, and precious furs, while the Catholic clergy accompanying the crusaders stole as many relics as they could find.

The Byzantine Empire now disintegrated into a series of petty states ruled by crusading barons and Byzantine princes. The chief state was the new Latin Empire of Constantinople led by Count Baldwin of Flanders as emperor. The Venetians seized the island of Crete and secured domination of Constantinople's trade. Why had the western crusaders succeeded so easily when Persians, Bulgars, and Arabs had failed for centuries to conquer Constantinople? Although the crusaders were no doubt motivated by greed and a lust for conquest, they were also convinced that they were acting in God's cause. After all, a Catholic patriarch (a Venetian) had now been installed in Constantinople, and the reconciliation of Eastern Orthodoxy with Catholic Christianity had been accomplished. Nor should we overlook the military superiority of the French warriors and the superb organizational skills of the Venetians; together, they formed a union of great effectiveness and power.

Revival of the Byzantine Empire Although he protested the diversion of the crusade from the Holy Land, Pope Innocent III belatedly accepted as "God's work" the conversion of Greek Byzantium to Latin Christianity. Some have argued that Innocent did realize, however, that the use of force to reunite the churches virtually guaranteed the failure of any permanent reunion. All too soon, this proved correct. The west was unable to maintain the Latin Empire, for the western rulers of the newly created principalities were soon engrossed in fighting each other. Some parts of the Byzantine Empire had managed to survive under Byzantine princes. In 1259, Michael Paleologus, a Greek military leader, took control of the kingdom of Nicaea in western Asia Minor, led a Byzantine army to recapture Constantinople two years later, and then established a new Byzantine dynasty, the Paleologi.

The Byzantine Empire had been saved, but it was no longer a Mediterranean power. The restored empire was a badly truncated entity, consisting of the city of Constantinople and its surrounding territory, some lands in Asia Minor, and part of Thessalonica. It was surrounded by enemies—Bulgarians, Mongols, Turks, and westerners, especially the resentful Venetians. And there was still internal opposition to Michael VIII. But the emperor survived and began a badly needed restoration of Constantinople.

Even in its reduced size, the empire limped along for another 190 years, and Constantinople remained an active economic center. Scholars continued to study the classics, and new churches and monasteries were built. Civil strife continued as rival claimants struggled over the throne. And enemies continued to multiply; the threat from the Turks finally doomed the aged empire.

The Ottoman Turks and the Fall of Constantinople

Beginning in northeastern Asia Minor in the thirteenth century, the Ottoman Turks spread rapidly, seizing the lands of the Seljuk Turks and the Byzantine Empire. In 1345, they bypassed Constantinople and moved into the Balkans. Under Sultan Murad, Ottoman forces moved through Bulgaria and into the lands of the Serbians; in 1389, at the Battle of Kosovo, Ottoman forces defeated the Serbs. By the beginning of the fifteenth century, what was left of the Byzantine Empire was mostly Constantinople, now surrounded on all sides by the Ottomans. When Mehmet II came to the throne in 1451 at the age of only nineteen, he was determined to capture Constantinople and complete the demise of the Byzantine Empire.

The siege began in April when Mehmet moved his forces—probably an army of about eighty thousand men—within striking distance of the 13-mile-long land walls along the western edge of the city. The pope and the Italian city-states of Venice and Genoa promised aid, but

CHRISTIAN CRUSADERS CAPTURE CONSTANTINOPLE

POLITICS & GOVERNMENT

Pope Innocent III inaugurated the Fourth Crusade after Saladin's empire began to disintegrate. Tragically, however, the crusading army of mostly French nobles was diverted to Constantinople to intervene in Byzantine politics. In 1204, the Christian crusaders stormed and sacked one of Christendom's greatest cities. This description of the conquest of Constantinople is taken from a contemporary account by a participant in the struggle.

Geoffrey de Villehardouin, *The Conquest of Constantinople*

The moment the knights aboard the transports saw this happen, they landed, and raising their ladders against the wall, climbed to the top, and took four more towers. Then all the rest of the troops started to leap out of warships, galleys, and transports, helter-skelter, each as fast as he could. They broke down about three of the gates and entered the city. The horses were then taken out of the transports; the knights mounted and rode straight towards the place where the Emperor had his camp. He had his battalions drawn up in front of the tents; but as soon as his men saw the knights charging towards them on horseback, they retreated in disorder. The Emperor himself fled through the streets of the city to the castle of Bucoleon.

Then followed a scene of massacre and pillage: on every hand the Greeks [Byzantines] were cut down, their horses, palfreys [saddlehorses], mules, and other possessions snatched as booty. So great was the number of killed and wounded that no man could count them. A great part of the Greek nobles had fled towards the gate of Blachernae; but by this time it was past six o'clock, and our men had grown weary of fighting and slaughtering. The troops began to assemble in a great square inside Constantinople... [and] decided to settle down near the walls and towers they had already captured....

That night passed, and the next day came.... Early that morning all the troops, knights and sergeants alike, armed themselves, and each man went to join his division. They left their quarters thinking to meet with stronger resistance than they had encountered the day before, since they did not know that the Emperor had fled during the night. But they found no one to oppose them.

The Marquis de Montferrat rode straight along the shore to the palace of Bucoleon. As soon as he arrived there the place was surrendered to him, on condition that the lives of all the people in it should be spared. Among these were very many ladies of the highest rank who had taken refuge there.... Words fail me when it comes to describing the treasures found in the palace, for there was such a store of precious things that one could not possibly count them....

The rest of the army, scattered throughout the city, also gained much booty; so much, indeed, that no one could estimate its amount or its value. It included gold and silver, table-services and precious stones, satin and silk, mantles of squirrel fur, ermine and miniver, and every choicest thing to be found on this earth. Geoffrey de Villehardouin here declares that, to his knowledge, so much booty had never been gained in any city since the creation of the world.

Everyone took quarters where he pleased, and there was no lack of fine dwellings in that city. So the troops of the Crusaders and the Venetians were duly housed. They all rejoiced and gave thanks to our Lord for the honor and the victory He had granted them, so that those who had been poor now lived in wealth and luxury. Thus they celebrated Palm Sunday and the Easter Day following, with hearts full of joy for the benefits our Lord and Saviour had bestowed on them. And well might they praise Him; since the whole of their army numbered no more than twenty thousand men, and with His help they had conquered four hundred thousand, or more, and that in the greatest, most powerful, and most strongly fortified city in the world.

Q *What does this document reveal about the crusading ideals and practices of the Europeans?*

Sophia, and ordered that it be converted into a mosque. He soon began the rebuilding of the city as the capital of the Ottoman Empire. The Byzantine Empire had come to an end.

The Crises of the Fourteenth Century

Q Focus Questions: What impact did the Black Death have on Europe and Asia in the fourteenth century? What problems did Europeans face during the fourteenth century, and what impact did they have on European economic, social, and religious life?

At the beginning of the fourteenth century, changes in global weather patterns ushered in what has been called a "little ice age." Shortened growing seasons and disastrous weather conditions, including heavy storms and constant rain, led to widespread famine and hunger. Soon an even greater catastrophe struck.

The Black Death: From Asia to Europe

In the mid-fourteenth century, a disaster known as the Black Death struck in Asia, North Africa, and Europe. Bubonic plague was the most common and most important form of plague in the diffusion of the Black Death and was spread by black rats infested with fleas who were host to the deadly bacterium *Yersinia pestis.*

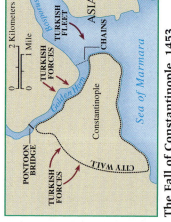

The Fall of Constantinople, 1453

Role of the Mongols This great plague originated in Asia. After disappearing from Europe and the Middle East in the Middle Ages, bubonic plague continued to haunt areas of southwestern China. In the early 1300s, rats accompanying Mongol troops spread the plague into central China and by 1331 to northeastern China. In one province near Beijing, it was reported that 90 percent of the population died. Overall, China's population may have declined from 120 million in the mid-1300s to 80 million by 1400.

In the thirteenth century, the Mongols had brought much of the Eurasian landmass under a single rule, which in turn facilitated long-distance trade, particularly along the Silk Road, now dominated by Muslim merchants from Central Asia (see Chapter 10). The spread of people and goods throughout this Eurasian landmass also facilitated the spread of the plague.

In the 1330s, the plague had spread to Central Asia; by 1339 it had reached Samarkand, a caravan stop on the Silk Road. From Central Asia, trading caravans brought the plague to Caffa, on the Black Sea, in 1346 and to Constantinople by the following year (see the

---

most of it was too little and too late. The city probably had six to eight thousand soldiers mobilized for its defense. On April 2, Emperor Constantine XI (1449–1453), the last Byzantine emperor, ordered that a floating chain or boom be stretched across the Golden Horn, the inlet that forms the city's harbor, in order to prevent a naval attack from the north. Mehmet's forces, however, took control of the tip of the peninsula north of the Golden Horn and then pulled their ships overland across the peninsula from the Bosporus and placed them into the water behind the chains. The Ottoman fleet in the Horn built a pontoon bridge and set up artillery, forcing the Byzantines to defend the city on all sides.

The Ottomans' main attack, however, came against the land walls. On April 6, the artillery onslaught began. The Ottoman invaders had a distinct advantage with their cannons. One of them, constructed by a Hungarian engineer, had a 26-foot barrel that fired stone balls weighing 1,200 pounds. It took sixty oxen and two thousand men to pull the great cannon into position. On May 29, Mehmet decided on a final assault, especially against the areas where the walls had been breached. When Ottoman forces broke into the city, the emperor became one of the first casualties (see the box on p. 379). Irregular Ottoman forces began to loot the city before regular troops were able to stop them. About four thousand defenders were killed, and thousands of the inhabitants were sold into slavery. Early in the afternoon, Mehmet II rode into the city, exalted the power of Allah from the pulpit in the cathedral of Hagia

comparative essay "The Role of Disease in History" on p. 380). Its arrival in the Byzantine Empire was noted in a work by Emperor John VI, who lost a son: "Upon arrival in Constantinople she [the empress] found Andronikos, the youngest born, dead from the invading plague, which...attacked almost all the sea coasts of the world and killed most of their people."[7] By 1348, the plague had spread to Egypt and also to Mecca and Damascus and other parts of the Middle East. The Muslim historian Ibn Khaldun, writing in the fourteenth century, commented, "Civilization in the East and West was visited by a destructive plague which devastated nations and caused populations to vanish. It swallowed up many of the good things of civilization and wiped them out."[8] Egypt was particularly devastated by the plague; it has been estimated that it was not until the nineteenth century that the population of Egypt returned to pre-1347 levels.

The Black Death in Europe

The **Black Death** of the mid-fourteenth century was the most devastating natural disaster in European history, ravaging Europe's population and causing economic, social, political, and cultural upheaval. Contemporary chroniclers lamented how parents abandoned their children; one related the words: "Oh, father, why have you abandoned me?...Mother where have you gone?"[9]

The plague reached Europe in October 1347 when Genoese merchants brought it from Caffa to the island of Sicily off the coast of Italy. One contemporary wrote, "As it happened, among those who escaped from Caffa by boat, there were a few sailors who had been infected

THE FALL OF CONSTANTINOPLE

Few events in the history of the Ottoman Empire are more dramatic than the conquest of Constantinople in 1453. In this excerpt, the conquest is described by Kritovoulos, a Greek who later served in the Ottoman administration. Although the author did not witness the conquest itself, he was apparently well informed about the event and provides us with a vivid description.

Kritovoulos, *Life of Mehmed the Conqueror*

So saying, he [the Sultan] led them himself. And they, with a shout on the run and with a fearsome yell, went on ahead of the Sultan, pressing on up to the palisade. After a long and bitter struggle they hurled back the Romans [Byzantines] from there and climbed by force up the palisade. They dashed some of their foe down into the ditch between the great wall and the palisade, which was deep and hard to get out of, and they killed them there. The rest they drove back to the gate.

He had opened this gate in the great wall, so as to go easily over to the palisade. Now there was a great struggle there and great slaughter among those stationed there, for they were attacked by the heavy infantry and not a few others in irregular formation, who had been attracted from many points by the shouting. There the Emperor Constantine [Constantine XI Paleologus], with all who were with him, fell in gallant combat.

The heavy infantry were already streaming through the little gate into the City, and others had rushed in through the breach in the great wall. Then all the rest of the army, with a rush and a roar, poured in brilliantly and scattered all over the City. And the Sultan stood before the great wall, where the standard also was and the ensigns, and watched the proceedings. The day was already breaking....

The soldiers fell on them [the citizens] with anger and great wrath. For one thing, they were actuated by the hardships of the siege. For another, some foolish people had hurled taunts and curses at them from the battlements all through the siege. Now, in general they killed so as to frighten all the City, and to terrorize and enslave all by the slaughter.

When they had had enough of murder, and the City was reduced to slavery, some of the troops turned to the mansions of the mighty, by bands and companies and divisions, for plunder and spoil. Others went to the robbing of churches, and others dispersed to the simple homes of the common people, stealing, robbing, plundering, killing, insulting, taking and enslaving men, women, and children, old and young, priests, monks—in short, every age and class....

After this the Sultan entered the City and looked about to see its great size, its situation, its grandeur and beauty, its teeming population, its loveliness, and the costliness of its churches and public buildings and of the private houses and community houses and those of the officials.... When he saw what a large number had been killed, and the ruin of the buildings, and the wholesale ruin and destruction of the City, he was filled with compassion and repented not a little at the destruction and plundering. Tears fell from his eyes as he groaned deeply and passionately: "What a city we have given over to plunder and destruction...."

As for the great City of Constantine, raised to a great height of glory and dominion and wealth in its own times, overshadowing to an infinite degree all the cities around it, renowned for its glory, wealth, authority, power, and greatness, and all its other qualities, it thus came to its end.

Q What was the strategy used by the Turkish forces to seize the city of Constantinople? Compare this description of the capture of Constantinople to the one 250 years earlier described on p. 377. What are the similarities? What are the differences?

COMPARATIVE ESSAY
THE ROLE OF DISEASE IN HISTORY

© Snark/Art Resource, NY

Mass Burial of Plague Victims. The Black Death had spread to northern Europe by the end of 1348. Shown here is a mass burial of victims of the plague in Tournai, located in modern Belgium. As is evident in the illustration, at this stage of the plague, there was still time to make coffins for the victims' burial. Later, as the plague intensified, the dead were thrown into open pits.

INTERACTION & EXCHANGE

When Hernán Cortés and his fellow conquistadors arrived in Mesoamerica in 1519, the local inhabitants were frightened of the horses and the firearms that accompanied the Spaniards. What they did not know was that the most dangerous enemies brought by these strange new arrivals were invisible–the disease-bearing microbes that would soon kill them by the millions.

Diseases have been the scourge of animal species since the dawn of prehistory, making the lives of human beings, in the words of the English philosopher Thomas Hobbes, "nasty, brutish, and short." With the increasing sophistication of forensic evidence, archaeologists today are able to determine from recently discovered human remains that our immediate ancestors were plagued by such familiar ailments as anemia, arthritis, tuberculosis, and malaria.

With the explosive growth of the human population brought about by the agricultural revolution, the problems posed by the presence of disease intensified. As people began to congregate in villages and cities, bacteria settled in their piles of refuse and were carried by lice in their clothing. The domestication of animals made humans more vulnerable to diseases carried by their livestock. As population density increased, the danger of widespread epidemics increased with it.

As time went on, succeeding generations gradually developed partial or complete immunity to many of these diseases, which became chronic rather than fatal to their victims, as occurred with malaria in parts of Africa, for example, and chickenpox in the Americas. But when a disease was introduced to a particular society that had not previously been exposed to it, the consequences were often devastating. The most dramatic example was the famous

Black Death, the plague that ravaged Europe and China during the fourteenth century, killing one-fourth to one-half of the inhabitants in the affected regions (and even greater numbers in certain areas). Smallpox had the same impact in the Americas after the arrival of Christopher Columbus, and malaria was fatal to many Europeans on their arrival in West Africa.

How were these diseases transmitted? In most instances, they followed the trade routes. Such was the case with the Black Death, which was initially carried by fleas living in the saddlebags of Mongol warriors as they advanced toward Europe in the thirteenth and fourteenth centuries and thereafter by rats in the holds of cargo ships. Smallpox and other diseases were brought to the Americas by the conquistadors. Epidemics, then, are a price that humans pay for having developed the network of rapid communication that has accompanied the evolution of human society.

 What role has disease played in human history?

through Spain, France, and the Low Countries and into Germany. By the end of that year, it had moved to England. By the end of the next, the plague had reached northern Europe and Scandinavia. Eastern Europe and Russia were affected by 1351.

Mortality figures for the Black Death were incredibly high. Especially hard hit were Italy's crowded cities, where 50 to 60 percent of the people died. One citizen

with the poisonous disease. Some boats were bound for Genoa, others went to Venice and other Christian areas. When the sailors reached these places and mixed with the people there, it was as if they had brought evil spirits with them."[10] The plague quickly spread to southern Italy and then to southern France by the end of the year (see Map 13.3). Diffusion of the Black Death followed commercial trade routes. In 1348, it spread

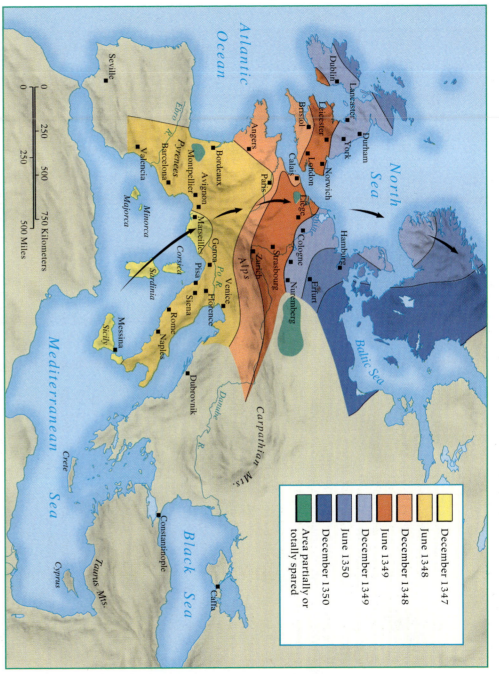

MAP 13.3 Spread of the Black Death. The plague entered Europe through Sicily in 1347 and within three years had killed between one-quarter and one-half of the population. Outbreaks continued into the early eighteenth century, and it took Europe two hundred years to return to the population level it had before the Black Death.

Q Is there a general pattern between distance from Sicily and the elapsed time before a region was infected with the plague?

December 1347
June 1348
December 1348
June 1349
December 1349
June 1350
December 1350
Area partially or totally spared

of Florence wrote, "A great many breathed their last in the public streets, day and night; a large number perished in their homes, and it was only by the stench of their decaying bodies that they proclaimed their deaths to their neighbors. Everywhere the city was teeming with corpses."11 In England and Germany, entire villages simply disappeared. It has been estimated that out of a total European population of 75 million, as many as 38 million people may have died of the plague between 1347 and 1351.

The attempt of contemporaries to explain the Black Death and mitigate its harshness led to extreme sorts of behavior. To many, either the plague had been sent by God as a punishment for humans' sins, or it had been caused by the devil. Some, known as the flagellants, resorted to extreme measures to gain God's forgiveness. Groups of flagellants, both men and women, wandered from town to town, flogging each other with whips to beg the forgiveness of a God who, they felt, had sent the

plague to punish humans for their sinful ways. One contemporary chronicler described their activities:

The penitents went about, coming first out of Germany. They were men who did public penance and scourged themselves with whips of hard knotted leather with little iron spikes. Some made themselves bleed very badly between the shoulder blades and some foolish women had cloths ready to catch the blood and smear it on their eyes, saying it was miraculous blood. While they were doing penance, they sang very mournful songs about the nativity and the passion of Our Lord. The object of this penance was to put a stop to the mortality, for in that time...at least a third of all the people in the world died.12

The flagellants created mass hysteria wherever they went, and authorities worked overtime to crush the movement.

An outbreak of virulent anti-Semitism also accompanied the Black Death. Jews were accused of causing the plague by poisoning town wells. The worst **pogroms** (massacres) against this minority were carried out in Germany, where more than sixty major Jewish communities

The Cremation of the Strasbourg Jews

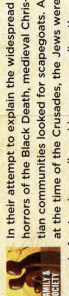

In their attempt to explain the widespread horrors of the Black Death, medieval Christian communities looked for scapegoats. As at the time of the Crusades, the Jews were accused of poisoning wells and hence spreading the plague. This selection by a contemporary chronicler, written in 1349, gives an account of how Christians in the town of Strasbourg in the Holy Roman Empire dealt with their Jewish community. It is apparent that financial gain was also an important factor in killing the Jews.

Jacob von Königshofen, "The Cremation of the Strasbourg Jews"

In the year 1349 there occurred the greatest epidemic that ever happened. Death went from one end of the earth to the other.... And from what this epidemic came, all wise teachers and physicians could only say that it was God's will.... This epidemic also came to Strasbourg in the summer of the above-mentioned year, and it is estimated that about sixteen thousand people died.

In the matter of this plague the Jews throughout the world were reviled and accused in all lands of having caused it through the poison which they are said to have put into the water and the wells—that is what they were accused of—and for this reason the Jews were burnt all the way from the Mediterranean into Germany....

[The account then goes on to discuss the situation of the Jews in the city of Strasbourg.]

On Saturday ... they burnt the Jews on a wooden platform in their cemetery. There were about two thousand people of them. Those who wanted to baptize themselves were spared. [Some say that about a thousand accepted baptism.] Many small children were taken out of the fire and baptized against the will of their fathers and mothers. And everything that was owed to the Jews was canceled, and the Jews had to surrender all pledges and notes that they had taken for debts. The council, however, took the cash that the Jews possessed and divided it among the workingmen proportionately. The money was indeed the thing that killed the Jews. If they had been poor and if the feudal lords had not been in debt to them, they would not have been burnt....

Thus were the Jews burnt at Strasbourg, and in the same year in all the cities of the Rhine, whether Free Cities or Imperial Cities or cities belonging to the lords. In some towns they burnt the Jews after a trial; in others, without a trial. In some cities the Jews themselves set fire to their houses and cremated themselves.

It was decided in Strasbourg that no Jew should enter the city for a hundred years, but before twenty years had passed, the council and magistrates agreed that they ought to admit the Jews again into the city for twenty years. And so the Jews came back again to Strasbourg in the year 1368 after the birth of our Lord.

Q *What charges were made against the Jews in regard to the Black Death? Can it be said that these charges were economically motivated? Why or why not? How did the anti-Semitism of towns such as Strasbourg lead to the establishment of large Jewish populations in eastern Europe?*

---

had been exterminated by 1351 (see the box above). Many Jews fled eastward to Russia and especially to Poland, where the king offered them protection. Eastern Europe became home to large Jewish communities.

Economic Dislocation and Social Upheaval

The death of so many people in the fourteenth century also had severe economic consequences. Trade declined, and some industries suffered greatly. Florence's woolens industry, one of the giants, had produced 70,000 to 80,000 pieces of cloth in 1338; in 1378, it was yielding only 24,000 pieces.

Both peasants and noble landlords were also affected. A shortage of workers caused a dramatic rise in the price of labor, while the decline in the number of people lowered the demand for food, resulting in falling prices. Landlords were now paying more for labor at the same time that their rental income was declining. Concurrently, the decline in the number of peasants after the Black Death made it easier for some to convert their labor services to rent, thus freeing them from serfdom. But

there were limits to how much the peasants could advance. They faced the same economic hurdles as the lords, who also attempted to impose wage restrictions and reinstate old forms of labor service. New governmental taxes also hurt. Peasant complaints became widespread and soon gave rise to rural revolts.

Although the peasant revolts sometimes resulted in short-term gains for the participants, the uprisings were relatively easily crushed and their gains quickly lost. Accustomed to ruling, the established classes easily combined and stifled dissent. Nevertheless, the revolts of the fourteenth century had introduced a new element to European life; henceforth, social unrest would be a characteristic of European history.

Political Instability

Famine, plague, economic turmoil, and social upheaval were not the only problems of the fourteenth century. War and political instability must also be added to the list. And of all the struggles that ensued, the Hundred Years' War was the most violent.

382 CHAPTER 13 THE BYZANTINE EMPIRE AND CRISIS AND RECOVERY IN THE WEST

The Hundred Years' War In the thirteenth century, England still held one small possession in France known as the duchy of Gascony. As duke of Gascony, the English king pledged loyalty as a vassal to the French king, but when King Philip VI of France (1328–1350) seized Gascony in 1337, the duke of Gascony—King Edward III of England (1327–1377)—declared war on Philip.

The war began in a burst of knightly enthusiasm. The French army of 1337 still relied largely on heavily armed noble cavalrymen, who looked with contempt on foot soldiers and crossbowmen, whom they regarded as social inferiors. The English, too, used heavily armed cavalry, but they relied even more on large numbers of paid foot soldiers. Armed with pikes, many of these soldiers had also adopted the longbow, invented by the Welsh. The longbow had greater striking power, a longer range, and greater speed of fire than the crossbow.

The first major battle of the war occurred in 1346 at Crécy, just south of Flanders. The larger French army followed no battle plan but simply attacked the English lines in a disorderly fashion. The arrows of the English archers decimated the French cavalry. As the chronicler Froissart described it, "The English [with their long-bows] continued to shoot into the thickest part of the crowd, wasting none of their arrows. They impaled or wounded horses and riders, who fell to the ground in great distress, unable to get up again without the help of

© The Bridgeman Art Library

The Battle of Crécy. This fifteenth-century manuscript illustration depicts the Battle of Crécy, the first of several military disasters suffered by the French in the Hundred Years' War, and shows why the English preferred the longbow to the crossbow. At the left, the French crossbowmen stop shooting and prime their weapons by cranking the handle, while English archers continue to shoot their longbows (a skilled archer could launch ten arrows a minute).

several men."[13] It was a stunning victory for the English and the foot soldier.

The Battle of Crécy was not decisive, however. The English simply did not possess the resources to subjugate all of France, but they continued to try. The English king, Henry V (1413–1422), was especially eager to achieve victory. At the Battle of Agincourt in 1415, the heavy, armor-plated French knights attempted to attack across a field turned to mud by heavy rain; the result was a disastrous French defeat and the death of fifteen hundred French nobles. The English had become the masters of northern France.

The seemingly hopeless French cause fell into the hands of the dauphin Charles, the heir to the throne, who governed the southern two-thirds of French lands. Charles's cause seemed doomed until a French peasant woman quite unexpectedly saved the timid monarch. Born in 1412, the daughter of well-to-do peasants, Joan of Arc was a deeply religious person who came to believe that her favorite saints had commanded her to free France. In February 1429, Joan made her way to the dauphin's court and persuaded Charles to allow her to accompany a French army to Orléans. Apparently in-spired by the faith of the peasant girl known as "the Maid of Orléans," the French armies found new confidence in themselves and liberated the city. Joan had brought the war to a decisive turning point.

But she did not live to see the war con-cluded. Captured in 1430, Joan was turned over by the English to the Inquisition on charges of witchcraft. In the fifteenth century, spiritual visions were thought to be inspired by either God or the devil. Joan was condemned to death as a heretic and burned at the stake in 1431. To the end, as the flames rose up around her, she declared "that her voices came from God and had not deceived her." Twenty-five years later, a new ecclesiastical court exonerated her of these charges, and five centuries later, in 1920, she was made a saint of the Roman Catholic Church.

Joan of Arc's accomplishments proved decisive. Although the war dragged on for an-other two decades, defeats of English armies in Normandy and Aquitaine led to French victory by 1453. Important to the French success was the use of the cannon, a new weapon made possible by the invention of gunpowder. The Chinese had invented gunpowder in the eleventh century and devised a simple cannon by the thirteenth. The Mongols greatly improved this technology, developing more accurate cannons and cannonballs; both spread to the Middle East in the thirteenth century and to Europe by the fourteenth. The use of gunpowder even-tually brought drastic changes to European warfare by making castles, city walls, and ar-mored knights obsolete.

BONIFACE VIII'S DEFENSE OF PAPAL SUPREMACY

One of the most remarkable documents of the fourteenth century was the exaggerated statement of papal supremacy issued by Pope Boniface VIII in 1302 in the heat of his conflict with the French king Philip IV. Ironically, this strongest statement ever made of papal supremacy was issued at a time when the rising power of the secular monarchies made it increasingly difficult for the premises to be accepted. Not long after issuing it, Boniface was taken prisoner by the French. Although he was freed by his fellow Italians, the humiliation of his defeat brought his death a short time later.

Pope Boniface VIII, *Unam Sanctam*

We are compelled, our faith urging us, to believe and to hold—and we do firmly believe and simply confess—that there is one holy catholic and apostolic church, outside of which there is neither salvation nor remission of sins.... In this church there is one Lord, one faith, and one baptism.... Therefore, of this one and only church there is one body and one head.... Christ, namely, and the vicar of Christ, St. Peter, and the successor of Peter. For the Lord himself said to Peter, feed my sheep....

We are told by the word of the gospel that in this His fold there are two swords—a spiritual, namely, and a temporal.... Both swords, the spiritual and the material, therefore, are in the power of the church; the one, indeed, to be wielded for the church, the other by the church; the one by the hand of the priest, the other by the hand of kings and knights, but at the will and sufferance of the priest. One sword, moreover, ought to be under the other, and the temporal authority to be subjected to the spiritual....

Therefore if the earthly power err it shall be judged by the spiritual power; but if the lesser spiritual power err, by the greater. But if the greatest, it can be judged by God alone, not by man, the apostle bearing witness. A spiritual man judges all things, but he himself is judged by no one. This authority, moreover, even though it is given to man and exercised through man, is not human but rather divine, being given by divine lips to Peter and founded on a rock for him and his successors through Christ himself whom he has confessed; the Lord himself saying to Peter: "Whatsoever thou shalt bind, etc." Whoever, therefore, resists this power thus ordained by God, resists the ordination of God....

Indeed, we declare, announce, and define that it is altogether necessary to salvation for every human creature to be subject to the Roman pontiff.

Q *What claims does Boniface VIII make in Unam Sanctam? To what extent are these claims a logical continuation of the development of the papacy in the Middle Ages? If you were a monarch, why would you object to these claims?*

CENGAGENOW. *To read another of Boniface VIII's writings, enter the documents area of the World History Resource Center using the access card that is available for World History.*

Political Disintegration By the fourteenth century, the feudal order had begun to break down. With money from taxes, kings could now hire professional soldiers, who tended to be more reliable than feudal knights anyway. Fourteenth-century kings had their own problems as well. Many dynasties in Europe were unable to produce male heirs, while the founders of new dynasties had to fight for their positions as groups of nobles, trying to gain advantages for themselves, supported opposing candidates. Rulers encountered financial problems too. Hiring professional soldiers left them always short of cash, adding yet another element of uncertainty and confusion to fourteenth-century politics.

The Decline of the Church

The papacy of the Roman Catholic Church reached the height of its power in the thirteenth century. But problems in the fourteenth century led to a serious decline for the church. By that time, the monarchies of Europe were no longer willing to accept papal claims of temporal supremacy, as is evident in the struggle between Pope Boniface VIII (1294–1303) and King Philip IV (1285–1314) of France. In his desire to acquire new revenues, Philip expressed the right to tax the clergy of France, but Boniface VIII claimed that the clergy of any state could not pay taxes to their secular ruler without the pope's consent. In no uncertain terms he argued that popes were supreme over both the church and the state (see the box above).

Philip IV refused to accept the pope's position and sent a small contingent of French forces to capture Boniface and bring him back to France for trial. The pope escaped but soon died from the shock of his experience. To ensure his position and avoid any future papal threat, Philip IV engineered the election of a Frenchman, Clement V (1305–1314), as pope. Using the excuse of turbulence in the city of Rome, the new pope took up residence in Avignon on the east bank of the Rhone River.

From 1305 to 1377, the popes resided in Avignon, leading to an increase in antipapal sentiment. The city of Rome was the traditional capital of the universal church. The pope was the bishop of Rome, and it was unseemly that the head of the Catholic church should reside in Avignon instead of Rome. Moreover, the splendor in which the pope and cardinals were living in Avignon led to highly vocal criticism of both clergy and papacy. At last, Pope Gregory XI, perceiving the disastrous decline in papal prestige, returned to Rome in 1377.

The Great Schism and Cries for Reform

Gregory XI (1370–1378) died in Rome the spring after his return. When the college of cardinals met to elect a new pope, the citizens of Rome, fearful that the French majority would choose another Frenchman who would move the papacy back to Avignon, threatened that the cardinals would not leave Rome alive unless a Roman or an Italian were elected pope. Wisely, the terrified cardinals duly elected the Italian archbishop of Bari as Pope Urban VI (1378–1389). Five months later, a group of dissenting cardinals—the French ones—declared Urban's election invalid and chose one of their number, a Frenchman, who took the title of Clement VII and promptly returned to Avignon. Because Urban remained in Rome, there were now two popes, beginning what has been called the Great Schism of the church.

The Great Schism divided Europe. France and its allies supported the pope in Avignon, whereas France's enemy England and its allies supported the pope in Rome. The Great Schism was also damaging to the faith of Christian believers. The pope was widely believed to be the true leader of Christendom; when both lines of popes denounced the other as the Antichrist, people's faith in the papacy and the church were undermined. Finally, a church council met at Constance, Switzerland, in 1417. After the competing popes resigned or were deposed, a new pope was elected who was acceptable to all parties.

By the mid-fifteenth century, as a result of these crises, the church had lost much of its temporal power. Even worse, the papacy and the church had also lost much of their moral prestige.

Recovery: The Renaissance

Focus Question: What were the main features of the Renaissance in Europe, and how did it differ from the Middle Ages?

People who lived in Italy between 1350 and 1550 or so believed that they were witnessing a rebirth of classical antiquity—the world of the Greeks and Romans. To them, this marked a new age, which historians later called the **Renaissance** (French for "rebirth") and viewed as a distinct period of European history, which began in Italy and then spread to the rest of Europe.

Renaissance Italy was largely an urban society. The city-states became the centers of Italian political, economic, and social life. Within this new urban society, a secular spirit emerged as increasing wealth created new possibilities for the enjoyment of worldly things.

The Renaissance was also an age of recovery from the disasters of the fourteenth century, including the Black Death, political disorder, and economic recession. In pursuing that recovery, Italian intellectuals became intensely interested in the glories of their own past, the Greco-Roman culture of antiquity.

A new view of human beings emerged as people in the Italian Renaissance began to emphasize individual ability. The fifteenth-century Florentine architect Leon Battista Alberti expressed the new philosophy succinctly: "Men can do all things if they will."[14] This high regard for human worth and for individual potentiality gave rise to a new social ideal of the well-rounded personality or "universal person" (*l'uomo universale*) who was capable of achievements in many areas of life.

The Intellectual Renaissance

The emergence and growth of individualism and secularism as characteristics of the Italian Renaissance are most noticeable in the intellectual and artistic realms. The most important literary movement associated with the Renaissance is humanism.

Renaissance humanism was an intellectual movement based on the study of the classics, the literary works of Greece and Rome. Humanists studied the liberal arts—grammar, rhetoric, poetry, moral philosophy or ethics, and history—all based on the writings of ancient Greek and Roman authors. We call these subjects the humanities.

Petrarch (1304–1374), who has often been called the father of Italian Renaissance humanism, did more than any other individual in the fourteenth century to foster its development. Petrarch sought to find forgotten Latin manuscripts and set in motion a ransacking of monastic libraries throughout Europe. He also began the humanist emphasis on the use of pure classical Latin. Humanists used the works of Cicero as a model for prose and those of Virgil for poetry. As Petrarch said, "Christ is my God; Cicero is the prince of the language."

In Florence, the humanist movement took a new direction at the beginning of the fifteenth century. Fourteenth-century humanists such as Petrarch had described the intellectual life as one of solitude. They rejected family and a life of action in the community. However, the humanists who worked as secretaries for the city council of Florence took a new interest in civic life. They came to believe that it was the duty of an intellectual to live an active life for one's state. Humanists came to believe that their study of the humanities should be put to the service of the state. It is no accident that humanists served as secretaries in Italian city-states or at courts of princes or popes.

Also evident in the humanism of the first half of the fifteenth century was a growing interest in Classical Greek civilization. One of the first Italian humanists to gain a thorough knowledge of Greek was Leonardo Bruni, who became an enthusiastic pupil of the Byzantine scholar Manuel Chrysoloras, who taught in Florence from 1396 to 1400.

Some women in Italy were also educated in the humanist fashion and went on to establish their own literary careers. Isotta Nogarola, born to a noble family in Verona, mastered Latin and wrote numerous letters and treatises

A WOMAN'S DEFENSE OF LEARNING

As a young woman, Laura Cereta was proud of her learning but condemned by a male world that found it unseemly for women to be scholars. One monk said to her father, "She gives herself to things unworthy of her—namely, the classics." Before being silenced, Laura Cereta wrote a series of letters, including one to a male critic who had argued that her work was so good it could not have been written by a woman.

Laura Cereta, *Defense of the Liberal Instruction of Women*

My ears are wearied by your carping. You brashly and publicly not merely wonder but indeed lament that I am said to possess as fine a mind as nature ever bestowed upon the most learned man. You seem to think that so learned a woman has scarcely before been seen in the world. You are wrong on both counts....

I would have been silent.... But I cannot tolerate your having attacked my entire sex. For this reason my thirsty soul seeks revenge, my sleeping pen is aroused to literary struggle, raging anger stirs mental passions long chained by silence. With just cause I am moved to demonstrate how great a reputation for learning and virtue women have won by their inborn excellence, manifested in every age as knowledge....

Only the question of the rarity of outstanding women remains to be addressed. The explanation is clear: women have been able by nature to be exceptional, but have chosen lesser goals. For some women are concerned with parting their hair correctly, adorning themselves with lovely dresses, or decorating their fingers with pearls and other gems. Others delight in mouthing carefully composed phrases, indulging in dancing, or managing spoiled puppies. Still others wish to gaze at lavish banquet tables, to

rest in sleep, or, standing at mirrors, to smear their lovely faces. But those in whom a deeper integrity yearns for virtue, restrain from the start their youthful souls, reflect on higher things, harden the body with sobriety and trials, and curb their tongues, open their ears, compose their thoughts in wakeful hours, their minds in contemplation, to letters bonded to righteousness. For knowledge is not given as a gift, but [is gained] with diligence. The free mind, not shirking effort, always soars zealously toward the good, and the desire to know grows ever more wide and deep. It is because of no special holiness, therefore, that we [women] are rewarded by God the Giver with the gift of exceptional talent. Nature has generously lavished its gifts upon all people, opening to all the doors of choice through which reason sends envoys to the will, from which they learn and convey its desires. The will must choose to exercise the gift of reason....

I have been praised too much; showing your contempt for women, you pretend that I alone am admirable because of the good fortune of my intellect.... Do you suppose, O most contemptible man on earth, that I think myself sprung [like Athena] from the head of Jove? I am a school girl, possessed of the sleeping embers of an ordinary mind. Indeed I am too hurt, and my mind, offended, too swayed by passions, sighs, tormenting itself, conscious of the obligation to defend my sex. For absolutely everything—that which is within us and that which is without—is made weak by association with my sex.

Q *How does Cereta explain her intellectual interests and accomplishments? Why were Renaissance women rarely taken seriously in their quest for educational opportunities and recognition for their intellectual talents? Were any of those factors unique to the Renaissance era?*

---

that brought her praise from male Italian intellectuals. Cassandra Fedele of Venice, who learned both Latin and Greek from humanist tutors hired by her family, became prominent in Venice for her public recitations of orations. Laura Cereta was educated in Latin by her father, a physician from Brescia. Laura defended the ability of women to pursue scholarly pursuits (see the box above).

The Artistic Renaissance

Renaissance artists sought to imitate nature in their works of art. Their search for naturalism became an end in itself: to persuade onlookers of the reality of the object or event they were portraying. At the same time, the new artistic standards reflected the new attitude of mind in which human beings became the focus of attention, the "center and measure of all things," as one artist proclaimed.

The frescoes by Masaccio (1401–1428) in Florence have long been regarded as the first masterpieces of Early Renaissance art. With his use of monumental figures, a more realistic relationship between figures and landscape, and the visual representation of the laws of perspective, a new realistic style of painting was born. Onlookers became aware of a world of reality that appeared to be a continuation of their own.

This new Renaissance style was absorbed and modified by other Florentine painters in the fifteenth century. Especially important were two major developments. One emphasized the technical side of painting—understanding the laws of perspective and the geometrical organization of outdoor space and light. The second development was the investigation of movement and anatomical structure. The realistic portrayal of the human nude became one of the foremost preoccupations of Italian Renaissance artists.

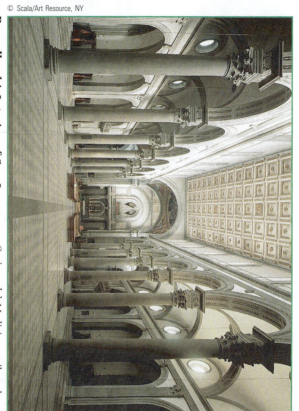

© Scala/Art Resource, NY

Brunelleschi, Interior of San Lorenzo. Cosimo de' Medici contributed massive amounts of money to the rebuilding of the Church of San Lorenzo. As seen in this view of the nave and choir of the church, Brunelleschi's architectural designs were based on the basilica plan borrowed by early Christians from pagan Rome. San Lorenzo's simplicity, evident in its rows of slender Corinthian columns, created a human-centered space.

A new style in architecture also emerged when Filippo Brunelleschi (1377–1446), inspired by Roman models, created an interior in the Church of San Lorenzo in Florence that was very different from that of the great medieval cathedrals. San Lorenzo's classical columns, rounded arches, and coffered ceiling created an environment that did not overwhelm the worshipers physically

and psychologically, as Gothic cathedrals did, but comforted them as a space created to fit human, not divine, measurements. Like painters and sculptors, Renaissance architects sought to reflect a human-centered world.

By the end of the fifteenth century, Italian artists had mastered the new techniques for scientific observation of the world around them and were now ready to move into new forms of creative expression. This marked the shift to the High Renaissance, which was dominated by the work of three artistic giants, Leonardo da Vinci (1452–1519), Raphael (1483–1520), and Michelangelo (1475–1564). Leonardo carried on the fifteenth-century experimental tradition by studying everything and even dissecting human bodies in order to see how nature worked. But Leonardo stressed the need to advance beyond such realism and initiated the High Renaissance's preoccupation with the idealization of nature, an attempt to generalize from realistic portrayal to an ideal form.

At twenty-five, Raphael was already regarded as one of Italy's best painters. He was acclaimed for his numerous madonnas, in which he attempted to achieve an ideal of beauty far surpassing human standards. He is well known for his frescoes in the Vatican Palace, which reveal a world of balance, harmony, and order—the underlying principles of the art of Classical Greece and Rome.

Michelangelo, an accomplished painter, sculptor, and architect, was fiercely driven by a desire to create, and he

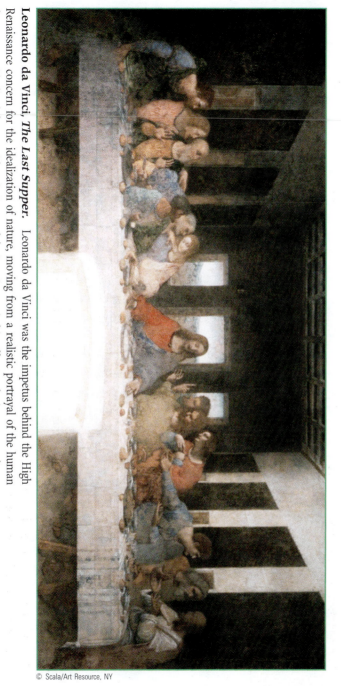

© Scala/Art Resource, NY

Leonardo da Vinci, The Last Supper. Leonardo da Vinci was the impetus behind the High Renaissance concern for the idealization of nature, moving from a realistic portrayal of the human figure to an idealized form. Evident in Leonardo's Last Supper is his effort to depict a person's character and inner nature by the use of gesture and movement. Unfortunately, Leonardo used an experimental technique in this fresco, which soon led to its physical deterioration.

worked with great passion and energy on a remarkable number of projects. Michelangelo was influenced by Neoplatonism, especially evident in his figures on the ceiling of the Sistine Chapel. These muscular figures reveal an ideal type of human being with perfect proportions. In good Neoplatonic fashion, their beauty is meant to be a reflection of divine beauty; the more beautiful the body, the more God-like the figure. Another manifestation of Michelangelo's search for ideal beauty was his David, a colossal marble statue commissioned by the government of Florence in 1501 and completed in 1504.

The State in the Renaissance

In the second half of the fifteenth century, attempts were made to reestablish the centralized power of monarchical governments after the political disasters of the fourteenth century. Some historians called these states the "new monarchies," especially those of France, England, and Spain (see Map 13.4).

The Italian States   The Italian states provided the earliest examples of state building in the fifteenth century. During the Middle Ages, Italy had failed to develop a centralized territorial state, and by the fifteenth century, five major powers dominated the Italian peninsula: the duchy of Milan, the republics of Florence and Venice, the Papal States, and the kingdom of Naples.

Milan, Florence, and Venice proved especially adept at building strong, centralized states. Under a series of dukes, Milan became a highly centralized territorial state in which the rulers devised systems of taxation that generated enormous revenues for the government. The maritime republic of Venice remained an extremely stable political entity governed by a small oligarchy of merchant-aristocrats. Its commercial empire brought in vast revenues and gave it the status of an international power. In Florence, Cosimo de' Medici took control of the merchant oligarchy in 1434. Through lavish patronage and careful courting of political allies, he and his family dominated the city at a time when Florence was the center of the cultural Renaissance.

Italian States in the Middle Ages

© Scala/Art Resource, NY

Michelangelo, David. This statue of David, cut from an 18-foot-high piece of marble, exalts the beauty of the human body and is a fitting symbol of the Italian Renaissance's affirmation of human power. Completed in 1504, David was moved by Florentine authorities to a special location in front of the Palazzo Vecchio, the seat of the Florentine government.

As strong as these Italian states became, they still could not compete with the powerful monarchical states to the north and west. Beginning in 1494, Italy became a battlefield for the great power struggle between the French and Spanish monarchies, a conflict that led to Spanish domination of Italy in the sixteenth century.

Western Europe   The Hundred Years' War left France prostrate. But it had also engendered a certain degree of French national feeling toward a common enemy that the kings could use to reestablish monarchical power. The development of a French territorial state was greatly advanced by King Louis XI (1461–1483), known as the Spider because of his wily and devious ways. Louis strengthened the use of the **taille**—an annual direct tax usually on land or property—as a permanent tax imposed by royal authority, giving him a sound, regular source of income, which created the foundations of a strong French monarchy.

The Hundred Years' War had also strongly affected the English. The cost of the war in its final years and the losses to the labor force strained the English economy. At the end of the war, England faced even greater turmoil when a civil war, known as the War of the Roses, erupted and aristocratic factions fought over the monarchy until 1485, when Henry Tudor established a new dynasty.

As the first Tudor king, Henry VII (1485–1509) worked to establish a strong monarchical government. Henry ended the petty wars of the nobility by abolishing their private armies. He was also very thrifty. By not overburdening the nobility and the middle class with taxes, Henry won their favor, and they provided him much support.

Spain, too, experienced the growth of a strong national monarchy by the end of the fifteenth century. During the Middle Ages, several independent Christian kingdoms had emerged in the course of the long reconquest of the Iberian peninsula from the Muslims. Two of the strongest were Aragon and Castile. When Isabella of Castile (1474–1504) married Ferdinand of Aragon (1479–1516) in 1469, it was a major step toward unifying Spain. The two rulers worked to strengthen royal control of government. They filled the royal council, which supervised the administration of the government, with middle-class lawyers. Trained in Roman law, these officials operated on the belief that the monarchy embodied the power of the state. Ferdinand and Isabella also reorganized the military forces of Spain, making the new Spanish army the best in Europe by the sixteenth century.

Central and Eastern Europe Unlike France, England, and Spain, the Holy Roman Empire failed to develop a strong monarchical authority. The failure of the German emperors in the thirteenth century ended any chance of centralized authority, and Germany became a land of hundreds of virtually independent states. After 1438, the position of Holy Roman Emperor was held by members of the Habsburg dynasty. Having gradually acquired a number of possessions along the Danube, known

collectively as Austria, the house of Habsburg had become one of the wealthiest landholders in the empire and by the mid-fifteenth century had begun to play an important role in European affairs.

In eastern Europe, rulers struggled to achieve the centralization of the territorial states. Religious differences troubled the area as Roman Catholics, Eastern Orthodox Christians, and other groups, including the Mongols, confronted each other. In Poland, the nobles gained the upper hand and established the right to elect their kings, a policy that drastically weakened royal authority.

Since the thirteenth century, Russia had been under the domination of the Mongols. Gradually, the princes of Moscow rose to prominence by using their close relationship to the Mongol khans to increase their wealth and expand their possessions. During the reign of the great Prince Ivan III (1462–1505), a new Russian state was born. Ivan annexed other Russian principalities and took advantage of dissension among the Mongols to throw off their yoke by 1480.

MAP 13.4 Europe in the Second Half of the Fifteenth Century. By the second half of the fifteenth century, states in western Europe, particularly France, Spain, and England, had begun the process of modern state building. With varying success, they reined in the power of the church and nobles, increased the ability to levy taxes, and established effective government bureaucracies.

Q What aspects of Europe's political boundaries help explain why France and the Holy Roman Empire were often at war with each other?

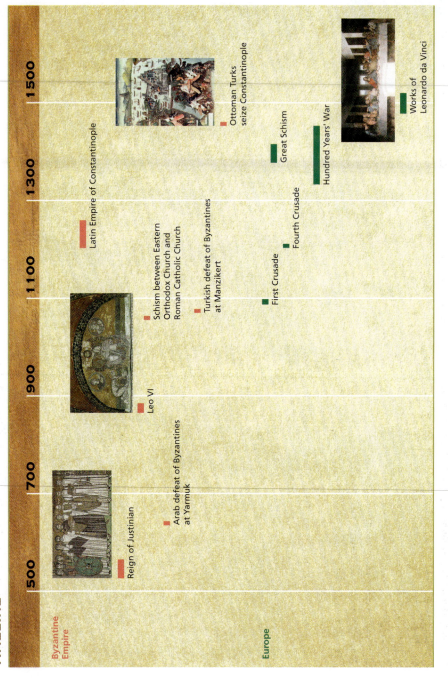

Byzantine Empire

Reign of Justinian

Arab defeat of Byzantines at Yarmuk

Leo VI

Schism between Eastern Orthodox Church and Roman Catholic Church

Turkish defeat of Byzantines at Manzikert

Latin Empire of Constantinople

Ottoman Turks seize Constantinople

500 · 700 · 900 · 1100 · 1300 · 1500

Europe

First Crusade

Fourth Crusade

Great Schism

Hundred Years' War

Works of Leonardo da Vinci

CONCLUSION

After the collapse of Roman power in the west, the Eastern Roman Empire, centered on Constantinople, continued in the eastern Mediterranean and eventually emerged as the Byzantine Empire, which flourished for hundreds of years. While a new Christian civilization arose in Europe, the Byzantine Empire created its own unique Christian civilization. And while Europe struggled in the Early Middle Ages, the Byzantine world continued to prosper and flourish. Especially during the ninth, tenth, and eleventh centuries, under the Macedonian emperors, the Byzantine Empire expanded and achieved an economic prosperity that was evident to foreign visitors who frequently praised the size, wealth, and physical surroundings of the central city of Constantinople.

During its heyday, Byzantium was a multicultural and multiethnic empire that ruled a remarkable number of peoples who spoke different languages. Byzantine cultural and religious forms spread to the Balkans, parts of central Europe, and Russia. Byzantine scholars spread the study of the Greek language to Italy, expanding Renaissance humanism with an interest in Classical Greek civilization. The Byzantine Empire also interacted with the world of Islam to its east and the new European civilization of the west. Both interactions proved costly and ultimately fatal.

Although European civilization and Byzantine civilization shared a common bond in Christianity, it proved incapable of keeping them in harmony politically. Indeed, the west's Crusades to Palestine, ostensibly for religious motives, led to western control of the Byzantine Empire from 1204 to 1261. Although the empire was restored, it limped along until its other interaction—with the Muslim world—led to its demise when the Ottoman Turks conquered the city of Constantinople and made it the center of their new empire.

While Byzantium was declining in the twelfth and thirteenth centuries, Europe was achieving new levels of growth and optimism. In the fourteenth century, however, Europe too experienced a real time of troubles as it was devastated by the Black Death, economic dislocation, political chaos, and religious decline. But in the fifteenth century, while Constantinople and the remnants of the Byzantine Empire finally fell to the world of Islam, Europe experienced a dramatic revival. Elements of recovery in the Renaissance made the fifteenth century a period of significant artistic, intellectual, and political change in Europe. By the second half of the fifteenth century, as we shall see in the next chapter, the growth of strong, centralized monarchical states made possible the dramatic expansion of Europe into other parts of the world.

CHAPTER NOTES

1. Quoted in P. Cesaretti, *Theodora: Empress of Byzantium*, trans. R. M. Frongia (New York, 2004), p. 197.

2. Procopius, *Buildings of Justinian* (London, 1897), pp. 9, 6–7.

3. Procopius, *Secret History*, trans. R. Atwater (Ann Arbor, Mich., 1963), p. 3.

4. Quoted in J. Harris, *Constantinople: Capital of Byzantium* (New York, 2007), p. 40.

5. Quoted in ibid., p. 118.

6. A. Cameron, *The Byzantines* (Oxford, 2006), p. 45.

7. Quoted in C. S. Bartsocas, "Two Fourteenth-Century Descriptions of the 'Black Death,'" *Journal of the History of Medicine* (October 1966), p. xiii.

8. Quoted in M. Dols, *The Black Death in the Middle East* (Princeton, N.J., 1977), p. 111.

9. Quoted in D. J. Herlihy, *The Black Death and the Transformation of the West*, ed. S. K. Cohn Jr. (Cambridge, Mass., 1997), p. 9.

10. Quoted in R. Horrox, *The Black Death* (Manchester, England, 1994), p. 16.

11. G. Boccaccio, *The Decameron*, trans. F. Winwar (New York, 1955), p. xiii.

12. J. Froissart, *Chronicles*, ed. and trans. G. Brereton (Harmondsworth, England, 1968), p. 111.

13. Ibid., p. 89.

14. Quoted in J. Burckhardt, *The Civilization of the Renaissance in Italy*, trans. S. G. C. Middlemore (London, 1960), p. 81.

SUGGESTED READING

General Histories of the Byzantine Empire For comprehensive surveys of the Byzantine Empire, see T. E. Gregory, *A History of Byzantium* (Oxford, 2005), and W. Treadgold, *A History of the Byzantine State and Society* (Stanford, Calif., 1997). See also C. Mango, ed., *The Oxford History of Byzantium* (Oxford, 2002). Brief but good introductions to Byzantine history can be found in J. Haldon, *Byzantium: A History* (Charleston, S.C., 2000), and W. Treadgold, *A Concise History of Byzantium* (London, 2001). For a thematic approach, see A. Cameron, *The Byzantines* (Oxford, 2006).

The Early Empire (to 1025) Byzantine civilization in this period is examined in M. Whitow, *The Making of Orthodox Byzantium, 600–1025* (Berkeley, Calif., 1996), and W. Treadgold, *The Byzantine Revival, 780–842* (Stanford, Calif., 1988). On Justinian, see J. Moorhead, *Justinian* (London, 1995), and J. A. S. Evans, *The Age of Justinian* (New York, 1996). On Theodora, see P. Cesavetti, *Theodora, Empress of Byzantium*, trans. R. M. Frongia (New York, 2001). On Leo VI, see S. Tougher, *The Reign of Leo VI: Politics and People* (Leiden, Netherlands, 1997). On Constantinople, see J. Harris, *Constantinople: Capital of Byzantium* (London, 2007). The role of the Christian church is discussed in J. Hussey, *The Orthodox Church in the Byzantine Empire* (Oxford, 1986). Women in the Byzantine Empire are examined in C. L. Connor, *Women of Byzantium* (New Haven, Conn., 2004), and J. Herrin, *Women in Purple: Rulers of Medieval Byzantium* (Princeton, N.J., 2001). On economic affairs, see A. Harvey, *Economic Expansion in the Byzantine Empire, 900–1200* (Cambridge, 1990). Art is examined in T. F. Mathews, *The Art of Byzantium: Between Antiquity and the Renaissance* (London, 1998).

The Late Empire (1025–1453) On the eleventh and twelfth centuries, see M. Angold, *The Byzantine Empire, 1025–1204*, 2d ed. (London, 1997). The impact of the Crusades on the Byzantine Empire is examined in J. Harris, *Byzantium and the Crusades* (London, 2003). The disastrous Fourth Crusade is examined in J. Philips, *The Fourth Crusade and the Sack of Constantinople* (New York, 2004). The revival of Byzantium after the Latin Empire is discussed in D. Nicol, *The Last Centuries of Byzantium, 1261–1453*, 2d ed. (Cambridge, 1993). On the fall of Constantinople, see D. Nicolle, J. Haldon, and S. Turnbull, *The Fall of Constantinople: The Ottoman Conquest of Byzantium* (Oxford, 2007).

Crises of the Fourteenth Century On the Black Death, see J. Kelly, *The Great Mortality* (New York, 2005); and D. J. Herlihy, *The Black Death and the Transformation of the West*, ed. S. K. Cohn Jr. (Cambridge, Mass., 1997). A worthy account of the Hundred Years' War is A. Curry, *The Hundred Years' War*, 2d ed. (New York, 2004). On Joan of Arc, see M. Warner, *Joan of Arc: The Image of Female Heroism* (New York, 1981).

The Renaissance General works on the Renaissance in Europe include P. Burke, *The European Renaissance: Centres and Peripheries* (Oxford, 1998); M. L. King, *The Renaissance in Europe* (New York, 2004); and J. R. Hale, *The Civilization of Europe in the Renaissance* (New York, 1994). For beautifully illustrated introductions to the Renaissance, see G. Holmes, *Renaissance* (New York, 1996), and M. Aston, ed., *The Panorama of the Renaissance* (New York, 1996). A brief introduction to Renaissance humanism can be found in C. G. Nauert Jr., *Humanism and the Culture of Renaissance Europe*, 2d ed. (Cambridge, 2006). Good surveys of Renaissance art include R. Turner, *Renaissance Florence: The Invention of a New Art* (New York, 1997), and J. T. Paoletti and G. M. Radke, *Art, Power, and Patronage in Renaissance Italy*, 3d ed. (Upper Saddle River, N.J., 2003). For a general work on the political development of Europe in the Renaissance, see C. Mulgan, *The Renaissance Monarchies, 1469–1558* (Cambridge, 1998). A good study of the Italian states is J. M. Najemy, *Italy in the Age of the Renaissance, 1300–1550* (Oxford, 2004).

WORLD HISTORY RESOURCE CENTER

Enter the Resource Center using either your CengageNOW access card or your separate access card for the World History Resource Center. Organized by topic, this Website includes quizzes; images; over 350 primary source documents; interactive simulations, maps, and timelines; movie explorations; and a wealth of other resources. You can read the following documents, and many more, at the World History Resource Center:

The Hundred Years' War in the High Court of Parlement

Visit the *World History Companion* Website for chapter quizzes and more:

www.cengage.com/history/Duiker/Worlde

Enter CengageNOW using the access card that is available with this text. CengageNOW will help you understand the content in this chapter with lesson plans generated for your needs, as well as provide you with a connection to the Wadsworth World History Resource Center (see description below for details).

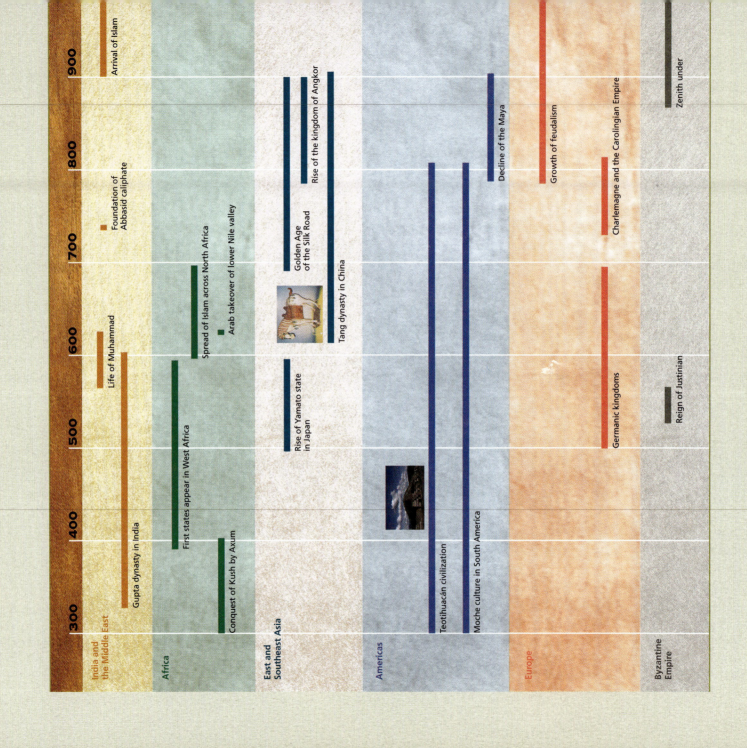

PART II REVIEW TIMELINE

	300	400	500	600	700	800	900

India and the Middle East
- Gupta dynasty in India
- Life of Muhammad
- Foundation of Abbasid caliphate
- Arrival of Islam

Africa
- Conquest of Kush by Axum
- First states appear in West Africa
- Spread of Islam across North Africa
- Arab takeover of lower Nile valley

East and Southeast Asia
- Rise of Yamato state in Japan
- Golden Age of the Silk Road
- Tang dynasty in China
- Rise of the kingdom of Angkor

Americas
- Teotihuacán civilization
- Moche culture in South America
- Decline of the Maya

Europe
- Germanic kingdoms
- Growth of feudalism
- Charlemagne and the Carolingian Empire

Byzantine Empire
- Reign of Justinian
- Zenith under

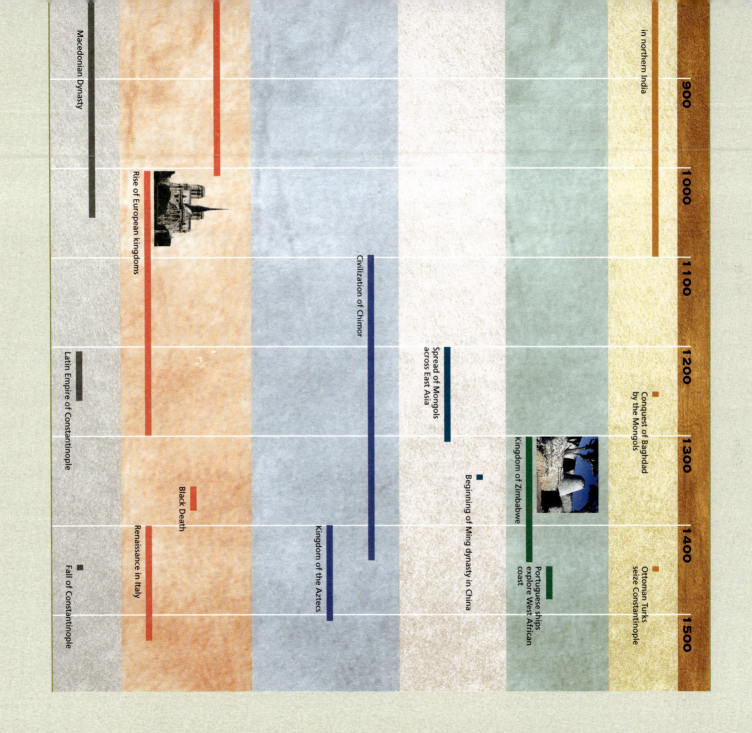

900

1000

1100

1200

1300

1400

1500

Macedonian Dynasty

Rise of European kingdoms

Latin Empire of Constantinople

Fall of Constantinople

Black Death

Renaissance in Italy

Civilization of Chimor

Kingdom of the Aztecs

Spread of Mongols across East Asia

Beginning of Ming dynasty in China

Kingdom of Zimbabwe

Portuguese ships explore West African coast

in northern India

Conquest of Baghdad by the Mongols

Ottoman Turks seize Constantinople

abbess   the head of a convent or monastery for women.

abbot   the head of a monastery.

absolutism   a form of government in which the sovereign power or ultimate authority rested in the hands of a monarch who claimed to rule by divine right and was therefore responsible only to God.

Abstract Expressionism   a post–World War II artistic movement that broke with all conventions of form and structure in favor of total abstraction.

abstract painting   an artistic movement that developed early in the twentieth century in which artists focused on color to avoid any references to visual reality.

Agricultural (Neolithic) Revolution   the shift from hunting animals and gathering plants for sustenance to producing food by systematic agriculture that occurred gradually between 10,000 and 4000 B.C.E. (the Neolithic or "New Stone" Age).

Amerindians   earliest inhabitants of North and South America. Original theories suggested migration from Siberia across the Bering Land Bridge; more recent evidence suggests migration also occurred by sea from regions of the South Pacific to South America.

Analects   the body of writing containing conversations between Confucius and his disciples that preserves his worldly wisdom and pragmatic philosophies.

anarchists   people who hold that all governments and existing social institutions are unnecessary and advocate a society based on voluntary cooperation.

ANC   the African National Congress. Founded in 1912, it was the beginning of political activity by South African blacks. Banned by politically dominant European whites in 1960, it was not officially "unbanned" until 1990. It is now the official majority party of the South African government.

anti-Semitism   hostility toward or discrimination against Jews.

apartheid   the system of racial segregation practiced in the Republic of South Africa until the 1990s, which involved political, legal, and economic discrimination against nonwhites.

appeasement   the policy, followed by the European nations in the 1930s, of accepting Hitler's annexation of Austria and Czechoslovakia in the belief that meeting his demands would ensure peace and stability.

Aramaic   a Semitic language dominant in the Middle East in the first century B.C.E.; still in use in small regions of the Middle East and southern Asia.

aristocracy   a class of hereditary nobility in medieval Europe; a warrior class who shared a distinctive lifestyle based on the institution of knighthood, although there were social divisions within the group based on extremes of wealth.

Arthasastra   an early Indian political treatise that sets forth many fundamental aspects of the relationship of rulers and their subjects. It has been compared to Machiavelli's well-known book *The Prince* and has provided principles on which many aspects of social organization have developed in the region.

Aryans   Indo–European-speaking nomads who entered India from the Central Asian steppes between 1500 and 1000 B.C.E. and greatly affected Indian society, notably by establishing the caste system. The term *Aryan* was later adopted by German Nazis to describe their racial ideal.

asceticism   a lifestyle involving the denial of worldly pleasures. Predominantly associated with the Hindu, Buddhist, and Christian religions, adherents perceive their practices as a path to greater spirituality.

ASEAN   the Association for the Southeast Asian Nations, formed in 1967 to promote the prosperity and political stability of its member nations. Currently, Brunei, Indonesia, Laos, Malaysia, Myanmar, the Philippines, Singapore, Thailand, and Vietnam are members. Other countries in the region participate as "observer" members.

assimilation   the concept, originated in France, that the colonial peoples should be assimilated into the parent French culture.

association   the concept developed by French colonial officials that the relationship between France and its colonial societies should be one of association, rather than assimilation. Under that concept, colonial peoples would be permitted to retain their precolonial cultural traditions.

Ausgleich   the "compromise" of 1867 that created the dual monarchy of Austria–Hungary. Austria and Hungary each had its own capital, constitution, and legislative assembly but were united under one monarch.

authoritarian state   a state that has a dictatorial government and some other trappings of a totalitarian state but does not demand that the masses be actively involved in the regime's goals as totalitarian states do.

bakufu   the centralized government set up in Japan in the twelfth century. See shogunate system.

banners   originally established in 1639 by the Qing empire, the eight banners were administrative divisions into which all Manchu families were placed. Banners quickly evolved into the basis of Manchu military organization, with each required to raise and support a prescribed number of troops.

Bao-jia system   the Chinese practice, reportedly originated by the Qin dynasty in the third century B.C.E., of organizing families into groups of five or ten to exercise mutual control and surveillance and reduce loyalty to the family.

bard   in Africa, a professional storyteller.

Baroque   a style that dominated Western painting, sculpture, architecture, and music from about 1580 to 1730, generally characterized by elaborate ornamentation and dramatic effects. Important practitioners included Bernini, Rubens, Handel, and Bach.

Bedouins   nomadic tribes originally from northern Arabia who became important traders after the domestication of the camel during the first millennium B.C.E. Early converts to Islam, their values and practices deeply affected Muhammad.

Berbers   an ethnic group indigenous to western North Africa.

bey   a provincial governor in the Ottoman Empire.

bhakti   in Hinduism, devotion as a means of religious observance open to all persons regardless of class.

Black Death   the outbreak of plague (mostly bubonic) in the mid-fourteenth century that killed from 25 to 50 percent of Europe's population.

Blitzkrieg   "lightning war." A war conducted with great speed and force, as in Germany's advance at the beginning of World War II.

bodhi   wisdom. Sometimes described as complete awareness of the true nature of the universe.

bodhisattva   in some schools of Buddhism, an individual who has achieved enlightenment but, because of his great compassion, has chosen to renounce Nirvana and to remain on earth in spirit form to help all human beings achieve release from reincarnation.

Bolsheviks a small faction of the Russian Social Democratic Party who were led by Lenin and dedicated to violent revolution; seized power in Russia in 1917 and were subsequently renamed the Communists.

bonsai the cultivation of stunted trees and shrubs to create exquisite nature scenes in miniature. Originating in China in the first millenium B.C.E. and known there as *penzai*, bonsai was imported to Japan between 700 and 900 C.E.

Brahman the Hindu word roughly equivalent to God; the divine basis of all being; regarded as the source and sum of the cosmos.

brahmin a member of the Hindu priestly caste or class; literally "one who has realized or attempts to realize Brahman." Traditionally, duties of a brahmin include studying Hindu religious scriptures and transmitting them to others orally. The priests of Hindu temples are brahmins.

Brezhnev Doctrine the doctrine, enunciated by Leonid Brezhnev, that the Soviet Union had a right to intervene if socialism was threatened in another socialist state; used to justify the use of Soviet troops in Czechoslovakia in 1968.

Buddhism a religion and philosophy based on the teachings of Siddhartha Gautama around 500 B.C.E. Principally practiced in China, India, and other parts of Asia, Buddhism has 360 million followers and is considered a major world religion.

Burakumin a Japanese minority similar to *dalits* (untouchables) in Indian culture. Past and current discrimination has resulted in lower educational attainment and socioeconomic status for members of this group. Movements with objectives ranging from "liberation" to integration have tried over the years to change this situation.

Bushido the code of conduct observed by samurai warriors; comparable to the European concept of chivalry.

caliph the secular leader of the Islamic community.

calpulli in Aztec society, a kinship group, often of a thousand or more, that served as an intermediary with the central government, providing taxes and conscript labor to the state.

capital material wealth used or available for use in the production of more wealth.

cartel a combination of independent commercial enterprises that work together to control prices and limit competition.

Cartesian dualism Descartes's principle of the separation of mind and matter (and mind and body) that enabled scientists to view matter as something separate from themselves that could be investigated by reason.

caste system a system of rigid social hierarchy in which all members of that society are assigned by birth to specific "ranks" and inherit specific roles and privileges.

Catholic Reformation a movement for the reform of the Catholic Church in the sixteenth century.

caudillos strong leaders in nineteenth-century Latin America who were usually supported by the landed elites and ruled chiefly by military force, though some were popular; they included both modernizers and destructive dictators.

censorate one of the three primary Chinese ministries, originally established in the Qin dynasty, whose inspectors surveyed the efficiency of officials throughout the system.

centuriate assembly the chief popular assembly of the Roman Republic. It passed laws and elected the chief magistrates.

chaebol a South Korean business structure similar to the Japanese *keiretsu.*

Chan Buddhism a Chinese sect (Zen in Japanese) influenced by Daoist ideas, which called for mind training and a strict regimen as a means of seeking enlightenment.

chinampas in Mesoamerica, artifical islands crisscrossed by canals that provided water for crops and easy transportation to local markets.

chivalry the ideal of civilized behavior that emerged among the European nobility in the eleventh and twelfth centuries under the influence of the church; a code of ethics knights were expected to uphold.

Christian humanism an intellectual movement in northern Europe in the late fifteenth and early sixteenth centuries that combined interest in the classics of the Italian Renaissance with an interest in the sources of early Christianity, including the New Testament and the writings of the church fathers.

civil disobedience a tactic designed by the Indian nationalist leader Mohandas Gandhi to resist British colonial rule by adopting illegal but nonviolent means. The concept would later be adopted by nationalist and liberation forces in many other countries.

civilization a complex culture in which large numbers of humans share a variety of common elements, including cities; religious, political, military, and social structures; writing; and significant artistic and intellectual activity.

civil rights the basic rights of citizens, including equality before the law, freedom of speech and press, and freedom from arbitrary arrest.

civil service examination an elaborate Chinese system of selecting bureaucrats on merit, first introduced in 165 C.E., developed by the Tang dynasty in the seventh century C.E., and refined under the Song dynasty; later adopted in Vietnam and with less success in Japan and Korea. It contributed to efficient government, upward mobility, and cultural uniformity.

class struggle the basis of the Marxist analysis of history, which says that the owners of the means of production have always oppressed the workers and predicts an inevitable revolution. See Marxism.

Cold War the ideological conflict between the Soviet Union and the United States between the end of World War II and the early 1990s.

collective farms large farms created in the Soviet Union by Stalin by combining many small holdings into large farms worked by the peasants under government supervision.

collective security the use of an international army raised by an association of nations to deter aggression and keep the peace.

commercial capitalism beginning in the Middle Ages, an economic system in which people invested in trade and goods in order to make profits.

common law law common to the entire kingdom of England; imposed by the king's courts beginning in the twelfth century to replace the customary law used in county and feudal courts that varied from place to place.

communalism in South Asia, the tendency of people to band together in mutually antagonistic social subgroups; elsewhere used to describe unifying trends in the larger community.

commune in medieval Europe, an association of townspeople bound together by a sworn oath for the purpose of obtaining basic liberties from the lord of the territory in which the town was located; also, the self-governing town after receiving its liberties.

Communist International (Comintern) a worldwide organization of Communist parties, founded by Lenin in 1919, dedicated to the advancement of world revolution; also known as the Third International.

Confucianism a system of thought based on the teachings of Confucius (551–479 B.C.E.) that developed into the ruling ideology of the Chinese state. See Neo-Confucianism.

conquistadors "conquerors." Leaders in the Spanish conquests in the Americas, especially Mexico and Peru, in the sixteenth century.

conscription a military draft.

conservatism an ideology based on tradition and social stability that favored the maintenance of established institutions, organized religion, and obedience to authority and resisted change, especially abrupt change.

consuls the chief executive officers of the Roman Republic. Two were chosen annually to administer the government and lead the army in battle.

consumer society a term applied to Western society after World War II as the working classes adopted the consumption patterns of the middle class and installment plans, credit cards, and easy credit made consumer goods such as appliances and automobiles widely available.

containment a policy adopted by the United States in the Cold War. Its goal was to use whatever means, short of all-out war, to limit Soviet expansion.

Continental System Napoleon's effort to bar British goods from the Continent in the hope of weakening Britain's economy and destroying its capacity to wage war.

Contras in Nicaragua in the 1980s, an anti-Sandinista guerrilla movement supported by the U.S. Reagan administration.

Coptic a form of Christianity, originally Egyptian, that has thrived in Ethiopia since the fourth century C.E.

cosmopolitanism the quality of being sophisticated and having wide international experience.

cottage industry a system of textile manufacturing in which spinners and weavers worked at home in their cottages using raw materials supplied to them by capitalist entrepreneurs.

council of the plebs a council only for the plebeians. After 287 B.C.E., however, its resolutions were binding on all Romans.

creoles in Latin America, American-born descendants of Europeans.

Crusade in the Middle Ages, a military campaign in defense of Christendom.

Cubism an artistic style developed at the beginning of the twentieth century, especially by Pablo Picasso, that used geometric designs to re-create reality in the viewer's mind.

cultural relativism the belief that no culture is superior to another because culture is a matter of custom, not reason, and derives its meaning from the group that created it.

cuneiform "wedge-shaped." A system of writing developed by the Sumerians that consisted of wedge-shaped impressions made by a reed stylus on clay tablets.

Dadaism an artistic movement in the 1920s and 1930s by artists who were revolted by the senseless slaughter of World War I and used their "anti-art" to express contempt for the Western tradition.

daimyo prominent Japanese families who provided allegiance to the local shogun in exchange for protection; similar to vassals in Europe.

dalits commonly referred to as untouchables; the lowest level of Indian society, technically outside the caste system and considered less than human; renamed harijans ("children of God") by Gandhi, they remain the object of discrimination despite affirmative action programs.

Dao a Chinese philosophical concept, literally "the Way," central to both Confucianism and Daoism, that describes the behavior proper to each member of society; somewhat similar to the Indian concept of dharma.

Daoism a Chinese philosophy traditionally ascribed to the perhaps legendary Lao Tzu, which holds that acceptance and spontaneity are the keys to harmonious interaction with the universal order; an alternative to Confucianism.

decolonization the process of becoming free of colonial status and achieving statehood; occurred in most of the world's colonies between 1947 and 1962.

deconstruction a system of thought, formulated by Jacques Derrida, that holds that culture is created in a variety of ways, according to the manner in which people create their own meaning. Hence, there is no fixed truth or universal meaning.

deficit spending the concept, developed by John Maynard Keynes in the 1930s, that in times of economic depression, governments should stimulate demand by hiring people to do public works, such as building highways, even if this increased public debt.

deism belief in God as the creator of the universe who, after setting it in motion, ceased to have any direct involvement in it and allowed it to run according to its own natural laws.

demesne the part of a manor retained under the direct control of the lord and worked by the serfs as part of their labor services.

denazification after World War II, the Allied policy of rooting out all traces of Nazism in German society by bringing prominent Nazis to trial for war crimes and purging any known Nazis from political office.

depression a very severe, protracted economic downturn with high levels of unemployment.

destalinization the policy of denouncing and undoing the most repressive aspects of Stalin's regime; begun by Nikita Khrushchev in 1956.

détente the relaxation of tension between the Soviet Union and the United States that occurred in the 1970s.

developed nations a term used to refer to rich nations, primarily in the Northern Hemisphere, that have well-organized industrial and agricultural systems, advanced technologies, and effective educational systems.

developing nations a term used to refer to poor nations, mainly in the Southern Hemisphere, that are primarily farming nations with little technology and serious population problems.

devshirme in the Ottoman Empire, a system (literally, "collection") of training talented children to be administrators or members of the sultan's harem; originally meant, by the seventeenth century it had degenerated into a hereditary caste.

dharma in Hinduism and Buddhism, the law that governs the universe and specifically human behavior.

diocese the area under the jurisdiction of a Christian bishop; based originally on Roman administrative districts.

direct representation a system of choosing delegates to a representative assembly in which citizens vote directly for the delegates who will represent them.

direct rule a concept devised by European colonial governments to rule their colonial subjects without the participation of local authorities. It was most often applied in colonial societies in Africa.

divination the practice of seeking to foretell future events by interpreting divine signs, which could appear in various forms, such as in the entrails of animals, in patterns in smoke, or in dreams.

divine-right monarchy a monarchy based on the belief that monarchs receive their power directly from God and are responsible to no one except God.

domino theory the belief that if the Communists succeeded in Vietnam, other countries in Southeast and East Asia would also fall (like dominoes) to communism; a justification for the U.S. intervention in Vietnam.

dualism the belief that the universe is dominated by two opposing forces, one good and the other evil.

dyarchy during the Qing dynasty in China, a system in which all important national and provincial administrative positions were shared equally by Chinese and Manchus, which helped consolidate both the Manchus' rule and their assimilation.

dynastic state a state in which the maintenance and expansion of the interests of the ruling family are the primary consideration.

economic imperialism the process in which banks and corporations from developed nations invest in underdeveloped regions and establish a major presence there in the hope of making high profits; not necessarily the same as colonial expansion in that businesses invest where they can make a profit, which may not be in their own nation's colonies.

El Niño periodic changes in water temperature at the surface of the Pacific Ocean, which can lead to major environmental changes and may have led to the collapse of the Moche civilization in what is now Peru.

emir "commander" in Arabic, a title used by Muslim rulers in southern Spain and elsewhere.

empiricism the practice of relying on observation and experiment.

encomienda a grant from the Spanish monarch to colonial conquistadors; see encomienda system.

encomienda system the system by which Spain first governed its American colonies. Holders of an encomienda were supposed to protect the Indians as well as use them as laborers and collect tribute but in practice exploited them.

encyclical a letter from the pope to all the bishops of the Roman Catholic Church.

enlightened absolutism an absolute monarchy in which the ruler follows the principles of the Enlightenment by introducing reforms for the improvement of society, allowing freedom of speech and the press, permitting religious toleration, expanding education, and ruling in accordance with the laws.

Einsatzgruppen in Nazi Germany, special strike forces in the SS that played an important role in rounding up and killing Jews.

Enlightenment an eighteenth-century intellectual movement, led by the philosophes, that stressed the application of reason and the scientific method to all aspects of life.

entrepreneur one who organizes, operates, and assumes the risk in a business venture in the expectation of making a profit.

Epicureanism a philosophy founded by Epicurus in the fourth century B.C.E. that taught that happiness (freedom from emotional turmoil) could be achieved through the pursuit of pleasure (intellectual rather than sensual pleasure).

eta in feudal Japan, a class of hereditary slaves who were responsible for what were considered degrading occupations, such as curing leather and burying the dead.

ethnic cleansing the policy of killing or forcibly removing people of another ethnic group; used by the Serbs against Bosnian Muslims in the 1990s.

Eucharist a Christian sacrament in which consecrated bread and wine are consumed in celebration of Jesus' Last Supper; also called the Lord's Supper or communion.

eunuch a man whose testicles have been removed; common in the Chinese imperial system, the Ottoman Empire, and the Mughal dynasty, among others.

existentialism a philosophical movement that arose after World War II that emphasized the meaninglessness of life, born of the desperation caused by two world wars.

fascism an ideology that exalts the nation above the individual and calls for a centralized government with a dictatorial leader, economic and social regimentation, and forcible suppression of opposition; in particular, the ideology of Mussolini's Fascist regime in Italy.

Final Solution the Nazis' name for their attempted physical extermination of the Jewish people during World War II.

Five Pillars of Islam the core requirements of the faith, observation of which would lead to paradise: belief in Allah and his prophet, Muhammad; prescribed prayers; observation of Ramadan; pilgrimage to Mecca; and giving alms to the poor.

feminism the belief in the social, political, and economic equality of the sexes; also, organized activity to advance women's rights.

fief a landed estate granted to a vassal in exchange for military services.

filial piety in traditional China, in particular, a hierarchical system in which every family member has his or her place, subordinate to a patriarch who has certain reciprocal responsibilities.

folk culture the traditional arts and crafts, literature, music, and other customs of the people; something that people make, as opposed to modern popular culture, which is something people buy.

foot binding an extremely painful process, common in China throughout the second millennium C.E., that compressed girls' feet to half their natural size, representing submissiveness and self-discipline, which were considered necessary attributes of an ideal wife.

five relationships in traditional China, the hierarchical interpersonal associations considered crucial to social order, within the family, between friends, and with the king.

Four Modernizations the radical reforms of Chinese industry, agriculture, technology, and national defense instituted by Deng Xiaoping after his accession to power in the late 1970s.

free trade the unrestricted international exchange of goods with low or no tariffs.

functionalism the idea that the function of an object should determine its design and materials.

fundamentalism a movement that emphasizes rigid adherence to basic religious principles; often used to describe evangelical Christianity; it also characterizes the practices of Islamic conservatives.

genin landless laborers in feudal Japan, who were effectively slaves.

genro name applied to the ruling clique of aristocrats in Meiji Japan.

geocentric theory the idea that the earth is at the center of the universe and that the sun and other celestial objects revolve around the earth.

glasnost "openness." Mikhail Gorbachev's policy of encouraging Soviet citizens to openly discuss the strengths and weaknesses of the Soviet Union.

global civilization human society considered as a single worldwide entity in which local differences are less important than overall similarities.

global economy an interdependent economy in which the production, distribution, and sale of goods is accomplished on a worldwide scale.

globalization a term referring to the trend by which peoples and nations have become more interdependent; often used to refer to the development of a global economy and culture.

global warming the increase in the temperature of the earth's atmosphere caused by the greenhouse effect.

good emperors the five emperors who ruled from 96 to 180 (Nerva, Trajan, Hadrian, Antoninus Pius, and Marcus Aurelius), a period of peace and prosperity for the Roman Empire.

Good Neighbor policy a policy adopted by the administration of President Franklin Roosevelt to practice restraint in U.S. relations with its Latin American neighbors.

Gothic a term used to describe the art and especially architecture of Europe in the twelfth, thirteenth, and fourteenth centuries.

Gothic literature a form of literature used by Romantics to emphasize the bizarre and unusual, especially evident in horror stories.

Grand Council the top of the government hierarchy in the Song dynasty in China.

grand vezir the chief executive in the Ottoman Empire, under the sultan (also spelled vizier).

Great Leap Forward a short-lived, radical experiment in China, started in 1958, that created vast rural communes in an attempt to replace the family as the fundamental social unit.

Great Proletarian Cultural Revolution an attempt to destroy all vestiges of tradition in China in order to create a totally egalitarian society; launched by Mao Zedong in 1966, it devolved into virtual anarchy and lasted only until Mao's death in 1976.

greenhouse effect the warming of the earth caused by the buildup of carbon dioxide in the atmosphere as a result of human activity.

green revolution the introduction of technological agriculture, especially in India in the 1960s, which increased food production substantially but also exacerbated rural inequality because only the wealthier farmers could afford fertilizer.

guest workers foreign workers employed temporarily in European countries.

guided democracy the name given by President Sukarno of Indonesia in the late 1950s to his style of government, which theoretically operated by consensus.

guild an association of people with common interests and concerns, especially people working in the same craft. In medieval Europe, guilds came to control much of the production process and to restrict entry into various trades.

guru teacher, especially in the Hindu, Buddhist, and Sikh religious traditions, where the term is an important honorific.

Hadith a collection of the sayings of the Prophet Muhammad, used to supplement the revelations contained in the Qur'an.

harem the private domain of a ruler such as the sultan in the Ottoman Empire or the caliph of Baghdad, generally large and mostly inhabited by the extended family.

Hegira the flight of Muhammad from Mecca to Medina in 622, which marks the first date on the official calendar of Islam.

heliocentric theory the idea that the sun (not the earth) is at the center of the universe.

Hellenistic literally, "to imitate the Greeks"; the era after the death of Alexander the Great when Greek culture spread into the Near East and blended with the culture of that region.

helots serfs in ancient Sparta who were permanently bound to the land that they worked for their Spartan masters.

heresy the holding of religious doctrines different from the official teachings of the church.

hieroglyphics a highly pictorial system of writing most often associated with ancient Egypt. Also used (with different "pictographs") by other ancient peoples such as the Maya.

high culture the literary and artistic culture of the educated and wealthy ruling classes.

Hinayana the scornful name for Theravada Buddhism ("lesser vehicle") used by devotees of Mahayana Buddhism.

Hinduism the main religion in India; it emphasizes reincarnation, based on the results of the previous life, and the desirability of escaping this cycle. Its various forms feature both asceticism and the pleasures of ordinary life and encompass a multitude of gods as different manifestations of one ultimate reality.

Holocaust the mass slaughter of European Jews by the Nazis during World War II.

hominids the earliest humanlike creatures. They flourished in East and South Africa as long as three to four million years ago.

Hopewell culture a Native American society that flourished from about 200 B.C.E. to 400 C.E., noted for large burial mounds and extensive manufacturing. Largely based in Ohio, its traders ranged as far as the Gulf of Mexico.

hoplites heavily armed infantry soldiers used in ancient Greece in a phalanx formation.

Hundred Schools (of philosophy) in China around the third century B.C.E., a wide-ranging debate over the nature of human beings, society, and the universe. The schools included Legalism and Daoism, as well as Confucianism.

hydraulic society a society organized around a large irrigation system.

iconoclasm an eighth-century Byzantine movement against the use of icons (pictures of sacred figures), which was condemned as idolatry.

iconoclast a member of an eighth-century Byzantine movement against the use of icons (pictures of sacred figures), which it condemned as idolatry.

ideology a political philosophy such as conservatism or liberalism.

imam an Islamic religious leader. Some traditions say there is only one per generation; others use the term more broadly.

imperialism the policy of extending one nation's power either by conquest or by establishing direct or indirect economic or cultural authority over another. Generally driven by economic self-interest, it can also be motivated by a sincere (if often misguided) sense of moral obligation.

Impressionism an artistic movement that originated in France in the 1870s. Impressionists sought to capture their impressions of the changing effects of light on objects in nature.

indirect representation a system of choosing delegates to a representative assembly in which citizens do not choose the delegates directly but instead vote for electors who choose the delegates.

indirect rule a colonial policy of foreign rule in cooperation with local political elites; implemented in much of India and Malaya and parts of Africa, it was not feasible where resistance was greater.

individualism emphasis on and interest in the unique traits of each person.

indulgence the remission of part or all of the temporal punishment in purgatory due to sin; granted for charitable contributions and other good deeds. Indulgences became a regular practice of the Christian church in the High Middle Ages, and their abuse was instrumental in sparking Luther's reform movement in the sixteenth century.

infanticide the practice of killing infants.

inflation a sustained rise in the price level.

intendants royal officials in seventeenth-century France who were sent into the provinces to execute the orders of the central government.

interdict in the Catholic Church, a censure by which a region or country is deprived of receiving the sacraments.

intervention the idea, after the Congress of Vienna, that the great powers of Europe had the right to send armies into countries experiencing revolution to restore legitimate monarchs to their thrones.

intifada the "uprising" of Palestinians living under Israeli control, especially in the 1980s and 1990s.

Islam the religion derived from the revelations of Muhammad, the Prophet of Allah; literally, "submission" (to the will of Allah); also, the culture and civilization based on the faith.

isolationism a foreign policy in which a nation refrains from making alliances or engaging actively in international affairs.

Jainism an Indian religion, founded in the fifth century B.C.E., that stresses extreme simplicity.

Janissaries an elite core of eight thousand troops personally loyal to the sultan of the Ottoman Empire.

jati a kinship group, the basic social organization of traditional Indian society, to some extent specialized by occupation.

jihad in Islam, "striving in the way of the Lord." The term is ambiguous and has been subject to varying interpretations, from the practice of conducting raids against local neighbors to the conduct of "holy war" against unbelievers.

Jomon the earliest known Neolithic inhabitants of Japan, named for the cord pattern of their pottery.

joint-stock investment bank a bank created by selling shares of stock to investors. Such banks potentially have access to much more capital than private banks owned by one or a few individuals.

joint-stock company a company or association that raises capital by selling shares to individuals who receive dividends on their investment while a board of directors runs the company.

justification by faith the primary doctrine of the Protestant Reformation; taught that humans are saved not through good works but by the grace of God, bestowed freely through the sacrifice of Jesus.

Kabuki a form of Japanese theater that developed in the seventeenth century C.E.; originally disreputable, it became a highly stylized art form.

kami spirits worshiped in early Japan that resided in trees, rivers, and streams. See Shinto.

karma a fundamental concept in Hindu (and later Buddhist, Jain, and Sikh) philosophy, that rebirth in a future life is determined by actions in this or other lives; the word refers to the entire process, to the individual's actions, and also to the cumulative result of those actions (for instance, a store of good or bad karma).

keiretsu a type of powerful industrial or financial conglomerate that emerged in post–World War II Japan following the abolition of zaibatsu.

khanates Mongol kingdoms, in particular the subdivisions of Genghis Khan's empire ruled by his heirs.

kokutai the core ideology of the Japanese state, particularly during the Meiji Restoration, stressing the uniqueness of the Japanese system and the supreme authority of the emperor.

kolkhoz a collective farm in the Soviet Union, in which the great bulk of the land was held and worked communally. Between 1928 and 1934, some 26 million family farms were reconfigured into 250,000 kolkhozes.

kshatriya originally, the warrior class of Aryan society in India; ranked below (sometimes equal to) brahmins, in modern times often government workers or soldiers.

laissez-faire French for "leave it alone." An economic doctrine that holds that an economy is best served when the government does not interfere but allows the economy to self-regulate according to the forces of supply and demand.

lay investiture the practice in which a layperson chose a bishop and invested him with the symbols of both his temporal office and his spiritual office; led to the Investiture Controversy, which was ended by compromise in the Concordat of Worms in 1122.

latifundia large landed estates in the Roman Empire (singular: *latifundium*).

Lebensraum "living space." The doctrine, adopted by Hitler, that a nation's power depends on the amount of land it occupies; thus a nation must expand to be strong.

Legalism a Chinese philosophy that argued that human beings were by nature evil and would follow the correct path only if coerced by harsh laws and stiff punishments. Adopted as official ideology by the Qin dynasty, it was later rejected but remained influential.

legitimacy the idea that after the Napoleonic wars, peace could best be reestablished in Europe by restoring legitimate monarchs who would preserve traditional institutions; guided Metternich at the Congress of Vienna.

Leninism Lenin's revision of Marxism that held that Russia need not experience a bourgeois revolution before it could move toward socialism.

liberal arts the seven areas of study that formed the basis of education in medieval and early modern Europe. Following Boethius and other late Roman authors, they consisted of grammar, rhetoric, and dialectic or logic (the trivium) and arithmetic, geometry, astronomy, and music (the quadrivium).

liberalism an ideology based on the belief that people should be as free from restraint as possible. Economic liberalism is the idea that the government should not interfere in the workings of the economy. Political liberalism is the idea that there should be restraints on the exercise of power so that people can enjoy basic civil rights in a constitutional state with a representative assembly.

limited liability the principle that shareholders in a joint-stock corporation can be held responsible for the corporation's debts only up to the amount they have invested.

limited (constitutional) monarchy a system of government in which the monarch is limited by a representative assembly and by the duty to rule in accordance with the laws of the land.

lineage group the descendants of a common ancestor; relatives, often as opposed to immediate family.

Longshan a Neolithic society from near the Yellow River in China, sometimes identified by its black pottery.

maharaja originally, a king in the Aryan society of early India (a great raja); later used more generally to denote an important ruler.

Mahayana a school of Buddhism that promotes the idea of universal salvation through the intercession of bodhisattvas; predominant in north Asia.

majlis a council of elders among the Bedouins of the Roman era.

mandate of Heaven the justification for the rule of the Zhou dynasty in China; the king was charged to maintain order as a representative of Heaven, which was viewed as an impersonal law of nature.

mandates a system established after World War I whereby a nation officially administered a territory (mandate) on behalf of the League of Nations. Thus France administered Lebanon and Syria as mandates, and Britain administered Iraq and Palestine.

Manichaeanism an offshoot of the ancient Zoroastrian religion, influenced by Christianity; became popular in central Asia in the eighth century C.E.

manor an agricultural estate operated by a lord and worked by peasants who performed labor services and paid various rents and fees to the lord in exchange for protection and sustenance.

Marshall Plan the European Recovery Program, under which the United States provided financial aid to European countries to help them rebuild after World War II.

Marxism the political, economic, and social theories of Karl Marx, which included the idea that history is the story of class struggle and that ultimately the proletariat will overthrow the bourgeoisie and establish a dictatorship en route to a classless society.

mass education a state-run educational system, usually free of charge and compulsory, that aims to ensure that all children in society have at least a basic education.

mass leisure forms of leisure that appeal to large numbers of people in a society, including the working classes; emerged at the end of the nineteenth century to provide workers with amusements after work and on weekends; used during the twentieth century by totalitarian states to control their populations.

mass politics a political order characterized by mass political parties and universal male and (eventually) female suffrage.

mass society a society in which the concerns of the majority—the lower classes—play a prominent role; characterized by extension of voting rights, an improved standard of living for the lower classes, and mass education.

materialism the belief that everything mental, spiritual, or ideal is an outgrowth of physical forces and that truth is found in concrete material existence, not through feeling or intuition.

matrilinear passing through the female line—for example, from a father to his sister's son rather than his own—as practiced in some African societies; not necessarily or even usually combined with matriarchy, in which women rule.

megaliths large stones, widely used in Europe from around 4000 to 1500 B.C.E. to create monuments, including sophisticated astronomical observatories.

Meiji Restoration the period during the late nineteenth and early twentieth centuries when fundamental economic and cultural changes occurred in Japan, transforming it from a feudal and agrarian society to an industrial and technological one.

mercantilism an economic theory that held that a nation's prosperity depended on its supply of gold and silver and that the total volume of trade is unchangeable; therefore advocated that the government play an active role in the economy by encouraging exports and discouraging imports, especially through the use of tariffs.

Mesoamerica the region stretching roughly from modern central Mexico to Honduras, in which the Olmec, Maya, Aztec, and other civilizations developed.

Mesolithic Age the period from 10,000 to 7000 B.C.E., characterized by a gradual transition from a food-gathering and hunting economy to a food-producing economy.

mestizos the offspring of intermarriage between Europeans, originally Spaniards, and native American Indians.

Middle Passage the journey of slaves from Africa to the Americas as the middle leg of the triangular trade.

Middle Path a central concept of Buddhism, which advocates avoiding extremes of both materialism and asceticism; also known as the Eightfold Way.

mihrab the niche in a mosque's wall that indicates the direction of Mecca, usually containing an ornately decorated panel representing Allah.

militarism a policy of aggressive military preparedness; in particular, the large armies based on mass conscription and complex, inflexible plans for mobilization that most European nations had before World War I.

millet an administrative unit in the Ottoman Empire used to organize religious groups.

ministerial responsibility a tenet of nineteenth-century liberalism that held that ministers of the monarch should be responsible to the legislative assembly rather than to the monarch.

Modernism the artistic and literary styles that emerged in the decades before 1914 as artists rebelled against traditional efforts to portray reality as accurately as possible (leading to Impressionism and Cubism) and writers explored new forms.

monasticism a movement that began in early Christianity whose purpose was to create communities of men and women who practiced a communal life dedicated to God as a moral example to the world around them.

monk a man who chooses to live a communal life divorced from the world in order to dedicate himself totally to the will of God.

monotheism having only one god; the doctrine or belief that there is only one god.

muezzin the man who calls Muslims to prayer at the appointed times; nowadays often a tape-recorded message played over loudspeakers.

mulattoes the offspring of Africans and Europeans, particularly in Latin America.

multiculturalism a term referring to the connection of several cultural or ethnic groups within a society.

multinational corporation a company with divisions in more than two countries.

mutual deterrence the belief that nuclear war could best be prevented if both the United States and the Soviet Union had sufficient nuclear weapons so that even if one nation launched a preemptive first strike, the other could respond and devastate the attacker.

mystery religions religions that involve initiation into secret rites that promise intense emotional involvement with spiritual forces and a greater chance of individual immortality.

nationalism a sense of national consciousness based on awareness of being part of a community—a "nation"—that has common institutions, traditions, language, and customs and that becomes the focus of the individual's primary political loyalty.

nationalization the process of converting a business or industry from private ownership to government control and ownership.

nation in arms the people's army raised by universal mobilization to repel the foreign enemies of the French Revolution.

nation-state a form of political organization in which a relatively homogeneous people inhabits a sovereign state, as opposed to a state containing people of several nationalities.

natural rights certain inalienable rights to which all people are entitled; they include the right to life, liberty, and ownership of property; freedom of speech and religion; and equal treatment under the law.

natural selection Darwin's idea that organisms that are most adaptable to their environment survive and pass on the variations that enabled them to survive while less adaptable organisms become extinct; known by the shorthand expression "survival of the fittest."

NATO the North Atlantic Treaty Organization; a military alliance formed in 1949 in which the signatories (Belgium, Canada, Denmark, France, Great Britain, Iceland, Italy, Luxembourg, the Netherlands, Norway, Portugal, and the United States) agreed to provide mutual assistance if any one of them was attacked; later expanded to include other nations, including former members of the Warsaw Pact—Poland, the Czech Republic, and Hungary.

natural law a body of laws or specific principles held to be derived from nature and binding on all human society even in the absence of positive laws.

Nazi New Order the Nazis' plan for their conquered territories; it included the extermination of Jews and others considered inferior, ruthless exploitation of resources, German colonization in the east, and the use of Poles, Russians, and Ukrainians as slave labor.

négritude a philosophy shared among African blacks that there exists a distinctive "African personality" that owes nothing to Western values and provides a common sense of purpose and destiny for black Africans.

neocolonialism the use of economic rather than political or military means to maintain Western domination of developing nations.

Neo-Confucianism the dominant ideology of China during the second millennium C.E.; it combined the metaphysical speculations of Buddhism and Daoism with the pragmatic Confucian approach to society, maintaining that the world is real, not illusory, and that fulfillment comes from participation, not withdrawal. It encouraged an intellectual environment that valued continuity over change and tradition over innovation.

Neolithic Revolution the development of agriculture, including the planting of food crops and the domestication of farm animals, around 10,000 B.C.E.

New Course a short-lived, liberalizing change in Soviet policy to its eastern European allies instituted after the death of Stalin in 1953.

New Culture Movement a protest launched at Beijing University after the failure of the 1911 revolution, aimed at abolishing the remnants of the old system and introducing Western values and institutions into China.

New Deal the reform program implemented by President Franklin Roosevelt in the 1930s, which included large public works projects and the introduction of Social Security.

New Democracy the initial program of the Chinese Communist government, from 1949 to 1955, focusing on honest government, land reform, social justice, and peace rather than on the utopian goal of a classless society.

New Economic Policy a modified version of the old capitalist system introduced in the Soviet Union by Lenin in 1921 to revive the economy after the ravages of the civil war and war communism.

new imperialism the revival of imperialism after 1880 in which European nations established colonies throughout much of Asia and Africa.

new monarchies the governments of France, England, and Spain at the end of the fifteenth century, where the rulers were successful in reestablishing or extending centralized royal authority, suppressing the nobility, controlling the church, and insisting on the loyalty of all peoples living in their territories.

Nirvana in Buddhist thought, enlightenment, the ultimate transcendence from the illusion of the material world; release from the "wheel of life."

Nok culture in northern Nigeria, one of the most active early ironworking societies in Africa, artifacts from which date back as far as 500 B.C.E.

Nonaligned Movement an organization of neutralist nations established in the 1950s to provide a counterpoise between the Socialist Bloc, headed by the Soviet Union, and the capitalist nations led by the United States. Chief sponsors of the movement were Jawaharlal Nehru of India, Gamal Abdul Nasser of Egypt, and Sukarno of Indonesia.

nongovernmental organizations (NGOs) organizations that have no government ties and work to address world problems.

northern Renaissance humanism see Christian humanism.

nuclear family a family group consisting only of father, mother, and children.

nun female monk.

old regime/old order the political and social system of France in the eighteenth century before the Revolution.

oligarchy rule by the few.

Open Door Notes a series of letters sent in 1899 by U.S. Secretary of State John Hay to Great Britain, France, Germany, Italy, Japan, and Russia, calling for equal economic access to the China market for all states and for the maintenance of the territorial and administrative integrity of the Chinese Empire.

opium trade the sale of the addictive product of the poppy, specifically by British traders to China in the 1830s. Chinese attempts to prevent it led to the Opium War of 1839–1842, which resulted in British access to Chinese ports and has traditionally been considered the beginning of modern Chinese history.

orders/estates the traditional tripartite division of European society based on heredity and quality rather than wealth or economic standing, first established in the Middle Ages and continuing into the eighteenth century; traditionally consisted of those who pray (the clergy), those who fight (the nobility), and those who work (all the rest).

organic evolution Darwin's principle that all plants and animals have evolved over a long period of time from earlier and simpler forms of life.

Organization of African Unity founded in Addis Ababa in 1963, a group intended to represent the interests of all the newly independent countries of Africa and provided a forum for the discussion of common problems until 2001, when it was replaced by the African Union.

Oriental despotism a theory identified with the Sinologist Karl Wittfogel that traditional societies organized on the basis of large-scale irrigation networks—many of them in eastern Asia—often possessed tendencies to create autocratic political systems.

Paleolithic Age the period of human history when humans used simple stone tools (c. 2,500,000–10,000 B.C.E.).

pan-Africanism the concept of African continental unity and solidarity in which the common interests of African countries transcend regional boundaries.

pan-Arabism a movement promoted by Egyptian president Gamal Abdul Nasser and other Middle Eastern leaders to unify all Arabic peoples in a single supra-national organization. After Nasser's death in 1971, the movement languished.

pantheism a doctrine that equates God with the universe and all that is in it.

pariahs members of the lowest level of traditional Indian society, technically outside the class system itself; also known as untouchables.

pasha an administrative official of the Ottoman Empire, responsible for collecting taxes and maintaining order in the provinces; later, some became hereditary rulers.

paterfamilias the dominant male in a Roman family whose powers over his wife and children were theoretically unlimited, though they were sometimes circumvented in practice.

patriarchal family a family in which the man (husband and father) dominates his wife and children.

patriarchy a society in which the father is supreme in the clan or family; more generally, a society dominated by men.

patricians great landowners who became the ruling class in the Roman Republic; in Early Modern Europe, a term used to identify the ruling elites of cities.

patrilinear passing through the male line, from father to son; often combined with patriarchy.

patronage the practice of awarding titles and making appointments to government and other positions to gain political support.

Pax Romana "Roman peace," the stability and prosperity that Roman rule brought to the Mediterranean world and much of western Europe during the first and second centuries C.E.

peaceful coexistence the policy adopted by the Soviet Union under Khrushchev in 1955 and continued by his successors that called for economic and ideological rivalry with the West rather than nuclear war.

peon in Latin America, a native peasant permanently dependent on the landowners.

people's democracies a term invented by the Soviet Union to define a society in the early stage of socialist transition, applied to Eastern European countries in the 1950s.

perestroika "restructuring," the term applied to Mikhail Gorbachev's economic, political, and social reforms in the Soviet Union.

permissive society a characterization of Western society after World War II to reflect its sexual freedom and the emergence of the drug culture.

Petrine supremacy the doctrine that the bishop of Rome, the pope, as the successor of Saint Peter (traditionally considered the first bishop of Rome), should hold a preeminent position in the church.

pharaoh the most common title used for Egyptian kings. Pharaohs possessed absolute power and were seen as divine.

philosophes intellectuals of the eighteenth-century Enlightenment who believed in applying a spirit of rational criticism to all things, including religion and politics, and who focused on improving and enjoying this world rather than on the afterlife.

phalanx a rectangular formation of tightly massed infantry soldiers.

plebeians the class of Roman citizens who included nonpatrician landowners, craftspeople, merchants, and small farmers in the Roman Republic. Their struggle for equal rights with the patricians dominated much of the Republic's history.

pogroms organized massacres of Jews.

polis an ancient Greek city-state encompassing both an urban area and its surrounding countryside; a small but autonomous political unit where all major political and social activities were carried out in a central location (plural: *poleis*).

political democracy a form of government characterized by universal suffrage and mass political parties.

polygyny the practice of having more than one wife at a time.

polytheism having many gods; belief in or the worship of more than one god.

popular culture as opposed to high culture, the unofficial written and unwritten culture of the masses, much of which was passed down orally; centered on public and group activities such as festivals. In the twentieth century, the entertainment, recreation, and pleasures that people purchase as part of mass consumer society.

popular sovereignty the doctrine that government is created by and subject to the will of the people, who are the source of all political power.

portolani charts of landmasses and coastlines made by navigators and mathematicians in the thirteenth and fourteenth centuries.

Post-Impressionism an artistic movement that began in France in the 1880s. Post-Impressionists sought to use color and line to express inner feelings and produce a personal statement of reality.

Postmodernism a term used to cover a variety of artistic and intellectual styles and ways of thinking prominent since the 1970s.

Poststructuralism a theory formulated by Jacques Derrida in the 1960s, holding that there is no fixed, universal truth because culture is created and can therefore be analyzed in various ways.

praetorian guard the military unit that served as the personal bodyguard of the Roman emperors.

praetors the two senior Roman judges, who had executive authority when the consuls were away from the city and could also lead armies.

Prakrit an ancient Indian language, a simplified form of Sanskrit.

predestination the belief, associated with Calvinism, that God, as a consequence of his foreknowledge of all events, has predetermined who will be saved (the elect) and who will be damned.

price revolution the dramatic rise in prices (inflation) that occurred throughout Europe in the sixteenth and early seventeenth centuries.

primogeniture an inheritance practice in which the eldest son receives all or the largest share of the parents' estate.

principate the form of government established by Augustus for the Roman Empire; continued the constitutional forms of the Republic and consisted of the princeps ("first citizen") and the senate, although the princeps was clearly the dominant partner.

proletariat the industrial working class. In Marxism, the class that will ultimately overthrow the bourgeoisie.

Protestant Reformation the western European religious reform movement in the sixteenth century C.E. that divided Christianity into Catholic and Protestant groups.

psychoanalysis a method developed by Sigmund Freud to resolve a patient's psychic conflict.

purdah the Indian term for the practice among Muslims and some Hindus of isolating women and preventing them from associating with men outside the home.

Pure Land a Buddhist sect, originally Chinese but later popular in Japan, that taught that devotion alone could lead to enlightenment and release.

Puritans English Protestants inspired by Calvinist theology who wished to remove all traces of Catholicism from the Church of England.

quipu an Inka record-keeping system that used knotted strings rather than writing.

raj the British colonial regime in India.

raja originally, a chieftain in the Aryan society of early India, a representative of the gods; later used more generally to denote a ruler.

Ramadan the holy month of Islam, during which believers fast from dawn to sunset; because the Islamic calendar is lunar, Ramadan migrates through the seasons.

rationalism a system of thought based on the belief that human reason and experience are the chief sources of knowledge.

Realism in medieval Europe, the school of thought that, following Plato, held that the individual objects we perceive are not real but merely manifestations of universal ideas existing in the mind of God. In the nineteenth century, a school of painting that emphasized the everyday life of ordinary people, depicted with photographic realism.

Realpolitik "politics of reality." Politics based on practical concerns rather than theory or ethics.

reason of state the principle that a nation should act on the basis of its long-term interests and not merely to further the dynastic interests of its ruling family.

reincarnation   the idea that the individual soul is reborn in a different form after death; in Hindu and Buddhist thought, release from this cycle is the objective of all living souls.

relativity theory   Einstein's theory that holds, among other things, that space and time are not absolute but are relative to the observer and interwoven into a four-dimensional space-time continuum and that matter is a form of energy; expressed by the equation $E = mc^2$.

relics   the bones of Christian saints or objects intimately associated with saints that were considered worthy of veneration.

Renaissance   the "rebirth" of classical culture that occurred in Italy between c. 1350 and c. 1550; also, the earlier revivals of classical culture that occurred under Charlemagne and in the twelfth century.

Renaissance humanism   an intellectual movement in Renaissance Italy based on the study of the Greek and Roman classics.

rentier   a person who lives on income from property and is not personally involved in its operation.

reparations   payments made by a defeated nation after a war to compensate another nation for damage sustained as a result of the war; required from Germany after World War I.

revisionism   a socialist doctrine that rejected Marx's emphasis on class struggle and revolution and argued instead that workers should work through political parties to bring about gradual change.

revolution   a fundamental change in the political and social organization of a state.

revolutionary socialism   the socialist doctrine espoused by Georges Sorel, who held that violent action was the only way to achieve the goals of socialism.

rhetoric   the art of persuasive speaking; in the Middle Ages, one of the seven liberal arts.

Rococo   a style, especially of decoration and architecture, that developed from the Baroque and spread throughout Europe by the 1730s. While still elaborate, it emphasized curves, lightness, and charm in the pursuit of pleasure, happiness, and love.

Romanesque   a term used to describe the art and especially architecture of Europe in the eleventh and twelfth centuries.

Romanticism   a nineteenth-century intellectual and artistic movement that rejected the emphasis on reason of the Enlightenment. Instead, Romantics stressed the importance of intuition, feeling, emotion, and imagination as sources of knowing.

ronin   Japanese warriors made unemployed by developments in the early modern era, since samurai were forbidden by tradition to engage in commerce.

rural responsibility system   post-Maoist land reform in China, under which collectives leased land to peasant families, who could consume or sell their surplus production and keep the profits.

sacraments   rites considered imperative for a Christian's salvation. By the thirteenth century, they consisted of the Eucharist or Lord's Supper, baptism, marriage, penance, extreme unction, holy orders, and confirmation of children; Protestant reformers of the sixteenth century generally recognized only two—baptism and communion (the Lord's Supper).

Sanskrit   an early Indo-European language, in which the Vedas were composed, beginning in the second millennium B.C.E. It survived as the language of literature and the bureaucracy in India for centuries after its decline as a spoken tongue.

sans-culottes   the common people who did not wear the fine clothes of the upper classes (sans-culottes means "without breeches") and played an important role in the radical phase of the French Revolution.

samurai   literally, "retainers"; similar to European knights. Usually in service to a particular shogun, these Japanese warriors lived by a strict code of ethics and duty.

sati   the Hindu ritual requiring a wife to throw herself on her deceased husband's funeral pyre.

satori   enlightenment, in the Japanese (especially Zen) Buddhist tradition.

satrap   a governor with both civil and military duties in the ancient Persian Empire, which was divided into satrapies, or provinces, each administered by a satrap.

satrapy   one of the provinces of the ancient Persian Empire, each ruled by a satrap.

satyagraha   the Hindi term for the practice of nonviolent resistance, as advocated by Mohandas Gandhi; literally, "hold fast to the truth."

scholar-gentry   in Song dynasty China, candidates who passed the civil service examinations and whose families were nonaristocratic landowners; eventually, a majority of the bureaucracy.

scholasticism   the philosophical and theological system of the medieval schools, which emphasized rigorous analysis of contradictory authorities; often used to try to reconcile faith and reason.

School of Mind   a philosophy espoused by Wang Yangming during the mid-Ming era of China, which argued that mind and the universe were a single unit and knowledge was therefore obtained through internal self-searching rather than through investigation of the outside world; for a while, a significant but unofficial rival to neo-Confucianism.

scientific method   a method of seeking knowledge through inductive principles; it uses experiments and observations to develop generalizations.

Scientific Revolution   the transition from the medieval worldview to a largely secular, rational, and materialistic perspective; it began in the seventeenth century and was popularized in the eighteenth.

secularization   the process of becoming more concerned with material, worldly, temporal things and less with spiritual and religious things.

self-determination   the doctrine that the people of a given territory or a particular nationality should have the right to determine their own government and political future.

self-strengthening   a late-nineteenth-century Chinese policy under which Western technology would be adopted while Confucian principles and institutions were maintained intact.

senate   the leading council of the Roman Republic; composed of about three hundred men (senators) who served for life and dominated much of the political life of the Republic.

separation of powers   a doctrine enunciated by Montesquieu in the eighteenth century that separate executive, legislative, and judicial powers serve to limit and control each other.

sepoys   native troops hired by the East India Company to protect British interests in South Asia, who formed the basis of the British Indian Army.

serf   a peasant who is bound to the land and obliged to provide labor services and pay various rents and fees to the lord; considered unfree but not a slave because serfs could not be bought and sold.

Sharia   a law code, originally drawn up by Muslim scholars shortly after the death of Muhammad, that provides believers with a set of prescriptions to regulate their daily lives.

sheikh   originally, the ruler of a Bedouin tribe; later, also used as a more general honorific.

Shi'ite   the second largest tradition of Islam, which split from the majority Sunni soon after the death of Muhammad in a disagreement over his succession; especially significant in Iran and Iraq.

Shinto   a kind of state religion in Japan, derived from beliefs in nature spirits and until recently linked with belief in the divinity of the emperor and the sacredness of the Japanese nation.

shogun   a powerful Japanese leader, originally military, who ruled under the titular authority of the emperor.

shogunate system   the system of government in Japan in which the emperor exercised only titular authority while the shogun (regional military dictators) exercised actual political power.

Sikhism   a religion, founded in the early sixteenth century in the Punjab, that began as an attempt to reconcile the Hindu and Muslim traditions and developed into a significant alternative to both.

sipahis   in the Ottoman Empire, local cavalry elites who held fiefdoms and collected taxes.

Slavophiles   in the nineteenth century, Russian intellectuals who believed that Russia's tsarist system, peasant villages, and Orthodox religious faith were superior to any Western ideals.

social Darwinism   the application of Darwin's principle of organic evolution to the social order; led to the belief that progress comes from the struggle for survival as the fittest advance and the weak decline.

socialism   an ideology that calls for collective or government ownership of the means of production and the distribution of goods.

socialized medicine   health services for all citizens provided by government assistance.

social security   government programs that provide social welfare measures such as old-age pensions, accident, and disability insurance.

Socratic method   a form of teaching that uses a question-and-answer format to enable students to reach conclusions by using their own reasoning.

Sophists   wandering scholars and professional teachers in ancient Greece who stressed the importance of rhetoric and tended toward skepticism and relativism.

soviets   councils of workers' and soldiers' deputies formed throughout Russia in 1917; played an important role in the Bolshevik Revolution.

sphere of influence   a territory or region over which an outside nation exercises political or economic influence.

squadristi   in Italy in the 1920s, bands of armed Fascists used to create disorder by attacking Socialist offices and newspapers.

Star Wars   nickname of the Strategic Defense Initiative, proposed by President Reagan, which was intended to provide a shield that would destroy any incoming missiles; named after a popular science-fiction movie series.

State Confucianism   the integration of Confucian doctrine with Legalist practice under the Han dynasty in China, which became the basis of Chinese political thought until the modern era.

subinfeudation   the practice in which a lord's greatest vassals subdivided their fiefs and had vassals of their own, and those vassals in turn subdivided their fiefs and so on down to simple knights, whose fiefs were too small to subdivide.

stateless societies   the pre-Columbian communities in much of the Americas that developed substantial cultures without formal nation-states.

Stoicism   a philosophy founded by Zeno in the fourth century B.C.E. that taught that happiness could be obtained by accepting one's lot and living in harmony with the will of God, thereby achieving inner peace.

sudras   the classes that represented the great bulk of the Indian population from ancient times, mostly peasants, artisans, or manual laborers; ranked below brahmins, kshatriyas, and vaisyas but above the pariahs.

Sublime Porte   the office of the grand vezir in the Ottoman Empire.

suffrage   the right to vote.

suffragists   those who advocate the extension of the right to vote (suffrage), especially to women.

Sufism   a mystical school of Islam, noted for its music, dance, and poetry, which became prominent in about the thirteenth century.

sultan   "holder of power"; a title commonly used by Muslim rulers in the Ottoman Empire, Egypt, and elsewhere; still in use in parts of Asia, sometimes for regional authorities.

Sunni   the largest tradition of Islam, from which the Shi'ites split soon after the death of Muhammad in a disagreement over his succession.

Supreme Ultimate   according to Neo-Confucianists, a transcendent world distinct from the material world in which humans live but to which humans may aspire; a set of abstract principles, roughly equivalent to the Dao.

Surrealism   an artistic movement that arose between World War I and World War II. Surrealists portrayed recognizable objects in unrecognizable relationships in order to reveal the world of the unconscious.

Swahili   a mixed African-Arabian culture that developed by the twelfth century along the east coast of Africa; also, the national language of Kenya and Tanzania.

syncretism   the combining of different forms of belief or practice, as when two gods are regarded as different forms of the same underlying divine force and are fused together.

Taika reforms   the seventh-century "great change" reforms that established the centralized Japanese state.

taille   a French tax on land or property, developed by King Louis XI in the fifteenth century as the financial basis of the monarchy. It was largely paid by the peasantry; the nobility and the clergy were exempt.

Tantrism   a mystical Buddhist sect that emphasized the importance of magical symbols and ritual in seeking a path to enlightenment.

tariffs   duties (taxes) imposed on imported goods; usually imposed both to raise revenue and to discourage imports and protect domestic industries.

theocracy   a government based on a divine authority.

Theravada   a school of Buddhism that stresses personal behavior and the quest for understanding as a means of release from the wheel of life, rather than the intercession of bodhisattvas; predominant in Sri Lanka and Southeast Asia.

three-field system   in medieval agriculture, the practice of dividing the arable land into three fields so that one could lie fallow while the other two were planted in winter grains and spring crops.

three kingdoms   Koguryo, Paekche, and Silla, rivals but all under varying degrees of Chinese influence, which together controlled virtually all of Korea from the fourth to the seventh centuries.

three obediences   the traditional duties of Japanese women, in permanent subservience: child to father, wife to husband, and widow to son.

tithe   a tenth of one's harvest or income; paid by medieval peasants to the village church.

Tongmenghui   the political organization—"Revolutionary Alliance"—formed by Sun Yat-sen in 1905, which united various revolutionary factions and ultimately toppled the Manchu dynasty.

totalitarian state   a state characterized by government control over all aspects of economic, social, political, cultural, and intellectual life; subordination of the individual to the state; and insistence that the masses be actively involved in the regime's goals.

total war   warfare in which all of a nation's resources, including civilians at home and soldiers in the field, are mobilized for the war effort.

trade union   an association of workers in the same trade, formed to help members secure better wages, benefits, and working conditions.

transnational corporation   another term for "a multinational corporation," or a company with divisions in more than two countries.

trench warfare   warfare in which the opposing forces attack and counterattack from a relatively permanent system of trenches protected by barbed wire; characteristic of World War I.

tribunes of the plebs   beginning in 494 B.C.E., Roman officials who were given the power to protect plebeians against arrest by patrician magistrates.

tribute system   an important element of Chinese foreign policy under which neighboring states paid for the privilege of access to Chinese markets, received legitimation, and agreed not to harbor enemies of the Chinese Empire.

Truman Doctrine   the doctrine, enunciated by Harry Truman in 1947, that the United States would provide economic aid to countries that said they were threatened by Communist expansion.

twice-born   the males of the higher castes in traditional Indian society, who underwent an initiation ceremony at puberty.

tyranny   rule by a tyrant.

tyrant   in an ancient Greek polis (or an Italian city-state during the Renaissance), a ruler who came to power in an unconstitutional way and ruled without being subject to the law.

uhuru "freedom" in Swahili; a key slogan in African independence movements, especially in Kenya.

uji a clan in early Japanese tribal society.

ulama a convocation of leading Muslim scholars, the earliest of which shortly after the death of Muhammad drew up a law code, called the *Shari'a*, based largely on the Qur'an and the sayings of the Prophet, to provide believers with a set of prescriptions to regulate their daily lives.

umma the Muslim community as a whole.

uncertainty principle a principle in quantum mechanics, posited by Heisenberg, that holds that one cannot determine the path of an electron because the very act of observing the electron would affect its location.

unconditional surrender complete, unqualified surrender of a nation.

uninterrupted revolution the goal of the Great Proletarian Cultural Revolution launched by Mao Zedong in 1966.

utopian socialists intellectuals and theorists in the early nineteenth century who favored equality in social and economic conditions and wished to replace private property and competition with collective ownership and cooperation; deemed impractical and "utopian" by later socialists.

vaisya the third-ranked class in traditional Indian society; usually merchants.

varna Indian classes or castes. See caste system.

vassal a person granted a fief, or landed estate, in exchange for providing military services to the lord and fulfilling certain other obligations such as appearing at the lord's court when summoned and making a payment on the knighting of the lord's eldest son.

veneration of ancestors the extension of filial piety to include care for the deceased, for instance, by burning replicas of useful objects to accompany them on their journey to the next world.

vernacular the everyday language of a region, as distinguished from a language used for special purposes. For example, in medieval Paris, French was the vernacular, but Latin was used for academic writing and for classes at the University of Paris.

vezir see vizier.

viceroy the administrative head of the provinces of New Spain and Peru in the Americas.

Vietnam syndrome the presumption, from the 1970s on, that the U.S. public would object to a protracted military entanglement abroad, such as another Vietnam-type conflict.

vizier (also, vezir) the prime minister in the Abbasid caliphate and elsewhere, a chief executive.

war communism Lenin's policy of nationalizing industrial and other facilities and requisitioning the peasants' produce during the civil war in Russia.

War Guilt Clause the clause in the Treaty of Versailles that declared Germany (and Austria) responsible for starting World War I and ordered Germany to pay reparations for the damage the Allies had suffered as a result of the war.

Warsaw Pact a military alliance, formed in 1955, in which Albania, Bulgaria, Czechoslovakia, East Germany, Hungary, Poland, Romania, and the Soviet Union agreed to provide mutual assistance. Dissolved in 1991, most former members eventually joined NATO.

welfare state a social and political system in which the government assumes primary responsibility for the social welfare of its citizens by providing such things as social security, unemployment benefits, and health care.

well field system the theoretical pattern of land ownership in early China, named for the appearance of the Chinese character for "well," in which farmland was divided into nine segments and a peasant family would cultivate one for its own use and cooperate with seven others to cultivate the ninth for the landlord.

wergeld "money for a man." In early Germanic law, a person's value in monetary terms, which was paid by a wrongdoer to the family of the person who had been injured or killed.

White Lotus a Chinese Buddhist sect, founded in 1133 C.E., that sought political reform; in 1796–1804, a Chinese peasant revolt.

Westernizers in the nineteenth century, Russian intellectuals who believed that Western ways were the solution to Russia's problems.

women's liberation movement the struggle for equal rights for women, which has deep roots in history but achieved new prominence under this name in the 1960s, building on the work of, among others, Simone de Beauvoir and Betty Friedan.

world-machine Newton's conception of the universe as one huge, regulated, and uniform machine that operated according to natural laws in absolute time, space, and motion.

Yangshao a Neolithic society from near the Yellow River in China, sometimes identified by its painted pottery.

Young Turks a successful Turkish reformist group in the late nineteenth and early twentieth centuries.

zaibatsu powerful business cartels formed in Japan during the Meiji era and outlawed following World War II.

zamindars Indian tax collectors who were assigned land from which they kept part of the revenue; the British revived the system in a misguided attempt to create a landed gentry.

Zen (in Chinese, Chan or Chan) a school of Buddhism particularly important in Japan, some of whose adherents stress that enlightenment (satori) can be achieved suddenly, though others emphasize lengthy meditation.

ziggurat a massive stepped tower on which a temple dedicated to the chief god or goddess of a Sumerian city was built.

Zionism an international movement that called for the establishment of a Jewish state or a refuge for Jews in Palestine.

Zoroastrianism a religion founded by the Persian Zoroaster in the seventh century B.C.E., characterized by worship of a supreme god, Ahuramazda, who represents the good against the evil spirit, Ahriman.

Abbasid uh-BAH-sid or AB-uh-sid
Abd al-Rahman ub-duh-rahkh-MAHN
Abu al-Abbas uh-BOOL-uh-BUSS
Abu Bakr uh-boo-BAHK-ur
Achebe, Chinua ah-CHAY-bay, CHIN-wah
Achilles uh-KIL-eez
Addis Ababa AD-iss uh-BAY-buh
Adenauer, Konrad AD-uh-now-ur
Aegospotami ee-guh-SPOT-uh-mee
Aeolians ee-OH-lee-unz
Aeschylus ESS-kuh-luss
Aetius ay-EE-shuss
Afrikaners ah-fri-KAH-nurz
Agincourt AH-zhen-koor
Aguinaldo, Emilio ah-gwee-NAHL-doh, ay-MEEL-yoh
Ahuramazda uh-hoor-uh-MAHZ-duh
Aix-la-Chapelle ex-lah-shah-PELL
Ajanta uh-JUHN-tuh
Akhenaten ah-khuh-NAH-tun
Akhetaten ah-khuh-TAH-tun
Akkadians uh-KAY-dee-unz
Alaric AL-uh-rik
al-Maʾmun al-muh-MOON
Alberti, Leon Battista al-BAYR-tee, LAY-un buh-TEESS-tuh
Albuquerque, Afonso de AL-buh-kur-kee, ah-FAHN-soh day
al-Fatah al-FAH-tuh
al-Hakim al-hah-KEEM
Alia, Ramiz AH-lee-uh, rah-MEEZ
al-Khwarizmi al-KHWAR-iz-mee
Allah AH-lah
al-Maʾmun al-muh-MOON
Almeida, Francesco da ahl-MAY-duh, frahn-CHAYSS-koh
al-Sadat, Anwar ah-sah-DAHT, ahn-WAHR
Aidoo, Ama Ata ah-EE-doo, AH-mah AH-tah
Amaterasu ah-muh-teh-RAH-suh
Amenhotep ah-mun-HOH-tep
Anasazi ah-nuh-SAH-zee
Andropov, Yuri ahn-DRAHP-awf, YOOR-ee
Anjou AHN-zhoo
Antigonid an-TIG-uh-nid
Antigonus Gonatus an-TIG-oh-nuss guh-NAH-tuss
Antiochus an-TY-uh-kuss
Anyang ahn-YAHNG
Aquinas, Thomas uh-KWY-nuss
Arafat, Yasir ah-ruh-FAHT, yah-SEER
Arawak AR-uh-wahk
Archimedes ahr-kuh-MEE-deez
Aristarchus ar-iss-TAR-kus
Aristotle AR-iss-tot-ul
Arjuna ahr-JOO-nuh
Arsinoë ahr-SIN-oh-ee
Aryan AR-ee-un
Ashikaga ah-shee-KAH-guh
Ashoka uh-SHOH-kuh
Ashurbanipal ah-shur-BAH-nuh-pahl
Ashurnasirpal ah-shur-NAH-zur-pahl

Assyrians uh-SEER-ee-unz
Atahualpa ah-tuh-WAHL-puh
audiencias ow-dee-en-SEE-uss
Auerstadt OW-urr-shtaht
Augustine AW-guh-steen
Aum Shinri Kyo awm-shin-ree-KYO
Aung San Suu Kyi AWNG-sawn-soo-chee
Aurelian aw-REEL-yun
Auschwitz-Birkenau OW-shvitz-BEER-kuh-now
Ausgleich OWSS-glykh
Austerlitz AWSS-tur-litz
Australasia awss-TRAY-zhuh
Australopithecines aw-stray-loh-PITH-uh-synz
Avalokitesvara uh-VAH-loh-kee-TESH-vuh-ruh
Avicenna av-i-SENN-uh
Avignon ah-veen-YOHNN
Ayacucho ah-ya-KOO-choh
Ayodhya ah-YOHD-hyah
Ayuthaya ah-yoo-TY-yuh
Azerbaijan az-ur-by-JAN

Baʾath BAHTH
Baader-Meinhof BAH-durr-MYN-huff
Babur BAH-burr
Bach, Johann Sebastian BAKH, yoh-HAHN suh-BASS-chun
Bai Hua by HWA
bakufu buh-KOO-foo or Japanese bah-KOO-fuh
Balboa, Vasco Nuñez de bal-BOH-uh, BAHS-koh NOON-yez day
Ban Zhao bahn ZHOW
Bandaranaike, Sirimavo bahn-dur-uh-NY-uh-kuh, see-ree-MAH-voh

Bao-jia BOW-jah
Barbarossa bar-buh-ROH-suh
Baroque buh-ROHK
Basho BAH-shoh
Bastille bass-STEEL
Basutoland buh-SOO-toh-land
Batista, Fulgencio bah-TEES-tuh, full-JEN-see-oh
Bauhaus BOW-howss
Bayazid by-uh-ZEED
Beauvoir, Simone de boh-VWAR, see-MUHN duh
Bechuanaland bech-WAH-nuh-land
Begin, Menachem BAY-gin, muh-NAH-khum
Beijing bay-ZHING
Belarus bell-uh-ROOSS
Belisarius bell-uh-SAH-ree-uss
benefice BEN-uh-fiss
Benin bay-NEEN
Bernhardi, Friedrich von bayrn-HAR-dee, FREED-reekh fun
Bernini, Gian Lorenzo bur-NEE-nee, JAHN loh-RENT-zoh
Bhagavad Gita bah-guh-vahd-GEE-tuh
Bharata Janata BAR-ruh-tuh JAH-nuh-tuh
Bhutto, Zulfikar Ali BOO-toh, ZOOL-fee-kahr ah-LEE
Bismarck, Otto von BIZ-mark, OH-toh fun
Blitzkrieg BLITZ-kreeg

Boer BOOR or BOR
Boleyn, Anne BUH-lin or buh-LIN
Bolívar, Simón boh-LEE-var, see-MOHN
Bologna boh-LOHN-yuh
Bolsheviks BOHL-shuh-viks
Bora, Katherina von BOH-rah, kat-uh-REE-nuh fun
Borobudur boh-roh-buh-DOOR
Bosnia BAHZ-nee-uh
Bosporus BAHSS-pruss
Botswana baht-SWAH-nuh
Brahe, Tycho BRAH, TY-koh
Brahmo Samaj BRAH-moh suh-MAHJ
Brandt, Willy BRAHNT, VIL-ee
Brest-Litovsk BREST-li-TUFFSK
Brétigny bray-tee-NYEE
Brezhnev, Leonid BREZH-neff, lyee-oh-NYEET
Briand, Aristide bree-AHNH, ah-ruh-STEED
Broz, Josip BRAWZ, yaw-SEEP
Brunelleschi, Filippo BROO-nuh-LESS-kee, fee-LEE-poh
Bund Deutscher Mädel BOONT DOIT-chur MAY-dul
Bushido BOO-shee-doh
Cabral, Pedro kuh-BRAL, PAY-droh
Cai Yuanpei TSY yoo-wan-PAY
Calais ka-LAY
caliph KAY-liff
caliphate KAY-luh-fayt
Callicrates kuh-LIK-ruh-teez
Cambyses kam-BY-seez
Camus, Albert ka-MOO, ahl-BAYR
Can Vuong kahn VWAHNG
Canaanites KAY-nuh-nytss
Cannae KAH-nee
Cao Cao TSOW-tsow
Capet, Hugh ka-PAY, YOO
Capetian kuh-PEE-shun
Caracalla kuh-RAK-uh-luh
Cárdenas, Lázaro KAHR-day-nahss, LAH-zah-roh
Carolingian kar-uh-LIN-jun
Carthage KAHR-thij
Carthaginian kahr-thuh-JIN-ee-un
Casa de Contratación KAH-sah day KOHN-trah-tahk-SYOHN
Castro, Fidel KASS-troh, fee-DELL
Çatal Hüyük chaht-ul hoo-YOOK
Catharism KATH-uh-riz-um
Catullus kuh-TULL-uss
Cavendish, Margaret KAV-un-dish
Cavour, Camillo di kuh-VOOR, kuh-MEEL-oh dee
Ceaușescu, Nicolae chow-SHES-koo, nee-koh-LY
celibacy SELL-uh-buh-see
cenobitic sen-oh-BIT-ik
Cereta, Laura say-RAY-tuh, LOW-ruh
Cerularius, Michael sayr-yuh-LAR-ee-uss
Chacabuco chahk-ah-BOO-koh
Chaeronea ker-uh-NEE-uh
Chaldean kal-DEE-un
Chamorro, Violeta Barrios de chah-MOH-roh, vee-oh-LET-uh bah-REE-ohss day
Chandragupta Maurya chun-druh-GOOP-tuh MOWR-yuh
Chang'an CHENG-AHN
Chao Phraya chow-PRY-uh
Charlemagne SHAR-luh-mayn
Chauvet shoh-VAY
Chavín de Huántar chah-VEEN day HWAHN-tahr
Chechnya CHECH-nyuh
Cheka CHEK-uh

Chennai CHEN-ny
Chen Shuibian CHEN-shwee-BYAHN
Chiang Kai-shek CHANG ky-SHEK
Chichén Itzá chee-CHEN-eet-SAH
Chimor chee-MAWR
Chirac, Jacques shee-RAK, ZHAHK
Chongqing chung-CHING
Chrétien, Jean kray-TYEN, ZHAHNH
Chrysoloras, Manuel kriss-uh-LAWR-uss, man-WEL
Cicero SIS-uh-roh
Cincinnatus sin-suh-NAT-uss
Cistercians sis-TUR-shunz
Cixi TSEE-chee
Clairvaux klayr-VOH
Cleisthenes KLYSS-thuh-neez
Clemenceau, Georges kluh-mahn-SOH, ZHORZH
Clovis KLOH-viss
Colbert, Jean-Baptiste kohl-BAYR, ZHAHN-bap-TEEST
Commenus kahm-NEE-nuss
concilium plebis kahn-SILL-ee-um PLEE-biss
Concordat of Worms kun-KOR-dat uv WURMZ or VORMPS
Confucius kun-FYOO-shuss
conquistador kahn-KEESS-tuh-dor
consul KAHN-sull
conversos kohn-VAYR-sohz
Copán koh-PAHN
Copernicus, Nicolaus kuh-PURR-nuh-kuss, NEE-koh-lowss
Córdoba KOR-duh-buh
Corinth KOR-inth
Corpus Iuris Civilis KOR-pus YOOR-iss SIV-i-liss
corregidores kuhr-reg-uh-DOR-ayss
Cortés, Hernán kor-TAYSS or kor-TEZ, hayr-NAHN
Courbet, Gustave koor-BAY, goo-STAHV
Crassus KRASS-uss
Crécy kray-SEE
Credit Anstalt KRAY-deet AHN-shtahlt
Croatia kroh-AY-shuh
Croesus KREE-suss
Curie, Marie kyoo-REE
Cyrenaica seer-uh-NAY-uh-kuh
Dadaism DAH-duh-iz-um
daimyo DYM-yoh
Dai Viet dy VYET
Dalí, Salvador dah-LEE, sahl-vah-DOR
Dandin DUN-din
Dao de Jing DOW-deh-JING
Darius duh-RY-uss
Darmstadt DARM-shtaht
dauphin DAW-fin
de Gaulle, Charles duh GOHL, SHAHRL
Dei-Anang DAY-ah-NAHNG
Deir el Bahri dayr-ahl-BAH-ree
Delacroix, Eugène duh-lah-KRWAH, oo-ZHEN
demesne duh-MAYN
Deng Xiaoping DENG-show-PING
Desai, Anita dess-SY
descamisados dayss-kah-mee-SAH-dohss
Descartes, René day-KART, ruh-NAY
détente day-TAHNT
devshirme dev-SHEER-may
dharma DAR-muh
dhoti DOH-tee
Dias, Bartholomeu DEE-ush, bar-toh-loh-MAY-oo
Diaspora dy-ASS-pur-uh
Diderot, Denis dee-DROH, duh-NEE

Diem, Ngo Dinh DYEM, GOH din
Ding Ling DING LING
Diocletian dy-uh-KLEE-shun
Disraeli, Benjamin diz-RAY-lee
Djibouti juh-BOO-tee
Djoser ZHOH-sur
Domesday Book DOOMZ-day book
Dopolavoro duh-puh-LAH-vuh-roh
Dorians DOR-ee-unz
Doryphoros doh-RIF-uh-rohss
Dreyfus, Alfred DRY-fuss
Du Bois, W. E. B. doo-BOISS
Dubček, Alexander DOOB-chek
Duma DOO-muh
Duong Thu Huong ZHWAHNG too HWAHNG
Ebert, Friedrich AY-bayrt, FREE-drikh
ecclesia ek-KLEE-zee-uh
Einsatzgruppen YN-zahtz-group-un
Einstein, Albert YN-styn
Ekaterinburg i-kat-tuh-RIN-burk
Emecheta, Buchi ay-muh-CHAY-tuh, BOO-chee
encomienda en-koh-MYEN-duh
Engels, Friedrich ENG-ulz, FREE-drikh
Enki EN-kee
Enlil EN-lil
Entente Cordiale ahn-TAHNT kor-DYAHL
entrepôt ahn-truh-POH
Ephesus EFF-uh-suss
Epicureanism ep-i-kyoo-REE-uh-ni-zum
Epicurus ep-i-KYOOR-uss
equestrians i-KWES-tree-unz
Erasmus, Desiderius i-RAZZ-mus, dez-i-DEER-ee-uss
Eratosthenes er-uh-TAHSS-thuh-neez
eremitical er-uh-MIT-i-kul
Estonia ess-TOH-nee-uh
Etruscans i-TRUSS-kunz
Euclid YOO-klid
Euripides yoo-RIP-uh-deez
exchequer EKS-chek-ur
Eylau Y-low
Fang Lizhu FAHNG lee-ZHOO
fasces FASS-eez
Fatimid FAT-i-mid
Flaubert, Gustave floh-BAYR, goo-STAHV
Fontainebleau FAWNH-ten-bloh
Freud, Sigmund FROID, SIG-mund or ZIG-munt
Friedan, Betty free-DAN
Friedland FREET-laht
Friedrich, Caspar David FREED-rikh, kass-PAR dah-VEET
Fu Xi foo SHEE
Fu Xuan foo SHWAHN
fueros FWYA-rohss
Führerprinzip FYOOR-ur-prin-TSEEP
Fujiwara foo-jee-WAH-rah
Galilei, Galileo GAL-li-lay, gal-li-LAY-oh
Gama, Vasco da GAHM-uh, VAHSH-koh dah
Gandhi, Mohandas (Mahatma) GAHN-dee, moh-HAHN-dus (mah-HAHT-muh)
Garibaldi, Giuseppe gar-uh-BAHL-dee, joo-ZEP-pay
Gaugamela gaw-guh-MEE-luh
Genghis Khan JING-uss or GENG-uss KAHN
genin gay-NIN
Gentileschi, Artemisia jen-tuh-LESS-kee, ar-tuh-MEE-zhuh
gerousia juh-ROO-see-uh
Gilgamesh GILL-guh-mesh
Girondins juh-RAHN-dinz

glasnost GLAHZ-nohst
Gokhale, Gopal GOH-ku-lay, goh-PAHL
Gomulka, Wladyslaw goh-MOOL-kuh, vlah-DIS-lahf
Gorbachev, Mikhail GOR-buh-chof, meek-HAYL
Gouges, Olympe GOOZH, oh-LAMP
Gracchus, Tiberius and Gaius GRAK-us, ty-BEER-ee-uss and GY-uss
Gropius, Walter GROH-pee-uss, VAHL-tuh
Guan Yin gwahn-YIN
Guangdong gwahng-DUNG
Guangxu gwahng-SHOO
Guangzhou gwahng-JOH
Guaraní gwahr-uh-NEE
Guise GEEZ
Gujarat goo-juh-RAHT
Guomindang gwoh-min-DAHNG
Gustavus Adolphus goo-STAY-vus uh-DAHL-fuss
Gutenberg, Johannes GOO-ten-bayrk, yoh-HAH-nuss
Habsburg HAPS-burg
Hadith huh-DEETH
Hadrian HAY-dree-un
Hagia Sophia HAG-ee-uh soh-FEE-uh
haji HAJ
Hammurabi hahm-uh-RAH-bee
Han Gaozu HAHN gow-DZOO
Han Wudi HAHN woo-DEE
Handel, George Friedrich HAN-dul
Hankou HAHN-kow
Hannibal HAN-uh-bul
Hanukkah HAH-nuh-kuh
Harappa huh-RAP-uh
Harun al-Rashid huh-ROON ah-rah-SHEED
Hassan ben Sabbah khah-SAHN ben shah-BAH
Hatshepsut hat-SHEP-soot
Havel, Vaclav HAH-vul, VAHT-slahf
Haydn, Franz Joseph HY-dun, FRAHNTS YO-zef
Hedayat, Sadeq hay-DY-yaht, sah-DEK
Hegira hee-JY-ruh
Heian hay-AHN
Hellenistic hel-uh-NIS-tik
helots HEL-uts
Heraclius he-ruh-KLY-uss or huh-RAK-lee-uss
Herculaneum hur-kyuh-LAY-nee-um
Herodotus huh-ROD-uh-tuss
Herzegovina HAYRT-suh-guh-VEE-nuh
Herzl, Theodor HAYRT-sul, TAY-oh-dor
Heshen HEH-shen
Hesse, Hermann HESS-uh, hayr-MAHN
Heydrich, Reinhard HY-drikh, RYN-hart
Hideyoshi, Toyotomi hee-day-YOH-shee, toh-yoh-TOH-mee
hieroglyph HY-uh-roh-glif
Hildegard of Bingen HIL-duh-gard uv BING-un
Hindenburg, Paul von HIN-den-boork, POWL fun
Hiroshima hee-roh-SHEE-muh
Hisauchi, Michio hee-sah-OO-chee, mee-CHEE-OH
Hitler Jugend HIT-luh YOO-gunt
Ho Chi Minh HOH CHEE MIN
Höch, Hannah HURKH
Hohenstaufen hoh-en-SHTOW-fen
Hohenzollern hoh-en-TSULL-urn
Hokkaido hoh-KY-doh
Hokusai hoh-kuh-sy
Homo sapiens HOH-moh SAY-pee-unz
Honecker, Erich HOH-nek-uh, AY-reekh
Hong Xiuquan HOONG shee-oo-CHWAHN

hoplites HAHP-lyts
Horace HOR-uss
Hosokawa, Mirohiro hoh-soh-KAH-wah, mee-roh-HEE-roh
Höss, Rudolf HURSS
Huang Di hwahng-DEE
Huayna Inca WY-nuh INK-uh
Huê HWAY
Huguenots HYOO-guh-nots
Huitzilopochtli WEET-see-loh-POHCHT-lee
Humayun hoo-MY-yoon
Husák, Gustav HOO-sahk, goo-STAHV
Ibn Saud ib-un-sah-OOD
Ibn Sina ib-un SEE-nuh
iconoclasm y-KAHN-uh-claz-um
Ictinus ik-TY-nuss
Ife EE-fay
Ignatius of Loyola ig-NAY-shuss uv loi-OH-luh
Il Duce eel DOO-chay
Île-de-France EEL-duh-fronhss
imperator im-puh-RAH-tur
imperium im-PEER-ee-um
Irigoyen, Hipólito ee-ree-GOH-yen, ee-POH-lee-toh
Isis Y-sis
Issus ISS-uss
Iturbide, Agustín de ee-tur-BEE-day, ah-goo-STEEN dat
Itzamna eet-SAHM-nuh
Izanagi ee-zah-NAH-gee
Izanami ee-zah-NAH-mee
Izvestia iz-VESS-tee-uh
Jacobin JAK-uh-bin
jati JAH-tee
Jena YAY-nuh
Jiang Qing jahng-CHING
Jiang Zemin JAHNG zuh-MIN
Jiangxi JAHNG-shee
jihad jee-HAHD
Jinnah, Mohammed Ali JIN-uh, moh-HAM-ed ah-LEE
Joffre, Joseph ZHUFF-ruh, zhoh-ZEFF
Juana Inés de la Cruz, Sor HWAH-nuh ee-NAYSS day lah KROOZ, SAWR
Judaea joo-DEE-uh
Judas Maccabaeus JOO-dus mak-uh-BEE-uss
Jung, Carl YOONG
Junkers YOONG-kurz
Jupiter Optimus Maximus JOO-puh-tur AHP-tuh-muss MAK-suh-muss
Jurchen roor-ZHEN
Justinian juh-STIN-ee-un
Juvenal JOO-vuh-nul
Ka'aba KAH-buh
Kádár, János KAH-dahr, YAH-nush
Kalidasa kah-lee-DAH-suh
kamikaze kah-mi-KAH-zee
Kanagawa kah-nah-GAH-wah
Kanchipuram kahn-CHEE-poo-rum
Kandinsky, Wassily kan-DIN-skee, vus-YEEL-yee
Kang Youwei KAHNG yow-WAY
Kangxi GANG-zhee
Kanishka kuh-NISH-kuh
Kant, Immanuel KAHNT, i-MAHN-yoo-el
Karisma Kapoor kuh-RIZ-muh kuh-POOR
Karlsbad KARLSS-baht
Kautilya kow-TIL-yuh
Kazakhstan ka-zak-STAN or kuh-zahk-STAHN
Kemal Atatürk, Mustafá kuh-MAHL ah-tah-TIRK, moos-tah-FAH

Kenyatta, Jomo ken-YAHT-uh, JOH-moh
Kerensky, Alexander kuh-REN-skee
Keynes, John Maynard KAYNZ
Khadija kaha-DEE-jah
Khajuraho khah-joo-RAH-hoh
Khanbaliq khahn-bah-LEEK
Khomeini, Ayatollah Ruholla khoh-MAY-nee, ah-yah-TUL-uh roo-HUL-uh
Khrushchev, Nikita KHROOSH-chawf, nuh-KEE-tuh
Khubilai Khan KOO-bluh KAHN
Kikuya ki-KOO-yuh
Kilwa KIL-wuh
Kim Dae Jung kim day JOONG
Kim Il Sung kim il SOONG
Kirghiz keer-GEEZ
Knesset kuh-NESS-it
Koguryo koh-GOOR-yoh
Kohl, Helmut KOHL, HEL-moot
Koizumi, Junichero koh-ee-ZOO-mee, joo-nee-CHAY-roh
kokutai koh-kuh-TY
Kolchak, Alexander kul-CHAHK
Kollantai, Alexandra kul-lun-TY
Kongzi koong-SHEE
Königgrätz kur-nig-GRETS
Kornilov, Lavr kor-NYEE-luff, LAH-vur
Koryo KAWR-yoh
Kosovo KAWSS-suh-voh
Kostunica, Vojislav kuh-STOO-nit-suh, VOH-yee-slav
Kosygin, Alexei kuh-SEE-gun, uh-LEK-say
Kraft durch Freude KRAHFT doorkh FROI-duh
Krishna KRISH-nuh
Kristallnacht kri-STAHL-nahkht
Kukulcan koo-kul-KAHN
kulaks KOO-lahks
Kundera, Milan koon-DAYR-uh, MEE-lahn
Kursk KOORSK
Kushanas koo-SHAH-nuz
Kwasniewski, Aleksander kwahsh-NYEF-skee
Kyangyi kyang-YEE
Kyoto KYOH-toh
Kyushu KYOO-shoo
laissez-faire less-ay-FAYR
Lancaster LAN-kas-tur
Lao Tzu LOW-dzuh
La Rochefoucauld-Liancourt, duc de lah-RUSH-foo-koh-lee-ahnh-KOOR, dook duh
latifundia lat-i-FOON-dee-uh
Latium LAY-shum
Latvia LAT-vee-uh
Launay, marquis de loh-NAY, mar-KEE duh
Laurier, Wilfred LOR-ee-ay
Lazar lah-ZAR
Lebensraum LAY-benz-rowm
Lee Kuan-yew LEE-kwahn-YOO
Les Demoiselles d'Avignon lay dem-wah-ZEL dah-vee-NYOHNH
Lévesque, René lay-VEK, ruh-NAY
Leviathan luh-VY-uh-thun
Leyster, Judith LESS-tur
Liège lee-EZH
Li Su lee SOO
Li Yuan lee YWAHN
Li Zicheng lee zee-CHENG
Liaodong LYOW-doong
Licinius ly-SIN-ee-uss
Liliuokalani LIL-ee-uh-woh-kuh-LAH-nee
Lin Zexu LIN dzeh-SHOO

Lindisfarne LIN-dis-farn
List, Friedrich LIST, FREED-rikh
Lithuania lith-WAY-nee-uh
Liu Bang lyoo BAHNG
Liu Ling lyoo LING
Liu Shaoqi lyoo show-CHEE
Livy LIV-ee
Longshan loong-SHAHN
l'Ouverture, Toussaint loo-vayr-TOOR, too-SANH
Lu Xun loo SHUN
Ludendorff, Erich LOO-dun-dorf
Luftwaffe LOOFT-vahf-uh
l'uomo universale LWOH-moh OO-nee-vayr-SAH-lay
Luoyang LWOH-yahng
Lützen LURT-sun
Lyons LYOHNH
Maastricht MAHSS-trikht
Maat MAH-ut
Macao muh-KOW
Machiavelli, Niccolò mahk-ee-uh-VEL-ee, nee-koh-LOH
Maginot Line MA-zhi-noh lyn
Magna Graecia MAG-nuh GREE-shuh
Magyars MAG-yarz
Mahabharata muh-hahb-huh-RAH-tuh
maharaja mah-huh-RAH-juh
Mahavira mah-hah-VEE-ruh
Mahayana mah-huh-YAH-nuh
Mahfouz, Naguib mahkh-FOOZ, nah-GEEB
Mahmud of Ghazni MAHKH-mood uv GAHZ-nee
Maimonides my-MAH-nuh-deez
Malaysia muh-LAY-zhuh
Malaya muh-LAY-uh
Malenkov, Georgy muh-LEN-kuf, gyee-OR-gyee
Mamallapuram muh-MAH-luh-poor-um
Manchukuo man-CHOO-kwoh
Manetho MAN-uh-thoh
Mao Dun mow DOON
Mao Zedong mow zee-DOONG
Marconi, Guglielmo mahr-KOH-nee, gool-YEL-moh
Marcus Aurelius MAR-kuss aw-REE-lee-uss
Marie Antoinette muh-REE an-twuh-NET
Marius MAR-ee-uss
Marquez, Gabriel Garcia mar-KEZ
Marseilles mar-SAY
Masaccio muh-ZAH-choh
Maya MY-uh
Mazarin maz-uh-RANH
Mazzini, Giuseppe maht-SEE-nee, joo-ZEP-pay
Megasthenes muh-GAS-thuh-neez
Mehmet meh-MET
Meiji MAY-jee
Mein Kampf myn KAHMPF
Meir, Golda may-EER
Menander muh-NAN-dur
Mencius MEN-shuss
Mendeleyev, Dmitri men-duh-LAY-ef, di-MEE-tree
Mensheviks MENS-shuh-viks
Mercator, Gerardus mur-KAY-tur, juh-RAHR-dus
Merian, Maria Sibylla MAY-ree-un
Merovingian meh-ruh-VIN-jee-un
Mesopotamia mess-uh-puh-TAY-mee-uh
mestizos mess-TEE-zohz
Metternich, Klemens von MET-ayr-nikh, KLAY-menss fun
Mexica meh-SHEE-kuh
Michelangelo my-kuh-LAN-juh-loh
Mieszko MYESH-koh

millet mi-LET
Milošević, Slobodan mi-LOH-suh-vich, sluh-BOH-dahn
Miltiades mil-TY-uh-deez
Minamoto Yoritomo mee-nah-MOH-toh, yoh-ree-
TOH-moh
Minseito MEEN-say-toh
Mishima, Yukio mi-SHEE-muh, yoo-KEE-oh
missi dominici MISS-ee doh-MIN-i-chee
Mitterrand, François MEE-tayr-rahnh, frahnh-SWAH
Moche moh-CHAY
Moctezuma mahk-tuh-ZOO-muh
Mogadishu moh-guh-DEE-shoo
Mohács MOH-hach
Mohenjo-Daro mo-HEN-jo-DAH-roh
Moldova mohl-DOH-vuh
Moldavia mohl-DAY-vee-uh
Molière, Jean-Baptiste mohl-YAYR, ZHAHNH-bah-TEEST
Molotov, Vyacheslav MAHL-uh-tawf, vyich-chiss-SLAHF
Mombasa mahm-BAH-suh
Monet, Claude moh-NEH, KLOHD
Mongkut MAWNG-koot
Montesquieu MOHN-tess-kyoo
Montessori, Maria mahn-tuh-SOR-ee
Morisot, Berthe mor-ee-ZOH, BAYRT
Mozambique moh-zam-BEEK
Mozart, Wolfgang Amadeus MOH-tsart, VULF-gahng
ah-muh-DAY-uss

Muawiya moo-AH-wee-yah
Mudéjares moo-theh-KHAH-rayss
Mughal MOO-gul
Muhammad moh-HAM-ud or moh-HAHM-ud
Mühlberg MURL-bayrk
Mukden MOOK-dun
mulattoes muh-LAH-tohz
Mumbai MUM-by
Murad moo-RAHD
Musharraf, Pervaiz moo-SHAHR-uf, pur-VEZ
Muslim MUZ-lum
Mutsuhito moo-tsoo-HEE-toh
Myanmar MYAN-mahr
Mycenaean my-suh-NEE-un
Nabonidas nab-uh-NY-duss
Nabopolassar nab-uh-puh-LASS-ur
Nagasaki nah-gah-SAH-kee
Nagy, Imry NAHJ, IM-ray
Nanjing nan-JING
Nantes NAHNT
Nara NAH-rah
Nasrin, Taslima naz-REEN, tah-SLEE-muh
Nasser, Gamal Abdul NAH-sur, juh-MAHL ahb-DOOL
Navarre nuh-VAHR
Nebuchadnezzar neb-uh-kud-NEZZ-ur
Nehru, Jawaharlal NAY-roo, juh-WAH-hur-lahl
Nero NEE-roh
Netanyahu, Benjamin net-ahn-YAH-hoo
Neumann, Balthasar NOI-mahn, BAHL-tuh-zahr
Neustria NOO-stree-uh
Nevsky, Alexander NYEF-skee
Nguyen NGWEN
Nimwegen NIM-vay-gun
Ninhursaga nin-HUR-sah-guh
Nkrumah, Kwame en-KROO-muh, KWAH-may
Nobunaga, Oda noh-buh-NAH-guh, OH-dah
Nogarola, Isotta noh-guh-ROH-luh, ee-ZAHT-uh
Novotny, Antonin noh-VAHT-nee, AHN-toh-nyeen
nuoc mam NWAHK MAHM

Nyame NYAH-may
Oaxaca wah-HAH-kuh
Octavian ahk-TAY-vee-un
Odoacer oh-doh-AY-sur
Odysseus oh-DISS-ee-uss
Oe, Kenzaburo OH-ay, ken-zuh-BOO-roh
Olmec AHL-mek or OHL-mek
Omar Khayyam OH-mar ky-YAHM
Ometeotl oh-met-tee-AH-tul
Oresteia uh-res-TY-uh
Orkhan or-KHAHN
Osaka oh-SAH-kuh
Osama bin Laden oh-SAH-muh bin LAH-dun
Osiris oh-SY-russ
Ostpolitik OHST-poh-lee-teek
Ostrogoths AHSS-truh-gahthss
Ovid OH-vid
Pacal pa-KAL
Pachakuti pah-chah-KOO-tee
Paekche bayk-JEE
Pagan puh-GAHN
Paleologus pay-lee-AWL-uh-guss
Pankhurst, Emmeline PANK-hurst
papal curia PAY-pul KYOOR-ee-uh
Parti Québécois par-TEE kay-bek-KWAH
Pasternak, Boris PASS-tur-nak, buh-REESS
Pasteur, Louis pass-TOOR, LWEE
Pataliputra pah-tah-lee-POO-truh
paterfamilias pay-tur-fuh-MEEL-yus
Pepin PEP-in or pay-PANH
perestroika per-uh-STROI-kuh
Pergamum PUR-guh-mum
Pericles PER-i-kleez
Perpetua pur-PET-choo-uh
Petrarch PEE-trark or PET-trark
philosophe fee-loh-ZAWF
Phoenicians fuh-NEE-shunz
Photius FOH-shuss
Picasso, Pablo pi-KAH-soh
Pietism PY-uh-tiz-um
Pisistratus puh-SIS-truh-tuss
Pizarro, Francesco puh-ZAHR-oh, frahn-CHESS-koh
Planck, Max PLAHNK
Plantagenet plan-TAJ-uh-net
Plassey PLASS-ee
Plato PLAY-toh
polis POH-liss
Polybius puh-LIB-ee-uss
Pompeii pahm-PAY
Pompey PAHM-pee
Popul Vuh puh-PUL VOO
Potosí poh-toh-SEE
Potsdam PAHTS-dam
praetor PREE-tur
Prakrit PRAH-krit
Pravda PRAHV-duh
primogeniture pree-moh-JEN-i-chur
princeps PRIN-seps
Principia prin-SIP-ee-uh
Procopius pruh-KOH-pee-uss
procurator PROK-yuh-ray-tur
Ptolemaic tahl-uh-MAY-ik
Ptolemy TAHL-uh-mee
Pugachev, Emelyan poo-guh-CHAWF, yim-yil-YAHN
Punic PYOO-nik
Putin, Vladimir POO-tin

Pyongyang pyawng-YANG
Pythagoras puh-THAG-uh-russ
Qajar kuh-JAHR
Qianlong CHAN-loong
Qin CHIN
Qin Shi Huangdi chin shee hwang-DEE
Qing CHING
Qiu Jin chee-oo-JIN
Qu CHOO
Quetzelcoatl KWET-sul-koh-AHT-ul
Quraishi koo-RY-shee
Qur'an kuh-RAN or kuh-RAHN
Rabe'a of Qozdar rah-BAY-uh uv kuz-DAHR
Rajput RAHJ-poot
Rama RAH-mah
Ramayana rah-mah-YAH-nah
Ramcaritmanas RAM-kah-rit-MAH-nuz
Rameses RAM-uh-seez
Raphael RAFF-ee-ul
Rasputin rass-PYOO-tin
Realpolitik ray-AHL-poh-lee-teek
Reichstag RYKHSS-tahk
Rembrandt van Rijn REM-brant vahn RYN
Rémy, Nicholas ray-MEE, nee-koh-LAH
rentier rahn-TYAY
Rhee, Syngman REE, SING-mun
Ricci, Matteo REE-chee, ma-TAY-oh
Richelieu REESH-uh-lyuh
Rig Veda RIK-vee-duh
Rimbaud, Arthur ram-BOH, ar-TOOR
Riza-i-Abassi ree-ZAH-yah-BAH-see
Robespierre, Maximilien ROHBZ-pyayr, mak-see-meel-YENH
Rococo ruh-KOH-koh
Rocroi roh-KRWAH
Rommel, Erwin RAHM-ul
Romulus Augustulus RAHM-yuh-luss ow-GOOS-chuh-luss
Rousseau, Jean-Jacques roo-SOH, ZHAHNH-ZHAHK
Rus ROOSS or ROOSH
Saikaku sy-KAH-koo
Sakharov, Andrei SAH-kuh-rawf, ahn-DRAY
Saladin SAL-uh-din
Samnite SAM-nyt
Samudragupta suh-mood-ruh-GOOP-tuh
samurai SAM-uh-ry
San Martín, José de san mar-TEEN, hoh-SAY day
Sandinista san-duh-NEES-tuh
Sarraut, Albert sah-ROH, ahl-BAYR
Sartre, Jean-Paul SAR-truh, ZHAHNH-POHL
Sassanid suh-SAN-id
sati suh-TEE
satrap SAY-trap
satrapy SAY-truh-pee
Schleswig-Holstein SHLESS-vik-HOHL-shtyn
Schlieffen, Alfred von SHLEE-fun, AHL-fret fun
Schliemann, Heinrich SHLEE-mahn, HYN-rikh
Schmidt, Helmut SHMIT, HEL-moot
Schönberg, Arnold SHURN-bayrk, AR-nawlt
Schröder, Gerhard SHRUR-duh, GAYR-hahrt
Scipio Aemilianus SEE-pee-oh ee-mil-YAY-nuss
Scipio Africanus SEE-pee-oh af-ree-KAY-nuss
Sejm SAYM
Seleucid suh-LOO-sid
Seleucus suh-LOO-kuss
Seljuk SEL-jook
Septimius Severus sep-TIM-ee-uss se-VEER-uss

Shakuntala shah-koon-TAH-lah
Shandong SHAHN-doong
Shang SHAHNG
Sharia shah-REE-uh
Shen Nong shun-NOONG
Shi'ite SHEE-YT
Shidehara shee-de-HAH-rah
Shiga Naoya SHEE-gah NOW-yah
Shikoku shee-KOH-koo
Shimonoseki shee-moh-noh-SEK-ee
Shiva SHIV-uh
Shotoku Taishi shoh-TOH-koo ty-EE-shee
Sichuan SEECH-wahn
Siddhartha Gautama si-DAR-tuh GAW-tuh-muh
Sieveking, Amalie SEE-vuh-king, uh-MAHL-yuh
Sigiriya see-gee-REE-uh
Silla SIL-uh
Silva, Luís Inácio Lula de LWEES ee-NAH-syoh LOO-luh duh-SEEL-vuh
Sima Qian SEE-mah chee-AHN
sipahis suh-PAH-heez
Sita SEE-tuh
Slovenia sloh-VEE-nee-uh
Socrates SAHK-ruh-teez
Solon SOH-lun
Solzhenitsyn, Alexander sohl-zhuh-NEET-sin
Somme SUM
Song Taizu SOONG ty-DZOO
Soong, Mei-ling SOONG, may-LING
Sophocles SAHF-uh-kleez
Spartacus SPAR-tuh-kuss
squadristi skwah-DREES-tee
Srebrenica sreb-bruh-NEET-suh
Stasi SHTAH-see
Stoicism STOH-i-siz-um
Stresemann, Gustav SHTRAY-zuh-mahn, GOOS-tahf
Sturmabteilung SHTOORM-ap-ty-loonk
Sudetenland soo-DAY-tun-land
sudra SOO-druh or SHOO-druh
Suger soo-ZHAYR
Suharto soo-HAHR-toh
Sui Wendi SWEE wen-DEE
Sui Yangdi SWEE yahng-DEE
Sukarno soo-KAHR-noh
Sukarnoputri, Megawati soo-kahr-noh-POO-tree, meg-uh-WAH-tee
Suleiman SOO-lay-mahn
Suleymaniye soo-lay-MAHN-ee-eh
Sulla SUL-uh
Sumerians soo-MER-ee-unz or soo-MEER-ee-unz
Summa Theologica SOO-muh tay-oh-LAH-jee-kuh
Sun Yat-sen SOON yaht-SEN
Suttner, Bertha von ZOOT-nuh, BAYR-tuh fun
Swaziland SWAH-zee-land
Taban lo Liyong tuh-BAN loh-lee-YAWNG
Tacitus TASS-i-tuss
Tahuantinsuyu tuh-HWAHN-tin-SOO-yoo
Taika TY-kuh
taille TY
Taiping ty-PING
Tanganyika tang-an-YEE-kuh
Tanizaki, Junichiro tan-i-ZAH-kee, jun-i-CHEE-roh
Tanzania tan-zuh-NEE-uh
Temuchin TEM-yuh-jin
Tenochtitlán tay-nawch-teet-LAHN
Teotihuacán tay-noh-tee-hwa-KAHN

Texcoco tess-KOH-koh
Thales THAY-leez
Theocritus thee-AHK-ruh-tuss
Theodora thee-uh-DOR-uh
Theodoric thee-AHD-uh-rik
Theodosius thee-uh-DOH-shuss
Theravada thay-ruh-VAH-duh
Thermopylae thur-MAHP-uh-lee
Thucydides thoo-SID-uh-deez
Thutmosis thoot-MOH-suss
Tiananmen TYAHN-ahn-men
Tianjin TYAHN-jin
Tiberius ty-BEER-ee-uss
Tikal tee-KAHL
Tito TEE-toh
Titus TY-tuss
Tlaloc tuh-lah-LOHK
Tlaltelolco tuh-lahl-teh-LOH-koh
Tlaxcala tuh-lah-SKAH-lah
Toer, Pramoedya TOOR, pra-MOO-dyah
Tojo, Hideki TOH-joh, hee-DEK-ee
Tokugawa Ieyasu toh-koo-GAH-wah ee-yeh-YAH-soo
Tongmenghui toong-meng-HWEE
Topa Inca TOH-puh INK-uh
Topkapi tawp-KAH-pee
Tordesillas tor-day-SEE-yass
Touré, Sékou too-RAY, say-KOO
Trajan TRAY-jun
Trevithick, Richard TREV-uh-thik
Trotsky, Leon TRAHT-skee
Troyes TRWAH
Trudeau, Pierre troo-DOH, PYAYR
Tughluq tug-LUK
Tulsidas tool-see-DAHSS
Tutankhamun too-tang-KAH-mun
uhuru oo-HOO-roo
uji OO-jee
Ulbricht, Walter OOL-brikht, VAHL-tuh
Ulianov, Vladimir ool-YA-nuf
Umayyads oo-MY-adz
Unam Sanctam OO-nahm SAHNK-tahm
universitas yoo-nee-VAYR-see-tahss
Utamaro OO-tah-mah-roh
Uzbekistan ooz-BEK-i-stan
vaisya VISH-yuh
Vajpayee, Atal Behari VAHJ-py-ee, AH-tahl bi-HAH-ree
Valois val-WAH
Van de Velde, Theodore vahn duh VEL-duh, TAY-oh-dor
van Eyck, Jan vahn YK or van AYK, YAHN
van Gogh, Vincent van GOH
Venetia vuh-NEE-shuh
Verdun vur-DUN
Versailles vayr-SY
Vespucci, Amerigo vess-POO-chee, ahm-ay-REE-goh
Vesuvius vuh-SOO-vee-uss
Vichy VISH-ee
Vierzehnheiligen feer-tsayn-HY-li-gen
Virgil VUR-jul
Vishnu VISH-noo
Visigoths VIZ-uh-gathz
Volk FULK
Voltaire vohl-TAYR
Wahd WAHFT
Walesa, Lech vah-WENT-sah, LEK
Wallachia wah-LAY-kee-uh
Wang Anshi WAHNG ahn-SHEE

Wang Shuo wahng-SHWOH
Wang Tao wahng-TOW
Wannsee VAHN-zay
Watteau, Antoine wah-TOH, AHN-twahn
wergeld WUR-geld
Winkelmann, Maria VINK-ul-mahn
Witte, Sergei VIT-uh, syir-GYAY
Wittenberg VIT-ten-bayrk
Wojtyla, Karol voy-TEE-wah, KAH-rul
Wollstonecraft, Mary WULL-stun-kraft
Wu Zhao woo-ZHOW
Würzburg VURTS-boork
Xavier, Francis ZAY-vee-ur
Xerxes ZURK-seez
Xhosa KHOH-suh
Xia SHEE-ah
Xian SHEE-ahn
Xiangyang SHYAHNG-yahng
Xinjiang SHIN-jyahng
Xiongnu SHYAHNG-noo
Xui Tong shwee-TOONG
Yahweh YAH-way
Yan'an yuh-NAHN
Yang Guifei yahng gwee-FAY
Yangshao yahng-SHOW

Yangtze YANG-tsee
Yayoi yah-YO-ee
Yeltsin, Boris YELT-sun
Yi Jing yee-JING
Yi Song-gye YEE song-YEE
Yuan Shikai yoo-AHN shee-KY
Yudhoyono, Susilo yood-hoh-YOH-noh, soo-SEE-loh
Yue yoo-EH
zaibatsu zy-BAHT-soo or Japanese DZY-bahtss
Zanj ZANJ
Zanzibar ZAN-zi-bar
Zemsky Sobor ZEM-skee suh-BOR
zemstvos ZEMPST-vohz
Zeno ZEE-noh
zeppelin ZEP-puh-lin
Zeus ZOOSS
Zhang Zhidong JANG jee-DOONG
Zhao Ziyang JOW dzee-YAHNG
Zhenotdel zhen-ut-DEL
Zia ul-Haq, Mohammad ZEE-uh ool-HAHK
ziggurat ZIG-uh-rat
Zoroaster ZOR-oh-ass-tur
Zuanzong zwahn-ZOONG
Zuni ZOO-nee
Zwingli, Ulrich TSFING-lee, OOL-rikh

MAP CREDITS

The authors wish to acknowledge their use of the following books as reference in preparing the maps listed here:

MAP 3.1 Geoffrey Barraclough, ed., *Times Atlas of World History,* (Maplewood, N.J.: Hammond Inc., 1978), p. 63.

MAP 5.4 Hammond Past Worlds: *The Times Atlas of Archeology,* (Maplewood, N.J.: Hammond Inc., 1988), pp. 190–191.

MAP 5.5 Conrad Schirokauer, *A Brief History of Chinese and Japanese Civilizations,* 2d ed. (San Diego: Harcourt Brace Jovanovich, 1989), p. 52.

MAP 6.3 Michael Coe, Dean Snow and Elizabeth Benson, *Atlas of Ancient America* (New York: Facts on File, 1988), p. 144.

MAP 6.4 Geoffrey Barraclough, ed., *Times Atlas of World History,* (Maplewood, N.J.: Hammond Inc., 1978), p. 47.

MAP 6.5 Phillipa Fernandez-Arnesto, *Atlas of World Exploration,* (New York: Harper Collins, 1991), p. 35.

MAP 6.6 Geoffrey Barraclough, ed., *Times Atlas of World History,* (Maplewood, N.J.: Hammond Inc., 1978), p. 47.

MAP 7.3 Geoffrey Barraclough, ed., *Times Atlas of World History,* (Maplewood, N.J.: Hammond Inc., 1978), pp. 134–135.

MAP 7.4 Geoffrey Barraclough, ed., *Times Atlas of World History,* (Maplewood, N.J.: Hammond Inc., 1978), p. 135.

MAP 8.1 Geoffrey Barraclough, ed., *Times Atlas of World History,* (Maplewood, N.J.: Hammond Inc., 1978), pp. 44–45.

MAP 8.4 Geoffrey Barraclough, ed., *Times Atlas of World History,* (Maplewood, N.J.: Hammond Inc., 1978), pp. 136–137.

MAP 9.2 Michael Edwardes, *A History of India* (London: Thames and Hudson, 1961), p. 79.

MAP 10.1 John K. Fairbank, Edwin O. Reischauer, and Albert M. Craig, *East Asia: Tradition and Transformation* (Boston: Houghton Mifflin, 1973), p. 103.

SPOT MAP, PAGE 279 Albert Hermann, *An Historical Atlas of China* (Chicago: Aidine, 1966), p. 13.

MAP 11.1 John K. Fairbank, Edwin O. Reischauer, and Albert M. Craig, *East Asia: Tradition and Transformation* (Boston: Houghton Mifflin, 1973), p. 363.